AF555927

GENDER JUSTICE
AND
WOMEN EMPOWERMENT

An Integrated Approach

GENDER JUSTICE AND WOMEN EMPOWERMENT

An Integrated Approach

Editors

SARBJEET SINGH

PANKAJ DODH

Foreword by

DR. JASPAL SINGH

Vice-Chancellor

Punjabi University, Patiala, Punjab

REGAL PUBLICATIONS

New Delhi - 110 027

Foreword

Equality between men and women is both a human right as well as a Millennium Development Goal in its own right. It is now widely accepted fact that gender equality and women's social, economic and political empowerment is a pre-requisite for inclusive growth, sustainable development, pro-poor growth and realisation of the Millennium Development Goals (MDGs).

United Nations Secretary-General, Ban Ki-moon points out that, women are not just the target of special measures to promote development. They are also the driving force to overcome poverty, reduce hunger, fight illiteracy, heal the sick, prevent the spread of disease and promote stability. Gender equality and women's empowerment are considered to be a desirable by-product of human development. Therefore, to achieve these goals, it is essential to close the gender-gap in education, employment, and political participation.

Amartya Sen (1999) transformed the discourse on development when he argued that development is not only about raising people's incomes or reducing poverty, but rather it involves a process of expanding freedoms equally for all people. Viewed from this perspective, gender equality is intrinsically valued coupled with empowerment of women would be the catalysts for multiplying development efforts. Women often face multiple discrimination and exclusion in all spheres of life.

A growing body of empirical literature from around the world demonstrates that promoting gender equality is of immense value to enhance a country's ability to compete in an increasingly globalised environment. *World Development Report, 2012* acknowledges gender equality as 'smart economics'.

Indeed, the existing literature infers that greater gender equality in endowments, access to economic opportunities and agency can contribute to higher productivity, sustainable income growth, poverty reduction and improve the opportunities and outcomes for the next generation.

The contributions to this book have been made by experts from diversified fields from all over India. I am confident that academic works of this nature will definitely pave-way for the planners, policy-makers and researchers to suggest strategies for empowering women socially, economically, psychologically and politically. This book has succeeded in identifying multiple issues related to gender equality, gender justice and women empowerment, while presenting a comprehensive scenario of the socio, economic, legal and political status of women and discrimination against women at all stages of life. These studies may provide a basis to suggest a multi-pronged and integrated approach for empowering women and provide inspiration and guidance to those already working for gender equality and empowerment.

DR. JASPAL SINGH
Vice-Chancellor
Punjabi University,
Patiala, Punjab

Preface

This book is culmination of efforts to provide an integrated analysis of the dynamics of gender justice and women empowerment. Today, Indian society is at the cusp of a paradigm change, reorienting and restructuring its general perception regarding the position and status of women. The western enlightenment discourse and its cascading impact on the socio-economic and political transformation have incubated some of the underdeveloped societies of the world, including India.

India stands firmly in her tryst to become a major power of the world in the next few decades. Only a vibrant and dynamic society, enriched with liberal ideas of gender equality, freedom for all and the highest regard for justice can realise the dream of becoming a peaceful, stable and developed nation. Gender equality and empowerment of women play an important role in development through a multiplier process; an empowered woman not only empowers her family but empowers the society as well. Women hold up half the sky in demographic sense but their visibility in various spheres continues to be ignored and underestimated.

Women's empowerment is a complex and evolving concept that is constantly being defined, redefined, elaborated, sharpened and clarified. It is deeply inter-linked with gender equality and equity which appear to be the ultimate goals of women's empowerment. Gender justice entails to eliminate man-made inequalities and discrimination, and extend equal opportunities to women.

The book attempts to analyse various dimensions of gender justice, gender equality and women empowerment by applying a multi-disciplinary perspective. Major focus remains on transforming the status of women through enhancing socio-economic security supported with effective statutory and political enforcement and ensuring greater participation of women in decision making process based on the universal values of equality, justice and honour.

The book spotlights various historical, cultural, socio-economic, psychological, political and legal dimensions of women emancipation. A contextual and textual approach to conflate various interconnected aspects concerned with women empowerment and gender equality has been followed. In a nutshell, the book provides an inquisitive perspective to various strands of women empowerment and gender justice and discusses the existing inequalities and discrimination against women in the wider public arena.

SARBJEET SINGH
PANKAJ DODH

About the Contributors

1. Dr. Anupama, Professor, Department of Economics, Punjabi University, Patiala, Punjab.
2. Dr. Arup Jyoti Sarma, Assistant Professor, Department of Philosophy, Tripura University, Tripura.
3. Dr. Baldev Singh Negi, Project Officer, Research Institute of Integrated Himalayan Studies (UGC Centre of Excellence), Himachal Pradesh University, Shimla.
4. Dr. Barasa Deka, Assistant Professor, Department of Political Science, Gauhati University, Assam.
5. Dr. Gauri Sharma, Associate Professor in History, Department of Evening Studies, Panjab University, Chandigarh.
6. Dr. Gian Singh, Professor, Department of Economics, Punjabi University, Patiala, Punjab.
7. Dr. Gurinder Kaur, Professor, Department of Geography, Punjabi University, Patiala, Punjab.
8. Dr. Jasdeep Singh Toor, Assistant Professor, Department of Economics, Punjabi University, Patiala, Punjab.
9. Dr. K.R. Nayar, Professor, Centre of Social Medicine and Community Health, Jawaharlal Nehru University, New Delhi.
10. Dr. Kamalini Mukhopadhyaya, Research Officer, Kusuma Foundation, New Delhi.
11. Dr. Mast Ram, Assistant Professor, Shyam Lal College, Delhi University, New Delhi.
12. Dr. Naorem Arunibala Devi, Centre of Social Medicine and Community Health, Jawaharlal Nehru University, New Delhi.
13. Dr. Neeraj Sharma, Associate Professor in Economics, Department of Evening Studies, Panjab University, Chandigarh.
14. Dr. Pankaj Dodh, Research Associate, National Maritime Foundation, New Delhi.

15. Dr. Prithpal Kaur, Assistant Registrar of Trade Marks and Geographical Indications in Trade Marks Registry, Ministry of Commerce and Industry, New Delhi.
16. Dr. R.K. Mahajan, Professor in Department of Economics, Post-Graduate Studies, Punjabi University Regional Centre, Bathinda, Punjab.
17. Dr. Ramna, Assistant Professor in Economics, Vallabh Government College, Mandi, Himachal Pradesh.
18. Dr. Ravita, Assistant Professor, Department of Economics, Punjabi University, Patiala, Punjab.
19. Dr. Sanjay Sindhu, Associate Professor, Department of Law, H.P. University, Shimla, Himachal Pradesh.
20. Dr. Sanjeev Kumar, Senior Research Officer, Institute of Integrated Himalayan Studies (UGC Centre of Excellence), Himachal Pradesh University, Shimla.
21. Dr. Sarbjeet Singh, Assistant Professor, Department of Economics, Punjabi University, Patiala, Punjab.
22. Dr. Veena Kumari, Assistant Professor, UILS, HP University Ava Lodge, Chaura Maidan, Shimla, Himachal Pradesh.
23. Dr. Vivek Negi, Assistant Professor in English, Government Degree College, Paonta Sahib, District Sirmour, H.P.
24. Mr. Anubhab Sarmah, Department of Political Science, Gauhati University, Assam.
25. Mr. Bhagwant Singh, Research Scholar, Department of Economics, Punjabi University, Patiala, Punjab.
26. Mr. Dharam Pal, Research Scholar, Department of Economics, Punjabi University, Patiala, Punjab.
27. Mr. Jagdev Singh, Research Scholar, Department of Economics, Punjabi University, Patiala, Punjab.
28. Mr. Ranvir Singh, Research Scholar, Centre of Social Medicine and Community Health, School of Social Sciences, Jawaharlal Nehru University, New Delhi, India.
29. Mr. Shishir Kumar Yadav, Junior Research Fellow, Centre of Social Medicine and Community Health, School of Social Sciences, Jawaharlal Nehru University, New Delhi, India.
30. Ms. Apra, Assistant Professor in Economics, Apeejay College of Fine Arts, Jalandhar, Punjab.
31. Ms. Kusam Kumari, Ph.D. Scholar, Department of Political Science, Himachal Pradesh University, Shimla.
32. Ms. Sonal Pandey, Senior Research Fellow, Department of Humanities and Social Sciences, Indian Institute of Technology, Kharagpur, U.P.

Introduction

SARBJEET SINGH

> *"Social, political and economic equality for women is integral to the achievement of all Millennium Development Goals. Until women and girls are liberated from poverty and injustice, all our goals—peace, security, sustainable development—stand in jeopardy."*
>
> *—U.N. Secretary-General, Ban Ki-moon, June 2010*

An enlightened woman in a society is recognised as a key agent to accelerate the developmental processes which are sustainable. Any civilised society, modern polity or developing economy cannot ignore the aspirations of women as well as their rights in the society. Gender equality is at the very heart of a country's development process. Empowered women and girls contribute to the health and productivity of families and communities which improve prospects for the next generation.

Gender equality and women's empowerment is one of the eight United Nations Millennium Development Goals. According to United Nations Secretary-General Ban Ki-moon, women are not just the target of special measures to promote development, but are also the driving force to overcome poverty, reduce hunger, fight illiteracy, heal the sick, prevent the spread of disease and promote stability (Teneja, *et al.*, 2009).

Gender equality is not about parity; it is about providing an equal as well as enabling environment for the growth and prosperity for both sexes. The relationship between the sexes should be based on mutual respect for each other's roles, capabilities and sensibilities. Millions of women in the villages, especially in northern and western India, experience widespread discrimination and prejudice on account of entrenched conservatism. It is these poor women who need the support of the government and society. The concept of gender equality needs to be re-evaluated and reinterpreted (Mukundarajan, 2010).

Gender equality does not necessarily mean equality of outcomes for males and females. World Development Report (2006) defines gender equality as equal access to the "opportunities that allow people to pursue a life of their own choosing and to avoid extreme deprivations in outcomes"—that is, gender equality in rights, resources, and voice. Equality of rights refers to equality under the law, whether customary or statutory. Equality of resources refers to equality of opportunity, including equality of access to human capital investments and other productive resources and to markets. Equality of voice captures the ability to influence and contribute to the political discourse and the development process (World Bank, 2007).

Gender equality and women's empowerment are considered to be a desirable by-product of human development. Therefore, in order to achieve these goals, it is essential to reduce the gender inequality and empowerment gaps in education, employment and political participation. According to United Nations Development Programme, "gender inequality is an obstacle to progress, a roadblock on the path of human development" (UNDP, 2002).

Women are among those who shoulder the brunt of globalisation's drawbacks; however, women are also the world's greatest untapped resource for turning the tide on economic injustice. Research has shown that providing equal access to education, credit, property and employment for women, will ensure economic justice and sustainability for all (World WYCA and UNFPA, 2006). Since empowerment is a complex issue with varying interpretations in different societal, national and cultural contexts, the indicators of empowerment at the level of the individual woman and her household, community and national level may be useful (UNESCO Institute for Education, 1995).

Women's empowerment is a complex and evolving concept that is constantly being defined, redefined, elaborated, sharpened and clarified. It is deeply inter-linked with gender equality and equity which appear to be the ultimate goals of women empowerment. It has been associated with the structural transformation of society through land and labour reforms, educational opportunities, access to resources, autonomy, the right to decision-making, control over fertility and women's own control over their bodies, sexuality, and reproduction. Empowerment is context-dependent, and one vague and abstract notion of empowerment cannot be imposed on all contexts across space and time. It is a malleable concept which can signify different things in varying and multiple contexts: thus it eludes a clear and concise definition (Saigol, 2011). The Commission on Women and Development (2007) has defined four aspects of empowerment assets (power to); knowledge and know-how (power to); will (internal power) and capacity (informal power and power with).

A problematic aspect of women's empowerment is the question of how to measure and quantify this abstract and intangible concept. The UNDP's Human Development Report of 1995 introduced two new complementary indices: the Gender-related Development Index (GDI) and the Gender Empowerment Measure (GEM). The GDI indicator measures the inequalities between men and women in terms of access to basic needs. GEM evaluates women's access to political and economic posts. In 2010, HDR, GDI and GEM indices were superseded by the Gender Inequality Index (GII), a composite measure reflecting inequality in achievements between women and men in three dimensions: reproductive health, empowerment and the labour market (UNDP, 2010).

There is a need to ensure equality of opportunities, resources and outcomes to both male and female in an unbiased manner. Gender equality and empowerment of women play a critical role in development through a multiplier process; an empowered woman not only empowers her family, she empowers the society as well. However, women's empowerment does not merely mean their upliftment and providing opportunities to them in the context of basic human rights; it is an environment, which ensures the full freedom to make use of these opportunities and in which equality with men can be enjoyed by all women everywhere (Chakrabarti and Biswas, 2012).

Gender justice entails to eliminate man-made inequalities and discrimination by extending equal opportunities to socio-economic and political resources to women. It entails ending the inequalities between women and men that are produced and reproduced in the family, community, market and the State. It also requires the gender mainstreaming in institutions—from justice to economic policy-making, which are accountable for tackling injustice and discrimination against poor and marginalised women (UNIFEM, 2010).

The most substantive aspect of gender justice demands not only emancipation but also ensuring social security as well as safeguarding the modesty and integrity of women through an effective constitutional, institutional and social awareness mechanism. Violence against women cuts across all regions, religions, races, castes, classes and communities.

However, the atrocities and ill-treatment experienced by women in comparison to their male counterparts is one of the biggest challenges in developing societies including that of India. A woman has been treated merely as a commodity and has not only been faced challenges for her dignity and pride in the wider public space but, has been equally harassed and ill-treated for varieties of reasons within the narrow confines of her own house. Women have been deliberately marginalised in their inherent socio-economic and political prerogatives under the pretext of male dominated stereotype mindset. Despite the fact that women nurture the society as a *Janani* (mother), they are made to suffer social preclusion. This exclusion leads to their socio-economic deprivation as well as political marginalisation.

Indian social system is still predominantly based on patriarchal norms. It is mainly ruled by an ideology of female subordination (the Confucian Three Bonds of Obedience—to father when young, to husband when married, and to son when old—are the same and as abiding as the tenets of Manu, the ancient codifier of Hindu social laws). This system accordingly compose patriarchal families, with the economic controls (of land, capital, and the labour processes of women and children) firmly in male hands (Bardhan, 1985).

The most cherished universal values of liberty, equality, justice and human rights have remained only in theory with their very little implementation in practice. Discrimination against women in comparison to men, in terms of distribution of social entitlements, values, resources, capabilities and honours remain one of the most substantive issues in a society. Gender-based fair and equitable assurance of justice in socio-economic and political domain remains a great challenge that women face from womb to tomb.

Amartya Sen (1999) transformed the discourse on development when he argued that development is not only about raising people's incomes or reducing poverty, but rather, it involves a process of expanding freedom equally for all people. Viewed from this perspective, gender equality is intrinsically valued. The near-universal ratification and adoption of the Convention on the Elimination of All Forms of Discrimination against Women (CEDAW) 2—and the subsequent commitment of the international community to Millennium

Development Goals 3 and 5—underscores a near-global consensus that gender equality and women's empowerment are development objectives in their own rights (World Bank, 2012).

According to Oxfam analysis, gender inequality and lack of women empowerment are key causes of poverty worldwide, which seriously constrains the futuristic wealth creation (Oxfam, 2010). In India, poverty reduction, participation and women empowerment has transcending impacts on one another. Empowering women is an important pre-requisite to poverty reduction in India. The experience of Self-Help Groups (SHGs) has been quite encouraging to empower women, and economic development and increased economic profile further enabled women to increase presence in the decision-making processes (Reddy and Reddy, 2008). Increased deliberative presence in political decision-making would further empower women and add to poverty reduction.

There have been increased efforts from central as well as state governments to increase the participation of women in various spheres of socio-economic and political domain. More women in politics will bring a new culture and discipline into politics, which in turn, will encourage greater participation by women. More women in power at all levels will ensure that women's needs get higher priority. The need to have better representation of women in decision-making bodies is to advance their struggle for basic rights including food, work and a life free from violence inside and outside the home. The increasing number of women representatives in the Parliament and State Legislative Assemblies (SLAs) will make the dreams of the founders of our Constitution come true.

In many developing countries (especially in South Asia), one strategy which has been found to be promising for women empowerment is participatory institution building in the self-help groups, often coupled with savings and micro-credit loans (ESCAP, 2003). Swain and Wallentin (2007) identified two mechanisms through which micro-finance leads to women empowerment—direct and indirect empowerment effects. The direct empowerment through micro-finance takes place, when women become members of a group and/or when they are exposed to training or workshops leading to greater awareness creation. Micro-finance also leads to an increase in women empowerment through indirect channels.

Further, the supposed success of SHGs in empowering women has supplanted other empowering strategies by government and non-government actors. When implemented in its ideal form, such programmes do have the potential to empower women to varying degrees. However, this potential is limited by the persistence of a top-down orientation in SHG programme application (Jakimow and Kilby, 2006). Economic empowerment provides incentives to change the pattern of traditional behaviour to which a woman is bound as a dependent member of the household. Economic empowerment provides incentives to change the pattern of traditional behaviour to which a woman is bound as a dependent member of the household (UNFPA, 2005).

Rising percentage of women in political decision-making ingrass-root institutions resonate the importance of constitutional and statutory amendments such as 73rd amendment in transforming the women's stature to a more constructive and creative level (Mohanty, 1995). Though, it is a paradox that while the percentage of women participation has increased but they are still far from the actual decision-making process (Singh and Bakshi, 2007).

In addition, there is a need to ensure greater participation of women in public sphere through active welfare policy formation and implementation through institution level. Presently, there are a large numbers of women-centered welfare policies in both rural and urban sectors which need focused strategy to accrue desired result. The National Policy for the empowerment of women (2001) aims to bring about the advancement, development and empowerment of women in socio-economic and political arena. The policy objectives primarily highlight exploring an environment through positive economic and social policies for full development of women to enable them to realise their full potential; ensuring equal access to health care, ensuring quality education at all levels; and elimination of discrimination and all forms of violence against women and girl child (Nayak, 2012).

More importantly, the focus on women empowerment has to be aimed at rural development. Rural India holds a bedrock position in transforming the national economy to a formidable and self-reliant level. Agriculture and allied sectors are the backbone of rural economy and women play significant role in these sectors. Therefore, the role of women needs to be addressed with adequate attention, while considering their valuable shares, which is not included and counted.

Women contribution to the socio-economic and political sphere is eminent and inalienably significant. Women constitute almost half of the total global population. However, the actual participation of women in all spheres of human interactions has been extremely poor. The percentage of women in organised work-force is highly negligible.

Women contribute to 66 percent of the world's work, produce 50 percent of the global food, but receive only 10 percent of the income output and own just one percent of the property (UNICEF, 2007).

In the case of India, the scenario is quite dismal as the participation of women in socio-economic and political domain is extremely minimal and marginalised. Women are primarily employed in unorganised sector than organised sector. The highly restrictive culture of Indian society has been a major factor for low participation of women in public sector. Women are predominantly engaged in agricultural and informal household labour. A woman is also a real incubator of rural economy, which serves as the backbone of Indian economy. Women constitute 32.2 percent of the total workforce and among them 72.8 percent are employed in agriculture as against 48.8 percent men. Women workers are predominantly in the informal sector with a share of about 91.2 percent. Women contribute 23.4 percent of the GDP in the informal sector and 16.2 percent in the formal sector. The overall contribution of women to the GDP remains about 19.8 percent (Raveendran, 2010).

According to Understanding Gender Equality in India—2012 Report, it is not just at home that women face discrimination. Our Constitution is not spared either. Women occupy less than 8 percent of the Cabinet positions, less than 9 percent of seats in high courts and Supreme Court and less than 12 percent of administrators and managers are women. The issue of multidimensional poverty is extremely contextual to the status of women in India because although a lot of work has been done on the condition of women, the position of women still remains unaddressed (Dhar, 2012).

India, after independence, was set to move ahead with liberal democratic model with focus on social welfare economy. The constitution of India made various statutory provisions to empower women by providing equal rights and opportunities to them. The constitution of India not only guarantees equality to women but also authorises the state governments to initiate protective measures against women discrimination. These measures are well defined in Preamble, Fundamental Rights, Fundamental Duties and Directive Principles which extend enough safeguards and opportunities to ensure equality and justice to women. Article 14 of the Constitution of India guarantees equality before law; Article 15 prohibits discrimination on the grounds of sex; Article 16 provides equality of opportunity for all citizens in matters relating to employment. In the institutional domain too, women empowerment has remained a key issue of concern before the successive state and central government (Bakshi, 2005).

However, in practice the entire gamut of women empowerment remained too far from desired ends. Though, women participation in socio-economic and political milieu has increased in recent times but they are still far from decision-making processes. The patriarchal values and gender based social alienation in many parts of rural India are still prevalent. However, up to certain extent, the constitutional and institutional efforts have succeeded in changing the face of rural women while providing access to education, health-care facilities and legal protection against domestic violence.

In nutshell, women empowerment is a multi-faceted and multi-dimensional phenomenon where one aspect of empowerment has transcending impacts on others. There is a need for more rigorous research to further boost-up the campaign for women empowerment in the 21st century. Empowering women essentially needs a critical transformation of social values through a wider participation and support from civil society organisations, NGOs, community participation, mass media and community itself. Finally, political empowerment through increased participation in decision-making in local, state and central level is also vital for the realisation of gender justice while understanding the diverse contour of gender main-streaming.

In a progressive and developed society, women must enjoy equal social, economic and political status. The empowerment of women is a pre-requisite for achieving sustainable development, pro-poor growth as well as, achieving all the Millennium Development Goals. Gender equality and empowered women are catalysts for multiplying the development efforts. Thus, it can be concluded that no nation can achieve its goals while discriminating against half of the human race.

The present book is an attempt to analyse diverse facets of women empowerment by applying an integrated approach towards achieving the desired end. The volume covers a whole array of social, economic, political, legal and psychological aspects of women empowerment and gender justice.

Pankaj Dodh, in his paper, examines the gravity of theoretical contribution that Feminist literature (both from Eastern and Western world) has/had extended to the liberation and empowerment of women from the supposedly male dominated modern rationality cult. The paper analyses the theoretical and conceptual application of feminism to the actual liberation and emancipation of women from contemporary socio-economic and political discourses. Reconstruction and rationalisation of socially constructed public and private spheres of action is central to the contemporary debate on feminist emancipation. The study proceeds with the analysis of predominant feminist strands and their preferred understandings regarding gender equality.

R.K. Mahajan in his paper focuses on the enhanced capabilities and participation of women in microfinance sector through Self-Help Groups (SHGs). The study underpins the conceptual framework of microfinance, SHGs and women empowerment in Punjab. The paper analyses the impact of the microfinance programme on social, political and psychological empowerment of women. The study highlights how microfinance programme is an innovative method of providing collateral free micro loans to the poor rural women. The present study shows that microfinance programme has empowered women economically, socially, psychologically and politically more as compared to the non-participants. The beneficiaries of the programme have higher levels of employment, income and participation in household financial decision-making leading to their economic empowerment. In the nutshell, the author avers that the emergence of microfinance in India and its applicability through SHGs has immensely contributed in empowering women socially, economically and politically. He also highlights that lack of proper guidance, skill training, supervision and marketing facilities has restricted the impact of microfinance programme on women empowerment.

Neeraj Sharma analyses the role of microfinance, self-help groups in empowement of women in the rural areas. His study highlights that empowerment is a social action process that promotes participation of people, organisations and communities in gaining control over their lives in their community. Empowering of women pre-supposes a dynamic and democratic change in the perception and expectations from women in our society. Mobilisation of women through SHGs is considered a major strategy of development and empowerment of women both by policy-makers and social scientists. The study highlights that despite a formal banking system in the rural areas, a large number of poor remain outside their preview and thus need was felt to have an alternative mechanism to meet the requirements of rural poor especially women. The limitations of the formal and informal financial sector in providing financial services to the needy and poor rural women have led to the emergence and extension of micro-credit programmes in the developing countries like India. The author demonstrates that micro-finance has become one of the most effective interventions for economic empowerment of the women. It plays a very important role in simultaneously addressing both poverty alleviation and women's empowerment. The empowerment of women through SHGs gives benefits not only to the individual women but also to the entire family and community. The paper suggests that the SHGs empower women both socially and economically. They not only mobilise and organise women at grass root level and provide access to supportive activities, but also prepare women to take up challenging tasks. It is through creating livelihood opportunities for the rural women that they can be empowered and the micro-finance and self-help groups can become a better means through which their living conditions can be improved.

Ramna's paper evaluates the impact of MGNREGS in empowering women in the rural areas. The study highlights that in India more than four-fifth of all working women in the rural areas are engaged in agriculture but their contribution is not documented. Rural female unemployment has also been on the rise, and is higher than rural men's unemployment rate. The paper elucidates the fact that MGNREGA has provided an opportunity for women to work in their villages and get equal minimum wages. It appears that while men often manage to move out into other activities or migrate to other areas in search of work, women have fewer options. They remain as a flexible labour force in agriculture—as own account workers, casual agricultural labour or unpaid family workers. There are so many reasons like socio-cultural norms around women's work, mobility and intra household allocations of roles and responsibilities, individual household factors like levels of care responsibilities and number of adult women in the house, health status, opportunity costs, other market opportunities and market wages for men and women, efficiency of implementation and information flows to and within households etc., which are responsible for different women's participation across states. The author suggests that in order to make MGNREGS more effective, government should increase the minimum wage rate paid under it.

In his paper, Arup Jyoti Sharma emphasises upon the important linkage between globalisation and gendered dimensions of poverty and proposes several steps for facilitating the empowerment of women in a globalised world. In order to systematise the discussion, the author has divided the paper into different parts. In Part-I, the author discusses about the women centred or so called *feminist* approach towards globalisation. Part-II highlights the policies for implementation to promote gender equality in general and women empowerment in particular. Finally, the Part-III emphasises on the question—how far the country has achieved 'women empowerment'? Is it still a dream or reality? The author expresses his optimism while saying, women empowerment is not a myth but, still a lot needs to be done from all quarters to achieve gender equality and women empowerment.

Gurinder Kaur attempts to study the declining child sex ratio in India. The paper pinpoints that a decline in the child sex ratio for the age group 0-6 years has crossed all the limits and has remained alarmingly at its lowest as per 2011 census. The decline in child sex ratio was pronounced only in the north-western states in 2001 but according to the 2011 census this phenomenon has spread to all of the states and union territories of the country. The child sex ratio has declined to 914 in 2011, whereas it was 927 in 2001. The author highlights that the main reasons for decline in the child sex ratio are many, but the most important are the presence of strong son preference, law of inheritance in the favour of girls, small size of family and huge demand of dowry. Some policy implications have been outlined for the improvement in child sex ratio in the country to bring the girls into the main stream of child population. The study suggests that mind set-up of the society needs to be changed towards the girl child along with providing free education for the female child to make her self-reliant.

Anupama in her paper focuses on gender discrimination in labour market. The paper has observed the quantitative as well as qualitative changes in participation of female workforce in India during last one and a half decade and found that the work participation rate for women has remained very low in India and these opportunities further constrained during the period of crisis. The study highlights that gender-bias was common in the labour market and conditions are unfavourable towards women. The paper pinpoints fact that women were paid less as compared to men even in same type of work and there was a negative shift in occupational structure against women as their share in non-agricultural occupations has declined. The author highlights the fact that the patriarchal societies should invest more and more in health and education in general and that of women in particular. At the same time there should be more emphasis on reducing the gender gap in access to such facilities. The author argued that any type of crisis in the economy pushes further the already marginalised groups including women to the margins of the margins. So, there is need to mitigate the social inequalities in order to achieve economic equalities.

Apra's paper deals with gender inequalities in employment in unorganised manufacturing sector of India. The paper is divided into five sections. Introduction and review of related literature have been discussed in Sections I and II respectively and Section III deals with sources and methodology. Section IV discusses the gender inequalities in employment in the unorganised manufacturing sector and Section V presents conclusions drawn from the analysis. The study highlighted that unorganised sector provides employment to more than 90 percent of the total work force and increasingly large portion of women are absorbed by this sector. The study reveals that although the female labour force participation has increased and sex segregation of total employment has declined in the unorganised manufacturing sector of India, yet their access to decent economic opportunities is frequently constrained, particularly in paid employment category. The women have larger share in unpaid and part time jobs in the unorganised manufacturing sector of India. The author analyses that no doubt, female employment has been increasing with the gigantic growth of unorganised sector, but the type of jobs they are getting are far low in quality than the male workers.

Sanjay Sindhu and Veena Kumari discuss the gender justice and status of women under the Constitution of India. The gender-based discrimination represents the ugly face of the society. This issue is global with varying degree and very old. It is a travesty of all cannons of social justice and equality that woman who constitute half of the world's population and who work two-third of the world working hours should earn just one-tenth of the world's property and also should remain victim of inequality and injustice. This all indicated towards the gender injustice. The question of gender injustice is a very old and burning problem of the world. In this paper, the authors made sincere attempt to highlight the status of women under the constitution of India, 1950. The constitution of India safeguards women's rights by putting her at par with man socially, economically and politically. The principle of the gender equality is enshrined in the constitution in its Preamble, Fundamental Rights, Directive Principles of State Policy and Fundamental Duties, with some other provisions like right to vote, reservation in local self-government. Still there is a very wide gap between the goals enunciated in the constitution, legislature, programmes and related mechanism on the one hand and situational reality of the status of women in India on the other. The authors pinpoint that no doubt the women are empowered by the constitution as well as many other laws in India but ironically, most of them are limited to books only. They suggested that all these provisions should be implemented strictly for achieving gender justice as well as for enhancing the socio-economic status of women.

Gauri Sharma analyses the social, economic, political and cultural perspectives of women in ancient and medieval India. This study points out that in the Vedic period they enjoyed a pride place in the society. They shared an equal, if not a higher, status than their men folk enjoying liberty that had societal sanction. The dishonorable place of the women in the society started in the post-Vedic period. These sources indicate that the world of women during this time started becoming restricted on account of the existing patriarchal set-up. The age is marked by marginalisation of their role in society and nothing but, implicit obedience and subordination was expected from her which finally led to her seclusion. They were treated as subordinates to men. During Islamic period, they had legal and inheritance rights and they were confined to purdah, polygamy and harem but the women of royal descent were more powerful than ordinary Muslim women. She highlighted that no doubt the socio-economic and political status of women has undergone various changes from ancient to medieval but while studying the position of women status at present, the past cannot be ignored.

Vivek Negi's paper, "Vedanta: Key to Empowerment" is an experiment to discover and rouse the latent storehouse of power in the man and the woman. The iconographic depiction of Lord Siva being awakened with the touch of foot of Goddess Kali in Indian mythological aesthetics emphasises the fact that unless one experiences the topsy-turviness of life, one cannot attain the state of *Annubhuti* (realisation). The woman can find the thrust of power inside her only if she establishes perfection in her anima and animus, or the eros and her logos. Being deeply feminine within she must act like Siva outside—slow to anger but once roused, going hammers and tongs after the evil in the world. She has to be the voyager undertaking the Campbellion journey of the hero. She will have to fit all the stages of the hero archetype. The initiation falls in 'Ego Dissolution', followed by 'Ego-Shadow Resolution' by encountering the opposites and shadows in herself. These encounters will make her strive towards 'Anima Recognition' and finally attain 'Wholeness'.

Prithpal Kaur highlights in her paper that violence against women is a permanent phenomenon form medieval to present era. The study has pinpointed that violence against women was basically due to assumption of superior position of men to women. The study reveals that historically the women were subjected to various kinds of deprivation and discrimination. The areas of discrimination include health, education and other aspects of social-economic life. The situation is worse in the rural areas as compared to urban areas. Despite their contribution in various fields, very little has been done or given to encourage women to emerge from the society. There is no dearth of laws to protect women's right but the implementation part is quite weak. The study points out that during medieval period due to the fear of invaders, Indian women started using 'Pardah' which further deteriorated their status. The use of technologies like amniocentesis and ultrasound to know the sex of the foetus has resulted into problem of declining sex-ratio. Government has introduced various laws to protect the women like Prenatal Diagnostic Technique Act but implementation of these rights is weak. The study suggested that gender development required sensitisation and political will.

Ravita and Jagdev Singh highlight that discrimination against women has been an important factor for female vulnerability in the society. The authors point out that the adverse female-to-male sex ratio in India has attracted considerable academic and policy concern in the recent years. The phrase "missing women", coined by Amartya Sen, refers to the observation that in parts of the developing world, the ratio of women to men is suspiciously low. In India, where no generalisation apply to nation's regional, religious and social and economic groups, issue of improving health, empowerment of women, gender discrimination and violence against women has great importance. The paper points out that poor gender ratio continue to be a challenge to planners and policy-makers.

Shishir Kumar Yadav and Sonal Pandey in their paper attempt to explore the major factors leading to the vulnerability of the women to disasters. The popular disaster discourse presents the 'victims' as a univariate category, thus downplaying the role of social constructs such as caste, class or gender in aggravating the vulnerability to disasters popularly known as the 'social vulnerability'. The paper evaluates that universally, women and children are the most vulnerable in disaster situation as the afflicted world in which we live is characterised by deeply unequal sharing of the burden of adversities between women and men. Sprawling inequalities persist in their access to education, health care, physical and financial resources and opportunities in the political, economic, social, and cultural spheres. The authors claim that 'vulnerability of women' should be understood to be primarily cultural and organisational rather than biological or physiological. According to the 'Social Vulnerability Approach', disaster does not create specific vulnerability for women but exacerbate the pre-existing gender inequality. The paper demonstrates that, all women are not universally or identically impacted by disasters. Adolescents, pregnant women, lactating mothers, the disabled, and the aged make up particularly vulnerable groups in emergencies.

Kamalini Mukhopadhyaya in her paper tries to locate the health goals of MDGs in the genealogy of discourses of women's health in India, and analyses whether MDGs as an international commitment are relevant for the Third World, especially India, as is often claimed. The author attempts to show the narrow and restricted understanding of the MDGs by engaging with the goal concerning maternal mortality. The paper begins by tracing the concern for maternal health and interventions in the field from the colonial period. There was a clear demarcation in the availability of the services to the rich and to the poor women. Even after independence, this differential provision of health services exists. Maternal mortality needs to be addressed as part of women's overall health, which in turn is determined by her social and economic location. Thus, a much more comprehensive strategy will be a strong primary health care along with necessary welfare services, employment, minimum wages and food security. It will not only help in reducing extreme poverty and hunger, but will also address the very cause of the determinants of all mortality including that of maternal mortality.

Dharma Pal and Gian Singh in their paper have tried to analyse the socio-economic conditions and occupational structure of women labourers from 498 sample households in rural Punjab during 2010-11. The paper reveals that the socio-economic conditions of the women labourers in rural Punjab are very miserable. Majority of the sampled women labourers (47.59 percent) fall in the age group of 30 to 44 years. Almost three-fourths (72.89 percent) of the women labourers are illiterate and about 80 percent belong to the scheduled caste category. The pattern and composition of sectoral employment of the women labourers reveals that the majority of women labourers in rural Punjab are not able to find sufficient amount of work in agriculture sector alone and employed in non-agriculture sectors also. In agriculture sector, the women labourers get on an average 70.44 days of employment in a year. They get only seasonal employment in agriculture sector. The women labourers are involved only in crop production activities. The field survey reveals that the labourers work for 10-12 hours per day in the busy season, while in slack season; they worked for 7-8 hours per day. Moreover, in non-agriculture sector, the women labourers adopt the occupation of domestic servant, brick kiln, construction and other activities such as vending vegetables/fruits, helping in shoe-making or white-washing, etc. Some of them are engaged in local industries and

MGNREGS. The author suggests that Quality education should be provided to the children of the women labourers so that they may get jobs in the non-agriculture sectors and help their family members in improving their socio-economic conditions. The government and non-government agencies should take necessary steps to organise skill development programmes for women labourers to enhance their earning capacity.

The analysis of Sanjeev Kumar and Kusum Kumari provides a vivid explanation of changing dynamism in socio-economic and political empowerment of women in Panchayati Raj Institutions (PRIs). The study concentrates on empowering women through increased participation of women in PRIs. The paper emphasises to find out the participation and involvement of women in the grassroot politics. The paper seeks to do this in the context of the socio-economic and political profile of these new 'representatives' of rural women. More emphasisingly, the study is to cover the socio-economic and political profile of women in grassroot politics in the state of Himachal Pradesh in general and the Kangra district in particular. The authors are of the opinion that, the institutional diffusion, especially the 73rd amendment, has been a major catalyst to transform the socio-economic and political status of women in India.

The analysis of Baldev Negi and Mast Ram initiates the discussion with generalising gender empowerment as an academic discipline and the need to strengthen the concept of women empowerment and gender justice in practical sphere. The authors argue that the definition of women's status is measured using different indicators in different frameworks. The frameworks used to study status were defined more by default than discourse: the parameters used by a given study or analysis become the *de facto* definition of the framework to study status. The paper concentrates on sectoral approach for analysing the situation of women *vis-à-vis* men in some key sectors such as demographic, economic and work, education, health and political status. The major highlights of the study remain on analysing socio-economic and political empowerment of women through increased female participation in public domain in Himachal Pradesh.

Naorem Arunibala Devi and K.R. Nayar's paper underpins women's multiple contribution in managing their household in the state, Manipur and whether or not their valuable services are counted or left uncounted due to several reasons among the women weavers. In the context of this study, the socio-cultural aspects and the role of the government towards the welfare of the weavers have been emphasised.

The authors are of the view that, the Women's economic participation is a way which saves them from complete dependency and this has been reported by the women respondents as well. However, without having any power to bargain and negotiate their interest with others, within and outside the household, their earnings still remain too weak to achieve the level of empowerment among these women weavers who are toiling hard to sustain the livelihood of the whole family. The authors infer that work participation and income generation cannot be considered as magic bullets for women's empowerment within a society such as Manipur where patriarchy still rules.

The analysis of Barasa Deka and Anubhab Sarmah proceeds with the theoretical generalisation about achieving gender equality in India. The evaluation of authors draws that the patriarchal structures and the values legitimising gender inequality has raised various questions regarding the availability of public space for women in our society or how well they are able to capitalise this space in order to become agents of change and empower themselves. The paper tries to analyse the status of women in North-East India. The paper argues that, inspite, the absence of age old social evils of Indian society like; casteism, dowry and child marriage that women enjoy a degree of autonomy in economic and social sphere. Women of North-East suffer from patriarchal domination in all spheres of life. As the women are caught into this kind of conflict situation specially perpetrated by the intra-state actors, what kind of victimhood and suffering they undergo and how do they take initiatives to overcome this situation are the major thrust of the paper. The paper attempts to discuss the role of women in conflict situation and their initiative to bring peace. Thus, it is an attempt to see their journey from victimhood to agency. The authors argue that this agency in terms of giving them a public space to negotiate peace is no way a guarantee of gender equality in the societies of North-East India.

Jasdeep Singh Toor, Ranvir Singh and Bhagwant Singh in their paper evaluate the racial discrimination experienced by the women from north- east India. The authors have tried to analyse various factors responsible for gender discrimination against north-east women in major metropolitan cities of India. The study highlights how the historical, geographic, demographic and socio-economic distinctiveness serve as vital factors responsible for discrimination against women of north-east. The study also focuses on the lack of a stringent legal and administrative mechanism to protect women from criminals and offenders. Finally, the emphasis remained on the preventive and curative measures in which strengthening of security architecture, rapid judicial action against the lawbreakers and to create greater awareness to fight the scourge of discrimination against women through civil society participation.

References

Bakshi, P.M. (2005), *The Constitution of India*, New Delhi: Universal Law Publishing Company.

Bardhan, Kalpana (1985), "Women's Work, Welfare and Status: Forces of Tradition and Change in India", *Economic and Political Weekly*, Vol. 20, No. 50, pp. 2207-20.

Chakrabarti, Snigdha and Chaiti Sharmab Biswas (2012), "An Exploratory Analysis of Women's Empowerment in India: A Structural Equation Modelling Approach", *Journal of Development Studies*, 48:1, pp.164-80.

Commission on Women and Development (2007), "The Women Empowerment Approach: A Methodological Guide", 'Gender and Indicators' Working Group, June 2007.

Dhar, Aarti (2012), "Some Poignant Pointers", *The Hindu*, March 27.

ESCAP (2003), 'Social Safety Nets for Women', United Nations Publication.

Gavey, N. (1989), "Feminist Post-structurism and discourse Analysis: Contribution to Feminist Psychology", *Psychology of Women Quarterly*, Vol. 13, No. 4, pp. 459-75.

Jakimow, Tanya and Patrick Kilby (2006), "Empowering Women: A Critique of the Blueprint for Self-Help Groups in India", *Indian Journal of Gender Studies*, 13:3, pp. 375-400.

Mohanty, B. (1995), "Panchayati Raj, 73rd Constitutional Amendment and Women", *Economic and Political Weekly*, Vol. 30, No. 52, pp. 3346-50.

Mukundarajan,V.N. (2010), "Gender Equality is Passé, Let Us Usher in Gender Partnership", *The Hindu*, September 26.

Nayak, A.P. (2012), "Women Empowerment: Myth and Reality" Online Web: http://EzineArticles.com/?expert=Ashok_Priyadarshi_Nayak Accessed on August 11, 2012.

OECD (2010), Accelerating Progress Towards the MDGs through Pro-Poor Growth: Policy Messages from the DAC Network on Poverty Reduction, Paris: OECD.

Oxfam (2010), Women Empowerment: Mainstreaming and Networking, The Hague.

Raveendran, G. (2010), "Contribution of Women to the National Economy", *ILO Asia-Pacific Working Paper Series*, ILO Sub-Regional Office for South Asia, New Delhi.

Rawls, J. (1999), "A Theory of Justice," United States: Harvard University Press.

Reddy, C.S. and Reddy, M.B.S. (2008), "Poverty Reduction and Women Empowerment: Role of SHG Federations in Urban Areas", *National Workshop on Urban Poverty Eradication Strategies,* Regional Center for Urban and Environmental Studies, Osmania University, Hyderabad.

Saigol, Rubina (2011), "Women's Empowerment in Pakistan: A Scoping Study", Aurat Foundation, with the financial support of United States Agency for

International Development (USAID).

Selden, R. *et al.*, (2005), *A Reader's Guide to Contemporary Literary Theory*, 5th Edition, United Kingdom: Pearson Education Limited.

Sen, Amartya (1999), *Development as Freedom*, Oxford: Oxford University Press.

Singh, S. and Bakshi, S. (2007) "Impact of 73rd Amendment Act on Women Empowerment—A Study of Punjab and Haryana", *Guru Nanak Journal of Sociology*, Vol. 28, No. 1-2, pp. 56-57.

Swain, Ranjula Bali and Fan Young Wallentit (2007), "Can Microfinance Empower Women? Self-Help Groups in India", ADA Dialogue, No. 37, May 2007, pp. 61-82.

Taneja, Sonia, Pryor, Mildred Golden and Humphreys John (2009), "Empowerment from the Gender Perspective", *Delhi Business Review*, Vol. 10, No. 2, pp.17-26.

UNDP (2002), *The Human Development Report, 2002,* New York and Oxford: Oxford University Press

UNESCO Institute for Education (1995), "Women, Education and Empowerment: Pathways towards Autonomy", edited by Carolyn Medel Anonuevo, Report of the International Seminar held at UIE, Hamburg, Germany.

UNFPA (2005), "Women's Economic Empowerment: Meeting the Needs of Impoverished Women", Workshop Report, *United Nations Population Fund,* New York.

UNICEF (2007), "Gender Equality—The Big Picture," Online Web: http://www.unicef.org/gender/index_bigpicture.html Accessed on August 11, 2012.

UNIFEM (2010), Gender Justice: Key to Acheving the Millennium Development Goals, New York, USA. Available at: www.unwomen.org/wp-content/uploads/2010/on/UNIFEM-MDG-Brief-2010.pdf.

United Nations (2008), *The Millennium Development Goals Report, 2008,* United Nations Department of Economic and Social Affairs, New York.

United Nations Development Programme (2010), *Human Development Report, 2010—The Real Wealth of Nations: Pathways to Human Development*, New York.

World Bank (2007), *Global Monitoring Report, 2007,* Washington, DC.

World Bank (2012), *Toward Gender Equality in East Asia and the Pacific: A Companion to the World Development Report,* Conference Edition. Washington, DC.

World WYCA and UNFPA (2006), "Empowering Young Women to Lead Change: A Training Manual", Geneva.

Theorising Gender: A Way to Women Empowerment and Gender Justice

Pankaj Dodh

Introduction

Gender equality remains a key theoretical and operational paradigm in the contemporary socio-economic and political discourses. 'Women hold up half of the sky', yet, their visibility have been considerably low and marginalised in the wider public domain. The historically, socially and culturally constructed value system predominantly emanates the prevalence of the patriarchal dominance in all spheres of human life. Women, as a biological sex, have been denied to their essential human rights under the enlightenment discourses of rationality.

A woman, through the myopic subjectively posturing of modernity, as the post-modernists argue, has been stereotyped as kind, affectionate, submissive and emotional, which could hardly run the affairs in the wider public sphere. A man, in contrast, was supposed to be more rational who is capable to lead and dictate command in socio-economic and political arena. Women were deliberately kept out of pubic life in the gender biased patriarchal society. The socially and culturally constructed male and female value dichotomy has led to the exploitation of women in different spheres of life.

Similarly, in the academic world, the contribution of women, in the growth and expansion of political theory, has been marginalised and the history is embedded with the exagerated male theoretic prejudice. The observations of Shanley and Pateman show that the ideas of William Godwin and Jean Paul Sartre figure prominently in the courses of political theory than, equally important Liberal feminist work of their partners; Mary Wollstonecraft and Simone de Beauvoir (Mckinnon, 2008).

However, the spread of modern education and democratisation of political institution in the 18th Century Europe, and, the emergence of the United States of America as a catalyst to challenge exploitation of women in domestic and public life has invoked a new realisation toward feminist emancipation in the developed world. The spread of public institutions, mass media and the reformism in the West, has essentially galvanised the feminist movement in the European world. The increased visibilities of women in the political life further intensified the efforts towards socio-economic and political inclusion of women.

The patriarchal and misogynist mind-set of the society received scything protest and criticism with the advent of democratic regimes in all parts of the world today. The continues subjugation of women, over the extended period of history, received sharp resistance as, the democratic values of the universal human rights, individual rationality and equality, received wider acceptability in the civil society. The prevailing discriminatory social norms were fervently challenged in both theoretical and practical stand-points especially, in the 20th Century (Ramaswamy, 2003). The gradual expansion of democratic rights, women participation in various political activities and the universalisation of modern education worked as a major catalyst toward women empowerment in the contemporary era.

On the theoretical perspective, feminist theory seeks to portray a realistic picture of a woman's condition in the so-called patriarchal society. The feminists are reluctant to accept that, inequality is natural and, hold that women are equal to men in terms of intellectual capacity and creative capabilities. The early feminists, most notable; the Liberal feminists, seek to eliminate all forms of discrimination against women through institutional and legal reforms.

The Liberal feminists strive for greater equality and freedom for women in both public and private spheres. Similarly, the Social feminists emphasise to increase greater harmony between private and public domain. This strand of feminism holds that, both private and public spheres are equally important in their pursuit to a stable and sustained society. Therefore, it is important to strike a proper balance and ensure greater autonomy between two distinctive concepts.

Development of Gender in the Theoretical Domain and Women Empowerment

Feminist scholarship exerts an enormous impact on the emancipation of women from the male dominated socio-economic and political structure of the society. The Feminist theories have struck a very justified and defensive reaction against prevailed gender bias in the society. The feminist theoretical assault against all forms of gender discriminations, inspired women, to strike a collective and organised offensive against their subjugation and exploitation in diverse spheres of human relationships. The gravity of feminist thoughts and its fervent desire for equality, justice and respect for the basic human rights of women inspired the political elites in the developed world (now in the developing world) to ensure a more gender sensitised institutional and systemic mechanism.

However, the issue of gender equality remained a low priority till the down of renaissance and reformism in the European world. The ancient Greek philosophers, Plato and Aristotle were greatly obsessed to explore the idea of a perfect form of government, which could ensure security and stability in the Greek city states. Subsequently, both the Greek thinkers transferred the authority to rule the state to a very few competent citizens (Okin, 1979). Therefore, the scope for gender equality remained a non-priority issue in the earliest political establishments. The middle age further worsen the scope for women emancipation amid the frequent clashed among the autocratic monarchs, powerful Feudal lords and religious clerics.

Similarly, the social contract theorists, most notably; Thomas Hobbes, John Locke and Jean Jacques Rousseau, were more inclined to justify their respective hypothesis concerned to the evolution of state and society. Gender equality continues to remain a non-priority issue in the political thinking of these philosophers. Though, Locke and Rousseau have supported the rights of equality and liberty in general term, rather than, gender specific dimension. Locke, however, rejects the divine rights of the King, but, legitimised patriarchy as divine. He made a clear distinction between public and private sphere. Patriarchal authority, as a private sphere, was deemed to be divine whereas, political power, as a public sphere, was deemed to resonate from the governed.

The public-private distinction of Locke essentially provided theoretical and operational ground for the entrenchment of patriarchal authority in both private and public spheres, which further marginalised the cause for women emancipation (Binion, 1995). Rousseau, even, excludes women from the right to citizenship (Mckinnon, 2008).

Moreover, the feminist scholarship, as an intellectual discipline, appeared in its nascent stage in the 18th and the 19th Century, primarily, in the developed countries. The expansion of modern education and establishment of democratic regimes by uprooting monarchist and authoritative rulers, led to increased participation in the public spaces in the West. The Liberal feminism, as mentioned earlier, initiated its earliest inroads against the exploitation and subjugation of women in the society. Similarly, in the socialist and Communist countries, most notable, in Cuba and Venezuela women actively participated in their respective national liberation movements. The advent of radical feminism in the 1960s further invigorated the feminist movement.

However, it was J.S. Mill, the Utilitarian thinker, who clearly supported the equal political rights for women. J.S. Mill remained a major inspiration in laying-down the foundation of Liberal feminism. Liberal feminism, along with the Marxist and the Socialist feminism continue to aspire for a society based on gender equality and the liberation of women from male dominated socio-economic and political structure of the society till the first half of the 20th Century.

Similarly, the emergence of Youth Left activists along with the Gay Liberation and the colored feminist strands in Western Europe in the early 1970s further widened the scope for women emancipator in both theoretical and practical label (Jackson and Jones, 1998).

The present study focuses broadly on various theoretical and conceptual disciplines that present their respective agenda for women emancipation over the extended period of human relationships.

Liberal Feminism

Liberal feminism, also known as first wave feminism, strives to ensure a more equitable and gender inclusive structural changes in the society. This school of thought seeks women empowerment through various legal and administrative reforms. Liberal feminism strives for the grater participation of women in the public realm. Liberal feminists, such as, Sylvya, Emmeline, Mary Wollstonecraft, Sojourner and J.S. Mill focuse their study on the legal and political rights of women (Mckinnon, 2008). This discipline demonstrates the idea of equality before law and equal representation of women in democratic institutions. Liberal feminism has tried to explain and analyse the unjustified restrictions imposed upon women in the male dominated socio-economic and political order the society. The Liberal feminism has inspired women to come out from private sphere to public life, to ensure greater participation in order to secure more power in political realm (Ostrander, 1989).

Similarly, Margret Mead's analysis focuses on the biological equality and cultivated talent of each sex. Mead seeks an equal participation of women in the areas of law and governance, religion, art and science. Her focus remains to ensure the equitable and purposeful participation of women in the fields that were historically and culturally supposed to be dominated by men (Komarovsy, 1991). One of the important objectives of liberal feminism remains to rescind the gender bias in the domain of art and aesthetics. A numbers of liberal theorists are critical to the role of art in demonstrating and perpetuating female inferiority. Women are generally considered an object of art rather than a rational and creative being, to create and evaluate the aesthetical parameters (Musgrave, 2003).

It is therefore, imperative to demonstrate that the liberal feminist scholarship dared to strike its earliest assault against the exploitation of women in both private and public sphere. Liberal feminism initiated a very fervent criticism against the persistent inequality and discrimination in the society. Consequently, public institutions were reformed and made more inclusive, democratic and egalitarian in both structural as well as functional level.

Marxist and Socialist Feminism

Marxist and Socialist feminism focuses primarily on the economic aspects of women exploitation. Marx and Engels tried to understand women operation and exploitations in terms of the nature of material production and the concept of alienation. Marxist thinking about women exploitation is essentially analogous to the alienation of the working class in a capitalistic mode of production. The powerful capitalistic exploitative culture not only prevails in the economic sphere, but is equally implied to the exploitation of women in the narrow confine of household affairs.

Engels vividly painted the picture of women subjugation in parallel to the emergence of the private property over an extending period of history. Due to the expansion of the civilization and material possessions, male succeeded to assert greater control over the exchange value of produced goods. This was further fortified with the emergence of the family, a primary unit of the society. Exclusive controls of the male over the domestic affairs as an owner of private property further worsen the condition of women. Women were complexly marginalised in socio-economic and political life. Engels therefore, suggested for the complete demolition of 'private domestic labour' and the supported the spread of 'public industry' for the liberation of women (Donovan, 2006).

Moreover, Juliet Mitchell's 'Women Estate' follows the Marxist perception regarding the exploitation of women especially, in the European world (Mitchell, 1971). One of the central themes of the Marxist feminism is that, it tries to integrate women's emancipation in the wider context of a class struggle against the capitalistic society. This strand of feminism envisages that an accumulation of wealth in the hands of few is the root causes behind an exploitation of both the proletariat and women by the dominant bourgeois. In comparison, Radical feminism refuses the Marxist's women and class alliances approach and advocates autonomy of the feminist movement (Jackson and Jones, 1998). Though, Radical feminism accepts the theoretical foundation of Marxist feminism, as, the former agrees to the latter's analysis that the exploitation of women is systematically planned and is socially constructed. Radical feminists, like Marxists, hold that inequality is not natural, but is created (Jackson, 1998).

The Neo-Marxian feminist strand galvanises the orthodox Marxism/ Marxist feminism while insisting on the significance of non-waged labour that sustain and produces labour, mostly done by women workers. Neo-Marxist demonstrates that, the patriarchal structure is not constructed only through class exploitation, but is also structured through non-waged domestic labour, prominently undertaken by women. More importantly, in the later stages, women have been employed by the capitalists in some of the gender specified labour market with far cheaper wage structure than their male counterpart. The exploitation of women in both non-waged domestic labour and gender segregated labour market provides much more capital surplus to the capitalists than male (Chafetz, 1997).

Radical Feminism and the Universalisation of the Feminist Movement

The real thrust for feminist emancipation comes from Radical strand of feminism which emerged in 1960s and continue to stimulate the gender movement till the emergence of another dominant theoretical feminist strand, Post-modernist feminism, in the 1980s (Crow, 2000). The Radical feminism tries to bridge the difference between 'public sphere' and 'private sphere'. The Radical feminists, most notably; Patterson and Okin hold that, the 'public sphere' continue remains to be controlled and regulated by the male. Similarly, 'private sphere', the family, is equally controlled by the male through patriarchal customs, and the male dominated rules and regulations in the family affairs (Millett, 1970). The prominent Radical feminists, Andrew Dworkin,

Germaine Greer, Catherine Mackinnon, S. Firestone and Mary Daly carry forward a powerful theoretical protest against the patriarchal cruelty meted upon their female counterparts. The discipline seeks a complete emancipation of women on the sex-gender variation.

The foundation of Radical feminism lies in the establishment of an egalitarian society. Radical feminism strives to obliterate the gender based public-private division of function. The public-private distinction not only prevents women from participation in public life, but also ignores the issue of domestic violence against them. Jean Grimshaw, in her article, 'Autonomy and Identity in Feminist Thinking' (1988), has expressed the similar desire, as, she said "to engage with those theories which deconstruct the distinction between the 'individual' and the 'social'; which recognise the power of desire and fantasy and the problem of supposing any 'original' unity in the self, while at the same time preserving its concern with lived experience and the practical and material struggles of women to achieve more autonomy and control in their lives" (Ahmed, 1996).

More importantly, Radical feminism not only demonstrates the idea of fair equality of opportunity, but also seeks equality of entitlements, treatment and honour (Elshtain, 1975). The observation of Juliet Mitchell, (1973) reveals the similar fact, as she demonstrates, not to conquer privilege, but to eliminate distinction. Radical feminism rejects the traditional sex-role stereotype as, boys are more active and girls are passive. Similarly, an adult male is more capable to control complex socio-economic and political conditions, whereas, the female as affectionate, caring and submissive, could better be honored as mother and wives (Komarovsky, 1991).

The main thrust for enlightenment rationality and values-related orientation received considerable influence from 17th Century French philosopher, Rene Descartes. Descartes postulates his own parameters for rationality and the level of reasoning. He divides the world dualistically into *res cogitans* and *res extensa*. *Res cogitans* demonstrates the powerful qualities as, reason, mind, spirit, objectivity, universality and logic; whereas, *Res extensa*, the extended, mechanistic world, was connected with subjectivity, emotions and intuition (Dolfsma and Hoppe, 2003). The much practiced gender bias in the modernity discourses, demonstrates the cognitive connection of *res cogitans* with the masculinity and *res extensa* with the femininity, where the latter one was undervalued as inferior to the former (Perlich, 1992).

The Radical feminists aver that, the gender inequality is not nurtured through biological sex, but is historically and culturally constructed.

Julie Nelson, (1992) highlights the existence of similar gender bias in the economic sector. Nelson asserts that the predominant characteristic of economics is metaphorically linked with the hierarchical, dualistic conception of gender and a privileging of a particular conception of masculinity. Nelson is therefore, critical to the metaphorically embedded historical and cultural value dualism that undermines the feminine qualities, constructively and rationality. Nelson defines gender distinctions as follows:

> "gender distinctions are cognitive organizers built on an experience of sexual dimorphism. As such, I see them not as created by society in order to maintain some particular order, but formed as a part of the development of human mental organization in early childhood" (Nelson, 1994).

Radical feminism seeks to eventually deconstruct the patriarchal power prevalence in both public and private spaces. Radical feminism makes a clear distinction between gender and sex. Sex stands for biological difference; while, gender is a historically and socially constructed idea. The sublime virtues of care, affection, nurture and motherliness were deliberately overshadowed by the patriarchal rationality and power. The artificially allotted 'submission' to women; and men desire to exert exclusive control over the nature, has led to the construction of a patriarchal culture, value system and an economic and political structure, as a historical process (Hierro and Marquez, 1994).

The Radical feminist thinkers want to destroy the socially constructed parameters of gender differences. The principle articulated by Catherine MacKinnon, "to see the personal as political is to see the private and political", inspire the reorientation in personal, emotive, and socio-economic and political activities of women. The reconfiguring of public and private dichotomy would ensure greater equality in personal and political domain (Ostrander, 1989).

Post-modern Feminism: A Deconstruction to Positivist Notion of Objectivity

Feminism and the Post-modernism have their own distinctive ontological, epistemological and rationality postulations with considerable divergence from Positivist school of thought. Both the theories exhibit a great deal of divergences than convergences. Feminism and the Post-modernism represent a similar Post-positivist methodological reaction against Positivist orientation. Both the school of thoughts represents critical, emancipatory and deconstructionist views against the prevailing theoretical order.

Feminism, as mentioned earlier, constructed its early intellectual foundation on the line of enlightenment discourses. The Liberal feminism is predominantly constructed by the efforts of highly educated middle class theorists in Europe and the United States of America. In the sense, feminism is essentially a product of enlightenment premise. The Feminism emerges with in modernism, and, is thus, rooted in the enlightenment narratives of self, knowledge and rationality. However, the feminist dilemma is that, it could not accept dominance of the patriarchal rationality founded by the modernist epistemology. Therefore, feminism especially, the Radical and the Marxist feminism, have been critical to enlightenment prejudice and discrimination against women in the society (Gudorf, 2004).

More interestingly, the feminist critique to gender discrimination which is legitimised in the modernity discourse provides ideological foundation to the post-modernism that is equally critical to the Positivists rationality prejudice. The post-modernism and feminist intellectual and political perceptions also reconcile in their respective skepticism regarding the notion of rationality and the universality of knowledge (Jackson and Jones, 1998). Judith Butler, a prominent post-structuralist scholar, rejects the Modernists discourses of self, subjectivity, and rationality. Butler denies any autonomous priori characteristic of self, as the Modernists demonstrates. One's 'self' is constructed and formed throughout the relational interaction with others in the society, and within the reigning power discourses (Beste, 2006). In the sense, the feminist scholarship receives a theoretical perspective from Butler to reject the Modernists orientation regarding the gender bias, rationality, self and subjectivity which is essentially patriarchal in nature.

Moreover, Feminism repudiates the post-modernism's disattachment from the 18th century European enlightenment discourses. The Post-modernist's objection of the universality of knowledge and values or the possibility of an objective science could not win place in feminist political discourses, as it, (Post-modernist's critique on the universality of knowledge and objectivity serving as vested interests) could erode the feminist contribution to women emancipation and empowerment in an historic and political perspective. Similarly, feminism differs from post-modernism on their respective understanding about identity, self and subjectivity. The Feminism perceives 'self' as continuous and embodied, a consciousness developed in relationship to others. Post-modernism, in comparison, is skeptical not only to the biological sexuality, but also rejects the very existence of the concept 'continuous self,' perpetuated by the Post-modernist feminism (Gudorf, 2004).

However, the Radical feminist reconciles with the post-modernism in their rejection and incredulity to universal truth claims of the enlightenment discourses. Feminists defy the enlightenment discourses of universalisation of the white middle class male dominance and supposedly, parochial perception of objectivity (Waugh, 1998). It is quite interesting that both the Feminism and the Post-modernism represent some of the startling similarities in their respective assault against the Positivist ontological, epistemological and methodological foundations.

The Feminism, more specifically, focuses on enlightenment and modernity value perception, subjectivity and the rationality parameters, which according to feminists scholarships, essentially, represents gender bias. The Feminists, most notably, Radical feminism and post-modern feminism rejects the socially, culturally and historically constructed sex and gender dichotomy, which prejudicially establishes male domination in the society. The feminist scholarship rejects the hypothesis that inequality of capability is natural and a man exhibits superior qualities in comparison to a woman.

Similarly, the Post-modernism provides a contextual assistance to the feminist scholarship, as, it rejects the myopic demonstration of objectivity, self and scientific knowledge presented by the modernity discourses. Post-modernism rejects the Euro-Atlantic notion of rationality which demonstrates a specific class, race and gender bias. In other words, Post-modernism apply multiple methodology instead of monologues methodology to provide an accessible platform for the silenced voices to come out onto the stage and join the discussion over a varieties of issue in the social laboratory and to egalitarianise the mainstream Positivist voice (Agger, 1991). In brief, Post-modernism extends a general assistance to a more specific gender centred feminist revolution.

Conclusion

After making a detailed analysis about the conditions of women in a theoretical standpoint, it can be concluded that, there have been growing sensitisation towards women emancipation in all parts of the world today. The drive towards the empowerment of women started in the West in the form of greater participation of women in the socio-economic and political life. The development of democratic institutions, inclusiveness in public institutions, modern education, spread of information technology and the globalisation are some of the major determinants in inspiring the modern world to ensure greater gender equality, freedom and justice.

The emergence of feminist scholarship remains a major ideological tool towards crafting a global sensitisation towards achieving freedom and justice for women. The spread of various feminist strands provides their distinctive contribution to the liberation of women and to inspire them to ensure a place of honour and dignity in a civilised society. It is the impact of powerful thoughts and ideas that has led to growing representation of women in the socio-economic and political realm. Similarly, the increased legal and statutory institutions are working as an effective guardian of the basic human rights of women.

It is equally concerning that the feminist movement lacks coherence of objectives in both the developed and the developing countries. Feminist theories, indeed, implies to the industrial world whereas, the socialistic world and the third world remains unrepresented by the most feminist theoretical imprints (Bruno, 2006). In addition, the Feminist movement lacks the unity of thoughts, actions and objectives. The absence of an organisational coherence is also a major limitation in this regard. Feminist organizations lack any global, regional and national solidarity, and are therefore fragmented in various small groups pursuing their narrow specific goals rather to concentrate on the common concerns of women empowerment.

Nevertheless, it is imperative to demonstrate that, the feminist movement holds an important place in the contemporary debate towards achieving the goal of social justice and gender equality. The growing participation of women in political decision-making and their increasing claims over the distribution of earth's resources emanates the success of feminist scholarship and empowerment of the subaltern groups in the contemporary social order. Women, not only in developed world, but also in the developing world, is emerging as a new social force working towards ensuring a better world, with respect to essential human rights, equality, justice and honour for the marginalised sections of the society. The recent Nobel peace prize conferred to the Liberian President, Ellen Johnson Sirleaf, her compatriot Leymah Gbowee and Yemeni Arab Spring activist Tawakul Karman, demonstrates the growing contribution of women in their pursuit to establish a society that is essentially embedded with the values of peace, dignity and justice.

The Norwegian Nobel Committee President, Thorbjoern Jagland, said on the occasion, "you represent one of the most important motive forces for change in today's world: the struggle for human rights in general and the struggle for wòmen for equality and peace in particular," (*The Hindu*, December 11, 2011). To sum up with an optimism that a new era of peace, progress, equality, justice and respect for human rights would prevail in the foreseeable future where women would enjoy equal socio-economic and political rights as compared to men.

References

Agger, B. (1991), "Critical Theory, Post-structuralism, Post-modernism: Their Sociological Relevance", *Annual Review of Sociology*, Vol. 17, pp. 105-31.

Ahmed, S. (1996), "Beyond Humanism and Post-modernism: Theorising a Feminist Practice", *Hypatia*, Vol. 11, No. 2, pp. 71-93.

Beste, J. (2006), "The Limits of Post-structuralism for Feminist Theology", *Journal of Feminist Studies in Religion*, Vol. 22, No. 1, pp. 5-19.

Binion, G. (1995), "Human Rights: A Feminist Perspective", *Human Rights Quarterly*, Vol. 17, No. 3, pp. 509-26.

Bruno, J.P. (2006), "Third World Critiques of Western Feminist Theory in the Post-Development Era", University of Texas at Austin.

Chafetz, J.S. (1997), "Feminist Theory and Sociology: Underutilized Contributions for Mainstream Theory", *Annual Review of Sociology*, Vol. 23 (1997), pp. 97-120.

Crow, B.A. (eds.), (2000), "Radical Feminism: A Documentary Reader", NYU Press.

Dolfsma, W. and Hoppe, H. (2003), "On Feminist Economics", *Feminist Review*, No. 75, pp. 118-28.

Donovan, J. (2006), "Feminist Theory: The Intellectual Traditions", New York: The Continuum Publishing.

Elshtain, J.B. (1975), "The Feminist Movement and the Question of Equality", *Polity*, Vol. 7, No. 4, pp. 452 77.

Gudorf, C.E. (2004), "Feminism and Post-modernism in Susan Frank Parsons" *The Journal of Religious Ethics*, Vol. 32, No. 3 (Winter, 2004), pp. 519-43.

Hierro, G. and Marquez, I. (1994), "Gender and Power", *Hypatia*, Vol. 9, No. 1, pp. 173-83.

Jackson, S. (1998), "Feminist Social Theory" in Jones, J. (eds.), *Contemporary Feminist Theories*, Edinburgh: Edinburgh University Press.

Jackson, S. and Jones, J. (1998), "Thinking of Ourselves: An Introduction to Theorizing Feminist Theory", in Jones, J. (eds.), *Contemporary Feminist Theories*, Edinburgh: Edinburgh University Press.

Komarovsky, M. (1991), "Some Reflections on the Feminist Scholarship in Sociology", *Annual Review of Sociology*, Vol. 17, pp. 1-25.

McKinnon, C. (2008), "Issues in Political Theory", New York: Oxford University Press.

Millett, K. (2000), "Sexual Politics", United States: University of Illinois Press.

Mitchell, J. (1973), "Woman's Estate", New York: Vintage Books.

Musgrave, L.R. (2003), "Liberal Feminism, from Law to Art: The Impact of Feminist Jurisprudence on Feminist Aesthetics", *Hypatia*, Vol. 18, No. 4, pp. 214-35.

Nelson, J.A. (1994), "More Thinking about Gender: Reply', *Hypatia,* Vol. 9, pp. 199-205.

Okin, S.M. (1979), "Women in Western Political Thought", United Kingdom: Princeton University Press.

Ostrander, S.A. (1989), "Feminism, Voluntarism and the Welfare State: Toward a Feminist Sociological Theory of Social Welfare", *The American Sociologist,* Vol. 20, No. 1, pp. 29-41.

Perlich, P.S. (1992), "The Political Economy of the Informal Sector: A Feminist Critique of Development Economics", Ann Arbor, MI: Bell & Howell.

Ramaswamy, S. (2003), "Political Theories: Ideas and Concepts", New Delhi: Macmillan India Ltd.

The Hindu, (2011), "Three 'Peace Warrior' Receives Their Nobel Prize", December 1, 2011, New Delhi.

Waugh, P. (1998), "Postmodernism and Feminism", in Jones, J. (eds.), *Contemporary Feminist Theories,* Edinburgh: Edinburgh University Press.

Microfinance, Self-Help Groups and Women Empowerment: A Case Study

R.K. MAHAJAN

Introduction

Most of the development and poverty alleviation programmes in India in post-independence years till 1980s were based on trickle-down effect and hardly took into consideration the gender inequality. Women constitute almost 50 percent of the total population and they are vulnerable section of the society. Women had been shadowed with male dominated development schemes since long and contributed little in the overall development of the country. Recently, most of the development schemes give equal opportunities of participation.

Microfinance programme functioning through Self-Help Groups (SHGs) is dominated by women. Keeping in view the success of microfinance programme in Bangladesh, the programme has been formally introduced in India in the year 1992. The focus of the microfinance programme on women is right step because in most of the developing countries women have a low socio-economic status. As a result the women remained laggard and less participative in the development process of the country.

Investing in women capabilities empower them to stand on their own feet and allow them to make choices independently which are warranted for growth and development. It is veritable truth that women take care of most of the familial problems and an empowered women results in higher well-being of the family. Thus women empowerment gives power or authority to challenge submissive social condition or status of the women. There is no dearth of studies conducted in Bangladesh which has given evidence that microfinance has helped in the empowerment of women.

The present paper is a modest attempt to study the microfinance, SHG and women empowerment in Punjab. The specific objectives of the study are:

1. To discuss the conceptual framework of microfinance, SHGs and women empowerment.
2. To examine the impact of the programme on social, political and psychological empowerment.
3. To prepare a composite index of empowerment.
4. To find out the determinants of women empowerment.

Self-Help Groups (SHGs) and Microfinance

The origin of SHGs is originated by Grameen Bank of Bangladesh, which was founded by Mohammed Yunus. In India, the real effort to form SHGs was made after 1991-92 from the linkage of SHGs with the banks. A SHG is a small economically homogeneous affinity group of the rural poor voluntarily coming together to save small amount regularly, which are deposited in a common fund to meet members emergency needs and to provide collateral free loans decided by the group (Abhaskumar Jha, 2000). In most of the cases these SHGs comprises of women. A monthly meeting is organised of this SHG, where apart from disbursal and repayment of loan, formal and informal discussions are held. Women share their experiences in these groups. The minutes of these meetings are documented and the accounts are written.

SHG is an organisation with the development of saving habit among women, enhances the equality of status of women, promote women as decision maker and beneficiaries in the democratic, economic, social and cultural spheres of life. (Ritu Jain, 2003) The basic principles of the SHGs are group approach, mutual trust, organisation of small and manageable groups, group cohesiveness, sprit of thrift, demand-based lending, collateral free women-friendly loan, peer group pressure in repayment, skill training capacity building and empowerment (Lalitha, 2000).

A Brief History of Microfinance in India

The concern about the development of poor in India has been the hallmark of the development strategy in India. That is why the banks were nationalised in 1969 and 1980 to help the rural poor and agricultural development. It has been observed in post-nationalisation period that a substantial amount of resources being earmarked towards meeting the credit needs of the poor. There were several objectives for the bank nationalisation strategy including expanding the outreach of financial services to neglected sectors (Singh, 2005).

In the early 1980s, Integrated Rural Development Programme (IRDP) was started with a sole aim of poverty alleviation in rural areas, which made available government subsidized credit through banks to the poor. It was aimed that the poor would be able to use the inexpensive credit to finance themselves over the poverty line.

However, most of the studies conducted by NABARD pointed towards the increase in financial exclusion. These studies also showed that the existing banking policies, systems and procedures, and deposit and loan products were perhaps not well suited to meet the most immediate needs of the poor. It was found that poor really needed was better access to credit services and products, rather than cheap subsidized credit. Against this background, the access of the poor to microfinance was made rather than just micro credit. Microcredit is loaned to a micro-entrepreneur by a bank or other institution and can be offered, often without collateral, to a group or an individual. Recently, microfinance has come to be recognised as one of the new development paradigm for alleviating poverty and economic empowerment. Over time, the microfinance industry recognised that the poor who lack access to traditional formal financial services required a variety of financial products to meet their needs, not just microcredit. So microcredit evolved into microfinance. Microfinance includes a broader range of services, such as loans, savings, insurance and transfer services (remittances) targeted at low-income clients.

Microfinance Involving Credit Linkage with Banks

(i) *SHG-Bank Linkage Model:* This model involves the SHGs financed directly by the banks viz., Commercial Banks (Public Sector and Private Sector), RRBs and Cooperative Banks.

(ii) *MFI-Bank Linkage Model:* This model covers financing of Micro Finance Institutions (MFIs) by banking agencies for on-lending to SHGs and other small borrowers.

NABARD has been playing a pivotal role in this movement of self-help groups. The SHG-Bank linkage programme which commenced as pilot programme in 1992 by NABARD with 500 SHGs has now grown exponentially over two decades. Up till March 2011, 97 million households have regular access to saving through 74.6 lakh SHGs linked to different banks. Of these, about 48 lakh SHGs also have direct access to credit from banks. As much as 82 percent of SHGs already linked with banks are exclusively women group. (NABARD, 2011)

Other than SHGs, the Joint Liability Groups have been promoted for financing to the group on the whole.

Financing of Joint Liability Groups (JLGs)

JLGs are informal groups of 4-10 members (can go up to 20, if need be) who are engaged in similar activities like crop production and who are willing to jointly undertake to repay taken by the groups from the banks. Unlike SHGs, JLGs are intended basically a credit group for tenant farmers and small farmers who do not have proper title of their farm land. Financing of JLGs was introduced as a pilot project in 2004-05 by NABARD in 8 states with the support of 13 RRBs. Amount of Rs. 24.74 crore was sanctioned as grant for promotion of 1.25 lakh JLG across the country till 31st March, 2011.

A Harsh Fact about Microfinance

There has been a lot of debate on the exorbitant rates of interest charged under microfinance programme. The 30 suicides in 45 days as Business Insider (Oct., 2010) in Andhra Pradesh have brought the operations of microfinance institutions (MFIs) a bad name. It is well documented by both print and electronic media that these debt-driven suicides were due to high rates of interest and coercive methods of loan recovery used by commercial MFIs. The commercial MFIs operate as profit-making non-banking financial corporations (NBFCs) in India. Different studies point to the interest rates to MFI members' range from 24 percent to 48 percent or more. The Reserve Bank has capped interest rates charged by microfinance institutions from small borrowers at 26 percent. Contrary to public posturing that MFIs are saviors of the poor and charge reasonable interest rates, several big MFIs in Andhra Pradesh have been charging very high interest rates, closer to the ones charged by traditional moneylenders (Singh, 2010).

Microfinance and Women Empowerment: Process and Review of Literature

The measurement of the impact of microfinance on empowerment

Lending Norms of Banks to MFIs and MFIs to Members (Reddy and Parhlada, 2011)

	Norms	*Banks to MFIs*	*MFI to Members*
1.	Loan term	12-60 months depending on loan size	12 months irrespective of loan size
2.	Colume	Depends on loan cycles; loan size varying from Rs. 50,000 to Rs. 5 lakhs per group depending on linkage; single loan; rarely housing loans	Depends on loan cycles; Loan up to Rs. 30,000 per member; other loans 3-4 weeks even before clearing previous loan; multiple loans
3.	Instalments	Monthly Instalment	Weekly Instalment
4.	Rate of interest	9 to 12 percent per annum; diminishing rate of interest; entitled for interest subsidies	24 to 36 percent per annum; flat rate of interest; no interest subsidies
5.	Mode of repayment	Mostly fixed amount includes both principal and interest	Fixed amount includes both principal and interest
6.	Collateral/ surety	No collateral; inter-se agreement between bank and groups; informal collateral- large funds in SB account, FDs	No collateral; formal agreement between MFI and JLG; informal collaterals-signed blank cheques and promissory notes
7.	Penalties	Compound interest for every 3 months	Heavy fines and zero tolerance Problems and Issues

is somewhat a tedious exercise. It is mainly because of the fact that collection of both qualitative as well as quantitative data is difficult to handle. Most of the studies point towards caution of taking care of drawing conclusions towards the level of empowerment of the women. Hashemi *et al.* (1996) concluded that credit contributes significantly to the magnitude of the economic position of women. It is observed that assets holdings in the name of women had increased; they had money with them to spend and their political and legal awareness had also increased. The access to credit had increased the levels of mobility, political participation and involvement in 'major decision-making'.

Basically, microfinance is more than a credit programme and the process of forming SHG, savings, group meetings, investment decisions, etc. develops the personality of the participant of the microfinance programme. Kabeer (1998) in a study of microfinance programme found that the women as the members of SHGs feel changes in the form of increased self-worth. Since woman started contributing economically at the household level, she became an important member in the family who improved her status and position. Women often reported the feeling of an increase in affection and consideration within the household with longer programme membership.

The involvement of women in the microfinance programme has also given her non-economic benefits such as increased status in the family/society, increased self-confidence, decreased domestic violence and increased participation in domestic decision-making. In a study by Cheston and Kuhn (2002), it is found that 68 percent of its members were making decisions on buying and selling property, sending their daughters to school, negotiating their children's marriage, and planning their family. Earlier, the husband used to make these decisions. MkNelly and Dunford (1998) in a study of Bolivia and Ghana indicate that programme participation led to increase in self-confidence in women and improved status within the community. Participants in Ghana played a more active role in community life and community ceremonies, while participants in Bolivia were actively involved in local governments.

Banu *et al.* (2001) conceptualised empowerment as the capacity of women to reduce their socio-economic vulnerability and their dependency on their husbands or other male counterparts. The household surveys were conducted on 1072 households from 125 village organisation. The study concentrated on before and after type of comparison of members over time. In order to assess the impact over time the members were categorised in three groups according to the length of membership in BRAC, such as 1 to 11 months, 12 to 17 months, and 48 months or above. Women used their income for a variety of personal and household uses but they had yet to reach a stage where they can take independent decision regarding the use of this income. The economic dependence of women on their husbands was reduced. Women had begun to acquire positive self-perceptions of their own interests. They had become more confident in travelling and in dealing with other members of the society. It was found that empowerment was continuous process of change that was greatly influenced by the length of time a woman had been involved in BRAC.

Myrada (2002) studied the impact of SHGs on the empowerment status of women members in southern India. The objective of the study was to establish whether and to what extent the membership in SHGs had an impact on the social status and empowerment of the women members of such groups. The study is based on 190 SHGs members. The results of the study showed that in matured or old groups the income level is higher than the new groups. It was also concluded that members of old groups were more confident, more aware regarding their health and hygiene, more technically skilled, financially more secure, more in control of their lives and in a stronger position *vis-à-vis* their family members as compared to young group members. Hence, it was concluded that if responses from the new groups were taken as benchmark, the process of empowerment seemed to have started in old groups.

Tracey *et al.* (2006) in their study examined the personal and economic empowerment of rural Indian women through self-help group participation. Data was collected from 100 rural women from the Udaipur district of the state of Rajasthan in India. The study was based on both the quantitative and qualitative data which was collected through questionnaires, informal interviews and discussions. The quantitative data found that working women reported enhanced meaningfulness in their daily lives, increased personal control over spending, enhanced social networks, reduced boredom, increased decision-making power in home and enhanced independence. The inclusion of women in income-generating activities gave support to their personal and economic empowerment.

Ranjula Bali Swain (2007) in an article concluded that many strides have been made in the right direction and women are in the process of empowering themselves and NGOs that provide support in financial services and specialised training, have a greater ability to make a positive impact on women empowerment.

Sarumathi and Mohan (2011) in their study found that

microfinance through Self-Help Group (SHG) has been recognised internationally as the modern tool to combat poverty and empowering women. Microfinance in women's empowerment are considered into three dimensions namely psychological, social and economical. The study is undertaken in rural areas of Pondicherry region. Both primary and secondary data's are used. Analysis showed that there is a definite improvement in psychological well being and social empowerment among rural women as a result of participating in micro finance through SHG programme.

Microfinance, SHGs and Women Empowerment: A Case Study of Punjab

In Punjab there were approximately 40,919 SHGs upto March 2011, whereas there were only 12,000 self-help groups upto March 2006. These groups are mainly financed (79 percent) by the public sector commercial banks and rest of them by co-operative and regional rural banks. The role of regional rural banks (RRBs) is very limited (only 6 percent)

Different agencies are involved in promoting the microfinance programme in Punjab. These are Child Development Project Officer (CDPO), District Rural Development Agency (DRDA), Chief Agriculture Officer, National Cooperative Union of India (NCUI), Forest Department, Milk Union and Department of Soil & Water Conservation (DSWC). Almost all these agencies are government or government-sponsored agencies. Recently, some of the NGOs, e.g., SKS Finance and Ujjivan Financial Services, have entered in Punjab with microfinance programme. However, so for, the role of NGOs is very small in the process of promoting microfinance scheme in Punjab.

Most of the self-help groups formed in rural Punjab comprises of women. Microfinance is helping them in increasing their family income, employment and empowerment. In the subsequent pages an empirical study is conducted in the study area to discuss in detail the impact of microfinance on women empowerment.

Methodology

In the present study, the impact will be determined by comparing two groups: participant women of the programme (henceforth called as *participants*) and non-participants. Participants are the members of the SHG who have been benefited from the scheme and are credit linked up to March 2006. Non-participants are those households in the same area who are eligible for the microfinance scheme but did not access credit up to the time of the survey, i.e., October 2007-March 2008.

The present study is based on primary data. The primary data is collected from participants and non-participants of the sample households. The study is conducted in the Punjab. The administrative division of the state is into 20 districts. A multistage random sampling method is used. In the first stage Punjab is divided into three parts:

1. Alluvial Plains

It comprises the districts of Amritsar, Jalandhar, Kapurthala, Nawashahr, Ludhiana, Patiala, Fatehgarh Sahib, Taran Taran, Sangrur and Batala tehsil of district Gurdaspur.

2. Hilly Sub-Mountainous Strip

This is north-eastern region of Punjab which includes Hoshiarpur, Gurdaspur, Ropar and Mohali districts.

3. Sandy Region or South-Western Region

South-Western region of Punjab is sandy and dry. This part includes districts of Bathinda, Mansa, Faridkot, Moga, Muktsar, Ferozepur and Barnala. One district is selected from each region having sufficiently large number of credit linked SHGs under the microfinance programme. As a result, Jalandhar district from alluvial plains, Hoshiarpur district from sub-mountainous region and Bathinda district from sandy region is selected for the purpose of study. In the second stage, 5 percent of the credit linked self-help groups in these three districts are selected and in the last stage three members from each group are interviewed randomly. For the purpose of selection of sample households, three blocks from each of these districts are selected where there are the highest number of credit linked SHGs (Table 3.1). Sample households are selected proportionately from these blocks. The detail of the sample is shown in the table.

It is clear from the table that 90, 74 and 26 participants are surveyed from Jalandhar, Hoshiarpur and Bathinda districts, respectively. Matching number of non-participants of the programme, who are otherwise eligible, are selected randomly from the same areas. The data is collected with the help of a schedule specially prepared and pre-tested for this study.

The basic objective of this paper is to find out the impact of microfinance on the empowerment of women. Therefore, empowering activities are recorded during the collection of data, which are divided into economic, social, political and psychological. These activities are

Table 3.1: Sample Frame for the Study

S. No.	Region	District Selected	No. of groups surveyed	Block Selected	Total No. of SHGs in 2006	Surveyed	
						Groups	Participants
1.	Alluvial Plains	Jalandhar (595)	30	Jalandhar East	163	11	33
				Jalandhar West	156	11	33
				Nakoder	125	8	24
				Total	**444**	**30**	**90**
2.	Hilly Sub-Mountainous Strip	Hoshiarpur (492)	25	Garhshankar	123	11	33
				Hoshiarpur-1	104	9	27
				Bhunga	49	5	15
				Total	**276**	**25**	**74**
3.	South-Western Region	Bathinda (184)	09	Nathana	77	5	14
				Sangat	38	3	9
				Bathinda	21	1	3
				Total	**136**	**9**	**26**

Figures in the parentheses show total No. of credit linked SHGs in respective districts.

assigned arbitrary values (see Appendix Table 3.1). On the basis of these values a composite empowerment index (CEI) is prepared both for participants and non-participants of the programme. Chi-square (χ^2) method is used to find out the significance of the difference between the values of participants and non-participants.

The data collected from the field is edited and presented in tables. Simple average and percentage are used to summarise the data. A multiple regression technique is applied to find out the determinants of women empowerment. The following regression analysis is used to measure the effect of key indicators on CEI.

$$CEI = b_0 + b_1 AGE + b_2 EDU + b_3 GAGE + b_4 PROLOAN + b_5 EMPL + b_6 HHINC + b_7 MOBTY + u_i$$

where: CEI = Composite empowerment index
AGE = Age of the participant in years
EDU = Education level of the participant
GAGE = Group age to know the maturity of the group
PROLOAN = Amount of loan used for productive purpose in rupees
EMPL = Employment in person days in Post-SHG
HHINC = Household income of the participant in rupees
MOBTY = Level of mobility of the participant

It is observed from the above equation that independent variables are measured at different units. Therefore, there is need to standardize the regression coefficients to compare the strength of the relationship between dependent and independent variables. This is done by standardising the coefficients with the help of the formula $\beta_i = b_i * SD_y / SD_{bi}$, where b_i are the unstandardised regression coefficients; β_i are the standardised coefficients; SD_y is the standard division of regression equation; and SD_{bi} are the standard division of regression coefficients. These standardized coefficients will help in comparing directly to determine which variable has the largest impact on the dependent variable.

Results and Discussion

General Characteristics of Microfinance Programme

In Punjab most of the SHGs are formed and supervised by the village *Aanganwadi* workers under the overall supervision of Child Development Project Officer (CDPO) at block levels. These workers are not specially trained for the process of group formation. They are also not following any particular criteria for selecting women as SHG members. Table 3.2 shows the general characteristics of microfinance programme in the study area.

Table 3.2: General Characteristics of Groups under Microfinance Programme

Total No. of groups surveyed	64
No. of participants surveyed	190
No. of participants actively involved in group functioning	60
Average membership of the group	14
Average amount of loans (Rs.) per group	107163
Average amount of loans (Rs.) per participant	17638
Average amount of savings (per month) per participant	100

In the present study 190 members from 64 SHGs are interviewed to study the impact of the programme on women empowerment. Perusal of Table 3.2 shows that the average amount of loans received by the group is Rs. 1,07,163 and the average amount of loan received by the group members is Rs. 17,638. On an average, group members save Rs. 100 per month. It is also observed that out of 190 participants surveyed just 60 participants are actively involved in group functioning, i.e., maintaining accounts, attending meetings with higher officials, visiting to the banks to receive and repay the group loans, etc. In this way these groups are not democratically managed and the empowerment process is hindered.

General Characteristics of the Sample Households in Study Area

Age is a crucial variable for adopting a programme. If a person is in young age, he/she can take the risk and initiative to adopt the innovative programme. The present study shows that more than 60 percent of the participants belong to less than 40 years of age. However, the non-participants of the programme also belong to the same age group and they are only waiting for credit link.

Most of the poor in rural areas belong to the scheduled caste category. The perusal of Table 3.3 shows that microfinance programme in the study area has been helping to the scheduled caste and backward class women.

Most of the participants of the programme are married. The table shows that 89 percent participants are married. It has been observed that for stability of membership, unmarried girls are not selected as group members. It is also observed that 73 percent of the participants

Table 3.3: General Characteristics of the Sample Households

Characteristic	Category	Participants				Non-participants			
		Jal.	*Hsp.*	*Bti.*	*Pun.*	*Jal.*	*Hsp.*	*Bti.*	*Pun.*
Caste-wise distribution of sample units	S.C.	66 (73)	46 (62)	11 (42)	**123 (65)**	79 (88)	55 (74)	14 (54)	**148 (78)**
	B.C.	7 (8)	5 (7)	4 (16)	**16 (8)**	4 (4)	8 (11)	4 (15)	**16 (8)**
	General	17 (19)	23 (31)	11 (42)	**51 (27)**	7 (8)	11 (15)	8 (31)	**26 (14)**
Age-wise distribution of sample units	Below 25	6 (7)	2 (3)	-	**8 (4)**	13 (15)	11 (15)	7 (27)	**31 (16)**
	26 to 40	50 (55)	43 (58)	15 (58)	**108 (57)**	53 (59)	38 (51)	13 (50)	**104 (55)**
	41 to 60	32 (35)	28 (38)	9 (34)	**69 (36)**	22 (24)	22 (30)	5 (19)	**49 (26)**
	Above 60	2 (2)	1 (1)	2 (8)	**5 (3)**	2 (2)	3 (4)	1 (4)	**6 (3)**
Marital status	Married	79 (88)	65 (88)	26 (100)	**170 (89)**	69 (77)	63 (85)	23 (88)	**155 (81)**
	Widow	7 (8)	8 (11)	-	**15 (8)**	9 (10)	5 (7)	-	**14 (8)**
	Unmarried	4 (4)	1 (1)	-	**5 (3)**	12 (13)	6 (8)	3 (12)	**21 (11)**
Level of education	Illiterate	24 (27)	11 (15)	16 (61)	**51 (27)**	28 (31)	22 (30)	15 (58)	**65 (34)**
	Up to middle	34 (38)	42 (56)	7 (27)	**83 (44)**	34 (38)	33 (44)	5 (19)	**72 (38)**
	Matric	27 (30)	16 (21)	1 (4)	**44 (23)**	19 (21)	16 (22)	5 (19)	**40 (21)**
	Above Matric	5 (5)	6 (8)	2 (8)	**12 (6)**	9 (10)	3 (4)	1 (4)	**13 (7)**

Figures in the parentheses are percentages.

Legends: Jal. = Jalandhar Bti. = Bathinda Hsp. = Hoshiarpur Pun. = Punjab and 66 percent of the non-participants are literate. 67 percent of the participants and the 59 percent of the non-participants have studied up to Matric level. Most of the participants as well as non-participants are illiterate in Bathinda district. The most of the beneficiaries of the programme in Jalandhar and Hoshiarpur districts are scheduled castes.

Nature of Economic Activities Undertaken by the Participants

Microfinance programme has helped the participants in adopting various economic activities. Table 3.4 shows the nature of economic activities undertaken by microfinance programme participants.

The perusal of the table shows that rearing of milch animal is a popular activity of the sample households. Twenty-two percent of the participants and 12 percent of the non-participants are engaged in raising milch animal and they generate income by selling milk. The main reason of choosing this activity may be that most of the households are already engaged in this activity and at the same time it does not require any special skill.

Stitching and embroidery is the second popular activity that is preferred by participants. The table shows that 12 percent of the participants are doing stitching and embroidery work. Some of the participants are involved in stitching of the school bags, traveling bags, bed covers, etc. which has a good market in the village itself. The discussion with the participants shows that the reason of adopting and expanding these traditional and less profitable activities is the lack of marketing support to sell other non-traditional products.

It is also observed that 27 percent of participants are engaged in manufacturing and small business activities like petty shops, dairy, garland-making, rope-making, surf-making, running STD/PCOs, etc. as compared to just 2 percent by non-participants. This shows that microfinance programme participants are attracted towards these non-traditional activities due to some skill training and motivation provided to them under this scheme. The table also shows that none of the non-participants and just 2 percent of the participants are involved in agriculture. It may be because of the fact that most of the participants and non-participants are landless households.

The impact of microfinance programme on women empowerment can be observed from the comparison of occupational difference of participants and the non-participants. It is observed during the field survey that the football sewing is an activity where workers are paid very low wage against their hard work. Eleven percent of the non-participants are involved in this occupation as compared to 6 percent

Table 3.4: Nature of Economic Activities Undertaken by Microfinance Programme

S.No.	*Activity*	*Participants*				*Non-participants*			
		Jal.	*Hsp.*	*Bti.*	*Pun.*	*Jal.*	*Hsp.*	*Bti.*	*Pun.*
1.	Milch animals	13 (14)	20 (27)	9 (34)	42 (22)	5 (6)	8 (11)	9 (35)	22 (12)
2.	Stitching & embroidery	9 (10)	14 (19)	0 (0)	23 (12)	1 (1)	5 (7)	-	6 (3)
3.	Rope-making/Garland-making	1 (1)	8 (11)	2 (8)	11 (6)	1 (1)	1 (1)	1 (4)	3 (1)
4.	Petty shop	10 (11)	6 (8)	6 (23)	22 (12)	1 (1)	1 (1)		2 (1)
5.	Labour/Domestic aid	5 (6)	5 (6)	2 (8)	12 (6)	9 (10)	11 (15)	3 (11)	23 (12)
6.	Agriculture	2 (2)	2 (3)	-	4 (2)	-	-	-	0 (0)
7.	Service	4 (4)	2 (3)	-	6 (3)	5 (6)	3 (4)	3 (11)	11 (6)
8.	Dairy/STD/PCOs	2 (2)	2 (3)	2 (8)	6 (3)	-	-	-	0 (0)
9.	Football Sewing	12 (14)	-	-	12 (6)	21 (23)	-	-	21 (11)
10.	Soap/Surf-making	12 (14)	-	-	12 (6)	1 (1)	-	-	0 (0)
11.	Others	-	1 (1)	-	1 (1)	-	2 (3)	1 (4)	4 (2)
	Total	70 (78)	60 (81)	21 (81)	151 (79)	44 (49)	31 (42)	17 (65)	92 (48)
	Not involved in any activity	20 (22)	14 (19)	5 (19)	39 (21)	46 (51)	43 (58)	9 (35)	98 (52)
	Total	90	74	26	190	90	74	26	190

Figures in the parentheses are percentages.

of the participants. It is also found that only 6 percent participants are engaged in domestic aid as compared to 12 percent of non-participants. Domestic aid is considered to be a socially degraded job and participants with the availability of micro loans want to get rid of it. With the help of loans they have started micro enterprises of their own. This has given them economic independence. However 21 percent of the participants and 52 percent of the non-participants are not involved in any economic activity.

Economic Empowerment of Women and Microfinance Programme

Microfinance through SHGs has linked poor rural women with formal credit delivery system and has encouraged them to start micro-enterprises. This programme has helped in increasing economic prospects of the beneficiaries and economically empowered them. The increase in level of the employment and income of the participant are the good indicators of economic empowerment.

Impact on Employment

The study shows that the microfinance programme has helped the participants in increasing the employment. The perusal of Table 3.5 shows that 79 percent of the participants and 48 percent of non-participants are engaged in some income generating activities at the time of the survey. Even the employment condition of the participants has improved from pre-SHG to post-SHG level.

It is not only that the participants are employed, but they are also engaged in the job throughout the year. The perusal of Table 3.6 shows that the average employment of the participants is 160 person-days per annum, whereas the non-participants are employed only for 78 person-days per annum. The increase in employment will certainly help in increasing the income of the beneficiaries of the programme.

Training enhances skill and interest of the participants which thereby increases their level of employment. Table 3.7 shows that the trained participants are employed for 192 PDs per annum while untrained participants are employed for just 145 PDs per annum.

Impact on Income

The study also shows that the microfinance programme has helped the women participants to increase their contribution to the household income. Table 3.8 shows that various income generating activities have increased the average income per month of participants. Average income of the participants is Rs. 1746 per month in post-SHG as compared to

Table 3.5: Employment Status of Participants and Non-Participants

Employment	*Participants*								*Non-participants*			
	Pre-SHG				*Post-SHG*				*Jal.*	*Hsp.*	*Bti.*	*Pun.*
	Jal.	*Hsp.*	*Bti.*	*Pun.*	*Jal.*	*Hsp.*	*Bti.*	*Pun.*				
Employed	38 (42)	44 (59)	12 (46)	**94 (49)**	70 (78)	60 (81)	21 (81)	**151 (79)**	44 (49)	31 (42)	17 (65)	**92 (48)**
Unemployed	52 (58)	30 (41)	14 (54)	**96 (51)**	20 (22)	14 (19)	5 (19)	**39 (21)**	46 (51)	43 (58)	9 (35)	**98 (52)**
Total	90	74	26	**190**	90	74	26	**190**	90	74	26	**190**

Figures in the parentheses are percentages.
Chi-square (χ^2) = 22.22; Table value at 5% and 1% in 1 d.f. = 3.84 and 6.63 respectively.

Table 3.6: Number of Person Days (PDs) Employment Generated in a Year

District	Average employment generated			
	Participants			Non-Participants
	Pre-SHG	Post-SHG	Increment	
Jalandhar	79	163	84	85
Hoshiarpur	83	153	70	61
Bathinda	73	166	93	99
Punjab	80	160	80	78

Table 3.7: Impact of Training on Employment

Type of the participants	No. of participants	Average employment in PDs
Trained	56 (29)	192
Untrained	134 (71)	145

Figures in the parentheses are percentages.

Rs. 718 per month in pre-SHG situation. The average income of non-participants is only Rs. 638 per month. It shows that the income of the participant women have increased substantially. The contribution to the family income helps women to become economically independent and a decision-maker in the household expenditure.

Table 3.8: Average Income Generated Per Month (in Rs.)

Particulars	Average Income of Participants			Non-Participants
	Pre-SHG	Post-SHG	Increment	
Jalandhar	657	1557	900	646
Hoshiarpur	772	1952	1180	573
Bathinda	773	1813	1040	799
Punjab	718	1746	1028	638

Figures in the parentheses are percentages.

Role of Microfinance in Decision-making

In this male dominant society, female is always on the recipient end because she does not contribute to family income. However, microfinance programme has raised the status of women from mere a consumer to a producer and from economically dependent to independent.

The perusal of Table 3.9 shows that 21 percent of the participant women and only 11 percent of non-participants dominate in household financial decisions. However, in a majority of cases, both husband and wife jointly take the household decisions. This shows that microfinance programme has helped women in increasing their income and now they feel more economically empowered. The Chi-square (χ^2) test also shows a significant difference between participants and non-participants in household financial decision-making.

Banking Habits

Microfinance programme has also developed the banking habits of self-help group members who contribute to the group savings fund in fixed installments at regular intervals. This develops the habit of thrift and banking. The perusal of Table 3.10 shows that 54 percent of the participants have saving account with banks as compared to only 37 percent of the non-participants. It is observed from the table that 30 percent of the participants deposit money regularly in their saving bank account as compared to 18 percent of the non-participants.

Social and Psychological Empowerment

Confidence in Traveling

The self-help groups encourage and offer an opportunity to their members to visit to other places for getting skills, training and exhibiting their products in various fairs and exhibitions. They have to purchase raw materials and sell final products of their micro enterprise in the market. Exposure of the members in the programme increases their confidence in traveling to other places. However, some of the women are hesitant and do not take these activities themselves.

Table 3.11 shows the confidence of self-help group members to visit a city, nearest town and another village. It has been observed that only 46 percent of the participants are more confident to visit in a city. However, 79 percent participants are confident to visit the nearest town as compared to 69 percent of non-participants. It is clear from the table that participants of the programme are more confident in visiting cities and towns than non-participants. Chi-square test shows very significant differences among participants and non-participants regarding their confidence in traveling to city.

Confidence in Dealing with Other Members of Society

It is very important to conduct confidently in a group. The self-

Table 3.9: Role of Women in Household Financial Decision-making

Financial decision-making	*Participants*				*Non-participants*			
	Jal.	*Hsp.*	*Bti.*	*Pun.*	*Jal.*	*Hsp.*	*Bti.*	*Pun.*
Self-dominate	21 (23)	19 (26)	-	40 (21)	11 (12)	8 (11)	2 (8)	21 (11)
Husband-dominate	4 (5)	3 (4)	3 (12)	10 (5)	12 (13)	7 (10)	4 (15)	23 (12)
Jointly by self & husband	63 (70)	52 (70)	23 (88)	138 (73)	63 (70)	55 (74)	19 (73)	137 (72)
Other members dominate	2 (2)	-	-	2 (1)	4 (5)	4 (5)	1 (4)	9 (5)
Total	90	74	26	190	90	74	26	190

Figures in the parentheses are percentages.
Chi-square (χ^2) = 8.67 which is significant at 5% level.

Table 3.10: Banking Habits of Participants and Non-participants

Indicator		*Participants*				*Non-participants*			
		Jal.	*Hsp.*	*Bti.*	*Pun.*	*Jal.*	*Hsp.*	*Bti.*	*Pun.*
Saving bank account	Yes	56 (62)	36 (49)	10 (38)	102 (54)	36 (40)	28 (38)	7 (27)	71 (37)
	No	34 (38)	38 (51)	16 (62)	88 (46)	54 (60)	46 (62)	19 (73)	119 (63)
Deposit in bank regularly	Yes	25 (28)	24 (32)	8 (31)	57 (30)	12 (13)	19 (26)	4 (15)	35 (18)
	No	65 (72)	50 (68)	18 (69)	133 (70)	78 (87)	55 (74)	22 (85)	155 (82)

Figures in the parentheses are percentages.
Chi-square (χ^2) = 5.84 and 3.94; Table value at 5% and 1% in 1 d.f. = 3.84 and 6.63 respectively.

Table 3.11: Confidence in Traveling to Various Places

Level of Confidence		*Participants*				*Non-participants*			
		Jal.	*Hsp.*	*Bti.*	*Pun.*	*Jal.*	*Hsp.*	*Bti.*	*Pun.*
Traveling to city	More Confident	39 (43)	43 (58)	6 (23)	**88 (46)**	11 (12)	12 (16)	3 (12)	**26 (14)**
	Less Confident	30 (33)	22 (30)	5 (19)	**57 (30)**	56 (62)	36 (49)	9 (34)	**101 (53)**
	Can't go	21 (24)	9 (12)	15 (58)	**45 (24)**	23 (26)	26 (35)	14 (54)	**63 (33)**
Traveling to nearest town	More Confident	72 (80)	66 (89)	12 (46)	**150 (79)**	65 (72)	52 (70)	15 (58)	**132 (69)**
	Less Confident	16 (18)	6 (8)	9 (35)	**31 (16)**	23 (26)	18 (24)	8 (31)	**49 (26)**
	Can't go	2 (2)	2 (3)	5 (19)	**9 (5)**	2 (2)	4 (6)	3 (11)	**9 (5)**
Traveling to another nearest village	More Confident	86 (96)	71 (96)	24 (92)	**181 (95)**	84 (93)	65 (88)	21 (81)	**170 (89)**
	Less Confident	3 (3)	2 (3)	1 (4)	**6 (3)**	4 (5)	6 (8)	5 (19)	**15 (8)**
	Can't go	1 (1)	1 (1)	1 (4)	**3 (2)**	2 (2)	3 (4)	0 (0)	**5 (3)**

Figures in the parentheses are percentages
Chi-sq. (χ^2) = 24.86, 3.06 and 2 668 respectively, Table values at 5% and 1% in 2 d.f. = 5.99 and 9.21.

Table 3.12: Confidence in Dealing with Other Members of Society

Level of Confidence		*Participants*				*Non-participants*			
		Jal.	*Hsp.*	*Bti.*	*Pun.*	*Jal.*	*Hsp.*	*Bti.*	*Pun.*
Dealing with other persons	More Confident	64 (71)	62 (84)	15 (58)	**141 (74)**	26 (29)	18 (25)	8 (31)	**52 (27)**
	Less Confident	26 (29)	11 (15)	10 (38)	**47 (25)**	64 (71)	55 (74)	18 (69)	**137 (72)**
	Cannot say	-	1 (1)	1 (4)	**2 (1)**	-	1 (1)	-	**1 (1)**

Figures in the parentheses are percentages.
Chi-square (χ^2) = 44.66, Table values at 5% and 1% in 2 d.f. = 5.99 and 9.21.

help group members have to arrange meetings weekly or fortnightly, visit other villages, interact with important local people, go to banks and meet various government officials. This requires a good level of confidence in dealing with officials, group members and other members of the community.

Table 3.12 shows that 74 percent of the participants and just 27 percent of the non-participants are more confident in dealing with the other members of the society. There is very significant difference among participants and non-participants regarding their confidence in dealing with other members of society.

Political Empowerment

Self-confident and conscious women are capable of taking part in election process and village polity. The study shows that along with the economic and social empowerment, microfinance programme has also led to the political empowerment of the women participants. The participants feel they are in the mainstream of the village life, therefore, they play an important role in village polity.

The perusal of Table 3.13 shows that both participants and non-participants are aware of local polity. It is found that almost all the participants and non-participants are aware of their voting rights and the name of their village *sarpanch*. However, when participants are asked to name the chief minister of Punjab and prime minister of India, 52 percent of the participants know the name of chief minister of the state and 34 percent know the name of prime minister as compared to 39 and 13 percent of non-participants, respectively.

The study also tried to find the role of women in *panchayat* meetings for decisions regarding village development. The respondents, participants and non-participants, are asked whether they attend the *panchayat* meetings and participate in them. Fifty-eight percent of the participants respond positively as compared to 43 percent of the non-participants.

Composite Empowerment Index

The impact of microfinance programme on women empowerment can be better understood by preparing a composite empowerment index (CEI). The index combines both quantitative and qualitative data relating to empowerment. The scores of 21 indicators are added together. The participants who score between 0-10 are classified as not empowered. Similarly, the scores between 11-20, 21-30 and 31-40 are

Table 3.13: Political Indicators of Empowerment

Indicator		*Participants*				*Non-participants*			
		Jal.	*Hsp.*	*Bti.*	*Pun.*	*Jal.*	*Hsp.*	*Bti.*	*Pun.*
Casting votes in village,	Yes	90 (100)	73 (99)	26 (100)	**189 (99)**	89 (99)	74 (100)	25 (96)	**188 (99)**
state and center elections	No	-	1 (1)	-	**1 (1)**	1 (1)	-	1 (4)	**2 (1)**
Know the name of village	Yes	87 (97)	67 (91)	24 (92)	**178 (94)**	83 (92)	71 (96)	24 (92)	**178 (94)**
sarpanch	No	3 (3)	7 (9)	2 (8)	**12 (6)**	7 (8)	3 (4)	2 (8)	**12 (6)**
Know the name of state	Yes	51 (57)	38 (51)	10 (38)	**99 (52)**	44 (49)	23 (31)	8 (31)	**75 (39)**
chief minister	No	39 (43)	36 (49)	16 (62)	**91 (48)**	46 (51)	51 (69)	18 (69)	**115 (61)**
Know the name of	Yes	32 (36)	26 (35)	6 (23)	**64 (34)**	14 (16)	7 (9)	3 (12)	**24 (13)**
prime minister	No	58 (64)	48 (65)	20 (77)	**126 (66)**	76 (84)	67 (91)	23 (88)	**166 (87)**
Attended and participated	Yes	52 (58)	47 (34)	12 (46)	**111 (58)**	40 (44)	31 (42)	10 (38)	**81 (43)**
in *panchayat* meetings	No	38 (42)	27 (36)	14 (54)	**79 (42)**	50 (56)	43 (58)	16 (62)	**109 (57)**

Figures in the parentheses are percentages.

classified as low, medium and highly empowered, respectively. The results are shown in Table 3.14.

The perusal of the Table 3.14 shows that 76 percent participants are in the range of medium and highly empowered, whereas only 48 percent non-participants are in this category. The Chi-square (χ^2) test shows a significant difference between the empowerment of the participants and non-participants of the microfinance programme.

Determinants of Empowerment (Regression Analysis)

A linear multiple regression is used to determine the variables influencing women empowerment. Table 3.15 shows the coefficients of these variables. The measure of best fit, i.e., the coefficient of determination (R^2) shows that the variables selected for the study explain the 78 percent of the variations.

The results of the table show that all the coefficients have positive values except variables of age and loan used for productive purposes in Bathinda. The coefficients of regression variables e.g. age, education, group age, household income, employment, amount of loans used for productive purposes and spatial mobility of the participants are playing an important and significant role in women empowerment. Education is an important variable of women empowerment. It provides more knowledge, confidence and awareness to make better and timely decisions. The maturity of the group (Group age) is also an important factor. As the group grows older the participants develop more confidence, mutual faith, co-ordination and credibility of getting loans. The mature groups also spend their loans for productive purposes. Household income provides a financial base for contribution in group saving as well as to start micro-enterprises. The mobility also increases the opportunities for participants and further increase the sources of betterment and hence more empowerment. More employment days leads to more income, confidence and respect in the family and the society, thus contributing significantly to women empowerment. However, participant's age is a positive coefficient but is not very significant. In Bathinda district the variables of age and loans spent for productive usage are showing negative sign. However, these coefficients are not statistically significant.

Summary and Conclusion

Microfinance programme is an innovative method of providing collateral free micro loans to the poor rural women. Microfinance through SHGs has contributed in empowerment of women. The present

Table 3.14: Composite Empowerment Index (CEI) of Participants and Non-participants

Level of Empowerment	*CEI Score*	*Participants*				*Non-participants*			
		Jal.	*Hsp.*	*Bti.*	*Pun.*	*Jal.*	*Hsp.*	*Bti.*	*Pun.*
Highly empowered	(31–40)	23 (26)	21 (28)	6 (23)	**50 (26)**	4 (4)	4 (5)	1 (4)	**9 (5)**
Medium empowered	(21–30)	43 (47)	44 (60)	8 (31)	**95 (50)**	39 (43)	34 (46)	8 (31)	**81 (43)**
Less empowered	(11–20)	23 (26)	8 (11)	9 (35)	**40 (21)**	42 (47)	29 (39)	13 (50)	**84 (44)**
Not empowered	(0–10)	1 (1)	1 (1)	3 (11)	5 (3)	5 (6)	7 (10)	4 (15)	**16 (8)**
	Total	90	74	26	**190**	90	74	26	**190**

Figures in the parentheses are percentages.
Chi-square (χ^2) = 25.16; Table value at 5% and 1% in 3 d.f. = 7.81 and 11.3 respectively

Table 3.15: The Determinants of Women Empowerment

Variables	*Standardised Coefficients*			
	Jalandhar	*Hoshiarpur*	*Bathinda*	*Punjab*
Constant	1.606	0.683	9.263	**2.291**
AGE	0.058 (1.026)	0.109 (1.401)	(-)0.201 (2.088)**	**0.021** (0.550)
EDU	0.459 (7.686)*	0.355 (4.362)*	0.216 (1.967)**	**0.374** (8.910)*
GAGE	0.113 (1.877)	0.238 (2.990)**	0.020 (0.156)	**0.153** (3.775)*
PROLOAN	0.059 (1.040)	0.089 (1.223)	(-)0.115 (0.968)	**0.063** (1.641)
EMP	0.192 (2.984)*	0.205 (2.465)**	0.249 (2.019)**	**0.196** (4.611)*
HHINCOME	0.135 (2.453)**	0.057 (0.763)	0.266 (2.036)**	**0.107** (2.797)*
MOBILITY	0.467 (8.932)*	0.309 (5.280)*	0.581 (4.888)*	**0.476** (12.499)*
R-Square	0.799	0.717	0.854	0.780

The figures in parentheses are t-values. * Significant at 1 percent level. ** Significant at 5 percent level.

study shows that microfinance programme has empowered women economically, socially, psychologically and politically as compared to the non-participants. The beneficiaries of the programme have higher levels of employment, income and participation in household financial decision-making leading to their economic empowerment. It is also found that the beneficiaries are more confident in traveling and in dealing with the other members of the society. They are more participative in the social development activities and are more politically aware as compared to non-beneficiaries. The study also reveals that all the participants are not fully empowered even after availing the benefits of microfinance programme for at least past two years.

It is found that the impact of the programme on the participants is not fully observed even after availing the benefits of the microfinance programme for at least past two years. One of the major reasons of less impact of the programme may be the inactive involvement of NGOs. In Punjab, this programme is run by the government and government functionaries mainly through *Aanganwadi* workers. These workers are not specifically trained in the process of group formation to select poor women as SHG beneficiaries. Therefore, this programme seems to be just like many other schemes run by the government. It has been observed that skill development training to the participants leads to more employment, but only 29 percent of the participants are provided this training. The entire thrust is on formation and bank linkage of the SHGs and a little attention is paid towards their sustainable functioning. Lack of proper guidance, supervision, skill training and marketing facilities has restricted the impact of the microfinance programme on women empowerment. The regression analysis shows that education of the participants, maturity of the group, employment level, household income and mobility are the significant variables to determine empowerment of the participants.

Recommendations

(a) In order to achieve higher levels of women empowerment the group loans must be backed by the guidance to start profitable activities, skill training, regular supervision, marketing support and performance appraisal.

(b) The local level officials involved in the process of group formation must be fully trained in the process of group formation and its sustained functioning. The NGOs having unselfish record must be encouraged to support this programme.

(c) As per the regression results, initiatives must be taken by promoting agencies to improve women's education, mobility, group leadership and easy availability of large amounts of loans for productive purposes.

The author thankfully acknowledges Dr. Deepty Bansal for the use of data in this paper collected by her for her Ph.D. thesis, 'Impact of Microfinance on Poverty, Employment and Women Empowerment in Rural Punjab' submitted and degree awarded by Punjabi University, Patiala.

References

Abhaskumar Jha (2000), "Lending to Poor: Designs for Credit", *Economic and Political Weekly*, Vol. 35, No. 8.

Ackerly, Brooke A. (1995), "Testing the Tools of Development: Credit Programmes, Loan Involvement, and Women's Empowerment", *IDS Bulletin*, Vol. 26, No. 3, pp. 56-68.

Amin, R. Becker, S. and Bayes, A. (1998), "NGO-Promoted Micro Credit Programs and Women's Empowerment in Rural Bangladesh: Quantitative and Qualitative Evidence", *The Journal of Developing Areas,* Vol. 32, No. 2, pp. 221-36.

APMAS (2007), *SHG-Bank Linkage Programme: A Recurrent Study in Andhra Pradesh,* Communication Division of APMAS Published the Draft Report of the Study.

______ (2010), *Status of SHG Savings: A Study with Reference to SHGs in Andhra Pradesh,* In-house Research Study of APMAS.

Banu, Dilruba, *et al.* (2001), "Empowering Women in Rural Bangladesh: Impact of Bangladesh Rural Advancement Committee's (BRAC's) Programme", *Journal of International Women's Studies,* Vol. 2, No. 3, p. 24.

Batliwala, Srilatha (1994), "The Meaning of Women's Empowerment: New Concepts from Action", in G. Sen; A. Germain; and L.C. Chen (eds.), *Population Policies Reconsidered: Health, Empowerment and Rights,* Cambridge: Harvard University Press, pp. 127-38.

Business Insider (Oct. 2010), Online Web: http://articles.businessinsider.com/2010-10-19/wall_street/30025181_1_microfinance-institutions-lenders-new-laws#ixzz1w8B26l5J Accessed on 25 October, 2010.

Chambers, Robert (1997), *Whose Reality Counts? Putting the First Last,* London: ITDG Publishing.

Goetz, Anne Marie and Gupta, Rina Sen (1996), "Who Takes the Credit? Gender, Power, and Control Over Loan Use in Rural Credit Programs in Bangladesh", *World Development,* Vol. 24, No. 1, pp. 45-63.

Hannover Wolfgang (2005), *Impact of Microfinance Linkage Banking in India on the Millennium Development Goals,* Report to NABARD.

Hashemi, Syed M. *et al.* (1996), "Rural Credit Programs and Women's Empowerment in Bangladesh", *World Development,* Vol. 24, No. 4, pp. 635-53.

Human Development Report (1995), *United Nations Development Programme,* New York: Oxford University Press.

John Snow, Inc. (1990), "Empowerment of Women Program", John Snow, Inc., Arlington, VA.

Kabeer, N. (1994), *Reversed Realities: Gender Hierarchies in Development Thought,* London, Verso.

____ (1999), "The Conditions and Consequences of Choice: Reflections on the Measurement of Women's Empowerment", *Discussion Paper, No. 108,* United Nations Research Institute for Social Development, Geneva.

____ (2001), "Conflict over Credit: Re-evaluating the Empowerment Potential of Loans to Women in Rural Bangladesh", *World Development,* Vol. 29, No. 1, pp. 63-84.

Kumar, Prahlad and Paul, Tinku (2007), "Empowerment of Women: Concept, Policy Approach and Implications", Paper Presented at a Seminar on Gender Issues and Empowerment of Women, *Indian Statistical Institute,* Kolkata, 1-2 February.

Lalitha, N. (2000), "Women thrift and credit Groups—Breaking the barriers at the Gross Roots", *Peninsular Economist,* Vol. 12, No. 2.

Longwe, S.H. (1999), "Women's Empowerment (Longwe) Framework" in Candida March; Inés A. Smyth; and Maitrayee Mukhopadhyay (eds.), *A Guide To Gender-Analysis Frameworks,* OXFAM GB, Oxford, pp. 92-101.

Longwe, S.H. and Clarke, R. (1994), "Women in Development, Culture and Youth: Workshop Readings", Longwe Clarke and Associates, Lusaka, Zambia.

Malhotra, A., Schuler, S.R. and Boender, C. (2002), *Measuring Women's Empowerment as a Variable in International Development,* World Bank, Washington, DC.

Mayoux, Linda (2000), "Micro-finance and the Empowerment of Women—A Review of the Key Issues", International Labor Organisation, Geneva. Available at: http://www.ilo.org/wcmsp5/groups/public/-ed_emp/documents/publication/wcms_ 117993.pdf Accessed on 29 December, 2009.

Mizan, A.N. (1994), *In Quest of Empowerment: The Grameen Bank Impact on Women's Power and Status,* Dhaka: University Press Limited.

MkNelly Barbara and Christopher Dunford (1998), "Impact of Credit with Education on Mothers and Their Young Children's Nutrition: Lower Pra Rural Bank Credit with Education Program in Ghana", *Research Paper No. 4,* Davis, California: Freedom from Hunger.

NABARD (2006), SHG Bank Linkage Programme, Available at http://nabard.org/pdf/stmt3.pdf Accessed on 9 December, 2009.

NABARD (2007), SHG Bank Linkage Programme, Available at http://nabard.org/pdf/stmt1.pdf Accessed on 2 December, 2009.

NABARD (2011), *Status of Microfinance in India, 2010-11,* Mumbai, India.

Page, N., and Czuba, C.E. (1999), "Empowerment: What is it?", *Journal of Extension,* Vol. 37, No. 5, Online web: Available at: http://www.joe.org/joe/1999october/comm1.html

Pillai, J.K. (1995), *Women and Empowerment,* New Delhi: Gyan Publishing House, pp. 23-24.

Rahman, A. (1999), "Micro-credit Initiatives for Equitable and Sustainable Development: Who Pays?", *World Development,* Vol. 27, No. 1, pp. 67-82.

Ranjula Bali Swaina and Fan Yang Wallentin (September 2009), Does microfinance empower women? Evidence from self-help groups in India, '*International Review of Applied Economics*', Vol. 23, No. 5, 541-56, http://pdfserve.informaworld.com/ 595379_758077589_913075296.pdf.

Ritu Jain (2003), "Socio-Economic impact through Self-Help Groups", *Yojana,* Vol. 47, No. 7.

Reddy K. Raja *et al.* (2011), 'SHG-Bank Linkage Programme: A Study On Loan Default And Recovery, Online Web: http://www.apmas.org/pdf/SHG-%20Bank%20Linkage%20-%20Study%20on%20Loan%20Default%20and%20 Recovery. pdf Accesses on 13 October, 2009.

Rowlands, J. (1997), 'Questioning Empowerment: Working with Women in Honduras', Oxford, U.K.: Oxfam Publishing.

Sarumathi, S. and Mohan, K. (2011), "Role of Microfinance in Women's Empowerment (An Empirical study in Pondicherry region rural SHG's)", *Journal of Management and Science,* Vol. 1, No. 1, pp. 1-10, Sep.

Sen, Amartya (1999), *Development as Freedom,* Oxford University Press, Oxford.

Singh, Kavaljit (2005), Banking Sector Liberalisation in India: Some Distributing Trends, ASED, August 29.

____ (2010), "Taming The Wild West" of Microfinance", Countercurrents.org, 25 December.

Stromquist, Nelly P. (1995), "The Theoretical and Practical Bases for Empowerment", in Carolyn Medel-Anonuevo (ed.), *Women, Education and Empowerment: Pathways Towards Autonomy,* United Nations Educational, Scientific and Cultural Organisation (UNESCO), Hamburg, Germany.

Tracey, L. Moyle *et al.* (2006), "Personal and Economic Empowerment in Rural Indian Women: A Self-Help Group Approach", *International Journal of Rural Management,* Vol. 2, No. 2, pp. 245-66.

Wallerstein, N. (1992), "Powerlessness, Empowerment and Health: Implications for Health Promotion Programs", *American Journal of Health Promotion,* Vol. 6, pp. 197-205.

World Bank (2001), *Engendering Development: Through Gender Equality in Rights, Resources and Voice,* World Bank Policy Research Report, Oxford University Press, Oxford.

Appendix Table 3.1: Table Used for Calculating Women Empowerment Index

S.No.	*Particulars*		*Score*
1.	Woman's monthly contribution to the H.H. income (in Rs.)	No income	0
		Up to 1000	1
		1000-2000	2
		2000-3000	3
		3000-4000	4
		Above 4000	5
2.	Woman's participation in H.H. decision-making	No Participation	0
		Joint participation	1
		Independent in decision-making	2
3.	Woman owns house	No	0
		Yes	1
4.	Woman owns land	No	0
		Yes	1
5.	Maintaining HH records	No	0
		Yes	1
6.	Visit market to make small purchases	Not confident	0
		Less confident	1
		More confident	2
7.	Having a saving bank account in her own name	No	0
		Yes (irregular deposit)	1
		Yes (regular deposit)	2
8.	Recognise count and read numbers	Not able	0
		Some difficulty	1
		No difficulty	2
9.	Able to do basic calculations	Not able	0
		Some difficulty	1
		No difficulty	2
10.	Able to fill bank forms	Not able	0
		Some difficulty	1
		No difficulty	2
11.	Able to understand basic banking operations	Not able	0
		Some difficulty	1
		No difficulty	2
12.	Ability to keep A/C of loans received and repaid	Not able	0
		Some difficulty	1
		No difficulty	2
	Social Empowerment		
13.	Participation in *gram-sabha/ gram-panchayat* meetings	No	0
		Yes	1

(*Contd.*)

S.No.	*Particulars*		*Score*
14.	Helping others in resolving conflicts	No	0
		Yes	1
	Political Empowerment		
15.	Casting votes in *gram-panchayats* and state elections	No	0
		Yes	1
16.	Knowledge of local polity	No knowledge	0
		Know village *sarpanch* name	1
		Know *sarpanch* and CM name	2
		Sarpanch, CM and PM name	3
	Psychological Empowerment		
17.	Confidence in dealing with members of the society	No confidence	0
		Less confident	1
		More confident	2
18.	Confidence in traveling	Can't go outside	0
		Can visit another village	1
		Can visit other village and nearest town	2
		Can visit other village, nearest town and city	3
19.	Reading newspaper	Never	0
		Occasionally	1
		Regularly	2
20.	Able to write name	Not able	0
		Some difficulty	1
		No difficulty	2
21.	Husband became helpful after joining SHG	Remained same	0
		Help Increased	1

Micro-Finance, Self-Help Groups and Economic Empowerment of Rural Women

NEERAJ SHARMA

Introduction

Micro-financing is about provisioning of thrift, credit and other financial services and products of very small amounts to the poor in rural, semi-urban or urban areas for enabling them to raise their income level and to improve their living standards. These financial services may include savings, credit, insurance, leasing, money transfer, etc. that is any type of financial service provided to customers to meet their normal financial needs. Despite the expansion of the organised banking system into rural areas, it was found that large number of poor continued to remain outside the fold of formal banking system. Need was felt for an alternative delivery mechanism which would meet the requirements of the poor and especially the women members of such households. The success of Grameen Bank in Bangladesh has established the fact and several literatures in this regard also acknowledge the fact that poor are bankable in terms of capacity to save and repay the loans, provided the same are collected at their door steps in small amounts and at frequent intervals. The experience of India shows that provision of small financial services and products to the poor people through bank linkage of self-help groups has contributed to the process of rural development by creating conditions that are conducive to human development. It has a strong gender orientation. More than 85 percent of the self-help groups linked to banks are reported to be of women. Through these groups, women empowerment is taking place. It is thought that easy access to credit facilities and equal share in employment opportunities will ultimately lead to women empowerment. Their participation in economic activities and decision-making at the household and security level is increasing and is making the process of rural development participatory, democratic and sustainable.

Origin of Microfinance

The origin of micro-finance could be traced back to the beginning of the co-operative movement in Germany. The movement was started in 1944 in the field of co-operative based credit system by the Raiffeisen Societies as well as Rochdale Pioneers in England. Similarly, the enactment of the Co-operative Credit Societies Act, 1904 could be considered as the beginning of micro-finance in India. Micro-finance was started with the origination of the Grameen Bank in Bangladesh by renowned Prof. Mohammed Yunus, an economist. The U.N. year of Micro Credit, 2005, was a turning point for micro-finance as the private sector banks began to take more interest in micro-finance. Studies reveal that micro-finance now reaches about 80 million families and approximately 20,000 micro-finance institutions are now operating in developing countries of Asia, Africa, Europe and Latin America with an aim to eradicate poverty. India is home to growing and innovative sector of micro-finance. With a large proportion of world's poor, India is likely to have a large potential demand for micro-finance.

Micro-finance and Empowerment of Women

"Empowerment is an active multi-dimensional process which should enable women to realise their full identity and power in all spheres of life. It would consist of greater access to knowledge and resources, greater autonomy in decision-making, greater ability to plan their lives, have greater control over the circumstances that influence their lives and free them from shackles imposed on them by custom, belief and practice" (Soni, 2001). Micro-credit has been advocated as new panacea for reduction of poverty and economic empowerment of rural women. Its mission is to help the poor people to help themselves to overcome poverty. It is targeted to the poor, particularly poor women. It can effectively generate employment and sustain the income of the households by giving them opportunities to work. The formal credit mechanisms have not been successful in providing adequate credit to the rural poor.

Though the vast network of branches is available for rural credit, the outcome is not encouraging. Rural poor lack collateral, steady employment and a verifiable credit history and, therefore, cannot meet even the most minimal qualifications to gain access to traditional credit. Micro-credit is a tool for socio-economic development. Most distinctive feature of micro-credit is that it is not based on any collateral. It is based on trust and not on legal procedures and system. Micro-credit is the extension of very small loans to the entrepreneurs and to others living in poverty that are not considered bankable. It provided services at the door steps of the poor based on the principle that people should not go to the bank but the bank should go to the people. Dr. Mohammad Yunus explains the role of micro-credit in facilitating women potential as women have plans for their children, for their homes and for their meal. Micro-credit programmes extend small loans to very poor people for self-employment projects that generate income, allowing them to care for themselves and their families.

Micro-finance programmes are currently being promoted as a key strategy for simultaneously addressing both poverty alleviation and women's empowerment. Where financial service provision leads to the setting-up or expansion of micro-enterprises there are a range of potential impacts including:

- Increasing women's income levels and control over income leading to greater levels of economic independence.
- Access to networks and markets giving wider experience of the word outside the home, access to information and possibilities for development of other social and political roles.
- Enhancing perception of women's contribution to household income and family welfare, increasing women's participation in household decisions about expenditure and other issues and leading to greater expenditure on women's welfare.
- More general improvements in attitudes to women's role in the household and community.

Micro-finance programmes targeting women have been a welcome corrective to previous neglect of women's productive role. Micro finance programmes have indeed set in motion a process of empowerment where all the above elements have been mutually reinforcing.

Role of Self-Help Groups

SHGs have emerged as a powerful tool that aimed at empowering women and eradicating poverty in a sustainable manner. Self-Help-Groups are voluntary associations of 10-20 disadvantaged people formed to attain a collective goal. The SHGs are essentially informal. People who are homogeneous with respect to social background, occupation, etc. come together with the clear objective of brining about positive changes in the situation in which they find themselves through self-help and self-reliance. Such group is called SHG. Group members agree to form themselves into group and function in an organised manner with the specific objective of pooling their savings so as to be able to give credit to its members for meeting their consumption and production needs.

The main objectives of the groups are to improve the economic and social status of the members in terms of their needs and interest. The SHG provides savings mechanism which suits the needs of the members. It also provides a cost effective delivery mechanism for small credit to its members. The SHGs are the platform or forum to the members to come together for emergency, disaster, social reasons, economic support to each other have ease to conversation, social interactions and economic activities. Some of the common characteristics in the functioning of these groups are:

- The Group creates a common fund by contributing small savings on a regular basis.
- Periodic meetings are held where competing claims on the limited resources are settled by consensus.
- Loans are granted for the production as well as for consumption needs of the members.
- Loan is granted on a mutual trust without any security or any very minimal documentation.
- Rate of interest is generally higher than that is charged by the formal credit agencies but lower than that is charged by rural money lenders/commission agents.
- Default rates are low due to the pressure of the group and informal monitoring of the group members.

Review of Literature

Hashemi *et al.* (1996) worked out the impact of credit on a number of indicators of empowerment: (i) the reported magnitude of women's economic contribution; (ii) their mobility in the public domain;

(iii) their ability to make large and small purchases; (iv) ownership of productive assets, including house or homestead land and cash savings; (v) involvement in major decision-making; (vi) freedom from family domination, including the ability to make choices concerning how their money was used, the ability to visit their natal home when desired and a say in decision relating to the sale of their jewellery or land or to taking up outside work; (vii) political awareness such as knowledge of key national and political figures and the law on inheritance and participation in political action of various kinds; and (viii) a composite of all these indictors. They found that women's access to credit was a significant determinant of the magnitude of economic contributions reported by women: an increase in asset holdings in their own names; an increase in their purchasing power; their political and legal awareness and their composite empowerment index. The study also found that access to credit was associated with an overall reduction of the incidence of violence against women: women's participation in the expanded set of social relationships as a result of membership of credit organisations rather than increases in their productivity *per se* were responsible for reductions in domestic violence.

Gaiha (2001) has conducted a study to review the Maharashtra Rural Credit Project (MRCP)-a micro credit scheme, by focusing on the process of implementation and its implications for the empowerment of women and trade off between coverage of the poorest and sustainability of this scheme. It was found that the effectiveness of a micro-credit scheme such as the MRCP was likely to depend on whether it has flexibility to induce the participation of the poorest and whether it enables them to acquire the basic skills to benefit them. Dadhich (2001) observed that properly designed and effectively implemented micro-finance could be a means not only to alleviate poverty and empower women but also be a viable economic and financial proportion.

Eswaram (2002) concluded that the micro-credit has provided the rural poor access to finance without the burden of collateral through Self-Help Groups which have empowered the women folk economically and socially. Reddy (2002) reported that after the onset of SHGs women had better access to assets and resources and were able to tackle the issues of injustice and family violence. Manimekalai and Rajeshwari (2002) in their study of SHGs in Tamil Nadu found that SHG women who took up their own enterprise like tailoring, animal husbandry, petty shops, etc. were contributing more than 50 percent of their earnings to the households. Sudha Rani, Uma Devi and Surendra (2003) concluded that the increasing participation of women in Self-Help Groups enriched the empowerment of women. Pitt Khandkar and Cartwright (2003) in their findings mentioned that women's participation in micro credit programmes helps to increase women's empowerment. Credit program participation leads to women taking a greater part in household decision-making, having greater access to financial and economic resources, having greater social networks, having greater bargaining power *vis-à-vis* their husbands, and having greater freedom of mobility. Female credit also tended to increase spousal communication in general about family planning and parenting concerns.

Punithavanty Pandran & Shylendra (2004) stated that through linkage programme NABARD would like to realise the vision of empowering rural pool by improving their access to the formal credit system in an effective and sustainable manner to reach the goal of 100 million poor through one million SHGs by 2008. Nirmala *et al.* (2004) studied the empowerment of rural women through SHGs in Pondicherry by examining the changes with certain indicators. They found that due to SHGs there was an increase in income level of women, improvement in access to credit facilities and reduction in workload. Besides, the authors also observed positive changes in the status and decision-making power of women. Ramesh (2004) in his study of Shadnagar Mandal of Mehbub Nagar district (A.P.) found that access and availability of micro-credit through SHGs has not only resulted in higher incomes of women but also developed better leaderships skills, awareness regarding health and education aspects, communication skills and improved financial literacy among women. Narayanaswami (2005) worked out that out of 100 SHGs, 98 groups are only of women engaged with micro-enterprises because they are the main key to close the poverty. The basic principles of SHGs are group approach, mutual trust organisation of small and manageable groups, group cohesiveness, spirit of thrift, demand-based lending, collateral free, women-friendly loan, peer group pressure in repayment, skill training, capacity building and empowerment.

Ratna Ravi Kumar (2006) stated that SHG is a medium group for the development of saving habit among women. These SHGs come to the rescue of women and they enhance the quality and status of women as participants, decision makers and beneficiaries in the demographic, economic, social and cultural spheres of life. Khandelwal (2007) regarded micro-financing programmes as potentially very significant contributor to gender equality and propose development. Swaminathan

(2007) observed that by providing micro-credit to the "poorest of the poor" the gap in the formal rural credit sector can be filled. T. Ramachandran and S. Balakrishan (2008) conducted a study in Kanyakumari district by selecting 120 respondents. The study revealed that before joining Self-Help Groups, 34.17 percent of the respondents had no income and none of the respondents had income of above Rs. 1200. After joining Self-Help Groups, no respondent is without any income and 8.33 percent of them have income above Rs. 1200. SHGs have the power to create a socio-economic revolution in the rural areas of the country. In the study area SHGs have served the cause of women empowerment, social solidarity and socio-economic betterment of the poor.

The study suggested periodical training at regular intervals to group members on self-management aspect may be imparted with the help of experienced resource persons. Attendance at meeting should be made mandatory to inculcate the group cohesiveness among all the members. The NGOs and government should take necessary steps for marketing of the goods produced by SHGs. Richard Rosenberg (2010) studied whether or not the micro-finance movement was right to stress loans for micro enterprises, or had it been too slow to embrace savings and other services. He concluded that irrespective of how micro-credit loans were used, borrowers appreciated the fact that relative to almost all their other financial partners, micro-finance providers were reliable. People not only took loans, but they also repaid them with high reliability. Clients found micro-finance services so valuable that they were typically willing to pay high rate of interest on loans and accepted minimum or no return on their savings.

The true advantage of micro finance was not that each "dose" was more powerful, but rather that each dose cost much less in subsidies. Social programmes like primary education and healthcare usually required large continuing subsidies but micro-finance was different when it was done right, relatively small up-front subsidies led to permanent institutions that can continue providing services year after year with no further subsidy needed. Micro-credit helped in producing sustainable delivery year after year of highly valued services that helped hundreds of millions of people to keep their consumption stable, finance major expenses and cope shocks despite incomes that are low, irregular and unreliable. The main findings of these studies are:

- Micro-finance helps poor people to meet their basic consumption and production requirement.

- Micro-financing is leading to empowerment of women and thus helping in bringing gender-equity.
- SHGs have fostered a credit culture among its members, resulting in the growth of assets and income in full has improved the status of women in the rural households.
- SHGs have promoted thrift among the poor people, resulting in the improvement of self-reliance and self-financing.
- SHGs have promoted entrepreneurial skills among the members specially women.
- SHGs are a forum in which women can critically analyze their situations and devise collective strategies to overcome their difficulties.

Linking SHGs with Banking System

First official interest in informal group lending in India took shape during 1986-87 on the initiative of the NABARD. As a part of this broad mandate, NABARD initiated certain research projects on SHGs as a channel for delivery of micro-finance in the late 1980s. In 1988-89 in collaboration with some of the member institutions of the Asia Pacific Rural and Agricultural Credit Association, NABARD undertook a survey of 43 NGOs in 11 states in India, to study the functioning of micro-finance, SHGs and their collaboration possibilities with the formal banking system. Both these research projects conveyed encouraging possibilities and the NABARD initiated schemes with a view to evolve credit strategies for reaching the unreached poor in the rural areas. NABARD has been working as a catalyst in promoting and linking more and more SHGs to the banking system.

The pioneering efforts in this direction were made by NABARD in 1991-92; a pilot project for linking about 500 Self-Help Groups with banks was launched by NABARD in consultation with the RBI. It is considered as a landmark development in banking for the poor as it has been covering poorest of the poor who were so far neglected by the formal financial sector. Under the SHG-bank linkage model, usually the focus is on the poor, especially women. SHG's are assessed by banks for bank credit after six months of their functioning. If the Self-Help Groups are found to be functioning well the bank gives credit four times the savings of the SHG's.

In India, two major SHG Networks have access to institutional credit. One is NABARD sponsored SHG-bank linkage and second is Swarnajayanti Gram Swarozgar Yojana (SGSY).

Linkage Model of Micro-Finance

There are essentially three models of SHG-bank linkage in India

Model I

In this model, Self-Help Group promotion is done by some NGO and the group is brought in contact with the bank for savings and credit linkage. This is the largest model in India, covering 72 percent of the total of about 3.50 million groups—that are linked to banks.

Model II

In this model, the group promotion is done by bank staff themselves and the group is linked with the bank. This model covers about 20 percent of the total groups linked to banks in India.

Model III

This model is known as bulk lending model, wherein the groups are promoted by NGO-MFI that encourage the groups as well as play the role of intermediary. In this model, the NGO-MFI receives bulk loan from the bank. The bank, in turn, delivers the same to groups and in the process charges some service fee from SHGs. This model covers about 8 percent of the total groups and is expected to grow in future. Recognising their importance, both the Reserve Bank and NABARD have been spearheading the promotion and linkage of SHGs to the banking system by initiating proactive policies and systems. NABARD has been extending refinance support to the banking system and promotional grant support to NGO's and developing capacity building outreach of various partners.

Micro-Enterprise Promotion by SHGs through SGSY

Looking at the success that the SHG-bank linkage programme achieved, the Government of India developed the concept of SHG under the Government subsidy driven programme SGSY. On April 1, 1999 after merging six rural development programmes viz. Integrated Rural Development Programme (IRDP), Training of rural Youth for Self-Employment (TRYSEM), Development of Women and Children in Rural Areas (DWCRA), Supply of Improved Tool Kits for Rural Artisans (SITRA), Million Wells Schemes (MWS) and Ganga Kalyan Yojana (GKY) the government launched Swarnajayanti Gram Swarozgar Yojana (SGSY). SGSY is conceived as a holistic programme of micro enterprise development in rural areas with emphasis on organising the rural poor into Self-Help Groups, capacity building, planning of activity clusters, infrastructure support, technology, credit and marketing linkages.

It seeks to provide a network of agencies, namely, the District Rural Development Agency (DRDA), line departments of State Governments, Banks, Non-Government Organisations and Panchayati Raj Institutions for implementations of the programme. The programme recognises the need to focus on the key activities and the importance of activity clusters. The members of Self-Help Groups have to save regularly and convert their savings into a common fund known as the Group Corpus. The fund is used among the members through borrowing which is known as internal lending. The Group Corpus is supplemented with Revolving fund sanctioned as cash credit limit by the banks. The Group has to take up economic activity of their choice for income generation. The programme has inbuilt safeguards for the weaker sections. It insists that 50 percent of the SHGs must be formed exclusively by women and that 50 percent of the benefits should flow to scheduled castes and scheduled tribes.

There has also been a provision for disabled beneficiaries. The programme is credit driven and subsidy is back-ended. Subsidy under the SGSY to individuals is uniform at 30 percent of the project cost subject to a maximum of Rs. 7,500 in respect of scheduled castes and scheduled tribes, to a maximum of Rs. 10,000. For groups of Swarozgar the subsidy is 50 percent of the cost of the project, subject to a ceiling of Rs. 1.25 lakh as back end subsidy. There is no monetary limit as subsidy for irrigation projects.

SHG Movement and Progress of Micro-Finance in India

Micro-finance has made tremendous strides in India. It has become a household name in view of the variety of benefits reaped by the poor from micro-finance services. Self-Help Groups (SHGs) have become the common vehicle of development process, converging all development programmes, SHG-Bank Linkage Programme launched by NABARD way back in 1992 synthesising formal financial system and informal sector has become a movement throughout the country. It is considered as the largest micro-finance programme in terms of outreach in the world and many other countries are keen to replicate this model. At present a large number of Self-Help Promoting Institutions (SHPIs), all the banking agencies and Micro-Finance Institutions (MFIs) are pursuing this programme for upliftment of the poor. The RBI also recognised this as part of priority sector lending and normal banking business.

It has removed the interest rate cap for the final beneficiaries under the MF investment. The Micro-finance programme in India has emerged as not only the largest in the world having covered about 8.6 crore poor households as on 31 March 2009 but also the main contributor towards financial inclusion in the country. As on 31 March 2009, 61.21 lakh SHGs maintained bank savings of Rs. 5,545.62 crore and 42.24 lakh SHGs had loan outstanding of Rs. 22,679.84 crore. During the year 2009-10, while 16.09 lakh groups availed of bank credit of Rs. 12,253.51 crore. 581 Micro-Finance Institutions (MFIs) availed of Rs. 3,732.33 crore of bank credit. As on 31 March 2010, 1.915 MFIs had loan outstanding of Rs. 5,00.09 crore. The share of SHG loan to Ground Level Credit (GLC) increased to 4.07 percent in 2008-09 from 3.8 percent in 2007-08.

During 2009-10 an amount of Rs. 20.49 crore was released as grant support for SHG promotional activities and Rs. 60.42 crore to MFIs for capital support Revolving Fund Assistance (RFA) as against Rs. 18.73 crore and Rs.15.93 crore in the previous year respectively. During 2009-10 grant assistance of Rs. 28.78 crore was sanctioned to various agencies for promoting 71,268 SHGs, taking the cumulative assistance sanctioned to Rs. 107.66 crore for 4,92,746 groups as on 31 March 2010. The cumulative disbursement was Rs. 40.38 crore for 2,36,683 SHGs. An expenditure of Rs. 9.93 crore was incurred for capacity building initiatives for all stakeholders in the SHG segment.

During the year 2009-10, grant support of Rs. 6.76 lakh was given for the rating of five MFIs. During the year capital support of Rs. 6.87 crore was sanctioned to 10 agencies taking the cumulative support to Rs. 27.87 crore for 33 agencies and RFA amounting to Rs. 23 crore was sanctioned to 13 agencies taking the cumulative credit sanctioned to Rs. 74.02 crore to 42 agencies.

As on 31 March 2010, 116 Women Development Cells (WDC) were supported in 58 RRBs. 55 co-operative banks and three State Cooperative Agriculture and Rural Development Banks (SCARDBs) to address gender discrimination in credit and support services. A sum of Rs. 40.39 lakh was disbursed till 31 March 2010 Under Marketing of Non-Farm Products of Rural Women (MAHIMA) and Assistance to Rural Women in Non-Farm Development (ARWIND) schemes, grant support of Rs. 6.92 lakh and Rs. 17.56 lakh respectively were released as on 31 March 2010.

The programme is also the main contributor towards financial inclusion in the country. As on 31 March 2009, there were more than 61.21 lakh savings linked SHGs and more than 42.24 lakh credit linked SHGs and thus about 8.6 crore poor households have been covered in

Table 4.1: Progress of the Micro-Finance Programme (As on 31st March 2009)

S.No.	Particulars	Self-Help Groups				Micro-Finance Institutions (MFIs)*			
		2008		2009		2008		2009	
		Number	Amount	Number	Amount	Number	Amount	Number	Amount
1.	Loan disbursed during the year	12,27,770 (2,46,649)	8,849.26 (1,857.74)	16,09,586 (2,64,653)	12,253.51 (2,015.22)	518	1970.15	581	3732.33
2.	Loans Outstanding	36,25,941 (9,16,978)	16,999.90 (4,816.87)	42,24,338 (9,76,887)	22,679.84 (5,861.73)	1109	2748.84	1915	5009.09
3.	Savings accounts with banks	50,09,794 (12,03,070)	3,785.39 (809.51)	61,21,147 (15,05,581)	5,545.62 (1,563.39)	-	-	-	-

Figures in parenthesis indicate the share of SHGs covered under SGSY.

* Actual number of MFIs provided with bank loans would be lower, as several MFIs availed loans from more than one bank.

the programme. The share of SHG loan to Ground Level Credit (GLC) increased from 3.8 percent in 2007-08 to 4.07 percent in the 2008-09. The overall progress of the micro-finance programme is given in Table 4.1.

Recent Initiatives by NABARD

A. Micro-Finance Development and Equity Fund (MFDEF)

The micro-finance development and equity fund is being utilised for promotion of various micro-finance activities such as formation and linkage of SHGs through SHPIs, training and capacity building of stake holders, capital and soft loan assistance to MFIs, livelihood propagation, studies, documentation, etc. During 2009-10 an amount of Rs. 80.91 crore was released of which Rs. 20.49 crore was grant support far promotional activities and Rs. 60.42 crore was for capital support. Revolving Fund Assistance (RFA) to MFIs as against Rs. 18.73 crore and Rs. 15.93 crore in the previous year respectively.

B. Support to Partner Agencies

NABARD continued to extend grant support to NGOs, RRBs, DCCBs, FCs and Individual Rural Volunteers (IRVs) for promoting and nurturing quality SHGs. New SHPIs were identified even while supporting the existing ones. During 2009-10 grant assistance of Rs. 2,878.17 lakh was sanctioned to various agencies for promoting 71,268 groups taking the cumulative assistance sanctioned to Rs. 10,766.07 lakh for 4,92,746 groups. As on 31 March 2010, Rs. 4,037.74 lakh was released and 2,36,683 SHGs credit linked to banks.

C. Capacity Building of Partner Agencies

To fine tune the strategies for up scaling support to the microfinance sector NABARD conducted many awareness creation and sensitisation programmes and arranged exposure visits for SHG members, NGOs. Bankers, Trainers, Panchayat Raj Institution (PRI) representatives. NABARD officials, IAS officers and micro-entrepreneurs throughout the year, entailing an expenditure of Rs. 9.93 crore as against Rs. 11.18 crore in the previous year.

D. Support to Micro-Finance Institutions

Micro-Finance Institutions (MFIs) registered in various legal forms are supplementing the efforts of the formal banking network In providing credit support to the unreached clients for inclusive growth recognising their role as a tool for financial inclusion. NABARD has been supporting them through grant and soft loan assistance:

(i) Support to Banks and MFIs

NABARD continued to provide grant assistance to commercial banks and RRSs for getting the MFls rated by accredited rating agencies (CRISIL, M-CRIL, ICRA, CARE and Planet Finance) Under the scheme professional fees charged by the rating agency are reimbursed to the bank/MFI concerned subject to a maximum of Rs. 3 lakh. The assistance is available for the first rating of MFIs with loan outstanding higher than Rs. 50 lakh and less than Rs. 10 crore. During the year, the scheme for providing grant assistance to MFls for their rating was revised. During the year, rating support amounted to Rs. 676 lakhs for five agencies.

(ii) Capital Support and Revolving Fund Assistance MFIs

Capital Support is given to MFIs to leverage capital so that commercial and other funds required for providing financial services at affordable cost to the poor and achieving sustainability in credit operations over a period of 3-5 years, could be easily accessed from banks. During the year, capital support of Rs. 6.87 crore was sanctioned to 10 agencies taking the cumulative support to Rs. 27.87 crore for 33 agencies. Revolving Fund Assistance (RFA) is provided to MFIs, on selective basis, for on-lending to the unreached poor. The idea behind such selective assistance is to experiment with various MF models for innovating the alternative credit delivery systems and for drawing lessons for sustainability and replicability. During the year, RFA amounting to Rs. 23 crore was sanctioned to 13 agencies, taking the cumulative credit sanctioned to Rs. 74.02 crore for 42 agencies. During the year, the scheme for Capital/RFA support to MFIs was thoroughly revised to give more support to startup MFIs and at a cheaper cost, so as to make them sustainable over a period of time.

E. Scaling-up of Micro-Finance Programmer: Special Initiative

Support to Activity-Based Groups (ABG)

NABARD continued to support the scheme for small-scale activity-based groups wherein capacity building, credit and market-related support will be extended. The focus is on forming and nurturing groups engaged in similar economic activities, i.e., farmers, hand loom weavers, craftsmen, fishermen, etc. to improve production and realising better

Table 4.2: Grant Assistance Extended to various Partners in SHG-Bank Linkage Programme (as on 31st March 2010) (Rs. Lakh)

Agencies	*Sanctions during the year*			*Cumulative sanctions*			*Cumulative Progress*		
	No.	*Amount*	*No. of SHGs*	*No.*	*Amount*	*No. of SHGs*	*Amount released*	*SHGs formed*	*SHGs linked*
Co-operative Banks	7	63.23	5230	102	626.36	59105	252.95	44618	29075
RRB	4	40.14	3395	117	429.44	47985	189.23	54271	36155
NGO	306	2620.10	53393	2624	9025.81	345173	3469.69	244367	157831
Farmers' Clubs	-	-	-	-	-	-	61.96	14858	7986
IRVs	2	154.70	9250	68	684.46	40483	63.91	9991	5636
Total	319	2878.17	71268	2911	10766.07	492746	4037.74	368105	236683

NABARD: Annual Report, 2009-10.

price for produce The scheme has both grant and loan components. While grant support would cover group formation training, extensions services, establishing market linkages, etc., bank loans would cover investment and working capital needs of the groups, could draw refinance for the loans provided to activity-based groups like SHGs. In select cases, NABARD may provide loans directly to registered groups or through agencies promoting the group, to establish a few initial projects where none exists.

(i) ***Grant Assistance to Self-Help Promoting Institutions (SHPIs) for Promotion and Credit Linkage of SHGs—Revision of Existing Guidelines.***
The promotional grant assistance given to various agencies for forming, nurturing, linking and stabilising credit linkage of SHGs has been enhanced with special focus on hilly tough districts and resource poor regions. To ensure that SHGs develop self-expertise in managing themselves an additional handholding support for one year, over and above three years has also been allowed subject to certain conditionalities.

(ii) ***Micro-Enterprise Development Programme***
NABARD had launched the Micro-Enterprise Development Programme (MEDP) during 2005-06 for skill upgradation and development of sustainable livelihoods venturing into micro-enterprise, by matured SHG members. During the year 1530 MEDPs were conducted for 38,313 SHG members on location—specific farm, non-farm and service sector activities like bee-keeping, soyabean and mushroom cultivation, organic farming, horticulture and floriculture agarbatti-making, tailoring, beauty parlor, plate-making from areca-nut crafts, screen printing, crochet and chikan work, mandap decoration, motor coil rewinding, lantana basket-weaving, etc., Cumulatively, as on 31 March 2010, 2,843 MEDPs had been conducted covering 71,518 participants.

The Shortcomings

Besides the positive impacts of micro-financing the researchers have also pointed out some of the drawbacks of micro-financing in India. Raghav Gaiha (2001) observed that very high rates of interest are charged under micro credit. This high rate of interest is a burden for the poor borrower, given the low capacity intensity of investment through micro credit and the resultant low profit margins. Madheswaru & Dharanadaikary (2001) found that micro-financing programme is working very effectively, but a major challenge for this programme is the viability of non-farm economic activities. There are two major problems, first, to find an economic activity that will yield a rate of profit necessary to cover the interest rate on the loan. Second, marketing of the produce is a problem.

The main market for non-farm activities is in the urban areas, hence when these activities are taken up by rural women the products cannot meet standards of urban market. Srinivasan (2002) observed the margin for the bank varies from 2.5 percent to 6.5 percent, for the NGO it varies from 6 percent to 24 percent and the final rates of interest to the borrower turns out to be in the range of 24.36 percent per annum. Ramachandran and Swaminathan (2002) found the cost of credit under micro credit programmes is also in line with the informal sources. They observed that the high cost of credit under micro-credit programme is due to the margins at different levels charged over the market rate of interest. Shah Mihir, *et al.* (2007), observed that there is a great lack of transparency and potentially exploitative situation is experienced in the recovery and repayment of loans. People are reported to have had to borrow from the money-lenders in order to repay MFIs.

S. Ramachandran *et al.* (2008) in their study of Thirunelveli district of Tamil Nadu observed that unfortunately the mobilisation and organisation of women through SHGs could not eradicate the disempowering effect of patriarchy but they could show the sign of improving the power of women. The study probed into the economic empowerment of women in terms of their ownership and control over household income, savings, debt and assets.

Though, the SHGs have not contributed much to improve the women's share in income and assets which are mostly men controlled. They could increase the share of women in household savings and debt. V. Sucharita (2008) observed in a study conducted in Andhra Pradesh that although conscious efforts were made to form groups and provide loans to reach targets on the paper. However, there were no deliberate attempts like sensitising them about gender discrimination, freedom from violence, knowledge of legal rights, etc. to empower women. But women are being empowered to some extent as observed through various changes at individual, family and village levels. However, these changes reflect only the functional aspect of empowerment.

There has not been any visible structural change like control over their assets, credit, involvement in decision-making in the family, etc. Suresh Karuppasamy (2010) studied the problems faced by the members of SHGs while marketing their products. The author concluded that the produced products were mainly sold in village, town and district. They were not concentrated on state level marketing. It may be because of non co-operation from the other states or lack of finance. So the central government should give appropriate co-ordination to SHGs to get loans from the nationalised banks and also each and every state should co-operate themselves to allow the sales of products of other state SHGs. Most of the SHGs were following direct selling method to sell the products. It may be because of the non-preference by the shopkeepers. The government can give subsidies to the shopkeepers and also other purchasers. It may increase the sales of products. Government should assure the purchase of certain products such as Sericulture, handicrafts, etc., which may increase income of SHG members.

The observations made by most of the researchers clearly indicate that interest cost of the loans under micro-credit programmes to the poor borrowers is a cause of concern. The interest rates charged by the micro-credit institutes are very high as compared to those charged by the formal credit sources. Another problem faced by SHGs is regarding the marketing of the products produced by these SHGs. Also, due to lack of monitoring and supervision of loans the funds are not used for their real purposes of production. Generally, people divert these funds during emergency and in order to meet out their social and religious obligations.

Besides, the poorest particularly rural women have various constraints such a very low income with limited resources, illiteracy, ill health and lack of entrepreneurial ability which prevent them from taking loans and investing in any high return activity. Some researchers argue that micro-finance programmes divert the attention of women from other more effective strategies for empowerment. Evidence suggests that even in financially successful micro finance programmes, actual contribution to empowerment is often limited (Mayoux, 2010).

- Most women remain confined to a narrow range of female low-income activities.
- Many women have limited control over income and/or what little income they earn may substitute for former male household contributions, as men retain more of their earnings for their own use.
- Women often have greater workloads combining both production and reproductive tasks.
- Women's expenditure decisions may continue to prioritize men and male children while daughters or daughters-in-law bear the brunt of unpaid domestic work.

- Where women actively press for change, this may increase tensions in the household and the incidence of domestic violence.
- Women remain marginalised in local and national level political processes. This is not just a question of lack of impact, but may also be a process of disempowerment.
- Credit is also debt, savings and loan interest or insurance payments divert resources which might otherwise go towards necessary consumption or investment.
- Putting the responsibility for savings and credit on women may absolve men of responsibility for the household.
- Where group meetings focus only on savings and credit, this uses up women's precious work and leisure time, cutting programme costs but not necessarily benefitting women.

Main Challenges in Micro-Finance

A major contention is that micro-credit programmes do not reach the poorest. A large number of poor people are not acquainted with the activities and advantages of the SHGs. Although the outreach has touched a respectable level, the challenge that still remains is to identify the poor specially women and to cover them all. Another challenge is promotion of individual and group enterprises with strong backward and forward linkages. Micro-finance institutes also face challenges regarding sustainability of various micro-finance operations viz., how to lower the interest rate and transaction cost so that it is economical for both providers and clients and how to shift from self-employment to employment generation through micro enterprises.

Conclusion and Suggestions

Micro-finance is fast emerging as an effective solution to the problem of poverty. Micro-finance has a significant role to play for boosting micro-entrepreneurial activities for creating productive assets and for generating gainful employment opportunities for rural women. It is proved as an important liberating force in societies, where women in particular have to struggle against social and economic conditions. The SHG movement in India has led to empowerment of rural women both economically and in terms of more equitable gender relations. Self-Help Group bank linkage programme is responsible for developing banking habits among the rural poor women. It helps in building up their self-confidence through community action. Interactions in the group meetings and collective decision-making enables poor women to identify and prioritize their needs and resources. They become aware of the policies and programmes of the government through the Self-Help Group movement. The impact of the micro finance on poverty reduction is sustainable but much more is needed to be done to achieve better results.

In order to enforce effectiveness of micro-finance for better sustainability it is suggested:

- Credit institutions should develop schemes in which provisions be made to get marketing finances so that distress sales may be avoided.
- SHGs should be provided infrastructural support for marketing of their products.
- Proper training should be provided to the members to understand banking operations and also to maintain records properly.
- There should be proper monitoring of evaluation of SHGs through different agencies like bankers, NGOs and Government Officials, etc.
- To adopt flexible repayment schedule to suit borrowers cash flow.
- There should be co-ordination among all the micro-credit institutions.
- Trained staff should be involved and the policies should be implemented properly.
- Government should encourage exports of goods which are produced by the groups.
- Delays in sanctioning loans and also red-tapism in the banks must be curbed.
- Group activities should be promoted by officials. Training workshops should be organised.
- Keeping in view the indebtedness and increasing farmers' distress, the government should think of increasing support to micro-finance institutions so that they may reduce the rate of interest.

No doubt micro-finance programmes have proved an effective instrument for eradication of poverty and economic empowerment of rural women. SHGs are sustainable, stimulate savings and help the borrowers to come out of the vicious circle of poverty. SHGs have served the cause of women empowerment, social harmony and socio-economic betterment of rural poor women. Noeleen Heyzer, co chair UN council, Micro-credit summit, rightly pointed out, "Micro-credit is much more than access to money. It is about women gaining control over the means to make a living. It is about women lifting themselves out of poverty and vulnerability. It is about women achieving economic and political empowerment within their homes, their villages, their countries". SHG movement shall be able to achieve its objective of women's economic empowerment if intervened with social awareness generation. Problems related to women can be effectively tackled only by bringing social awakening. Therefore, increasing people's participation and awareness as well as suitable and more effective policies of the government are essential for the success of the programme.

References

Ahirrao Jitendra (2009), "Rural Women Empowerment through Micro-finance", *Kurukshetra,* Vol. 57, No. 4, pp. 23-25.

Dadhieh, C.L. (2001), "Micro-finance, A Panacea for Poverty Alleviation: A Case Study of Oriental Grameen Project in India", *Indian Journal of Agricultural Economics,* Vol. 56, No. 3, pp. 419-26.

Gaiha Raghav (2001), "Micro-credit and the Rural Poor: A Review of the Maharashtra Rural Credit Project", *Journal of Micro-Finance,* Vol. 3, No. 2, pp. 125-53.

Government of India (2009), *Economic Survey,* 2008-09, Ministry of Finance, New Delhi.

Haque Imamul, S.M. (2009), "Micro-Finance—An Answer to Poverty", *Professional Banker,* pp. 11-15.

Hashemi, S.M., Schuler, S.R., and Riley, A.P. (1996), "Rural credit programs and women's empowerment in Bangladesh", *World Development,* Vol. 24, No. 4.

Karuppasamy, Suresh (2010), Marketing of Products Produced by Self-Help Groups.

Khandelwal, A.K. (2007), "Micro-Finance Development Strategy for India", *Economic and Political Weekly,* Vol. XLII, No. 13, March 31-April 6, pp. 1127-35.

Lokhande Murlidhar, A. (2009), "Micro-finance Initiatives in India", *Kurukshetra,* Vol. 57, No. 4, pp. 16-18.

Madheswaran, S. and A. Dharmadhikary (2001), "Empowering Rural Women through Self-Help Groups: Lessons from Maharashtra Rural Credit Project", *Indian Journal of Agricultural Economics,* Vol. 56, No. 3, pp. 427-43.

Malyadri, P. (2010), "Empowerment of Rural Women through Panchayati Raj Institutions", *Kurukshetra,* Vol.58, No.12, p. 49.

Malhotra, Meenakshi (2004), *Role of Micro-Finance in Women Empowerment: In Empowerment of Women* (ed.), Isha Books, Delhi, pp. 1-57.

Manimekalai, N., Rajeshwari, G. (2002), Grassroots Entrepreneurship through SHGs, SEDME 29.2.

Mansuri, B.B. (2009), "Self-Help Group Approach to Rural Development: An Appropriate Alternative", *Udyog Yug,* Vol. 30, No. 7, pp. 10-17.

NABARD Annual Report, 2009-10.

Narayanaswami (2005), "Micro-Credit and Rural Enterprises", *Journal of Rural Development,* Vol. 24, No. 3, pp. 353-76.

Nirmala, V. *et al.* (2004), "SHGs for Poverty Alleviation in Pondicherry", *Journal of Rural Development,* Vol. 23, No. 2.

Pandian Punithavanty and R. Eswaram (2002), "Empowerment of Women through Micro-Credit", *Yojana,* Vol. 46, pp. 47-50.

Pitt, M.M., Khandker, S.R. and Cartwright, J. (2003), Does Micro-Credit Empower Women? Evidence from Bangladesh, *World Bank Policy Research Working Paper 2998.*

Purushotham, P. (2004), Micro-Credit for Micro-Enterprise, in Rural Non-Farm Employment, NRID, Rajendranagar.

Raju, Hema Sundra K., M. Muni Reddy and B. Bhagwan Reddy (2009), "Outreaching Unbanked Rural Marginalised Groups", *Kurukshetra,* Vol. 54, No. 4, pp. 10-12.

Ramachandran, S., S. Sasikumar and E. Kanagaraj (2008), *Self-Help Groups and Economic Empowerment of Women in Thirunelveli district of Tamil Nadu in Micro-finance and Poverty Eradication* (ed.), New Delhi: New Century Publication, pp. 544-51.

Ramachandran, T. and S. Balakrishnan (2008), "Impact of Self-Help Groups on Women's Empowerment—A study in Kanyakumari District", *Kurukshetra,* Vol. 57, No. 2, pp. 31-34.

Ramachandran, V.K. and M. Swaminathan (2002), "Rural Banking and Landless Labour Households: Institutional Reforms and Rural Credit Markets in India", *Journal of Agrarian Change,* Vol. 2, No. 4.

Ramesh D. (2004), Transformation of Rural Women through Micro-Credit, SEDME 31.4.

Ratna Ravi Kumar (2006), "A Premier on Micro-Finance—The Paradox of Poverty in Plenty", *Journal of Chartered Accountant,* Vol. 54, No. 11, pp. 1631-33.

Rosenberg, Richard (2010), Does Micro-credit Really Help Poor People?, Focus note 59, Washington, DC, CGAP.

Shah Mihir, Rangu Rao, P.S. Vijayshankar (2007), "Rural Credit in 20th Century India: Overview of History and Perspectives", *Economic and Political Weekly,* Vol. XLII, No. 15, pp. 1356-62.

Sharma, K.C. (2009), "Micro-Finance in India—Status and Challenges", *Professional Banker,* Vol. IX, Issue-7, pp. 17-19.

Shylendra (2004), "The SHG Bank Linkage Programme", *Journal of Rural Development,* Vol. 23, No. 4, pp. 411-50.

Soni, Balbir (2001), *Reform Prospects for Rural Development,* Vol. 2, Ch. 1, Empowerment of Women, New Delhi: Dominant Publishers and Distributors.

Srinivasan, Girija (2002), "Linking Self-Help Groups with Banks in India, SEDME—Small Enterprises Development", *Management and Extension Journal.*

Sudha Rani, K., D. Uma Devi and G. Surendra (2003), "SHGs, Micro-credit and Empowerment", *Social Welfare,* Vol. 48, No. 11, pp. 18-22.

Swaminathan, M. (2007), "The Micro-Credit Alternative?", *Economic and Political Weekly,* Vol. XLII, No. 13, March 31-April 6, pp 1171-75.

Vasimali, M.P.V. and K., Narendra (2007), "Micro-Finance for Poverty Reduction: The Kalanjiam Way", *Economic and Political Weekly,* Vol. XLII, No. 13, March 31-April 6, pp. 1192-95.

Women's Empowerment in Rural India: A Study Based on MGNREGA

RAMNA

Introduction

In India, more than four-fifths of all women working in rural areas are engaged in agriculture. They work and contribute to the economy in one form or another but much of their work is not documented or accounted for in official statistics. Women plough fields and harvest crops while working on farms; women weave and make handicrafts while working in household industries; women sell food and gather wood while working in the informal sector.

Additionally, women are traditionally responsible for the daily household chores (e.g., cooking, fetching water, and looking after children). In this country, everyone ranked relative to others according to their caste, class, wealth, and power due to its hierarchical nature. There are different standards of behaviour for men and women that carry over into the work environment. Women are expected to be chaste and especially modest in all actions which may constrain their ability to perform in the workplace on an equal basis with men. Another related aspect of life in India is veiling and seclusion of women. Fewer women, especially younger women, observe veiling today, but those who still do face constraints beyond those already placed on them by other hierarchical practices. These cultural rules place some Indian women, particularly those of lower caste, in a paradoxical situation: when a family suffers economically, people often think that a woman should go out and work, yet at the same time the woman's participation in employment outside the home is viewed as "slightly inappropriate, subtly wrong, and definitely dangerous to their chastity and womanly virtue". When a family recovers from an economic crisis or attempts to improve its status, women may be kept at home as a demonstration of the family's morality and as a symbol of its financial security.

As in many other countries, working women of all segments of Indian society face various forms of discrimination including sexual harassment. Although the cultural restrictions women face are changing, women are still not as free as men to participate in the formal economy. In the past, cultural restrictions were the primary pediments to female employment; now, however, the shortage of jobs throughout the country contributes to low female employment as well. Women account for a small proportion of the formal Indian labour force, even though the number of female main workers has grown faster in recent years than that of their male counterparts.

Labour Participation Rates by Gender and Age

Table 5.1 reveals that in no cohort the female Labour participation rates were over half of the male rates, and repeatedly much lower, especially among the 20-24 and the 60-64 of age. As for trends, the table shows that between 2000-08 the labour participation rates for the 15-19-year-olds have fallen for both genders by respectively

Table 5.1: Labour Participation Rates by Gender and Age Group in India (2000 and 2008)

Age Group	*2000*			*2008*		
	All	*Women*	*Men*	*All*	*Women*	*Men*
15-19	35.9	23.1	47.6	33.4	20.6	45.0
20-24	58.3	30.9	83.6	57.8	29.3	82.3
25-29	67.3	36.4	95.7	68.0	37.7	95.9
30-34	71.0	41.6	97.8	71.1	42.9	97.1
35-39	72.2	44.4	97.6	73.8	47.9	97.7
40-44	72.4	45.1	97.4	72.3	46.3	96.5
45-49	71.2	43.2	96.8	71.9	45.8	96.3
50-54	67.5	39.9	93.8	67.4	39.6	93.4
55-59	61.6	34.8	87.9	60.5	35.4	84.8
60-64	42.2	10.6	74.7	39.9	7.8	72.7
Total 15-64	61.1	35.2	85.2	61.0	35.7	84.6

Source: ILO Laborsta.

2.5 percent points for females and 2.6 percent points for males. Table also reveals that between 2000-08 the LPRs for both genders aged 25-29 slightly went up.

Employment by Industry and Gender

It is clear from Table 5.2 that women spent maximum time (56.9 percent) in community, social, personal services because they are traditionally responsible for the daily household chores (e.g., cooking, etching water, and looking after children, followed by manufacturing (18.7 percent) and agriculture, forestry, fishing (9.6 percent) while they spent minimum time in wholesale, retail, restaurants, hotels (1.0 percent) because due to cultural restrictions women are still not as free as men to participate in the formal economy.

Table 5.2: Employment by Industry and Gender, Employees (organised sector), India, 2005

(*in percent*)

	All	*Women*	*Men*
Agriculture, forestry, fishing	5.6	9.6	4.7
Mining	4.1	1.5	4.7
Manufacturing	21.3	18.7	22.2
Utilities	3.4	1.1	4.0
Construction	3.6	1.3	4.1
Transport, storage communication	10.7	3.8	12.3
Wholesale, retail, restaurants, hotels	2.1	1.0	2.4
Finance, real estate, business services	7.3	6.0	7.6
Community, social, personal services	41.9	56.9	38.3
Total	100.0	100.0	100.0

Source: ILO Laborsta.

Unemployment

We now turn to unemployment. Between 2000-06, the period for which detailed figures are available, official unemployment fluctuated between 39.3 million and 42.0 million, the 2006 average was 41, 47 million unemployed of 14 years and older, making up approximately 9.5 percent of the economically active population, and that of 2008 39, 11 million unemployed, or about 8.3 percent of the economically active population: 26, 78 million men (about 7.9 percent) and 12, 33 million women (about 9.4 percent). Table 5.3 also shows nearly equal unemployment rates for females and males.

Categories by far most affected by unemployment were the young women and men aged 14-19 and 20-29. In 2006, the official unemployment rates for the girls aged 15-19 and the young women aged 20-29 were respectively 21 and 17 percent. In 2006 there were on average 8, 21 million female unemployed 14 to 29-year-olds, bringing their joint unemployment rate at 18.0 percent. These young unemployed females accounted for 70 percent of all unemployed women and 20 percent of all unemployed.

Table 5.3: Unemployment Rates by Gender and Age Group, India, 2006

Age group	*Total*	*Male*	*Female*
14-19	21.9	22.3	21.2
20-29	15.8	15.3	17.0
30-39	8.9	9.0	8.5
40-49	2.3	2.2	2.4
50-59	0.5	0.4	0.6
60+	0.1	0.1	0.1
Total	9.5	9.5	9.6

Source: ILO, Laborsta.

Addressing the challenge of low labour absorption capacity of traditional agricultural and organised industrial sector for women, several programs have been started by the government of India to provide employment to them and Mahatma Gandhi National Rural Employment Guarantee Scheme (MGNREGS) is one of them which has been launched on February 2, 2006 under the national rural employment guarantee act on September 7, 2005. On going, programmes of Sampoorana Grameen Rozgar Yojana (SGRY) and National Food for Work Programme (NFWP) subsumed within the MGNREGA in the 200 districts identified in the initial stage and expanded to 330 districts during 2007-08 and coverage was extended to all rural districts of the country in 2008-09. At present 619 districts are covered under MGNREGA.

Data Sources and Methodology

Like other public employment programmes, Mahatma Gandhi National Rural Guarantee Programme is also based on Keynesian aggregate demand strategy. There are several provisions which are made in the Operational Guidelines for the NREGA seek to encourage women's effective participation in the programme both as workers and as managers of the programme. The guidelines spell out clear instructions for equal payment of wages for men and women and that at least one-third of the beneficiaries shall be women who have registered and requested for work under the scheme. A crèche is to be provided if there are more than five children under 6 years of age and that payment to the crèche in charge will not be included as part of the work measurement. As per the guidelines, each work shall be monitored by a local Vigilance and Monitoring Committee which shall be composed of members from the immediate locality or village where the work is undertaken, to monitor the progress and quality of work. The Gram Sabha is expected to ensure that women are represented on this Committee. The guidelines mention a social audit forum to be convened by the Gram Sabha every 6 months as part of the continuous auditing process, and that the timing of the forum should be convenient in particular for NREGP workers, women and marginalised communities. By recognising single persons as a 'household', the act makes it possible for widows and other single woman to access this work.

To promote women's participation in the NREGA, some state governments have introduced specific features to the scheme. Kerala and Himachal Pradesh pay the minimum wages based on a day's work, not piece rated, which has enabled women to attain stipulated minimum wages more easily than under a piece rated system. Some states such as: Andhra Pradesh, Bihar and West Bengal have introduced different (reduced) task rates for women. Andhra Pradesh and Orissa were the first to pay wages through a bank account to ensure that leakages are minimized. Since September 2008, the government has made it mandatory to switch to bank payments to minimize corruption, although the roll out of this provision is contingent on the speed with which individual bank accounts can be opened.

In Himachal Pradesh 'Mahatma Gandhi National Rural Guarantee Act' has made effective w.e.f. 2nd February, 2006. In the first phase, this scheme introduced in district Chamba and Sirmaur on the same date. In the second phase, it was started in districts Kangra and Mandi w.e.f. 1.4.2007. In the third phase all the remaining eight districts of the state have been covered under the scheme w.e.f. 1.4.2008. In the present study in order to analyse the performance of MGNREGA, secondary source of data has been used. Data has been collected from related books, journals and publications of different departments', e.g. Planning department, economic and statistics department, rural development department, Annual plans of Himachal Pradesh as well as India's Annual Administrative Reports. Main purpose of this study is to examine at what extent this programme has been succeeded in generating employment opportunities for women in Himachal Pradesh.

Review of Literature

There are so many studies which have been supported the fact that MGNREGA has positivity affected the living of women by ensuring better responsiveness of local government to community needs and rejuvenating natural resources and by stopping the local population from migration to the cities. Malhotra (2005) stated that employment guarantee related works would have positive effect on household income by raising agriculture wage and investment in human capital. Dreze (2005) stated that the main purpose of the employment guarantee is to protect rural households from economic insecurity. Aiyar (2006) has analysed the superiority of employment guarantee act in providing or strengthening social security and community mobilisation. Puri (2006) concluded that the main objective of rural employment guarantee scheme is to rejuvenate natural resources to stimulate the local economy and to stop population from migration to the cities. Singh (2006) stated that MGNREGA is not only towards poverty alleviation but also for empowerment of those who are living at the margins.

It is a significant achievement for the rural poor. Mathur (2007) examined the performance of MGNREGA and worked out that some 'backward' states have done better than several of the progressive ones. Narayanan (2008) worked out that this scheme has brought about major change in the lives of women. There are so many other studies such as: Jha (2008), Vanaik (2008), Siddartha (2008), Mehrotra (2008), Khera (2008), Afridi (2008), Khera (2009), Adhikari (2010) and Champatiray (2010) have appreciated MGNREGA in one way or the other that it has become a beacon of light in the rural areas and contributed substantially for the increasing living and economic conditions by reducing income imbalance in the rural area. It has contributed to the reduction of migration from rural area to urban area for searching petty jobs.

Some of them have also appreciated the transfer of wages into workers bank account. But some studies such as: Louis (2006), Dater (2007) and Vanaik (2008) have observed the under utilisation of funds in some states and payment through bank accounts could not eliminate corruption under the scheme.

Results and Discussion

The basic aim of MGNREGA scheme is to improve livelihood, security of the households in rural areas of the state by providing 100 days of generated wage employment in every financial year to every household whose adult member is volunteer to do unskilled manual work. And the 33 percent reservation for women workers together with the effort to create women-friendly worksites by providing child care at the sites certainly are reasons for increased women's participation. Another potentially important impact is on women's wages, since women's market wages, especially, are usually lower than minimum wages.

Year-wise Percentage Share of Employment Generated for Women under MGNREGA at National Level

Table 5.4 shows that in the year 2006-07 and 2007-08, out of total mandays generated, Tamil Nadu has shown highest percentage of mandays generated for women followed by Kerala, Rajasthan and Karnataka, etc. But between 2008-11, Kerala has shown highest percentage of mandays generated for women followed by Tamil Nadu, Puducherry and Andhra Pradesh in 2008-09, by Chandigarh, Tamil Nadu, Rajasthan, Puducherry and Andhra Pradesh in 2009-10 and Puducherry, Tamil Nadu, Dadar and Nagar Haweli, Goa, Rajasthan and Andhra Pradesh in 2010-11. There are some states where percentage of person days generated for women is greater than their percentage share in total population include Kerala, Tamil Nadu, Rajasthan, Andhra Pradesh, Karnataka, Goa, Tripura (2006-07 and 2008-09), Himachal Pradesh (2011-12) and U.Ts like Puducherry, Dadar and Nagar Haveli, Chandigarh (2010-11) and Andeman and Nichobar (2010-11 and 2011-12). Except these states, the percentage of person days generated for women is lower than their percentage share in total population.

There are so many reasons like socio-cultural norms around women's work, mobility and intra-household allocations of roles and responsibilities, individual household factors like levels of care responsibilities and numbers of adult women in the house, health status, opportunity costs, other market opportunities and market wages for men and women, efficiency of implementation and information flows to and within households, etc. which are responsible for different women's participation across states.

Year-wise percentage Share of Employment Generated for Women under MGNREGA in Himachal Pradesh

In Himachal Pradesh, all twelve districts have been covered under MGNREGA in 2008. There are some districts like Kinnaur, Mandi, Hamirpur, Lahaul-Spiti, Kangra, Kullu, Una (2010-11) in which percentage Share of Employment Generated for Women Under

Table 5.4: Year-wise Percentage Share of Employment Generated for Women under MGNREGA at National Level

Name of the States	*State-wise percentage share of women in Total Population*	*Year-wise percentage Share of Employment Generated for Women Under MGNREGA at National Level*					
		2006-07	*2007-08*	*2008-09*	*2009-10*	*2010-11*	*2011-12*
Andhra Pradesh	49.79	54.79	57.75	58.15	58.09	57.05	57.69
Arunachal Pradesh	47.90	30.02	29.75	26.13	17.25	33.26	28.57
Assam	48.81	31.67	30.85	27.16	27.90	26.50	25.33
Bihar	47.80	17.38	26.62	30.02	30.04	28.50	28.68
Gujarat	47.86	28.70	46.55	42.82	47.55	44.23	46.23
Haryana	46.73	30.60	34.42	30.65	34.81	35.62	36.54
Himachal Pradesh	49.33	12.24	30.10	30.01	46.09	48.25	58.87
Jammu & Kashmir	48.46	4.46	0.01	5.76	6.67	7.46	14.21
Karnataka	49.19	50.56	50.27	50.42	36.79	46.01	45.56
Kerala	52.01	65.62	71.39	85.01	88.19	90.39	93.15
Madhya Pradesh	48.19	43.24	41.67	43.28	44.23	44.40	42.52
Maharashtra	48.07	37.07	39.99	46.22	39.65	45.88	47.02
Punjab	47.17	37.76	16.29	24.61	26.29	33.84	44.16
Rajasthan	48.09	67.14	68.99	67.11	66.89	68.34	68.99
Sikkim	47.07	24.79	36.74	37.66	51.22	46.68	46.58
Tamil Nadu	49.88	81.11	82.00	79.67	82.90	82.60	75.65
Tripura	49.01	75.00	44.51	51.01	41.09	38.55	38.29
Utter Pradesh	47.59	16.55	14.53	18.11	21.67	21.42	17.29
West Bengal	48.62	18.28	16.99	26.53	33.42	33.69	32.17
Chhattisgarh	49.77	39.32	42.05	47.43	49.21	48.63	45.75
Jharkhand	48.64	39.47	27.17	28.51	34.25	33.47	30.91
Uttarakhand	49.05	30.47	42.77	36.86	40.28	40.30	41.12
Manipur	49.67	50.89	32.80	45.92	47.98	35.07	33.17
Meghalaya	49.64	19.40	30.87	41.35	47.20	43.92	43.07
Mizoram	49.37	33.37	33.62	36.58	34.99	33.93	23.93
Nagaland	48.21	29.97	29.35	36.70	43.53	35.02	00.00
Odisha	49.46	35.60	36.39	37.58	36.25	39.40	38.74
Puducherry	50.94	-	-	67.07	63.51	80.39	79.32
Andeman & Nichobar	46.75	-	-	0.39	44.85	47.39	47.17
Lakshadweep	48.61	-	-	40.66	37.59	34.33	40.24
Chandigarh	44.98	-	-	00.00	00.00	85.11	00.00
Dadar & Nagar Haweli	43.66	-	-	79.17	87.14	68.38	00.00
Daman & Dew	38.20	-	-	00.00	00.00	00.00	00.00
Goa	49.19	-	-	00.00	62.16	68.37	75.21
Total		40.65	42.52	47.88	48.10	47.73	49.60

Table 5.5: Year-wise percentage Share of Employment Generated for Women under MGNREGA in Himachal Pradesh

Name of the Districts	*District-wise percentage share of women in Total Population*	*Year-wise percentage Share of Employment Generated for Women Under MGNREGA at State Level*		
		2009-10	*2010-11*	*2011-12*
Chamba	49.73	38.56	41.70	37.48
Sirmaur	47.79	12.07	17.22	20.27
Kangra	50.33	55.84	59.89	65.08
Mandi	50.30	70.74	73.49	72.36
Bilaspur	49.53	46.85	49.52	61.45
Hamirpur	52.29	64.64	69.37	74.63
Kinnaur	45.00	71.75	75.46	75.78
Kullu	48.72	49.06	54.12	59.75
Lahaul-Spiti	47.81	63.71	61.89	57.33
Shimla	47.81	42.85	47.71	48.58
Solan	46.91	37.91	39.51	42.94
Una	49.42	46.15	53.49	59.04
Total	49.33	52.47	55.67	58.64

Source: Government of India, Ministry of Rural Development, Department of Rural Development, Monthly Progress Report under Mahatma Gandhi National Rural Employment Guarantee Act (MGNREGA), Part-VIB, 2009-10, 2010-11 and 2011-12.

MGNREGA in 2009-10 and 2010-11 is greater than their percentage share in Total Population. But in 2011-12 except Sirmaur, Chamba and Solan, in all other districts, the percentage Share of Employment Generated for Women under MGNREGA is greater than their percentage share in Total Population. And if we compare this data with stipulated 33 percent, person days of work created for women is greater than this 33 percent in all other districts except Sirmaur. It is clear from Table 5.5 that out of total Person days which have been generated in Himachal Pradesh in the financial year 2009-10, 52.47 percent person days have been generated for women.

District Kinnaur has leaded in all districts by generating 71.75 percent person days for Women followed by district Mandi (70.74 percent), Hamirpur (64.64 percent) Lahaul-Spiti (63.71) and Kangra (55.84 percent). In district Chamba, out of total only 38.56 percent Person days have been generated for Women followed by district Solan (37.91 percent) and Sirmaur (12.07 percent) in the same financial year. In the financial year 2010-11, out of total person days generated, 55.67

percent have been generated for women. In this financial year again Kinnaur has leaded in generating maximum cumulative persondays for women followed by district Mandi (73.49), Hamirpur (69.37percent), Lahaul-Spiti (61.89 percent) and Kangra (59.89).

District Sirmaur is again in the bottom in generating lowest percentage (17.22) of total Person days for women. Out of total person days which have been generated in the financial year 2011-12 (till date), 58.64 percent person days have been generated for women. Districts Kinnaur, Hamirpur, Mandi and Kangra are again leading in generating maximum person days for women. District Sirmaur is again in the bottom with lowest percentage (20.27) of total Person days generated for Women. But it is clear from this table that the percentage of person days generated for Women is showing an increasing tendency.

Concluding Remarks

It can be concluded from the above study that MGNREGA has succeeded in providing employment for women in Himachal Pradesh. This programme provides an opportunity for women to work in their villages, and secondly since it is supposed to be at minimum wages, it has an impact on wages/earnings of women. It appears that while men often manage to move out into other activities or migrate to other areas in search of work, women have fewer options. They remain as a flexible labour force in agriculture—as own account workers, casual agricultural labour or unpaid family workers. Rural female unemployment has also been on the rise, and is higher than rural men's unemployment rate.

States where person days of work created for women has been greater than the stipulated 33 percent include Kerala, Tamil Nadu, Rajasthan, Sikkim (except in 2006-07), Andhra Pradesh, Tripura, Chhattisgarh, Karnataka, Meghalaya (except in 2006-07), Maharashtra, Manipur, Madhya Pradesh, Orissa, Uttarakhand (except in 2006-07), Mizoram (except in 2011-12), Himachal Pradesh (in 2006-07), Gujarat (except in 2006-07).

States where the share is lower include Bihar, Jharkand, Haryana, Assam, West Bengal, Punjab, Uttar Pradesh, Arunachal Pradesh, Jammu and Kashmir. There are so many reasons like socio-cultural norms around women's work, mobility and intra household allocations of roles and responsibilities, individual household factors like levels of care responsibilities and number of adult women in the house, health status, opportunity costs, other market opportunities and market wages for men and women, efficiency of implementation and information flows to and within households, etc. which are responsible for different women's participation across states.

MGNREGA provides a statutory guarantee of wage employment. It provides a right-based framework for the wage employment. Employment is dependent upon the worker exercising the choice to apply for registration, obtain a job card, and seek employment for the time and duration that the workers want. Unlike the earlier wage employment programs that were allocation-based, MGNREGA is demand driven. Resource transfer under MGNREGA is based on the demand for employment and this provides another critical incentive to states to leverage the act to meet the employment needs of the poor.

But in order to make this programme more effective, government should increase the minimum wage rates paid under MGNREGA scheme to increase standard of living of poor. More employment must be given to poorest people of the rural area. Unemployment allowances should be increased under this scheme. To control the migration from rural to urban area, non-manual work should also be considered under this scheme. MGNREGA fund should be used in right way. Government should be launched different programmes to aware the poor people under this scheme. Special awareness should be given to illiterate people (especially to SC/ST and Women) to handle bank procedures.

References

Adlikri, Anindita and Kartika Bhatia (2010), "NREGA Wage Payment: Can be Bank on the Banks", *Economic and Political Weekly*, January 2, 2010, Vol. XLV, No. 1, pp. 32-37.

Affridi, Farzana (2008), "Can Community Monitoring Improve the Accountability of Public Officials", *Economic and Political Weekly*, October 18, 2008, Vol. XLIII, No. 42, pp. 35-40.

Aiar, Yamini and Salimah Samji (2006), "Improving the Effectiveness of National Rural Employment Guarantee Act", *Economic and Political Weekly*, Vol. XLI, No. 4, Delhi, January 8, pp. 320-26.

Anish Vanaik, Siddharatha (2008), "CAG Report on NREGA: Fact and Fiction", *Economic and Political Weekly*, June 21, Vol. XLII, No. 25, pp. 39-44.

Daisy, Dwyer and Judith Bruce, (eds.) (1988), *A Home Divided: Women and Income in the Third World*, Stanford, CA.

Datar, Chhaya (2007), "Failure of National Rural Employment Guarantee Scheme in Maharashtra", *Economic and Political Weekly*, August 25, 2007, Vol. XLII, No. 34, pp. 3454-57.

Dreze, Jean (2005), "Employment Guarantee Act Premise and Demise", *Kurukshetra*, Vol. 53, No. 7, May, 2005, pp. 9-13.

Government of Himachal Pradesh, Draft of Ninth Plan, 1997-2002 and Annual Plan, 2001-02, Shimla, p. 58.

Government of India, Ministry of Rural Department, Department of Rural Development, Monthly Progress Report Under National Rural Employment Guarantee Act.

Government of India, Draft of Eighth Five Year Plan (1992-97) and Annual Plan 1992-93, Planning Department, India.

Government of India, Planning Commission, Eleventh Five Year Plan, New Delhi, 2007-12, p. 6.

Heitzman, James and Robert L. Worden, (eds.) (1996), *Area Handbook Series, India–A Country Study,* Washington, DC.

International Labour Office (1997), Yearbook of Labour Statistics, 1997, Geneva.

Joanna, Liddle and Rama Joshi (1986), *Daughters of Independence: Gender, Caste and Class in India,*

Khera, Ritika (2008), "Employment Guarantee Act", *Economic and Political Weekly,* 30 August, Vol. XLII, No. 35, pp. 8-10.

Khera, Ritika and Nandini Nayak (2009), "Women Work as and Perceptions of National Rural Development Guarantee Act", *Economic and Political Weekly,* 24 October, Vol. XLIV, No. 43, pp. 48-57.

Leela, Dube and Rajni Palriwala, (eds.) (1990), *Structures and Strategies: Women, Work, and Family,* New Delhi.

Madhu, Kishwar and Ruth Vanita (eds.) (1985), *In Search of Answers: Indian Women's Voices from Manushi,* London.

Manohar Puri (2006), "The NREGA: Rural People to Grow with the Nation", *Kurukshetra,* May 2006, Vol. 54, No. 7, pp. 17-19.

Mathur, Lalit (2007), "Employment Guarantee Progress so Far", *Economic and Political Weekly,* December 29, 2007, Vol. XLII, No. 52, pp. 17-20.

Mehrotra, Dr. Santosh (2005), "Employment Guarantee", *Yojna,* Vol. 49, April 2005, pp. 11-13.

Mehrotra, Santosh (2008), "NREGA Two Years on: Where Do We Go from Here", *Economic and Political Weekly,* 2 August, Vol. XLII, No. 31, pp. 27-35.

Narayanan, Sudha (2008), "Employment Guarantee Women's Work and Children", *Economic and Political Weekly,* March 1, Vol. XLIII, No. 9, pp.10-12.

National Commission for Women in India (1993), "Proceedings of the National Workshop on Employment, Equality and Impact of Economic Reforms on Women," New Delhi.

National Sample Survey Organisation (1994), *Sarvekshana,* Vol. 17, No. 3, January-March.

New Brunswick, *et al.* (1996), "Occupational Segregation and Earnings Differentials by Sex: Evidence from India," *Artha Vijnana,* Vol. 8, No. 4, pp. 372-86.

Pinaki Chakraborty, "Implementation of Employment Guarantee: A Preliminary Appraisal", *Economic and Political* Weekly, February 17, 2007, Vol. XLII, No. 7, pp. 548-52.

Prakash Louis (2006), "NREGA Implementations-II—Birth Pages in Bihar", *Economic and Political Weekly,* December 2, 2006, Vol. XLI, No. 48, pp. 4946-47.

Raghbendra Jha *et al.* (2008), "Reviewing the National Employment Guarantee Program", *Economic and Political Weekly,* 15 March, 2008, Vol. XLII, No. 11, pp. 44-49.

Registrar General and Census Commissioner (1993), Census of India, 1991, Final Population Totals: Brief Analysis of Primary Census Abstract, Series 1, New Delhi.

Sibabrata Champatisay (2010), "MGNREGA Helps Villages Build Road to Happiness", *Kurukshetra*, August, Vol. 58, No. 10, pp. 47.

Singh, Balbinder (2006), "National Rural Development Guarantee Act as a Half Step Towards Right to Work/Live", *Labour and Development*, Vols. 11-12, No. 2 and 1 June, 2006, pp. 150-56.

The World Bank (1991), *Gender and Poverty in India,* Washington, DC.

Vanaik, Anish and Siddharatha (2008), "Bank Payments: End of Corruption in NREGA", *Economic and Political Weekly*, April 26, 2008, Vol. XLIII, No. 17, pp. 33-39.

Empowering Women in a Globalised World

Arup Jyoti Sarma

Introduction

Globalisation is not a new phenomenon since the process has been stirring for ages. The term 'globalisation' was first used by Theodore Levitt in 1983 in an article published in the *Harvard Business Review* (Sinha, 2006). The process of globalisation overcomes all sorts of limitedness, or blind attachment to fixed boundaries. It makes us open, fluid, accommodative. To be global is to embrace the world as a whole. According to Roland Robertson, a leading theoretician of globalisation asserts that, "Globalisation as a concept refers both of the compression of the world and the intensification of the consciousness of the world as a whole" (Robertson, 1992).

The process of globalisation is popularly described as a gradual removal of barriers to trade and investment between nations. It aims to achieve economic efficiency through competitiveness, while seeking the broader objectives of economic and social development. Mainstream analyses of globalisation are embedded in a belief in the 'free market', and particularly informed by acceptance of the notions of 'comparative advantage' and a 'level playing field' (Bisnath, 2001). These analyses remove the roles of political and social institutions and power relations in powering economic activities in the micro, macro-levels, as well as the material realities of women and men living in the poverty line. Furthermore, it also discards the proposal that unevenness in levels of development, coupled with asymmetrical power relations both within and outside the national and international economic spheres, constitute situations where countries and individuals do not enter, or participate in markets on equal terms (Bisnath, 2001).

In other words, economic globalisation is represented as an apolitical force, whereby the economic and political institutions through which it is facilitated are positioned as seemingly neutral in gender, class and race relations, through which it is mediated, are and assumed to be without relevance to the functioning of the global market place. Another important aspect of the economic globalisation is the *situatedness* of the gender within the process of production and reproduction. Reproductive or caring work is also crucial for the maintenance of the economy. Moreover, the gendered implications of economic liberalisation are partly influenced by women's and men's locations within the process of production and reproduction, and their countries position within the international economic and political orders.

In this paper, I shall emphasise upon the link between globalisation and gendered dimensions of poverty and propose several steps for facilitating the empowerment of women in a globalised world. In order to systematise my discussion, I shall divide my paper into the following parts. In Part-I, I shall discuss about the women centred or so called *feminist* approach towards globalisation. In Part-II, I shall discuss about the policies for implementation to promote gender equality in general and women empowerment in particular. In Part-III, I shall conclude my paper by stressing on the question—how far we have achieved 'women empowerment'? Is it still a dream or reality? And my conclusion will be that attaining women empowerment is not a myth. But still a lot needs to be done from all quarters to achieve gender equality and women empowerment.

PART I

The formation of the multilateral trading regime, the implementation of the Uruguay Round agreements, and the facilitation of the economic liberalisation are resulting in a more decisive shift in the planning focus of, and the roles of the state in developing the potential in revealing (1) the contributions of women and men in the economy —through productive and caring labour, and (2) to empower women in the society.

A feminist approach towards globalisation has to reveal the ways in which economic institutions, processes and relations are not outside of, or prior to, the political and the social but constitutive of it, and gendered; and bring into historical visibility of women's and men's participation in economic activities—this entails empirical studies, as well as discussions of their roles in, and the links between reproductive and productive work, and the gendered effects of the public/private divide (Bisnath, 2001). Such analysis definitely helps us in giving us a proper understanding of the causes of growth, development and poverty, and result in more effective and gender awareness policies aimed at improving the material realities of women and men living in a society.

In order to address issues that is related to the empowerment of women, analyses of linkages and feedbacks between macro-policies, such as those influencing labour markets, and meso-level institutions such as firms and social service agencies, and the material realities of women and men are necessary.

It is important to recognise that at the macro and the meso-levels, laws, norms and rules that govern markets and public services are not gender neutral, and that men and women, in part because of their differing entitlements, are positioned differently in their interactions with these institutions (Bisnath, 2001) The latter point is very important because feminist models for analysing the effects of globalisation must have the capacity to reveal the ways in which gendered structures of production are linked to gender bias in access to resources, for example, education. This linkage, depending on the sector in question, may pose opportunities or constraints on the export market at the national level, or result in the marginalisation of specific groups of women and/or men, as a result of job displacement, because of the importation of certain products. Within this context, it is also important to understand the market, not in isolation, but within their political and cultural contexts. This point is highlighted by Karl Polanyi (1944).

Polanyi analysed the roles of the market in partially constituting economic, political and social relations in 19th century Europe. He formulated a framework for understanding the 'self-regulating market', not as a natural phenomenon, but as a political and economic construct. He argued that the market was represented as both separated from the society and self-managing, and perceived as such via the ideological view of economic liberalism. As a result, the different ways in which market forces influenced and informed everyday political and individual decision-making were obscured.

Polanyi's analysis of the market as a social construct enables a partial analytic framing of the multiple and contradictory ways in which gender relations, as well as roles and norms, are reconstituted as women formally and or informally participated in the global economy, or are marginalised from it. An example, in this case may be taken from Bisnath to highlight this point. Bisnath here cites an example stating that the promotion of the tourism industry in the Caribbean is leading to an increase in employment, a need for training, the privatisation of public spaces, the trafficking of women, as well as a rise in female and male prostitution. It also enables an understanding of the fact that while market expansion in many instances build on and reinforces pre-existing gender relations, it may also destabilise such relations, and open up new spaces for feminist actions.

Therefore, we may come to a point that women's positioning varies depending on their race, class, age and their countries structural position in the international economic and political orders, and are partially reconstituted through their relations with economic, political and socio-cultural institutions and processes. In addition to this, women's *choices* and *preferences* are formed by their position in society. Thus, uneven development and asymmetrical power relations within global and national markets constitute situations where nation-states and women and men do not enter into, or participate in, the market on equal terms. For instance, within the neo-liberal framework, labour is considered to be mobile.

However, this assumption cancels the fact that skill labour tends be more mobile than unskilled labour. It does not differentiate between the differences in the ability and cultural acceptability of female and male workers to move from one type of job to another type of job, or to move from one spatial location to another in the pursuit of a lob. In many countries particularly in the South-East Asian countries, women are often discouraged or forbidden from working night duties, mainly to alert/protect them from insecurities. This type of protective labour legislation has the paradoxical result of protecting men's jobs and reinforces violence against women, primarily because it forecloses discussions of men using violence, such as sexual assault, to regulate women's rights, and also to maintain their privilege in an insecure labour market (Bisnath, 2001).

Thus, women centred analysis of globalisation has to be framed by the ideas that:

(1) the market is a gendered, social construction;
(2) production and reproduction are intrinsically linked and reconstituted through relations of power,

(3) women and men often enter and participate in markets on differential terms, and
(4) nation-states have differential levels of development, in addition to being unevenly developed within their national boundaries (Bisnath, 2001).

These discussions can give us an idea (if not the whole!) of the fundamental problems of women and the need to implement some of the policies to empower women. In the next section, I shall take up the issue of women empowerment through implementation of certain policies.

PART II

The term 'empowerment' has been a buzz word in our times. Empowerment is "now increasingly seen as a process by which the one's without power gain greater control over their lives. This means control over material assets, intellectual resources and ideology. It involves power to, power with and power within" (Chandra). It may again be defined as a process of awareness and conscientisation, of capacity building leading to greater participation, effective decision-making power and control leading to transformative action. This involves ability to get what one wants and to influence others on our concerns. With reference to women, the power relation that has to be involved includes their lives at multiple levels, family, community, market and the state (Chandra).

Now the question arises—why do we think of the idea of 'women empowerment'? More precisely, why do we want to *empower* women in a society? Certainly, there must be *gendered inequality* in the society, where a woman is suppressed in the household activities; there is neither space for freedom of expression, nor space for exercising basic rights. They usually have less access than men to medical care, property ownership, credit, training and employment. They are far less likely than men to be politically aware and far more likely to be victims of domestic violence. In this condition, we have to give proper emphasis upon *gender equality* and our focus must be on women empowerment.

Gender equality implies a society in which women and men enjoy the same opportunities, rights and obligations in all spheres of life. Equality between men and women exists where they can share equality in the distribution of power, financial independence; enjoy equal access to education and the opportunity to develop personal ambitions. A crucial aspect of promoting gender equality is the empowerment of women, with a focus on identifying and redressing power imbalances and giving women more autonomy to manage their own lives. Women's empowerment is vital to sustainable development and exercise human rights for all. Successful empowerment strategies also require the direct employment of women in the planning and implementation of projects.

Women's empowerment is presumed to be attainable through different points of time, including political mobilisation, conscious raising and education. In addition to this, changes where and when necessary in laws, civil codes, systems of property rights, and the social and legal institutions that underwrite male control and privilege are assumed to be essential for the achievement of women's equality. According to Srilatha Batliwala (1994), "...the goals of women's empowerment are to challenge patriarchal ideology (male domination and women subordination); transform the structures and institutions that reinforce and perpetuate gender discrimination and social inequality (the family, caste, class, religion, educational processes and institutions, the media, health practices and systems, laws and civil codes, political processes, development models, and government institutions); and enable women to gain access to, and control of, both material and informational resources" (Batliwala, 1944).

Nelly P. Stromquist (1995), in her article on *Educational Empowerment for Women*, which appeared in Carolyn Medel-Anonuevo (ed.), *Women, Education and Empowerment: Pathways Towards Autonomy*, interprets empowerment as a socio-political concept that goes beyond formal political participation and consciousness raising. She argues that a full definition of empowerment must include cognitive, psychological, political and economic components. She explains that—

(a) The *cognitive dimension* refers to women having an understanding of the conditions and causes of their subordination at the micro and macro-levels. It involves making choices that may go against cultural expectations and norms.

(b) The *economic component* requires that women have access to, and control over productive resources, thus ensuring some degree of financial autonomy. However, changes in the economic balance of power do not necessarily alter traditional gender roles or norms.

(c) The *political element* entails that women have the capability to analyze, organise and mobilise for social change.

(d) The *psychological dimension* includes the belief that women can act at personal and societal levels to improve their individual realities and the society in which they live (Bisnath, 2001).

United Nations Population Fund (UNFPA) refers to some of the ways to establish gender equality in general and promote women's empowerment in particular—

Empowering through Education

"Education is one of the most important means of empowering women with the knowledge, skills and self-confidence necessary to participate fully in the development process." (ICPD programme of Action, paragraph 4.2). Education is important for everyone, but especially more important for girls and women. Proper education has direct effects within the family, society and across generations. Education helps women to know their rights and to gain self-confidence. Girls who have proper education are most likely married later and have smaller and healthier families. Educated women can recognise the importance of health care and know-how to seek it for themselves and their children. The 1994 Cairo consensus recognised education especially for women as a force for social and economic development. Closing the gender gap in education by 2015 is also one of the benchmarks for the Millennium Development Goals. However, women's literacy rates are significantly lower than men's in many developed countries. UNFPA advocated widely for universal education and has been instrumental in advancing legislation in many countries to reduce gender disparities in schooling. The 2003 UNFPA global survey on ICPD+10 most programmed countries formally recognise the importance of reducing the gender gap in education. UNFPA supports a variety of educational programmes, from literacy projects to curricula development with a focus on reproductive and sexual health.

Women's Work and Economic Empowerment

In many countries, women work for many hours than men, but they are usually paid less and are more likely to live in poverty. In subsistence economies, women spend more of the time performing tasks to maintain the household, such as carrying water and collecting fuel wood. Again, in many countries, women are also busy in agricultural production and selling. Unpaid domestic work-from food preparation to care giving, directly affects the health and overall well-being and quality of life of children and other household members. Women's work is statistically less visible, non-monetized and relegated to subsistence production and domestic side, this counts for 60% of unpaid family work and 98% of domestic work (Chandra, 2001).

The non-paid work includes domestic chares like cooking, cleaning, child care and care for the elderly; these are traditionally understood to be women's work. Subsistence activities like pitches gardening post harvest processing, feeding farm hands, live stock maintenance, gathering of fuel, forest products are done by women. Restriction on women's mobility, complete child care responsibility ideology of female seclusion, vulnerability to abuse, low access to information and mass media, low literacy, assumption that women's supplementary and confinement to largely manual untrained tasks leads to women's poor access to income.

The differences in the work patterns of men and women, and the 'invisibility' of work that is not included in national accounts, lead to lower entitlements to women. Women's lower access to resources and the lack of attention to gender in macro-economic policy adds to the inequality which in turn, perpetuates gender gaps.

UNFPA is committed to actions to attack poverty and powerless, especially among women. About half of the UNFPA programme countries have developed strategies to provide women with economic opportunities. The fund has supported economic empowerment and micro-credit initiatives in Bangladesh, Chad, Kenya, and Morocco, Palestine and other countries. UNFPA strongly supports addressing the feminisation of poverty through the integration of gender concerns in macro-economic policy and in poverty reduction strategies.

Political Empowerment

Women's political participation has been recognised as one of the important steps for political empowerment. Throughout the world, women's equality is undermined by historical imbalances in decision-making power and access to resources, rights, and entitlements for women. Women in many countries deprive their basic rights to—own land and to inherit property, obtain access to credit, attend and stay in school, earn income and move up in their work, free from job discrimination. Moreover, women are still not fully represented in decision-making either in the household matters or in the public sphere.

Addressing these inequalities through laws and public policy is a way of formalising the goal of gender equality. Legal changes may often regarded as a necessary step to institute gender equality. It is also now often pointed out that women's empowerment must be seen as a process wherein we must consider women's awareness consciousness, choices with live alternatives, resources at their disposal, voice, agency and participation. These are all related to enhancement of women's capabilities and decision they take individually or collectively for themselves (Chandra, 2001).

Effective advocacy requires partnership and coalition building. UNFPA alone is a relatively small agency, but when it works together with other international agencies and non-governmental organisations to address gender biases in laws and policies at the national level, it can be very effective. Formal international agreements, such as the ICPD programme of action and the Millennium Development Goals, provide key areas for policy changes. With its development partners, UNFPA advocates widely for legislation to advance gender equality, to eliminate all forms of discrimination based on gender, and to prevent gender-based violence and increased penalties for those who inflict it. The fund has established partnerships with parliamentarians in developing countries for political and legislative support for population and development challenges, of which the empowerment of women is central.

Improving Reproductive Health

Women for both physiological and social reasons are more vulnerable than men to reproductive health problems. Reproductive health problems including maternal mortality and morbidity represent a major but preventable cause of death and disability for women in developing countries, Failure to provide informations, services and conditions to help women protect their reproductive health therefore constitutes gender-based discrimination and a violation of women's rights to health and life. Reproductive health encompasses key areas of the UNFPA vision—that every child is precious, every birth is safe, every person is free from HIV diseases, and that every girl and women is treated with dignity and respect.

The critical importance of reproductive health to development has been widely acknowledged at the highest level. At the 2005 World Summit, world leaders added universal access to reproductive health as a target in Millennium Development Goals Framework. UNFPA is fully committed to mobilising support and scaling up efforts to make reproductive health for all a reality by 2015.

PART III

Enough we have said about globalisation and women empowerment and the strategies for implementing women empowerment. But the question still arises to our mind—how far women empowerment is attainable? Is it a reality or a dream? The reason behind posing this question is that women's rights and liberties have been violated in every spheres of life. The birth of a female child is an unwelcome event in many countries, particularly in traditional Indian society. Right from birth, there is discrimination in the bringing up of a female child. Females are generally treated as a 'weaker sex'. Because of this discrimination, enactments and judicial pronouncements in favour of women have failed to bring the desired results. Only enactments and judicial pronouncements cannot bring about a change. There must be a social environment conducive to it. If female children are continued to be brought up in the same traditional manner, there are very few chances of improvement in the conditions of women's human rights (Karia, 2003).

Women's Human Rights are being violated in the fields of marriage, divorce, adoption and succession. In other words, women's rights in these fields are limited in comparison to those of their male counterparts. The main reason behind these is that these enactments are largely based upon religion and its traditions. Again, it is a common experience of working women to be harassed at their working places. Sexual harassment is a violation of human rights. Most of the cases of sexual harassment are also not reported to the police.

Dowry deaths are common in some parts of India. In spite of the Dowry Prohibition Act, 1961, the increase in dowry deaths has continued unabated. Sometimes, family circumstances compel housewives to commit suicide. There is also an increase of the rape cases now days. Compulsory pregnancy, birth of an unwanted child, torture and sexual harassment to female members of the family violate women's human rights.

Under all these circumstances just mentioned, can we speak about achieving 'women empowerment in a globalise world?' Is it still a myth? The answer although negative, but still a lot needs to be done for women's empowerment. We can particularly mention here the role of the United Nations Development Fund for Women (UNIFEM), United Nations Population Fund (UNFPA), United Nations International Children's Emergency Fund (UNICEF), United Nations Development Programme (UNDP), etc. for promoting gender equality and taking measures for women empowerment.

The Inter-Agency Network on Women and Gender Equality (IANWGE) brings together representatives of gender units, gender specialists and gender specialists organisations of the multilateral systems. Network members promote gender equality throughout the United Nations system and in follow-up to the Fourth World

Conference on Women in Beijing in 1995 and the twenty-third special session of the General Assembly (Beijing+5) in 2000. The Network monitors the mainstreaming of gender perspectives in the normative and operational work of the UN system. It works through *ad hoc* task forces with designated task managers and through informal inter-sessional meetings (UNIFEM, 2005).

The Task Force on Gender Mainstreaming in the Common Country Assessment and United Nations Development Assistance Framework (CCA/UNDAF) of the IANWGE is coordinated by UNIFEM and composed of the United Nations Development Programme (UNDP), the United Nations Children Fund (UNICEF), the United Nations Population Fund (UNFPA) and the Division for the Advancement of Women (DAW). It aims to develop a common and coherent UN agency approach to gender mainstreaming in the CCA/UNDAF process.

Beijing Conference on Women: Some Highlights

The Beijing Declaration and Platform for Action, approved in September 1995 at the Fourth World Conference on Women, is a global commitment for achieving equality, development and peace for women worldwide. As defined in the Mission Statement of the 123-page document:

> The Platform for Action is an agenda for women's empowerment. It aims at...removing all the obstacles to women's active participation in all sphere of public and private life through a full and equal share in economic, social, cultural and political decision-making....at home, in the workplace and in the wider national and international communities. Equality...is a matter of human rights and a condition for social justice...

To achieve equality, the Platform for Action emphasises the need for women to work together and in partnership with men towards the common goal of gender equity worldwide.

Although the Beijing Declaration and Platform for Action is a stand-alone document, it builds upon consensus and progress made at earlier UN conferences/summits, particularly the Conference on Women in Nairobi in 1985 which developed the Nairobi Forward-looking Strategies for the Advancement of Women.

The Beijing Platform focuses on 12 "critical areas of concern" that must be addressed to achieve gender quality and women's empowerment:

- women and poverty

- education and training of women
- women and health
- violence against women
- women and armed conflict
- women and the economy
- women in power and decision-making
- institutional mechanisms for the advancement of women
- human rights of women
- women and the media
- women and the environment
- the girl child

To address each of the above concerns, specific strategic objectives were identified along with actions to be implemented by governments, financial and development institutions such as the World Bank, national and international NGOs (non-governmental groups) and women's groups, and the private sector.

The Beijing Declaration and Platform for Action was approved unanimously by representatives from 189 countries attending the Fourth World Conference on Women, held during the 50th anniversary year of the founding of the United Nations.

Throughout the discussion, we can come to the point that achieving gender equality and women empowerment is no more a dream. We have achieved a lot during the last 50 years but still a lot of effort requires from all sides in gaining greater progress and height.

References

Batliwala, S. (1944), "The Meaning of Women Empowerment: New Concepts from Actions", Gita Sen, Adrienne Germain and Lincoln C. Chen (eds.), *Population Policies Reconsidered: Health, Empowerment and Rights,* Harvard University Press, quoted from Bisnath, Savitri (2001), "Globalisation, Poverty and Women's Empowerment", *United Nations Division for the Advancement of Women, op cit.*, p. 12.

Bisnath, S. (2001), "Globalisation, Poverty and Women's Empowerment," *United Nations Division for the Advancement of Women,* Expert Group Meeting on "empowerment of women throughout the life cycle as a transformative strategy for poverty eradication," 26-29 November, 2001, New Delhi, India, p. 1.

Chandra, R., *Women Empowerment in India—Milestones and Challenges,* Lucknow: University of Lucknow, p. 1.

Karia, A.N. (2003), *Human Rights,* Mumbai: C. Jamnadas and Company, p. 91.

Poanyi, K. (1944), *The Great Transformation: The Political and Economic Origins of our Times, Beacon.*

Robertson, R. (1992), *Globalisation: Social Theory and Global Culture*, London: Sage Publications, p. 8.

Sinha, A.K. (2006), "Globalisation: The Linguistic Perspective," in B.N. Patnaik and S. Imtiaz Hassain (eds.), *Globalisation: Language, Culture and Media*, Shimla: Indian Institute of Advanced Study, p. 17.

UNIFEM (2005), Resource Guide for Gender Theme Groups, United Nations Development Fund for Women (UNIFEM).

Internet Sources

http://www.unfpa.org/gender/empowerment.htm, Accessed on 13 January, 2012.

http://womensissues.about.com/od/internationalwomensrights/f/BeijingDeclaration.htm, Accessed on 17 January, 2012.

http://womensissues.about.com/od/internationalwomensrights/f/BeijingDeclaration.htm, Accessed on 17 January, 2012.

http://womensissues.about.com/od/internationalwomensrights/f/BeijingDeclaration.htm, Accessed on 19 January, 2012.

http://womensissues.about.com/od/internationalwomensrights/f/BeijingDeclaration.htm, retrieved on Accessed on 19 January, 2012

Declining Child Sex Ratio in India

GURINDER KAUR

Sex composition is one of the most important demographic characteristics as it directly affects the incidence of birth, death and marriage. It is used as a basis of distinction in almost every aspect of social structure. There are different tools to measure gender equity in population. Sex ratio is one such widely used tool for cross-sectional analysis to measure gender balance. Sex ratio is the number of females per 1000 males. Sex ratio is an index of the socio-economic conditions of an area and it is also a composite indicator of women's status in the society. An understanding of sex ratio of an area is important for different types of planning and for comprehending demographic dynamism in terms of natality, mortality, migration, marital status, economic characteristics and so forth (Chandna, 1986).

India is one of the few countries in the world where there are more males than females (Table 7.1). India's general sex ratio throughout the 20th century and as well as in the 21st century reflects a masculine sex ratio. In 1901, the Indian general sex ratio was 972; it declined steadily in the decades from 1901 to 1971 with a negligible increase of only one point in 1951. It improved marginally to 934 in 1981 from 930 in 1971. In 1991, there was again a decrease in the sex ratio and it recorded 927 females per thousand males. However, a marginal increase of 6 females (933) was recorded in the year 2001. There is a further improvement in the general sex ratio with 940 females in 2011 (Table 7.2).

Table 7.1: Sex Ratio of Selected Countries, 2011

S. No.	*Country*	*Sex Ratio*	*S. No.*	*Country*	*Sex Ratio*
1.	China	926	7.	Nigeria	987
2.	India	940	8.	Russian Fed.	1167
3.	U.S.A.	1025	9.	Pakistan	943
4.	Indonesia	1004	10.	Sri Lanka	1034
5.	Brazil	1042	11.	Nepal	1014
6.	Japan	1055	12.	Myanmar	1048

* *Note:* Rates have been worked out for India based on the provisional Census 2011 and those of Indonesia and Brazil round of Census.

Source: 2011, World Population Prospects 2008 revision UN.

Table 7.2: General and Child Sex Ratio in India: 1961-2011

Year	*General Sex Ratio*	*Change in General Sex Ratio*	*Child Sex Ratio*	*Change in Child Sex Ratio*
1961	941	—	976	
1971	930	–11	964	–12
1981	934	+4	962	–2
1991	927	–7	945	–17
2001	933	+6	927	–18
2011	940	+7	914	–13
Change 1961-2011		–1		–62

Source: Census of India, General Population Tables of 1961, 1971, 1981, 1991, 2001 and 2011.

The change in the general sex ratio during the period 2001 to 2011 is marginal, but appreciable. This increase is due to greater life span of females as compared to males. They tend to live longer if they are not subjected to incapacitating forms of discrimination in nutrition and health care (www.livepunjab.com/articles/only-914 girls-1000males-census-2011-reports-2051303/27/2011). However, the happiness over the increase of general sex ratio will not remain for long. If not in the next decade but after two or more decades the census would show an abysmal sex ratio disfavouring women. This is because of the fewer girls (0-6 years) now and their number is on the decrease (*The Hindu*, 2011).

The general sex ratio as highlighted in Figure 7.1 presents an encouraging picture in India, while the same is not true in the case of female children in the age-group of 0-6 years.

The child sex ratio in the country has witnessed a decline with more

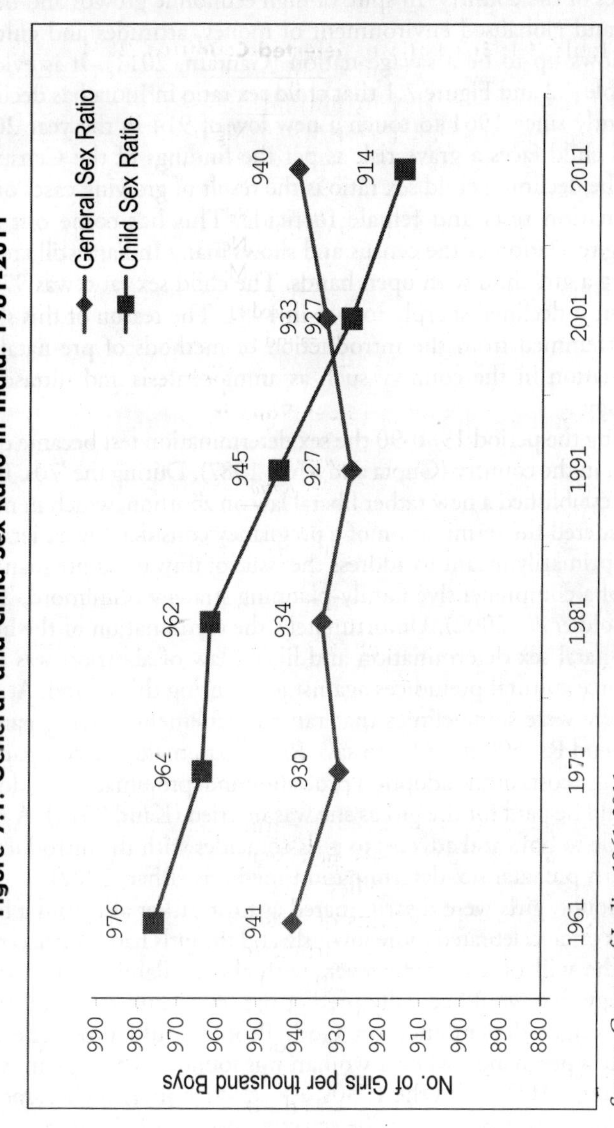

Figure 7.1: General and Child Sex Ratio in India: 1961-2011

Source: Census of India: 1961-2011

preference being given to the male child in all the states and union territories of the country. In spite of high economic growth and better literacy and globalised environment of money, attitudes and culture, India shows up to be a savage nation (Gautam, 2011). It is evident from Table 7.2 and Figure 7.1 that child sex ratio in India has declined consistently since 1961 to touch a new low of 914 in the year 2011. The girl child faces a grave risk as per the findings of the Census of 2011. The declining child sex ratio is the result of growing cases of sex determination tests and female foeticide. This has come out as a shocking revelation of the census and shows many Indians still are not accepting a girl child with open hands. The child sex ratio was 976 in 1961, but it declined sharply to 945 in 1991. The reason of this sharp decline stemmed from the introduction of methods of pre-natal sex determination in the country such as amniocentesis and ultrasound technology.

During the period 1980-90 the sex determination test became quite common in the country (Gupta and Bhat, 1987). During the '70s, India had also established a new rather liberal law on abortion, which in many cases rendered the termination of a pregnancy considerably easier. The law was primarily meant to address the issue of unwanted pregnancies, as part of a comprehensive family-planning strategy (Guilmoto, 2007 and Arnold *et al.*, 2002). Unfortunately, the combination of the both, i.e., pre-natal sex determination and liberal law of abortion was used to reinforce cultural prejudices against girls during this period. At that time, there were some clinics that ran advertisements, saying parents could spend Rs. 500 in order to save Rs. 5 lakh, making a comparison between the costs of the adoption procedure and, presumably, the dowry that would be paid for the girl as she was married (Kaur, 2011). A ratio favourable to boys and adverse to girls coincides with the introduction of modern prenatal sex-determination methods (Bhat, 2002).

No doubt, girls were discriminated against earlier also, and a boy's birth was often celebrated more joyously and the girls had been accepted as just the will of God. However, with the availability of medical technology that would actually predict the sex of unborn child, there was no longer dependence on God. People could intervene and terminate a pregnancy, when a woman was found to be pregnant with a girl (Kaur, 2011). From the 1980s, sex-selective abortion became the primary method used to alter the sex composition of children (Gupta and Bhat, 1987). An alarming decline in the proportion of girls during the period 1981 to 1991 (Table 7.2 and Figure 7.1) was observed due to terrifying number of female foetuses began to be routinely aborted (Gupta, 2005).

As a result, the law banning the sex determination test came into force in 1994. The All India Democratic Women's Association and the National Commission for Protection of Child Rights were also behind the call to enforce a ban against sex-selective abortion. The law saw certain amendments. It declared sex determination an illegal activity; anyone who breaks this law is subject to prosecution (Kaur, 2011).

Despite the PC & PNDT Act, the Census of 2001 registered further lower child sex ratio. During this decade (1991-2001) the child sex ratio declined by 18 points and only in two decades (1981-2001) this decline recorded 35 points as a whole. It showed that modern techniques, therefore, set the new regime apart from the older discrimination strategies of girl child (Bora and Tyagi, 2008). Finding a declining trend in the number of girl children in the age group of 0-6 years, the Government of India again revised the PC & PNDT Act in 2003.

However, the child sex ratio further deteriorated during the period 2001 to 2011 in the country. It is again favourable to boys and adverse to girls. There is a further decline of 13 points in the number of girls in 2011 and it is now only 914 girls per thousand boys of the same age group (0-6 years) as sex-selective abortions have become more easier during the last one decade, enabling people to determine the foetus just by purchasing modern and portable ultrasound machines.

Every census has documented a decline in the child sex ratio since 1981 (Table 7.3 and Maps 7.1 to 7.4) signalling a ubiquitous trend. Map 1 show that all the states and union territories of the country recorded child ratio above 900 and it is pertinent to note that 24 states and union territories had recorded child sex ratio above 950 during this decade (Table 7.4). After the introduction of modern pre-natal sex-determination test in 1980s, the decline in child sex ratio was firstly observed in the states of Punjab & Haryana and the union territory of Chandigarh in the north-western parts of the country in 1991. Elsewhere in India, apparently no large scale deterioration was observed in child sex ratio which by and large remained above 900. However, it was important to note that the area and the number of states those observing child sex ratio below 950 had widened their circle in 1991 and there was a reduction in the number of states and union territories observing child ratio above 950 (Map 7.2).

There has been a decline in the number of states and union territories having child sex ratio of 950 and above since 1981. According to 1981 Census, 24 states and union territories observed child sex ratio above 950, but their number declined to 22 in 1991, 18 in 2001 and only

10 in 2011 (Table 7.4 and Maps 7.1 to 7.4).

Table 7.3: Trends of Child Sex Ratio in India, 1981-2011

Country/States	*1981*	*1991*	*2001*	*2011*
India	962	945	927	914
Haryana	902	879	819	830
Himachal Pradesh	971	951	896	906
Jammu & Kashmir	964	N.A.	941	859
Punjab	908	875	798	846
Rajasthan	954	916	909	883
Gujarat	947	928	883	886
Maharashtra	956	946	913	883
Goa	965	964	938	920
Chandigarh	907	899	845	867
Delhi	926	915	868	866
Uttrakhand	N.A.	949	908	886
Uttar Pradesh	935	927	916	890
Bihar	981	953	942	933
Madhya Pradesh	977	941	932	912
Chhatisgarh	N.A.	984	975	964
Jharkhand	N.A.	979	965	943
Orissa	995	967	953	934
West Bengal	981	967	960	950
Kerala	970	958	960	959
Karnataka	975	960	946	943
Tamil Nadu	967	948	942	946
Andhra Pradesh	992	975	961	943
Assam	N.A.	975	965	957
Arunachal Pradesh	997	982	964	960
Meghalaya	991	986	973	970
Manipur	986	974	957	934
Nagaland	988	993	964	944
Sikkim	978	965	963	944
Tripura	972	967	966	953
Mizoram	986	969	964	971
Andaman & Nicobar	978	973	957	966
Dadra & Nagar Haveli	995	1013	979	924
Daman & Diu	N.A.	958	926	909
Lakshdweep	964	941	959	908
Puducherry	965	963	967	965

Source: Census of India, General Population Tables, 1981, 1991, 2001 and 2011.

Map 7.1

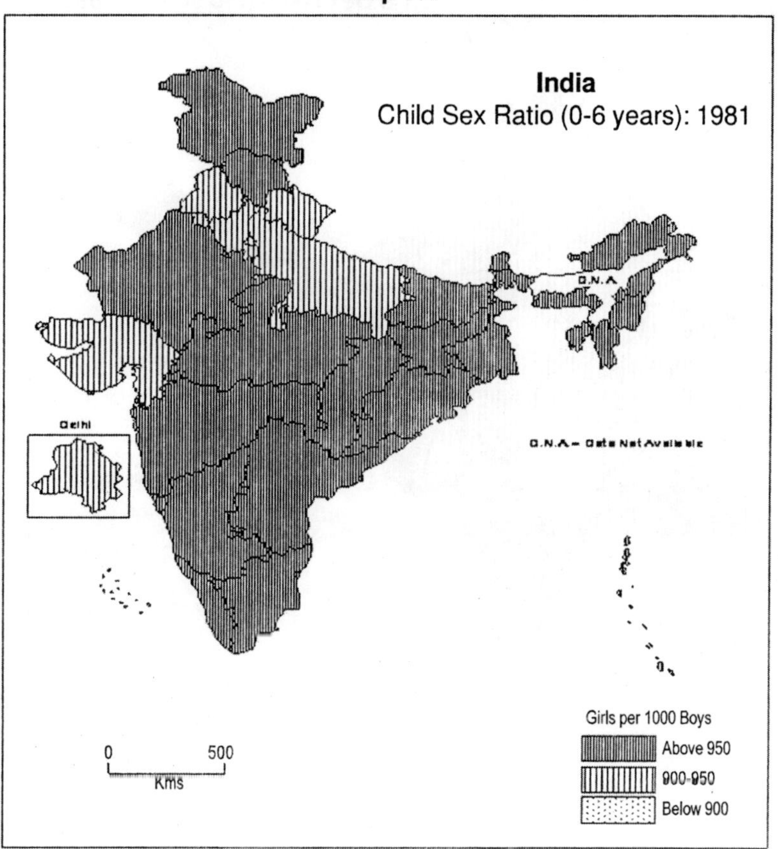
India
Child Sex Ratio (0-6 years): 1981
D.N.A.
Delhi
D.N.A. – Data Not Available
0
500
Kms
Girls per 1000 Boys
Above 950
900-950
Below 900

Map 7.2

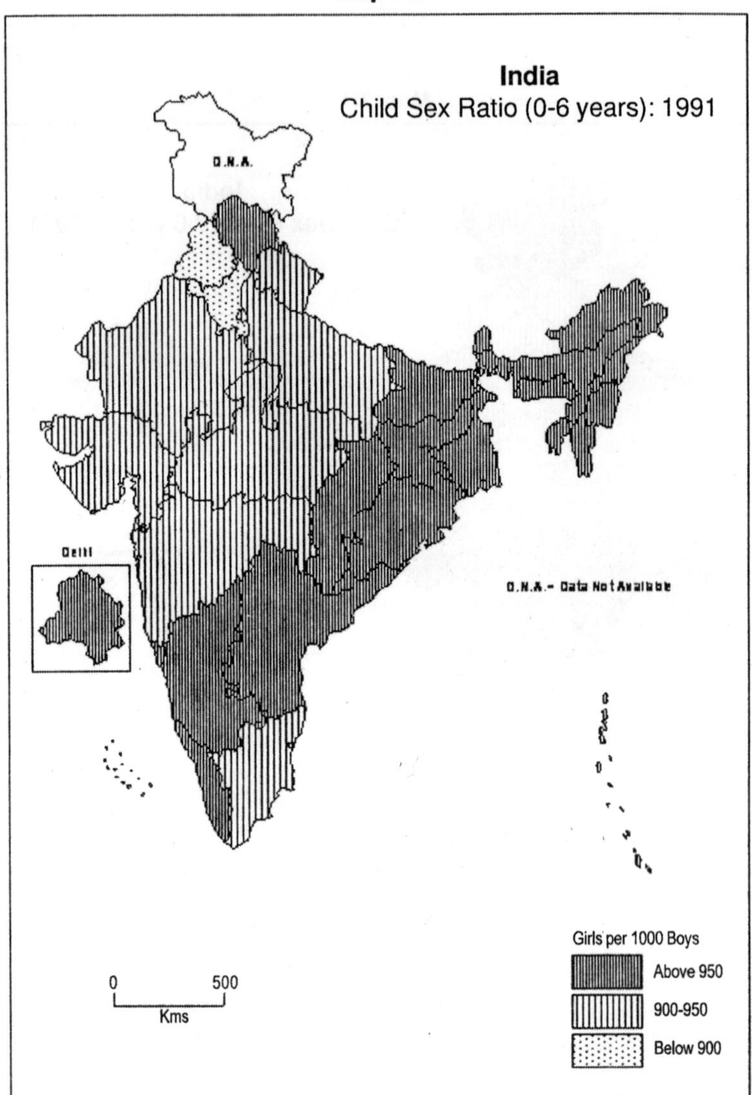
India
Child Sex Ratio (0-6 years): 1991
D.N.A.
Delhi
D.N.A.- Data Not Available
0
500
Kms
Girls per 1000 Boys
Above 950
900-950
Below 900

Map 7.3

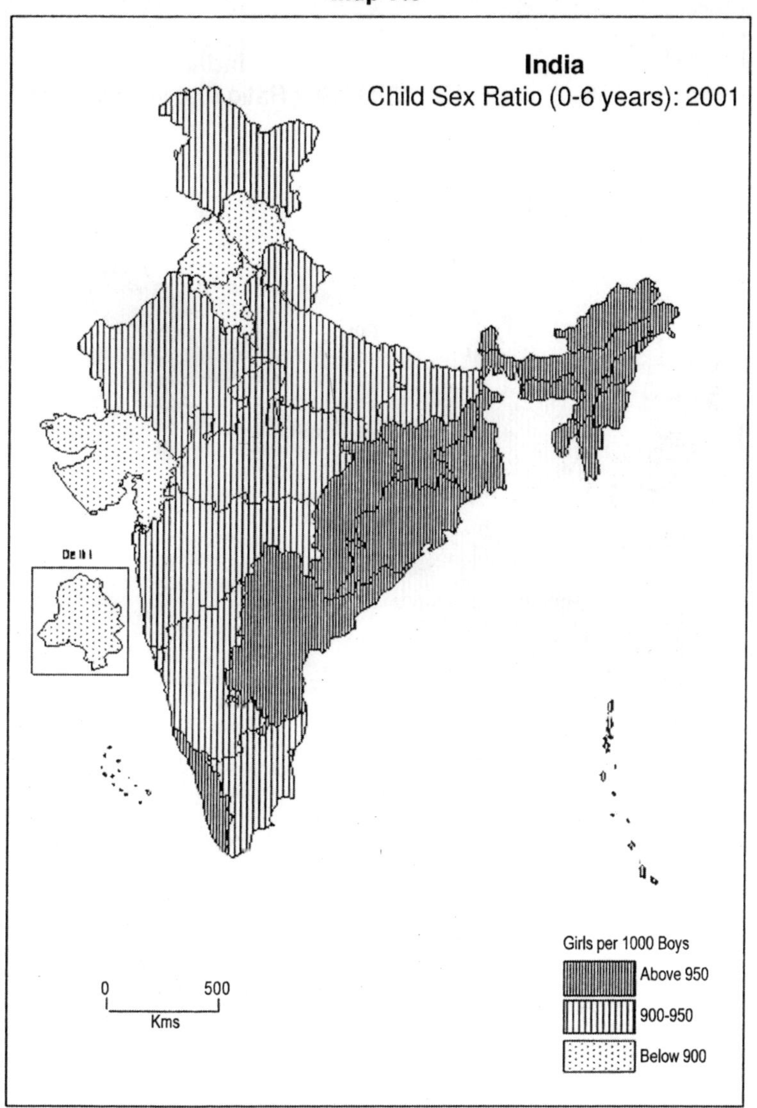
India
Child Sex Ratio (0-6 years): 2001
Delhi
0
500
Kms
Girls per 1000 Boys
Above 950
900-950
Below 900

Map 7.4

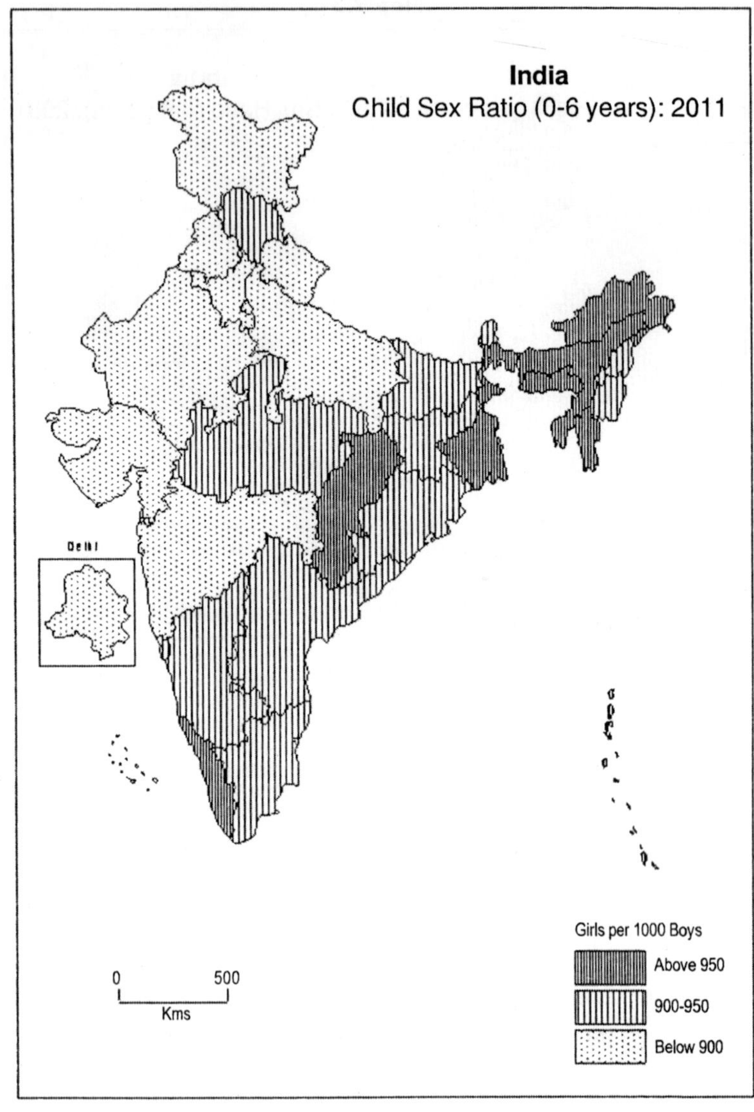
India
Child Sex Ratio (0-6 years): 2011
Delhi
0 500
Kms
Girls per 1000 Boys
Above 950
900-950
Below 900

Table 7.4: Range of Child Sex Ratio in India, 1981-2011

Value	*Number of States/Union Territories*			
	1981	*1991*	*2001*	*2011*
Below 900	0	3	6	11
900-950	6	9	11	14
Above 950	24	22	18	10
	30*	34**	35	35

Notes: *In 1981, Uttaranchal, Jharkhand, Chhatisgarh and Daman & Diu were included in their respective states Uttar Pradesh, Bihar, Madhya Pradesh and Goa.

**Census was not conducted in Assam and Jammu & Kashmir.

Source: Census of India, General Population Tables of 1981, 1991, 2001 and 2011.

On the other hand, the number of states and union territories has increased in the other two categories. In 1981, there was not even a single state and union territory where the child sex ratio was below 900. However, in 2011, their number rose to 11 under this category. A similar increase in the number of states and union territories was observed in the category where sex ratio ranged between 900 and 950.

The deterioration of child sex ratio had been limited in some of the states and union territories only in 1991. These were Punjab, Haryana and Chandigarh. This can be attributed to the reason that Punjab was the first state to start the commercial use of sex determination and sex pre-selection test as early as in 1979 (Patel, 2011). However, this phenomenon gradually widened its circle. According to the latest Census of 2011, this trend has appeared in 11 states and union territories starting from Jammu & Kashmir in the North-West to Maharashtra in the South-West and Uttar Pradesh in the East (Map 7.4).

It is sad to note that Kerala, with its high literacy and traditionally matrilineal Nair Society; and the state of Meghalaya presently having matrilineal society also have reported a decline in their child sex ratio. It is alarming to find that we do not have even a single state where the girls outnumber the boys. These results point out that there is an intensification of the girl's deficit areas in the country with the each successive decade.

The indiscriminate abortion of female fetuses is the main reason for the skewed child sex ratio. If abortions could have been avoided, we may have about 952 girls born for 1000 boys. The exact number of abortions done in India, for obvious reasons, is not known (*The Hindu*,

2011). This can evidently be judged from the growth of female child population as compared to male child population (Table 7.5). The data on child population in the age group of 0-6 years is primarily intended for calculating the literacy rates.

It also allows us to broadly analyse possible linkages with the growth of population in this age group (Census of India, 2011). It is heartening to see that all the states (except Jammu & Kashmir) and union territories have recorded a decline in the growth of child population. However, on the other side of it, there have been more declines in the proportion of female children than male children in all the states and union territories with few exceptions only. It clearly indicates that the growth of child population is controlled by the sex-selective abortions. The small size of the family is the outcome of the adoption of the darker side of family planning through the termination of female child before birth with the help of new methods and technology.

The declining child sex ratio and declining growth of girl population highlights that Indian people still prefer sons to their daughters. Education exposure and affluence have not brought value such as gender equality rather it has brought consumerism and commoditisation of relationship (Vasudev, 2003).

Table 7.5: Growth Rate and Distribution of Child Population, 2011

Country/States	*Total*	*Males*	*Females*
India	13.12	13.30	12.93
Jammu & Kashmir	16.01	16.21	15.77
Nagaland	14.44	14.34	14.54
Mizoram	15.17	15.20	15.14
Manipur	12.98	13.34	12.61
Goa	9.57	9.81	9.32
Meghalaya	18.75	18.91	18.60
Tripura	12.10	12.15	12.04
Chandigarh	11.18	10.89	11.54
Puducherry	10.25	10.64	9.89
Himachal Pradesh	11.14	11.53	10.74
Kerala	9.95	10.59	9.36
Tamil Nadu	9.56	9.80	9.32
Andaman & Nicobar Islands	10.40	9.93	10.92
Bihar	17.90	17.75	18.07
Daman & Diu	10.65	9.03	13.28
Karnataka	11.21	11.36	11.07
Punjab	10.62	10.89	10.32
Assam	14.47	14.45	14.50
Gujarat	12.41	12.62	12.18

	Total	*Males*	*Females*
Jharkhand	15.89	15.92	15.85
Orissa	12.00	12.28	11.73
Maharashtra	11.43	11.69	11.16
Haryana	13.01	13.34	12.62
NCT of Delhi	11.76	11.76	11.76
Uttarakhand	13.14	13.67	12.58
Chhattisgarh	14.03	14.23	13.84
Andhra Pradesh	10.21	10.46	9.95
West Bengal	11.07	11.05	11.09
Madhya Pradesh	14.53	14.67	14.38
Rajasthan	15.31	15.67	14.92
Dadra & Nagar Haveli	14.35	13.24	15.78
Lakshadweep	11.00	11.22	10.77
Arunachal Pradesh	14.66	14.36	15.00
Uttar Pradesh	14.90	14.97	14.82
Sikkim	10.05	9.77	10.37

Note: The figures represent the percentages.
Source: Census of India, 2011, Provisional Population Tables.

A strong son preference has been found in the Indian society (Gupta *et al.*, 2003; Pande and Astone, 2007). Son preference is due to a variety of social and economic factors which interact to make females less valuable to their families (Bora, 2007).

Table 7.6 carries the data showing son preference attitude among males and females in all the states of India. The table shows that more than twenty-two percent of women prefer sons than daughters, but only 2.6 percent have their preference for daughters. Similarly, in the case of males, 20.0 percent have their preference for sons, while only 2.0 percent for daughters. The son preference exists among both the males and females in all the states. The son preference tends to be stronger among both the males and females in most of the northern parts, viz. Punjab and Haryana; and poverty stricken states, namely, Bihar, Uttar Pradesh, Rajasthan, Madhya Pradesh, Chhatisgarh and Jharkhand. Other states with a high son preference above national average include Arunachal Pradesh, Manipur, Mizoram, Jammu & Kashmir and Gujarat. The weakest son preference is found in the states of Tamil Nadu (5.7 percent), Goa (8.7 percent), Andhra Pradesh (9.3 percent), Kerala (11.0 percent) and Karnataka (11.6 percent).

Meghalaya and Mizoram make an exception where both the females and males have greater preference for daughters. In all the states except Meghalaya and Mizoram, not more than 5 percent of males prefer daughters. It is interesting to note that males in Meghalaya have less

Table 7.6: Sex Preference by State, 2005-06

Country/States	*Percentage who want more sons than daughters*		*Percentage who want more daughters than sons*	
	Males	*Females*	*Males*	*Females*
India	20.0	22.4	2.0	2.6
Delhi	11.7	11.7	1.5	2.1
Haryana	18.4	22.0	2.2	1.2
Himachal Pradesh	9.2	11.8	1.1	2.0
Jammu & Kashmir	23.9	23.4	2.2	3.1
Punjab	13.4	17.7	1.5	1.6
Rajasthan	24.0	34.3	1.8	1.5
Uttarakhand	13.6	20.7	1.3	2.1
Madhya Pradesh	27.9	30.8	2.4	1.8
Chhatisgarh	24.8	32.8	1.0	3.6
Uttar Pradesh	27.8	33.5	1.2	1.7
Bihar	38.5	39.2	1.7	1.2
Jharkhand	24.6	28.1	3.7	2.3
Orissa	20.3	24.2	1.6	2.4
West Bengal	16.6	16.5	2.1	3.5
Arunachal Pradesh	30.3	28.3	3.2	5.0
Assam	17.9	24.1	2.8	2.1
Manipur	34.7	28.5	3.3	4.2
Meghalaya	21.5	11.9	13.5	22.7
Mizoram	43.5	29.0	14.7	17.0
Nagaland	28.4	21.4	5.0	9.8
Sikkim	17.1	15.5	4.2	5.9
Tripura	15.2	17.7	2.2	3.4
Goa	11.4	8.7	2.1	4.1
Maharashtra	14.3	14.1	2.2	2.9
Gujarat	20.0	22.7	1.6	2.3
Andhra Pradesh	12.0	9.3	2.0	2.6
Karnataka	12.7	11.6	2.7	4.6
Kerala	11.8	11.0	3.8	5.7
Tamil Nadu	7.9	5.7	1.8	3.1

Source: National Family Health Survey, Vol. 1.

preference for sons. In the case of Punjab and Haryana, there is need to further investigate the preference for sons as both these states are occupying the bottom ranks of child sex ratio in 2011.

A son is preferred for the main reasons that he tends support to his parents in their old age; he fetches a handsome amount of dowry at the time of his marriage; the amount spent on his brining up and career results in multiplication of their money; and as per the Hindu belief, he is required to perform the last rites of his parents.

The decline in the child sex ratio is alarming in the sense that it poses a serious threat to the existence of the society itself. The decline in number of girl children is unbalancing the ratio between girls and boys. This deficit leads to the shortage of brides for the marriageable boys and this is already being felt in many pockets of Haryana and Punjab, where young men face many difficulties in finding the brides (Kaur, 2004). In such a situation, the number of males is increasing resorting to unusual solutions such as import of brides from other areas, sharing of wife and trafficking of women.

The scarcity of females has led to the re-emergence of 'bride price', the system of paying money to obtain a wife and polyandry system. The reports in the national and local media have also been highlighting the increasing incidents of 'sale of girls' in the states of Haryana and Punjab from the states of West Bengal, Assam, Orissa and even from the southern states of the country. The difficulties and inability in finding a female partner would lead to social tension, particularly manifested in crime against women. It would increase the incidences of rape, prostitution and violence against women. The crime against women is rising in the country as India is designated as the fourth most unsafe country all over the world for women to live in (Thomson, 2011) and India also stands at the third place where it comes to rape cases in the world (Economic Times, 2008).

Besides, a number of relations and festivals those are related with girls in our country will slowly and gradually be eliminated from the social life of the Indians and will be a part of history.

The decline in the child sex ratio suggests that marked improvements in the economy and literacy rates do not seem to have had any impact on this index. However, the following measures based on the findings of this study would help to improve the child sex ratio in the country:

1. The first and foremost need is the complete change in the mind set of the society toward the girl child. Unless the citizens of India themselves wake up to the need, the evil of female foeticide and other malpractices targeting the Indian girls shall not be done away.
2. It is required that every girl child gets the right to be born, extended the same love and affection as to the boys, provided tender care and nourishment without any discrimination against them, and given equal opportunities for education as to the boys. The evil of dowry needs to be abolished from the society in order to empower the women and make them independent in their decisions.

3. The Pre-Conception and Pre-Natal Diagnostic Techniques Act and the Dowry Prohibition Act should be implemented effectively and stringently. The doctors, nurses and others found guilty should be punished hard such as cancellation of their licenses. The license for medical practice once cancelled should not be restored under any circumstances. The parents found guilty of any act leading to termination of female foetus should be given exemplary punishment. Legislation needs to be enacted to the effect that a bride shall have equal right on the property of her husband immediately after the marriage.
4. Free and compulsory education for the female child is required to make her self-reliant. The formulation of various schemes promoting vocational training and skill development can help to generate employment opportunities and increase the income of women.
5. The empowerment of women through reservation of jobs in public as well as private sector institutions would improve their status in the society. This would also increase their decision-making skills and would be helpful in opposing the family's direction for sex-selection related abortion.
6. The couples having a single female child should be provided free medical care and handsome old age pension. Those in the government service should be given some additional annual increments for greater care of the female child.

Some of these measures could go a long way in removing the deeply entrenched prejudice against the girls.

References

Arnold, F. Kishor, S. and Roy, T.K. (2002), "Sex-Selective Abortions in India", *Population and Development Review*, 28(4) pp. 759-85.

Bhat, P.N. (2002), "On the Trail of 'Missing' Indian Females: Search and Clues", *Economic and Political Weekly*, 37(51), pp. 5105-18.

Bora, R.S. (2007), "Imbalance in Child Sex Ratio: Trends, Causes and Emerging Issues", www.iegindia.org/workpap/ wp280.pdf.

Bora, R.S. and Tyagi, R.P. (2008), "Socio-Economic and Cultural Explanation for Declining Child Sex Ratio: A Study of North-Western States in India", *Demography India*, 37 (1).

Census of India (1961), *General Population Tables.*

Census of India (1971), *General Population Tables.*

Census of India (1981), *General Population Tables.*

Census of India (1991), *General Population Tables.*

Census of India (2001), *General Population Tables.*

Census of India (2011), *Provisional Population Totals.*

Chandna, R.C. (1986), *A Geography of Population,* New Delhi: Kalyani Publishers, p. 103.

Economic Times (2008), "India Ranks Third in Rape Cases", articles.economictimes. indiatimes.com>collections>India, December, 9.

Gautam, C. (2011), "To Help our Daughters Survive, Give Economic Empowerment to Women", *Hindustan Times,* 4 November.

Guilmoto, C.Z. (2007), "Characteristics of Sex Ratio Imbalance in India and Future Scenario", 4th *Asia Pacific Conference on Reproductive and Sexual Health and Rights,* Hyderabad, Oct. 29-31, pp. 11-12.

Gupta, D.M. *et al.* (2003), "Why is Son Preferences so Persistent in East and South Asia? A Cross-Country Study of China, India and Republic of Korea", *Journal of Development Studies,* 40(2), pp. 153-87.

Gupta, D.M. and Bhat, P.N. (1987), "Selective Discrimination Against Female Children in Punjab, North India", *Population and Development Review,* 13(1), pp. 77-100.

Gupta, D.M. (2005), "Explaining Asia's Missing Women: A New Look at the Data", *Population and Development Review,* 31(3), pp. 529-35.

Kaur, G. (2011), "Don't Lift that Ban; Let Baby Girls be Born", *Daily Post,* 17 November.

Kaur, R. (2004), "Across Region Marriages: Poverty, Female Migration and Sex Ratio", *Economic and Political Weekly,* 39(25), pp. 2595-2630.

Pande, R. and Astone, N. (2007), "Explaining Son Preference in Rural India: The Independent Role of Structural Versus Individual Factors", *Population Research and Policy Review,* 26(1), pp. 1-29.

Patel, V. (2011), "A Long Battle for the Girl Child", *Economic and Political Weekly,* Vol. XLVI, No. 21, p. 19.

The Hindu (2011), "Boom Economy without Women", Online Web: www.hindu. com/op/2011/06/12/stories/2011061250081200.htm Accessed on 12 December, 2011.

The Hindu (2011), "It's Murder, Pure and Simple", www.hindu.com/op/2011/06/ 12/ stories/2011061250061200.htm Accessed on 12 December, 2011.

Thomson, Reuters (2011), "Fact Box—The World's Most Dangerous Countries for Women", http://in.reuter.com/article/ 2011/06/15/idinindia_57704120110615.

Vasudev, S. (2003), "Missing Girl Child", *India Today,* Nov. 10, p. 15.

For more details see, www.livepunjab.com/articles/only-914girls-1000males-census-2011-reports-2051303 /27/2011.

Gender Discrimination in Indian Labour Market

ANUPAMA

Introduction

Gender asymmetry is a commonplace in the labour market in which women suffer multiple disadvantages and also face constraints in terms of sectors of economic activity in which they would like to work and working conditions to which they aspire. These opportunities become more limited in time of any crisis. Their tendency to be placed in low paid insecure jobs increases in such circumstances.

Recent trends in world of work have witnessed two opposite tendencies, particularly in developing economies. Early 90s experienced an increase in opportunities due to globalisation and liberalisation of these economies and more recently a gloomy picture is being painted due to wide spread global crisis. Though, initially, it was generally argued that Indian economy would not be significantly affected by the crisis due to its strong regulatory system in the financial market (Kamath, 2008) yet now, it is officially being admitted that it do had its toll on the Indian economy (NCEUS, 2009a). It is being worried that the unfolding of this crisis would adversely affect its workers due to changes in domestic aggregate demand, flow of credit and so due to fall in new and existing employment opportunities. In such a scenario, it becomes imperative to observe how it affects the vulnerable sections of society, particularly, women.

Though, the era of globalisation has witnessed the 'feminisation of labour' force every where in the world (ILO, 2004 and Chen *et al.*, 2005) yet the feminisation of labour force is also being associated with low quality informal jobs. This has led to coincidence of the terms 'informalisation', 'feminisation of labour force' and 'feminisation of poverty' in many studies (e.g. Chen, Vanek and Heintz, 2006).

Thus, during the era of globalisation when cost effectiveness is the catchword of the business, cheapness of labour along with flexibility of employment easily match with women labour force. Now, let us observe the second scenario, when globalisation has resulted in to global spread of the crisis mainly initiated in the developed countries (to start with the US sub-prime crisis). In such a scenario, the jobs become scarce, the employed being retrenched due to recession and in situations of scarcity, the women are being further marginalised in the labour market. It seems that the 'U-curve' showing feminisation of labour force is now going to take the inverted shape.

Though, the labour market is always being discriminated against women in patriarchal societies of developing countries, yet, these differences can never be desirable in a competitive global economy as a discriminatory labour market neither results in 'efficiency optimum' (from employers' point of view) nor in 'welfare optimum' (from female workers or disadvantaged employees' point of view). Despite all the theories of economic rationality, gender discrimination has always prevailed in the labour market. This discrimination is reflected both in the choice of occupations and the wages among men and women.

There are many theories that depict these gaps. The *status attainment* model, a descendant of the economists' human capital theory, looks at what individuals bring to the marketplace—that is, occupational aspirations, education, values, attitudes, and experiences—and assesses which variables affect the attainment of high status (Stockard and Johnson, 1980). It assumes that men and women compete in the same job market; the extent to which women lose is attributed to factors that make women less desirable as employees, that is, marital status, number of children, previous work experience, and so on. Once these factors are controlled, the model argues, lesser achievement by women in the marketplace can be attributed to discrimination. Thus the model assumes a "rational" marketplace; it does not address capitalism or patriarchy as cultural ideologies with structural consequences, i.e. the differential placement of men and women (Richardson, 1988). On the other hand, the *dual market* model argues that there are two distinct labour markets: one for men—the primary or core market—and one for women—the secondary or peripheral market. This model maintains that even if the "supply" characteristics of women were changed, unless the market structure were changed, women would see little relief (Acker, 1980).

In India like all the developing economies in the world, this is a naked reality that the discrimination against women exists to a large extent. The statement of the status attainment model that the differences due to different human capabilities of men and women are justifiable can not be a valid justification of gender discrimination as regarding this there works a vicious cycle of discrimination (Fig. 8.1) (Makkonen, 2002) which perpetuates fragmented labour market conditions. Actually, due to these stereotypes, the families invest less in women education, leading them to be less productive. Their emphasis on family duties leads them to more absenteeism and even withdrawal from the labour force, leading to lower experience. This leads the employers to have a bias against female workers (Becker, 1971; Anker, 1995).

Figure 8.1: Vicious Circle of Discrimination

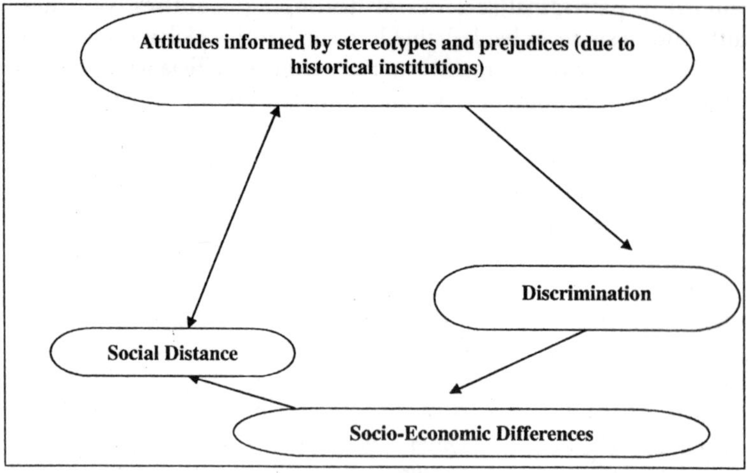

Source: Makkonen, 2002.

Thus, both the demand and supply side constraints may be working against women in choice of jobs in the labour market. But during the crisis, the women are further excluded from the labour market-making them more vulnerable and so would be the foremost sufferers of the crisis. Hence, the social and cultural values often intervene with the economic conditions. In this perspective it would be quite imperative to explore how the crisis has affected the women workers in India who already have been facing discrimination in the labour market. For this purpose, present paper has been divided into five sub sections. Apart from present introductory section, section II would deal with data and methodology. Section III would give the gendered analysis of employment in India since liberalisation, section IV would analyse the gender discrimination in wages in the Indian labour market with special focus on the crisis period and finally, section V would give the conclusions and suggestions on basis of the study.

Data and Methods

This study is based upon the secondary data. For this purpose, the data has been taken from NSSO (National Sample Survey Organisation) surveys on 'Employment and Unemployment Situation in India'. NSSO provides quinquennial data on the extent and various characteristics of employment in India. For analysing the impact of crisis on employment of women workers, the focus would on two Rounds of NSSO, viz. 55th Round (2004-05) and the latest 64th Round (2007-08). Though, the picture on the impact of crisis on employment in India would be clearer from the 66th Round for which only key indicators are available till now, yet the trends of this situation could also be observed from the 64th Round. For analysing the impact of crisis on women workers, simple averages, percentage shares have been calculated. The degree of segregation in Indian labour market during this period has been shown with help of simple index of dissimilarity (ID) as suggested by Watts (1998). The simple ID is given as follows:

$$ID = \frac{1}{2}\sum_{j=1}^{n} |(f_j / f - m_j / m)| * 100$$

where, f_j and m_j denote the number of female and male employees in the jth occupation and f and m are total female and male employment, respectively. The index denotes the fraction of total employment that would have to be relocated between occupations to achieve zero gender segregation. Overtime, both the occupational shares and overall gender shares of employment typically change. In such a case, the index of Dissimilarity can be further decomposed to recognise the sex composition effect and occupational effect separately (Blau and Hendricks, 1979). This decomposition of the ID is given as follows:

$$S = 1/2[\sum_i |(f_{i2}T_{i1} / \sum_i f_{i2}T_{i1}) - (m_{i2}T_{i1} / \sum_i m_{i2}T_{i1})| -$$
$$- \sum_i |(f_{i1}T_{i1} / \sum_i f_{i1}T_{i1}) - (m_{i1}T_{i1} / \sum_i m_{i1}T_{i1})|]$$

$$O = 1/2[\sum_i |(f_{i1}T_{i2} / \sum_i f_{i1}T_{i2}) - (m_{i1}T_{i2} / \sum_i m_{i1}T_{i2})| -$$
$$- \sum_i |(f_{i1}T_{i1} / \sum_i f_{i1}T_{i1}) - (m_{i1}T_{i1} / \sum_i m_{i1}T_{i1})|]$$

$$Residual = Change\ in\ ID - S - O$$

Here, *S*—stands for sex composition effect, holding constant the size of occupations within the unorganised manufacturing sector. *O*—stands for occupation effect, which measures change in segregation due to changes in occupational composition, holding constant the sex composition for the given period. f_i, m_i, T_i are respectively percentage of female workers, male workers and total number of workers in i^{th} occupation. The subscripts 1 and 2 belong to the initial time period and the latest time period.

Further, for disaggregating the wage differentials into the explained (i.e. due to difference in human capabilities and other individual characteristics of men and women) and unexplained variation (i.e. due to pure discrimination) the simple Blinder-Oaxaca decomposition technique has been used (Blinder, 1973 and Oaxaca, 1973). In this methodology the sample average wage difference between, say, males and females, is broken into two parts. One part measures the impact of differences in the male/female parameters of the wage determination equation, and the other part measures the impact of male/female endowment differences. The former part is referred to as that part due to discrimination. This technique is easy to apply and only requires coefficient estimates from linear regressions for the outcome and sample means of independent variables used in regressions. Calculation of this measure is undertaken in three steps:

(1) Running a regression on the male data,
(2) Running a regression on the female data, and
(3) Using these regression results and average values of various capabilities defining differences, we may compute the two parts of the wage discrimination described above.

Suppose the wage determination function for the males is given as

$$W_m = X_m \beta_m + \varepsilon_m$$

where w is an $N_m \times 1$ vector of observations on wages of N_m individuals,

X is an $N \times K$ matrix of observations on K explanatory variables, β is a $K \times 1$ vector of parameters, and ε is an $N \times 1$ vector of errors. The m subscript denotes males; the wage determination function for females is written by replacing the m subscript with an f subscript.

$$W_f = X_f \beta_f + \varepsilon_f$$

Because the regression line passes through the average of the observations,

$$\overline{W}_m = \overline{X}_m \hat{\beta}_m \text{ and } \overline{W}_f = \overline{X}_f \hat{\beta}_f$$

where the bar denotes average and the hat denotes the ordinary least square estimate.

The error term disappears because the sum of the ordinary least squares errors is zero.

From this the difference between the male and female average wages in the sample can be written as

$$\overline{W}_m - \overline{W}_f = \overline{X}_m \hat{\beta}_m - \overline{X}_f \hat{\beta}_f$$

Subtracting and adding $\overline{X}_m \hat{\beta}_f$ we get

$$\overline{W}_m - \overline{W}_f = \overline{X}_m \left(\hat{\beta}_m - \hat{\beta}_f\right) + \left(\overline{X}_m - \overline{X}_f\right) \hat{\beta}_f \qquad ...(1)$$

This decomposes the sample male/female average wage difference into two parts, one due to differences in the specification parameters and the other due to differences in endowments. The former is the discrimination measure. Often they are reported as a percentage of their sum.

When producing equation (1) above we could have subtracted and added $\overline{X}_f \hat{\beta}_m$ instead of $\overline{X}_m \hat{\beta}_f$, obtaining an alternative measure

$$\overline{W}_m - \overline{W}_f = \overline{X}_f \left(\hat{\beta}_m - \hat{\beta}_f\right) + \left(\overline{X}_m - \overline{X}_f\right) \hat{\beta}_m \qquad ...(2)$$

Gendered Analysis of Employment in India

Table 8.1 shows the trends in labour force participation rate and work force participation rate in India since liberalisation. We can observe from this table that the labour force participation rate and the work force participation rate among women has always remained much below than that of the men. But the gap in these two indicators which was being reduced after liberalisation seems to be widening during the period of crisis. The table also points out that the period 1993-94 to 1999-2000 has observed a decline in work force participation rate both for men and women, showing an era of job less growth, but during the period 1999-2000 to 2000-04, Indian economy experienced an increase in work force participation rate both for men and women. Interestingly, the period 2004-05 to 2007-08 seems to be discriminating among the male and female workers as both in rural and urban areas for every type of status of employment, the work force participation rate among men has increased while for women it has declined considerably. The year 2009-10 has shown further decline in female work participation rate in rural areas.

At usual principal and subsidiary status, it has declined from 32.7 percent during 2004-05 to 26.1 percent only in 2009-10. On the other hand, the male work force participation rate has increased slightly from 54.6 percent to 54.7 percent during the same time period. One can easily observe an inverted-U trend in case of female work participation rate in rural India since 1999-2000, i.e., during the last decade. The table shows that the job losses by women workers has been much higher than that of the job gains by the male workers, showing that the overall decline in the job market has taken whole of its brunt on the female labour force.

It can also be noted from the table that in the rural areas, the increase in male work participation rate is higher in case of current weekly and daily status as compared to the principal status while the female work force participation rate has declined in both the cases. This shows that during the period of crisis not only the regular jobs have become scarce for females but the casual or irregular jobs have also contracted.

Similar trends could be observed in urban areas as far as female work participation is concerned. But, in urban areas, the male work participation rate has also declined sharply during 2009-10 as compared to the year 2007-08, yet the proportion of unemployed (which is defined as persons unemployed per thousands of persons and here it can be calculated as difference of labour force participation rate and work force participation rate) has declined in case of males as the decline in male work participation rate has been lower than that of the labour force participation rate. On the other hand, in case of females we can observe an increasing rate of urban unemployment in principal status and weekly status while no change can be observed on usual principal and subsidiary status and daily status (in rural areas, we can observe an

Table 8.1: Trends in Labour Force Participation Rate (and Work Force Participation Rate) Among Men and Women (per '000)

Status of Employment	*Male*					*Female*				
	1993-94	*1999-2000*	*2004-05*	*2007-08*	*2009-10*	*1993-94*	*1999-2000*	*2004-05*	*2007-08*	*2009-10*
Rural										
Usual (PS)	549 (538)	533 (522)	546 (535)	551 (538)	548 (537)	237 (234)	235 (231)	249 (242)	220 (216)	208 (202)
Usual (PS+SS)	561 (553)	540 (531)	555 (546)	559 (548)	556 (547)	330 (328)	302 (299)	333 (327)	292 (289)	265 (261)
Current Weekly Status	547 (531)	531 (510)	545 (524)	547 (525)	548 (531)	276 (267)	263 (253)	287 (275)	245 (237)	231 (223)
Current Daily Status	534 (504)	515 (478)	531 (488)	536 (490)	536 (501)	232 (219)	220 (204)	237 (216)	204 (187)	197 (182)
Urban										
Usual (PS)	538 (513)	539 (513)	566 (541)	573 (550)	556 (539)	132 (121)	126 (117)	148 (135)	126 (118)	128 (119)
Usual (PS+SS)	543 (521)	542 (518)	570 (549)	576 (554)	556 (543)	165 (155)	147 (139)	178 (166)	146 (138)	146 (138)
Current Weekly Status	538 (511)	539 (509)	566 (537)	572 (545)	556 (536)	152 (139)	138 (128)	168 (152)	138 (129)	141 (130)
Current Daily Status	532 (496)	528 (490)	561 (519)	568 (529)	550 (522)	132 (120)	123 (111)	150 (133)	125 (113)	129 (117)

PS—Principal status, SS—Subsidiary status. Figures in bracket show the work force participation rate.
Source: NSSO (2006, 2010 and 2011).

increase in unemployment rate for women on UPS, UPSS and CDS).

Further Table 8.2 shows the sectoral distribution of workforce in India. The theories of structural change have argued that as an economy grows the share of agriculture in total employment falls and that of the other sectors increases (Kuznets, 1966; Chenery, 1979). In Table 8.2 these trends can be observed even within the time span of 16 years. The table shows that during this period in rural areas, about 12 percent of total male workforce has shifted itself from agriculture to be occupied in other occupations, while this fall is less than 8 percentage points for females (a bigger shift, i.e., of 5 percentage points can be observed during last two years only).

On the other hand, in urban areas, this decline is greater in case of females as compared to the males. But still the percentage of female workers employed in agriculture is greater than that of the males. Currently, 78.8 percent of the female work force in rural areas and 11.8 percent in the urban areas is employed in agriculture, while this percentage is respectively, 62.0 percent and 5.6 percent in case of males. In urban areas, outside agriculture, male workers are mainly employed in manufacturing, trade, hotels and business, etc., while females are mainly employed in services, followed by manufacturing.

During the period of crisis, we can observe the decline in the share of workers employed in manufacturing in rural as well as urban areas. Though, this decline in similar in rural areas both for males and females but in urban areas the decline in share of female workers in manufacturing is greater than that of the males. On the other hand, rapidly increasing number of women seems to be finding jobs in other services during this period. An overview of the table shows the slower occupational shifts of both the male and female workers during the period 2004-05 to 2007-08 as compared to previous time periods. But the year 2009-10 has shown sharper shifts from agriculture to non-agricultural sector in which the construction and transport, storage and communications seem to be the major drivers of this change.

Actually, it has been observed that the period of globalisation and liberalisation has increased the rate of informality in jobs. Since 1993-94 almost the entire additional employment has been absorbed by the informal sector of the economy. Even in the organised sector, new jobs were mainly informal in character, which is being termed as 'informalisation of the formal sector' in India (NCEUS, 2009b) where any employment increase consists of regular workers without social security benefits, job contract, etc.

This fact can also be observed from the fact that the employment

Table 8.2: Distribution of Usually Employed Persons by Broad Industry Division

Sector	*Male*					*Female*				
	1993-94	*1999-2000*	*2004-05*	*2007-08*	*2009-10*	*1993-94*	*1999-2000*	*2004-05*	*2007-08*	*2009-10*
					Rural					
Agriculture	74.1	71.4	66.5	66.5	62.0	86.2	85.4	83.3	83.5	78.8
Mining and Quarrying	0.7	0.6	0.6	0.6	0.8	0.4	0.3	0.3	0.3	0.3
Manufacturing	7.0	7.3	7.9	7.7	7.1	7.0	7.6	8.4	7.4	7.6
Electricity, Water, etc.	0.3	0.2	0.2	0.2	0.2	0.0	0.0	0.0	0.0	0.0
Construction	3.2	4.5	6.3	7.7	11.4	0.9	1.1	1.5	2.0	4.2
Trade, Hotel and Restaurant	5.5	6.8	8.3	7.6	7.2	2.1	2.0	2.5	2.3	3.1
Transport, Storage and Communications	2.2	3.2	3.8	4.0	5.0	0.1	0.1	0.2	0.2	0.5
Other Services	7.0	6.1	5.9	5.7	4.8	3.4	3.7	3.9	4.3	3.5
					Urban					
Agriculture	9.0	6.6	5.1	5.8	5.6	24.7	17.7	18.1	15.3	11.8
Mining and Quarrying	1.3	0.9	0.9	0.6	0.7	0.6	0.4	0.2	0.3	0.3
Manufacturing	23.5	22.4	23.5	23.5	21.9	24.1	24.0	28.2	27.5	25.9
Electricity, Water, etc.	1.2	0.8	0.8	0.7	0.7	0.3	0.2	0.2	0.2	0.4
Construction	6.9	8.7	9.2	9.5	11.5	4.1	4.8	3.8	4.3	5.1
Trade, Hotel and Restaurant	21.9	29.4	28.0	27.8	27.0	10.0	16.9	12.2	12.8	12.4
Transport, Storage and Communications	9.7	10.4	10.7	10.9	17.7	1.3	1.8	1.4	1.8	6.6
Other Services	26.4	21.0	20.8	21.0	14.6	35.0	34.2	35.9	37.8	47.6

Source: NSSO (2006, 2010 and 2011).

scenario of India, is dominated by self employed workers (which comprises own account workers, employers and the unpaid family workers) followed by the casual workers and then the least share is comprised of the regular salaried workers. over a period of time, almost similar trends could be observed regarding change in this composition both for males and females and the overall composition seems to be approaching perfect equality (particularly in urban areas). Since 2004-05, much of the decline in self-employment has been absorbed by the casual jobs and the rural females seem to be the worst sufferers. We can observe from the table that of the total decline of 8 percentage points of self-employed female workers (between 2004-05 to 2009-10) in rural areas, only 0.7 percent have joined the regular jobs and 7.3 percent have gone to casual jobs. But, in urban areas, though, the increase in casual jobs for female workers has been greater than that of the males, yet the increase in regular jobs for females is also greater *vis-à-vis* males.

Thus, in the post crisis period we can observe deterioration in rural labour market but an improvement in quality of jobs in urban labour market for the female workers. On the other hand the decomposition of the self-employed into own account workers, employers and unpaid

Table 8.3: Distribution of Usual Status Workers by Status of Employment (percent)

	Male			*Female*		
	Self-Employed	*Regular Wage/ Salaried*	*Casual Labour*	*Self-Employed*	*Regular Wage/ Salaried*	*Casual Labour*
			Rural			
1993-94	57.7	8.5	33.8	58.6	2.7	38.7
1999-2000	55.0	8.8	36.2	57.3	3.1	39.6
2004-05	58.1	9.0	32.9	63.7	3.7	32.6
2007-08	55.4	9.1	35.5	58.3	4.1	37.6
2009-10	53.5	8.5	38.0	55.7	4.4	39.9
			Urban			
1993-94	41.7	42.0	16.3	44.8	29.2	26.1
1999-2000	41.5	41.7	16.8	45.3	33.3	21.4
2004-05	44.8	40.6	14.6	47.7	35.6	16.7
2007-08	42.7	42.0	15.4	42.3	37.9	19.9
2009-10	41.1	41.9	17.0	41.1	39.3	19.6

Source: NSSO (2006 and 2010).

family workers further shows that, the majority of self employed males are own account workers and employers, while majority of self-employed females are unpaid family workers. This can be observed from Table 8.4.

Table 8.4 shows that the decline in self-employed workers in the period 2004-05 to 2007-08 has mainly been due to the decline in the unpaid family labour both for males and females but still the share of female workers working as unpaid workers is very high as compared to the males as it has been about 45 percent in rural areas and about 21 percent of total female workers in urban areas in the year 2007-08. This percentage is only 14.01 and 7.41 for males, in rural and urban areas, respectively.

Table 8.4: Distribution of Self-Employed Workers

Year	*Male*			*Female*		
	Own Account and Employers	*Unpaid Family Workers*	*Total Self-Employed*	*Own Account and Employers*	*Unpaid Family Workers*	*Total Self-Employed*
			Rural			
1993-94	40.39	17.36	57.74	16.31	42.31	58.62
2004-05	41.50	16.59	58.09	15.74	47.98	63.92
2007-08	41.41	14.01	55.42	13.37	44.93	58.30
			Urban			
1993-94	33.38	8.27	41.65	24.16	20.66	44.82
2004-05	36.40	8.42	44.82	24.14	23.55	47.69
2007-08	35.32	7.41	42.73	21.51	20.83	42.34

Source: NCEUS (2009) and unit level records of NSSO (2010) 64th Round.

Above differences in access to labour market and the types of jobs among men and women lead to differences in outcomes (i.e. the wages) because if women are placed in low paid, casual and unpaid activities then their average wages would be lower than that of the males. These tendencies can be examined in the following section.

Gender Discrimination in Wages in India during Crisis

The existence of gender differences in wages can be found nearly in all countries in the world, irrespective of the level of economic growth therein. India is also no exception in this case. Various studies on gender gap in India have shown that the unexplained differences in wages of male and females is 50-66 percent of total differences (Duraisamy and

Duraisamy, 1996; Kingdon and Unni, 2001; Datta and Reilly, 2008 and many more). The gender based wage inequalities in India have not been bridged even after fruits of economic growth are being realised in shape of increasing incomes (Dev, 2002). These differences could arise due to difference in human capabilities and due to differential access to occupations.

Actually, women are more likely to be employed in low paid jobs, particularly in developing countries (Anker and Hein, 1986; Lee and Nagraj, 1995; Chen and Heintz, 2006). The matter of fact is that gender segregation of occupations and pay differentials are nearly the same things. As we find the answers of occupational segregation in the neo-classical human capital model and non-economic feminist theories which find the patriarchal system being the main cause of sex stereotyping of occupations, so is the case with male-female pay differentials. If the differences in education and other individual characteristics can not explain the entire wage differentials between females and males, discrimination is present in the labour market. Many studies have suggested that human capital is not the only factor explaining the earnings gap between genders (Blau, 1996; Blau and Kahn,1994; Horrace and Oaxaca, 2001).

If the differences in wages arise even after controlling the differences in wages and productivity, then these differences are purely due to discrimination which may arise due to differences in race, gender, social status or simply biases of the employers (personal biases are again reflection of the cultural attitudes for a particular group/class). In this perspective, here an attempt has been made to analyse the wage discrimination in Indian labour market in recent years. For this purpose first of all we will focus on the sex composition of occupations and see if any dissimilarity exists in the Indian labour market. It can be observed from Table 8.5 that the dissimilarity has declined in 2009-10 as compared to the year 2004-05. But the rural-urban segregation shows that in rural areas, the dissimilarity has actually increased. Though, the urban areas have shown a decline in the value of index of dissimilarity, yet it is more than double the value in the rural areas. It can be observed that about 21 percent of workers in rural areas and 43.8 percent workers in urban areas need to be relocated to achieve perfect gender equality in the labour market.

The changes in value of ID during 2004-05 to 2007-08 and then during 2007-08 to 2009-10 can be further disaggregated into sex-composition effect and occupational effect. Interestingly, the table shows that out of total change in ID during 2004-05 to 2007-08, more of the increase in ID value has been due to occupational effect and the sex compositions of occupations has increased it by 0.01 percent only.

Table 8.5: The Index of Dissimilarity

Index of Dissimilarity (ID)	*Rural*	*Urban*	*Combined*
2004-05	20.62	43.98	29.59
2007-08	20.63	43.54	29.85
2009-10	21.0	43.8	29.5
Decomposition of ID Value			
	2004-05 to 2007-08		
Total Change in ID Value	0.01	-0.44	0.26
Sex Composition Effect	0.008	-1.12	0.01
Occupational Effect	0.082	-2.31	0.27
Residual	-0.08	2.99	-0.02
	2007-08 to 2009-10		
Total Change in ID Value	0.37	0.26	-0.35
Sex Composition Effect	0.053	-8.07	-0.30
Occupational Effect	-0.051	-6.20	-0.24
Residual	0.35	14.53	0.19

Source: Calculated from NSSO (2006 and 2010).

On the other hand, during the period 2007-08 to 2009-10, when the total value of the ID has declined by 0.35 percentage points, a greater decline has been due to change in sex compositions of occupations as compared to the occupational effect. However, the rural urban segregation of the results of ID show some interesting results. During 2004-05 to 2007-08, the ID has increased in case of rural areas and declined in the urban areas and in both the cases, the occupational effect had remained stronger as compared to the sex-composition effect. During 2007-08 to 2009-10, though the overall index has shown a decline in its value, yet we can observe an increase in the value of ID both in the rural and urban areas (this is quite possible as it is the property of the ID that as we go for more and more segregation of the data, the value may increase).

Here, two important trends can be noted in case of the change in the value of ID in rural areas. Firstly, the increase in ID value in rural areas has been greater than that of the urban areas and secondly, this increase has been due to sex-composition effect while the occupational effect seems to be reducing it. On the other hand, in urban areas both the sex composition effect and the occupational effect tend to reduce the dissimilarity in the labour market and some other factors seem to be responsible (shown by a positive residual) for a rise in the value of ID. Thus, we can say that though, the urban areas tend to be reducing the gender discrimination of occupations both by a change in the sex composition of the occupations and occupational structure but still the discrimination is higher as compared to the rural areas.

For a further exploration of the gender discrimination in Indian labour market, we can analyse the extent and determinants of discrimination in work as well as wages. For this purpose, we will be relying on data from 64th Round of NSSO (as for the 66th Round only Key Indicators are available and full report and unit level records are not yet available). Table 8.6 shows these differences in Indian labour market in 2007-08. The table shows that out of total workers, 75 percent are men and only 25 percent are women. This difference is more striking in urban areas where the women workers are only 16.54 percent of total workers as compared to 27.69 percent in rural areas. Most of men and women are employed in agriculture in rural areas. Out of total employment in agriculture, about 68 percent are men and 32 percent are women, but they comprise about 66 percent and 82 percent, respectively of total male and female workers employed in rural areas. In all other areas, the share of female workers is much below than their male counterparts, except in private households (in both the rural and urban areas) where women may be working as domestic servants.

Apart from it, more of women workers (out of total women workers) are employed in health and education services and traditional manufacturing (which is represented by manufacturing codes 15 to 22, the modern manufacturing, represented by codes 23 to 37 is more represented by men as compared to women). The gap is more prominent in urban areas as compared the rural ones. Some sectors like transport, storage, etc., public administration and mining and quarrying have a very nominal representation of women. It is obvious from the table that around 86 percent of women workers are concentrated in three sectors of agriculture, health and education services and traditional manufacturing. This shows the existence of sex-stereotyping of occupations in Indian labour market.

Women seem to be concentrated in low income jobs. In private households, which is the only sector, where the share of female workers is greater than that of the male workers, the female workers earn hardly 40 percent of male earnings for regular employment in this sector (this ratio is little higher for casual workers). This shows that women are paid less as compared to men even for same type of work. In regular

Table 8.6: Sectoral Distribution and Average Earnings in India (2007-08)

Sectors	Gender Distribution of Employment						Average Earnings (Contd.)			
	Rural		Urban		Combined		Rural			
	Male	Female	Male	Female	Male	Female	Regular Salaried		Casual Workers	
							Male	Female	Male	Female
1	2	3	4	5	6	7	8	9	10	11
Agriculture (01-05)	67.79	32.21	69.38	30.62	67.98	32.02	89.66	61.95 (0.69)	66.51	48.30 (0.72)
Mining & Quarrying (10-14)	79.67	20.33	90.97	9.03	81.82	8.18	270.38	154.01 (0.57)	90.65	58.28 (0.64)
Manufacturing (15-22)	66.20	33.80	75.15	24.85	70.0	30.0	121.21	62.65 (0.52)	83.21	46.32 (0.56)
Manufacturing (23-37)	84.34	15.66	91.32	8.68	88.14	11.86	139.10	58.01 (0.42)	88.95	64.82 (0.73)
Electricity, Gas and Water Supply (40-41)	100.0	0.0	94.63	5.37	100.0	0.0	262.76	326.62 (1.24)	100.17	69.54 (0.69)
Construction (45)	89.86	10.14	90.97	9.03	90.22	9.78	164.73	157.66 (0.96)	92.82	73.74 (0.79)
Trade, Hotels and Restaurants (50-55)	88.55	11.45	91.51	8.49	90.14	9.86	98.43	76.56 (0.78)	86.78	61.12 (0.70)

(Contd.)

Table 8.6 (*Contd.*)

1	*2*	*3*	*4*	*5*	*6*	*7*	*8*	*9*	*10*	*11*
Transport, Storage, etc. (60-64)	98.17	1.83	96.52	3.48	97.30	2.70	153.29	162.51 (1.06)	97.02	60.25 (0.62)
Public Administration, Defence, etc. (65-74)	90.14	9.86	87.10	12.90	86.75	13.25	245.10	131.31 (0.54)	75.29	138.37 (1.84)
Health, education and other Services (75-93)	74.02	25.98	70.76	29.24	71.92	28.08	256.45	131.62 (0.51)	86.08	42.64 (0.50)
Private Households with Employed Persons (95)	39.50	60.50	26.01	73.99	31.03	68.97	91.27	40.59 (0.45)	76.75	52.55 (0.69)
All	72.31	27.69	83.46	16.54	74.98	25.02	175.30	108.14 (0.62)	74.97	49.91 (0.67)

(*Contd.*)

Table 8.6 (Contd.)

Sectors	Average Earnings							
	Urban				Combined			
	Regular Salaried		Casual Workers		Regular Salaried		Casual Workers	
	Male	Female	Male	Female	Male	Female	Male	Female
1	12	13	14	15	16	17	18	19
Agriculture (01-05)	150.39	93.07 (0.62)	86.76	50.78 (0.59)	97.46	65.20 (0.67)	67.02	48.39 (0.72)
Mining & Quarrying (10-14)	421.83	238.05 (0.56)	113.59	119.94 (1.06)	361.21	202.63 (0.56)	93.14	63.93 (0.69)
Manufacturing (15-22)	170.71	100.25 (0.59)	90.54	50.58 (0.56)	154.84	85.74 (0.55)	86.29	48.14 (0.56)
Manufacturing (23-37)	243.63	203.00 (0.83)	109.96	52.57 (0.48)	213.23	151.32 (0.71)	96.30	60.85 (0.63)
Electricity, Gas and Water Supply (40-41)	441.46	306.75 (0.70)	98.27	100.00 (1.02)	360.47	310.09 (0.86)	99.64	81.18 (0.82)
Construction (45)	239.90	179.18 (0.75)	110.08	77.11 (0.70)	212.33	169.01 (0.80)	97.06	74.38 (0.77)
Trade, Hotels and Restaurants (50-55)	151.40	122.19 (0.81)	97.49	75.73 (0.78)	135.45	110.18 (0.81)	92.04	67.91 (0.74)

(Contd.)

Table 8.6 (Contd.)

1	*12*	*13*	*14*	*15*	*16*	*17*	*18*	*19*
Transport, Storage, etc. (60-64)	248.37	322.64 (1.30)	115.08	57.64 (0.50)	205.47	277.72 (1.35)	102.91	59.46 (0.58)
Public Administration, Defence, etc. (65-74)	509.14	441.45 (0.87)	107.19	63.57 (0.59)	469.20	389.03 (0.83)	92.96	66.65 (0.72)
Health, education and other Services (75-93)	348.89	239.42 (0.69)	109.70	59.02 (0.54)	308.63	191.64 (0.62)	95.65	50.57 (0.53)
Private Households with Employed Persons (95)	147.93	59.07 (0.40)	91.08	50.51 (0.56)	134.58	54.22 (0.40)	78.62	51.39 (0.65)
All	276.04	212.86 (0.77)	104.52	58.74 (0.56)	238.41	171.68 (0.72)	79.13	50.75 (0.64)

Source: Calculated from NSSO (2010). This shows that women workers in regular employment in urban areas are less discriminated as compared to women in casual employment in urban areas and rural women in both types of employment. It is only in the more organised sectors of transport, electricity, gas and water supply and modern manufacturing that female wages are either more than the male wages or the gap is much narrower as compared to other sectors. But these sectors employ a few number of female workers and in the female dominated occupations (where women get more representation as compared to their overall share in labour market) the male-female wage gap is much wider.

employment, the women workers in urban areas earn not only higher than their rural counterparts but also have a higher ratio of female to male wages. But same is not true for female workers in casual employment.

Thus, the employment of women is not only restricted to a few sectors but their earnings therein are also lower as compared to men. The reason of this discrimination may also be due to low productivity of women workers who have lower human capabilities and this may also be due to pure discrimination which finds its roots in traditions of the patriarchal society. To check these tendencies, firstly we will observe the ratio of female wages to male wages by sectors and by level of education. This can be examined from Table 8.7.

Though, no clear pattern emerges from this table but one thing is obvious that in main sectors of activity of the females in majority of the cases, the ratio of female wages to male wages has not only been very low but has also declined in 2007-08 as compared to 2004-05. Interestingly, this ratio has increased in case of traditional manufacturing in rural areas for illiterate women and for those who have attained less than middle level of education, while for women with higher level of education, it has declined to as low as 36 percent (approximately).

If we exclude the women workers who are graduate or have higher level of education (as this would show a different pattern depending upon the type of activity) we can observe a U-type pattern of the ratio of female to male wages, which means that the women with lower level of education earn closer to their male counterparts than the women with middle of higher secondary level of education. This ratio increases for the women with some diploma or certificate course, but that too, in sectors, where very few of them have been employed (e.g. in electricity, transport, storage and communications). Thus, in majority of the cases, the female to male wages has declined with increase in level of education, which points out that there may be some other determinants of wages apart from the human capital factor. For this purpose we will first see the relationship of wages with a few human capital factors and then we will decompose the wage discrimination among male and female workers during the period of crisis.

Here, we have taken the general wage determination equation as given below:

$$\log(wages) = \alpha + X_i \beta_i + \varepsilon_i$$

where, wages are income earned by male and female workers, β_is are respective coefficients of various independent variables included in the

Table 8.7: Female to Male Ratio of Average Wages of Regular Salaried Workers According to Sector of Activity and General Level of Education

Sector	*Rural*					*Urban*				
	Not Literate	*Literate and up to Middle*	*Secondary and Higher Secondary*	*Diploma/ Certificate Course*	*Graduate and Above*	*Not Literate*	*Literate and up to Middle*	*Secondary and Higher Secondary*	*Diploma/ Certificate Course*	*Graduate and Above*
Agriculture										
2004-05	85.50	82.10	90.10	347.40	52.57	80.78	103.95	40.76	0.00	95.02
2007-08	85.52	78.31	53.04	202.39	137.98	82.02	140.89	22.92	0.00	48.84
Mining and Quarrying										
2004-05	48.75	97.54	25.75	12.09	0.00	57.80	30.48	204.88	61.87	43.55
2007-08	47.99	85.82	0.00	0.00	0.00	79.72	36.57	182.73	0.00	156.61
Manufacturing 1										
2004-05	45.46	48.73	45.71	56.87	55.52	43.11	60.20	57.91	27.42	107.43
2007-08	61.68	63.60	39.80	36.78	101.20	70.85	69.75	65.61	83.08	77.23
Manufacturing 2										
2004-05	50.77	69.27	56.77	83.09	41.06	51.37	42.17	64.05	99.80	60.59
2007-08	58.91	50.23	45.44	49.88	40.39	99.73	77.59	63.46	104.48	73.08
Electricity, Gas and Water Supply										
2004-05	118.41	87.99	111.67	92.63	36.51	79.86	54.90	73.87	71.13	80.74
2007-08	120.12	54.37	33.64	107.51	118.37	40.26	75.17	59.38	99.73	138.83
Construction										
2004-05	96.55	44.13	91.56	133.82	61.00	85.25	106.06	138.65	48.89	67.36
2007-08	77.98	71.60	85.27	228.66	0.00	55.36	47.65	54.92	47.23	54.27

Trade, Hotels and Restaurants										
2004-05	53.13	61.05	77.98	112.71	125.95	78.17	70.19	84.73	60.66	98.03
2007-08	92.38	77.46	73.49	33.02	59.12	63.23	83.11	61.51	77.61	86.47
Transport, Storage and Communications										
2004-05	89.29	90.91	76.07	0.00	108.95	86.61	104.21	108.05	40.61	114.76
2007-08	120.32	81.03	75.46	32.06	125.29	119.75	75.18	83.84	50.83	111.82
Services 1										
2004-05	192.98	77.00	46.58	91.39	56.52	71.50	88.64	75.23	123.76	74.27
2007-08	0.00	103.48	49.25	25.96	47.59	292.99	115.32	91.03	59.37	70.76
Services 2										
2004-05	34.33	37.95	53.62	88.03	67.79	61.93	77.43	77.73	76.32	71.50
2007-08	49.67	34.99	48.40	72.83	69.60	52.69	50.85	64.02	65.16	75.28
Private Households with Employed Persons										
2004-05	57.51	51.14	62.29	0.00	0.00	48.50	47.62	82.08	0.00	41.21
2007-08	57.64	64.15	614.36	—	0.00	55.80	46.04	51.31	—	74.60

Source: Calculated from NSSO (2006 and 2010).

equation, X_i is matrix of human capabilities and other individual characteristics. These include age in years (as a proxy to experience) and age square, years of schooling, share of workers employed in non-agricultural occupations, nutritional status (expressed as monthly per capita expenditure, of which a big share is spent on food items) and family size; ε_i is the error term. The results of the equations computed separately for male and female workers are shown in Table 8.8.

Table 8.8: Regression Coefficients of Wage Equations for Males and Females

Independent Variables	*Males*	*Females*
Rural		
Constant	-0.571	0.410
Share in Non-agricultural Employment	0.001	-0.001
Years of Schooling	0.021	0.246**
Age	0.203	0.172
Age Square	-0.003	-0.004
Household Size	0.276*	0.244
Nutritional Status	0.002***	0.001
R^2	0.630	0.616
Urban		
Constant	2.267	9.849*
Share in Non-agricultural Employment	-0.003	0.003
Years of Schooling	0.120***	0.136*
Age	0.182	-0.521
Age Square	-0.003	0.010
Household Size	-0.021	0.177
Nutritional Status	0.0001	0.0004
R^2	0.431	0.331
Combined		
Constant	0.289	1.978
Share in Non-agricultural Employment	-0.001	0.005*
Years of Schooling	0.084*	0.178***
Age	0.248	0.077
Age Square	-0.005	-0.002
Household Size	0.107	0.201
Nutritional Status	0.001**	0.001
R^2	0.637	0.730

***99 percent level of significance.
**95 percent level of significance.
*90 percent level of significance.
Source: Calculated from NSSO (2010).

The results of the wage model given above shows that the

explanatory power of the included variables is considerably high as the value of R^2 is 0.637 for male workers and 0.730 for female workers (which shows that in case of male wages about 64 percent and case of female wages about 73 percent of total variation is depicted by the independent variables shown here). The results in above table show that for male workers, the general education status (shown by years of schooling) and the nutritional standard have significant positive impact on wages while in case of females, the workers with higher education are more likely to get higher wages. Interestingly, in rural areas, the male wages are also positively influenced by the house hold size as if the workers with bigger family size opt to work in jobs with higher wages.

As the table shows that education level is the significant factor influencing the wage level both in case of males and females, it needs to be explored whether, the difference in male and female wages is due to different access to education or it is due to pure discriminatory attitude of the employers. For this purpose, the male female wage differences are disaggregated into explained variation and the unexplained variation. As discussed in methodology part, the first term of equation 1, is the discriminatory measure and the second term shows the difference in wages due to difference in human capital attainments. The decomposition of the wage differentials is given in Table 8.9.

The table shows that out of total wage differences only 21.21 percent is depicted by the explained factors, i.e. the human capability differences and 78.79 percent of wage discrimination is purely due to discriminatory attitude. In urban areas the discriminatory attitude is visible to a greater extent as compared to the rural areas. The comparison of this table with Table 8.5 also shows that the urban areas discriminate against women to a greater extent not only in case of wages but also in case of sectoral distribution of jobs (as according to Table 8.5 about 20.63 percent of total workers in rural areas and 43.54 percent of total workers in urban areas need to be relocated to achieve gender equality in distribution of occupations among men and women). Thus, it can be easily deduced that the areas with unequal sectoral distribution are also the areas with greater degree of wage discrimination.

Conclusion and Suggestions

To sum up, we can say that the work participation rate for women has been very low in India and these opportunities are being further constrained during the period of crisis. This contraction in employment opportunities can not only be observed in quantitative terms but in

Table 8.9: Decomposition of Wage Differentials between Males and Females

	Rural		*Urban*		*Combined*	
	Calculated	*As percentage of total difference*	*Calculated*	*As percentage of total difference*	*Calculated*	*As percentage of total difference*
Total Wage Differential	1.36	100.0	7.82	100.0	1.97	100.0
Differences due to pure Discrimination (the unexplained Variation)	0.88	64.74	7.56	96.70	1.55	78.79
Difference due to Factor Endowments (explained variation)	0.48	35.26	0.26	3.30	0.42	21.21

Source: Calculated from NSSO (2010).

qualitative terms as well. We can observe that even during the short span of time, the shifts in occupational structure have gone against women as their share in major non-agricultural occupations has declined to a greater extent as compared to the males. So, during this period, women are more likely to be placed in low paid activities. Though, the employment situation in India is dominated by self-employed workers, but the share of this type of employment has been higher for females as compared to males. More worrisome is the fact that out of total self-employeds, majority of males are own account workers and employers, while majority of females are unpaid family workers. Such characteristics of male and female employment have led to wage discrimination.

But we can not simply isolate the economic discrimination from social discrimination as they are closely interwoven with each other. Results show that there is hardly any change in sex segregation of occupations during the analysis period and it has been closely associated with the wage discrimination, i.e. wherever the degree of occupational segregation is higher, we can observe a bigger gap in wages as well. But a major proportion of this gap is depicted by unexplained factors i.e. pure discriminatory attitude of the society. This leads us to the conclusion that any type of crisis in the economy pushes further the already marginalised groups to the margins of the margins. So, there is need to mitigate the social inequalities in order to achieve economic equalities. For this purpose, there is a need to change the attitude of the people and this can not be done without political will to bring the ideological revolution via education.

Having equal share in economic opportunities is not only the basic human right of these women but would also be efficiency enhancing as no society can grow at full potential by under exploiting the productive powers of half of its population. The argument generally goes that women being paid less and being offered limited activities is mainly due to the fact that they are less skilled and have low productivity. But in patriarchal societies which have a bias against investing in raising women's human capital, such behaviour would be like 'blaming the victim'. These societies should invest more and more in health and education in general and that of women in particular. At the same time there should be more emphasis on reducing the gender gap in access to such facilities.

References

Acker, Joan (1980), "Women and Stratification: A Review of Recent Literature", *Contemporary Sociology*, Vol. 9, pp. 25-35.

Anker, Richard (1995), "Labour Market Policies, Vulnerable Groups and Poverty", in H. Figueiredo and Z. Shaheed (eds.), *New Approaches to Poverty Analysis and Policy-II*, International Institute for Labour Studies, Geneva.

Anker, Richard and Hein, Catherine (1986), *Inequalities in Urban Employment in the Third World*, Macmillan, London.

Becker, G.S. (1971), *The Economics of Discrimination*, Chicago: University of Chicago Press.

Blau, Francine D. (1996), "Where Are We in the Economics of Gender? The Gender Pay Gap", *Working Paper No. 5664*, National Bureau of Economics Research.

Blau, Francine D., and Lawrence M. Kahn (1994), "Rising Wage Inequality and the U.S. Gender Gap", *American Economic Review*, 84(2), pp. 23-8.

Blinder, Alan S. (1973), "Wage Discrimination: Reduced Form and Structural Variables", *Journal of Human Resources*, Vol. 8, pp. 436-55.

Chen, Martha, Vanek, J., Lund, F., Heintz, J., Jhabwala, R. and Bonner, C. (2005), *Progress of World Women, 2005: Women, Work and Poverty*, UNIFEM, New York.

Chen, Martha, Vanek, J. and Heintz, J. (2006), "Informality, Gender and Poverty: A Global Picture", *Economic and Political Weekly*, 41(21).

Chenery, Hollis B. (1979), *Structural Change and Development Policy*, Baltimore: Johns Hopkins University Press.

Dev, S. Mahendra (2002), "Pro-Poor Growth in India: What do we Know about the Employment Effects of Growth, 1980-2000?" *Working Paper No. 161*, London: Overseas Development Institute.

Duraisamy, M. and P. Duraisamy (1996), "Sex Discrimination in Indian Labour Markets", *Feminist Economist*, 2(2), pp. 599-612.

Dutta, Puja V. and Barry Reilly (2008), "The Gender Pay Gap in the Era of Economic Change: Evidence from India, 1983 to 2004", *The Indian Journal of Labour Economics*, 51(3), pp. 341-66.

Horrace, William C. and Ronald L. Oaxaca (2001), "Inter-Industry Wage Differentials and the Gender Wage Gap: An Identification Problem", *Industrial and Labour Relations Review*, 54(3), pp. 611-18.

ILO (2004), *Global Employment Trends for Women, 2004*, Geneva: International Labour Office.

Kamath, K.V. (2008), 'Towards a Robust Indian Financial Sector', *The Economic Times*, October, 20.

Kingdon, G. and Jeemol Unni (2001), "Education and Women's Labour Market Outcomes in India", *Education Economics*, 9(2), pp. 173-95.

Kuznets, Simon (1966), *Modern Economic Growth: Rate, Structure and Spread*, New Haven: Yale University Press.

Lee, K.H. and Nagraj, Shyamala (1995), "Male-Female Earning Differentials in Malaysia", *The Journal of Development Studies*, 31(3).

Makkonen, Timo (2002), *Multiple, Compound and Intersectional Discrimination: Bringing the Experience of the Most Marginalised to the Fore*, Institute of Human Rights, Abo Akademi University.

NCEUS (2009a), *The Global Economic Crisis and the Informal Economy in India: Need for Urgent Measures and Fiscal Stimulus to Protect Incomes in the Informal Economy*, National Commission for Enterprises in the Unorganised Sector, Government of India, New Delhi.

NCEUS (2009b), *The Challenge of Employment in India: An Informal Economy Perspective, Volume-I,* National Commission for Enterprises in the Unorganised Sector, Government of India, New Delhi.

NSSO (2006), *Employment and Unemployment Situation in India, 2004-05,* NSS 61st Round (July 2004-June 2005), Part I and II, National Sample Survey Organisation, Ministry of Statistics and Programme Implementation, Government of India, New Delhi.

NSSO (2010), *Employment and Unemployment Situation in India, 2007-08,* NSS 64th Round (July 2007-June 2008), National Sample Survey Organisation, Ministry of Statistics and Programme Implementation, Government of India, New Delhi.

NSSO (2011), *Key Indicators of Employment and Unemployment Situation in India, 2009-10,* NSS 66th Round (July 2009-June 2010), National Sample Survey Organisation, Ministry of Statistics and Programme Implementation, Government of India, New Delhi, June.

Oaxaca, Ronald (1973), "Male-Female Wage Differentials in Urban Labour Markets", Vol. 14, October, pp. 693-709.

Richardson, Laurel (1988), *The Dynamics of Sex and Gender: A Sociological Perspective,* New York: Harper and Row.

Stockard, C. and M. Johnson (1980), *Sex Roles: Sex Inequality and Sex Role Development,* Englewood Cliffs, Prentice Hall, NJ.

Watts, M. (1998), "Occupational Gender Segregation: Index Measurement and Econometric Modelling", *Demography,* 35(4).

Gender Inequalities in Employment in Unorganised Manufacturing Sector of India

APRA

Introduction

Unorganised sector has become a perennial source of employment generation and its role in terms of its contribution to growth and income generation is gaining attention, especially in the developing countries. It is surprising to note that this sector absorbs more than 90 percent of the total work force in our country. The size of the unorganised sector has been substantial. This sector produces useful products and many organised sector industries depend on informal sector for the supply of raw materials.

Thus, the unorganised sector not only provides income earning opportunity to the poorer group of population but also has linkage with the industries of the country. In a heavily populated country like ours, it has established itself to be the only source of survival of a large segment of female work force in particular. An increasingly large portion of women has been absorbed by this sector and its role in absorbing the women workers is undeniable. The role of unorganised sector in terms of its contribution to employment and national income is vital. If we talk about the gender dimension of the employment we can say that any deliberation on this sector would be incomplete without a discussion on it. The adoption of stabilisation and structural adjustment policies could have also led enterprises to shift from regular wage employment to contract labour system and thereby created more demand for casual workers, particularly the women.

Importantly, when some of the large units experienced a decline, a large number of women got absorbed into small enterprises (employing less than 5 persons per unit) but under terms and conditions that were relatively unfavourable to women (Jose, 1987). During this process of globalisation, the industries generally demand cheap labour and female labour easily fall in this category. But the quality of the employment in these units may be exploitative (Rustagi, 1999).

The objective of this paper is to analyse the quantum and trends of women worker participation in the unorganised manufacturing sector. Here we try to find out whether the gender inequalities in employment in unorganised manufacturing sector in India have grown or declined after liberalisation .The paper is divided into five sections.

Apart from the ongoing introductory section, section II will give review of related literature, section III deals with sources and methodology, section IV discusses the gender inequalities in employment in the unorganised manufacturing sector and quality of female employment therein. In this section we compare the quality of male and female employment and also explore the type of work and enterprises where women participation is dominant or dormant. Section V gives conclusions drawn from the analysis.

Review of Literature

While it is true that jobs in unorganised manufacturing sector have changed the women's economic roles, it is also being increasingly realised that more women are engaged in activities that do not offer any income or employment security. While women constitute one-third of the total labour force in India, their productivity is severely constrained due to unfavourable conditions of work as well as discrimination.

Discrimination on the lines of gender is not always overt. It appears in very subtle forms such as in the nature of work performed, type of skills required to perform the work and the valuation of these skills and the technology used by men and women. It is often observed that women are discriminated against not only in terms of access to labour market but also while setting wages. The sexual division of labour in the society is also reflected in the division of labour in the workplace. This is argued that the activities or segments where the women are concentrated are low skilled.

During the last two decades though the work participation of women has increased, yet they are largely being placed in low paid, insecure and informal jobs (Ward, 1988), while the better paid supervisory and managerial jobs are reserved for men. So, it would be quite relevant here to observe how various types of jobs in unorganised manufacturing sector of India have been distributed among men and women

Bandyopadhyay and Hillary (1985) observed an increase in the participation of women in the Kolkata labour force, due to a combination of high male unemployment, falling urban living standards and some increase in employment of a semi or unskilled kind for which women workers are positively preferred. Saran and Sandhwar (1990) studied the problems of the women workers engaged in unorganised sector of brick kilns, quarries and mines of Bihar and West Bengal. It was revealed that the women working there were exploited, low paid, worked for long hours. Banerjee (1991) attempted to analyse the impact of new export-oriented industries on women workers in India. She had covered main industries viz. leather, garment, silk spinning, etc.

The conclusions drawn are that these women did unskilled works, worked for long erratic hours and under miserable working conditions and terms of work. During the phase of globalisation, opportunities for the women to be economically independent have considerably grown though the opportunities may vary (Cagatay and Ozler, 1995). Gajalakshmi (1998), Jhabvala (1998) and Rao (1998) empirically analysed women workers employed in unorganised sector at macro-level and concluded that they earned low income as compared to their male counterparts, live in poverty and work for long hours and explored the mechanism for social security provisions, insurance, social security funds for women in unorganised sector. Papola and Sharma (1999) conducted a study that there is marginal increase in labour force participation of women in unorganised sector.

The gender discrimination for work is more prevalent in unorganised sector labour market. Srinivasan (2000) looked into conceptual issues of the unorganised sector along with profile of women's employment and its trends. Many studies have shown gender gap in earnings even for same level of education, age and job tenure of women as compared to men (OECD, 2004; Mehra and Gammage, 1999). Since women have to devote more time to care work and less to remunerative activities than men, the total income from their employment falls (Chen *et al*, 2005; UNRISD, 2000; Beneria, 2003). This sexual division of labour that relegated the women to the lowest categories of work resulted in lower piece-rate wages and lower overall monthly incomes (Unni and Bali, 2002). As per NCEUS, 2008, it is observed that in most industry groups there is a hierarchy of jobs where the women are placed at the bottom.

Data Source and Methodology

This study is based upon secondary data. Source of the study is NSSO (National Sample Survey Organisation) surveys which provide extensive data on unorganised manufacturing sector. NSSO provides data for about 23 sub-sectors as per National Industrial Classification. All classification has been adjusted according to National Industrial Classification, 98 as per the concordance table provided by NSSO. This data is further disaggregated into various states and rural-urban segments.

The data provided by NSSO is classified into three types of enterprises namely, Own Account Manufacturing Enterprises (OAMEs), Non-directory Manufacturing Enterprises (NDMEs), Directory Manufacturing Enterprises (DMEs). NSSO defines OAMEs as those enterprises which operate with no hired worker on a fairly regular basis. NDMEs are those enterprises which employ less than six workers including household workers and DMEs employ six or more workers with at least one hired worker but not registered under the Factory Act, 1948 (NSSO, 2002).

For analysing the data, share of female employment out of total employment under various categories have been used to explore gender inequalities in type of work and enterprises in employment and wages in unorganised manufacturing sector of India in post-reform phase.

Gender Inequality and Quality of Employment in Unorganised Manufacturing Sector of India

The ever-changing, challenging and dynamic role of women in the current global scenario has forced the researchers and thinkers to explore the vistas of their new economic dimensions and find their contribution and conditions in the emerging socio-economic and cross-cultural world. In the recent growing, vibrant yet vulnerable global economic conditions unorganised manufacturing sector has become the bread provider of billions especially in emerging economies like ours. It is in this sense that the importance of focussing attention on this sector has become imperative and women empowerment so important.

Table 9.1 explains the percentage share of female workers in different types of enterprises, i.e. OAMEs, NDMEs and DMEs both in rural

Table 9.1: Share of Female Employment in Unorganised Manufacturing Sector by Type of Enterprise (percentage share)

Type of enterprise	*Rural*			*Urban*			*Combined*		
	1994-05	*2000-01*	*2005-06*	*1994-05*	*2000-01*	*2005-06*	*1994-05*	*2000-01*	*2005-06*
OAME	41.70	43.04	50.55	30.03	42.52	50.33	39.22	42.91	50.5
NDME	13.00	13.37	14.43	5.39	6.92	7.57	8.24	9.16	10.40
DME	28.33	26.89	27.79	10.07	12.76	10.98	17.99	19.12	18.34
All enterprises	37.84	38.69	43.92	17.46	24.58	27.26	31.05	33.70	37.98

Source: Calculated from NSSO 1998 (Report No. 433), NSSO 2002 (Report No. 479), NSSO 2008 (Report No. 525).

and urban areas. The percentage share of female workers has increased from 31.05 percent in 1994-95 to 37.70 percent in 2001-01 and to 37.98 percent in 2005-06. This increase is mainly due to the increased share of female workers in the OAMEs, i.e. from 39.22 percent in 1994-95 to 42.91 percent in 2000-01 and to 50.50 percent in 2005-06.

There has also been small increase in the share of female workers in NDMEs, i.e. from 8.24 percent in 1994-95 to 10.40 percent in 2005-06. In the case of DMEs, the share of female workers has increased from 17.99 percent in 1994-95 to 19.12 percent in 2000-01 but declined to 18.34 percent in 2005-06. The main reason for this increasing share of female workers in OAMEs is its home based and traditional nature.

Table 9.2 explains the percentage of female workers in different types of enterprises according to the nature of work, i.e., full time workers and part-time workers for the rural and urban areas. It is seen that at all India level the share of females in full time workers has remained stagnant at around 28 percent from 1994-95 to 2000-2001 and then increased to 32.26 percent in 2005-06. This increase is found both in the rural and urban areas. In rural areas the share has increased from 35.11 percent in 1994-95 to 38.85 percent in 2005-06.

While in the urban areas the share of female workers in full time jobs has increased from 16.39 percent in 1994-95 to 21.59 percent in 2005-06. As far as part-time workers are concerned, the share of female workers is very significant and was increasing over the period, i.e. from 52.53 percent in 1994-95 to 62.37 percent in 2000-01 and to 63.92 percent in 2005-06. In the rural area its share has increased from 54.75 percent in 1994-95 to 62.56 percent in 2005-06. In the urban areas, it has increased from 39.56 percent in 1994-95 to 68.28 percent in 2005-06. Thus, the analysis of percentage share of female workers according to nature of work shows the relative preference for part-time work by the women, particularly in urban areas.

The analysis of share of female workers by nature of work for different types of enterprises shows that in the OAMEs the female share has increased both for the full time and part time workers. In case of full time female workers it has increased from 37 percent from 1994-95 to 45.24 percent in 2005-06. In rural areas the share in full time jobs has increased from 38.92 percent in 1994-95 to 45.92 percent in 2005-06. In the urban areas the same has increased from 28.49 percent in 1994-95 to 43.15 percent in 2005-06. So in case of OAMEs the increase in the share of full time female workers is more prominent in urban areas in comparison to rural areas.

Table 9.2: Share of Women Employment in Unorganised Manufacturing Sector by Type of Enterprise and Nature of Work

	1994-95			*2000-01*			*2005-06*		
	Full time	*Part time*	*Total*	*Full time*	*Part time*	*Total*	*Full time*	*Part time*	*Total*
OAMEs									
Rural	38.92	56.08	41.70	37.46	62.39	43.04	45.92	64.42	50.55
Urban	28.49	53.52	30.02	35.72	76.51	42.52	43.15	76.61	50.33
Combined	36.50	55.84	39.22	37.03	65.03	42.91	45.24	67.01	50.50
NDMEs									
Rural	11.83	29.48	13.00	10.99	39.95	13.37	11.24	41.43	14.43
Urban	4.96	15.80	5.39	6.02	26.68	6.92	5.85	36.40	7.54
Combined	7.49	22.58	8.24	7.70	33.22	9.16	8.00	39.26	10.40
DMEs									
Rural	27.80	42.88	28.33	25.80	49.02	26.89	25.73	50.56	27.79
Urban	9.59	26.32	10.07	12.08	35.06	12.76	9.48	44.36	10.98
Combined	17.46	34.30	17.99	18.19	42.89	19.12	16.42	48.08	18.34
All Enterprise Type									
Rural	35.11	54.75	37.84	33.38	61.21	38.69	38.85	62.56	43.92
Urban	16.39	39.56	17.46	20.14	66.63	24.58	21.59	68.28	27.26
Combined	28.42	52.53	31.05	28.36	62.37	33.70	32.26	63.92	37.98

Source: Calculated from NSSO 1998 (Report No. 433), NSSO 2002 (Report No. 479), NSSO 2008 (Report No. 525).

So is the case with part time workers, where it has increased from 56.08 percent to 64.42 percent in rural areas and 53.52 percent to 76.61 percent in urban areas during the same period. However, the increase in the share of female part-time workers in urban areas is far greater than that of full time workers. Similar trends can be observed in NDMEs and DMEs. In NDMEs, the female share in full time jobs has increased from 7.49 percent in 1994-95 to 8 percent in 2005-06, while in case of part-time jobs it has increased from 22.58 percent to 39.26 percent.

The rural NDMEs have observed a decline in female share in full time jobs while the urban NDMEs have observed an increase from 4.96 percent in 1994-95 to 5.85 percent in 2005-06. On the other hand, in case of part-time jobs, the share of women has increased both in rural (from 29.48 percent to 41.43 percent) and urban areas (from 15.80 percent to 36.40 percent) but the relative increase in this share in urban areas is greater than that of the rural areas. The DMEs too, have observed a decline in the female share in full time jobs (from 17.46 percent to 16.42 percent) and an increase in their share in part-time jobs (34.30 percent to 48.08 percent) during 1994-95 to 2005-06. Again, the urban areas have registered higher increase in share of part-time jobs.

Table 9.3: Characteristics of Male/Female Workers in Various Types of Enterprises in Unorganised Manufacturing Sector in India (Share in percentage out of total)

	Male workers		*Female workers*	
	Full time	*Part time*	*Full time*	*Part time*
		1994-95		
OAMEs				
Rural	87.80	12.20	78.23	21.77
Urban	95.90	4.10	89.01	10.99
Combined	80.79	10.21	79.98	20.02
NDMEs				
Rural	94.63	5.37	84.98	15.02
Urban	96.42	3.58	88.20	11.80
Combined	95.78	4.22	86.30	13.70
DMEs				
Rural	97.21	2.79	94.71	5.29
Urban	97.64	2.36	92.48	7.52
Combined	97.48	2.52	94.00	6.00

(*Contd.*)

	Male workers		*Female workers*	
	Full time	*Part time*	*Full time*	*Part time*
All Enterprise Type				
Rural	89.80	10.20	79.79	20.21
Urban	96.61	3.39	89.52	10.48
Combined	92.52	7.48	81.61	18.39
		2005-06		
Rural	82.01	17.99	68.13	31.87
Urban	89.89	10.11	67.32	32.68
Combined	83.9	16.1	67.94	32.06
OAMEs				
Rural	92.75	7.25	69.59	30.11
Urban	96.13	3.87	72.92	27.08
Combined	94.80	5.20	71.02	28.98
NDMEs				
Rural	94.32	5.68	84.90	15.10
Urban	97.31	2.69	82.61	17.39
Combined	96.15	3.85	84.13	15.87
DMEs				
Rural	85.74	14.26	69.56	30.44
Urban	94.71	5.29	69.59	30.41
Combined	89.48	10.52	69.57	30.43

Source: Calculated from NSSO 1998 (Report No. 433), NSSO 2002 (Report No. 479), NSSO 2008 (Report No. 525).

Table 9.3 shows that the percentage of male workers working in full time jobs has always remained higher than that of the female workers, though this percentage has decreased from 92.52 percent in 1994-95 to 89.48 percent in 2005-06. On the other hand, in 1994-95 about 80 percent of female workers were working as full time workers and only 20 percent as part time workers, this composition changed to about 70 percent and 30 percent by the year 2005-06. If we move by the size (OAMEs being the smallest and DMEs as the largest enterprises), we can observe that more of male and female workers work in full time jobs as the size of enterprises increases. Further it can also be observed that the percentage of both male and female workers in full time jobs is higher in urban areas as compared to rural areas.

Table 9.4 shows the distribution of male and female workers in their own group, as per the type of workers. The table shows that more of the male workers are employed as working owners as compared to other types of workers. But if we exclude the OAMEs, we can see that a majority of male workers work as hired workers and this percentage is still higher for urban males.

Table 9.4: Characteristics of Male/Female Workers by Type of Workers in Respective Groups in Unorganised Manufacturing Sector in India

	Male workers			*Female workers*		
	Working owner	*Hired workers*	*Unpaid workers*	*Working owner*	*Hired workers*	*Unpaid workers*
			1994-95			
OAMEs						
Rural	70.71	.53	28.76	26.93	.43	72.64
Urban	64.80	1.28	33.92	35.13	.98	63.89
Combined	69.26	.72	33.02	28.26	.52	71.22
NDMEs						
Rural	35.10	53.99	10.91	9.71	45.74	55.45
Urban	31.90	59.71	8.39	15.24	49.33	35.43
Combined	33.04	57.68	9.28	11.94	47.19	40.87
DMEs						
Rural	14.07	74.72	11.21	1.43	83.12	15.45
Urban	13.85	77.91	8.24	4.41	79.63	15.96
Combined	13.94	76.79	9.37	2.35	82.03	15.62
All Enterprise Type						
Rural	59.48	16.06	24.46	24.32	8.58	67.10
Urban	38.70	43.40	17.90	28.24	17.90	53.66
Combined	51.24	26.91	21.85	25.09	10.32	64.5
			2000-01			
OAMEs						
Rural	78.41	0.65	20.94	55.39	0.45	44.16
Urban	74.01	1.57	24.42	61.92	0.41	37.67
Combined	77.36	.87	21.77	56.92	0.44	42.64
NDMEs						
Rural	38.44	53.76	7.80	23.08	43.95	33.01
Urban	33.33	59.26	7.41	27.14	48.87	23.99
Combined	35.02	57.43	7.54	25.08	46.37	28.55
DMEs						
Rural	14.87	76.39	8.74	3.85	83.88	12.27
Urban	16.29	77.09	6.62	6.57	81.56	11.89
Combined	15.71	76.81	7.48	4.85	83.02	12.13
All Enterprise Type						
Rural	64.68	17.64	17.68	50.15	8.68	41.17
Urban	41.99	44.99	13.02	51.41	15.62	32.97
Combined	55.56	28.63	15.81	50.48	10.47	39.05

(*Contd.*)

	Male workers			Female workers		
	Working owner	*Hired workers*	*Unpaid workers*	*Working owner*	*Hired workers*	*Unpaid workers*
			2005-06			
OAMEs						
Rural	76.37	0.19	23.44	58.36	0.10	41.54
Urban	71.35	0.60	28.05	62.61	0.04	37.35
Combined	75.17	0.29	24.54	59.37	0.09	40.54
NDMEs						
Rural	36.51	53.99	9.50	16.08	43.39	40.53
Urban	33.43	59.25	7.32	24.57	47.52	27.91
Combined	34.64	57.18	8.18	19.71	45.15	35.14
DMEs						
Rural	15.34	77.33	7.33	2.90	85.58	11.52
Urban	13.78	81.15	5.07	10.06	74.88	15.06
Combined	14.38	79.67	5.95	5.31	81.97	12.72
All Enterprise Type						
Rural	59.97	21.46	18.57	52.38	8.59	39.03
Urban	37.46	49.87	12.67	53.46	12.60	33.94
Combined	50.56	33.34	16.10	52.66	9.61	37.73

Source: Calculated from NSSO 1998 (Report No. 433), NSSO 2002 (Report No. 479), NSSO 2008 (Report No. 525).

On the other hand, in case of female workers, we can observe a shift from unpaid activities to working owners since 1994-95. The share of females working as unpaid family workers has declined from 64.59 percent in 1994-95 to 37.73 percent in 2005-06, meanwhile the share of female workers as working owners has increased from 25.09 percent to 52.66 percent. But this increase is mainly due to change in composition of female workers in OAMEs. It seems that those women, who were earlier working as unpaid family members, are likely to run the enterprises on their own, particularly when their percentage as hired workers is declining.

A comparative analysis of males and females shows that more of women work as unpaid workers as compared to men and more of men work as working owner and hired workers as compared to women and the difference is more overt in urban areas as compared to rural areas. At the enterprise level, it can be observed that the DMEs follow the least discriminatory practices.

Finally, the gender-wise distribution shows that although the share of female workers is increasing but this increase in female share is mainly due to increase in part time jobs. The women are mainly occupied in unpaid and part time jobs while their share in hired workers and full time jobs is very low *vis-à-vis* their overall share in total employment in the unorganised manufacturing sector of India.

Table 9.5 demonstrates that the share of females in total working owners has increased significantly from 18.22 percent in 1994-95 to 31.60 percent in 2000-01 and further to 38.94 percent in 2005-06. The same pattern has been observed in rural areas where this share has increased from 20.07 percent in 1994-95 to 32.85 percent in 2000-01 and to 40.62 percent in 2005-06. In the urban areas it has increased tremendously from 13.57 percent in 1994-95 to 28.53 percent in 2000-01 and then to 34.83 percent in 2005-06. So the share of women in working owners increased both in the rural and urban areas.

Though, the share of women in working owners has been the largest in OAMEs as compared to NDMEs and DMEs, yet, every type of enterprise has observed an increase in Women's share in working owners. In OAMEs, it increased from 20.95 percent in 1994-95 to 44.62 percent in 2005-06, in NDMEs it increased from 3.13 percent to 6.19 percent and in case of DMEs it increased from 3.67 percent to 7.65 percent during the same period of time. Though, both the rural and urban areas have registered the increase in women share in working owners, but it can be observed that the urban OAMEs and DMEs have registered a larger increase than their rural counterparts, while the increase is nearly similar for rural and urban NDMEs.

The share of females in hired workers has remained almost stagnant over the period. The enterprise level analysis shows that, the share of women in total hired workers has increased in NDMEs and declined in DMEs (here, analysis of OAMEs may not be significant as OAMEs do not employ hired workers on fairly regular basis). Though, in both types of enterprises, the share in rural areas is greater than that of urban areas, yet it can be observed that wherever this share has increased the increase has been sharper in urban areas and wherever it has declined, the decline has been smaller in urban areas as compared to rural areas.

On the other hand, women are heavily represented in unpaid activities. Their share has been as high as 57.37 percent in 1994-95 and 58.93 percent in 2005-06. Though, the female share in unpaid activities in rural areas has not changed very much (as it was 62.75 percent in 1994-95 and 62.20 percent in 2005-06), yet, in urban areas it has increased from 39.09 percent in 1994-95 to 50.11 percent in 2005-06. It can be observed from the table that the share of women in unpaid workers is the highest in OAMEs, while in NDMEs and DMEs,

Table 9.5: Share of Female Employment in Unorganised Manufacturing Sector in India by Type of Enterprise and Type of Worker (percentage share)

	1994-95			*2000-01*			*2005-06*		
	Working owners	*Hired workers*	*Unpaid workers*	*Working owners*	*Hired workers*	*Unpaid workers*	*Working owners*	*Hired workers*	*Unpaid workers*
OAMEs									
Rural	21.53	36.47	64.54	34.80	34.14	61.44	43.86	34.93	64.44
Urban	18.91	24.77	44.77	38.23	16.04	53.30	47.07	6.89	57.43
Combined	20.95	31.83	60.63	35.61	27.41	59.56	44.62	23.62	62.75
NDMEs									
Rural	3.99	11.29	38.02	8.46	11.18	39.56	6.91	11.93	41.85
Urban	2.60	4.42	19.12	5.71	5.78	19.41	5.68	6.16	23.80
Combined	3.13	6.82	28.26	6.73	7.52	27.62	6.19	8.40	33.28
DMEs									
Rural	3.95	31.11	35.89	8.70	28.77	34.05	6.78	29.87	37.70
Urban	3.49	10.39	18.02	5.76	13.40	20.80	8.27	10.22	26.82
Combined	3.67	19.42	27.30	6.80	20.35	27.70	7.65	18.77	32.45
All Enterprises									
Rural	20.07	24.70	62.75	32.85	23.69	59.50	40.62	23.86	62.20
Urban	13.57	8.10	39.04	28.53	10.16	45.22	34.84	8.65	50.11
Combined	18.22	14.86	57.37	31.60	15.67	55.68	38.94	15.01	58.93

Source: Calculated from NSSO 1998 (Report No. 433), NSSO 2002 (Report No. 479), NSSO 2008 (Report No. 525).

this share is the same. Interestingly, the year 2005-06, has observed an increase in the share of women in unpaid workers in every type of enterprise.

Though, this share has been greater in rural areas than the urban areas in every type of enterprise but interestingly this gap has been narrowing down since 1994-95. This is due to the greater increase in women share in unpaid activities in urban enterprises as compared to rural enterprises.

Conclusion

The above analysis shows that although the female labour force participation has increased and sex segregation of total employment has declined in the unorganised manufacturing sector of India, yet their access to decent economic opportunities is frequently constrained, particularly in paid employment category. The women have larger share in unpaid and part time jobs as compared to the jobs with positive characteristics under the unorganised manufacturing sector of India.

It is a fact that employment as well its quality is significant by which the benefits of development can trickle down to the grass root level and reduce poverty and misery of millions including women. It is observed that though, female employment has been increasing with the gigantic growth of unorganised sector, but the type of jobs they are getting are far low in quality than the male workers. They are largely employed in the enterprises requiring lower skills and unpaid jobs.

References

Bandyopadhyaya Bela and Standing Hillary (1985), "Women's Employment and Household—Some Findings from Calcutta", *Economic and Political Weekly*, Vol. 20, No. 7.

Banerjee, Nirmala (1991), *Indian Women in Changing Industrial Scenario*, New Delhi: Sage Publications.

Beneria, Lourdes (2003), *Gender, Development and Globalisation: Economics As if All People Mattered*, London: Routledge.

Cagatay, Nilufer and Özler, Sule (1995), "Feminisation of Labour Force: The Effect of Long-Term Development and Structural Adjustment," *World Development*, Vol. 23, No. 11.

Chen, Martha, Vanek, J., Lund, F., Heintz, J., Jhabwala, R. and Bonner, C. (2005), *Progress of World Women, 2005: Women, Work and Poverty*, UNIFEM, New York.

Gajalakshmi, N. (1998), *Problems and Prospective of Women Labour in India*, New Delhi: Mohit Publications.

Jhabvala, Renana (1998), "Social Security for Unorganised Sector", *Economic and Political Weekly*, Vol. 33, No. 22.

Jose, A.V. (1987), *Employment and Wages of Women Workers in Asian Countries: An Assessment"*, ILO/ARTEP.

Mehra, Rekha and Gammage, Sarah (1999), "Trends, Counter-Trends and Gaps in Women's Employment", *World Development*, Vol. 27, No. 3.

NSSO (1995), Tables with Notes on Survey of Unorganised Manufacture: Non-Directory Establishments and Own Account Enterprises, NSSO 45th Round (July 1989-June 1990), NSSO *Report No. 396*, Government of India, New Delhi.

_____ (1998a), "Unorganised Manufacturing Sector in India: Its Size, Employment and Some Key Estimates", NSSO 51st Round (July 1994-June 1995), NSSO *Report No. 433*, Government of India, New Delhi.

_____ (1998b), "Unorganised Manufacturing Enterprises in India: Salient Features", NSSO 51st Round (July 1994-June 1995), NSSO *Report No. 434*, Government of India, New Delhi.

_____ (2002a), "Unorganised Manufacturing Sector in India; 2000-01—Key Results", NSSO 56th Round (July 2000-June 2001), NSSO *Report No. 477*, Government of India, New Delhi.

_____ (2002b), "Unorganised Manufacturing Sector in India; 2000-01—Input, Output and Value Added", NSSO 56th Round (July 2000-June 2001), NSSO *Report No. 480*, Government of India, New Delhi

_____ (2008a), "Unorganised Manufacturing Sector in India; 2005-06—Key Results", NSSO 62nd Round (July 2005-June 2006), NSSO *Report No. 525*, Government of India, New Delhi.

Papola, T.S. and Sharma, Alakh (1999), (eds.), *Gender and Employment in India*, New Delhi: Vikas Publishing House.

OECD (2001), *OECD Employment Outlook, 2001*, Paris: Organisation for Economic Cooperation and Development.

Rao, R. (1998), "Women Workers in Beedi Industry", *Social Welfare*, Vol. 45, No. 5.

Rustagi, P. (1999), *The Structure and Dynamics of Indian Rural Labour Market*, Unpublished Ph.D. Thesis, Jawaharlal Nehru University, New Delhi.

Saran, A.B. and Sandhwar, A.N. (1990), *Problems of Women Workers in Unorganised Sector* (Brick Kilns, Quarries and Mines of Bihar and West Bengal), New Delhi: Northern Book Centre.

Srinivasan, M.V. (2000), "Women Workers in Unorganised Sector", *Women's Link*, Vol. 6, No. 4.

Unni, Jeemol and Bali, N. (2002), "Subcontracted Women Workers in the Garment Industry in India", in Radhika Balkrishnan (eds.), *The Hidden Assembly Line: Gender Dynamics of Sub-Contracted Work in a Global Economy*, Kumarian Press, Connecticut.

UNRISD (2005), *Striving for Justice in an Unequal World*, Geneva: United Nations Research Institute for Social Development.

Ward, K. (1988), "Women Workers and Global Restructuring", New York: ILR Press.

Concept of Gender Justice and Status of Women under the Constitution of India: An Introspection

Sanjay Sindhu and Veena Kumari

Introduction

Human beings are rational beings. They, by virtue of their being human, possess certain basic and inalienable rights which are commonly known as human rights. Since these rights belong to them because of their existence. Human rights being the birth rights are, therefore, inherent in all the individuals irrespective of their caste, creed, religion, sex and nationality. These rights are essentially for all the individuals as they are consonant with their freedom and dignity and are conducive to physical, moral, social and spiritual welfare. These rights are also necessary as they provide suitable conditions for the materials and moral uplift of the people. Because of their immense significance to human beings, these rights are also sometimes referred as fundamental rights, basic rights, inherent rights, natural rights and birth rights. The idea of human rights is bound up with human dignity. Thus, all those rights which are essential for maintenance of human dignity may be called human rights.[1]

Presently, gender-based discrimination represents the ugly face of the society. This issue is global with varying degree and very old. It is a travesty of all cannons of social justice and equality that woman who constitute half of the world's population and who work two third of the world working hours should earn just one tenth of the world's property and also should remain victim of inequality and injustice. This all indicated towards the gender injustice. The question of gender injustice is a very old and burning problem of the world. The words sex and gender are often interchangeably in everyday life, but literary these are frequently differentiated. The term sex is applied to those distinctions between men and women, which is based on biological differences, such as anatomy, physiology, hormones and chromosomes, and in this respect people are male and female.[2]

In simple words sex difference is natural, but gender difference is creative difference on the basis of sex, by putting gender bias. In this paper the authors made sincere attempt to highlight the status of women under the constitution of India 1950. The constitution of India safeguards women's right by putting her at par with man socially, politically and economically. The principle of the gender equality is enshrined in the constitution in its Preamble, fundamental rights, Directive Principles of State Policy and Fundamental Duties, with some other provisions like right to vote, reservation in local self-government. Still there is a very wide gap between the goals enunciated in the constitution, legislature, programmes and related mechanism on the one hand and situational reality of the status of women in India on the other.

A woman is the central figure in our society which inspires confidence in children, inculcates values in them and prepares them to pursue their goals relentlessly. The human rights of women are inalienable, integral and indivisible parts of human rights. The full and equal participation of women in political, civil, economic, social and cultural life at national and international levels and the eradication of all forms of discrimination on ground of sex are priority objectives of the international community, concluded by World Conference on Human Rights, 1993.[3] Advancement of rights of women has been the concern of world community since the end of Second World War. The Preamble, to the Charter of the United Nations Organisation mentions the determination of the people of the United Nations to reaffirm faith in fundamental human rights in the dignity and worth of the human person, in the equal rights of men and women and to employ international machinery for the promotion of the economic and social advancement of the people. Similarly, provisions are also incorporated in the Charter of the United Nations and other human rights instrument which provide for the protection and advancement of the rights of women.[4]

The principle of equal rights for men and women has been incorporated in the Universal Declaration of Human Rights, 1948. The principle of equal rights of men and women has found mention in International human rights instruments. For the promotion of status of women in various fields and to eliminate discrimination against women two organs have been established under the United Nations system, i.e., Commission on the Status of Women, and the Committee on the Elimination of Discrimination against Women.[5]

Status of Women under the Constitution of India, 1950

The Constitution of India guarantees to all its citizen equality before the law and the equal protection of law within the territory of India. All men and women are equal before the law and therefore, law protect them all. United Nations Declaration of Human Rights used both the expression, i.e., 'equal protection of law' and 'equality before law'; taken together, aim at establishing the 'equality of statuses as has been envisaged by the Preamble of the Constitution of India'.[6]

The principle of equality does not, of course, require that every law must have universal application, for the varying needs of different classes of persons often require separate treatment.[7] The classification permissible must be based on some real and substantial distinction bearing a just and reasonable relation to the objects sought to be attained and cannot be made arbitrary and without substantial basis.[8] The principle of equality as one of the milestones has been embodied in the Preamble of the Constitution of India. With respect to women, the Constitution assured that there shall be equality of opportunity for every citizen in fields of education and employment, and no one shall be discriminated against on the basis of sex and nothing shall prevent the state from making any special provision for women.[9]

The first fundamental right secured to the people of India is the 'Right to Equality' enshrined in Article 14 of the Constitution.[10] The concept of equality has been held basic to the rule of law and is regarded as the most fundamental postulate of republicanism.[11] In *Indira Nehru Gandhi v. Raj Narain*,[12] the Supreme Court held that the right to equality conferred by Article 14 is the basic structure of the Constitution and it is also an essential feature of democracy. In *Som Prakash v. Union of India*,[13] the court held that the equality before law embodied in Article 14 is not only formal equality before the law but is the real concept of substantive equality which strikes at the inequalities arising on account of vast social and economic differentiation and is an essential ingredient of social and economic justice.

Thus, two concepts are involved in Article 14, i.e., '*equality before law*' and '*equal protection of laws*'. In *Srinivasa Theater v. Govt. of Tamil Nadu*,[14] the Supreme Court has explained these two expressions 'equality before the law' and 'equal protection of law' do not mean the same thing even if there may be much in common between them. 'Equality before law' is a dynamic concept having many facets. One facet is that there shall be no privileged person or class and that none shall be above law. Another facet is "the obligation upon the state to bring about, though the machinery of law obligation upon the State to bring about, through the machinery of law, a mere equal society. In *Chiranjeet Lal v. Union of India*,[15] the Supreme Court observed that Article 14 prescribes equality before law. But it is a fact that all persons are not equal by nature, attainment or circumstances, and, therefore, a mechanical equality before the law may result in injustice.

The guarantee against the denial of equal protection of law does not mean that identically the same rules of law should be made applicable to all persons in spite of difference in circumstances or conditions. In *Air India v. Nargesh Merza*,[16] the Supreme Court struck down the Air India and Indian Airlines Regulations on the retirement and pregnancy bar on the services of Air Hostesses s unconstitutional on the ground that the conditions laid down were unreasonable and arbitrary. The condition that the services of Air Hostesses would be terminated on first pregnancy was the most unreasonable and arbitrary provision and liable to struck down and was, therefore, clearly violative of Article 14 of the Constitution. The Apex Court in *Githa Hariharan v. Reserve Bank of India*[17] invoked the rule of harmonious construction for securing the constitutional guarantee of gender equality. The court ruled that if one construction is given to a statute, the statute would become unconstitutional whereas on another construction, which might be open, the statute remained within the constitutional limits, the court would prefer the latter on the ground that the legislature was presumed to have acted in accordance with the Constitution and courts generally lean in favour of the constitutionality of the statutory provisions.

After enunciating the said rule, the Supreme Court upheld the validity of Section 6(a) of the Hindu Minority and Guardianship Act, 1956 and held that mother could act as natural guardian of minor even when father was alive. The court observed that the word 'after' in this section did necessarily not mean 'after the lifetime' but it meant 'in the absence of'. So, interpreted, the court held that if the father was absent from the care of minor's property or person for any reason whatever, though alive, mother of the minor being a recognised natural guardian, could act validly on behalf of the minor as a guardian.

Article 15(1) of the Constitution prohibits the state from making discrimination against any citizen on the ground of religion, race, caste, sex, place of birth or any of them. Article 15(2) provides that no citizen shall, on grounds only of religion, race, caste, sex, place of birth or any of them, be subject to any disability, liability, restriction or condition with regard to any access to shop, restaurants, hotels and place of entertainment. Article 15(3), being the exceptional clause of Article 15(1) and Article 15(2), declares that nothing under the provision shall prevent the state from making any special provision for women and children.[18] In *Government of Andhra Pradesh v. P.B. Vijayakumar,*[19] the Supreme Court explained the object for inserting clause (3) to Article 15.

The insertion of clause (3) to Article 15 in relation to women is recognition of the fact that for centuries women of this country have been socially and economically handicapped. As a result, they are unable to participate in the socio-economic activities of the nation on a footing of equality. It is in order to eliminate this socio-economic backwardness of women and to empower them in a manner that would bring about effective equality between men and women that Article 15(3) is placed in Article 15. Its object is to strengthen and improve the status of women. In *Anjali Roy v. State of West Bengal,*[20] the word 'for' in clause (3) signifies that special provision can be made 'in favour of women' and not against them. In *Vijay Lakshmi v. Panjub University and others,*[21] wherein a provision for reservation of posts of principal and teachers for women in colleges for girls colleges has been upheld as not violative of Articles 14, 15 and 16.

Section 125 of the Criminal Procedure Code, 1973, which requires the husband to maintain his wife and not vice-versa, in *Suvitaben Somabhai Bhatiya v. State of Gujarat,*[22] has been held not discriminatory, for it merely provides benefits and protection to women and children in certain circumstances. In *Thota Seshrathamma v. Thota Manikyama,*[23] the Supreme Court held that the section 14 of the Hindu Succession Act, 1956, absolutely vests the inherited property in women which was earlier held by them as limited estates, has been held to be protected from attack under Article 15(3). In *Yusuf Abdul Aziz v. State of Bombay,*[24] it was observed by the Supreme Court that Section 497 of the Indian Penal Code, 1860 which only punishes man for adultery and exempts women from punishment even though she may be equally guilty as an abettor was held to be valid since the classification was not based on the ground of sex alone. In *Danial Latifi v. Union of India*,[25] the Supreme Court uphold the validity of Muslim Women (Protection of Rights on Divorce) Act, 1986. The court has once again evaded the question whether existence of different personal laws is violative of Article 15(1). The Court held that the application of Section 125 of the Code of Criminal Procedure to women other than Muslim women and application of the Act of 1986 to the later did not create discrimination between them. Application of different laws to them did not constitute discrimination either in Articles 14 and 15.

In *Shamsher Singh v. State of Punjab*,[26] a rule granting a special allowance to the women principals working in a wing of the Punjab Educational Services was challenged on the ground that their male counterparts were not given the same benefit although both performed identical duties and were part of the same service. The constitutional validity of the rule was challenged under Article 16(2). The High Court upheld the impugned rule under Article 15(3), holding that even though the discrimination was based on the ground of sex, it was saved by Article 15(3). The court ruled that Article 15(3) could be invoked for construing and determining the scope of Article 16(2). Accordingly the court observed that Article 15(3) extends to the entire field of state activity, including the field of public employment which has been specifically dealt with in Article 16.

The court stated that if a particular provision squarely falls within the ambit of Article 15(3), it cannot be struck down merely because it may also amount to discrimination solely on the basis of sex. Articles 14, 15 and 16 being the constituents of a single code of constitutional guarantees, supplementing each other, clause (3) of Article 15 can be invoked for construing and determining the scope of Article 16(2). In the case of *C.B. Muthamma v. Union of India*,[27] Justice Krishna Iyer observed:

> We do not mean to universalise or degomatise that men and women are equal in all occupation in all situation and do not exclude the need to pragmatise where the requirements of particular employment, the sensitivities of sex or the handicaps of either sex may compel selectivity, but save where the difference in demonstrable, the rule of equality must govern.[28]

Therefore, making special provisions for women in respect of employment or posts under the state is an integral part of Article 15(3) and the power conferred under this clause is not whittled down in any manner by Article 16. Since Article 16 does not specifically permit special provisions for women being made by the State, it has been held that Article 16 could not, in any manner, derogate from the power conferred upon the State in this connection under Article 15(3). This power has been held to be wide enough to cover the entire range of State activity including employment under the State.[29]

Article 16(1) guarantees to all citizens equality of opportunity in matters relating to employment or appointment to any office under the State. Article 16(2) further strengthens the guarantee contained in clause (1) by declaring that "No citizen shall, on ground only of religion, race, caste, sex, descent, place of birth, residence or any of them, be ineligible for, or discriminated against in respect of, any employment or office under the state."[30] Article 16 is similar to Article 15 in one respect, i.e., both these provisions prohibit discrimination against citizens on specified grounds.

However, Article 15 is wider in operation than Article 16. While, Article 16 prohibits discrimination only in respect to one particular matter, i.e., relating to employment or appointment to posts under the State, Article 15 lays down general rule and prohibits discrimination in respect to all or any matters. In one respect, Article 16 is wider than Article 15, i.e., the grounds on the basis of which discrimination is prohibited. While Article 15 prohibits discrimination on any of the five grounds, i.e., religion, race, caste, sex or place of birth. Article 15 does not contain 'descent' and 'residence' as the prohibited grounds of discrimination. However, both these Articles can be invoked by citizens only.[31]

In *Gazula Dasaratha Rama Rao v. State of Andhra Pradesh*,[32] Das, J., explained the relative scope of Articles 14, 15 and 16 and observed, "Article 14 guarantees the general right of equality, Articles 15 and 16 are instances of the same right in favour of citizens in some special circumstances." In *Randhir v. Union of India*,[33] the court observed that the principle of equal pay for equal work is covered by equality of opportunity in Article 16(1). In *Uttarakhand Mahila Kalyan Parishad v. State of U.P.*,[34] the Supreme Court held that the difference in the pay scales and promotional avenues between male and female employees is also prohibited by Article 16(2). In *Govt. of Andhra Pradesh v. P.B. Vijaya Kumar*,[35] the legislation made by the State of Andhra Pradesh providing 30 percent reservation of seats for women in local bodies and in educational institutions was held valid by the Supreme court and the power conferred upon the state under Article 15(3) is so wide which would cover the power to make the special legal provisions for women in respect of employment or education.

Moreover, in *Associate Banks Officers Association v. State Bank of India,*[36] the Apex Court held that women workers are in no way inferior to their male counterparts, and hence there should be no discrimination on the ground of sex against women. Further in *Vijay Lakshmi v. Panjab University,*[37] it has been observed that rules 5 and 8 of the Panjab University Calendar, Vol. III, providing for appointment of a lady principal in a women's college or a lady teacher therein cannot be held to be violative of either Article 14 or Article 16 of the Constitution, because the classification is reasonable and it has a nexus with the object sought to be achieved.

Article 19(1)(g) of the Constitution guarantees that all citizens have the right to practise any profession or to carry on any occupation or trade or business. The right under Article 19(1)(g) must be exercised with human dignity. Sexual harassment in the exercise of this right at the work place amounts to its violation. In *Delhi Domestic Working Women's Forum v. Union of India,*[38] relating to rape and violence of working women, the court called for protection to the victims and provisions of appropriate legal representation and assistance to the complaints of sexual assault cases at the police station and in courts. In *Vishakha v. State of Rajasthan,*[39] the Supreme Court has laid down exhaustive guidelines to prevent sexual harassment of working women at their workplace. The court held that it is the duty of the employer or other responsible person to prevent sexual harassment of working women and to ensure that there is no hostile environment towards women at their working place. These guidelines were framed to protect the rights of working women to work with dignity under Articles 14, 19 and 21 of the Constitution of India. Their Lordships also observed, "Each incidence of sexual harassment of women at workplace results in violation of fundamental rights of 'gender equality' and the 'right to life and liberty'.

Under the Constitution of India, 1950, Article 21 of the Constitution says that "No person shall be deprived of his life or personal liberty except according to procedure established by law."[40] Prior to *Maneka Gandhi's*[41] decision, Article 21 guaranteed the right to life and personal liberty to citizens only against the arbitrary action of the executive and not from legislative action. The state could interfere with the liberty of citizens if it could support its action by a valid law. But after *Maneka Gandhi's* decision Article 21 protects the right of life and personal liberty to citizens not only from the executive action but from the legislative action also. A person can be deprived of his life and personal liberty if two conditions are complied with. First, there must be a law and secondly, there must be a procedure prescribed by that law, provided that the procedure is just, fair and reasonable.

In *A.K. Gopalan v. Union of India*,[42] for the first time meaning of the words, 'personal liberty' came up for consideration before the Supreme Court. A.K. Gopalan, petitioner was a communist leader who was detained under the Preventive Detention Act, 1950. The petitioner challenged the validity of his detention under the said Act on the ground that it was violative of his right to freedom of movement under Article 19(1)(d) of the Constitution which is the very essence of personal liberty guaranteed by Article 21 of the Constitution. The petitioner argued that the words 'personal liberty' include the freedom of movement also and therefore, the Preventive Detention Act, 1950 must also satisfy the requirement of Article 19(1)(d). It was argued that the Article 19(1)(d) and Article 21 should be read together because Article 19(1) deals with substantive rights and Article 21 deals with procedural rights.

It was also argued that reference in Article 21 to procedure established by law meant 'due process of law' and the impugned law does not satisfy the requirement of due process of law. Rejecting both the contentions, the Supreme Court held that 'personal liberty' in Article 21 means nothing more than the liberty of the physical body, that is, freedom from arrest and detention without the authority of law. In this case majority took the view that Articles 19 and 21 deal with different aspects of liberty.[43]

In fact, this case has acted as a catalytic agent for transformation of the judicial view on Article 21. Since then the Supreme Court has shown great, sensitivity to the protection of personal liberty. The court has re-interpreted Article 21 and practically overruled Gopalan in Maneka Gandhi's case which can be regarded as a highly creative judicial pronouncement on the part of the Supreme Court.[44] Since Maneka Gandhi's case, the Supreme Court has given Article 21, broader and broader interpretation so as to imply many more fundamental rights. In course of time, Article 21 has proved to be a very fruitful source of rights of the people.[45] In *Maneka Gandhi v. Union of India*,[46] section 10(3)(C) of the Passport Act authorises the passport authorities to impound a passport if it deems it necessary to do so in the interest of the sovereignty and integrity of India, the security of India, friendly relations of India with any foreign country, or in the interest of the general public. Maneka Gandhi's passport was impounded by the Central Government under the Passport Act in the interest of the general public. Maneka Gandhi filed a writ petition challenging the order on the ground of violation of her fundamental rights under Article 21.

One of the major grounds of challenge was that the order impounding the passport was null and void as it had been made without affording her an opportunity of being heard in her defence. It was held by the court that the mere prescription of some kind of procedure is not enough to comply with the mandate of Article 21.The procedure prescribed by law has to be fair, just and reasonable not fanciful, oppressive or arbitrary, otherwise, it should not be a procedure at all and all the requirements of Article 21 would not be satisfied. The procedure must be just, fair and reasonable law, i.e., which embodies the principles of natural justice. In *State of Punjab v. Gurmit Singh*[47] the court has consistently maintained that the offence of rape is violation of the right to privacy of the victim. The Apex Court observed that:

> It is a sad reflection on the attitude of indifference of the society towards the violation of human dignity of the victim of sex crimes. We must remember that a rapist not only violates the victim's privacy and personal integrity, but inevitably causes serious psychological as well as physical harm in the process. Rape is not merely a physical assault. It is often destructive of the whole personality of the victim. A murderer destroys the physical body of his victim; a rapist degrades the very soul of the helpless female.[48]

Sexual Harassment of Women at Working Place

Gender justice, in the Indian context, whatsoever the resolutions in the Constitution has yet to arm, the women with the confidence that in this country she matters as a free partner at home, in public places and offices, in opportunities of economic pursuit and social status, in family rights and participation in state processes.[49] In *Vishaka v. State of Rajasthan*,[50] the Supreme Court has declared sexual harassment of a working woman at her place of work as amounting to violative of rights of gender equality and right to life and liberty which is a clear violation of Articles 14, 15 and 21 of the Constitution. The petition was filed by a social worker by way of public interest litigation for the enforcement of rights of working women under Articles 14, 19 and 21 of the Constitution and the Supreme Court laid down exhaustive guidelines to prevent sexual harassment of working women in places of their work until a legislation is enacted for this purpose. The court held that it is the duty of the employer or other responsible person in work-places or other institutions, whether public or private, to prevent sexual harassment of working women.

Apparel Export Promotion Council v. A.K. Chopra,[51] was the first case in which the Supreme Court applied the law laid down in the case of *Vishaka v. State of Rajasthan* and upheld the dismissal from service of a superior officer of the Delhi based Apparel Export Promotion Council who was found guilty of sexual harassment of a subordinate female employee at the place of work on the ground that it violated her fundamental right guaranteed by Article 21 of the Constitution.[52]

The *Rupen Deol Bajaj v. K.P.S. Gill*[53] judgment is certainly a milestone, but a minor one to create a sense of security among the working class women. In *Apparel Export Promotion Council v. A.K. Chopra*[54] the court held that each incident of sexual harassment at the place of work, results in violation of the fundamental right to gender equality and the right to life and liberty the most precious fundamental rights guaranteed by the Constitution of India. It is surprising that such violations are taking place both in organised and unorganised sector. Sexual harassment occurs in government offices as frequently as in private organisations. Few of the glaring examples of incidence of sexual harassment are as such: In August 1989, Speaker of Goa Assembly, Dayanand Narvedkar sexually harassed a 19 year old employee, Sunita in his chamber.[55] In October, 1989, Mukti Dutt, Secretary to Jan Jagran Samiti, Delhi was harassed by the then Union Minister of Environment and Forest, Z.R. Ansari in his private office in Paryavaran Bhawan.[56]

In March 1992 a senior doctor of Bara Hindu Rao Hospital allegedly to molested two nurses of the hospital. There was an agitation by the nurses demanding justice.[57] Derupadi Bai, Sarpanch of Salheona village in Madhya Pradesh, was stripped naked during an extended panchayat meeting in the presence of the Block Development Officer when she refused to comply with demands of her male counterpart.[58] Lily Kujur, an employee of the Women and Child Development Department of the Chhattisgarh Government had leveled charges of sexual harassment since October 2001 against the Jashpur Collector, M.R. Sarthi. She had gone to extent of saying that she had been served a suspension notice when she resisted his moves. The victim, a tribal working as a supervisor, had moved to the Supreme Court alleging inaction against the accused by the State Government.[59] On July 30, 2003 Archana Gupta, a school Principal of Bhopal, lodged a complaint against city based journalist Sunder Swaroop Asthana. She alleged that Asthana has sexually exploited and blackmailed her.[60] A woman employee of Sahara Manoranjan, who has requested that her name be withheld, went public on 'sexual harassment' at her workplace. With the support of seven women's and human rights organisations in Mumbai, she narrated to the press the string of incidents in the last seven years that finally impelled her to seek justice.[61]

On July 17, 2004 a physician attached with Chittaranjan National Cancer Institute (CNCI), Kolkata had lodged a sexual harassment complaint against a senior doctor at Gariahat Police Station. The complainant holding several senior posts at CNCI had already complained about it to institute's acting Director Indira Chakraborty. The physician who holds top positions in the Anaesthesiology and Preventive Oncology Department had accused her.[62] Sexual harassment is also widespread in the legal profession itself indicating that the rules are broken even where they are made. Sangeeta Sharma's case is one of the example who was a women lawyer, committed suicide in Andhra Pradesh, reportedly due to sexual harassment by her senior.[63]

Right to Privacy

In India the law relating to right to privacy is not expressive. The Constitution of India does not guarantee right to privacy to any of its subjects or one of the fundamental rights in the absence of any constitutional and statutory provisions recognising the right to privacy. It was to be inferred from the judicial decisions. It has been clearly established by the Supreme Court of India that 'right to privacy' is a part of the fundamental rights guaranteed under Article 21 of the Constitution.[64] In *Govind v. State of Madhya Pradesh*,[65] for the first time the Apex Court commented upon the question relating to 'right to privacy'. It was held by the court that Article 21 of the Constitution protects the 'right to privacy' and promotes the dignity of the individual. The Supreme Court in this case observed that the right to personal liberty, the right to move freely and freedom of speech create an independent right of privacy as an emanation from them which can be characterised as fundamental right the 'right to privacy' would necessarily have to go through a process of case by case development."

In *State of Maharashtra v. Madhukar Narayan Mardikar*,[66] the Supreme Court pronounced a landmark judgement and observed that even a woman of easy virtue is entitled to privacy and no one can invade her privacy as and when he likes. So also it is not open to any and every person to violate her person as and when he wishes. She is entitled to protect her person if there is an attempt to violate it against her wish. She is equally entitled to the protection of law. In *State of Punjab v. Ramdev Singh*,[67] the Supreme Court held that the rape is a crime against basic human rights. Sexual violence apart from being a dehumanizing act is an unlawful intrusion on the right to privacy and sanctity of a female. It is a serious blow to her supreme honour and offends her self-esteem and dignity. In *State v. Gurmit Singh*,[68] the

Supreme Court held that a woman of easy virtue could not be raped by a person for that reason. The Supreme Court observed that—

> "Even if the prosecutrix has been promiscuous in her sexual behaviour earlier, she has a right to refuse to submit herself to sexual intercourse to anyone and everyone because she is not a vulnerable object or prey for being sexually assaulted by anyone and everyone."

It was further held by the Supreme Court that the trial of rape cases must be done invariably 'in camera' rather than in open court as envisaged under section 327(2) of the Criminal Procedure Code. It was also pointed out that it would be unlawful for any person to print or publish any mater in relation to the proceedings of such cases except with the previous permission of the Judge of the court as per provision of section 327(2) of Criminal Procedure Code. The further dictum of the Apex Court is that whenever possible, it would be desirable that sexual assault cases of women are tried by lady judges so that the victim can make her statement with greater ease and assist the court to properly discharge their duty without allowing the truth to be sacrificed.

In *V. Krishnan v. G. Rajan alias Madipur Rajan,*[69] the Madras High Court recognised the right to privacy with respect to procreation. In this case an application for direction, a writ of Habeas Corpus preferred by the father of a minor girl aged 16 years to terminate the pregnancy of the girl on the ground of her having been kidnapped and made pregnant and the girl resisting the father's application and pleading for normal continuance of pregnancy until delivery. The Madras High Court held that the fundamental rights can be enjoyed even by a minor and, therefore, the minor girl under Article 21 has a fundamental right to decide about her pregnancy. The court further held that it is the girl's fundamental right to have child having become pregnant.

In *Mr. 'X' v. Hospital 'Z'*[70] the Supreme Court held that the right to privacy is not absolute when this right is in conflict with the other rights of other person, it was further held by the court that the right which would advance public morality of public interest would alone be enforced through process of court. In Hospital 'Z' the appellant's blood was to be transfused to another. Therefore, a sample of his blood was taken for testing and was found to be HIV +ve. The hospital authorities disclosed this fact to one 'A' to whom the appellant was engaged to be married. On account of this disclosure, the marriage was called-off. He was also severely criticised and ostracised by the community.

The appellant contended that the hospital authorities had violated medical ethics by disclosing what they were required to keep secret. Further he also contended that his right to privacy was violated and, therefore, claimed compensation. The Supreme Court held that in view of the fact that the appellant was found to be HIV+ve its disclosure would not be violative either of the rule of confidentiality on right of privacy as 'A', whom the appellant was to marry, would have otherwise been infected by the deadly disease if the marriage had taken place and consummated. The court further held that where there is a clash of two fundamental rights as in the present case, namely the appellant's right to privacy as part of right to life and A's right to lead a healthy life which is her fundamental right under Article 21, the right which would advance public morality of public interest would alone be enforced through process of court.

In *Sheela Barse v. State of Maharashtra*,[71] a reputed journalist filed a petition against the custodial violence of Bombay city police. While disposing the petition, the Supreme Court issued certain directions to the police to follow. Some such directions relate to the right to protect the privacy of the women accused. Directions such are: (1) to keep the police lock up in good localities where only female suspects should be kept and they should be guarded by female constables, (2) the female suspects should not be kept in a lock-up in which male suspects were detained, (3) the interrogation should be carried out only in the presence of female police officer and female constables.

Besides this to safeguard and protect women against exploitation Article 23(1) of the Constitution of India prohibits traffic in human beings and beggar and other similar forms of forced labour. In *Raj Bahadur Singh v. Legal Remembrancer*,[72] the court held that the 'traffic in human beings' means selling and buying human beings as slaves and also includes immoral traffic in women and children for immoral or other purposes. In *Vishal Jeet v. Union of India*,[73] the Supreme Court held that the traffic in human beings includes devadasis and speedy and effective legal action should be taken against brothel keepers and the Supreme Court also directed the State Governments to instruct their law enforcing authorities to take action under the law to eradicate child prostitution. Dwelling on the scope of Article 23 of the Constitution Bhagwati, J. (as he then was) speaking for the court observed:[74]

> (Article 23) is clearly designed to protect the individual not only against the state but also against other private citizens. Article 23 is not limited in its application... The sweep of Article 23 is wide

and unlimited and it strikes at 'traffic in human beings and beggar and other similar form of forced labour' wherever they are found.[75]

In *Gaurav Jain v. Union of India*,[76] the question of rehabilitation of prostitutes and their children was brought before the Supreme Court through public interest litigation under Article 32 of the Constitution. A two Judge Bench took cognisance of the matter. The court issued several directions relating to the rehabilitation of the children of the prostitutes, child prostitutes and establishment of Juvenile Homes for them. In *Laxmi Kant Pandey v. Union of India*,[77] the Supreme Court accepted a letter as a writ petition, complaining of mal-practices indulged by non-government organisations and orphanages engaged in the work of offering Indian children, more specifically, female infants, in adoption to foreign parents. The Court observed that in the guise of adoption, Indian children of tender age were not only exposed to the long dreadful journey to distant foreign countries at great risk to their lives, but in case they survive, they were not provided proper care and shelter and were employed as slaves and in the course of time they become beggars or prostitutes for want of proper care and livelihood

Directive Principles of the State Policy and Status of Women

The Directive Principles of the State Policy contained in Part IV from Articles 36 to 51 of the Constitution set out the aims and objectives to be taken up by the States in the governance of the country. In *Kapila Hingorani v. State of Bihar*,[78] the Supreme Court laid down the objectives of the Directive Principles of State Policy as they are the ideals and objectives to be achieved by the state for setting up in India a social welfare state, as distinguished from a mere police state, which aims at social welfare and the common good and to secure to all its citizens justice social and economic. In *Air India Statutory Corpn. v. United Labour Union*,[79] the Supreme Court held that the basic aim of the Welfare State is the attainment of substantial degree of social, economic and political equalities, the assumption by community acting through the State, as its responsibility to provide the means, whereby all its members can reach minimum standard of economic good health. The Welfare State, therefore, should take positive measure to assist the community at large to achieve the above.

Article 39(a) of the Constitution says that the citizens, men and women equally have the right to adequate means of livelihood.[80] Keeping in view the objectives laid down in these Articles or provisions, various labour laws passed from time to time.[81] In *Olga Tellis v. Bombay*

Municipal Corporation,[82] it was held by the Supreme Court that the 'right to life' included the right to livelihood. The court held that the State shall direct its policy towards securing that the citizens men and women equally have the right to an adequate means of livelihood.

Article 39(d) of the Constitution lay down that there should be equal pay for equal work for both men and women.[83] In *Randhir Singh v. Union of India*,[84] the Supreme Court referred to Article 39(d) that the principle of 'equal pay for equal work' is not an abstract doctrine but one of substance. Though the principle is not expressly declared by the Constitution to be fundamental right yet it may be deduced by construing Articles 14 and 16 in the light of Article 39(d). The court held that the principle of 'equal pay for equal work though not a fundamental right' is certainly a constitutional goal and therefore, capable of enforcement through constitutional remedies under Article 32 of the Constitution.

Article 39(d) of the Constitution proclaims, 'equal pay for equal work for both men and women' as the Directive Principles of State Policy. Equal pay for equal work for both men and women means equal pay for equal work for everyone and as between sexes. Pursuant to Article 39(d), Parliament has enacted the Equal Remuneration Act, 1976. Directive Principles, as has been pointed out in some of the judgements of the courts have to be read into the fundamental rights as the matter of interpretation. Article 14 of the Constitution enjoins the States not to deny any person equality before the law or equal protection of laws and Article 16 declares that there shall be equality of opportunity for all citizens in matters relating to employment or appointment to any office under the State. These equality clauses of the Constitution must mean something to everyone.

Even if it does mean 'to each according to his need' it must at least mean 'equal pay for equal work'.[85] Article 39(e) of the Constitution lays down that the health and strength of workers, men and women, and the tender age of children are not abused and that citizens are not forced by economic necessity to enter avocation unsuited to their age or strength.[86] In *Bandhua Mukti Morcha v. Union of India*,[87] the Supreme Court read Articles 21 and 23 with such Directive principles as Article 39(e) and (f) and Articles 41 and 42 to secure the release of bonded labour and free them from exploitation, the court has observed that "this right to live with human dignity enshrined in Article 21 derives its breath from the Directive Principles of State Policy and particularly Articles 41 and 42." Article 39(e) is aimed at protecting the health and strength of workers, both men and women.

Article 39-A was added to the Constitution pursuant to the new policy of the government to give free legal aid to economically backward classes of people. Article 39-A directs the State to ensure that the operation of the legal system promote justice, on a basis of equal opportunities and shall in particular, provide free legal aid, by suitable legislation or schemes or in any other way, to ensure that opportunities for securing justice are not denied to any citizen by reason of economic or other disabilities.

Article 42 of the Constitution imposes an obligation upon the State to make provisions for securing just and human conditions of work and for maternity relief.[88] There are few legislations enacted for achieving the objectives of Article 42 of the Constitution are the Workmen's Compensation Act, 1923; the Employees State Insurance Act, 1948; the Minimum Wages Act, 1948; the Maternity Benefit Act, 1961; the Payment of Bonus Act, 1965, etc. In *Dattatraya v. State of Bombay*,[89] the Supreme Court held that legal provisions to give special maternity relief to women workers under Article 42 of the Constitution does not violate Article 15(1) of the Constitution. In *Municipal Corporation of Delhi v. Female Workers (Muster Roll)*,[90] the Supreme Court held that the benefits under the Maternity Benefits Act, 1961 extend to employees of the Municipal Corporation who are casual workers or workers employed on daily wages basis. Upholding, the claim of non-regularized female workers for maternity relief, the court has stated that since Article 42 specifically speaks of just and humane conditions of work, and maternity relief, the validity of an executive or administrative action in denying maternity benefit has to be examined on the anvil of Article 42 which though not enforceable at law, is nevertheless available for determining the legal efficacy of the action complained of.

Moreover, Article 44 of the Constitution provides for the uniform civil code for the citizens of India. India comprises of diverse religions, faith and beliefs and each of these religious denominations are governed by their distinct personal laws which vary from one another. In matters relating to marriage, divorce, adoption, maintenance and succession, different personal laws have treated and placed women on different levels. Due to these variations, people are being tempted to convert from one religion to another in order to seek the benefit under the guise of those personal laws.

In a historic judgement in *Sarla Mudgal v. Union of India*,[91] four petitions were filed, one by a registered society working for the welfare of women as public interest litigation, second by Meena Mathur who contended before the court that she was married to Jitendra in 1978 and they had three children and Jitendra solemnised second marriage with one Sunita Narula alias Fatima after marriage they converted to Islam, the petition was filed by Sunita alias Fatima contended that after her marriage with Jitendra Mathur her husband Jitendra Mathur has again reverted back to Hinduism, Sunita's grievance was that she still continued to be Muslim but not being maintained by her husband and has no protection under either of the personal law, third case was that one Gita Rani contended that she was married to one Pradeep Kumar according to Hindu rites in 1988 and 1991 she came to know that her husband ran away with one Deepa and after conversion to Islam married her, and fourth petition was of one Sushmita Ghosh who contended in the court that she was married to one G.C. Ghosh according to Hindu rites in 1984 and in 1992 her husband told her that he did not like her and he would embrace Islam and marry one Vinita Gupta. She prayed that her husband be restrained from entering into second marriage.

The court held that a Hindu husband married under Hindu law, after conversion to Islam, without dissolving the first marriage cannot solemnise a second marriage without getting a decree of divorce under any of the grounds of section 13 of the Hindu Marriage Act. The court held that such a marriage will be illegal and the husband can be prosecuted for bigamy under section 494 of the Indian Penal Code. In this case of Sarla Mudgal the Supreme Court has directed the Prime Minister to take fresh look at Article 44 of the Constitution which enjoins the State to secure a uniform civil code which according to the court is imperative for both protection of the oppressed and promotion of national unity and integrity. As regards the question of 'uniform civil code' the Division Bench said that since 1950 a number of Governments have come and gone but they have failed to make any efforts towards implementing the constitutional mandate under Article 44 of the Constitution. Consequently, the problem today is that many Hindus have changed their religion and have converted to Islam only for the purpose of escaping the consequence of bigamy. This is so because Muslim law permits more than one wife and to the extent of four. Kuldip Singh, J., said that Article 44 is based on the concept that there is no necessary connection between religion and personal law in a civilised society. Marriage, succession and like matters are of a secular nature and, therefore, they can be regulated by law. No religion permits deliberate distortions, the judges declared. Much apprehension prevails about bigamy in Islam itself. In many countries as in Syria, Tunisia,

Pakistan, Iran and other Islamic countries have codified their personal laws.

In *Noor Saba Khatoon v. Mohd. Quasim,*[92] the Supreme Court held that a divorced Muslim woman is entitled to claim maintenance for her children till they become major. The court held that both under the Muslim Personal Law and under section 125 of the Criminal Procedure Code, 1973 the obligations of the father was absolute when the children were living with the divorced wife.

In *Pragati Varghese v. Cyril George Varghese,*[93] Bombay High Court has struck down section 10 of the Indian Divorce Act under which a Christian wife had to prove adultery along with cruelty or desertion while seeking a divorce on the ground that it violates the fundamental right of a Christian woman to live with human dignity under Article 21 of the Constitution. In *Danial Latif and others v. Union of India,*[94] the Supreme Court upheld the constitutional validity of the Muslim Women (Protection of Rights on Divorce) Act, 1986 and held that a Muslim divorced woman has right to maintenance even after *iddat* period under the 1986 Act. The Court said that a Muslim husband is liable to make reasonable and fair provision for the future of the divorced wife which clearly extends beyond the *iddat* period in terms of section 3(1)(a) of the Act. The State has not yet made efforts to legislate the uniform civil code embodied under Article 44 of the Constitution. The Supreme Court in Sarla Mudgal and other cases has directed the government to report the measures taken by the Government for the implementation of the objectives enshrined in Article 44 of the Constitution in the interest of unity and integrity and for the welfare and benefit of women.

Fundamental Duties

By the 42nd Amendment, 1976 Article 51-A under the title of fundamental duties was added to the Constitution as Part IV-A. Article 51-A of the Constitution lays down certain fundamental duties upon citizen of India. Article 51-A(e) which relates to women, imposed a duty on Indian citizens 'to renounce practices derogatory to the dignity of women.' The duties under Article 51-A clause (e) are obligatory on citizens, but it is the duty of the courts to invoke such duties while deciding cases brought before the courts and it is also the duty of the State to keep in view such duties while legislating statutes and implementing laws.

Reservation of Seats for Women in Panchayats and Municipalities

Article 40 of the Constitution lays down duty on the state to take steps to organise village panchayats and endow them with such powers and authority as may be necessary to enable them to function as units of self-government. Reservation of seats for women in panchayats and municipalities have been provided with respect to Article 40 under Part IX and IX-A. Part IX under the title as 'The Panchayats' has been added by 73rd Amendment Act, 1992 and Part IX-A has been added by 74th Amendment Act, 1992 accordingly. Articles 243-D(3) lays down that not less than one-third (including the number of seats reserved for women belonging to the Scheduled Caste and Scheduled Tribes) of the total number of seats to be filled by direct election in every panchayat shall be reserved for women and such seats may be allotted by rotation to different constituencies in a panchayat.[95]

Article 243-T(3) of the Constitution lays down that not less than one-third (including the number of seats reserved for women belonging to Scheduled Castes and Scheduled Tribes) of the total number of seats to be filled by direct election in every Municipality shall be reserved for women and such seats may be allotted by rotation to different constituencies in Municipality.[96] Reservation of seats for women in panchayats and municipalities has been provided detailed scope in Article 243-A and Article 243-T of the Constitution of India.[97] The uplifting of women, empowerment of women becomes a question of uplift of a society, as a whole. Reservation of women can be a temporary sort of relief, as a mean to clear the backlog as far as possible but the greater aim of achieving complete equality between men and women demands a much broader political, social and economic policy.[98]

The voice of elected women bringing out anomalies in the system is like a whiff of fresh air. This has been possible because of the 73rd Amendment. Local Government are key promoters of the gender equality and can make a difference to the lives, and life chances of women. Increasing the number of women in local government and keeping the needs of women in mind when developing policies and services, is essential to achieving the goals of sustainable developments. It is also a question of justice and recognising gender equality as a human right.[99]

The present status of women in the Indian society is far from satisfaction. Reservation for women both in government jobs and democratic institutions would amount to a positive discrimination. But it might foster a sense of inferiority complex among the women that they have been provided with crutches to walk on, to struggle in the demanding world. In the present circumstances the intention of every political party is to talk in terms of reservation only, instead of hitting at the basic cause of such an inequality between men and women. Instead of providing any solution to this deep rooted problem, reservation for women may give rise to political, social as well as psychological tensions.[100]

As an extension, 73rd and 74th Amendment to the Constitution, the Constitution (81st Amendment) Bill was introduced in the Parliament way back in 1996 to reserve one-third of seats for women in the Lok Sabha and the State Assemblies. However, this Bill has not yet been brought into shape due to political overtures.

Besides these constitutional provisions other provisions have been made under various legislations. Several Commissions have been set-up by the government to look into the matter of status of women in the India society. Realising the need of setting up an agency to fulfil the needs, the government decided to set-up a Commission for women and enacted the National Commission for Women Act, 1990. The Central Government has enacted another important Act, i.e., the Protection of Human Rights Act, 1993. The Act gives a very wide and comprehensive definition of human rights as right relating to life, liberty, equality and dignity of the individual guaranteed by the Constitution. The Government of India, keeping in view the spirit of the Constitution has enacted several legislations,[101] which deals with women. These legislations seek to protect the rights of women against the oppression, unfair treatment and discrimination. The Protection of Women from Domestic Violence Act, 2005 has come into effect, where women bruised and battered physically and emotionally by their husbands and in laws will have a protective shield at their command. Their number may run into lakhs, if not crores.[102]

Earlier women could use only section 398-A of the Indian Penal Code, 1860 to file a complaint against an abusive spouse.[103] Further, keeping in view women as domestic workers, it is worthwhile to mention here that four million domestic workers in India are to be covered by the draft bill on *the Protection of women from sexual harassment at workplace*, which is now being examined by a parliamentary committee. If the bill gets the nod of the Parliament, the scope of workplace will be stretched beyond officers and factories; to homes and even vehicles used for ferrying women to and from their workplace.[104]

Thus, observations reveals that the constitution of India safeguards women's right by putting her at par with man socially, politically and economically. To sum up it is evident the women are empowered by the constitution and by many other laws in India. Ironically, most of them are limited to books only. All these provisions should be implemented strictly. Only then the aim of gender justice can be achieved in totality and status of women can be uplifted under Indian legal system.

Notes and References

1. Khan, Zubair Ahmad, Human Rights *vis-à-vis* Women Rights, *Civil and Military Law Journal,* (2007), Vol. 43, p. 42.
2. Malik and Raval, Law and Social Transformation (2007) at pp. 137-38.
3. See *Supra* Note 3.
4. Chauhan, S.S. and Mehta, P. L., Philosophy of Human Rights Jurisprudence: A Study With Special Reference to Women under United Nations Charter, *Civil and Military Law Journal,* (2004), Vol. 40, p. 99.
5. *Ibid.*
6. Sindhu, Sanjay, A Synoptic View of Legal Construction of Feministic Jurisprudence, *Civil and Military Law Journal,* (2007), Vol. 43, p. 24.
7. *Chiranjeetlal v. Union of India*, 1950 SCR 869.
8. See *supra* Note No 8.
9. Mishra, Jitendra, Right to Equality and Gender Justice, AIR 2004 Journal (Feb.), p. 48.
10. Kumar, Narender; *Constitutional Law of India*, 5th ed. (2006), p. 102.
11. *Ibid.*
12. AIR 1975 SC 2299.
13. AIR 1981 SC 212.
14. AIR 1992 SC 999.
15. AIR 1951 SC 41.
16. AIR 1981 SC 1829.
17. AIR 1999 SC 1149.
18. The Constitution of India, 1950; See Article 15.
19. AIR 1995 SC 1648.
20. AIR 1952 Cal. 825.
21. AIR 2003 SC 3331.
22. 2005 (3) SCC 636.
23. 1991 (4) SCC 412.
24. AIR 1954 SC 321.
25. 2001 (7) SCC 740; In *Air Cabin Crew Assn. v. Yeshas Winee Merchant,* 2003 (6) SCC 277, it was observed by the court that the twin Articles 15 and 16 prohibit a discriminatory treatment but not preferential or special treatment of women, which is a positive measure in their favour.
26. AIR 1970 P&H 372; also see *Raghubans Saudagar Singh v. State of Punjab*, AIR 1972 P&H 117, in which rule was made by Punjab Government rendering women ineligible for posting in the men's jails except for the posts of clerks and matrons. Thus, a woman could not be appointed as the Superintendent of Jails. This rule was challenged as being discriminatory on the ground of sex only.

The High Court rejected the challenge and observed "if the sex added a variety of other factors and considerations form a reasonable nexus for the object of classification then the bar of Articles 15 and 16(2) cannot possibly be attracted." The court said that, testing the proposition in reverse, the state may for identical considerations exclude men from the post of warden and other jail officials who have to come in direct and close contact with the women inmates of such a jail.

27. AIR 1979 SC 1868.
28. *Id.* at 1870.
29. See *supra* Note 12 at p 155.
30. For more details see The Constitution of India, 1950; Article 16.
31. See *supra* note 12 at p. 164.
32. AIR 1961 SC 564.
33. AIR 1982 SC 879.
34. AIR 1992 SC 1695.
35. AIR 1995 SC 1648.
36. AIR 1998 SC 32.
37. AIR 2003 SC 3331.
38. 1995 (1) SCC 14 .
39. AIR 1997 SC 3011.
40. For more details see The Constitution of India, 1950; Article 21.
41. AIR 1978 SC 597.
42. 1950 SC 27.
43. *Gopalan* case settled two major points in relation to Article 21. One, Articles 19, 21 and 22 were mutually exclusive and independent of each other and Article 19 was not to apply to a law affecting personal liberty to which Article 21 would apply. Two, a 'law' affecting life or personal liberty could not be declared unconstitutional merely because it lacked natural justice or due procedure. The legislature was free to lay down any procedure for this purpose. In course of time this rigid view came to be softened somewhat. The beginning of the new trend is to be found in the Bank Nationalisation case decided in 1970. Maneka Gandhi's case is a landmark case of the post-emergency period. This case shows how liberal tendencies have influenced the Supreme Court in the matter of interpreting fundamental rights, particularly Article 21. A great transformation has come about in the judicial attitude towards the protection of personal liberty after the traumatic experiences of the emergency during 1975 to 77 when personal liberty had reached its nadir, as became clear from the Supreme Court pronouncement in Shukla case. This case showed that Article 21 as has been interpreted in Gopalan's case could not play any role in providing any protection against any harsh law seeking to deprive a person of his life or personal liberty.
44. Jain, M.P., *Indian Constitutional Law*, 5th ed. (2006), p. 1085.
45. *Ibid.*
46. AIR 1978 SC 597.
47. AIR 1996 SC 1393.
48. *Ibid.*
49. Sadual, Manoj Kumar, Sexual Harassment of Women at Workplace: A Critique, CrLJ 2006 (3) 71.

50. AIR 1997 SC 3014.
51. AIR 1999 SC 625.
52. In male dominated societies, like ours, the sexual harassment of women is seen as the extension of patriarchal culture. The plight of Bhanwari Devi can be seen as a good example of such culture. Bhanwari Devi, a social activist, was threatened, harassed, ostracized and gang raped when she prevented two child marriages in her village in Rajasthan. Bhanwari Devi is not only single example who is subjected to harassment, torture and gang raped by the male patriarchy for her social activities. Each year we hear of hundreds of thousands of cases of gender exploitation, where women have been subjected to various kinds of harassment and exploitation both within and outside the family circle.
53. AIR 1996 SC 309.
54. AIR 1999 SC 625.
55. *The Indian Express*, 2nd September, 1989.
56. *The Times of India*, 21st October, 1989.
57. *The Hindustan Times*, 20th March, 1992.
58. *The Hindustan Times*, 5th November, 1996.
59. *The Hindu*, 25th November, 2002.
60. *The Hindustan Times*, 6th November, 2003.
61. *The Hindu*, 29th April, 2004.
62. *The Times of India*, 29th July, 2009.
63. *The Times of India*, 9th July, 2000.
64. Jayasree, L., The Right to Privacy of a Woman under Criminal Law, CrLJ 2003(5) at p. 145.
65. AIR 1975 SC 1378.
66. AIR 1999 SC 495.
67. 2004 (1) SCC 421; AIR 2004 SC 1290.
68. AIR 1996 SC 1393.
69. Madras L.W. 1994 (1) 89.
70. AIR 1999 SC 495.
71. 1983 CrLJ 642.
72. AIR 1953 Cal 522.
73. AIR 1990 SC 1412.
74. Jaswal, Nishtha, Role of the Supreme Court with Regard to the Right to Life and Personal Liberty, Ashish Publishing House, (1990) at p. 325.
75. *People's Union for Democratic Rights v. Union of India*, AIR 1982 SC 1473.
76. AIR 1997 SC 3021.
77. AIR 1984 SC 469.
78. Judgement Today, 2003 (5) SC 1.
79. AIR 1997 SC 645.
80. For more details see The Constitution of India, 1950; Article 39.
81. The Equal Remuneration Act, 1976; The Bounded Labour System (Abolition) Act, 1976; The Factories Act, 1948; The Mines Act, 1952; The Plantation Labour (Amendment) Act, 1981 and many other statutes.
82. AIR 1986 SC 180.
83. For more details see The Constitution of India, 1950; Article 39(d).
84. AIR 1982 SC 879.
85. Goswami, V.G., *Labour and Industrial Laws*, 7th ed., (1999) at p. 179.

86. For more detail see The Constitution of India, 1950; Article 39(e).
87. AIR 1984 SC 802.
88. For more details see The Constitution of India; Article 42.
89. AIR 1952 SC 181.
90. AIR 2000 SC 1274.
91. 1995 (3) SCC 635.
92. AIR 1997 SC 3280.
93. AIR 1997 Bom 349.
94. Judgement Today, 2001 (8)SC 218.
95. For more details see Article 243-D of the Constitution of India, 1950.
96. See The Constitution of India, 1950, Article 243-T.
97. Part IX and IXA have been added to the Constitution by the Constitutional Amendment Act, 1992 and the Constitution (74th Amendment) Act, 1992 popularly known as the Panchayat and Nagarapalika Constitution Amendment Acts, with Articles 243, 243-A to 243 D and Articles 243 P to 243 ZQ; for more details see Myneni, S.R., Women and Law, (2002) at p. 20.
98. Chawla, Monica, Role of Women in Panchayats and Local Government, *Civil and Military Law Journal,* 2005 (41) at pp. 141-42.
99. *Ibid.*
100. *Ibid.*
101. The Medical Termination of Pregnancy Act, 1972; The Hindu Adoption and Maintenance Act, 1956; The Maternity Benefits Act, 1961; The Equal Remuneration Act, 1976; The Prevention of Immoral Traffic Act, 1986; The Hindu Marriage Act, 1955; The Special Marriage Act, 1954; The Dowry Prohibition Act, 1961; The Child Marriage (Restrain) Act, 1933; The Hindu Succession Act, 1960, etc.
102. According to National Crime Record Bureau, 2005, 40 percent of Indian women are victims of domestic violence. A crime is committed against women in India every three minutes, for more details see Report of National Crime Record Bureau, 2005.
103. It is pertinent to mention here that under this legislation it is not only physical or sexual abuse which constitutes domestic violence but also 'verbal and emotional abuse' that includes insults, ridicule humiliation, name calling and insults or ridicule, especially with regard to not having a child or a male child. It is further pertinent to note that all this is not being said to underestimate the ordeal of the sufferance of domestic violence, but to ensure that there is no misuse of the law either.
104. For more details see the *Tribune*, Monday, December 12, 2011 at p. 8 (Bill to Protect Women).

Women in Ancient and Medieval India: An Overview of Social, Economic, Political and Cultural Perspective

Gauri Sharma

One of the best ways to understand the essence of any civilisation and to analyse its strengths and weaknesses is to study the position enjoyed by its women. The inherent relevance of the theme has made the analysis of position of women a subject of interest in recent decades. In all societies, cutting across geographical locations and cultures there has been considerable rethinking of the position accorded to women in all spheres of activity. This has led to a fresh assessment of their contributions in socio-economic, cultural and even political life in our historical past.

An important aspect of this assessment is that prejudice against women avowed or covert, institutionalised or personal dates back to the very ancient times and diverse cultures. According to Karen Leonard, any evaluation of women's role in Indian society explores women's position in many ways. They are often analysed as symbols of status and prestige whose seclusion and supervision are basic to the maintenance of family reputation. They have also been analysed as objects of exchange in terms of giving of women to men higher in status. They have also been analysed as productive capital assets, but basic to all these analyses is the fact that control of women at all stages of life was essential to the continuation of traditional family and societal patterns (Leonard, 1976).

Indians by and large whether they have had a formal education of history or not carry with them a sense of the past which they often internalise through popular beliefs and folklore. Formal history also percolates in a diluted form through writings and discussions in what may be called a 'dispersal effect'. So that elements of oral history pass down to us forming a medley of ideas and it is this medley of ideas that forms the basis of our perception of women in history.

As most of us would know, the position of women has not remained uniform in our past and has been changing in different points in time. In Vedic India, women occupied a very important position. Infect one that was sometimes considered to be superior to men. Vedic culture is one whose only symbol of strength and power are female, i.e., 'Shakti'. All male power coming from the feminine. No wonder the feminine forms of the Absolute and the popular Goddesses are believed to have taken shape in the later Vedic period. These female forms later came to represent different qualities and energies of Brahma–Goddess Kali portraying the destructive energy, Durga the protective, Lakshmi the nourishing and Saraswati the creative.

The Vedic age saw women enjoying a high place in society. They shared an equal if not a higher status than their men folk enjoying liberty that had societal sanction. Though the Vedic family was patriarchal, it never denied women certain privileges. Commenting on the status of women in the Vedic age *Will Durant* remarked:

> "Women enjoyed far greater freedom in the Vedic period than in the later ages. She had more to say in the choice of her husband, she appeared freely at feasts and dances and joined men in religious sacrifice. She could study, engage in philosophical disputation. If she was left a widow there was no restriction upon her marriage" (Durant, 1935).

The Manusmriti, often a parameter of studying the position of women, at one place says,

> "Women are worthy of worship. They are the fate of the household, the lamp of enlightenment that brings solace to the family. Gods reside in those households where women are worshipped and in households where women are slighted all efforts of improvement go in vain" (Manusmriti).

Women in Vedic period were epitomes of intellectuals and spiritual attainments. The Vedas have volumes to say about women who both complemented and supplemented their male partners. A shloka from Atharva Veda clearly states that the women leads the man: The Sun God follows the first illuminated and enlightened Goddess Usha (dawn) in the same manner as men emulate and follow women (Atharva Samhita).

Educational attainment and economic participation have always been the key issues in empowering women. The fact that Vedic age never denied education to its women shows the collective consciousness of a race which promulgated codes or laws which in turn contributed immensely to the creative force of its people (Ray Choudhri, 1978). If a woman wanted to acquire knowledge without getting married she had the freedom to pursue it without any constraints.

We have many sagacious and intellectually empowered women who rose to the position of *Rishi's* and encapsulated Vedic wisdom in myriad hyms (Majumdar, 1964). One of them, *Ghosha* had composed two hymns each containing fourteen verses which eulogise divine power and express her inner feelings and desires. The Rig Veda also records long conversations between the sage Agasthya and his wife *Lopmudra* that testifies to the intelligence and goodness of the latter. The Rig Veda also contains ten hymns accredited to *Maitreyi* a woman saint and philosopher. She is said to have contributed towards the enhancement of her sage husband *Yagyavalkya's* personality. *Gargi* was a saint and daughter of Vachaknu, who composed several hymns that questions the origin of all existence. She is even said to have participated in the Brahmayagya organised by King Janak of Videha.

In Vedic society, the practice of child marriage did not exist as there is nothing in the scriptures that promotes it, this also seems to suggest that since children were not married early they had some freedom to choose their partners in life (Joshi, 1978). There are references for preferences for sons over daughters, but society was free from evils like female infanticide and *sati*. The fact that widows had the right to remarriage is an indication of social dignity enjoyed by women. Women in Rig Vedic times were also known to have enjoyed economic independence to some extent. There are references of women taking up spinning and weaving. In one of hymns there is a senile in which night and dawn are compared to two young women engaged in weaving (Saran, 1957).

The dishonorable phase in the life of women began in the post-Vedic period. The *Brahmanas, Upanishads* and the Epics, the *Ramayana* and *Mahabharata* which despite their element of imagination hold value as social documents as well while throwing considerable light on status of women. *Kautilya's Arthasastra* is another valuable source on the socio-cultural ethos of the time. These sources indicate that the world of women during this time started becoming restricted on account of the existing patriarchal set-up. The age is marked by marginalisation of their role in society and nothing but, implicit obedience and subordination was expected from her which finally led to her seclusion. The Mahabharata, for instance offers a good reflection of the position of women.

The three key female characters of the *Mahabharata* can be taken as representatives of the age. *Gandhari,* wife of *Dhritrashtra* emerges as a farsighted and prudent person who constantly reminds her husband not to plunge the family into misfortune by acceding to the demands of their son *Duryodhana*, and despite her entreaties the prince carries on with his motive of depriving the *Pandavas* of their rightful share in the kingdom paving the way for the great war. This goes to show now insignificant and helpless women were in the decision-making processes of significance. We also have the example of *Kunti,* the mother of the *Pandavas,* who inspite of being married to a king was rendered homeless more than once. On one occasion she tells *Krishna* that she does not hold anybody but her father responsible for her misfortune, for having given her away to the kind Kuntibhoja like a donor gives away money to a beggar. She even goes on to say that she has been abandoned by her father and her inlaws (Adi parva). Another central female character *Draupadi,* the wife of the Pandavas emerges as well versed in many aspects of social life. Displaying intellectual equality to men, she challenges male ego at times and often resents and rejects what is imposed on her; yet there is a certain vulnerability in *Draupadi's* demeanor as well (Jhanji, 1996).

Similarly, the *Ramayana* is the story composed around the central character of *Sita* and the tribulations faced by her. Sita is seen as a *pativrata* (an ideal wife) by some, as victimised by others and as a liberated cherished wife of Rama by still others. She displayed greatness that comes with strength, truth and sincerity. Sita's character undoubtedly defines the limits of feminine resilience and endurance in her willingness to absorb, accept and accommodate to the demands of a patriarchal society.

Over a period of time as patriarchy became established as an acceptable system, the position of women was further marginalised. Henceforth, social customs and traditions which were reinforced by the law givers became attempts at working out what was believed to be a perfect social order (Thapar, 1966). These so called time tested rules not only pulled society backwards and deprived them of growth and development, but denied women her primary rights as an individual. In fact her condition can be described in what *Emily Dickinson* comments in one of her poems:

> *"They put me in the closet because they liked me still"* (Dickinson, 1890).

As a result Indian women also began perceiving themselves as subordinate and unable to untangle their true selves from the existing social roles. Thus the Rigvedic concept of '*Sahdharmini*' or equal partner slowly lost its relevance and was replaced by '*Pativrata Dharma*' or the duties of a chaste wife who would fulfil the wishes of her husband without questioning them.

The Buddhist interlude ranging from third century B.C. to sixth century A.D. brought about certain changes for the better. Although not a social reformer, Buddha believed in the essential man-woman equality as far as attainment of salvation was concerned and permitted them to join the monastic community and fully participate in it (Murcott, 2006). But various traditions within Buddhism hold different views as to the possibilities of women's spiritual attainments (Heng-Ching). Feminist scholars have also noted that even when a woman's potential for spiritual attainment is acknowledged records of such achievements may not have been kept or may be obscured by gender neutral language or mistranslation of original sources by western scholars. Despite this the influence of Buddhist ideology did leave a positive impact on man-woman equality as evidenced in the concept of marriage. It allowed women to marry men of their choice and child marriage was discouraged, Buddhism recognised the real meaning of '*dampati*' which etymologically meant joint owner of the house—Buddha even gave women the right to inherit property and showed compassion to widows.

However, Buddhism was unable to understand the position of women from the angle of social justice and never tried to abolish the existing social order. Therefore, many customs and traditions continued to be implicitly followed by majority of the people.

While studying the status of women in post-Buddha period it is imperative to focus on female royalty. Although exclusive historical accounts of the elite and royal women are scarce, traditional practices and social customs formally and informally supported monarchy and patriarchy and succession to the throne was confined to male descendants according to the law of primogeniture. Although available historical evidence does suggest that on a member of occasions women held position of power by way of royal lineage and were capable of influencing political decisions but women in the ancient period strongly internalised the ritualistic practices of patriarchy and gender hierarchy that had permeated the social structure of the times (Mitra & Knottnerus, 2004) and even when they could use their influence to challenge patriarchy and social convention they chose to perpetuate the dominant social order.

We could quote the example of *Kumaradevi* the *Lichchavi* princess who played an important role in the marriage between *Lichchavis* and *Guptas*. She could have exercised significant political influence on account of her role in this political alliance due to her parentage but used her position only to benefit her husband and enhance his position (Sharma, 1987).

There is the example of Kashmir dowager queen of Sankaravarman (883-902) Sugandhadevi, an energetic administrator, capable of retaining power but took the reins of government in her hands only to willingly give it to her son when he came of age. Similarly in 1028 A.D. Srilekha, queen of Hariraja who was not allowed to ascend the throne by her subjects and willingly denounced power in favour of an underage prince to avoid a civil war. Such incidents in our history would also suggest that women who mattered in political affairs were often made use of either by holders of power or by seekers of power.

With the coming of Islam in India started the 'medieval'phase of our history. Initially it was a struggle for power and economic supremacy between two systems, when for the first time in recorded history our religious and social traditions were faced with a system which was equally well developed and defined. This age is marked by better account of recorded history and women at least, the upper classes though confined, do find marginal representation in historical narratives. However, any attempt to locate the position of ordinary women in this age would find them only in servile positions. Their dependence on male relatives was a prominent feature of society. One can easily identify three dimensions to subordination of women, the political, the ideological and the economic which existed in different balances (Jeffrey, 1979).

Though Islam is theoretically considered to be gender friendly as compared to other religions in the world for granting a position of equality to women in terms of legal and inheritance rights; description of women in medieval Indian history has been confined to *purdah, polygamy, concubinage* and the *harem* which leads one to believe that women in the pre modern phase had no history. We cannot deny the prevalence of social evils like female infanticide, sati dowry, polygamy and *purdah* being enforced by medieval society, each of these being a reflection of her submissiveness, helplessness and inability to cope with the outside world. The preference for sons over daughters was widely prevalent in medieval society and assumed criminal proportions in the form of *female infanticide*. *Purdah* was part and parcel of social stratification in India and was strictly enforced after the coming of Islam; although it had existed among upper caste Hindus in the age of the *Dharmashastras*. One of the earliest references was found in the time of Ashoka. Panini refers to the phrase '*Asuryampashya-raja-darah*' which refers to those who do not see the sun, i.e. the wives of a king (Indra, 1955).

Dowry was another common evil. Actually meaning 'streedhana' it acquired huge dimensions with the bride losing all sense of selfworth. The condition of widows continued to be miserable with society imposing the denial of remarriage on her. The negative attitude towards widows and the feudal system prevalent in those times perpetrated *sati* the most inhuman crime against women. There is an interesting reference by the German Scholar Maxmullar, who in his study of the Vedic text says the Practice of Sati almost unheard of during Rig-Veda times was distorted to suit vested patriarchal and feudal interests where

अयः रोहनत आग्रे अयः रोहनत अग्ने

Where the first phrase says that after the death of the husband a woman should move forward (आग्रे) but at some stage got distorted to (अग्ने) meaning in fire. Reference should also be made of female slavery which was widely prevalent in medieval India. Though abominable, trading of female slaves was a lucrative preposition (Barani). However, despite this backdrop of a dismal and discouraging scenario, emerges a different image of women who displayed grit and talent. In the early phase of Islamic rule in India these are references of marriages between Hindu girls to members of Turkish royal families as part of strategy and political network formation (Mukhia, 2004).

Though women had little say in these alliances they were not only well received by both communities but fairly successful, with women making positive contributions to it. On the other hand, there are also examples of women who showed grit in refusing to follow their husband in conversion to a new faith. Sufi traditions refer to the case of a dacoit who converted to Islam on account of the influence of Shaikh Jalal-uddin-Tabrezi but his wife continued to follow Hinduism and separated from her husband (Hamid, 1952).

It is also interesting to find women taking interest in religion, piety and education in medieval times. Hagiographical literature provides interesting details about religious life of women in the sultanat period. We have women like *Bibi Sharifa* daughter of *Shaikh Farid-uddin-Ganjshakar* devoting herself to a life of religion and piety. Her father the renowned Sufi saint is said to have remarked: *"If other women had been like her, women would have taken precedence over men"* (Nizami, 1987). Here mention should also be made of women acquiring excellence in arts of music and dance. Barani refers to one *Nuzrat Khatoon* who sang with such sweetness that birds came down to hear her. There are references to *Nuzrat Bibi* and *Mahar Afroz* who were dancers par excellence and performed to entertain royal guests in the pleasure parties held by Sultan Jalal-uddin-Khilji (1290-1296) (Barani).

Contrary to the assumption that medieval Islamic civilisation was repressive towards women; well placed women had the opportunity of influencing socio cultural and political trends in their time. There is the example of *Illutimish's* widow *Shah Turkan* a politically (1210-1235) astute and ambitious lady who took control of administration in her hands because her son Ruknuddin Firuz had become neglectful of his duties. (Qureshi, 1996) There is reference to one of Illutimish's daughter who did not think it derogatory to seek divorce from her husband on grounds of temperamental incompatibility (Minhaj-i-Siraj).

Keeping in mind the patriarchal set up of the time, it is true that women could not really manipulate their position without the support of men but *Razia* (1236-1240) overcame the differences of opinion among Muslim theologians with regard to disqualification of women to become the temporal head of an empire and ascended the throne of Delhi. *Amir Khusrau* also refers to her leadership qualities and says she ruled successfully for three years before the nobles became fearful of her position and turned against her (Khusrau, trs.1917). Among other royal women of sultanat period we have the virtuous widow of Ghiasuddin Tughluq (1320-1326) Makhdum-i-Jahan who commissioned mosques, hospitals and sarais for the lesser privileged (Batuta).

During later medieval period we have *Babur*, the founder of magnificent mughal empire applauding the role of his mother *Aisan Daulat Begum* and his mother *Qutlugh Nigar Khanim* as very prime influences on him, nurturing his accomplishments as author, poet, empire-builder and his refined aesthetic sense. Babur's wife *Maham Begum* was astute enough to figure out and foil a conspiracy against the rightful accession of Humayun which if not carried out would have altered the course of our history. (Gulbadan Begum) Another example before us is that of *Gulbadan Begum* who was a symbol of mughal style and finesse and has left behind for us the *'HumayunNama'* which is a major source of information for the early part of mughal rule.

Akbar's mother, *Hamida Bano Begum* emerges as an empowered woman of her time. She was capable of taking political decisions in the interest of the state. A very significant aspect of her personality is revealed from the fact that she had an illustrated copy of the *Ramayana* in Persian in her personal possession (Asher & Talbot, 2006). A royal order issued by her gifting tax free land to the son of Vallabha, the founder of Krishna Bhakti movement is suggestive of her interest in religious traditions outside of Islam. Akbar's Rajput wives were not only successful in creating a space for themselves in the overall mughal patriarchal set-up but were a major influence on the emperor in his vision of a secular state in pre-colonial India (Dalal, 1999) and this aspect if studied in greater depth would add a new dimension to the socio-cultural life of the sixteenth century.

Nurjahan, Jahangir's ambitious wife is the well documented example of empowered women in our medieval history. A forceful lady who refused to follow tradition, Nurjahan's story is one of ambition, power, military and diplomatic skill. She knew how to work the system to her advantage. Her personal abilities extended well beyond political and economic into areas of art and architecture, literature and religion, travel and philanthropy that the range of her contributions to Indian culture remains unparalleled. Contemporary writers say there was nothing that she could and did not touch. A painting of Nurjahan with a rifle in her hands by Abul Hasan depicts her as a woman of undoubted power and is unprecedented in either Indian or Islamic art (Milo Beach, 1992).

Other Mughal princesses who emerge as empowered are Shah Jahan's daughters Jahanara and Roshanara. Jahanara showed great interest in mysticism and the arts particularly in architecture. The vast economic resources at her disposal gave her the freedom to follow her passion and enter what was generally considered to be a male prerogative. She is known to have commissioned. The *Jama Masjid* and the *Mullah Shahi Mosque* at Srinagar (Muhammad, 1896). Jahanara also had economic and commercial interests and is known to have possessed a fleet of ships and also freighted her goods in English and Dutch ships (Chandra, 2003).

Her literary and architectural endeavours and her political views (she opposed the re-imposition of Jaziya by Aurangzeb) provide us with a form of female voice emerging as a form of communication which brings to the fore an element of gender in the otherwise patriarchal set up of the mughals (Walther,1999). Her sister Roshanara also wielded tremendous political power and was the mastermined behind the accession of Aurangzeb in 1657 (Manucci). A leading woman of the court she virtually ruled the harem and advised her brother on political issues.

Aurangzeb's daughter Zebunissa's contribution to the cultural history of India has been overshadowed by the political and economic upheavals of Aurangzeb's reign. An exact opposite of her father's persona and political views, she wrote probably the largest body of poetry ever composed by a mughal princess under a concealed identity 'Makhfi' (Misra,1967). Her verses, most of them untranslated, speak of love, freedom and an inner experience. The fact that she could not come out and express her views in public also gives us an idea of the opulent yet sometimes stifling character of the mughal *Harem*. Despite this, her financial resources enabled her to set-up a library (bait-ul-ulum) to improve the lot of scholars (Sarkar), most royal women of the Mughal age emerge as empowered in some ways for despite being behind the veil, they could travel, hunt and make forceful statements through literary and architectural patronage giving us an idea of the ambiguity and richness of their lives. Further by representing themselves in ways reflective of their social roles within the prevailing culture they have enriched our history.

The foregoing account of women in our ancient and medieval past shows us the changes that women underwent over passing centuries. Any attempt to study the position of women in our present should not ignore the journey women have undergone in the past. In a collective assessment of women down the ages, despite the dominance of patriarchy, they appear as looking out of their windows ready to explore the outside world whenever given an opportunity. The limitations of south Asia's historical records can be seen in the indifference towards these women, who were neither a man's shadow nor his reflection, but part and parcel of social processes and therefore capable of influencing socio-cultural and economic trends.

References

Adi Parva, Chap. 168, *Slokas,* p. 15.

Amir Khusrau, *Deval Rani Khizr Khan (*Mathnavi), trs. Aligarh (1917), p. 49.

Asher, Catherine B. and Talbot Cynlhia (2006), *India before Europe*, p. 138.
Atharva Samhita, Part 2, Kand 27, Aukta 107, Shloka 5705.
Barani, *Tarikh-i-Firuzshahi*, pp. 373-74.
Barani, *Tarikh-i-Firuzshahi*, pp. 156-57.
Beach, Milo Cleveland (1992), *Mughal and Rajput Painting*, The New Cambridge History of India, p. 96.
Chandra, Satish (2003), *Essays on Medieval Indian History*, p. 239.
Dalal, Urvashi, Women's Time in the Havelis of North India, *Medieval History Journal*, (1999) p. 38
Durant, Will (1935), *Story of Civilisation: Our Oriental Heritage*, p. 401
Gulbadan Begum, *Humayun Nama*, p. 104.
Hamid Qalandar (1952), *Khair-ul-Majlis*, p. 192.
Heng-Ching Shih, *Women in Zen Buddhism, Chinese Bhikshunis in the Cha'n tradition.*
Ibn Batuta, *The Travels of Ibn Batuta*, Vol. 3, p. 736.
Jain (1971), *Labour in Ancient India*, p. 83.
Jeffrey Patricia (1979), *Frogs en the Well: Indian Women in Purdah*, p. 43.
Jhanji, Rekha (1996), *Women in the Mahabharata in Kiran Pawar* (ed.) *Women in Indian History*, p. 41.
Joshi, P.S. (1978), *Cultural History of India*, p. 6.
Latif, Muhammad (1896), *Agra—Historical and Descriptive*, p. 186.
Leonard, Karen (1976), *Women and Social Change in Modern India*, Feminist Studies, p. 51.
Majumdar, R.C. (1964), *History of Ancient India*, p. 44.
Manu Smriti, pp. 3-56
Manucci, *Storia Do Mogor*, Vol. III, p. 288.
Minhaj-i-Siraj, Tabaqat-i-Nasiri, Vol. I, p. 463.
Misra, Rekha (1967), *Women in Mughal India* (1526-1748), p. 91.
Mitra, Aditi and Knottnerus (2004), David, *Royal Women in Ancient India: The Ritualisation of Inequality in a Patriarchal Social Order*, p. 18.
Mukhia, Harbans (2004), *The Mughals in India*, p. 117.
Murcott Susan (2006), *The First Buddhist Woman: Poems and Stories on Awakening*, p. 4.
Nizami, K.A. (1987), *The Life and Times of Fariduddin-Ganj Shakar*, Delhi, p. 65.
Prof. Indra (1955), *Status of Women in Ancient Times*, p. 73.
Qureshi, I.H., *Socio-Political Role of Women in The Sultanat in Kiran Pawar (ed.) Women in Indian History*, p. 91.
Ray Choudhri, Tapan (1978), *Social, Cultural and Economic History of Ancient India*, p. 37.
Saqi Mustai'd Khan, *Maasir-i-Alamgiri*, trs. Jadunath Sarkar, p. 539.
Sharma, Tripat (1987), *Women in Ancient India from 320 A.D. to 1200 A.D.*, New Delhi, p. 143.
Thapar, Romilla (1966), *Ancient Indian History: Some Interpretations*, p.27.
The Complete Works of Emily Dickinson (1890), Boston, p. 302.
Walther Wicbke (1999), *Women in Islam: From Medieval to Modern Times*, p. 111.

Vedanta: Key to Empowerment

Vivek Negi

Empowerment of women has always been looked upon as an achievement, both by the men and women in the category of those who comprehend power as something different from what, being a woman is. Man's efforts in his world, to empower the 'power' are a pusillanimous attempt to play the role of the bestower. For aeons past India has been a fortunate witness of the power called woman. This cosmic creation is itself the various shades and attributes of the metaphor called 'Kali' which makes one feel the play of the power more emphatically than its description as a circle of birth, life and death. Who else, other than Vivekananda can mark the deeper knowledge of the voyager who begins to understand this power as the mother? The Kali is the magna mater. The play of the divine mother is that of a prophet who the guardian of the good is. Her role is not only to chide or chastise the astray but to smile in wrath whenever 'the jiva' inside in any form, deviates from the path of values. The common worldly child strains hard to understand the various plays of nature by discovering his inner identity. This yearning of the self to discover the mother is viewed as an intense longing of a voyager to embrace its mother. Various experiences and energies are encountered but the child is not able to comprehend them.

A unique symbol of godhead, Kali represents the totality of the universe: creation and destruction and pleasure; and all pairs of opposites. "Mother seems to black when viewed from a distance, like the water of the ocean: but to the intimate observer she is without colour, being one with Brahman, whose creative energy she represents." (Nikhilananda). The mystery of the shades deepens with her terrible aspect of the wrathful, punishing deity who wears a garland of human skulls: while on the other side she is gracious, blessing her devotees with the boom of prosperity and immortality.

The child or the voyager is a symbol of ignorance but the sages, seers and prophets too are bound by the play of the Mother. The sages, who outline the new development taking place in all fields of life whether economic, political or social, are unable to decipher the ways of the Mother. Vivekananda emphasises that whatever the flaws or deficiencies of the mind, they can be removed and the forces of nature assist in this process. A creative individual especially a woman is the representative of the universe in whom the unconscious creativity of nature becomes conscious creativity. Indian thought asks us to liberate ourselves from bondage. We must pass from sansara, life in time subject to discords to moksa or enlightenment or eternal life.... Freedom is used to develop wilfulness which breeds evils. To be good is to be capable of all evil and yet commit none. Each person is the result of his action and attitude which he can modify by the exercise of his will. (Recovery of Faith)

Sri Aurobindo also delineates four forms of the mother, namely, Maheshwari, Mahakali, Mahalaxmi and Mahasaraswati, the mother manifests from powers, wisdom, strength, harmony and perfection. These powers become four goddesses, through whom she descends the ladder of cosmic planes to carry out her work as the one who meditates and saves. Sovereign Maheshwari—Mother wisdom, intimately knows the nature of every being and becomes the inner guide, constrainer and educator. Golden Mahakali is to be distinguished from the dark and terrible Kali of vital level. Mahalaxmi is the mother of loveliness. She withdraws in 'divine disgust' when she meets gross passion or ascetic harshness but when she is invited she fills the heart and home with her felicity. Mahasarasvati displays the divine Mother's work power. Her one demand is sincerity. She takes the voyager in to total transformation. "Mahakali" would be the Terrible Mother experienced by the world in the times of change, vicissitudes, by the individuals caught between death-rebirth cycle. Mahalaxmi would be experienced as the great mother, Anima mundi, threatening and destructive for badly formed ego, while Mahasaraswati would be experienced as the celestial mother, Anima per excellence. Thus the mother's play as Mahakali is the goddess of the seers and the sages, as Mahalaxmi is of the heroes and Mahasaraswati is of the gurus.

Mother Kali is the liberator. Embodying in herself creation and destruction; love and terror; life and death; Kali is the symbol of total universe, the path towards the goals of life is lost in the material greed. The shade of mother as Kali is her most complex manifestation. The power is violent and in her madness destroys both the macro and the microcosm. This leads to not only wrenching but also cleansing of nature. The cleansing in present context is exemplified by the various revolutions that the history of world has witnessed.

The dark and the inscrutable in the world become the instruments to understand the 'One' behind all phenomenon. This universal power is in the Divine Mother. The turbulence is just a phase in the rhythm of the Mother's dance. The state where one loves misery and embraces death signifies a state where the ego is destroyed and the duality between misery and joy, life and death is demolished. It is the apprehension of this Vedantic oneness which resolves all contradictions. The intense desire to discover the self or reach the Divine is often viewed in terms of longing of a voyager to return to the embrace of its mother.

Further, Kali is not bliss as was for Sri Ramakrishna. She is Kali of action and of Karma. Kali is both elementary and transformative. As elementary she is the force of hunger and thirst, the drive of sexuality. In her transformative aspect she is the summon to the hero. She is so accelerative that she demands the work of several days to be done in trice.

Valorisation of strength and manliness is central to this experiment. Will is integral to strength and strength is the life force inhered in one's cultural samskaras. Whitman often declared that if one has faith in thirty thousand gods, but does not have faith in oneself, it is of no avail. Whereas one must exhort to valour and action like Siva; one must be deeply feminine within. Christs and Buddhas are to be discovered in the heart besides being worshipped. For a common householder the Divine is to be seen in the love of the beloved, in a handshake of a friend, in the smile of a child and in the kiss of a mother. Love, mercy, care, strength, force, reproof, help, etc. are Divine radiations. Perhaps this is 'nirvana' where the life of paradoxes is simplified into a journey of self-knowledge and a manifestation of Divine will.

The eternal cycle of the manifestation and non-manifestation of the universe is the breathing out and breathing in of this mother. Before creation she contains within her womb the seed of the universe which is left from the previous cycle. After the manifestation of the universe she becomes its preserver and nourishes and at the end the cycle she draws it back within herself and remains as the undifferentiated shakti, the creative power of Brahman. She is therefore the path to the realisation of the Absolute; She is the Absolute.

This 'wanderjhare' of the seeker where he tosses in the play of the mother and only then comes to the realisation of Siva—the Absolute, becomes an essential phenomenon to undergo. It awakens in him the proportionate existence of the eros and the logos; the anima and the animus; the Siva and the Shakti. Siva is realised only after the touch of the Shakti. This Campbellian voyage of tossing in the unresolved ego and finally transforming into an individuated whole, provides the material ruled world with an answer to the process called empowerment this realisation or 'annubhuti' will evoke in every human being a sense of respect and understanding towards feminity inside. Speaking in terms of Indian spiritual aesthetics no solution lies in empowering the feminine without resolving the 'ardhnarishwar'—the Siva and the Shakti within.

In the west the woman is wife. In India, the woman is mother Woman, thou shall not be conjoined with anything carnal. India has always emphasised on the empowerment of woman. But the neglect of education here can be accredited to the colonial rule. The colonial system produced mechanical slaves—a host of clerks, postmasters, operators and so on. Whereas, the Indian pursuit of knowledge aimed at freedom. The woman can solve their problems themselves. The faith in power and greatness lies latent in woman. This Shakti needs to be roused. If a woman's power is used for evil rather than for good; it is because she has been oppressed. Her suffering for ages has also given her infinite patience and infinite perseverance. A new race of superwomen will grow from the present day women. Even if this experiment fails; power initiative and self-responsibility will have been developed. The women of India will be gracious, loving, persevering a woman, great in heart and intellect, but greatest of all in spirituality.

References

Biswas, Mita (2005), *The Changing Concept of Culture in Indian English Poetry*, Shimla: IIAS.

Campbell, Joseph (1949), *The Hero with a Thousand Faces*, New York: Bollinger Foundation.

Chakraborti, Mohit (2001), *Swami Vivekananda, Vibrant Humanist*, New Delhi: Kanishka.

Edinger, E. (1972), *Ego and Archetype*, New York: Putham's Sons.

Gandhi, M.K. (1950), *Geeta Mata*, New Delhi: Sasta Literature Mandal.

Jung, C.G. (1979), *The Collected Works of C.G. Jung*, London: Routledge & Kegan Paul Ltd.

Muller, Max (2004), *Ramakrishna, His Lifestyle and Sayings*, New Delhi: Rupa & Company.

Nikhilananda, Swami (1982), *Vivekananda: A Biography*, Calcutta: Sri Ramakrishna Math.

Radhakrishnan, S. (1948), *The Bhagwad Geeta*, London: George Allan & Unvin.

Radhakrishnan, S. (1956), *Recovery of Faith*, New York: Harper Collins.

Ranchan, Som Pal (1984), *To Vivek Then I Came*, New Delhi: Vikas.

Ranchan, Som Pal (1996), *Kali, An Elusive Icon*, New Delhi: K.K. Publications.

Ranchan, Som Pal (2001), *Aurotherapy: An Alternate Therapy System*, Delhi: Indian Publications.

Whitman, Walt (1970), *Leaves of Grass*, New Delhi: Eurasia Publications.

13

Violence Against Women: Journey of Indian Women from Medieval to Present

Prithpal Kaur

"A Woman may live without a choice regardless of whether she is a little girl, a young lady or a mature woman. A young girl is under the command and choice of her father. A married woman is under the command and choice of her husband. A widow is under the command and choice of her male children and she may never become independent (after the death of her husband). A widow may never remarry after the death of her husband but rather she must neglect all that she likes in terms of food, clothes, and makeup until she dies. A woman may not own or possess anything as whatever she may gain or acquire shall go straight and immediately to the ownership of her husband".

—Manna Herma Sistra

Violence against women is partly a result of gender relations that assumes men to be superior to women. Given the subordinate status of women, much of gender violence is considered normal and enjoys social sanction. Manifestations of violence include physically aggregation such as blows of varying intensity, burns, attempted hanging, sexual abuse and rape, psychological violence through insults, humiliation, coercion, blackmail, economic or emotional threats and control over speech and actions (Altekar, 1962). In extreme but not unknown cases, death is the result. These expressions of violence take place in a man-woman relationship within the family and society. Usually, domestic aggression towards women and girls due to various reasons remain hidden.

The status of women in India has been subject to many great changes over the past few millennia. Scholars believe that in ancient India, the women enjoyed equal status with men in all fields of life. However, some others hold contrasting views. Works by ancient Indian grammarian such as Patanjali and Katyayana suggest that women were educated in the early Vedic period. Rigveda suggest that the women married at a mature age and were probably free to select their husband. In Indian society women were treated generally as maids or slaves as if they had no will or desire of their own. They had to follow their husbands in all matters (Agnew, 1979).

Cultural and social factors are interlinked with the development and propagation of violent behavior. With different processes of socialisation that men and women undergo, men take up stereotyped gender roles of domination and control whereas women take up that of submissions, dependence and respect for authority (Sha, 1993). The family socialises its member to accept hierarchical relations expressed in unequal division of labour between the sexes and power over the allocation of resources. The family and its operational unit is where the child is exposed to gender differences since birth and in recent times even before birth, in the form of sex-determination tests leading to foeticide and female infanticide. The home, which is supposed to be the most secure place, is where women are most exposed to violence (Astbury, 1999).

Violence against women has been clearly defined as a form of discrimination in numerous documents. The World Human Rights Conference in Vienna, first recognised gender-based violence as a human rights violation in 1993. In the same year, United Nations Declaration, 1993, defined violence against women as "any act of gender-based violence that results in, or is likely to result in, physical, sexual or psychological harm or suffering to a woman, including threats of such acts, coercion or arbitrary deprivations of liberty, whether occurring in public or private life" (Narasimhan, 1999).

India is one of the few countries where women enjoy a comparative better status than many women in other parts of the world. True Indian women face many problems and are subject to the same social pressures which women experience in other parts of the world. But relatively speaking, their situation is much better than what it used to be in the pre-independence era.

On the positive side women have made rapid strides in every aspect of modern life. The constitution guarantees equal opportunity and where necessary provides necessary safeguards from possible exploitation or injustice. Indian women of today are not afraid of voicing their opinions or joining forces with other women in the local community to fight against social maladies and injustice. They have opportunities to take bold decisions or lead unorthodox lives, which might and family pressures few decades ago. Undoubtedly, women of today in India enjoy better status and freedom than women in the past (Bakshi, 1995).

On the negative side, Indian women suffer from many disabilities and social injustices. This is true for all Indian women, to whatever religion they may belong except where their status, role and responsibilities are directly influenced by religious beliefs such as marriage and inheritance. Indian women rank high in terms of the number of prostitutes in the world, girl children neglected, abused or often sold purely for economic reasons as victims of AIDS and women living below the poverty line or forces to do physical labour even when they are pregnant or sick. Speaking of the sexual attitude of Hindu males, they are not much different from their counterparts in other religion (Chandra, 1999).

Today's girl is tomorrow's woman. Ladies first, this nicety has more of less a matter of social courtesy, limited perhaps to the higher strata of society Despite their contributions in various fields, Very little has been done or given to encourage women to emerge from the society. The triumphant march of democracy in all plants of the globe has aroused the collective conscience of the people to shed regimentation and unleash forces that have a liberating influence in society, polity and economy. It is this anchoring of modern life on democracy and the increasing exertion for equal rights for both man and woman that have paved the way for according top priority to women's issues in the global agenda.

The South Asian Association for Regional Cooperation (SAARC) had declared 1990 as the year of the girl child. Historically, the women were subjected to various kinds of deprivation and discrimination. The areas of discrimination include health, education and other aspects of social-economic life. The situation is worse in the rural areas as compares to the urban areas. Despite the pressure of society and systems women have in different period of Indian history, emerged to the forefront and proved their mettle (Devi, 1998).

Medieval Indian Women

Medieval India was not women's age it is supposed to be the 'dark age' for them. Medieval India saw many foreign conquests which resulted in the decline in women's status. When foreign conquerors like Muslims invaded India they brought with them their own culture. For them women was the sole property of her father, brother or husband and she does not have any will of their own (Government of India, 1985). This type of thinking also crept into the minds of Indian people and they also began to treat their own women like this. One more reason for the decline in women's status and freedom was that original Indians wanted to shield their women folk from the barbarous Muslim invaders (Desai and Krishnaraj, 1987).

As polygamy was a norm for these invaders they picked up any women they wanted and kept her in their 'harems'. In order to protect them Indian women started using 'Pardah' which covers body. Due to this reason their freedom also becomes affected. They were not allowed to move freely and this lead to the further deterioration of their status. These problems related with women resulted in changed mindset of people. Now they began to consider a girl as misery and a burden which has to be shielded from the eyes of intruders and needs extra care. Whereas a boy child will not need such extra care and instead will be helpful as an earning hand. Thus, a vicious circle started in which women was at the receiving end. All this gave rise to some new evils such as *Child Marriage, Sati, Jauhar and restriction on girl education* (Vorah and Sen, 1989).

Violence against Women

Domestic violence was common and a serious problem. In a survey by the National Family Health Survey releases during the year, 56 percent of the women said that domestic violence was justified. These sentiments combined with ineffective prosecution, made progress against domestic violence difficult. The issue of rape received increased political and social attention during the years. The only ten percent of rape cases were adjudicated fully by the courts and police typically failed to arrest rapists, thus fostering a climate of impunity. Several traditional practices that were harmful to women continued (Basu, 2009).

Technologies like amniocentesis and ultrasound used in most parts of the world, largely for detecting foetal abnormalities has been used in large parts of the Indian sub-continent for determining the sex of the foetus so that it can be aborted, it happens to be a female (Rani, 1978). The information of the sex of the unborn was being extensively misused. To prevent female foeticide and to restrict this misuse, the Prenatal Diagnostic Technique (Regulation and Prevention of Misuse) Act was passed on 20th September, 1994. The Act forbids the communication of the sex of the foetus, but the enforcement of this act is not easy (Coomaraswamy, 1994).

Medical Termination of Pregnancy Act (MTPA), 1971 allows abortion if the doctor is of the opinion that the continuance of the pregnancy would endanger the life of the pregnant woman or involve grave injury to her physical or mental health or there is substantial risk that the child would suffer from disabling physical or mental abnormalities. The anguish caused by pregnancy as a result of rape, or as a result of failure of any device or method used by a married couple for the purpose of limiting the number of children may be presumed to constitute a grave injury to the woman's mental health. The matter is thus purely between her and the medical practitioner and even the husband's consent becomes unnecessary (Sood, 1990).

In reality, however, a woman's right to abortion is very restricted and mostly it turns out to be family decision. Various court judgments have held that aborting a foetus without the husband's consent would amount to cruelty under the Hindu Marriage Act and hence ground for divorce. The procedure gets rampantly misused with the collaboration of the medical fraternity as an alternative in the case of couples who do not opt to practice family planning methods and who want to do away with the unwanted child (Mishra, 1997).

Since, the Constitution of India contains certain provisions that guarantee the welfare and development of children. The Indian Penal Code also has defined infanticide as murder. Female infanticide and foeticide has occurred not only in several cultures across history, but is known to occur in contemporary societies as well.

Statutory Provisions for Protecting the Rights of Women

India has made gigantic efforts to herald a better tomorrow for women. The Constitution of India guaranteed fundamental nights without any bar on count of sex. The Constitution frames were quite alive and fully aware to the problems of the weaker section of the society. Protective legislation to give them social security was considered to be judged by the standards by which it treats the weaker section of its polity. Equalitarian approach of the Constitution framers resulted in intensive legislative fiat in the post-independence era.

What woman has achieved after great struggle in Europe was well incorporated in the provisions of the Constitution itself. Fundamental rights guaranteed under Chapter III of the Constitution are for men and women alike. Article 15 clause (3) is most significant as it gives power to the State for making special provisions for women and children. The interests of women and children are carefully and clearly protected under the Constitution, as the women in India were accustomed to an excessive sheltered life and the situation further aggravated due to poverty and illiteracy which subject them to easy target for exploitation. The social security legislation has attempted much for the betterment of the women and tried to improve their position (The most important provision in this regard is Article 15 of the Constitution).

Article 23 provides prohibition of traffic in human being and forced labour and any contravention of this provision is an offence punishable in accordance with law. The expression 'traffic in human being' has been held to include not only slavery but also traffic in women for immoral purposes. With a view to protect the women, The Suppression of immoral Traffic in Women and Girls Bill was passed as early as 1956 which has been amended and renamed as immoral Traffic (Prevention) Act, 1986. The purpose of this enactment is to inhibit of abolish commercialised vice namely the traffic in person for the purpose of prostitution as an organised means of living it does not punish a person because he or she prostitutes himself. To live on the earnings of a prostitute is prohibited under the enactment (*Constitution of India*).

Instances of sexual abuse of children are ever increasing in the society. Today's society owes higher responsibility to do something effective to save children from incestuous relationships. Several enactments protecting the rights of women have been amended and passed in the recent years.

The Dowry Prohibition Act, 1961 was also amended in the year 1986. Under the Panchayat Raj Act, recently, women could successfully achieve the goal set under the Constitution to have and enjoy equality through 35% of reservation in their favour. This is an important step towards social justice (Immanuel, 1998).

While keeping in mind the constitutional requirements the Legislature has enacted from time to time a number of statutory provisions, protecting interests of children of tender age working as child labour. Child labour problem is the most glaring example of exploitation of children at the hands of employer. It is easier for the employer to exploit a female child labour. Children, undoubtedly need special legal protection, so that they do not fall victims of exploitation and cruelty at the hands of other members of the society.

Founding fathers of the Indian Constitution had complete awareness as to the weak position of children in poverty stricken illiterate society. Therefore, Article 24 reads as follows—no child below the age of fourteen years shall be employed to work in any factory or mine of engaged in any other hazardous employment.

The role of women in present society is being redefined. She is not confined to the boundaries of home. Today she is participating in decision-making and yet trying to preserve her own cultural heritage. She has become psychosocially competent and is trying to combine the instrumentalism of male and the expressive skills of female in a very unique and adaptive manner. She is actively approaching the idea off equalitarianism (Agnes, 1999). In the post-independence period the question of raising the legal status of women was taken up in right earnest.

Even so, discrimination as exercised by the general masses between boys and girls is a big hurdle in the process of development of women. Girls, from the very childhood, are denied nourishing food, proper clothing, education and other facilities. Even mother discriminates against her girl child, in providing proper education etc., as a lot of additional expenditure has to be made for her at the time of marriage. It is the mother who, if so wishes, may provide her daughter a right of inheritance und the present legal system. As early as in 1956 the Hindu Succession Act was enacted under which a daughter has the same right to inherit his father's property as a son has. (Relevant Sections are 14, 15 and 16 of the aforesaid Act). Under Muslim law daughters have their respective share in the father's property. Right of inheritance does exit there but how far it is enforced is a significant question to be tackled with.

There is no dearth of laws to protect women's right but the implementation part is quite weak. Right to equality and equal opportunities in life as provided to women under the Constitution is of little and exercise these freedoms. Is it not the failure of the right thinking people in the society that they are not capable of forming a strong opinion to stop such practices which result in the curtailment of basic fundamental rights of women who constitute the weaker section of the society? Why women are considered as slaves in the men-dominated society? Total outlook of the men is against women. Psychologically men require an immediate change in their behavioural pattern towards women. It's the moral duty of the father in the family to treat his daughter at par with the son. In various matters, parents are required, to give equal opportunities to the girl child so that her overall development is not adversely affected.

Why, despite so much protective legislation, is there hike in crime rates and atrocities against women? Why is there enormous increase in the number of rape cases in India? Why is there gradual decline in the sex ratio of women? Why is the primitive, barbarous institution of sati reviving? These are the problems which are raising heads so often. They are clear evidences of gender injustice in India. Public opinion has a significant and effective role to play in the present society. Sensitisation of people in general towards such situations gender discrimination is highly required.

Unless, they are made conscious of these the goal of equality will remain a dream for centuries to come. Aim and object of the Constitution framers can only be.realised through tremendous efforts in the right direction of educating masses. Legislative efforts must get social support to realise the ultimate goal gender justice (Jain, 1993).

In several States, sex determination and sex pre-selection tests and practices have come in handy as a way of concretising prejudices against girl child. In a single year of 1984, 40,000 female fetuses were aborted following amniocentesis tests in the city of Bombay alone. A survey conducted in Bombay showed that of the 8,000 cases of aforesaid test and abortion 7,999 aborted fetuses were female.

The disclosure of test figures and the implications of these practices galvanised women's organisations into action. Pressure was brought to bear on the Government of Maharashtra, which finally accepted the demand of these organisations to ban sex-determination and sex pre-selection tests by enactment of a law against it. Later, the Government of Goa too, banned the practice of sex-linked abortions. The struggle to get a similar law passed at the national continues. Female infanticide, though banned long ago, is still found in the States of Rajasthan and some parts of Tamil Nadu. The practices are taking away very right of female child to survive. This causes decline in sex ratio in the society, which may create many more problems like increase in the rate of crime and violence towards women.

Public opinion has a significant role to play in this matter of gender justice to a girl child. Once the public, is made aware of above discussed social evils through proper education, the goal to achieve success in eradicating such evils is not at all impossible. We have to create awareness among masses particularly amongst women that they should become literate and economically independent to serve due respect in the society.

By Setting up a National Commission on Women by an Act of parliament to prevent, among other things, discrimination against women and redress their grievances will not suffice. The very idea of gender justice will reign supreme on the psyche of people, provided, social workers, non-governmental organisations, electronic media etc, keep continue their struggle against inequality by educating masses through conducting seminars, nuckad nataks specially in rural area and fast spreading message to the general masses about the social evils resulting from gender inequalities.

Numerous laws exist to protect women's rights and to provide the equal status of women in the society. According to India's constitution, women are legal citizens of the country and have equal rights with men. Because of lack of acceptance from the male dominant society, Indian women suffer immensely. Women are responsible for baring children, yet they are malnourished and in poor health. Women are also overworked in the field and complete the all of the domestic work. Most Indian women are uneducated. Although the country's constitution says women have equal status to men, women are powerless and are mistreated inside and outside the home.

Suggestions and Recommendations

Gender equality and gender development are the key issues for the planners and policy-makers. Following are the issues which still require some concrete measures for the upliftment of women.

- There is need to involve the bureaucracy in the sensitisation process and to facilitate political will to look at the problem of violence.
- Women's rights based agendas have to be incorporated in the political process.
- Identification of functional shelter homes and support services and allocation of adequate resources to strengthen their work.
- Strategies have to be developed to raise awareness of the extent and impact of violence perpetrated against violence.
- Information dissemination on legal safeguards, rights, support services, health and accommodation. Women's groups should also inform other women about the available support services in the area and towns.
- Education of the youth is important. This is the time to develop healthy and respectful relationships. Schools can work with local communities to deliver anti-violence education.
- There is a need for societal responsibility, especially male

responsibility to mitigate violence against women. The society has to understand that women have as much of a right to a happy and violence-free life as anyone else.

- There should be effective and quick implementation of schemes like 'SWADHAR' an innovative intervention for women in difficult circumstances with a special focus on the rehabilitation of sex workers, bar dancers, jogins, women/girl in social and moral danger, destitute, etc.
- Removal of the gender gap in education at all levels.
- Pregnancy test and termination of pregnancy laws more strict and effective.
- Create an enabling environment for women to exercise their reproductive rights and choices freely.

Conclusion

The extent of violence against women is still not acknowledged and thus as a first step it is essential to study the trends in violence against women, analyse its causes and to gather to whatever extent possible, statistical figures on crimes against women. There is a need for research to be gender friendly and its analysis, sharp in order to engender the perspectives of social scientists. Building a constituent base is an important step in generating public support for addressing gender-based violence. This responsibility lies with the civil society on one hand and state agencies on the other.

However, women's organisations should be the facilitators in this process. The north-east region boasts of strong women's movements. It is important to build on this strong base to create coalitions by mobilising diverse groups. Community watch groups should be created and mobilisation of local government officials, legal advisors, community volunteers and survivors undertaken to establish procedures for reducing violence.

Initiating networks of women will encourage greater regional exchange on issues of gender equity, women's rights and empowerment of women. The network can also act as a base for service collaborations among domestic violence and sexual assault activists/organisations. They could also serve as important pressure groups to advocate for rights of women at the regional as well as national level. All this could go a long way in ensuring a violence-free life for women.

In this period of economic liberalisation and globalisation, the quality of women's employment will depend upon several factors. The foremost among these are access to education and opportunities for skill development. The solution lies in creating awareness among women about their legal rights and duties and by providing them adequate opportunities to upgrade their skill levels. The emphasis should be on effective enforcement of the Minimum Wages Act, 1948 and Equal Remuneration Act, 1976.

References

Agnes, F. (1999), *Law and Gender Inequality: The Politics of Women's Rights in India*, Oxford University Press, p. 56.

Altekar, A.S. (1962), *The Position of Women in Hindu Civilisation*, Motilal Banarsidass, Delhi, p. 45.

Astbury, I. (1999), *Promoting Women's Mental Health*, World Health Organisation, p. 29.

Agnew, V. (1979), *Elite Women in Indian Politics*, New Delhi: Vikas Publishing House, p. 76.

Bakshi, S.R. (1995), *Advanced History of Modern India*, Vol. 4, New Delhi: Anmol Publications, p. 33.

Basu, D. Das (2009), *Introduction to the Constitution of India*, New Delhi: Prentice Hall of India, p. 322.

Chandra, B. (1999), India after Independence, New Delhi: Penguin Books, p. 67.

Coomaraswamy, R. (1994), United Nations Economic and Social Council, *Preliminary Report submitted by the Special Rapporteur on Violence Against Women, its Causes and Consequences,* Commission on Human Rights Resolution, p. 42.

Desai, N. and Krishnaraj, M. (1987), *Women and Society in India*, New Delhi: Vohra Company, p. 23.

Devi, L. (1998), *Encyclopedia of Women's Development and Family Welfare*, Vol. 4, New Delhi: Anmol Publication, p. 89.

Government of India (1985), *Towards Equality*, Report of the Committee on the Status of Women in India, New Delhi.

Immanuel, M. (1998), *Women and Development*, Ahmedabad: Karnavati Publications, p. 24.

C.K. Jain (1993), *Women's Position in India*, New Delhi: Surjeet Publications, p. 89.

Mishra, S. (1997), *Women and 73rd Constitutional Amendment Act: A Critical Appraisal, Social Action*, Vol. 44, Law Library, pp. 16-30, p. 18.

Narasimhan, S. (1999), *Empowering Women: An Alternative Strategy from Rural India*, New Delhi: Sage Publications, p. 83.

Rani, K. (1978), *Role of Conflict in Working Women*, New Delhi: Chetna Publicatins, p. 98.

Sha, V. (1993), *Role of Women in Ancient India*, New Delhi: Surjeet Publications, p. 11.

Sood, S. (1990), *Violence against Women*, Jaipur: Arihant Publishers, p. 55.

Gender Discrimination Begins Before Birth: An Overview

Ravita and Jagdev Singh

Introduction

Women play a key role in development, both in the context of the family and society at large, including its economy as well as social system. The history of women's liberation movement all over the world shows that the importance of women's education was recognised as the most effective agent for improving their socio-economic status in the society. Promoting women's education would have a multiplier effect. It has been rightly said that the education of a man is the education of an individual and the education of a woman is the education of an entire family. Despite all the developmental measures and constitutional guarantees, women have lagged behind men in almost all walks of life.

Women status is changing in response to several emerging trends, on the positive side more girls are attending schools, delaying marriage and childbearing however diseases, malnutrition, low social status and gender inequalities are some of the challenges. Women's disproportionate poverty, low social status, limited access to health services and reproduction role expose them to high health risks and premature death. Declining life expectancy at birth of women below 1.0 in Asia is a sign of unfavourable socio-economic conditions particularly to women and girls (Tinker *et al.*, 2000). Demographic transition of India has played an important role in the socio-culture, economic and human development of India.

In the Developing country like India, the sex ratio of population (females), except of few states, is not satisfactory. The low female-male ratio (FMR) arises due to higher female over male mortalities that are largely a result of discrimination against women operating through unequal access to life sustaining inputs such as food, nutrition, education and health care (Visaria, 1971; Miller, 1981; Rosenzweig and Schultz, 1982; Kishor, 1993). Visaria and Visaria (1981) identified sex differentials in mortality as the main cause of the low FMRs, and Miller (1981) attributed the roots of these differentials to discrimination against women, and also emphasised greater bias in higher status and better-off households.

The adverse-to-females, FMRs have been commented on since before the first Indian Census in 1881 (Kantikar, 1991) the apparent deterioration in the sex ratio since then (Srinivasan, 1994) suggests that these problems may not disappear with development (Agnihotri, *et al*, 2002). The adverse female-to-male sex ratios in India have attracted considerable academic and policy concern in the recent years. The phenomenon of the missing women in India is a shortfall in the number of women relative to the number that would be expected. The phrase "missing women", coined by Amartya Sen, refers to the observation that in parts of the developing world the ratio of women to men is suspiciously low. The combined effect is a roughly equal proportion of men and women in the population as a whole (Anderson, 2010). Seven lakh girls are killed by parents every year in India even before they are born, While 1.72 million children die in India each year before the age of one, because of our gender bias, the mortality rate is even higher for girls than boys (One World Asia, 2012).

Even after 65 years of independence, the socio-economic conditions of women in the country in general, are not satisfactory. It is a fact that an Indian woman suffers from 'womb to tomb'. She suffers when she is in the womb of her mother in the form of foeticide and continues throughout life in the form of widowhood and social insecurity. In India, the government, society and all of us are responsible for missing women because we wordlessly see and tolerate the inequality without complaining or protesting against it. According to 'UN Human Development Report, 2011', India ranks a low, i.e., 134 among 187 countries in terms of the human development index.

The magnitude or the scale of maternal mortality and morbidity in the world and the huge disparities in their levels between developed and underdeveloped countries have been major concerns. Most countries in Asia and Africa have made commitments and pledges to reduce maternal mortality by interventions. However in spite, of well established protocols to treat complications arising from pregnancy and child birth still, more than half of million women worldwide die each year most of them in African and Asian Countries (Visaria, 2012).

Today, many countries have taken measures to ensure equal rights for women. Notwithstanding all these measures, declarations, global campaign for their socio-economic empowerment, women face discrimination at every step and in every walk of life. In India, where no generalisation applies to nation's regional, religious and socio-economic group, issue of improving health, empowerment of women, gender discrimination and violence against women has great importance. In the phase of economic development, the challenge of gender equality is remained there and in the context of declining child-sex ratio, new challenges have emerged.

The present paper aims to study the issues and trends of missing women in India as well as to give some suggestions for controlling discriminating which begins before their birth. For this purpose, secondary data has been collected from various census reports.

Sex Ratio at the World Level

It is observed from the table that at the world level, there is a significant imbalance in the female-male ratio. In the year 2001, India's female ratio was lowest whereas in 2011, China's female ratio was lowest at the world level. Further, it is clear that there is a positive trend of female ratio in India, Pakistan and Japan. There is a higher decline of female ratio in China in this decade. At the world level, the sex ratio

Table 14.1: Number of Females per 1000 Males (World and Selected Countries)

Country/World	*FMR (Number of females per 1000 males)*		
	2001	*2011*	*Change (2001-11)*
China	944	926	-18
India	933	940	+7
USA	1029	1025	-4
Indonesia	1004	988	-16
Pakistan	938	943	+5
Japan	1041	1055	+14
World	986	984	-2

Source: Census of India, 2001 and 2011.

has marginally declined from 986 to 984. Overall today world is suffering the problem of notable decline in the female population. This is the indication of future of world looking like plenty of nations without women (Bharti, 2012).

Child Sex Ratio in India: The Emerging Pattern

The child sex-ratio is a powerful index to examine the social response on female children. The child sex ratio of the age group 0 to 6 years shows the approach of society towards the girls. The discrimination in sex ratio of population existed because of the presence of the son preference in India and China (Fuege, 2010). It is interesting to look the number of girls at the time when population growth is declining and literacy rate among women is rising. According to the census of 2011, proportion of literate women has gone up to 65.46 percent. The gender gap in the spread of literacy has come down from 24.84 percent in 1991 to 16.68 percent in 2011. But the most disturbing aspect is growing imbalance between sexes.

Table 14.2: Trends in Sex Ratio and Child Sex Ratio in India

Year	*Sex ratio of total population*	*Change from the previous period*	*Child Sex ratio (0-6 years)*	*Change from the previous period*
1961	941	-	976	-
1971	930	-11	964	-12
1981	934	+4	962	-2
1991	927	-7	945	-17
2001	933	+6	927	-18
2011	940	+7	914	-13

Source: Census of India, Various Issues.

The decline in girl child population leads to serious demographic imbalance and adverse social consequences. The radical decline in child sex ratio is an issue of grave concern in India. Sex ratio has begun to improve from 927 in 1991 to 933 in 2001 and 940 in 2011. But when compared to most of countries in the world, India's sex ratio is anomalous (Visaria, 2011). The child sex ratio of children aged between 0-6 years has steadily declined from 976 in 1961 to 927 in 2001 and finally to 914 in 2011. This phenomenon has drawn worldwide attention to increasing practice of sex detection and female foeticides.

From the figure, it is clear that the overall sex ratio has increased in India. But there was continuously negative trend was observed in the

Figure 14.1: Sex Ratio at the World Level

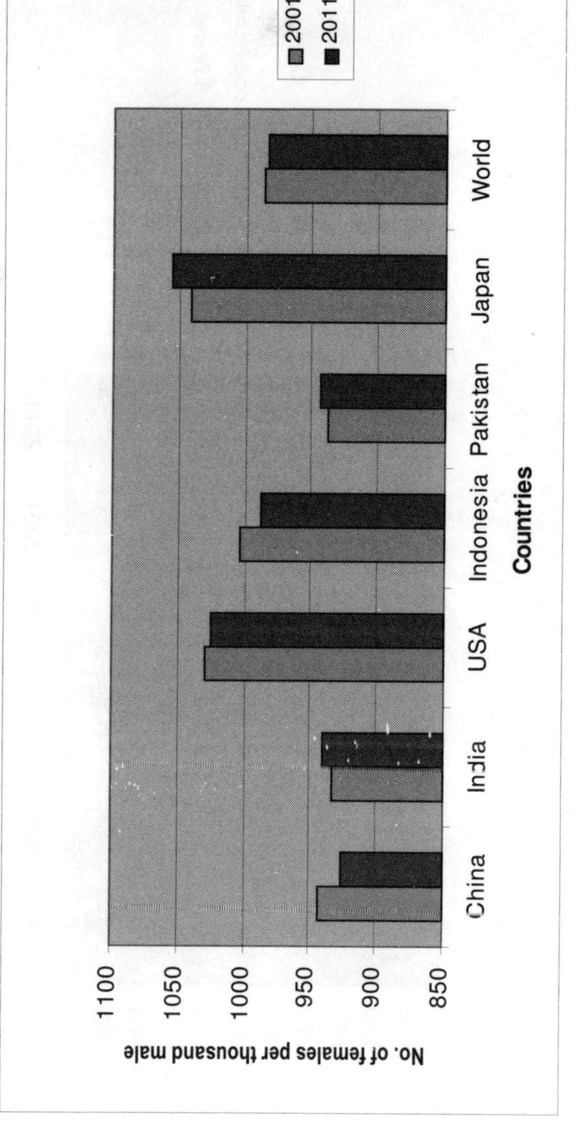

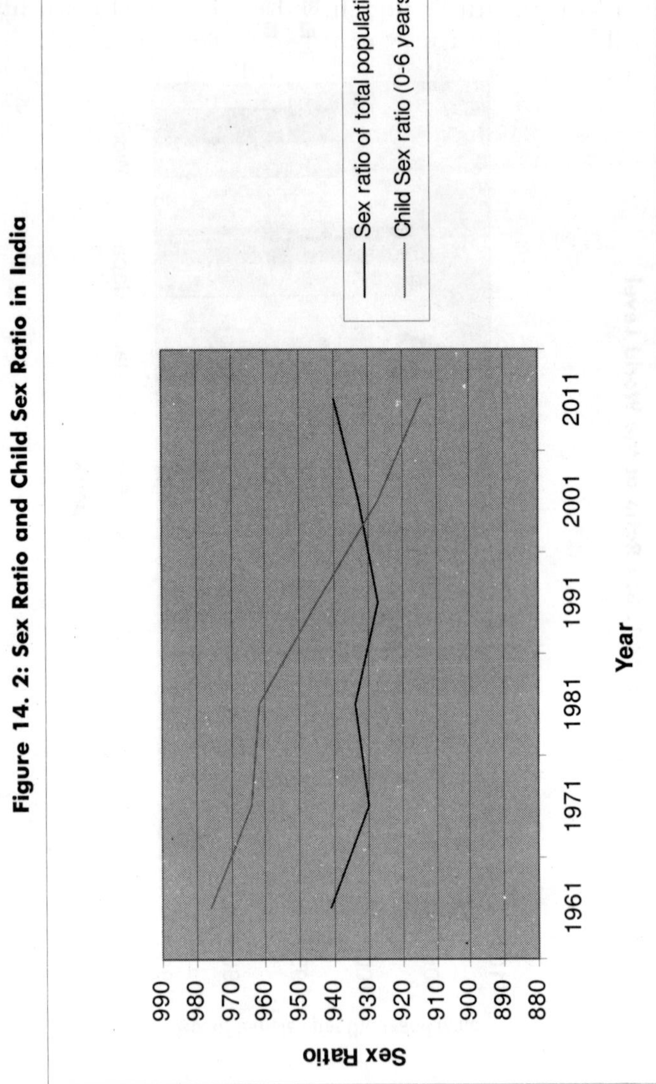

Figure 14. 2: Sex Ratio and Child Sex Ratio in India

sex ratio of the age group 0 to 6 years. It was highest in the year 2001. The Census of 2011 gives an important message because it is far away from a balanced gender ratio. In India, the birth of a daughter in generally regarded as burden on family. As a wife her position is also become worse. She is considered as plaything of her husband always playing second fiddle to him. Their masculinity seems to be jeopardised when they become bread winner (Sapru, 1989). The challenge is to an effort towards a balanced population and if these prejudices are to be overcome, the civil rights of women need to be protected. In order to generate the unbiased population, skill-building, health, education and opportunities for decision making and legal rights should be made available to women.

Child Sex Ratio at State Levels

In India, woman as a daughter is never welcome. The birth of even a fifth son is an occasion for congratulation, whereas the coming of even the first daughter plunges the whole household into disappointment (Sapru, 1989).

India has an exceptionally low female-male ratio or sex ratio. This problem is not, of course, equally acute in every region of India. The regional patterns of sex ratios are consistent with what is known as the character of gender relations in different parts of the country. The North-West states, for instance, are notorious for highly unequal gender relations, some symptoms of which include the continued practice of female seclusion, very low female labour-force participation rates, a large gender gap in literacy rates, extremely restricted female property rights, strong boy preference in the fertility decisions, widespread neglect of female children and drastic separation of a married women from her natal family. In all these respects, the social standing of women is somewhat better in the South India and Kerala, of course, has a distinguished history of a more liberated position of women in the society (Dreze and Murthi, 1996).

It is a fact that the number of females has been declining continuously after the 1981. Table 14.3 shows the child sex ratio in India at the state level. The break up of the states of the country is done to understand the status of the child sex ratio. The regions are North-west, North-central, West, East and South. At the India level, negative trend was observed. North-west India witnessed a positive child sex ratio than the other regions of India. Delhi experiences minor decline in child sex ratio during this time period. It is analysised from the table that there are improvements in this ratio in 2011 than 2001 in North-west states. The sharpest decline in child sex ratio has been observed in North-central states namely in Uttar Pradesh and Madhya Pradesh. Among the states, the drastic decline in child sex ratio has recorded in Rajasthan, Maharashtra, Goa, Bihar, Jharkhand, West Bengal, Nagaland, Orissa, Andhra Pradesh and Karnataka states.

Table 14.3: Child Sex Ratio (0-6 years) at State Level in India

State	*Females per 1000 males*		
	2001	*2011*	*Difference (2001-11)*
India	927	914	-13
North-West			
HP	896	906	+10
Punjab	798	846	+48
Haryana	819	830	+11
Chandigarh	845	867	+22
Delhi	868	866	-2
North-Central			
Uttar Pradesh	916	899	-17
Madhya Pradesh	932	912	-20
West			
Gujarat	883	886	+3
Rajasthan	909	883	-16
Maharashtra	913	883	-30
Goa	938	920	-18
East			
Bihar	942	933	-9
Jharkhand	965	943	-22
West Bengal	960	950	-10
Nagaland	964	944	-20
Orissa	953	934	-19
South			
Andhra Pradesh	961	943	-18
Karnataka	946	943	-3
Tamil Nadu	942	946	+4
Kerala	960	959	-1

Source: Census of India, 2001 and 2011.

The unfavorable sex ratio for the girl child (0-6 years) in states of India could be recognised to sex selective abortions and thereby interrupting natural history of reproduction. The deficit of women in India's population has been popular ever since the first decennial enumeration of people was conducted in the British-occupied parts of

India in the late 19th century (Dewan and Khan, 2009). Over the period of time, the deficit of women has progressively increased as obvious from the sex ratio of the states; the number of women per 1000 men more or less steadily declined from 2001 to 2011, partly because of population growth, the absolute gap between men and women increased. This deficit of women is known as the 'missing women'.

The increasing deficit of young girls is indicative of a strong possibility that traditional methods of neglect of female children are increasingly being combined with modem technology, and that girls are being prevented from being born. The socio-cultural factors that undervalue daughters have hardly changed over the years, nor has the patriarchal mindset that continues to sustain gender discrimination and inequity. Technology has contributed making this bias more manifest. When tradition and a discriminatory mindset meet with technology the offspring is male (UNFPA, 2005). Female infanticide was one of the main reasons for this highly skewed gender profile. Hence, there is a need for proper implementation of the Pre-natal Diagnostic Test Act which stipulated stringent punishment of those convicted of killing the girl children. Thus spreading awareness is the need of the hour if this menace is to be checked (*The Hindu*, 2012).

Child Sex Ratio in Rural and Urban Areas of India

The division of child sex ratio by residence shows the magnitude of change in the rural-urban areas. Data on child sex ratio in the rural and urban areas of India and Punjab is given in Table 14.4. It is clear from the table that the child sex ratio in India is higher in the rural areas as compared to urban areas. But the number of this ratio has been continuously declining in both the regions.

Table 14.4: Child Sex Ratio (0-6 years) by Residence in India

Year/Area→	*1991*		*2001*		*2011*	
	Rural	*Urban*	*Rural*	*Urban*	*Rural*	*Urban*
India	948	935	934	906	919	902
Punjab	878	866	799	796	843	851

Source: Census of India, 1991, 2001 and 2011, Provisional Population Tables. http://www.census2011.co.in/census/state/punjab.html.

Similar trend has been observed in the Punjab state. But it is clear from the figure that the child sex ratio in Punjab state has increased in the year 2011 in both the rural and urban areas. It is analysised from the table that though the child sex ratio is far worse in urban areas than the rural areas but the fall in child sex ratio in rural areas is greater than the urban areas. In fact the decline is steadier in urban areas. It is a fact that urban areas are usually connected with better medical, educational facilities, and higher per capita incomes. It shows that the level of education has little to do with female foeticide. A report on the missing females by the International Development Research Centre indicates that selective abortion of female foetuses is practiced more in families where the mothers are better educated. Anand (1998) writes that superior and so-called developed areas have a higher rate of female infanticide compared to the backward areas. The truth is that areas that are financially affluent have the highest female infanticide. There are many reasons that are responsible for the decline in the number of child sex ratio like sex selective abortions, son preference, mortality rate, female foeticide and neglect of the girl child.

There is considerable heterogeneity in the Indian experience, with serious evidence of gender imbalances in the North and the West of the country. These imbalances appear to be aggravated by recent technological developments permitting selective abortions, and will have important economic and social implications in the decades to come (Gupta and Bhaskar, 2007).

Literacy Rate in India

Before and at the time of independence, women literacy ratio in India was very low. But after the independence, women literacy rate shows remarkable change. Literacy rate of women has gone up from 8.86 percent in 1951 to 65.46 percent in 2011. It is clear from table and the figure that woman literacy rate increases with the passage of time. The increase in female literacy was 11.30 percent compared with 6.29 percent of male rate literacy in 2011. But the male literacy rate was 27.16 percent in 1951 and increased to 82.14 percent in 2011.

Table 14.5: Trends in Sex-wise Literacy Rate in India

(*in percent*)

Census Year	*Persons*	*Males*	*Females*	*Male-female gap in literacy rate*
1951	18.33	27.16	8.86	18.30
1961	28.30	40.40	15.35	25.05
1971	34.45	45.96	21.97	23.98
1981	43.57	56.38	29.76	26.62
1991	52.21	64.13	39.29	24.84
2001	64.84	75.26	53.67	21.59
2011	74.04	82.14	65.46	16.68

Source: Census of India, Various Issues.

Figure 14.3: Area-wise Child Sex Ratio in India

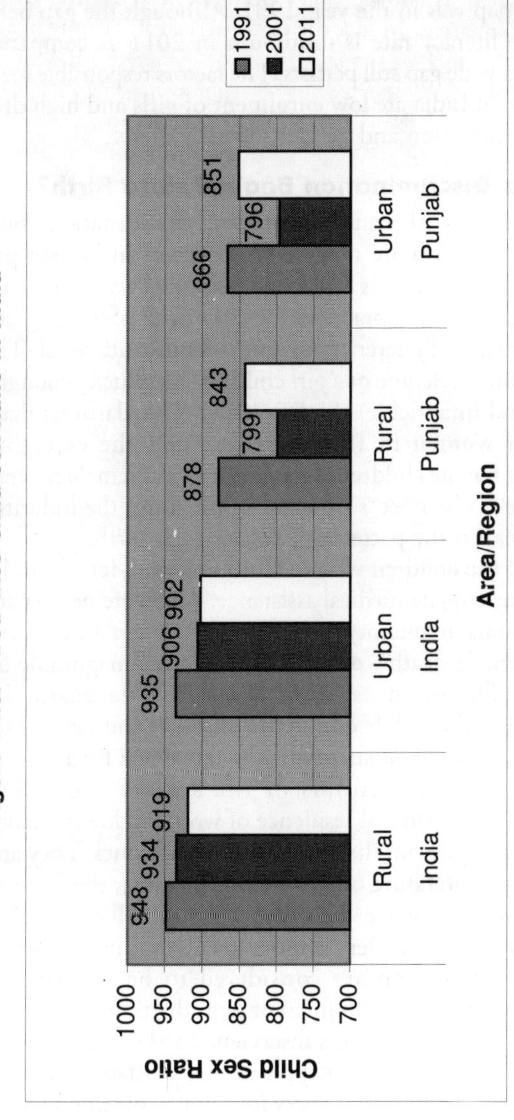

The male-female literacy gap has decreased after 1981 and the maximum gap was in the year 1981. Although the gap between male and female literacy rate is minimum in 2011 as compared to other census, yet a wide gap still persists. The factors responsible for low female literacy rate in India are low enrolment of girls and high dropout rate, social discrimination and gender inequality, etc.

Why does Discrimination Begin Before Birth?

In the absence of management, both the sex ratio at birth and the population sex ratio are remarkably constant in human populations. The son preference is clear in sex-selective abortion and in discrimination in care practices for girls, both of which lead to higher female mortality. Preference for son is almost universal. This leads to discriminatory welcome of a girl child (if she is lucky enough to survive foeticide and infanticide) (Sinha, 2011). The alarming decline in the number of women in India is a result of the emerging ways of eliminating female children. First is the excess female mortality during infancy itself. The next is prenatal elimination, the indicative signs of which appear in the patterns of sex ratios at birth.

Most of the children who die in infancy are female and this is due to lack or inadequate medical assistance, deliberate neglect and outright killing. In India, respiratory and infectious diseases are important sources of excess female deaths, of the same order of magnitude as maternal mortality. The main cause of excess female deaths in India is cardiovascular disease. It dominates all other sources of excess female mortality, and easily outstrips missing females at birth (Visaria, 2012).

Traditions and customs of the society too reflect gender discrimination. Patrilocal residence of women, dowry, veiling, sati like traditions emerge from the patriarchal social values. They are sustained by the art and literature of the society. In India, the fact remains that women is usually worse than that of men (Allahbadia, 2002), The difference between genders is more keenly felt in patriarchal societies like India where men are considered to be superior to women. Biologically they bear the burden of reproduction. Culturally, in India, women are expected to be subservient to the male members of the household and work for the happiness and satisfaction of men. Further, society expects them to play a very important role in providing informal health care to all the members of the family.

Crime against women is the important factor which is responsible for fewer girls in India. Dowry, sexual harassment and rape are some evils that are affecting the development of women. Some data on crime

Figure 14.4: Literacy Trends in India

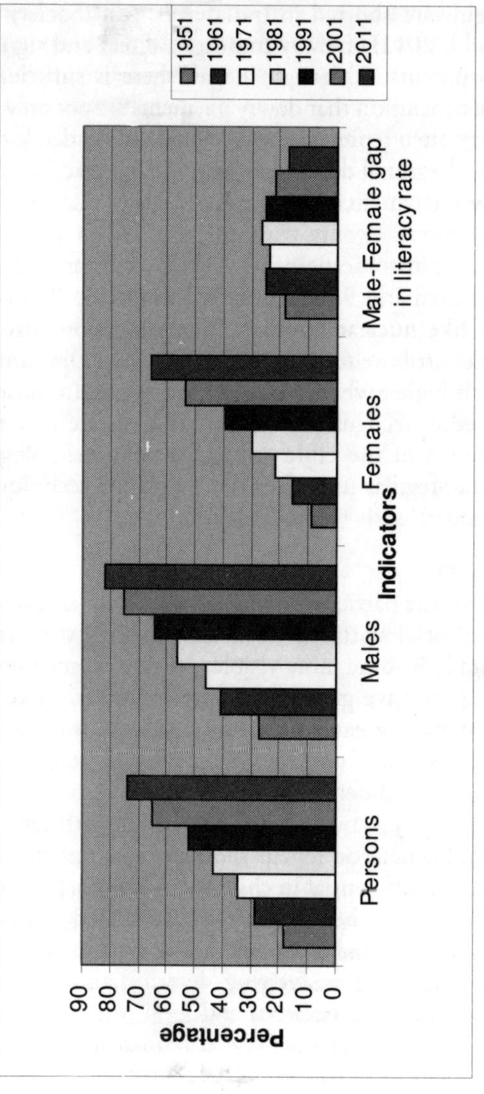

against women shows that there were 8,172 Dowry Deaths in India in 2008. While law exists to prevent selective sex tests and abortion still 7,50,000 girls are aborted in India every year (Society for Protection of Girl Child, 2011). Dowry imposes a direct and significant cost on the bride's parents. Although illegal, there is sufficient evidence to support the conclusion that dowry payments are not only still demanded but that they often represent a severe financial burden for the household of the bride. Regional differences in marriage practices and an increase in real dowry payments over the last decades may responsible for the observed sex ratios. Twenty-two percent of Indian men have committed sexual violence at some point in their lives, compared with 2 percent of Brazilian men and 9 percent of men in Chile (Bhayan, 2011).

Factors like nuclear families, high education cost and access to machinery contribute to it (UNESCO, 2012). Discrimination against girls is much higher where mothers are literate. In most cases, literacy is just curbed to recognised degrees; mindsets are ancient. It is easy to identify the sex of the child with improved technology and nuclear families make regular use of sex determination techniques to do away with "unwanted" girls (Jena, 2008).

Suggestions

- Women's participation in the workforce is also seen to increase the social status of women by making their contribution to family income more visible. Further, women who work for an income have greater access to resources, more independence and have greater exposure to the outside world. All these factors contribute to women's agency, thereby also having a positive influence on child health. This has been seen to be especially true in the case of the influence of women's employment on female mortality resulting in a decrease in the gender differential in child mortality (Chamarbogwala, 2005).
- The right to health has been articulated as an entitlement to an effective and integrated health system, encompassing health care and the underlying determinants of health which is responsible to national and local priorities and accessible to all. In this perspective, to reduce maternal mortality the entitlement to women include interventions such as emergency obstetric care, skilled birth attendant, education and information on sexual and reproductive health, safe absorption services, family planning and other health service. The measures like equal social and economic rights for males and

females must be guaranteed (Ministry of Women and Child Development, 2006).

- Basic health care should be available free of charge, so that parents are not deterred by the financial constraints from seeking health care for their daughters. Therefore, special supportive measures should be provided for families with no sons, to ensure protection for their parents in old age (Hesketh, and Xing, 2006)).
- In India, voiceless women who has no autonomy with respect to control over financial resources within household or freedom of mobility or decision-making power even on mundane and daily events with full understanding the interplay of various factors that influence the decision making powers, a mare medical solution is unlikely to help us to empower the women. The important role of socio-economic and cultural factors in accessing care by women needs much deeper understanding and research to solve the problem.
- Although formal and informal activities are quite different in nature in the rural areas, but most of these activities do not give them opportunities for employment, income, savings, pensions, insurances and better health facilities. If such facilities are extended to the rural areas, they will also need less financial support from their sons like urban parents. Such development will definitely improve the status of women in general and in rural areas in particular.
- Though there can never be any blueprint solution, steps can be taken to ensure the survival of women. Besides policing gender discriminating acts, implementing laws banning sex determination, and trying to bring down crime against women, the problem has to be addressed at the grassroots levels (*The Hindu*, 2002).

Concluding Remarks

Various social, economic and demographic indicators provide evidence of a gender bias as well as deep-rooted prejudice and discrimination against women and girl children. Inspite of various legislations to safeguard the constitutional rights of women, more and more female children are missing. In this regard, the 2011 Census, shows that the child sex ratio (CSR) for the age group 0-6 has crossed all limits and has remained alarmingly at the lowest.

It is widely agreed that sex ratio is a powerful indicator of the social health of any society. It conveys a great deal about the state of gender relations. Human development is not complete without gender equality. Deeply ingrained prejudices against women still persist in the modern society.

In nutshell, the declining sex ratio is not a problem restricted narrowly to the issue of decreasing birth of girl child but is central to women's rights, gender equity as well as gender justice. Therefore, the health planners, demographers and policy-makers should take this serious issue seriously. A multi-pronged strategy is required for solving this great menace at birth. So, it can be rightly conclude that *'So Kyo Manda Aakhaye, Jit Jamme Rajaan'.*

References

Agnihortri, S.B. (1995), "Missing Females: A Disaggregated Analysis", *Economic and Political Weekly,* Vol. 30, No. 33, pp. 2074-84.

Agnihotri, Satish, Jones, R.P. and Parikh, Ashok (2002), "Missing Women in Indian Districts: A Quantitative Analysis", *Structural Change and Economic Dynamics,* Vol. 13, pp. 285-314.

Allahbadia, Gautam N. (2002), "The 50 Million Missing Women", *Journal of Assisted Reproduction and Genetics,* Vol. 19, No. 9, pp. 411-16.

Anand, S. (1998), "Demographic Profile and Future Strategies for Development of the Girl Child", *Social Change.*

Anderson, Siwan and Debraj Ray (2010), "Missing Women: Age and Deceases", *Review of Economic Studies,* Vol. 77, p. 1.

Bharti, Deepak M. (2012), "Missing Women and Indian Cinema: 'Save The Girl Child", *Global Economic Research,* Vol. 1, No. 2, pp. 111-20.

Bhayan, Neha (2011), "Indian Men Lead to Sexual Violence, Worst on Gender Equality: Study", *Times of India,* New Delhi, May 7, 2011.

Census of India (2011), "Where the Girl Children", Available At: http:/ www.wikigender.org/index.php/census of India 2011: where are the girl children%3F, Accessed on 30 July 2012.

Chamarbagwela, Rubiana and Martin Ranger (2006), India's Missing Women: Disentangling Cultural, Political and Economic Variables, Centre for Applied Economics and Policy Research, *Working Paper No. 2006/21,* pp. 1-33.

Dewan, B.S. and Khan, A.M. (2009), "Socio-cultural Determinants of Female Foeticide", *Social Change,* Vol. 39, No. 3, pp. 388-405.

Dreze, Jean and Murthi, Mamta (1996), "Demographic Outcomes, Economic Development and Women's Agency", *Economic and Political Weekly,* Vol. 42, pp. 1739.

Fuege, Kan (2010), "Variations in attitudinal gender preference for children across 50 less developed countries", *Demographic Research,* Volume 23, Article 36, Nov 2010.

Gupta Bishnupriya and Bhaskar, V. (2007), "India's Missing Girls: Biology, Customs, and Economic Development", *Oxford Review of Economic Policy,* Vol. 23, No. 2, 2007, pp. 221-38.

Hausmann, Ricardo, Laura D. Tyson and Berkeley Saadia Zahidi (2011), *Global Gender Gap Report,* World Economic Forum, Geneva, Switzerland, p. 5.

Hesketh, Therese and Zhu Wei Xing (2006), "Abnormal Sex Ratios in Human Population: Causes and Consequences", *Proceeding of the National Academy of Sciences of the United States of America,* Vol. 103, No 36, pp. 13271-75.

Hicks, A. Douglas (2002), "Gender Discrimination and Capability: Insight from Amartya Sen", *Journal of Religious Ethics, Inc.,* pp. 137-54.

Human Development Report, 2011.

Jena, Krushna Chandra (2008), "Female Foeticide in India: A Serious Challenge for the Society", *Orissa Review,* Dec., pp. 8-17.

Kantikar, T. (1991), "The sex ratio in India: A Topic for Speculation and Research" *Journal of Family Welfare,* Vol. 37 (3), pp. 18-22.

Khera, Reetika and Nandi Nayak (2009), "Women Workers and Perceptions of the National Rural Employment Guarantee Act", *Economic and Political Weekly,* Vol. XXLV, No. 43, p. 50.

Kishor, S. (1993), "May God Give Sons to All, Gender and Child Mortality in India", *American Sociological Review,* Vol. 58, pp. 247-65.

Mari, Bhat, P. N. and A.J. Francis (2007), "Factors Influencing the Use of Prenatal Diagnostic Techniques and Sex Ratio at Birth in India", *Economic and Political Weekly,* Vol. 42, No. 24, pp. 2292-2303.

Miller, B.D. (1981), *The Endangered Sex,* Ithaca: Cornell University Press.

Ministry of Women and Child Development (2006), *Report of the Working Group on Empowerment of Women for Eleventh Plan,* Government of India, pp. 51-73.

One World Asia, (2012), "India: 700,000 unborn girls killed each year", Available At: http://southasia.oneworld.net/todaysheadlines/india-700-000-female-foeticides-taking-place-each-year Accessed on 30 July 2012.

Patel, Tulsi (2004), "Missing Girls in India", *Economic and Political Weekly,* Vol. 39, No. 9, pp. 887-889.

Rosenzweig, M., Schultz, T.P. (1982), "Market Opportunities, Genetic Endowment and Intra-Family Resource Distribution: Child Survival in Rural India", *American Economic Review,* Vol. 72, pp. 803-15.

Sapru, R.K. (1989), *Sex Equality in Socio-Economic Order: A Perspective,* New Delhi: A.S. Hish Publishing House, pp. 226-30.

Sharma, Swarn Lata (2001), *Gender Discrimination and Human Rights,* New Delhi: K.K. Publications, pp. 47-79.

Sinha, Dipa and Rosalinda (2011), The Invisible Half-Women's Status in Palanpur, LSE Asia Research Centre, *Working Paper No. 50,* pp. 12-14.

Society for Protection of the Girl Child (2011) *An Overview of Gendercide and Daughter Abuse in India,* available at www.protectgirls.org, Accessed on: 30 July 2012.

Srinivasan, K. (1994), "Sex Ratios: What They Hide and What They Reveal", *Economic and Political Weekly,* Vol. 30. No. 51, pp. 3233-34.

The Hindu (2012), "Help Curve Female Infanticides", April 21, 2012, Available At. www.thehindu.com,

The Hindu (2012), Our Missing Women, Monday, Dec. 9, 2012, Available At. www.thehindu.com,

Tinker, Anne *et al.* (2000), "Improving Women's Health: Issues and Interventions", *The World Bank,* Washington.

UNESCO (2012), "Key Messages and Data on Girls' and Women's Education and Literacy", Available at: http://www.uis.unesco.org/Education/Pages/gender education.aspx

United Nations Population Fund (2005), *Working from Within Culturally Sensitive Approaches in UNFPA Programming,* New York: UNFPA, pp. 15-17.

Visaria, Leela (2011), "India's 15th Population Census: Some Key Findings", *Yojana,* New Delhi.

Visaria, Leela (2012), *Maternal Mortality in India: Socio-Economic and Cultural Determinants,* Gujarat Institute of Development, Ahmedabad, pp. 1-20.

Visaria, P. (1971), The Sex Ratio of the Population of India, *Monograph No. 10,* Census of India, 1961, Office of the Registrar General, New Delhi.

Visaria, P. and Visaria, L. (1981), "Indian Population Scene after 1981 census," *Economic and Political Weekly,* Vol. 16, Nos. 44, 45 and 46, Special Number, pp. 1727-80.

MDGs and Maternal Mortality in a Historical Perspective

Kamalini Mukhopadhyaya

During the United Nations (UN) Millennium Summit in 2000, 147 heads of the states gathered and adopted the Millennium Development Goals (MDGs) to address extreme poverty in its many dimensions—income poverty, hunger, disease, lack of adequate shelter and exclusion—while promoting education, gender equality, and environmental sustainability, with quantitative targets for achieving the goals set for the year 2015. MDGs consist of eight goals, eighteen targets, and forty-eight indicators. Three of the eight MDGs are directly related to health: (i) reducing child mortality, (ii) improving maternal health, and (iii) combating HIV-AIDS, Malaria, and other diseases. The MDGs represent the widest international commitment in the modern era to address poverty and disease. It envisions massive transfer of technology from the First to the Third World countries and of sowing this technology in the latter. Interestingly, even while they are called "unachievable" and "unfeasible" by many because of the constraints in the basic MDG framework and allegedly they sustain the roots of income and health inequalities, majority of the development initiatives of 21st century are inevitably linked up to the MDGs. They do so either by the course of action or by their objectives. This chapter tries to locate the health goals of MDGs in the genealogy of discourses of women's health in India, and analyses whether MDGs as an international commitment are relevant for the Third World, especially India, as is often claimed.

One of the goals of the MDGs is reducing maternal mortality. The chapter attempts to show the narrow and restricted understanding of the MDGs by engaging with the goal concerning maternal mortality. The chapter begins by tracing the concern for maternal health and interventions in the field from the colonial period. During the British rule, there was a clear demarcation in the availability of the services to the rich and to the poor women. Even after independence, this differential provision of health services exists.

Post-independence, the understanding of health services for women have undergone a substantial change. The earlier broad understanding of women's health was now replaced by maternity health services, which placed family planning as its primary focus. Gradually, whatever public health services were available soon got replaced by market-driven neoliberal policies. Markets with narrow techno-centric interventions were supposed to be the answer to women's health problems and especially to curb maternal mortality. The goal of MDGs which follows the typical neoliberal agenda has not surprisingly found technical solutions to reduce maternal mortality through skilled birth attendants and emergency obstetric care. This chapter attempts to show the pitfalls of MDGs by analyzing the goal of maternal mortality.

Maternity Health Services in India

In India, historically the state's social policy and concern for the welfare of its women, especially women's health, has been through an emphasis on maternity health (Dhingra, 2001). These policies have been shaped by the interests of the developed countries, WHO's perception regarding health and illness, as well as its dependence on developed nations for funds. However, it has also been shaped at the country-level by its social dynamics and historical background.

The British ruling class paid attention to maternal and child health in their society, and consequently, it influenced British India's health policy towards the native poor women. In 1885, the National Association for Supplying Female Medical Aid to the Women of India, popularly known as the Lady Dufferin Fund was established. Initially, women missionaries from the USA, Britain and Canada came to India to open up dispensaries, hospitals and training schools for the midwives and nurses. Later on, by 1888, a considerable number of British women doctors were serving the Indian population. Thus, the colonial government encouraged the growth of institutionalised maternity care through these women doctors who were permitted to practise and run the hospitals and dispensaries. Nevertheless, their work was still considered as a philanthropic activity. Not only did the British gain good rapport with the local elites, who were only too eager to donate funds in order to gain respect from the natives, but their encouragement of the growing institutionalised maternity services became an opening for the western women doctors who found it difficult to break the male dominated professionals in their own countries. A number of women, unable to get into medical schools directly, first worked in India and later acquired their degrees and became eminent practitioners (Dhingra, 2001).Thus, social (health) welfare was still not a part of the direct governmental responsibility until the end of the 19th century.

The institutionalisation of medical care in India also brought about a discrediting of the traditional systems and practices of *dais* who were portrayed as being ignorant, vicious and careless. Thus, the colonial fund management system for health, instead of preserving the strengths of the traditional practices and improving on them, rejected them out right and set up training programmes based on the British medical curricula. Meanwhile, the Dufferin Fund's contribution was used in strengthening the British women doctors instead of using it to improve the conditions of public services for maternity care. Thus, three kinds of health services came into being. One was the state patronized voluntary hospital and dispensary system, the other was the private maternity health services that were run by the doctors of the voluntary hospitals that were availed by a few upper class women who could afford it; the third was that a huge section of the female population continued to depend on the traditional *dais* (Qadeer, 1998). Eventually, in 1911, the government of British India agreed to take some necessary action to provide adequate medical relief for large section of women. A huge grant was received by the Dufferin Fund, which was again used to improve the salaries and working conditions of the women professionals. Thus, even with the increase in subsidies and the establishment of women medical services, the maternity services continued to be a charity-based one as the provinces did not have adequate funds and the centre denied accepting responsibilities. In 1942, a national committee was set-up to examine the health issues in India. It strongly recommended the setting up of exclusive maternity and child health services under the commission of Maternity and Child Health (MCH). This went on to become the basis on which independent India's maternity and child health services was established (Qadeer, 1998).

Shifts in the Maternity Health Services in India

The post-independent India saw the Bhore and the Sokhey Committees, constituted before independence, influencing the five-year plan documents in health planning (National Planning Committee, 1948). The Bhore Committee was appointed by the Government of India in 1943, to make a broad survey of the then existing health conditions and statistics of ill health. The Committee placed emphasis on the high incidence of morbidity and mortality among mothers and children based on two broad principles, first, the provision of health services was the responsibility of the state, and second, comprehensive health care was the right of all, irrespective of the ability to pay. It, recommended that measures towards the reduction of these should be taken up by setting a high priority on preventive, primitive and curative care in maternal and child health (Government of India, 1946). Similarly, the Sokhey Committee, which was appointed in 1938, recommended a statutory body for the protection of motherhood and childhood, placing maternity and child health services over any other aspects of public health. The Committee, recognizing the importance of women's economic roles and concern for their health at their workplaces, recommended fixed working hours for women, including expectant mothers, establishment of crèches in factories and the formation of Maternity Benefit Act. It also recommended the setting up of infrastructural health facilities that included a need for training paramedical workers and traditional *dais* to provide natal, ante-natal and post-natal services. This in fact became the basis for a maternity and child health focus within India's general health services (Qadeer, 2002).

As a result, maternity health services were given priority in health planning during the first two five-year plans. However, soon after, the programme of family planning was attached to the maternal and child health programmes in the third five-year plan (Government of India, 1961). The family planning programme with its prime concern for population control recommended targets and incentives that became the centre of the health system, and maternity services began to be assessed by the number of sterilisations achieved, and not by the number of maternal and infant deaths it prevented (Qadeer, 1998). It was only in the fifth five-year plan that efforts were made to integrate the family planning programme, MCH and nutrition to provide a comprehensive welfare programme (Government of India, 1978). However, even before the trees of this welfare programme could bear its fruits, the State of Internal Emergency was imposed and resources of the Minimum Needs

Programme including nutrition were curtailed severely and family planning got all the attention of the health planners. It was only with the utter failure of the Family Planning Programme together with the change in the government that the family planning programme was announced as a voluntary programme to be integrated in a comprehensive policy along with education, health, MCH and nutrition to become a Family Welfare Programme (Rao, 1994). Subsequently, there was a small reduction in the resources for Family Planning Programme that was invested to strengthen the programmes against the communicable diseases. The national health policy and the Planning Commission Expert Group emphasised that in order to be more effective and acceptable the programme of family planning should be integrated with maternity and child health services (Government of India, 1983). Even though they expressed concern for high maternal mortality, the focus remained on child survival as women's health was not considered important for population control.

Such was the powerful impact of the population lobby that the subsequent five-year plans brought back the FPP to the forefront while investments in the general health services were simultaneously cut back. Attention to high mortality was not given importance until as late as 1992, with the launching of the Safe Motherhood Programme (Qadeer, 1998). Under this scheme, nutrition, immunisation and maternity care for pregnant women were consolidated and made a part of the government's child survival and Safe Motherhood Programme. Therefore, the initial conception of maternity health with its focus on communicable diseases and nutrition programmes was never actually implemented. Maternal health programmes were actually catering to the demands of the family planning interventions even though the latter could hardly make a difference in the high levels of mortality. There have never been any proper efforts made to assess maternal mortality at the national level. This is reflected in the absence of data on maternal mortality, which continues to be an estimated figure until today (Jhirad, 1959). The lopsided integration of family planning programmes within the general health services had two major implications for women: first, on maternal mortality, and second, on communicable diseases. In 1938, the Central Advisory Board of Health appointed a special committee. The committee's report on maternal mortality rate was nearly 20 per thousand live births (Government of India, 1946). Since then, however, there has been no national effort to assess the problem of MMR. From 1971 onwards, the model registration scheme provided insights into causes and time trends of maternal mortality in rural areas. It showed that over a period of 1970-90, maternal mortality had remained relatively stagnant as a proportion of total female deaths. It had also shown that deaths due to puerperal sepsis and toxaemia had consistently declined while deaths due to bleeding and anaemia had risen over time. It only revealed the poor state of the MCH services. While complications like sepsis was brought down with widespread use of antibiotics, anaemia that needed a rather simple intervention but a broad based one, continued to be the prime cause of maternal mortality (Soman, 1994).

The impact of communicable disease on women's health is another evidence of the overpowering influence of the family planning programmes on the health services. It has been seen through the five-year plans that while proportionate resource input into family planning has increased steadily, the disease control programmes have suffered in relative terms. The national data has indicated that of all the deaths among women, 65% are caused due to the disease groups which are predominantly infectious in nature whereas only 2.3% deaths are related to childbirth (Qadeer, 1998). Within the reproductive age group itself, deaths due to childbirth account for 12.5%. However, within this, around 4-6% of deaths are due to complications arising out of associated causes and not due to the process of childbirth itself. Among the associated causes are communicable diseases, anaemia, rheumatic heart disease and diabetes that can fully be controlled by a strong general health service system alone (Qadeer, 2002). The difference in the proportion of deaths due to communicable diseases, between groups of total female and females of reproductive age group was due to two reasons (Qadeer, 2005). First, among the reproductive group of females, deaths due to only major communicable diseases were taken into account. Second, the major portion of deaths and morbidity due to communicable diseases occurs among the younger population, especially girls (Qadeer, 2005). Thus, the Family Planning Programme lets a huge proportion of young girls suffer, while concentrating on a small group of women in the reproductive age group. In the process it excludes a large amount of morbidity and mortality in women who are not in the reproductive age group. Within the reproductive age group, too, concentration on mortality associated with childbirth (12.5%) ignores nearly 85% mortality associated with causes not related to childbirth (Qadeer, 2005).

In the process of its evolution, maternity health care, which was linked with the general health services, was overshadowed by the objectives of the population control. Consequently, while 'safe motherhood' strategies became a part of the broad-based family welfare programme, communicable disease control could never become a part of it. Thus, the child survival safe motherhood programme existed in isolation, at the most tackling the problem of vaccine preventable communicable diseases through immunisation only. Apart from this, there was always a shortage of women doctors in peripheral institutions, non-functioning Community Health Centres (CHCs) and Primary Health Centres (PHCs), poor referral services, lack of supply of drugs along with indifference of the senior health officials who were responsible for supervisory activities especially at the district and rural belts (Qadeer, 1998). All these limited the scope of other possibilities for women's health. The '90s saw the government policy acquire a different tone to solve the above problems. The term maternity health was replaced by 'reproductive health' (United Nations Population Fund, 1996). The argument given for this shift was that maternity health encompassed within itself too narrow a range that needed to be broadened to include other aspects of women's health. The components of reproductive health identified were safe motherhood and child survival, contraceptive services to prevent unwanted pregnancies, legal abortions, prevention and treatment of reproductive tract infections and sexually transmitted diseases, reproductive health services for adolescents, care of gynaecological problems including sterility, treatment of uterine and breast cancers and nutritional services. However, it was said that this package was too huge; therefore, a 'comprehensive package' was given as an alternative solution to the earlier. This 'comprehensive package' identified contraception, safe motherhood, child survival and reproductive tract infection and sexually transmitted diseases as the core services (Qadeer, 2001). At the implementation level, reproductive health had focused on fertility control with no concern for other aspects of health and used contraception as a key to reduce maternal mortality. In the process, it left out a significant intervention for maternal health-nutrition along with a range of other reasons for morbidity.

Markets and Maternal Mortality

The health sector reforms, introduced in 1990s, affected the health systems of a large number of developing countries. These reforms, which were driven by the neoliberal policies of the international financing institutions like the IMF and the World Bank, brought in changes in the health sector like cut backs in health spending, reduction of public spending, more private financing, more focus on cost-effectiveness analysis, development of 'essential packages' for health care, contracting out of services, introduction of user fees, etc. These changes were set into motion through the promotion of free-trade and free-market policies. Neoliberal trade agreements have reduced the livelihoods and ability to access food, clean water, sanitation, decent housing, quality education and a healthy working environment for many in the developing world. Since women tend to be economically more disadvantaged than men, they also tend to suffer more from the impact of the health sector reforms and the dominant market. The recent health sector reforms have resulted in a gross-marginalisation of the poor especially in the developing countries whose access to health care facilities have been greatly diminished. Surveys have found that widespread introduction of user fees, cost recovery schemes and privatisation of health care services have kept the poor away from hospitals and health centres (Sagar and Qadeer, 2003). It has resulted in the rise of women's poverty and ill health.

A large proportion of maternal and infant deaths in developing countries are due to very little or no accessibility of health services, dilapidated general health service system, under nutrition, anaemia and communicable diseases, food, poverty and inequity. The data on Infant Mortality Rate (IMR) shows stagnation in the rate of its decline over the '90s. Though no national statistics on time trends is available for MMR for the '90s, the aggressive Family Welfare Programme has affected lives negatively for many whose case reports have been recorded (Health-Watch, UP-Bihar, 2002).

- Chutki Devi of Barabanki district went to a health centre for an abortion. She was instructed to take pills and was told that the pregnancy was still in an early phase, so the abortion would be safe. After two days of taking the pills, she developed severe abdominal pain and died on her way to the health centre. The doctor at the district hospital said that she was four months pregnant and should not have undergone abortion.
- Leelawati, 29 years, went to her district hospital at Kushinagar for sterilisation. She died immediately after surgery, and the family was refused a death certificate.
- Dhokia had her abortion and then a tubectomy at the Manikpur government hospital. Just after the operation, she was thrown out by the doctor and the nurse and also badly beaten as she was complaining. Her stitches became septic and she had to spend Rs. 1500 for treatment.

Hence, any amount of the supply of contraceptives cannot compensate for the ill health among women.

In this respect, the Cairo Programme of Action, though mentions the reproductive rights of women, did so within the neoliberal market-oriented policies that had already widened income disparities and mortality and morbidity gaps between countries and within them (Qadeer, 2005). The only thing that the free market did was to take over our vertical health programmes that were managed through technological intervention and controlled by the [global] public-private partnerships. These interventions considered technological input as the solution to any health problem. Thus, the extremely important determinants of health, like access to water, food, housing, wages, employment, etc., were side-tracked. This over emphasis on techno-centric health interventions was due to the global politics, wherein through trade agreements and free markets, a huge market has been created in the developing countries for the powerful market forces to dump their technology. Hence, the advocates of reducing maternal mortality claim that managing emergency obstetric care is the most befitting way of reducing MMR (Qadeer, 2005). Incidentally, these same advocates run the global markets. It is not only in the field of maternal mortality but also for other diseases that such technology-driven interventions are being pushed forward even though their success is very limited. Interventions for diseases like polio, malaria, HIV/AIDS and tuberculosis have a very narrow techno-centric approach. In order to establish the legitimacy of the techno-centric programmes, concepts of 'perfect markets' have been used. This market seems to have a solution to any health problems irrespective of its applicability to 'health markets' of the developing countries (Qadeer, 2005).

ICPD and MDGs

The 1994 UN International Conference on Population and Development (ICPD), Cairo was considered as a leap forward and a paradigm shift in the discourse on population and development (UNPF, 1996). It has been projected to be a comprehensive international policy document promoting the concept of reproductive rights and reproductive health. According to ICPD programme recommendation, women's fertility will not drop till children survive well beyond their infancy and childhood as well as men take up their responsibility for contraception and women have social and political rights concluding that the policy was a highly "rights-based" one. However, it has been seen, that even after a decade have passed, the maternal mortality worldwide remains high. It is indicative of the fact that women still do not have social, political and cultural rights along with an access to comprehensive health services to help reduce their mortality. Even before the 1994 Cairo conference, influential policy-makers such as the World Bank had advocated for changes in the role of the government in financing, providing and regulating health services, etc. Advocating public health expenditure cuts, all they were doing was to create a "free market" in the health care sector. The World Bank's 1993 World Development Report, "*Investing in Health*" proposed that the public-sector should provide essential services only in the form of "clinical packages" and the rest of the services should be opened up for the market (UN Millennium Project, 2005). The intention of the World Bank was very clear. Through its narrowly defined packaged health services which were solely technology-driven, it conveniently sidelined the recognition of "Health for All", a declaration made at Alma-Ata in 1978.

The Cairo programme of action in a way consented with the World Bank approach (Nair *et al*, 2005). While accepting the neoliberal economic approach, which by itself was a detrimental factor to the "rights-based" agenda, the programme urged countries to introduce user fees in health services and social marketing schemes aimed at distributing contraceptives. It also encouraged governments to set-up private sector in health services and in the production and distribution of family planning commodities and contraceptives. In a way, this was actually supplementing those putting greater emphasis on only family planning services. There was a clear tone of neo-Malthusianism in the way sexual and reproductive health and rights was being discussed (Hartmann, 2005). Therefore, it is not surprising that various women organisations differed in their opinions regarding the ways in which women and sexual rights agenda were put forth in the conference. There was a clear divide between the Northern feminist groups who argued for a certain limited definition of "women's rights" while strengthening the neoliberal hold on the South and the Southern feminist group who were undermining those "women's rights" and battling against the Northern economic control (Hartmann, 2005). Despite its shortfalls, the 1994 ICPD of action did create a framework for the universal realisation of reproductive and sexual health and rights. Governments were asked to reject coercive measures regarding population control in favour of a new approach that was aimed at meeting the needs of individual woman to access a range of reproductive health services.

At a time when the political climate is harsh and bargains made especially for women are stringent, it was hoped that the gains made were laudable enough. The Cairo conference was centred on the gradual consolidation of the idea that human rights are central to the development discourse (Correa, 2005). There has been a positive shift at the conceptual level regarding reproductive health, which has been talked about keeping the "rights" agenda at the centre. This conceptual shift in the understanding of reproductive health around human rights agenda allowed for a much stronger political platform at the conference. However, one is reminded that the "rights" agenda is not a uniform one. Within governments and other women's organisations, there has been a dichotomy and confusion of agendas. Whereas the North stressed more on personal autonomy where the time was ripe for raising issues on personal choice of contraceptives, right over own body, abortion, etc., the Southern women's struggle was more focused on wages, labour rights, etc.

Therefore, debates revolving around the "rights" agenda among different women's groups, especially among those in the North and the South, had very different implications, which cannot be generalized as such. Together with this, the ICPD while concentrating on the "rights" based approach converted issues of women's health into isolated issues of "safe abortion" and "reproductive rights" and therefore undermined the holistic concept of women's health, which got translated into selective vertical programmes like reproductive child health (RCH) and family planning. Thus, the epidemiological basis for reproductive health has never really been cared for. Neither has it been realised why certain sections of women have remained silent over their reproductive health problems (Qadeer, 2005). It has been a continuous deprivation from their land rights, freedom from atrocities, food security, security system, minimum wages and communal harmony that have made these women silent on their reproductive health needs. In this restricted concept of reproductive health and rights, if one tries to perceive the conceptualisation of the MDGs, one realises how the latter even fails to live up to the narrow rights-based approach towards reproductive health of women, both conceptually and strategically.

Maternal Mortality Goal of MDGs

Maternal mortality has been considered to be one of the important indicators of a country's development, besides Infant Mortality Rate (IMR). However, progress in this indicator remains painfully low among many developing countries. It is estimated that each year, some eight million women suffer pregnancy-related complications and over 5 lakh women die, with 99% of these maternal deaths taking place in developing nations, mainly in sub-Saharan Africa and South Asia (WHO, 2003). There has also been a sharp contrast between the MMR of developed countries and that of developing countries. For example, in developing countries, one woman in 16 is at the risk of dying of pregnancy related complications, whereas in developed countries the risk is one woman in 2800 (WHO, 2003).

One of the MDGs' aims is to improve maternal health, with a target of reducing maternal mortality ratio by three quarters between 1990 and 2005. The goal is aimed at addressing the problems associated with reproductive health, safe motherhood and family planning.

Goal 5	*Targets*	*Indicators*
Improve maternal health	Reduce by ¾, between 1990 and 2015, the maternal mortality ratio	Maternal Mortality Ratios Proportion of births attended by skilled health personnel

Maternal mortality is justified as a MDG goal as proposed by the World Bank. According to the World Bank, there are precisely, three rationales for investing in maternal health (WHO, 2001). In line with that of the Commission for Macroeconomics and Health, it is assumed that death or illness among women in the reproductive age group has serious implications for a country's productive capacity, labour supply and economic well-being which in turn translate into economic loss and hardships at her family level. Poor maternal health, frequent and early pregnancies and the diseases associated with it contributes to her poverty. The second rationale given by the World Bank, for investment in maternal health is that now, since women's well-being is considered as an end in itself, deaths and illnesses associated with pregnancy and childbirth should be avoided as it undermines the human rights and social justice dimensions to it. The third rationale provided is that since a woman's health adversely affects that of the child (especially new-born), therefore, the survival of the child depends to a large extent on the maternal health. Poor nutritional status of pregnant women contributes to low birth weights among children. Apart from this, since women are care-givers in the family and especially for children, their death leaves the children in a more critical condition. Thus, investing in maternal health (or is it only preventing maternal deaths?) has been justified in these ways and the appropriate intervention tactics have also been evolved with time. Maternal deaths have been projected to be mostly due to obstetric complications and therefore strategies to combat it have been prioritized on skilled delivery care and management of complications to save women's lives. Skilled delivery care and management of complications have been tackled through technical interventions that include emergency obstetric care, skilled attendance, and management of unsafe abortions, focused antenatal care and family planning services (WHO, 2001). Thus, it is quite evident from the above that the underlying assumption is that maternal mortality can be achieved by neat technical operational strategies. As a consequence, maternal health has been picked out as an MDG goal in isolation from its roots, which lies in the socio-economic and political conditions of women in specific geographical areas apart from the health care services that they can access and placed in a highly medicalized environment where it is posed that it can be intervened best through technology.

The conceptualisation of the formation of the maternal health goal has deeper flaws in it than a mere concentration of technology. At the very outset, it has to be remembered that the MDGs have been formulated and implemented in the context of the structural adjustment programme (Qadeer, 2001). The MDGs seek to address poverty and other development goals in the context of intensified trade liberalisation. Women and men are located differently with respect to key economic and social resources like education, land and technology as well as their access to and their voice in the decision-making process (Qadeer, 2001). These asymmetries in gender go against the long-term social and economic empowerment of women in relation to men. Trade agreements at global level fail to critically examine the gender gaps and the consequent underpinning of trade and development (Williams, 2003). MDGs as a process, fails to critique the current multilateral trade regimes that undermine women's negotiation power within the trading system. Though the MDGs through millennium declaration affirms that a development agenda for economic and social goals cannot be separated from that of promotion and protection of human rights and gender equality, nevertheless, the highly technical approach aimed at economic growth to eradicate poverty does prove otherwise.

Reduction of hunger, improving of housing and health are mentioned without actually outlining a strategy to provide those. Their absence is often explained by the lack of rights and capabilities among the poor, thus diverting the issue of stratification, control over resources and power. Root issues like change that come about through transformation in power relations (specially economic and social) are never addressed within the MDGs. Rather a mere technical solution devoid of any alliances of power or politics makes the goal hardly impressive. It also explains why there is so much resistance in the area of gender equality as political commitment to change the power relations remains very difficult to attain (Antrobus, 2003). In this respect MDG-3, which refers to the promotion of equality and empowerment of woman as development goal, at the surface, seem, to address a range of social issues like income, health, education and environmental sustainability, all of which is within a framework of gender equality. However, a critical analysis of the goal shows a clear division between political and civil rights with that of economic and social rights (Antrobus, 2003). The indivisibility approach of this goal is clearly a detrimental factor for the achievement of gender equality and discrimination against women. The capacity of a women worker to enjoy her freedom to work, to earn an equal pay, to organise and be an active member in a worker's organisation, is governed and restricted by the roles and obligations that she needs to play within her family and community. Her social expectations to fulfil her role as a wife, housewife and mother with the cultural sanctions that impose restrictions on her mobility and ability to interact on equal terms with her male colleague in public spaces are detrimental to enhancing her capacity to become a leader in the worker's movement.

Empowering women in any one of the above areas without recognising the inter-linkages with others will hardly make a difference to the empowerment-related goal of the MDG. Hence, a lot of feminist groups have rightly critiqued that in an ever expanding era of privatisation and cuts in subsidies in the social sector together with a patriarchal model of maintaining power relations in the society, it is rather ironical that goals relating to universal primary education, maternal health and even child health are being placed in the context of women's empowerment (Williams, 2003). It only leaves us wondering about the kind of narrow definition of empowerment that is being achieved through this process. Even within the goal of empowerment, MDG-3 targets set to achieve the goal along with its indicator prove insufficient. In the absence of factors like access to and control of land, equality before the law, security against incidence of domestic violence and physical and sexual harassment and access to health and health services, the mere term "empowerment of women" remains only an ornamental one.

Another area in gender equity where the MDGs have fallen short surrounds the exclusion of internationally accepted ideas of reproductive rights acclaimed at ICPD. Though narrowly conceived at the ICPD, sexual and reproductive health is totally absent from the MDGs. Despite a widespread international recognition as well as efforts from governments, neither the MDGs nor their associated targets and indicators include specific mention of reproductive and sexual health and rights. A mere goal of maternal mortality without a mention of reproductive and sexual rights can be viewed as restricting and reducing the right to health of women as well as placing it within a purely biological role (Qadeer, 2005). This specific exclusion of the goal of women's sexual and reproductive rights reflects the power of certain regressive groups surrounding the ICPD conference that continued to gain strength in the context of the ongoing economic struggle of Southern feminist groups against the spread of neoliberalism. This together with the backlash against women's rights accounts for the spread of economic control through the WTO enforced trade agenda (Antrobus, 2003).

A focus on the targets to improve maternal health as a goal of MDG reveals that it depends on a technical base, which is highly individualised in its approach (Abeyesekera, 2000). Thus, the conceptualisation of maternal health and its causes is devoid of any social and structural complexities of the problem. Higher level of maternal mortality in developing countries have a far more complex inter linkages with its socio-economic and cultural dimensions than are portrayed through the MDGs which seems to pose the problem as that of typically medicalised one and therefore having interventions to control the situation medically. To further justify their point, for persisting with a narrow techno-centric approach towards maternal mortality, experience of China, Sri Lanka and even Kerala within India are cited where it is argued that levels of maternal mortality have diminished even where poverty levels are high (Qadeer, 2005). However, what arguments like this steer clearly away from is that though pure obstetric causes can be tackled through emergency obstetric management and an improved antenatal care, long-term results can only be obtained if the problem of maternal mortality is handled through economic, caste, religious, racial and gender inequality that perpetuates ill health among young girls and women (Sagar, 2002). A mere technical approach only suggests how the MDGs tries to simplify the complex phenomenon while trying to bring changes in the level of maternal mortality without addressing the need to have structural changes in the society. Whatever interventions have been called for at the social level, including legislation, family planning services, child care, improved access to health services for only some selected diseases and prevention of unsafe abortion does not take into account women's position in her family and society, her bargaining power *vis-à-vis* the men in the family and the social and cultural norms with which she is tied down to her family. There is also no mention about legislation pertaining to women's right to property, minimum wages as well as employment guarantee (Qadeer, 2005).Thus, the approach of MDG towards maternal mortality has been a fragmented and fractured one.

Before we discuss the larger context of maternal health, the issues within maternal mortality need to be understood. Maternal mortality constitutes around 12% of the female deaths in the reproductive age group. In addition, around 35% mortality in women of the reproductive age group and 40-42% of deaths in girls under 14 years of age are due to infectious diseases with around 4-6% girls dying due to anaemia. It is evident from the above that maternal mortality constitutes a small proportion of deaths even within the reproductive age group, not to talk of women in the other age groups. Thus, the goal of maternal mortality in the MDGs actually narrows down the understanding of deaths among women in general (Qadeer, 2005).

Causes such as haemorrhage, sepsis and unsafe abortion though having a medical side to it, are rooted deeply in the social context of women (Qadeer, 2005). The lack of care and support that women receive in patriarchal societies as well as their poverty-ridden conditions are the contributing factors for the deaths. Post-partum haemorrhage is said to be caused by the high prevalence of anaemia among women with poor nutrition, which is again due to their secondary status within their family that restricts their access to food. Post-partum infections are also a product of lack of care and poverty. Similarly, social norms forces unwed mothers to take recourse to unsafe abortions. On the other hand, abortions are also promoted as a means for family planning without ensuring adequate services (Abeyesekera, 2000).

Most young girls have critical morbid conditions that contribute to their mortality in their reproductive lives. Anaemia, malnutrition and infections are common among young girls in developing countries (Sagar, 2002). The MDG-5 seems to bypass this social context and limits itself to strategies to detect high-risk pregnancies or emergency maternal care. While not denying the fact that these interventions may be necessary as an overall strategy to curb mortality, it becomes highly questionable when these become the only strategies to reduce mortality. The uncritical acceptance of these strategies confirm the fact that the international powers as well as the domestic ones are not interested in addressing structural changes or power imbalances. They are rather providing for the so-called feasible strategies within their domain of power. It is a clear case of the strategies being pushed in isolation without bothering to realise whether these have a long-term impact on the development of people, especially when maternal mortality is an outcome of poor general health of women and socio-economic constraints. There is definitely an inadequate conceptualisation of the problem of maternal mortality as well as the legitimisation of a partially effective biomedical approach to it.

Concluding Remarks

The prevalence of high maternal mortality has been time and again found to be due to poor infrastructure along with lack of attention given to women in general themselves affecting their nutrition, access to services and particularly their requirements during the pregnancy. Therefore, if we look into the history of maternal mortality, countries with integrated health systems have fared much better in terms of mortality rates than those who treat health systems and health problems including Maternal Mortality Rate (MMR) in an isolated manner. The holistic understanding of women's health has been obliterated amidst all these developments, completely undermining the socio-cultural and economic factors along with power relations, which are so important in determining women's health. Addressing maternal mortality calls for a socially sensitive developmental strategy that recognises women's role in production. Maternal mortality needs to be addressed as part of women's overall health, which in turn is determined by her social and economic location. Thus, a much more comprehensive strategy will be a strong primary health care along with necessary welfare services, employment, minimum wages and food security. It will not only help in reducing extreme poverty and hunger, but will also address the very cause of the determinants of all mortality including that of maternal mortality.

References

Abeyesekera, Sunila (2000), "*Development and Women's Human Rights, Economic, Social and Cultural Rights, Section 3, Module*", International Human Rights Internship Programme and Forum Asia. *www.mdgender.net*

Antrobus, Peggy (2003), "MDGs—The Most Distracting Gimmick" in Contextualizing the MDGs *www.mdgender.net*

Correa, Sonia (2005), "Holding Ground: The challenges for sexual and reproductive rights and health: In dialogue with Sonia Correa", in *Development, Society for International Development*, Vol. 48(4), pp. 11-15.

Dhingra, Saroj (2001), *Women Doctors, Professionalism, Policies and the Emergence of Maternal Health Services in 19th Century India*; Ph.D. thesis, CSMCH (SSS), New Delhi.

Ministry of Health (1946), *Report of the Health Survey and Development Committee*, Government of India, New Delhi.

Planning Commission (1961), *Third Five Year Plan*, Government of India, New

Delhi.

Ministry of Health and Family Welfare (1983), *National Health Policy*, Government of India, New Delhi.

Planning Commission (1978), *Draft Five Year Plan*, 1978-83, Government of India, New Delhi.

Hartmann Betsy (2005), "Refuting Security Demographics: In Dialogue with Betsy Hartmann", *Development, Society for International Development*, Vol. 48(4), pp. 16-20.

Jhirad, J. (1959), "Survey of Trends in Maternal Mortality during the Past 20 Years", *Calcutta Medical Journal*, Vol. 56 (1), p. 59.

Nair, Sumati, and Preeti Kirbat, Sara Sexton (2005), "Population Politics and Women's Health in a Free Market Economy", *Development, Society for International Development*, Vol. 48 (4), pp. 43-51.

National Planning Committee (1948), *Sokhey Committee Report: Sub-Committee of the Indian National Congress*, Bombay.

Qadeer, Imrana (1998), "Our Historical Legacy in MCH Programmes" in Krishnaraj Maithreyi, Ratna M. Sudarshan, and Abusaleh Sheriff (eds.); *Gender, Population and Development*, Delhi, Oxford University Press, pp. 267-90.

Qadeer, Imrana (1998), "Reproductive Health; A Public Health Perspective," *Economic and Political Weekly*, pp. 2675-84.

Qadeer, Imrana (2001), "A Public Health Perspective for Reproductive Health of Women", *Focus*, Vol. IX.

Qadeer, Imrana (2002), "Women's Health Policies and Programmes: A Critical Review" in (eds.) Renu Khanna, Mira Shiva, and Sarala Gopalan, *Towards Comprehensive Women's Health Programmes and Policy* (SAHAJ), New Delhi.

Qadeer, Imrana (2005), "Maternal Mortality in South-East Asia", *Development, Society for International Development*, Vol. 48(4), pp.120-26.

Rao, Mohan (1994), "An Imagined Reality: Malthusianism, Neo-Malthusianism and Population Myth", *Economic and Political Weekly*, Vol. 29 (5), p. 40.

Sagar, Alpana (2002), "The Reproductive Health Package—A Chimera for Women's Health" in Renu Khanna, Mira Shiva, Sarala Gopalan (eds), *Towards Comprehensive Women's Health Programmes and Policy*, (SAHAT), New Delhi.

Sagar, A. and Imrana Qadeer (2003), 'Health', *Alternative Economic Survey*, Rainbow Publishers, Delhi, p.194.

Soman, Krishna (1994), "Trends in Maternal Mortality", *Economic and Political Weekly*, 29 (44), pp. 2859-60.

UN Millennium Project (2005), "*Investing in Development: A Practical Plan to Achieve the Millennium Development Goals*", New York.

United Nations Population Fund (1996), '*Programme of Action Adopted at the International Conference on Population and Development, Cairo, 5-13 September, 1994*'; New York, United Nations.

WHO (2001), "*Macroeconomics and Health: Investing in Health for Economic Development*, Report of the Commission on Macroeconomics and Health, Geneva.

WHO (2003), *Shaping the Future: The World Health Report*, Geneva.

Williams, Mariama (2003), "The MDGs in the Context of Gender and Trade" in *Emerging Perspectives and Approaches to Gender and Trade*, Centerfocus, Center of Concern, Washington, D.C.

Disaster, Gender and Vulnerability: A Review

Shishir Kumar Yadav and Sonal Pandey

Introduction

The vulnerability of any physical, structural or socio-economic systems to a natural hazard is its probability of being damaged, destroyed or lost (Birkmann, 2008; Pappenberger, Beven, Frodhsam, Romanowicz, and Matgen, 2007; Pistrika and Tsakiris, 2007; Dixit, 2003). Vulnerability, in the disaster context, is a person's or group's "capacity to anticipate, cope with, resist, and recover from the impact of a natural hazard" (Blaikie *et al.*, 1994 as cited in (McEntire, 2006; Pomeroy, Ratner, Hall, Pimoljinda, and Vivekanandan, 2006; Fothergill and Peek, 2004)). Vulnerability, as defined by inadequate capability, is linked to a specific group(s) of people or population. These people are perceived as vulnerable and thus it is difficult to protect them from a disaster. The degree of vulnerability is defined by factors such as: socio-economic status, differences in wealth, occupation, caste, ethnicity, gender, disability, health status, age, immigration status (legal or illegal), the nature and extent of social networks, and so on (Fothergill and Peek, 2004; Wisner, Blaikie, Cannon, and Davis, 1994). Vulnerable populations are more affected by the same disaster when compared to non-vulnerable populations. Moreover, among vulnerable population, the impacts of disasters vary depending on how vulnerable a person is.

For example, a person who is old, disabled, a single-mother, being an immigrant, and living in hazard prone areas will be more affected by a disaster than one who is only poor, or disabled, or being an immigrant, or old, or being a single-mother, or a non-vulnerable person who lives in hazard prone areas. Thus, a person who possesses more than one or all characteristics of vulnerability would be more susceptible to and affected by a disaster than one who possesses only one or fewer characteristics of vulnerability (Buttenheim, 2006).

The dominant theoretical perspectives, research strategies, and guiding questions in disaster social sciences are determinedly male oriented if not male dominated (Enarson and Meyreles, International Perspectives on Gender and Disaster: Differences and Possibilities, 2004). The popular disaster discourses present the 'victims' as a univariate category thus downplaying the role of social constructs such as caste, class or gender in aggravating the vulnerability to disasters better known as 'social vulnerability'. It is evident that disaster does not have an equal bearing on men and women instead women who have been invariably marginalised in the global domain are the worst sufferer during calamities. While, females are specifically prone to heightened risk to disasters, yet their voices are marginalised in the popular discourses. Regrettably, there is a particular lack of gender data specific victim information universally across the globe.

The present study attempts to explore the major factors leading to the vulnerability of the women to disasters.

Theoretical Framework for the Study

The structural paradigm perspective in disaster research asserts, disasters are "a products of a nature/society interface which intensify daily economic and social living problems" (Myers, 2005). According to this paradigm, pre-disaster social cultural configuration is an important predictor of post disaster hazards. Also, Tierney (2006) states, "Groups are differentially vulnerable ... in the face of disasters, depending upon their position in the stratification system" (Myers, 2005). This perspective is analogous to the Environmental Possibilism. There are no really generalised opportunities, and risks in nature, but instead there are sets of unequal access to opportunities unequal exposure to risks which are consequence of the socio-economic system (Hussain, 2004; Morrow, 1991). An important approach encompassed by the structural paradigm is the vulnerability approach, which focuses on the spatial dimensions of social and economic stratification in relation to disasters known as the 'social vulnerability approach' (Wiest,

Mocellin, and Motsisi, 1994). 'Social vulnerability' means complex set of characteristics that include initial well-being, livelihood resilience, social protection, and self-protection, social and political networks, and institutions (Cannon, 2001). The social vulnerability relates to differences in gender, age, social position, incomes, and many other potential factors that determine the ability to cope with adverse impact (Cutter, Boruff, and Shirley, 2003). It has been found that poor and impoverished and marginalised social groups, and individuals are more "at risk" in the wake of natural disasters (Wisner, Blaikie, Cannon, and Davis, 1994). Socio-economically disadvantaged or marginalised groups, including women, the elderly, racial/ethnic minorities, the poor, and those with lower levels of educational attainment, are often disproportionately affected by disasters.

Gender refers to "socially constructed roles and relationships, personality traits, attitudes, behaviours, values, relative power and influence that society ascribes to the two sexes on a differential basis" (Glossary of Gender Related Terms and Concept). According to the 'Social Vulnerability Approach' disaster does not create specific vulnerability for women but exacerbate the pre-existing gender inequality. Gender inequalities with respect to human rights, political and economic status, land ownership, housing conditions, exposure to violence, education and health, make women more vulnerable before, during and after disasters. Gender-biased attitudes and stereotypes can complicate and extend the time for women's recovery post disaster. Women's vulnerability to the impact of disasters is also increased by socially determined differences in roles and responsibilities of women and men and inequalities between them in access to resources and decision-making power (Gender and Health in Disaster, 2002). With the disruption of established male-dominated social control mechanisms, women and their children are the first to be neglected and/or abused. Women encounter strong institutional barriers to organisational efforts. Women are less likely to organise, either out of seclusion, lack of education, or outright threat.

Further, all women are not universally or identically impacted by disasters (Enarson, Gender Issues in Natural Disatsers: Talking Points and Research Needs, 2000). Adolescents, pregnant women, lactating mothers, the disabled, and the aged make up particularly vulnerable groups in emergencies (Hare, 2001). Further, the degrees of vulnerability among women in emergencies also differ considerably. For example, disabled, elder pregnant and lactating women and widows often require assistance on a longer-term while other women can be supported up to the point where they achieve food and economic self-sufficiency (Hare, 2001; Wiest, Mocellin, and Motsisi, 1994).

Results and Discussion

Universally, women and children are the most vulnerable in disaster situation (Flood Impact on Health and Hygiene of Rural Areas: Migration Options, 2004), as the afflicted world in which we live is characterised by deeply unequal sharing of the burden of adversities between women and men. Sprawling inequalities persist in their access to education, health care, physical and financial resources and opportunities in the political, economic, social, and cultural spheres (The Status of Women: A Reality Check, 2011). The "vulnerability of women" should be understood to be primarily cultural and organisational rather than biological or physiological (Hare, 2001; Wiest, Mocellin, and Motsisi, 1994). Further, all women are not universally or identically impacted by disasters (Enarson, Gender Issues in Natural Disatsers: Talking Points and Research Needs, 2000). Even amongst females, adolescents, pregnant women, single mothers, lactating mothers, the disabled, and the aged make up particularly vulnerable groups in emergencies (Khunwishit, 2007; Hare, 2001). The vulnerability of the women could be better discussed under the following heads:

Gender and Age

Throughout the world, women, children and elderly are disproportionately affected by disasters (Nelson, 2011; Flood Impact on Health and Hygiene of Rural Areas: Migration Options, 2004). Children are considered a high risk population in disasters and stress as because they are especially vulnerable to disruptions in their routines and settings, and they are dependent on adults' access to social institutions and the resources that sustain daily life. Gender discrimination in the allocation of resources, including those relating to nutrition and medicines, may put girls at greater risk than boys (Brody, Demetriades, and Esplen, 2008).

Bairagi (1986) reported that in rural Bangladesh the female children were more adversely affected by famine than were the boys (Neumayer and Plumper, 2007). Among children, boys are treated for illness more often than girls, and immunisation rates are higher for boys, indicating a relative neglect of girls' health needs (Hare, 2001). Also, males are favoured in the allocation of food within households, especially when it comes to diet quality (Neumayer and Plumper, 2007; Smith and

Bryon, 2005; Flood Impact on Health and Hygiene of Rural Areas: Migration Options, 2004). The increased household workload post-disaster has a direct toll on the girl's education, forcing many girls to drop-out of school to help with chores (Nelson, 2011; Brody, Demetriades, and Esplen, 2008). Many adolescent girls take on new responsibilities or share responsibilities with mothers and adolescent brothers (Flood impact on women and girls, 2002). A study in Cambodia (2002) reported older daughters often have to take on significantly increased responsibilities—usually from the mother or related to collection activities around the non-flooded or shallower parts of the village (fodder and firewood collection, small-scale fishing) (Flood impact on women and girls, 2002).

The life expectancy of women is usually longer than for men (Ollenburger and Tobin, 1998), which has an additive impact on the gendered vulnerability. Economics of aging place many women in extremely vulnerable positions that influences their abilities to cope with the unexpected consequences of a natural disasters. Half of all the elderly women living alone are officially classified as 'economically deprived' meaning thereby they are living on income at or below $9500 per annum (Neumayer and Plumper, 2007).

Elderly women are likely to be particularly vulnerable, especially in developing countries where resources are scant and social safety nets limited or non-existent (Brody, Demetriades, and Esplen, 2008). Elderly women may have heavy family and caring responsibilities which cause stress and fatigue while also preventing wider social and economic participation; and their incomes may be low because they can no longer take on paid work. They may also not understand their rights to access community and private sector services, such as local clinics. Even when they are aware of these services, even nominal amounts for clinic visits and drugs may not be affordable. Also, older women are more likely to suffer from health and mobility limitations, increasing their disaster vulnerability (Ollenburger and Tobin, 1998). Access is further restricted for older women living in rural areas, who are often unable to travel the long distances to the nearest health facility (Brody, Demetriades, and Esplen, 2008).

Gender and Class

Class is an economic concept; classes are not communities but exist where people share a specific component of their "life chances", especially as determined by their 'economic position' (Sharma, 1999 as cited in (Ray Bennett, 2009)). Class, in particular, plays a very important role in the creation of social inequality and it can make the influence of other sources of disparity (such as gender) much sharper (Sen, 2005 as cited in (Ray Bennett, 2009)). Class status is an important predictor of women's vulnerability to disasters (Enarson, Fothergill, and Peek, Gender and Disaster: Foundations and Directions, 2006; Neumayer and Plumper, 2007). Economically insecure, low-income and poor people are particularly vulnerable (Hubner, 2008; Neumayer and Plumper, 2007), and they are disproportionately women and their dependent children (Morrow, 1991). For instance, O'Hare (2001) found that the most vulnerable group affected by Hurricane 07B in the Godavari Delta in India was "migrant, scheduled (low) caste women" (Neumayer and Plumper, 2007). The poor women have low resilience to disasters as their pre-disaster impoverishment is further intensified (Enarson, Fothergill, and Peek, Gender and Disaster: Foundations and Directions, 2006). Poor women have difficult time recovering from disasters. They are also more likely than other women to depend on community-based services such as public transportation and health care, including crisis counseling and shelter from violence. Low income women also tend to live in housing that exposes them to harm, living more often than low income men in poorly maintained public housing, manufactured homes, and shelters and rental properties, and more often than men as low income single heads of household (Enarson, Fothergill, and Peek, Gender and Disaster: Foundations and Directions, 2006).

Gender and Economic Dependency

Women in developing counties have been called the 'invisible earners' (Wiest, Mocellin, and Motsisi, 1994). Women in comparison to men have restricted access to the formal and regulated labour market (Monzini, 2001). Women's productive work, particularly in child-rearing and other domestic work, as well as their enormous contribution to national food production requirements, is hidden in statistics (Chiu, 1982 as cited in (Wiest, Mocellin, and Motsisi, 1994)). Women are not only responsible for attending to the basic needs of their children and families, but also account significantly for productive and income-generating activities in their respective communities (Wiest, Mocellin, and Motsisi, 1994). This pre-disaster condition in many societies deny to women recognition for the work they actually carry out rendering them and their dependent children relatively more vulnerable than men (Hare, 2001).

The vulnerability of women stems from cultural, political, and economic conditions. Females generally have lower socio-economic status than males, and therefore, females are more sensitive to the possibility of resource loss (e.g., monetary loss) (Ho, Shaw, and Lin, 2005). Socio-cultural beliefs and practices often preclude women's ownership of land and other production technologies such as tractors or grinding mills (Wiest, Mocellin, and Motsisi, 1994). Statutory and/ or customary laws often restrict women's property and land rights and make it difficult for them to access credit and agricultural extension services (Brody, Demetriades, and Esplen, 2008). Low literacy coupled with very low levels of ownership of land and other productive assets makes women prone to destitution. Further, patrilocal residence, patrilineal descent, and the prohibition against women inheriting property tend to enforce the social norm that women are dependent on men from birth until death (Samarasinghe, 2008 as cited in (Locke, 2010)).

Gender and Women-headed Household

Woman-headed households are particularly vulnerable to disasters. The women-headed households refers a unit of residence or domestic consumption where the lead responsible individual is of women as bread earner (Chant, 1997). In these households, a woman is deemed responsible by members of the unit and by the community, and usually this person is the main income generator for the household. It consists of women with severely handicapped husbands and young children, handicapped women, widows, and young single women with no relatives.

Women-headed households are now an increasing phenomenon worldwide (Ray Bennett, 2009). Left as widows from disaster, abandoned by men in search of an alternative life, or forcefully separated in conflict—from a spouse induced disasters, women are more likely to remain behind in the disaster zones to attempt a reconstruction (Wiest, Mocellin, and Motsisi, 1994). Women-headed households may suffer from increased workloads and lack of access to resources where male household members out-migrate (Nelson, 2011), as women have to take on traditional male roles in disaster risk reduction (Neefjes *et al.*, 2009 as cited in (Nelson, 2011)). The post-disaster outmigration of males has an enormous impact in workloads both for those that migrate and crucially for those that remain behind and who have to take on responsibilities vacated by those that have migrated. In most families, these vacated responsibilities largely fall on the shoulders of mothers/ wives and adolescent daughters (Flood impact on women and girls, 2002). Further, women who become the primary breadwinners also have to play the socialising roles of both mother and father in providing material and emotional support to the children (Hare, 2001). Woman-headed households often have little control over resources (Nelson, 2011); have fewer resources to cope with and adapt to stresses of all kinds, and rely on more climate sensitive resources and livelihoods (Nelson, 2011) and the young dependent children of these households suffer disproportionately from malnutrition and from the added stress of prematurely having to contend with adult responsibilities (Hare, 2001). A study from Bangladesh reports instances of women in Bangladesh becoming destitute following a disaster as male relatives confiscated family land from a woman in the event of her husband's and son's deaths, leaving women and daughters poverty stricken and destitute. There were no legal provisions to protect women and their families against such problems (Gender and Health in Disaster, 2002).

Gender and Decision-making

One most striking common element between women in developing countries and those in disaster-prone areas is that of marginalisation due to lack of adequate decision-making power and control over resources (Taft, 1987 as cited in (Wiest, Mocellin, and Motsisi, 1994)). The social structure of most societies formally relegates women to inferiority and dependency, increasing their vulnerability through their disempowerment (Hare, 2001) in the household. Women are more likely than men to be absent from decision-making, whether in the household or at community, national or international levels—either because their contribution is not valued or because they do not have the time, confidence or resources to contribute (Brody, Demetriades, and Esplen, 2008). Major household decisions are the male prerogative and women generally have low decision-making power within households. This dependency is further aggravated during the emergency period, and the wife (or the females of the household) is (are) expected to take a supportive and submissive role. One study on a 1991 cyclone in Bangladesh noted that many women perished with their children at home as they had to wait for their husbands to return and make an evacuation decision (Gender and Health in Disaster, 2002). Women who are dependent on men in the household may also be kept in more passive 'victim' roles, with less of a voice in the recovery process in its male-gendered management structure. Also, low participation of women in planning and decision-making at the local, district and state levels is a considerable barrier to gender-sensitive disaster response, and results in insufficient attention to disaster-related violence (Gomez, 2006) in the communities.

Gender and Health

Disasters produce widespread psychological distress, physical health problems, and social disruptions among the general population (Pomeroy, Ratner, Hall, Pimoljinda, and Vivekanandan, 2006). Post-disaster mortality, morbidity, injury, and illness rates are often higher for girls and women (Neumayer and Plumper, 2007; Tunstall, Tapsell, Green, Floyd, and George, 2006; Enarson and Meyreles, International Perspectives on Gender and Disaster: Differences and Possibilities, 2004; Wiest, Mocellin, and Motsisi, 1994). According to a recent report from the World Conservation Union/Women's Environment and Development Organisation (IUCN/WEDO), women and children are 14 times more likely to die than men during disasters (IUCN/WEDO, 2007). Gender and age differentials in mortality rates were strikingly apparent in the aftermath of the Asian Tsunami where the largest numbers of fatalities were women and children under the age of 15 (Brody, Demetriades, and Esplen, 2008). Also, in an analysis of impacts of the flood, Del Niño and colleagues (2001), identified higher rates of stunting and wasting among flood exposed preschool children in and higher rates of chronic energy deficiency among flood exposed women in November 1998, two months after the flood waters receded (Buttenheim, 2006). Women are more generally responsible for water acquisition, and more often work with water in cooking and doing laundry. Consequently, they are at once more vulnerable to water-borne diseases, but are also transmitters of these diseases (Flood Impact on Health and Hygiene of Rural Areas: Migration Options, 2004; Wiest, Mocellin, and Motsisi, 1994). Also, being faced with the burden of caring for dependents while being obliged to travel further for water or firewood makes women and girls prone to stress-related illnesses and exhaustion (Brody, Demetriades, and Esplen, 2008).

Social taboos around menstruation and norms about appropriate behavior for women and girls are reported to contribute to health problems in young women in disaster situations (Gender and Health in Disaster, 2002). For example, during the 1998 floods in Bangladesh, adolescent girls reported perineal rashes and urinary tract infections because they were not able to wash out menstrual rags properly in private, often had no place to hang the rags to dry, or access to clean water. They reported wearing the still damp cloths, as they did not have a place to dry them (Gender and Health in Disaster, 2002). Further, women and girls are also more negatively affected by the often appalling health and hygienic conditions in refugee camps (Neumayer and Plumper, 2007). In addition, studies have also reported adverse reproductive out-comes following disasters, including early pregnancy loss, premature delivery, stillbirths, delivery-related complications and infertility (Gender and Health in Disaster, 2002). 24% of pregnant women exposed to isocyanides during the 1984 Bhopal explosion (India) had spontaneous abortions, as against 6% in a comparison group (Gender and Health in Disaster, 2002).

Further, women and girls also face barriers to accessing healthcare services due to a lack of economic assets to pay for healthcare, as well as cultural restrictions on their mobility which may prohibit them from travelling to seek healthcare (Brody, Demetriades, and Esplen, 2008).

Gender and Sexual abuse and Violence

There is increasing risk of emotional abuses and violence against women in the aftermath of disasters (Nelson, 2011; Enarson, Fothergill, and Peek, Gender and Disaster: Foundations and Directions, 2006; Karanci and Acarturk, 2005; Enarson, Gender Issues in Natural Disatsers: Talking Points and Research Needs, 2000), especially in low income countries. Following the 2004 Indian Ocean Tsunami, there were numerous media accounts of violence against women and sexual exploitation of girls (Nelson, 2011). Increasing instances of rape, abuse and social stigma have been reported in intermediate spaces like war camps and shelter camps formed during times of natural disasters (Neumayer and Plumper, 2007). A UNDP study (1994) reported girls are more vulnerable to sexual abuse and exploitation following disasters, especially displaced girls (Enarson, Fothergill, and Peek, Gender and Disaster: Foundations and Directions, 2006). The vulnerability to abuse and violence is aggravated in the aftermath of disasters, particularly when families have been displaced and are living in overcrowded emergency or transitional housing where they lack privacy. Disasters also increase the vulnerability of females to sex trafficking. Incidents have been reported of sale and purchase of females in the disaster affected areas where people sell their girls in exchange of cash and kinds (Nelson, 2011; Hameeda, Hlatshwayo, Tanner, Turker, and Yang, 2010; Sahara Group, 2004).

Gender and Social Support

Social support refers to social interactions that provide individuals with actual assistance and embed them into a web of social relationships perceived to be loving, caring, and readily available in times of need (Norris, Baker, Murphy, and Kaniasty, 2005). Gender had both main and interactive effects on post-disaster social support (Gender and

Health in Disaster, 2002), with women perceiving less social support and embeddedness than men, especially with regard to friend support (Norris, Baker, Murphy, and Kaniasty, 2005). Also, Bolin and Stanford (1999) suggested that women are particularly vulnerable to the effects of disaster because of their care giving roles and relative lack of power and status, and Hoffman (1999) argued that women tend to lose conflicts over scarce resources. These factors may have also contributed to women's lower levels of perceived social support (Norris, Baker, Murphy, and Kaniasty, 2005).

Summary and Conclusion

Women are particularly vulnerable to disasters across the globe. Women and girls' particular vulnerability is due to a combination of factors, such as economic dependency and lack of adequate financial resources, illiteracy, discriminatory cultural and social attitudes, physical infirmity, and so on. Women's and men's differential access to social and physical goods or resources is one of the key dimensions of gender inequality which is an important predictor of post-disaster vulnerability of the females. Gender inequality is a major factor contributing to the increased vulnerability of women and girls in disaster situations, which is further intensified in the aftermath of disasters.

Also, women continue to be discriminated in post-disaster relief and welfare programmes due to a gender bias in donor agencies and governments. Cultural norms have been found to inhibit women from visibly accessing relief centres, or they cannot leave their homes to go to relief centres due to child care responsibilities. Moreover, administrative gender bias has been particularly noteworthy in the context of refugee populations, and women have been openly discriminated against in the process of decision-making in assistance during the relief and reconstruction phases associated with disasters. Thus, there is an urgent need to reorient disaster prevention and mitigation policies. 'Gender' must be integrated into the disaster prevention and mitigation policies. A gender perspective should be integrated into all disaster risk management policies, plans and decision-making processes, including those related to risk assessment, early warning, information management, and education and training.

References

Birkmann, D.-I.J. (2008), "Approaches to Flood Vulnerability Assessment", *Guidelines for Flood Mapping*, United Nations University.

Brody, A., Demetriades, J., and Esplen, E. (2008), "Gender and climate change: mapping the linkages", A scoping study on knowledge and gaps, *Draft*,

London, Brighton, United Kingdom: Institute of Development Studies.

Buttenheim, A. (2006), "Flood Exposure and Child Health in Bangladesh", *Online Working Paper Series,* California, USA: California Centre for Population Research.

Cançado, V., Brasil, L., Nascimento, N., and Guerra, A. (2008), "Flood risk assessment in an urban area: Measuring hazard and Vulnerability", *11th International Conference on Urban Drainage,* Edinburgh, Scotland, UK.

Cannon, T. (2001), "Vulnerability Analysis and Disasters", In D.J. Parker (Ed.), *Floods,* London: Routledge.

Chant, S. (1997), "Gender Aspects of Urban Economic Growth and Development", *UN World Institute for Development Economics Research Working Paper No. 137,* Helinski, Finland: United Nations Organisation.

Cutter, S.L., Boruff, B.J., and Shirley, W.L. (2003), "Social Vulnerability to Environmental Hazards", *Social Science Quarterly,* 84 (2), 242-61.

Dixit, A. (2003), "Floods and Vulnerability: Need to Rethink Flood Management", *Natural Hazards,* 28, 155-79.

Enarson, E. (2000), "Gender Issues in Natural Disatsers: Talking Points and Research Needs", *ILO Infocus Programme on Crisis Response and Reconstruction Workshop,* Geneva, Switzerland, Europe: International Labour Organisation.

Enarson, E., and Meyreles, L. (2004), "International Perspectives on Gender and Disaster: Differences and Possibilities", *The International Journal of Sociology and Social Policy, 24* (10/11), 49-93.

Enarson, E., Fothergill, A., and Peek, L. (2006), "Gender and Disaster: Foundations and Directions", In H. Rodriguez, E.L. Quarantelli, and R. Dynes (Eds.), *Handbook of Disaster Research,* New York, Washington, USA: Springer Publishing, pp. 130-146.

Flood Impact on Health and Hygiene of Rural Areas: Migration Options (2004), Dhaka, Bangladesh: Ministry of Health and Family Welfare.

____(2002). *Flood impact on women and girls.* Cambodia: Care International.

Fothergill, A., and Peek, L.A. (2004), "Poverty and Disasters in the United States: A Review of Recent Sociological Findings", *Natural Hazards , 32,* 89-11.

Gender and Health in Disaster (2002), *Gender and Health,* Appia, Geneva, Switzerland: World Health Organisation.

Glossary of Gender Related Terms and Concept (n.d.), Retrieved May 12, 2012, from UN International Research and Training Institute for the Adavncement of Women: http://www.google.co.in/url?sa=tandrct=jandq=andesrc=sandsource =webandcd=2andved=0CFcQFjABandurl=http%3A%2F%2Funamid.unmissions. org%2FPortals%2FUNAMID%2FUNAMID%2520at%2520Work%2FGlossary %2520of%2520Gender-related%2520Terms% 2520 and %2520Concepts. docandei=XTrCT7TbJ8KJrAfHk5

Gomez, S. (2006), *Guidelines for Gender Sensitive Disaster Management,* Chian Mai: Asia Pacific Forum on Women, Law and Development (APWLD).

Hameeda, S., Hlatshwayo, S., Tanner, E., Turker, M., and Yang, J. (2010), *Human Trafficking in India: Dynamic, Current Efforts, and Intervention Opportunities for the Asia Foundation,* International Policy Studies, Stanford University.

Hare, G.O. (2001), "Hurricane 07B in the Godavari Delta, Andhra Pradesh, India: vulnerability, mitigation and the spatial impact", *The Geographical Journal, 167* (1), 23-28.

Ho, M.C., Shaw, D., and Lin, S. (2005), *Risk Perception of Flood and Landslide Victims in Taiwan,* Retrieved May 6, 2012, from www.iiasa.ac.at/Research/RMS/dpri2005/Papers/MingchouHo.pdf

Hubner, K. (2008), "Natural Disasters: Sudden Impact, Permanent Consequences on Income Inequality?", *2008 Pacific Development Conference JEL Classifications: O15, Q54, D39.*

Hussain, M. (2004), *Human Geography,* New Delhi: Rawat Publications.

Karanci, N.A., and Acarturk (2005), "Post-Traumatic Growth among Marmara Earthquake Survivors Involved in Disaster Preparedness as Volunteers", *Traumatology, 11* (4), 307-23.

Khunwishit, S. (2007), *Increasing Vulnerable Populations: Implications for Disaster Response in the U.S. Texas,* USA: University of North Texas.

Locke, R.A. (2010), Rescued, Rehabilitated, Returned: Institutional Approaches to the Rehabilitation of Survivors of Sex Trafficking in India and Nepal. Denver: University of Denver.

McEntire, D.A. (2006), "The Importance of Multi and Interdisciplinary Research on Disaster for Emergency Management", In *Disciplines, Disasters and Emergency Management: The Convergence and Divergence of Concepts, Issues and Trends from the Research Literature.*

Monzini, P. (2001), "Trafficking in Women and Girls and the Involvement of Organised Crime, with reference to the situation in Central and Eastern Europe", *First Annual Conference of the European Society of Criminology,* Lausanne, Switzerland.

Morrow, B.H. (1991), "Identifying and Community Vulnerability", *Disasters, 23* (1), 1-18.

Myers, C.A. (2005), *Poplulation Change and Social Vunlnerability in the Wake of Disasters: The Case of Hurricanes Katrina and Rita,* Louisiana, USA: The Department of Sociology.

Nelson, V. (2011), *Gender, Generations, Social Proctection and Climate Change: A Thematic Review,* University of Greenwich, London: National Resource Institute.

Neumayer, E., and Plumper, T. (2007), "The Gendered Nature of Natural Disasters: The Impact of Catastrophic Event on the Gender Gaps in Life Expectancy, 1981-2002", *Annals of the Association of American Geographers, 97* (3), 551-66.

Norris, F.H., Baker, C.K., Murphy, A.D., and Kaniasty, K. (2005), "Social Support Mobilisation and Deterioration after Mexico's 1999 Flood: Effects of Context, Gender, and Time", *American Journal of Community Psychology , 36* (1/2), 15-28.

Ollenburger, J.C., and Tobin, G.A. (1998), "Women and Post-Disaster Stress", In *Social Construction of Gendered Vulnerability,* pp. 95-107.

Pappenberger, F., Beven, K., Frodhsam, K., Romanowicz, R., and Matgen, P. (2007), "Grasping the unavoidable subjectivity in calibration of flood inundation models: A vulnerability weighted approach", *Journal of Hydrology , 333* (2-4), 275-87.

Pistrika, A., and Tsakiris, G. (2007), "Flood Risk Assessment: A Methodological Framework", *Water Resources Management: New Approaches and Technologies, European Water Resources Association* , 14-16, Chania, Crete, Greece.

Pomeroy, R.S., Ratner, B.D., Hall, S.J., Pimoljinda, J., and Vivekanandan, V.

(2006), "Coping with disasters: Rehabilitating coastal livelihoods", *Marine Policy, 30*, 786-93.

Ray Bennett, N.S. (2009), "The influence of Caste, Class and Gender in surviving multiple disasters: A case study from Orissa, India", *Envirionmental Hazards, 8*, 5-22.

Sahara Group (2004), *Best Practices on Rehabilitation and Reintegration of Trafficked Women and Girls.* Retrieved March 12, 2011, from www.childtrafficking.com: http://www.childtrafficking.com/Docs/sahara_jit_2004_best_pract.pdf

Smith, L.C., and Bryon, E.M. (2005), Is Greater Decision-making Power of Women Associated with Reduced Gender Discrimination in South Asia? *Food Consumpion and Nutritional Division Discussion Paper 200,* NW, Washington, USA: International Food Policy Research Institute.

The Status of Women: A reality check (2011), *Facts on Inequality and Crimes Against Women*, Kolkata: Swayam.

Tunstall, S., Tapsell, S., Green, C., Floyd, P.F., and George, C. (2006), "The health effects of flooding: social research results from England and Wales", *Journal of Water and Health , 4* (3), 365-80.

Violence against Women: Intimate partner and sexual violence against women (2011, September) Retrieved May 26, 2012, from World Health Organisation: http://www.who.int/mediacentre/factsheets/fs239/en/

Weist, R., Mocellin, J., and Motsisi, T. (1994), *The Needs of Women in Disasters and Emergencies.* Winnipeg: UNDP and Office of United Nations Disaster Relief.

Wiest, R.E., Mocellin, J.S., and Motsisi, D.T. (1994), *The Needs of Women in Disasters and Emergencies,* Winnipeg, Manitoba, USA: The University of Manitoba.

Wisner, B., Blaikie, P.T., Cannon, T., and Davis, I. (1994), *At Risk: Natural Hazards, People's Vulnerability and Disaster,* New York: Routledge.

Occupational Structure of Women Labourers in Rural Punjab

Dharam Pal and Gian Singh

After more than half a century of planned economic development and high levels of aggregate growth over the last two decades, the Indian economy still remains predominantly rural. According to Census 2011, 69 percent of people in India were rural. Within rural India, agriculture continues to still be the dominant occupation which provides more than half workforce employment. During the last two decades, especially since the early 1990s as a part of the neo-liberal wave of globalisation, there has been a general increasing tendency in the number of labour households. This is so because of the stagnation or slow growth of the agriculture sector and non-agriculture sectors and expanding labour force in the rural areas (Singh and Pal, 2011). One of the most distinguishing features of the rural economy of India has been the growth in the number of cultivators and agricultural labourers engaged in crop production. The phenomena of under-employment, under-development and surplus population are simultaneously manifested in the daily lives and living of the agricultural labourers. They usually get low wages, conditions of work put an excessive burden on them, and the employment which they get is extremely irregular (Padhi, 2007). Because of this, the income levels of the labour class continue to be very low. Many a times, the earning of the male workers is not enough to meet the basic necessities of the family. Consequently, women are pushed into labour market to supplement husband earnings. This is evident from the fact that even in a fairy high income state like Punjab, Female Work Participation Rate (FWPR) has increased nearly four and a half times in the recent past. It increased from 4.4 in 1991 to 18.7 percent (main workers 11.9 percent + marginal workers 6.8 percent) in 2001, and rural FWPR is 2.25 times that of urban FWPR. Out of the total female workers, 37.5 percent are engaged in agriculture sector (GoI, 2001). This higher participation of rural women is not accompanied by any other positive characteristic of the workforce. These rural females enjoy much lower occupational diversification, very poor employment status and high unemployment rate (Hirway and Roy, 1999).

Available empirical evidence indicates poor plight of the rural women labourers in India. Majority of them are poor, illiterate, unskilled and socially backward which force them to work in the unorganised sector at a low wages (GoI, 2008; Mishra, 2008; Rajasekhar *et al.*, 2007; Balakrishnan, 2005; Sandhu, 2002; Tuteja, 2000; Padma, 1999; Rani *et al.*, 1990). Very few opportunities are open for them in the high rewarding modern sector activities which are mainly skill and knowledge intensive in nature. Due to weak women labour organisations, many of them are subjected to various types of exploitation by their employers, which include long working hours, unhygienic working environment, discrimination in payment of wages and even non-payment of wages, economic and sexual exploitation and so on.

Objectives

In this paper, an endeavour has been made to analyse socio-economic conditions and occupational structure of the women labourers in rural Punjab. More specifically, the aims are:

(1) to examine the socio-economic conditions of women labourers in rural Punjab;
(2) to study about the living conditions of women labourers in rural Punjab;
(3) to examine the pattern and composition of women labourers employed in agriculture and non-agriculture sectors in rural Punjab; and
(4) to measure the season-wise employment of women labourers in agriculture in rural Punjab.

Data and Methodology

The present study is based on multi-stage systematic random sampling technique and related to the year 2010-11. In the first stage, the whole state is divided into three zones of districts on the basis of the work participation rate of rural women in Punjab (Table 17.1). In the second stage, three districts were selected one from each work participation zone. Sangrur district was selected from the high, Ludhiana district from the medium and Hoshiarpur district from the low work participation zones.

Table 17.1: District-wise Work Participation Rate of Rural Women in Punjab

Sl. No.	*Districts*	*Rural Women Workers*	*Total Rural Women Population*	*Work Participation Rate*
High Work Participation Zone				
1.	Nawanshahr	86,170	2,41,887	35.62
2.	Bathinda	1,33,494	3,87,423	34.46
3.	Sangrur	1,97,085	6,58,756	29.92
4.	Rupnagar	1,03,229	3,50,554	29.45
5.	Mansa	73,647	2,55,566	28.82
Medium Work Participation Zone				
6.	Muktsar	74,788	2,72,859	27.41
7.	Moga	91,179	3,36,892	27.06
8.	Faridkot	43,118	1,68,378	25.61
9.	Ludhiana	1,55,451	6,26,585	24.81
10.	Fatehgarh Sahib	40,751	1,79,013	22.76
11.	Firozpur	1,36,610	6,11,512	22.34
Low Work Participation Zone				
12.	Amritsar	1,86,529	8,79,171	21.22
13.	Patiala	1,14,426	5,57,591	20.52
14.	Hoshiarpur	1,11,678	5,77,987	19.32
15.	Kapurthala	39,303	2,42,021	16.24
16.	Jalandhar	75,721	4,91,696	15.40
17.	Gurdaspur	1,08,123	7,42,001	14.57
	Punjab	1,771,302	7,579,892	23.52

Source: Government of India, Census of India, 2001.

From the list of villages in each development block in each of the selected districts, one village was selected randomly. From these villages, a comprehensive list of the women labour households was prepared. From this list, 10 percent of the households were selected randomly. In all 498 households were selected for the survey. These 498 selected households were visited personally to collect information on the various socio-economic aspects of their families. Information was recorded by personal interview method on pre-tested structured questionnaire designed for the purpose. The results were analysed by using the mean values and percentages.

Results and Discussion

The first part of our study is related to the socio-economic conditions of the women labourers in rural Punjab. Table 17.2 depicts that out of total 498 sampled women labourers, 47.59 percent fall in the age group of 30 to 44 years. The fact responsible for this phenomenon is that the domestic chores are managed by their young daughters and so they are able to work in the agriculture and non-agriculture sectors. More than one-fourth (26.51 percent) of the women labourers are in the age group of 45 to 59 years. As many as 81 out of total women labourers (16.27 percent) fall in the age group of 15 to 29 years. In the age group of 60 years and above, 8.63 percent (43 out of 498) of the respondents have reported that they are working in the fields. Mostly women labourers in this age group are getting employment in MGNREGA. There are only 5 women labourers (1.00 percent) having age below 15 years who are working in the fields.

Table 17.2: Socio-Economic Background of Sampled Women Labourers in Rural Punjab

Age (in Years)						
Below 15		*15 to 29*	*30 to 44*	*45 to 59*	*60 & Above*	*Total*
5 (1.00)		81 (16.27)	237 (47.59)	132 (26.51)	43 (8.63)	498 (100.00)
Educational Status						
Illiterate	*Below Primary*	*Below Middle*	*Below Matric*	*Below Secondary*	*Secondary & Above*	*Total*
363 (72.89)	14 (2.81)	94 (18.88)	22 (4.42)	4 (0.80)	1 (0.20)	498 (100.00)
Caste						
Scheduled Castes		*Backward Castes*		*General Castes*		*Total*
398 (79.92)		94 (18.88)		6 (1.20)		498 (100.00)
Marital Status						
Married		*Unmarried*		*Widow/Divorced*		*Total*
441 (88.55)		8 (1.61)		49 (9.84)		498 (100.00)

No. of Children				
Up to 2	*2 to 4*	*4 to 6*	*6 & Above*	*Total*
158 (32.25)	193 (39.39)	121 (24.69)	18 (3.67)	490 (100.00)
Family Type				
Nuclear		*Joint*		*Total*
398 (79.92)		100 (20.08)		498 (100.00)

Note: Figures in parentheses are percentages.
Source: Field Survey, 2010-11.

Education provides awareness to women about their rights and prepares them for diverse occupation jobs (Bhatia and Dhindsa, 2009). The table reveals that almost three-fourths (72.89 percent) of the women labourers are illiterate and remaining (27.11 percent) are literate. Among the literate women labourers, majority of them (18.88 percent) have education below middle, 4.42 percent are below matric, 2.81 percent are below primary. A negligible small proportion of just 0.80 percent is below secondary. There is just a single women labourer (0.20 percent) in the sample who has passed secondary and above. For male workers, higher levels of education are indeed associated with higher WPR (work participation rate), both in rural and urban areas. But for women, WPR is higher for illiterate women than for women with higher levels of school education—a trend which reverses itself only for women with technical/vocational education or graduates (Srivastava and Srivastava, 2009).

Caste-wise distribution of women labourers shows that majority of the women labourers (79.92 percent) belong to the scheduled castes followed by backward castes (18.88 percent) and general castes (1.20 percent) categories. The WPR is the highest for scheduled tribe (ST) and scheduled caste (SC) women and the lowest for women from the other castes. The SCs and STs are the most marginalised sections in the economy and the most impoverished. Women from these groups have higher WPRs because extreme poverty leaves them with little choice but to work, and because they do not face social taboos that disapprove of work. The converse is true for women from other castes (Srivastava and Srivastava, 2009).

Further, out of total 498 sampled women labourers, majority of the women labourers (88.55 percent) are reported to be married and 1.61 percent of the respondents are unmarried. As many as 49 women labourers (9.84 percent) are widow/divorced. Most of the female Labourers have large families. The fact matches the empirical finding of another research study (Rani, 2010). Though most of the respondents (slightly less than 80 percent) belong to the nuclear families, but even than more than two-thirds (67.75 percent) have more than two children in their respective families. It implies that the majority of the women labourers are not aware about the advantages of small family.

As far as the housing conditions of these women labourers are concerned, Table 17.3 reveals that 401 respondents (more than 80 percent) have semi-*pacca* houses and 54 respondents (10.84 percent) are still living in *kacha* houses. Only 43 respondents (8.63 percent) have *pacca* houses. The table further revealed a disturbing fact that more than two-thirds (67.27 percent) of the total respondents are living in dilapidated conditions. As many as 25.91 percent live in moderate and only 4.82 percent are living in good conditions. Further, the table shows that more than half (52.01 percent) are using tap water followed by hand pump (19.68 percent) and submersible motor (2.01 percent). It is again very sad to note that more than one-fourth (26.30 percent) respondents have reported that they have no source of drinking water.

Table 17.3: Housing Conditions of Women Labourers in Rural Punjab

Type of House				
Kacha	Semi-*pacca*	*Pacca*		Total
54 (10.84)	401 (80.52)	43 (8.64)		498 (100.00)
Conditions				
Good	*Moderate*	*Dilapidated*		*Total*
24 (4.82)	139 (27.91)	335 (67.27)		498 (100.00)
Source of Drinking Water				
Hand pump	*Tap*	*Submersible Motor*	*No*	*Total*
98 (19.68)	259 (52.01)	10 (2.01)	131 (26.30)	498 (100.00)
Average No. of Rooms Available	*Families Having Access to Bathroom/Toilet*		*Houses Electrified*	
1.90	464 (93.17)		491 (98.59)	

Note: Figures in parentheses are percentages.
Source: Field Survey, 2010-11.

They have to bring it from neighbourers or common tab. Further, on an average 1.90 rooms are available in their respective families. As many as 93.19 percent of respondents have reported that they have access to bathroom/toilet. However, the field survey has revealed that the condition of bathroom/toilet used by the women labour households is of very poor quality. Punjab is regarded as one of the prosperous states, but there are still nearly 7 percent of the respondents who have no access even to poor quality bathroom/toilet. As many as 1.41 percent of the women labour households are found non-electrified.

The third part of our study is concerned about the employment pattern of the women labourers in rural Punjab. Table 17.4 highlights that 14.26 percent women labourers are employed only in agriculture and 8.23 percent only in non-agriculture sectors. The remaining (77.51 percent) are working both in agriculture and non-agriculture sectors. It is clear from this fact that the majority of women labourers in rural Punjab are not able to find sufficient amount of work in agriculture sector alone. They have to find it in both agriculture and non-agriculture sectors. The labour absorption capacity of agriculture has reached the upper limit and it is not able to keep the rural workers engaged throughout the year. The rural households also seek employment outside

Table 17.4: Sectoral Distribution of Women Labourers Working in and Out of Native Village in Rural Punjab

Sector	*Work Place*		*Total*
	In the Native Village	*Outside the Native Village*	
Agriculture	65 (18.37) [91.55]	6 (4.17) [8.45]	71 (14.26) [100.00]
Non-agriculture	18 (5.08) [43.90]	23 (15.97) [56.10]	41 (8.23) [100.00]
Both Agriculture and Non-agriculture	271 (76.55) [70.21]	115 (79.86) [29.79]	386 (77.51) [100.00]
Total	354 (100.00) [71.08]	144 (100.00) [28.92]	498 (100.00) [100.00]

Note: Figures in upper and lower brackets indicate column-wise and row-wise percentage share, respectively.

Source: Field Survey, 2010-11.

the agriculture sector to tide over the inter-year and intra-year variations in agricultural income (Bhakar *et al.*, 2007). Therefore, more than three-fourths (77.51 percent) of the women labourers are earning their livelihood in both agriculture and non-agriculture sectors.

The table further reveals the fact that nearly 29 percent of the women labourers are going out of their native villages in search of work. The remaining 71 percent, though work in the village, too, are not working in agriculture sector alone. About 70 percent of them are earning their livelihood both from agriculture and non-agriculture sectors. Out of total 354 women labourers working in the native villages, 18.37 percent are working in agriculture sector alone. Another 5.08 are working in non-agriculture sectors alone. As regards the sectoral composition of women labourers working outside the village only 4.17 percent are working in agriculture and 15.97 percent are in non-agriculture sectors. Slightly less than 80 percent are working in both agriculture and non-agriculture sectors.

The information regarding the season-wise employment of the women labourers in agriculture sector in rural Punjab is given in Table 17.5. The table shows that the women labourers get on an average 70.44 days of employment in agriculture sector in a year. The table and Figure 17.1 depicts that they get more employment during the *kharif* season (39.39 days) than *rabi* season (31.05 days).

Table 17.5: Season-wise Employment of Women Labourers in Agriculture Sector in Rural Punjab

Season	*Employment Days Per Labourer*	
	Days	*Percentage*
Kharif	39.39	55.92
Rabi	31.05	44.08
Total	70.44	100.00

Source: Field Survey, 2010-11.

In Punjab, the *kharif* season generally extends from the month of June to the first half of November. Table 17.6 shows that during this season, the women labourers get employment for 39.39 days. The table and Figure 17.2 depicts that they get maximum employment during the month of July (12.91 days) which accounted for 32.78 percent of total employment in the season. During the month of June, they get employment for 10.20 days (25.91 percent). However, they get few days of employment during the months of August (4.12 days),

Figure 17.1: Season-wise Employment of Women Labourers in Agriculture Sector in Rural Punjab

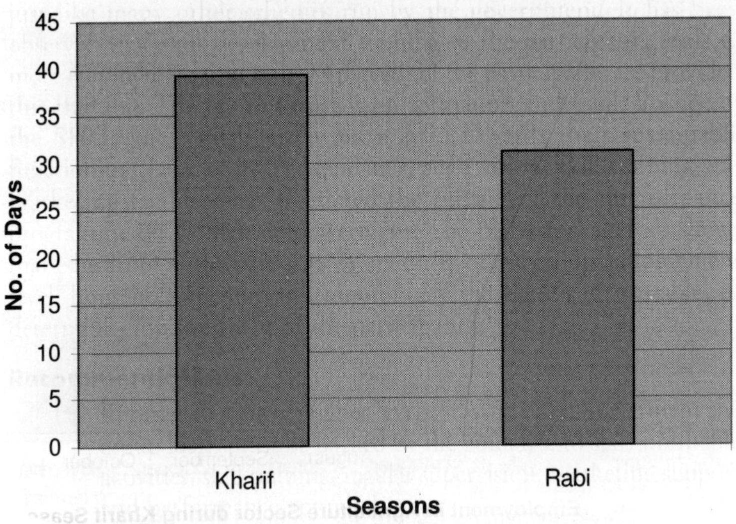

Note: Based on Table 17.5.

September (4.92 days), October (3.86 days) and first half of November (3.38 days).

Table 17.6: Employment of Women Labourers in Agriculture Sector during *Kharif* Season

Months	*Employment Days Per Labourer*	
	Days	*Percentage*
June	10.20	25.91
July	12.91	32.78
August	4.12	10.47
September	4.92	12.48
October	3.86	9.79
November (First Half)	3.38	8.57
Total	39.39	100.00

Source: Field Survey, 2010-11

In Punjab, the *Rabi* season generally extends from the second half of November to the month of May. Table 17.7 reveals that the women labourers get employment for 31.05 days in agriculture during this season. They get maximum employment during the month of April

Figure 17.2: Employment of Women Labourers in Agriculture Sector during *Kharif* Season

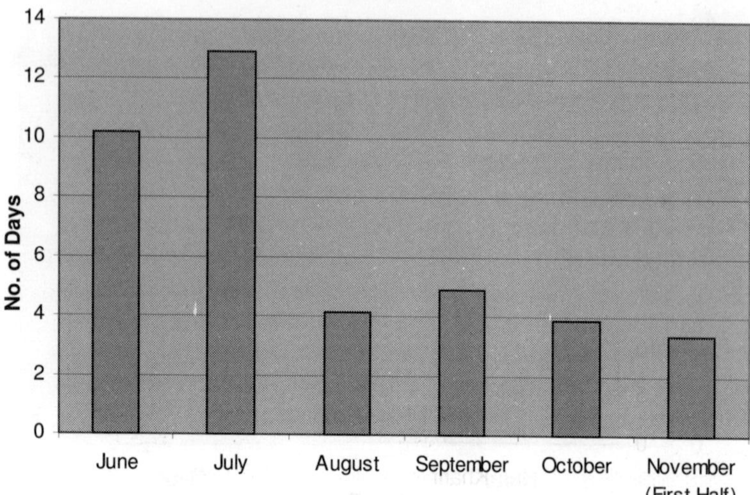

Note: Based on Table 17.6.

(11.35 days) which accounted for 36.57 percent of the total employment during the season. They get 6.70, 5.03, 4.34, 2.05, 0.91, 0.67 days of employment during the months of February, March, January, second half of November, December and May respectively.

Table 17.7: Employment of Women Labourers in Agriculture Sector during *Rabi* Season

Months	*Employment Days Per Labourer*	
	Days	*Percentage*
November (Second Half)	2.05	6.61
December	0.91	2.94
January	4.34	13.98
February	6.70	21.57
March	5.03	16.19
April	11.35	36.57
May	0.67	2.14
Total	31.05	100.00

Source: Field Survey, 2010-11.

The frequency of women labourers employed in agriculture sector is given in Table 17.8 and Figure 17.4. It is evident from the table and

Figure 17.3: Employment of Women Labourers in Agriculture Sector during *Rabi* Season

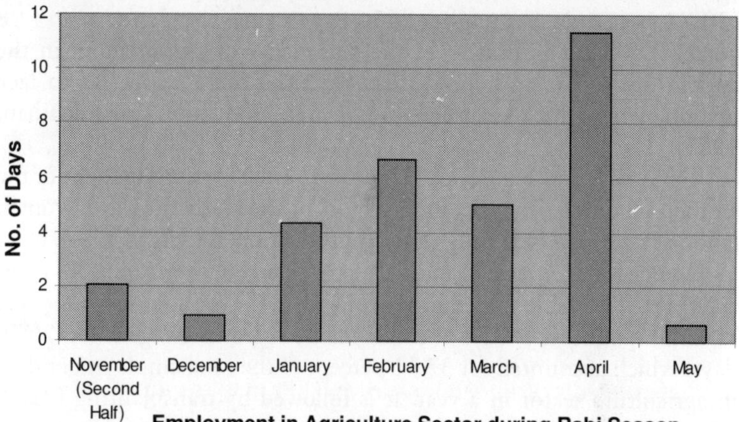

Note: Based on Table 17.7.

Table 17.8: Frequency of Women Labourers Employed in Agriculture Sector in Rural Punjab

Month	*Number of Women Labourers Employed*	*Percentage*
June	442	88.76
July	448	89.96
August	339	68.07
September	218	43.78
October	311	62.45
November	275	55.22
December	153	30.72
January	219	43.98
February	333	66.87
March	268	53.82
April	452	90.76
May	103	20.68
Sampled Women Labourers	498	100.00

Source: Field Survey, 2010-11.

figure that during the months of April (90.76 percent), July (89.96 percent) and June (88.76 percent), nine out of ten sampled women labourers get employment in agriculture sector. However, during the months of August (68.07 percent), February (67.87 percent), October (62.45 percent), November (55.22 percent) and March (53.82 percent), more than half of the total sampled women labourers get employment in agricultural activities. Lesser women labourers get employment in agriculture sector during the months of May (20.68 percent), December (30.72 percent), September (45.78 percent) and January (45.98 percent). This is indicative of the seasonality of employment in the agriculture sector and shows that the rural population has to face unemployment due to seasonal work in crop production (Swaminathan, 1981).

Table 17.9 and Figure 17.5 show the pattern of employment of the women labourers in agriculture sector. In the study area, the women labourers are involved only in crop production activities. There is no preference for age, caste or marital status in any of the crop production activities. The table and figure depict that the women labourers get maximum number of days of employment in growing vegetables (26.70 days) which accounted for 37.91 percent of the total employment days in agriculture sector in a year. It is followed by transplanting (22.48

Table 17.9: Operations Carried Out by Women Labourers in Crop Production

Sl. No.	*Operations*	*Wage (In Rs.)*	*Number of Days Worked*		*Total Days*
			Kharif	*Rabi*	
1.	Raising Nursery	130-150	0.67 (1.69)	-	0.67 (0.94)
2.	Transplanting	200-250	22.48 (57.06)	-	22.48 (31.91)
3.	Gap Filling	130-150	0.56 (1.41)	-	0.56 (0.79)
4.	Weeding	130-150	3.75 (9.53)	-	3.75 (5.33)
5.	Irrigation	-	-	-	-
6.	Harvesting and Threshing	200-250	4.55 (11.55)	9.50 (30.59)	14.05 (19.94)
7.	Winnowing and Sun Drying	200-250	2.23 (5.68)	-	2.23 (3.18)
8.	Growing Vegetables	80-100	5.15 (13.08)	21.55 (69.41)	26.70 (37.91)
	Total		39.39 (100.00)	31.05 (100.00)	70.44 (100.00)

Source: Field Survey, 2010-11.
Note: Figures in parentheses are percentages.

Figure 17.4: Frequency of Women Labourers Employed in Agriculture Sector in Rural Punjab

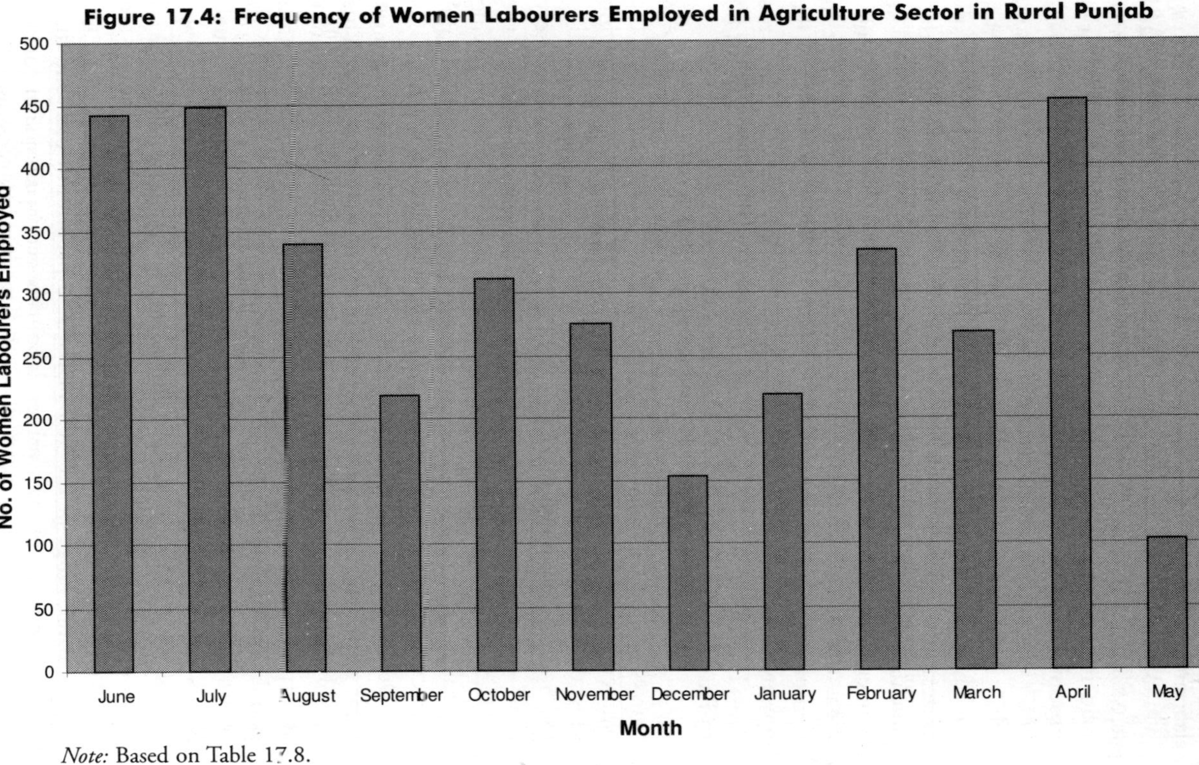

Note: Based on Table 17.8.

days) and harvesting and threshing (14.05 days) operations. The women labourers are also involved in other operations like weeding (3.75 days), winnowing and sun drying (2.23 days), raising nursery (0.67 days) and gap filling (0.56 days). There is not even a single woman in the sample who gets employment in irrigation operation in agriculture. It is observed from the field survey that the women labourers put in 10-12 hours of work per day in the agriculture sector during the busy season, while in slack season, they work for 7-8 hours per day.

The field survey also reveals that the women labourers mostly perform the different agricultural operations manually. For harvesting they use sickle. Weeding is done both by hand and by sickle/hoe. The women labourers receive wage in cash for all the operations. In the study area, the wage rate varies from Rs. 200 to Rs. 250 per day in transplanting and harvesting and threshing operations. However, in the operation of raising nursery, gap filling and weeding, the wage rate varies from Rs. 130 to Rs. 150 per day. The wage rate is in the range of Rs. 80 to Rs. 100 per day in the growing vegetables operations.

As far as the season-wise pattern of employment in agriculture is concerned, the table and figure show that during the *kharif* season, the women labourers are involved in transplanting (22.48 days), growing vegetables (5.15 days), harvesting and threshing (4.55 days), weeding (3.75 days), winnowing and sun drying (2.23 days), raising nursery (0.67 days) and gap filling (0.56 days). On the other hand, during the *rabi* season, the women labourers get maximum employment in growing vegetables (21.55 days) followed by harvesting and threshing (9.50 days) respectively.

During slack agricultural season, the women labourers depend on rural non-farm activities as the secondary source of income. This corroborates the Vaidyanathan's (1986) assertion that the labour absorption capacity of the agriculture was limited and the rural population was migrating from farm to non-farm activities. Table 17.10 shows that out of total, 410 women labourers get employment though MGNREGS. They get employment for 30-35 days in a year at a wage rate of Rs. 123 per day. The sampled women labourers also work as domestic servants. As many as 109 sampled women labourers are involved in this work. They work for 100-120 days and the wage rate is just in the range of Rs. 500 to Rs. 750 per month plus one time meal per day. Domestic women labourers get a paltry sum for the unpleasant work they perform. Some of them are exploited economically as well as physically (Balakrishnan, 2005).

Figure 17.5: Operations Carried Out by Women Labourers in Crop Production

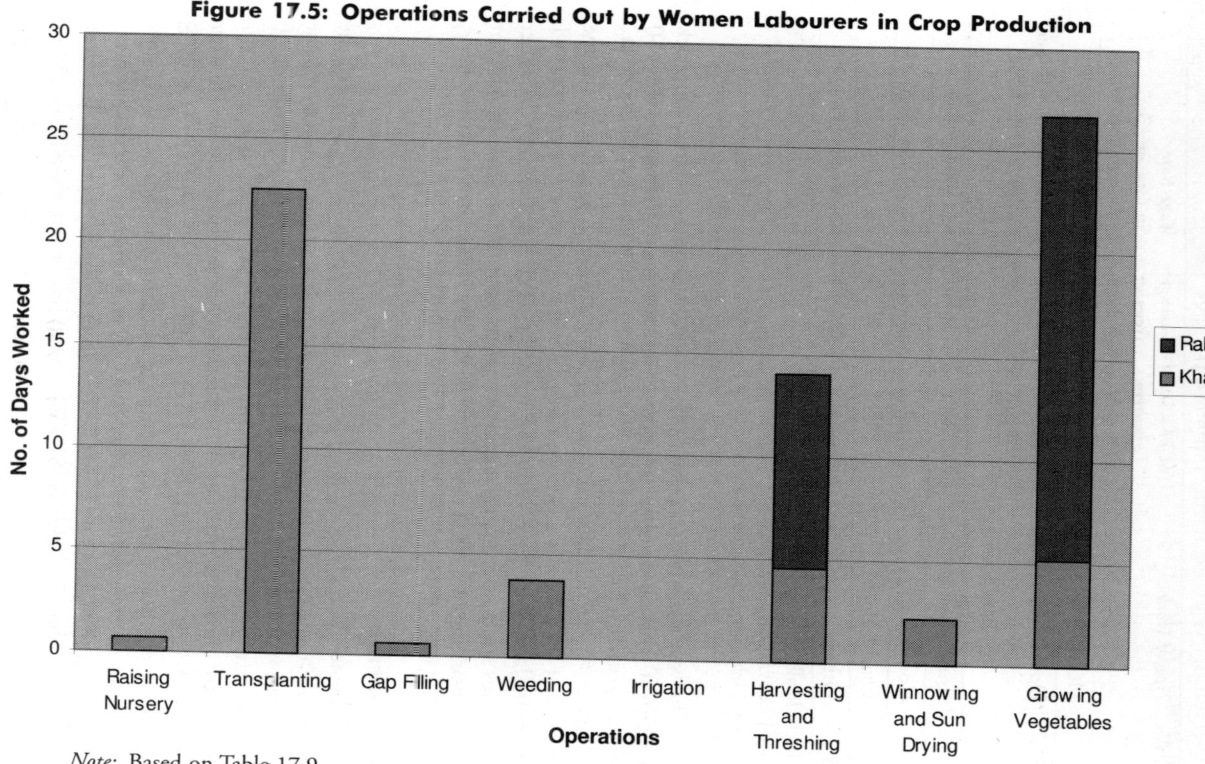

Note: Based on Table 17.9.

Table 17.10: Employment for Women Labourers in Non-Agriculture Sectors

S. No.	Type of Work	No. of Women Labourers Involved	Average Number of Days	Wage Rate (in Cash or Kind)
1.	MGNREGS	410	30-35	Rs. 123 per Day
2.	Domestic Servant	109	100-120	Rs. 500 to Rs. 750 per Month + One Time Meal Daily
3.	Brick Kiln	84	30-40	Rs. 150 per Day
4.	Construction	63	20-25	Rs. 135 per Day
5.	Local Industry	45	45-50	Rs. 112 per Day
6.	Others*	41	25-30	Rs. 95 per Day

*Include all types of work such as vending vegetables/fruits, helping in shoe-making or white-washing, etc.

Source: Field Survey, 2010-11.

The women labourers also work in brick kiln and construction work for 30-40 and 20-25 days respectively and earn on an average Rs. 150 per day in brick kiln and Rs. 135 per day in construction work. As many as 45 women labourers get employment in local industry for the period of 45-50 days at a wage rate of Rs. 112 per day. Out of total 41 women labourers have reported that they get employment in other activities such as vending vegetables/fruits, helping in shoe-making or white-washing, etc. for a period of 25-30 days. They earn, on an average, Rs. 95 per day from this work.

Conclusion

The above analysis shows that the socio-economic conditions of the women labourers in rural Punjab are very miserable. Majority of the sampled women labourers (47.59 percent) fall in the age group of 30 to 44 years. The fact responsible for this phenomenon is that the domestic chores are managed by their young daughters and so they are able to work in the agriculture sector. Almost three-fourths (72.89 percent) of the women labourers are illiterate and about 80 percent belong to the scheduled castes category. Though most of the respondents (slightly less than 80 percent) belong to the nuclear families, but even than more than two-thirds (67.75 percent) have more than two children in their respective families. It implies that the majority of the women labourers are not aware about the advantages of small family. The study reveals a disturbing fact that more than two-thirds (67.27 percent) of the total respondents are living in dilapidated conditions. It is again very sad to note that more than one-fourth (26.31 percent) respondents have reported that they have no source of drinking water. They have to bring it from neighbourers or common tab. Further, on an average 1.90 rooms are available in their respective families. Nearly 7 percent of the respondents who have no access to bathroom/toilet and 7 households out of 498 are found non-electrified.

The pattern and composition of sectoral employment of the women labourers reveal that the majority of women labourers in rural Punjab are not able to find sufficient amount of work in agriculture sector alone. They have to find it in both agriculture and non-agriculture sectors. In agriculture sector, the women labourers get on an average 70.44 days of employment in a year. They get more employment during the *kharif* season (39.39 days) than *rabi* season (31.05 days). This implies that women labourers get only seasonal employment in agriculture sector. The women labourers are involved only in crop production activities. There is no preference for age, caste or marital status in any of the crop production activities. The women labourers are mostly involved in transplanting, harvesting and growing vegetables activities which accounted for 87.52 percent of the total employment days in agriculture. It is observed from the field survey that the labourers work for 10-12 hours per day in the busy season, while in slack season, they work for 7-8 hours per day. Most of the agriculture operations are performed by manually. In non-agriculture sector, the women labourers adopt the occupation of domestic servant, brick kiln, construction and other activities such as vending vegetables/fruits, helping in shoe-making or white-washing, etc. Some of them are engaged in local industries and MGNREGS.

Policy Implications

The results of the study and field survey have some important implications. The central and state governments must take strong initiatives for creating sufficient employment opportunities and should effectively implement the policies for improving the economic condition of the women labour households in rural Punjab. To reduce the seasonal unemployment, government should effectively implement employment-oriented programmes especially during the off-season. Agro-based small-scale industries should be established in the rural areas on priority basis. There is an urgent need to create awareness about various employment programmes meant for the poor. Provision of loans at very low rate of interest for establishment of various income generating ventures would also help the women labourers. Quality education should be provided to the children of the women labourers so that they may get jobs in the non-agriculture sectors and help their family members in improving their economic condition. The government and non-government agencies should take necessary steps to organise skill development programmes for women labourers to enhance their earning capacity.

References

Balakrishnan, A. (2005), Rural Landless Women Labourers: Problems and Prospects, New Delhi: Kalpaz Publication.

Bhakar, R.; Banafar, K.N.S., Singh, N.P. and Gauraha, A.K. (2007), "Income and Employment Pattern in Rural Areas of Chhattisgarh: A Macro View", *Agricultural Economics Research Review,* Vol. 20, Jul.-Dec., pp. 395-406.

Bhatia, S. and Dhindsa, P.K. (2009), "Female Work Participation in the Emerging Labour Market—Case Study of Sarhali Village of Tarn-Taran District", *Journal of Development and Agricultural Economics,* Vol. 1 (6) September, pp. 127-31.

GoI, *Census of India*, Various Issues, Series-4, (Punjab).

GoI (2008), Socio-Economic Conditions of Women Workers in Selected Food Processing Industries including Sea Food and Marine Products, Shimla/ Chandigarh: Ministry of Labour & Employment Labour Bureau.

Hirway, I. and Roy, A.K. (1999), "Women in Rural Economy: The Case of India", *Indian Journal of Agricultural Economics,* Vol. 54, No. 3.

Mishra, S. (2008), "Life of Women Agricultural Labourers in Orissa", *Orissa Review,* November.

Padhi, K. (2007), "Agricultural Labour in India—A Close Look", *Orissa Review,* February-March, pp. 23-28.

Padma, K. (1999), "Changing Cropping Pattern and Employment Conditions of Women Workers: A Case Study", *The Indian Journal of Labour Economics,* Vol. 42, No. 4.

Rajasekhar, D., Suchitra, J.Y. and Manjula, R. (2007), "Women Workers in Urban Informal Employment: The Status of *Agarbathi* and Garment Workers in Karnataka", *The Indian Journal of Labour Economics,* Vol. 50, No. 4.

Rani, M. (2011), "Socio-Economic Conditions of Female Domestic Workers in Punjab: A Case Study", Women and Children Issues: National and International Perspectives, Women's Study Centre, Punjabi University, Patiala, Feb. 11-12, pp. 603-13.

Rani, P.S., Raju, V.T., Ram, P.R. and Naidu, M. (1990), "Wage Differentials and Factors Governing Employment of Women in Agriculture", *Agricultural Situation in India,* Vol. XLV, No. 4.

Sandhu, P. (2002), "Female Labour Force in Punjab: Socio-Economic Profile, Participation Rate and Problems Faced", *The Indian Journal of Social Work,* Vol. 63, No. 4.

Singh, G. and Pal, D. (2011), "Participation of Women Labourers in Household Income in Rural Punjab: District-wise Analysis", *Research Journal Social Sciences,* Vol. 19, No. 3, pp. 130-44.

Srivastava, N. and Srivastava, R. (2009), "Women, Work, and Employment Outcomes in Rural India", Paper presented at the FAO-IFAD-ILO Workshop on Gaps, Trends and Current Research in Gender Dimensions of Agricultural and Rural Employment: Differentiated Pathways out of Poverty, Rome, 31 March–02 April.

Swaminathan, M.S. (1981), "Indian Agriculture—Challenges for the Eighties", *Agricultural Situation in India,* Vol. 36(6), pp. 349-59.

Tuteja, U. (2000), "Female Employment in Agriculture: A District-wise Analysis of Haryana", *The Indian Journal of Labour Economics,* Vol. 43, No. 2.

Vaidynathan, A. (1986), "Labour Use in Rural India: A Case Study of Spatial and Temporal Variations", *Economic and Political Weekly,* Vol. 21 (52), December 27.

Dynamics of Socio-Economic and Political Background of Women Leadership in Panchayati Raj Institutions

SANJEEV KUMAR AND KUSAM KUMARI

Introduction

Women constitute about 50 percent of the country's population (Bhuyan, 2008). But they are the largest excluded category in almost all respects (Dutta, 2001). Women in India have been playing an important role in social life, since time immemorial. Evidently, women are not merely managing their houses but have shown their interest and ability to work for whole society, all segments and sectors of society. Their roles in economy are rather silent, but their invisible contribution in all economic activities can not be neglected. Indian old Sanskrit literature quotes, "Nari Sarvatr Pujyate" which means women are worshiped everywhere. It gives a place to women in a respectable position.

On the other hand women are ignored, and considered as ordinary household who can only work in house and farm, cook, wash and deliver child. But thanks to large pool of women, whose participation in social activities, Science and technology, political and economic and so forth and gave remarkable impetus to the women empowerment in India. There are numerous instances where women worked at par with men and in many cases they outraged men and are out fielding them (Kumar,

2008). Thus, the role of women in every sphere of socio-economic and political field, etc. has been remarkable. In the political field women are contributing a lot as a leader at the grassroots level.

Women Empowerment in the Post-73rd Amendment Scenario

After 73rd Amendment Act they are shaping the leadership pattern in Panchayti Raj Institution. Leadership is decision-making body in the present society (Sharma, 1997). The leadership of the developing countries has launched the centrally planned programmes of social development and transformation for the betterment of the people (Choudhary, 1981). The new leadership emerging in the countryside as a political consequence of Panchayati Raj is called "neo traditional", by many scholars in this field. The non-officials meaning in the Panchayati Raj bodies today represent the cumulative results of a process of change of the society, whose inspirational level they embody. The interest of these new leaders in village affairs is not causal nor do they quote caste, wealth and status to win election (Narian, 1964).

It was assumed that the villagers can do much for improving their belief only if they have leader who can bring dynamism in their lives. In the absence of such leadership, nothing substantial can be achieved. From another angle, the very success of PRIs depends largely only on the quality of leadership and its functioning in the PRIs. Thus the effective functioning of PRIs depends mainly on the quality of leadership available at the grassroots level (Sisikar, 1970).

Although, the efforts made by 73rd and 74th Amendment Acts are appreciable steps towards emergence of new leadership and particularly women and Dalit leadership, but the best quality of leadership is yet to be achieved. The rising concern and interest in the changing role and position of women in society has inspired a considerable number of innovative, important and scholarly work in the field of sociology, economy, anthropology and legal system. A large number of studies are devoted to the status of women in family and society, marriage system, education, status of working women. In India, little attention has been paid to the role of women in politics.

It still remains a least researched area despite the fact that no study in political area in a democratic set-up can be completed unless women are taken into account (Sharma and Sharma, 1987). The years soon after independence women were given a constitutional status which moved her to a position of equality with men in the social, economic and political life of the nation. It is of interest to see how the constitutional status has affected the lives of majority of Indian women across the diversity of regional background (D'Lima, 1983).

Since the passing of the 73rd Constitutional Amendment Act, the major change that took place in context of women functionaries of Panchayati Raj Institutions was political representation of women through reservation (Nupur, 2008). The 73rd Amendment Act has made a powerful impact on women by enabling them to enter into the decision-making sectors at the lowest level of democracy. Out of 5 lakh Indian villages encompassing more than 600 million people, this amendment has made possible 3,30,000 women to enter politics at the grassroots level. This percentage of women involved in political activity at this level has risen dramatically for 4-5 percent before the 73rd Amendment to 25-40 percent after the establishment of Panchayati Raj Institutions under the 73rd Amendment.

The reservation of seats in the 1993-94 elections have brought in about 8 lakh women into the political process in a single election (Dubey, 2002). Thus, 73rd Amendment Act provided opportunity for emergence of women leadership in the PRIs and rural women folk took active participation in the grassroots decision-making process.

The 73rd Constitutional Amendment by Himachal Pradesh Panchayati Raj Act, 1994 has ensured adequate representation to women at different levels of Panchayati Raj Institutions. In this act for the first time 33 percent reservation was given to women in the three tier Panchayati Raj Institutions in Himachal Pradesh. The present Government of Himachal Pradesh has further amended 73rd Amendment Act and the special provision of 50 percent reservation for women has recorded a remarkable in the history of Panchyati Raj System in Himachal Pradesh.

On April 8, 2008 Himachal Pradesh Panchayati Raj (Amendment) Bill was presented and passed in the house, and then Himachal became the third state after Rajasthan and Madhya Pradesh to give 50 percent reservation to women in Panchayats and local bodies. After the 27th August 2008 the Central Government also passed a bill on 50 percent reservation for women in Panchayati Raj Institutions. This will definitely help in empowering women and help in creating sensitivity to women-related development issues.

Study Area and Objective of Study

The present study was conducted in the district Kangra of Himachal

Pradesh which is merged area from Punjab into Himachal Pradesh. The district Kangra is situated between 31°41′ to 32°25′ east longitudes and 70°35′ to 77°5′ north latitudes. To the north it is bounded by Chamba district and Lahaul Spiti, to the east by Kullu and Mandi district, to the south by Hamirpur and Una district on the south-west by the district Hoshiarpur of Punjab.

The total geographical area of the district Kangra is 5739 sq. kms. which is 10.308 percent of total geographical area of the state. According to the 2011 Census, the total population of district Kangra is 15,07,223 person, out of which 7,48,559 are males and 7,58,664 are female, and the sex ratio for 1013 females per 1000 males. The density of population in the district is 263 per sq. km. The literacy rate is 86.49 percent. The male literacy rate is 92.55 percent and female literacy rate is 80.62 percent.

In the present study, an attempt has been made to find out the participation and involvement of women in the grassroot politics. The study seeks to do this in the context of the socio-economic and political profile of these new 'representatives' of rural women. The objective of the present study is to cover the socio-economic and political profile of women in grassroot politics. The present study has been conducted in the state of Himachal Pradesh, which has a Zila Parishad in each of the 12 districts headquarters. The district of Kangra has been identified for the study. This district is taken up for the study for the reason that they are highly populated and interestingly the female population in the district stands higher than male population as shown in Table 18.1 District Kangra consists of total fourteen developmental blocks viz. Baijnath, Bhawarna, Lambagaon, Panchrukhi, Kangra, Nagrota Bagwan, Rait, Dehra, Pragpur, Nagrota Surian, Nurpur, Indora, Fatehpur, Sulah. The Present study was conducted in two blocks of district Kangra, namely, Bhawarna and Nagrota Bagwan. Further, eight panchayats were selected purposively for survey out of which four panchayats falls in each block, i.e. Bhawarna and Nagrota Bagwan block.

Table 18.1: Detail of Total, Male and Female Population in District Kangra

District		*Population*
Kangra	Total	1507223
	Male	748559
	Female	758664

Source: Census of India, 2011.

The Socio-Economic and Political Profile of Women Leadership in Panchayati Raj Institutions

The introduction of 73rd Amendment Act has provided ample opportunity for emergence of women leadership in PRIs but changing patterns of socio-cultural, economic and political conditions of the society are prone dynamic. The emerging trends in women leadership pattern are influenced by her socio-economic and political background and various state and non-state actors which shape the behaviour of women leader and her capacity to involve in decision-making process. In order to study the leadership pattern of the village community, it is necessary to identify the leader of the community. So far as this study is concerned both the reputational and the positional theories have been adopted.

As far as positional theory concerned the elected women representatives have been selected for their interview. The social status of women leaders plays an important role in attaining leadership position and her capacity in decision-making as well as in leading PRIs. In the above background, the present study examines the socio-economic and political background of women leadership in PRIs.

Age

Age has been an important factor of determining the rural leadership. In the survey 53.85 percent women came from the age group of 31 to 40. However, a positive trend has been observed where 40.00 percent came from the age group of 21 to 30, and 6.15 percent of women come from the age group of 41 and above.

Table 18.2: Detail of Age-wise Composition of Respondents in District Kangra

S. No.	*Age*	*Name of District Kangra*	*Percentage*
1.	21 to 30	26	40.00
2.	31 to 40	35	53.85
3.	41 to above	04	6.15
	Total	65	100

Source: Primary Survey.

Thus, the trend shows that most of the women representatives are coming from younger strata of the society.

Marital Status

Marriage remains a very important indicator of socio-economic opportunities in India in the context of leadership, marital status and helps the leaders in identifying social roles. Through a set of official relation it also broadens his/her support network. In the above background marital status of women leaders is analysed (Indira and Kumar,1999).

Table 18.3: Marital Status of Elected Representative in District Kangra

S. No.	*Marital Status*	*Total*	*Percentage*
1.	Unmarried	00	00
2.	Married	59	90.77
3.	Widow	06	9.23
	Total	65	100

Source: Primary Survey.

The data collected regarding martial status showed that overwhelming majority (90.77 percent) of the respondents were married and remaining 9.23 percent were widows. The findings of the study indicate that married women have more acceptability as women leader in the society as compared to unmarried women leader.

Caste

Caste has its own important role in the Indian society. Caste is significant variable in the functioning of Indian Political system (Vidya, 1999). Caste believed to have played an important role in election (Majumda and Singh, 1996). Therefore, Indian Politics is under that threat of caste-ridden political trends and Himachal is no exception to this. The newly merged area in Himachal Pradesh has visible impact of caste factor as compared to old areas. Although the study area consists of two major castes, i.e., Brahmins and Rajputs, yet the number of schedule caste is quite high in the study area.

Table 18.4: Detail of Caste-wise Composition of the Respondents in District Kangra

Sl. No.	*Caste*	*Total*	*Percentage*
1.	General	30	46.15
2.	OBC	20	30.78
3.	SC	15	23.07
4.	ST	00	00
	Total	65	100

Source: Primary Survey.

Table 18.4 shows that one of the most important determinants of women participation is caste. The leadership pattern is dominated by General Caste which constitute 46.15 percent and is followed by OBCs (30.78 percent) and Scheduled Caste (23.07 percent) respectively.

Education

Women education is one of the most important preconditions for the inclusive growth and development of the society. The states which have given importance to women education, have shown phenomenal increase in all indicators of social progress, like a lower birthrate, higher health standards as well as a higher expectation of life at birth. Thus, women participation in public life and their leadership has direct link with the above factors (Singh, 2000). In the present study women were asked to reveal their educational background.

Table 18.5: Detail of the Educational Background in District Kangra

Sl. No.	*Educational Qualification*	*Total*	*Percentage*
1.	Illiterate	03	4.62
2.	Primary	05	7.69
3.	Middle	18	27.69
4.	High School	27	41.54
5.	College	10	15.38
6.	Post-Graduation	02	3.08
	Total	65	100

Source: Primary Survey.

It is clear from the table that literacy has gained importance in rural areas. Most of the women leaders are educated except 4.62 percent women who are illiterate. The study reveals that majority of the respondents were having matric or under-matric level of education. There are eighteen percent respondents who are graduate or post-graduate.

Occupation

Occupation to a large extent influences the economic resources, life style, behaviour patterns and one's status in the community (Singh, 2000). The occupation of elected panchayat members has been also important factor in determining the leadership pattern. Because through their occupation the contestants come in touch with each other and influence the voters. Apart from agricultural and horticultural activities, a large section of the respondents in the government jobs in Himachal Pradesh. In the present study attempts have been made to know about the occupation of the respondents in Table 18.6.

Table 18.6: Detail of Occupational Background of the Respondents in District Kangra

S. No.	*Occupation*	*Name of District Kangra*	*Percentage*
1.	Agriculture	38	58.46
2.	Housewife	16	24.61
3.	Service	09	13.85
4.	Other	02	3.08
	Total	65	100

Source: Primary Survey.

The Table 18.6 reveals that 58.46 percent respondents hails from agricultural background which is followed by housewife and in-service respondents. It is clear that rural leadership in India as well as in Himachal Pradesh is dominated by the agriculture class and particularly women leadership. This is due to the fact that the economy of H.P. is dependent upon agriculture and horticulture.

Income

Income is an important indicator of social status. In the rural areas it is hardly to expect people to talk about income in actual figures. Income status has been an important in selecting the women representatives. In other words, person having good economic status in the village is supposed to become member or Pradhan of the Panchayat (Vidya, 1999). In the Table 18.7 attempts have been made to know the economic status of the respondents.

Table 18.7: Stratification of Respondents on Income Basis in District Kangra

Sl. No	*Annual Income*	*Total*	*Percentage*
1.	Below Rs. 20000	15	23.08
2.	Below Rs. 40000	24	36.92
3.	Above Rs. 40000	26	40.00
	Total	65	100

Source: Primary Survey.

Out of the total sample major chunk of the respondents are having income less than forty thousands whereas only 40 percent respondents disclosed their income more than Rs. 40 thousands. The analysis reveals that most of the respondents belong to middle class or middle income group.

Party Politics and PRIs

The political parties along with state and national leadership, play an important role in the grassroots democracy. Villagers are much interested to become member of any political party. The political parties are important for working of democratic government. This is only from where people can raise their voice. The political parties are the soul of democratic system. The direct or indirect involvement of political parties in the affairs of Panchayat elections and functioning can not be denied. The interference of these political parties are increasing day-by-day and study tried to examine this fact by knowing the political affiliation of the respondents. In Table 18.8 the attempts have been made to know the party affiliation of the respondents.

Table 18.8: Party Affiliation of the Respondents in District Kangra

Sl. No.	*Political Parties*	*Total*	*Percentage*
1.	Congress	21	32.30
2.	BJP	22	33.85
3.	Other	22	33.85
	Total	65	100

Source: Primary Survey.

The Congress party and BJP are the main dominant parties in the state of Himachal Pradesh. The above table reveals that the respondents are equally affiliated with the BJP and Congress whereas remaining are independent or party-neutral respondents. This reveals that there is dominance of party politics in the grassroots institutions. Day-by-day, the indirect involvement of political parties is becoming direct interference in the grassroots politics and PRIs are not free from political parties.

Motivation for Contesting First Election

The survey questioned elected representatives about the factor that motivated them to contest their first Panchayat elections. While 20 percent claimed to be self-motivated, about 36.92 percent said that their spouse has inspired them. Out of total sample 33.85 percent are motivated by members of community group (such as Mahila Mandals, self-help groups, youth clubs, cooperatives, etc.). However, 9.23 percent of the elected representatives agreed the role of political parties in motivating them.

Table 18.9: The Essential Factors that can Motivate Women to take part in Election of PRI's in District Kangra

Sl. No.	*Factor Motivation*	*Total*	*Percentage*
1.	Self-Motivated	13	20.00
2.	Spouse	24	36.92
3.	Community Group	22	33.85
4.	Political Parties	06	9.23
	Total	65	100

Source: Primary Survey.

Male Dominance

Women have always been victims of male domination in all aspects of life throughout the history. Here, in this study we were concerned with dominant role played by male members in the decision making process. Mostly, women are dominated and guided by their male counterparts while taking the decision to contest the election in PRIs. The Table 18.10 presents the stratification the respondents regarding the issue of male dominance as follows:

Table 18.10: Detail of the Male Dominance in Decision-making Process in District Kangra

Sl. No.	*Response*	*Total*	*Percentage*
1.	Yes	42	64.62
2.	No	10	15.38
3.	No Opinion	13	20.00
	Total	65	100

Source: Primary Survey.

Thus, above table presents that most of the respondents agreed with the view that male dominate the decision-making process. It has been observed during the study that women are being dominated or influenced by the male members during decision-making process in Panchayati Raj Institutions. The study further finds that male interference in widely evident in the day-to-day activities of women while functioning at Panchayat level. The lack of experience, shortage of time due to their involvement in domestic affairs, etc., are the main factors for male's dominance over their sphere of activities.

Conclusion

Women participation in local government can best be understood within the context of a 'continuum of empowerment'. Women continue to face many constraints during their participation in local government. There constraints include; lack of experience, illiteracy, family responsibility, restrictive social norms, lack of an enabling environment, violence, including family violence trigged by their new position, harassment and character assignation. Despite these constraints, present research finds that socio-economic and political background of women leaders are the main determinate of women leadership pattern.

The study further reveals that young and educated women are emerging in the leadership pattern of PRIs. In the post 73rd Amendment Act further women leaders tend to come from agriculture background and middle income group. As far as direct or indirect involvement of political party are concerned, the study explores that majority of the women leaders are being influenced by political parties and they are duly affiliated with BJP or Congress Party. At the same time, these political parties are also motivating as well as inspiring actors for contesting the elections to PRIs at all levels.

The 73rd Amendment Act has some positive implications on the emergence of women leadership in PRIs. It has provided a political space to women and gave equal social status at par with a man which is good symbol for women empowerment. It has also provided opportunities for women leadership who are initiative, social, literate and provided political and administrative experience as well. The study analysed issues related to elected women representatives *vis-à-vis* their male counterparts.

It investigated their socio-economic characteristics, tracked their political career over the past three rounds of elections, and specifically examined the quality of their post-election participation in terms of performance of their roles, their synergy with the parallel bodies and Community Based Organisations. In nutshell, 50 percent reservations to women further strengthened their will to increase the level of participation in the democratic decentralisation process.

References

Bhuyan, D. (2008), "Women's Empowerment Participation in Panchayati Raj", *Yojana*, Vol. 52, October, p. 36.

Choudhary, D.S. (1981), *Emerging Leadership in an Indian State,* Rohtak: Manthan Publication, 1981, p. 1.

D'Lima, H. (1983), *Women in Local Government,* New Delhi: Concept Publishing Company, 1983, pp. 9-10.

Dubey, M.P. and Padaliya, Munni (2002), *Democratic Decentralisation of Panchayati Raj in India*, New Delhi: Anamika Publishers, p. 199.

Dutta, P. (2001), "Women in Panchayat", *Kurukshetra*, Vol. 50, No. 2, December, p. 35.

Indira, B., Kumar D. (1999), *Gender and Society in India*, Vol. II, New Delhi: Manak Publication, p. 106.

Kumar, S. (2008), *Women Empowerment Through Panchayati Raj Institutions in Himachal Himalaya*, Shimla: Institute of Himalayan Study, I.I.H.S., H.P.U., p. 3.

Majumda, A.K. (1996), *Panchayat Politics and Community Development*, New Delhi: Radha Publication, p. 39.

Narian, I. (1964), "Demoractic Decentralisation and Rural Leadership in India: The Rajasthan Experiment", *Asian Survey*, Vol. IV, Aug., pp. 1018-19.

Nupur (2008), "Women in Panchayati Raj", *The Indian Journal of Public Administration*, Vol. LIV, No. 1, Jan.-March, p. 34.

Sharma, R.K. (1997), *Rural Sociology, II*, New Delhi: Atlantic Publishers, pp. 212-15.

Sharma, U. and Sharma, B.M. (eds.) (1987), *Women and Society*, New Delhi: Common Wealth Publishers, 1987, pp. 17-18.

Singh, Raj (ed.) (2000), *New Panchayati Raj: A Functional Analysis*, New Delhi: Anmol Publication, p. 15.

Sisikar, V.M. (1970), *The Rural Elite in the Developing Society: A Study of Political Sociology*, New Delhi: Orient Longman Ltd., p. 1.

Vidya, K.C. (1999), *Political Empowerment of Women at Grassroots*, New Delhi: Kanishka Publishers, p. 137.

Socio-Economic Conditions of Women in Himachal Pradesh

Baldev Singh Negi and Mast Ram

"The human race is a two-winged bird. One wing is female, the other is male. Unless both wings are equally developed, the human race will not be able to fly. Now, more than ever; the cause of women is the cause of mankind."

—Boutros Boutros Ghali, Erstwhile Secretary General of the United Nations

Introduction

Gender equality is, first and foremost, a human right. A woman is entitled to live in dignity and in freedom from want and from fear. Empowering women is also an indispensable tool for advancing development and reducing poverty. Empowered women contribute to the health and productivity of whole families and communities and to improved prospects for the next generation. The importance of gender equality is underscored by its inclusion as one of the eight Millennium Development Goals. Gender equality is acknowledged as being a key to achieving the other seven goals.

Gender equality implies a society in which women and men enjoy the same opportunities, outcomes, rights and obligations in all spheres of life. Equality between men and women exists when both sexes are able to share equally in the distribution of power and influence; have equal opportunities for financial independence through work or through setting up businesses; enjoy equal access to education and the opportunity to develop personal ambitions.

Women's empowerment is vital to sustainable development and the realisation of human rights for all. Where women's status is low, family size tends to be large, which makes it more difficult for families to thrive. Population and development and reproductive health programmes are more effective when they address the educational opportunities, status and empowerment of women. When women are empowered, whole families benefit, and these benefits often have ripple effects to future generations (Shrivastva, 2009). Women's status has been considered as an important measure of social development in a community. It is a relevant tool for planning also.

The definition of women's status is measured using different indicators in different frameworks. The frameworks used to study status were defined more by default than discourse: the parameters used by a given study or analysis become the *de facto* definition of the frame work to study status. In the present study a sectoral approach for analysing the situation of women *vis-à-vis* men in some key sectors such as demography status, economic and work status, education status, health status and political status. Some studies include the parameter of the incidence and prevalence of violence against women (Anitha *et al.*, 1998).

Demography of Himachal Pradesh

Etymologically, the 'word' Himachal, the mountain of snow *('Him-snow, Anchal-mountain)*. The compact region, known as Himachal Pradesh was infact earlier divided in 30 odd principalities called as Punjab Hill States which gradually gained the status of a full-fledged state of Indian Union from 25th January, 1971. It is a northern state of India, bounded in north by Kashmir Valley, in south by Punjab and UP, Haryana and in north-east by Tibet. The altitudes of the state ranges from 350 meters to 6500 meters above main see level. The state has an area of 55673 sq. km. and constitutes 1.69 percent of India's area and 10.54 percent land mass. State is divided in 3 zone, 12 district, 52 sub-divisions, 109 tehsils and sub-tehsils, from development point of view, the Pradesh is divided into 75 developments blocks. The smallest unit for development-*cum*-administration is Panchayat and their number is 3243.

The State has a three-tier Panchayati Raj structure comprising of

12 Zila Parishads, 75 Panchayat Samitis and 3243 Gram Panchayats on the rural side; and 1 Municipal Corporation, 20 Municipal Councils and 28 Nagar Panchayats on the Urban side besides 7 Cantonment Boards. State is primarily rural, only one-eighth (13 percent) of households are in urban areas, and the remaining seven-eighths (87 percent) are in rural areas. On average, households in Himachal Pradesh are comprised of about five members. One-fifth (19 percent) of households are headed by women, with 16 percent of the population (Ministry of Health and Family Welfare, 2005-06).

According to the provisional census 2011, population-wise Kangra district contribute highest percentage, i.e., about 22 percent to the total population of the state followed by district Mandi (14.6 percent) and district Shimla (11.9 percent). On the other hand, district Lahaul and Spiti is the lowest populated (31,528 persons) among all the twelve districts of the state and contributes only 0.5 percent to the state's population (Table 19.1).

Table 19.1: District-wise Population Growth of Himachal Pradesh

Name	*Population*			*Growth Rate 2001-11*	*Density (per sq. km)*	
	Persons	*Males*	*Females*		*2001*	*2011*
Chamba	5,18,844	2,60,848	2,57,996	+12.58	71	80
Kangra	15,07,223	7,48,559	7,58,664	+12.56	233	263
Lahaul & Spiti	31,528	16,455	15,073	-5.10	2	2
Kullu	4,37,474	2,24,320	2,13,154	+14.65	69	79
Mandi	9,99,518	4,96,787	5,02,731	+10.89	228	253
Hamirpur	4,54,293	2,16,742	2,37,551	+10.08	369	406
Una	5,21,057	2,63,541	2,57,516	+16.24	291	338
Bilaspur	3,82,056	1,92,827	1,89,229	+12.08	292	327
Solan	5,76,670	3,06,162	2,70,508	+15.21	259	298
Sirmaur	5,30,164	2,76,801	2,53,363	+15.61	162	188
Shimla	8,13,384	4,24,486	3,88,898	+12.58	141	159
Kinnaur	84,298	46,364	37,934	+07.61	12	13
Himachal Pradesh	68,56,509	34,73,892	33,82,617	+12.81	109	123

Note: For calculation of sex-ratio, others have been considered as males.
Source: Series-3, Provisional Population Totals, Paper 1 of Census 2011.

Population growth of the state is plus 12.81 from census 2001 to 2011 (provisional). Among the districts highest growth rate plus 16.24 percent is recorded in district Una followed by Sirmour (+15.61 percent) and Solan (+15.21 percent). There is only one district in the state where

5.10 percent negative growth in population has been noticed in the provisional census 2011 (Table 19.1).

The density of the Himachal Pradesh was 109 per square kilometer according to census 2001 which now increased up to 123 per square kilometer in census, 2011. Among all the districts Hamirpur is highly dense where it was 369 per sq. km in 2001 now increased to 406 per sq. km in 2011 and here again district Lahaul and Spiti was the low density (2 per sq. km) and Kinnaur 12 and 13 per sq. km in censuses 2001 and 2011 respectively (Table 19.1).

Table 19.2 indicated the sex ratio over the period of time and it shows that decreasing sex ratio is a threat, since 1901 to 2011 it is below the average. It was 884 in 1901 in the state and now it has been gradually increased to 974 but then also it is below the average. According to the provisional census 2011, there are two districts *vis-a-vis* Solan (884) and Kinnaur (818) which are highly under critical situation where sex ratio is below 800. Shimla (916), Sirmaur (915) and Lahaul and Spiti (916) have also very low sex ratio. There are only two districts among the twelve in the state where sex ratio is above the average, namely, district Hamirpur (1096) and Mandi (1012).

Women and Health in Himachal Pradesh

Being a man or a woman has a significant impact on health, as a result of both biological and gender-related differences. The health of women and girls is of particular concern because, in many societies, they are disadvantaged by discrimination rooted in socio cultural factors. Some of the socio cultural and political factors that prevent women and girls to benefit from quality health services and attaining the best possible level of health include: an exclusive focus on women's reproductive roles; and potential or actual experience of physical, sexual and emotional violence. While poverty is an important barrier to positive health outcomes for both men and women, poverty tends to yield a higher burden on women and girls' health due to, for example, feeding practices (malnutrition) and use of unsafe cooking fuels.

Birth and Death Rate and Infant Mortality Rate

The mortality level in a population is an important indicator of its health and well-being. The infant mortality rate is an important measure of the well-being of infants, children, and pregnant women because it is associated with a variety of factors, such as maternal health, quality and access to medical care, socio-economic conditions, and public health practices. Table 19.3 shows that birth and death rates in the state is

Table 19.2: Sex-Ratios for State and Districts: 1901-2011

State/District	*1901*	*1911*	*1921*	*1931*	*1941*	*1951*	*1961*	*1971*	*1981*	*1991*	*2001*	*2011*
Chamba	903	897	893	910	874	894	876	945	936	949	959	989
Kangra	NA	900	930	917	916	936	964	1008	1016	1024	1025	1013
Lahul & Spiti	992	990	993	989	920	933	786	818	767	817	802	916
Kullu	NA	1009	1015	1006	930	941	945	920	918	920	927	950
Mandi	908	924	933	917	907	971	994	964	999	1013	1013	1012
Hamirpur	NA	900	930	917	916	936	1092	1118	1149	1105	1099	1096
Una	NA	900	930	917	916	936	978	1003	1028	1017	997	977
Bilaspur	840	862	874	900	938	948	952	993	1002	1002	990	981
Solan	725	723	645	724	736	800	879	923	929	909	852	884
Sirmaur	798	822	824	803	818	800	828	836	874	897	901	915
Shimla	853	881	842	886	867	875	852	869	878	894	896	916
Kinnaur	911	935	922	941	910	1070	969	887	885	856	857	818
Himachal Pradesh	**884**	**889**	**890**	**897**	**890**	**912**	**938**	**958**	**973**	**976**	**968**	**974**

NA = Not Available.

Source: Series-3, Provisional Population Totals, Paper 1 of Census 2011 and *Office of the Registrar General and Census Commissioner, India.*

significantly decreasing over the period of time. Birth rate in 1971 was 37.3 percent which decreased to 17.7 percent in 2008 and death rate decreased to 7.4 percent in 2008 from 15.6 percent in 1971. At the same time the difference between the birth and death rates also came down to 10.3 percent from 21.7 percent.

Table 19.3: Birth Rate and Death Rate in H.P and Comparative Data on Infant Mortality Rate

Year	*Birth Rate*	*Death Rate*	*Differential*	*Infant Mortality Rate (Per Thousand)*	
				Himachal	*All India*
1971	37.3	15.6	21.7	118	129
1981	31.5	11.1	20.4	71	110
1991	28.5	8.9	19.6	75	80
1999	23.8	7.3	16.5	62	70
2000	22.1	7.2	14.9	60	68
2001	21.2	7.1	14.1	54	66
2002	20.7	7.5	13.2	52	63
2003	20.6	7.1	13.5	49	60
2004	19.2	6.8	12.4	51	58
2005	20.0	6.9	13.1	49	58
2006	18.8	6.8	12.0	50	57
2007	17.4	7.1	10.3	47	55
2008	17.7	7.4	10.3	44	53

Source: Sample Registration System, Bulletin Registrar General, India.

Life Expectancy at Birth

Life expectancy at birth for a population cohort can be understood as the average number of years that a child born in the year is expected to live when exposed to the prevailing risks of death at various ages. It reflects and summarises the current age-specific death rates that in turn depend on the mortality profile. Life expectancy at birth is considered as a comprehensive measure of mortality, and is often used as a measure of health development. Both male and female Life expectancy at birth in Himachal Pradesh was high than the overall nation's life expectancy during the period from 1998-2002 to 2002-06 (Table 19.4).

Perinatal Mortality

Perinatal mortality, which includes stillbirths and very early infant deaths (in the first week of life), is estimated at 30 deaths per 1,000 pregnancies that lasted 7 months or more. Perinatal mortality is over two and half times higher in rural areas (32) than in urban areas (12).

Birth intervals also have a very strong effect on perinatal mortality. For pregnancies that take place less than 27 months after a previous birth, the perinatal mortality rate is 19 per 1,000, compared with only 7 per 1,000 when the interval is at least 39 months.

Table 19.4: Life Expectancy at Birth

Period	*Himachal Pradesh*		*India*	
	Male	*Female*	*Male*	*Female*
1998-2002	65.7	66.3	61.6	63.3
1999-2003	65.8	66.6	61.8	63.5
2000-04	66.1	66.8	62.1	63.7
2001-05	66.3	67.1	62.3	63.9
2002-06	66.5	67.3	62.6	64.2

Source: SRS, Registrar General of India, based Abridge Life Tables, 2002-06.

Mental Health: Antenatal Care

Among women who gave birth in the five years preceding the survey, 84 percent received antenatal care from a health professional (66 percent from a doctor and 18 percent from any other health professional). Five percent received antenatal care from a *dai* or traditional birth attendant (TBA). Women with more education, women in the highest wealth quintile, and women having their first child were more likely than other women to receive antenatal care. One in ten mothers received no antenatal care.

It is pertinent to note that despite a high level of antenatal care coverage in Himachal Pradesh, less than two-thirds of women in the state received at least three antenatal care visits for their last birth. Fifty-seven percent of women received antenatal care during the first trimester of pregnancy, as is recommended. Another 23 percent had their first visit during the fourth or fifth month of pregnancy. More than three in five mothers had three or more antenatal care visits; urban women were more likely to have three or more visits (76 percent) than rural women (61 percent). Although the coverage of three or more antenatal care visits is almost unchanged since NFHS-2, the proportion of women who received their first antenatal care visit in the first trimester of pregnancy has increased by 8 percentage points.

Delivery Care

Fifty-seven percent of births in the past five years in the state took place at home; more than two in five births took place in a health facility.

Institutional deliveries are less common among women who received no antenatal checkups, younger women, women with less education, women in the lower wealth quintiles, and births of higher order.

A little less than half of births during the five years preceding the survey (48%) took place with assistance from a health professional. Only 10 percent of home births were assisted by a health professional. A disposable delivery kit (DDK) was used for only one out of two home births.

The proportions of deliveries that take place in health facilities and deliveries that are assisted by a health professional have both risen over time. Among births in the three years before each survey, 45 percent of births in NFHS-3 were reported as delivered in a health facility, up from 17 percent in NFHS-1 and 29 percent in NFHS-2. A similar, though less sharp, increase is observed in deliveries assisted by a health professional.

In 94 percent of home births, a clean blade was used to cut the cord, as is recommended, but only 72 percent of home births followed the recommendation that the baby be immediately wiped dry and then wrapped without being bathed first. Women who gave birth at home were asked why they did not deliver in a health facility; by far the most common reason given was that they did not feel it was necessary to deliver in a facility (78 percent). Eleven percent of women said delivery in a health facility is too expensive. Sharp increase in institutional deliveries since NFHS-2 has been noticed.

Women's Nutritional Status

Adults in the state suffer from a dual burden of malnutrition; 3 in 10 adults are too thin, and 14 percent of women and 11 percent of men are overweight or obese. Only 60 percent of men and 57 percent of women are at a healthy weight for their height. Using iodized salt prevents iodine deficiency, which can lead to miscarriage, goitre, and mental retardation. Eighty-three percent of households in state were using sufficiently iodized salt at the time of the survey. This is 8 percentage points lower than the percentage in NFHS-2 (91 percent). However, a nationwide ban on non-iodised salt took effect just as the NFHS-3 fieldwork was being completed, so the effects of the new law could not be determined by the survey.

Anaemia

Anaemia is a major health problem among women and children. Anaemia can result in maternal mortality, weakness, diminished physical and mental capacity, increased morbidity from infectious diseases, prenatal mortality, premature delivery, low birth weight, and (in children) impaired cognitive performance, motor development, and scholastic achievement. Among children between the ages of 6 and 59 months, more than half (55 percent) are anaemic. This includes 26 percent, who are mildly anaemic, 27 percent who are moderately anaemic, and 2 percent who suffer from severe anaemia. Girls are slightly more likely than boys to have anaemia. Children of mothers who have anaemia are much more likely to be anaemic.

Over two-fifths of women in state have anaemia, including 32 percent with mild anaemia, 11 percent with moderate anaemia, and 1 percent with severe anaemia. Anaemia is particularly high among rural women, and women belonging to other backward classes. Women who are breastfeeding are more likely than pregnant or non-breastfeeding women to be anaemic. The prevalence of anaemia declined among children age 6-35 months over the past seven years from 70 percent in NFHS-2 to 62 percent in NFHS-3. By contrast, the prevalence of anaemia among ever-married women has increased by 3 percentage points.

Women and Education in Himachal Pradesh

Literacy and education becomes an important tool for the economic growth, for the effective decision-making and empowerment of the women. Quality of life and human development attainments invariably are high in the countries, which have invested heavily in education. In a country, which is in transition phase and is increasingly recognised as knowledge economy in the global market, education to women becomes of paramount importance, not to speak of basic right to access to education and determinant of worth of society by the literacy rates of women. Education as such, results in positive externalities. Not only does it have an intrinsic value in the sense of the joy of learning, reading, etc., but it also has instrumental, social and process roles.

Moreover, education may spread through interpersonal motivation. When one individual sends her child to school, her neighbour is likely to do so as well. Women's education too, often spreads this way, more specifically, through same sex effects, i.e., an educated woman is far more likely to send her daughter to school than an uneducated woman. Also, she is likely to maintain better conditions of nutrition and hygiene in her household and thereby improve her family's health (Sen, 1997). The presence of a larger number of female teachers may encourage parents to send their daughters to school. Thus education is a fundamental tool for women's empowerment.

The growth in literacy from 1961 to 2011 witnessed the tremendous growth in the state. However the growth in the nineties slowed down than a previous decade, because of wider base after the impressive growth results accumulated. In 1961 female literacy was just 9.49 percent and male literacy was 32.31 percent, however, census 2011 (provisional) is shows the growth in literacy in manifolds as female literacy has reached to 76.60 percent and male literacy is 90.83 percent. The growth rates for female have shown better attainment than their male counterparts, yet in absolute terms, females are less literate than males (Table 19.5).

Table 19.5: Literacy Rates by Sex from 1961-2011

Year	*Literacy in (%)*		
	Male	*Female*	*Total*
1961	32.31	9.49	21.26
1971	43.19	20.23	31.96
1981	64.29	37.72	51.18
1991	75.36	52.13	63.86
2001	86.02	68.08	77.13
2011	90.83	76.60	83.80

Source: Compiled from different government reports.

Table 19.6 depicts the decadal (2001-11) difference in literacy in India and Himachal Pradesh, difference in male literacy. It is 4.83 percent in the state and 6.14 percent is at the national level. However, the difference in female literacy rate is more than double, i.e., 8.5 percent in the state and 11.6 percent difference is at the national level. Further,

Table 19.6: Comparative Decadal Differences in Literacy: Himachal and India

		Himachal	*India*
Census 2001	Male Literacy	86.0	76.0
	Female Literacy	68.1	54.3
Gap in M-F literacy rate		17.9	21.7
Census 2011	Male Literacy	90.83	82.14
	Female Literacy	76.60	65.46
Gap in M-F literacy rate		14.23	16.68
Decadal difference in literacy rates	Male Literacy	4.83	6.14
	Female Literacy	8.5	11.16

Source: Registrar General & Census Commissioner, India (2001a:126f).

analysing the gap between male and female literacy, in 2001 it was 17.9 percent in Himachal Pradesh which has been reduced up to 14.23 percent in 2011 and the national level the gap in male female literacy it was about 4 percent bigger than Himachal Pradesh in 2001 which reduced to 16.68 percent in 2011.

Table 19.7 reveals the girls enrollment at the various stages, i.e., primary, upper primary, secondary and at higher education in the state during the years 2002-03 to 2007-08. In 2003-03 the girl's enrolment in primary level was 47.8 percent, at upper primary level 47.4 percent, secondary level 46.4 percent and at higher education level it was 42.7 percent. After five years, i.e., in 2007-08 girls enrollment at primary was 47.3 percent, at upper primary level 47.2 percent, secondary level 47.3 percent and at the higher education level it was 45.0 percent. Data of last five years shows that there has been a gradual fluctuation in the girl's enrolment at the various levels.

Table 19.7: Enrolments by Stages 2007-08 as on 30-09-2007

Year	*I-V*		*VI-VIII*		*IX-XII*		*Higher Education*	
	Girls	*Total*	*Girls*	*Total*	*Girls*	*Total*	*Girls*	*Total*
2002-03	47.8	720842	47.4	439613	46.4	365662	42.7	89714
2003-04	48.0	666938	47.9	419878	46.7	374276	43.6	94081
2004-05	47.7	670807	47.5	418802	46.7	690449	47.1	103628
2005-06	47.6	660960	47.4	410860	47.1	393337	46.5	104112
2006-07	47.3	676245	47.2	405596	45.7	414477	49.6	121865
2007-08	47.3	659579	47.2	424656	47.3	249283	45.0	161308

Source: Annual Reports 2004-05 to 2010-11, Department of School Education and Literacy, Department of Higher Education, Ministry of Human Resource Development, Government of India.

Dropout

Table 19.8 indicates the average dropout rate during 2002-03 to 2007-08 in the state. In 2002-03, the total dropout rate for classes I-V was 12.42 percent in which girls dropout percentage was 14.08 percent about 4 percent higher than the boys (10.82 percent). The dropout rate for class I-VIII was 9.56 percent in total and girls share was 11.32 percent, about 3.5 percent higher than the boys.

In the same year dropout rate for I-X classes was 29.95 percent and again the gap between girls and boys enrollment was notice up to 3-4 percent. As compare to the year 2002-03 to 2007-08 a significant decrease has been noticed in total and both in girls and boys dropout rate, as in 2007-08 dropout rate for the classes I-V was 2.9 percent with 4.4 percent girls and 1.6 percent boy's drop out. The dropout rate for the classes I-X was 30.2 percent with gap about 8 percent between girls and boys.

Table 19.8: Dropout Rates in Classes (I-V), (I-VIII) and (I-X)

Year	*I-V*			*I-VIII*			*I-X*		
	Boys	*Girls*	*Total*	*Boys*	*Girls*	*Total*	*Boys*	*Girls*	*Total*
2002-03	10.82	14.08	12.42	7.90	11.32	9.56	28.75	31.23	29.95
2003-04	15.87	18.15	16.98	13.29	15.32	14.28	31.85	33.03	23.42
2004-05	0.11	6.67	3.40	11.55	22.48	17.01	37.84	43.07	40.35
2005-06	10.3	11.40	10.69	8.70	13.02	10.82	25.68	32.47	29.00
2006-07	6.1	7.5	6.8	3.2	5.9	4.5	25.4	31.0	28.2
2007-08	1.6	4.4	2.9	0	0	0	26.1	34.2	30.2

Source: Annual Reports 2004-05 to 2010-11, Department of School Education and Literacy, Department of Higher Education, Ministry of Human Resource Development, Government of India

Above table reveals that women enrolment in post-graduate courses contributes 54.7 percent to the total enrolment (4611 students) in post-graduate courses in Himachal Pradesh. Among the post-graduate courses, women enrolment was noticed quite pathetic in some of the professional courses, e.g., it was only 15 percent in Engineering/Technology/Architecture/Design, 36 percent in Agriculture and Allied and only 39 percent in Medicine. High women enrolment was noticed only in Education/Teacher Training with 72.7 percent (Table 19.9).

As far as the under graduate course are concerned the out of the total enrolment the women share was 53.8 percent but, again the story was as similar as was in enrolment of post-graduation courses. Women enrolment in the professional under graduate courses much lower than the boys (Table 19.9).

Table 19.9: Enrolments in Higher Education by Level/Course (All Categories of Students)

Sl. No.	*Courses*	*Post-Graduate*		*Under-Graduate*	
		Total	*Women*	*Total*	*Women*
1.	Arts	2421	1547 (63.9)	45277	26474 (58.4)
2.	Commerce	68	39 (57.3)	6157	2223 (36.10)
3.	Science	523	268 (51.2)	12592	7195 (57.13)

(*Contd.*)

Sl. No.	*Courses*	*Post-Graduate*		*Under-Graduate*	
		Total	*Women*	*Total*	*Women*
4.	Engineering/Technology/ Architecture/Design	113	17 (15.0)	5273	995 (18.9)
5.	Medicine	133	52 (39.1)	3538	1463 (41.3)
6.	Agriculture & Allied	271	105 (38.7)	607	242 (39.9)
7.	Management/Hotel/Travel/ Tourism Management	352	128 (36.4)	1969	598 (30.4)
8.	Education/Teacher Training	55	40 (72.7)	5975	4804 (80.7)
9.	Law	49	32 (65.3)	1342	454 (33.8)
10	Other	596	297 (49.8)	3162	1222 (38.6)
	Total	4611	2525 (54.7)	84892	45670 (53.8)

Note: Enrolment in Open and Distance Learning has not been included.
Source: Statistics of Higher and Technical Education—2007-08. MoHRD, Bureau of Planning, Monitoring and Statistics, GOI, 2011.

The status of category-wise enrolment of women students in higher education was not encouraging as in post-graduate course enrolment of scheduled caste students was 13.9 percent, enrolment in under-graduate courses 14.2 percent and in M.Phil./Ph.D. it was 7.27 percent. In the same category the women students' enrollment it was 52.6 percent in post-graduate courses, 47.8 percent under graduate courses and 34.3 percent in M.Phil./Ph.D. courses. On the other hand, in scheduled tribe category total enrollment was 7.06 percent in post-graduate courses, 5.4 percent in under-graduate courses and 4.6 percent in M.Phil./Ph.D. courses.

While calculating the women students enrolment among scheduled tribe category, it was 47.6 percent in post-graduate courses, 48 percent in undergraduate courses and 40 percent in M.Phil./Ph.D. courses (Table 19.10). Here it is pertinent to mention that scheduled caste population contributes 24.70 percent and scheduled tribe contributes 4 percent to the total population of the state (HP). But the enrolment of the scheduled caste students in higher education has been noticed below the percentage of its population.

One of the most compelling arguments for increasing the number of women teachers in educational institutions relates to the positive impact that doing so has on girls' education. Table 19.11 indicates that during 2007-08 numbers of women teachers in the state (HP) was 49 percent to the total teacher's strength. On the other hand, in the same period women teacher's percentage in all India level was 48.2 percent (Table 19.11).

Table 19.10: Category-wise Women Students Enrolment in M.Phil./Ph.D., Post-Graduate and Under-Graduate Courses

Sl. No.	*Category*	*Post-Graduate*		*Under-Graduate*		*M.Phil./Ph.D.*	
		Total	*Women*	*Total*	*Women*	*Total*	*Women*
1.	Scheduled Castes	647 (13.9)	340 (52.6)	12033 (14.2)	5757 (47.8)	334 (7.27)	115 (34.3)
2.	Scheduled Tribes	328 (7.06)	156 (47.6)	4600 (5.4)	2207 (48.0)	112 (4.6)	45 (40.2)
	All Categories	4641	2525 (54.4)	84892	45670 (53.8)	2429	1044 (43.0)

Source: Statistics of Higher and Technical Education, 2007-08, MoHRD, Bureau of Planning, Monitoring and Statistics, GOI, 2011.

Note: Enrolment in Open and Distance Learning has not been included.

Table 19.11: Number of Teachers in Educational Institutions—2007-08

(Primary/Junior, Middle/Sr. Basic, High/Post Basic and Higher Secondary)

States/UTs	*Total*	*Women*
Himachal Pradesh	69431	34079
India	5270252	2539067

Source: Department of Education, Ministry of Human Resource, Government of India, Dehli.

Women and Work Force Participation in Himachal Pradesh

Human Development is viewed as composite of indices, namely, economic empowerment, health and educational status. Women economic empowerment, their participation in the work is an important component towards measuring the Gender equality or inequality. Since per capita income continues to be important indicator of economic well-being, the data constraints make it unable to estimate the per capita income of women in the state, another data gap if looked at from the gender perspective. Further a large number of women work in the farms, agricultural lands and their own orchards, where their wages are not measurable in absence of time use surveys or economic estimations in the state. Nevertheless the workforce numbers indicate the increasing healthy trend of increased female participation in the workforce. There has been gradual increase in the proportion of women to the total workforce and gender disparity has reduced over the decades. While in 1981, females made up the 37.07 percent of total work force, in 1991 and 2001 this proportion has increased to 40.15 percent and 43.66 percent respectively. Compound growth of main and females marginal workers was 3.38 percent as compared to 1.96 percent of males (Table 19.12)

Table 19.12: Gender Disparity in Terms of the Share of Females in Total Workforce and its Compound Growth Rate of Himachal Pradesh (1981–2001)

Census year	*Main workers*		*Marginal workers*		*Main & marginal workers*	
	Males	*Females*	*Males*	*Females*	*Males*	*Females*
1981	73.15	26.85	19.11	80.89	62.93	37.07
1991	72.21	27.79	9.35	90.65	59.85	40.15
2001	67.92	32.08	34.19	65.81	56.34	43.66
Compound Growth 1981-2001	1.08	2.36	8.76	4.55	1.96	3.38

Source: Computed from the Census 1981 and 2001 data.

Women Participation in PRI's and the State Legislature in the State

Women participation in politics is an important step towards social equality, economic development of any society. Hitherto women have been denied equality of status and opportunities in the social, economic and political spheres. Despite constituting more than half of the country's population, women have remained marginal to the democratic process. Women have been remained inadequately represented in various policy and decision-making bodies at various levels, which so vitally influence their lives. Perhaps the main reasons for this deep-rooted gender biased are social attitudes and practices and lack of organisation to voice their concern.

The continued low level non-representation of women in the democratic institutions was called for affirmative action at the highest levels. The enactment of the 73rd Constitutional Amendment in 1993, which clearly mandates 33.3 percent reservation of seats for them in the local bodies, has brought about a radical change and women participation and representation at the grass root level has increased considerably. This landmark constitutional amendment has paved the way for women finding a prominent place among the Panchayat representatives. Reservation of seats at the grassroot level, i.e., Gram Panchayats has opened a new era of opportunities for the women, previously only the women hailing from privileged sections of the society had the chance to participate in the decision-making processes. The 73rd Constitutional Amendment has proved to be a boon for women especially the rural women enabling them to contribute in their own way to the society, thus enabling them to think beyond their home and hearth.

There are 68 constituencies in the state legislative assembly comprising 49 general, 16 or scheduled caste and 3 for scheduled tribe. Women voters are playing a very important and decisive role for the government formation in the state. Table 19.13 showing the percentage of women electors among the total electors in Himachal Pradesh since 1977 to 2003. During the assembly election 1977 there was 19,97,405 voters out which 48.6 percent (9,69,744) were women electors. The percentage of women electors increased to 50.2 percent in the election of 1982 and 1985. In the latest state assembly election, i.e., 2007 assembly election there was 49.2 percent women electors (Table 19.13).

In the voting percentage table is further revealing the fact that though women vote percentage in the state was not much encouraging till the state assembly election 1993 as compare to the men. But after the assembly election 1998 it was noticed uninterruptedly increasing till the latest assembly election held in 2007. In the assembly election 2007 women vote percentage was about 5 percent higher than the men in the state. It was all because of women empowerment and growing awareness among the women towards their rights, duty and importance in the nation-building (Table 19.13).

Women reservation (33 percent) has been provided by the amendment in Panchayat Raj Act, 1994, and Himachal Pradesh Panchayati Raj Amendment Act, 2008 has provided 50 percent reservation of seats for women in PRIs and urban local bodies which is a historical step for the political empowerment of women. The experiment of 50 percent reservation of seats for women in PRIs and urban local bodies has been successful in the State. Before 1995, women's representation in local self-governments was up to two women in all the bodies. After 1995, it has increased to minimum 33 percent and

Table 19.13: Women Electors, Voting percentage and Representation of Women of Vidhan Sabha Elections

Years	*No. of Seats*	*No. of Electors*		*Voting Percentage*			*Difference between men & women voting percentage*	*Representation of Women*		
		Women	*Total*	*Men*	*Women*	*Total*		*Total Contes-tants*	*Women Contestants (%age to the total contestants)*	*Seats Won by Women (%age to the Total Seats)*
1972	-	-	-	49.95	-	-	-	-	5*	5 (7.35)
1977	68	969744	1997405	58.57	62.16	54.76	- 7.40	330	9(2.72)	1 (1.47)
1982	68	1109961	2211524	71.06	73.29	68.85	- 4.44	441	9(2.04)	3 (4.41)
1985	68	1183713	2356932	70.36	71.91	68.83	- 3.08	294	8(2.72)	3 (4.41)
1990	68	1511087	3058394	67.73	69.48	65.97	- 3.51	454	17(3.74)	4 (5.88)
1993	68	1624429	3267725	71.72	72.21	71.21	- 1.00	416	16(3.85)	4 (5.88)
1998	68	1801571	3628864	71.23	70.24	72.32	+ 1.99	369	25(6.78)	7 (10.29)
2003	68	2019973	4101093	74.51	73.14	75.92	+ 2.78	408	31(7.60)	4 (5.88)
2007	68	2267604	4604443	71.61	69.67	74.55	+ 4.88	336	25(7.44)	5 (7.35)

Reports on General Elections to Himachal Pradesh State Legislative Assembly from 1972 to 2007, Chief Electoral Officer and Financial Commissioner, Govt. of H.P., Shimla.

*One woman member was elected in the bye-election.

Source: Compiled from the various reports of HP State Election Commission, Shimla.

now 50 percent since 2010 elections to the PRIs and urban local bodies. Table 19.14 reveals the performance of women participation in the PRI election 2011. Data of 2347 gram pachayats shows that there were total 1286 (54.8 percent) women elected pradhan (president) against the reservation of 50 percent. Out of 402 gram panchayats there were 314 elected up-pradhan (vice-presidents) in the state.

Table 19.14: Total Number of Women Elected in PRIs in the Panchayat Election, 2011

Elected women for the post of	*No. of Gram Panchayat*	*Elected*				
		GEN (W)	*SC (W)*	*ST (W)*	*OBC (W)*	*Total*
Ward member	2710	5015	2852	631	602	9050
Up-Pradhan	402	175	44	34	61	314
Pradhan	2347	690	344	69	183	1286

Note: Data of Panchayat Smiti Tissa, Bhoran, Tihra Sujanpur, Panchrukhi, Lahaul, Nahan and Nalagrah, not included in the table.
Source: State Election Commission, Himachal Pradesh.

Crimes and Security

In the security related issues, Himachal Pradesh is rank high state in crimes against women, while the totals numbers of crimes have gone down from 920 reported cases in 2002 to 881 in 2006, overall it ranks 5th in the country under this category. Another noteworthy feature of social security is the care for female headed households. The underlying reasons for the greater incidence of female headed households are two-folds: *de-jure*, due to widowhood, being abandoned etc., de-facto, due to long-term migration, economic crises, refugees status abandonment. Next to Kerala, Himachal has the highest number of female headed households. However, domestic violence is high, but unreported and socially accepted. Number of girl child labourers in Himachal Pradesh is 8 times higher than in Kerala and Punjab.

Concluding Remarks

Findings of the above writings reveals that Himachal Pradesh has set example of fast mover in being gender empowered state in the country, yet there are certain constraints which have locked horns with the gender mainstreaming or the women empowerment. In spite of the various legal provisions and women's specific developmental programmes, the gender bias and deep-rooted prejudices still persist. The continuously declining child sex ratio over time is a glaring example of gender bias and is a matter of serious concern.

There has been noticed gap between male female literacy, meanwhile, female literacy has recorded an unprecedented increase but, despite sharp increase it is still far below the male literacy percentage. In a hilly state like Himachal Pradesh women's life is extremely busy from early morning to late evening and sometimes even till late at night. Women work side by side with men in every sphere of life. But while analysing the situation of girls' enrolment at the higher education level there again biasness has clearly occurred especially girls' enrolment in professional courses was negligible as comparative to the boys. Women work force participation is an important component towards measuring the gender equality or inequality. Data of various censuses shows higher involvement of males in full time work and that of females in seasonal work. Low literacy rate among females is the main reason for their non-participation in full time work or jobs of professional nature.

It also speaks of their less freedom in work choice. Various reports of NFHS further reveals that the health status of women in state has not been sufficiently maintained. For example, very few deliveries are being conducted in the health institutions and negligible numbers of women who delivered received post-natal check-ups. Notwithstanding the status of empowerment of women in health care decision-making, in accessibility of health centers, because of the topography, poor infrastructure facilities and frequent transfer of grassroots health workers may be the reasons for lower maternal health status of women. Also there are number of issues which needs a perfect women empowerment policy to be prepared by the state to integrate women effectively into the process of development and a holistic approach is necessary to consider all the aspects of women empowerment, social, economic, political, cultural, security and decision-making.

References

Anitha, B.K. *et al.* (1998), "Status of Rural Women in Karnataka", *Institute of Advanced Studies*, Bangalore.

Bhasin, V. (1991), "Status of women in the Himalayas: A case of Gaddis", *J. Hum. Ecol.*, 2(2), pp. 107-16.

Bhasin, V. (1988), *Himalayan Ecology, Transhumance and Social Organisation. Gaddis of Himachal Pradesh*, New Delhi: Kamla-Raj Enterprises.

Elementary Education in India, Progress Towards UEE, Flash Statistics, 2008-09, National University of Education Planning and Administration, New Delhi.

Government of Himachal Pradesh (2003), *An Overview of Planning in Himachal Pradesh*, Planning Department, Shimla.

Government of Himachal Pradesh (2005), *Economic Survey of Himachal Pradesh, 2004-05*, Economics & Statistics Department, Shimla.

Government of Himachal Pradesh, *Evaluation of Gandhi Kutir Yojana in Himachal*

Pradesh, Planning Department, Shimla.

Government of India (2010), *Report to the People on Education, 2009-10,* Ministry of Human Resource Development, New Delhi.

Government of India, *Annual Report, 2003-04, 2004-05, 2005-06, 2006-07, 2007-08 and 2009-10,* Department of Secondary & Higher Education, Ministry of Human Resource Development, New Delhi.

Government of India, Himachal Pradesh (2006), *National Family Health Survey (NFHS-3), 2005-06,* International Institute of Population Science, Mumbai, Ministry of Health and Family Welfare.

Government of Himachal Pradesh (2001), *Human Development Report-2001,* Planning Department, Shimla.

Kelkar, G. (1991), "Violence Against Women in India: Perspectives and Strategies", *Asian Institute of Technology,* Bangkok.

Ministry of Health and Family Welfare (2005-06), Government of India, *National Family Health Survey (NFHS-3), Himachal Pradesh,* International Institute of Populaiton Science, Mumbai.

Mukharjee, Mukul A. (2004), Situational Analysis of Women and Girls in West Bengal, *National Commission for Women,* New Delhi.

Research on ICDS: an Overview (2008), National Institute of Public Cooperation and Child Development, Vol. 3, 1996-2008, New Delhi.

Srilatha, B. *et al.* (1998), Status of Rural Women in Karnataka, *National Institute of Advanced Studies,* Bangalore.

Srivastava, Meetika, Essay on Women Empowerment (October 4, 2009). Available at SSRN: http://ssrn.com/abstract=1482560

Vaidya, V. (2004), "A Situational Analysis of Women and Girls in Himachal Pradesh", *National Commission for Women,* New Delhi.

Online Sources

www.educationhp.org
www.education.nic.in
www.hp.gov.in
http://himachal.nic.in/economics/
http://himachal.nic.in/hipa/
http://hprural.nic.in/
http://hphealth.nic.in/
http://hppanchayat.nic.in/
http://himachal.gov.in/welfare/

Questioning Women's Labour: Women in Manipur

NAOREM ARUNIBALA DEVI AND K.R. NAYAR

Introduction

North-east region of India has its natural beauty which is marred by poor development in many sectors. This is combined with extremely uncertain political scenario with insurgency playing an important role in all spheres of community life. It is undoubtedly the common people, the poor and the marginalised are the ones who suffer the most in this scenario. Even among these, women and children are affected the most. It appears that government of Manipur is more focused on tackling the problem of insurgent uprising than fighting social issues including the problems of women who are the backbone of the welfare of the family and the society.

It is normally assumed that women in north-east region are relatively more empowered as compared with their fellow women citizens in other regions of the nation. Leaving aside the existing matriarchal social structure in the state of Meghalaya where the women are expected to be the owners of the ancestral property, women in rest of the states in the region face discrimination based on gender similar to other patriarchal social structures. In fact, there have been changes even within the matrilineal structure among the Khasis (Nongbri, 1984 quoted in Biswas, 2008). Even in a situation where a woman is expected to inherit the ancestral property, studies have revealed that women do not possess the right to dispose-off the property on their own (Biswas). Women in Meghalaya face 'double negative effects': (a) discrimination based on gender, and (b) women have rights over the wealth which becomes largely pseudo depiction of women having power and this deviates the policy attention to ensure their rights (Chhakchhauk, cited in Biswas).

More often, Manipur has been misconceived as a matriarchal society where women are considered to be empowered if not equals in all forms. This happens due to the existing matrilineal structures in two communities, i.e., Khasi-Jaintia and Garo in Meghalaya State (Sharma, 2008). Manipur is a patriarchal social set-up, and it directly or indirectly indicates that subordination of women does exist in Manipur too which is predominantly found in all the patriarchal societies. It is important to highlight this because women's issues should be dealt carefully and their needs to be addressed in the policy planning. To quote Agarwal, equality of women is the basic condition of development of the nation (Agarwal, 2002).

From the mid-1980s onwards, many studies highlight women's role in the developmental process in which women's economic participation is given prime importance, intended to empower women. In due process, gender inequality is expected to reduce within the family and in the society through the process of empowerment. Against this scenario, this study explores women's level of work participation in the weaving sector, their role in decision-making process of the family and examines whether their perceived contribution towards the survival and livelihood of the family is converted into power. It is informed by Sen (1990) that there is a positive relationship between high perceived contribution and one's bargaining power over the conflicting interest among the members in the family.

Gender inequality and female deprivation can be characterised as the negative aspects in the process of women's empowerment. The study examines the complex relationship between women's work participation, empowerment and well-being. With this, we would be able to delineate the assumption of women's economic participation and its positive implications for women's life. Like in any other patriarchal society, in Manipur too, the gender roles have been clearly defined despite their 'value added services' to the family income. However, women could not gain due recognition out of their economic contribution in their families which was clearly revealed in the study among the women involved in pottery work in Manipur though majority of them were the main income earners in their families (Naorem, 2007). Home has become the work place thereby women handle their domestic chores side-by-side. As Donahoe says, one major problem with the labour force concept is that household or domestic work is not defined as economic activity because it is of use value rather than exchange value (Donahoe, 1999).

The authors further add that there is a thin line between housework and primary production. Therefore, women may not report economic activity that they consider part of their domestic duties. The fundamental question is what constitutes work. Feminists posed on the question of work women performed as a housework which is normally described as non-productive in relation to the production process and market system. This indicates that the 'values' of women have been ignored in the society and are marginalised even when they contribute economically.

In Manipur, Meitei women's active role in the market economy as well as in public domain has been documented academically. However, it is important for us to understand the linkages between their economic contribution and their level of empowerment. In this study, the authors will make an attempt to draw linkages between female work participation, economic contribution and empowerment in Manipur by focusing on women weavers who contribute economically to not only the family but the society as well. Most studies in the field of gender indicate the unequal power relation between men and women in the society and especially in the patriarchal social set-up.

To examine gender roles critically remain significant because we cannot ignore its impact on health of the women in the long-run. It is necessary to understand the social factors which aid women's oppression along with perceptual factors such as how women feel about it. Given this background, this study advances a hypothesis that the invisibility that is observed regarding the household labour of women is also extended to the economic sectors where women work for their livelihood as the women have no control and autonomy with regard to the income earned by women and is also unrecognised. The continuation of such oppression needs to be contextualised within the present paradigm of development which strongly focuses on the intent that women be made inclusive or equal partners in the process of development.

Methodological Framework

Study Area

The study was undertaken in three districts-Imphal East, Imphal West and Bishnupur depending on the concentration level of weavers among the nine districts in the state, Manipur. All these three districts under the study are in the valley areas and majority of the population belong to Meitei community. Nine villages were covered under these three districts depending on the concentration level of the women weavers. The three different organisations in production process were chosen based on women weavers' relationship with marketing of their finished products. They are as follows:

1. Category I: Household Level of Production (HLP)

Weavers involved in household level of production (HLP, hereafter) are hereby categorised as Category I (Cat. I, hereafter). Due to the situation and context of the field, snow balling technique was adopted to gather the data. With the help of this technique, the researchers were able to collect informations on marketing channel of the products; their relationship with the middle women and mode of payment; their choices and freedom in their occupation as well as their lives; their level of empowerment; health perceptions and livelihood strategies adopted by the women weavers keeping in view the socio-political situation in Manipur at present. In Cat. I, the authors studied the culture of weaving in household level of production. In this category, women weave in their own homes and also they have their own looms. The areas covered in this group are Kongba Ucheckkon, Wangkhei, Huirem (Bamon Kampu), Chanam Sandrok and Heigrujam.

2. Category II: Women Weavers under "NC"

The second Category (Cat. II, hereafter) of weavers belong to a NGO based in Imphal West district of Manipur. The name of this organisation is '*Women's Worth Organisation*'[1] (NC group, hereafter) based in Nagamapal, Imphal West in the heart of the main market '*Ima* Keithel'. A group of weavers in this organisation from Moidangpok in Imphal West was selected for the study. The selection of the organisation and its member weavers was purposive. The organisation is working mainly for the social upliftment of the women and girls in the rural areas through income generation. Based on the organisation's imperative towards women and girls in the society, the issues covered for the study were security level of the weavers; the mode of payment and their relationship with the organisation; any upliftment through their involvement with the organisation; their role in the family maintenance and perception about their health. Weavers covered under this category also work in their own homes except one group of women weavers working under the work shed built by the organisation in 2006. In this work shed, 12 weavers were working together. The products of the weavers under 'NC' in this village and to some extent from nearby village were brought together to the work shed then finally collected by the organisation based in Imphal ('NC').

3. *Category III: Women Weavers under Organisation for Rural Improvement (ORI)*

The selection of the organisation[2] was purposive and the list of the women weavers was collected. The organisation is called *'Organisation for Rural Improvement'* (ORI group, hereafter) based in Nambol working under the principle of micro-credit finance. There were number of villages covered by this organisation. The authors had chosen Irom Meijrao, Kakyai, Utlou and Heigrujam among other villages. Some of the queries were on why did they seek financial support from this organisation? What do they feel about the organisation and their help? Do they see any improvement in their lives by involving themselves? What is their level of freedom in relation to the production process? The pattern of selling their products was also examined.

Except loans provided by the organisation to the women in rural areas irrespective of their own business ventures, the organisation works independently from the production process as well as from marketing the products. One of the greatest contributions by this organisation is their successful orientation of these helpless women workers towards positive life approach. Workers of varied occupation exclusively of women in rural areas take loans from the organisation and sustain their livelihood. The researchers selected the women weavers who were also taking loans from the organisation and supporting their families. The data from the field was collected by attending the weekly meetings hold by the organisation with the women workers in different villages. The researchers were informed about the next meeting and also the timing of the meetings by the organisation which helped in accessing the information from the respondents from these villages covered in the study. A similar trend to Cat. I was found that weavers in this category too weave in their own homes and market their products through the middle women.

Objectives of the Study

The following are the objectives of the study:

I. To study the organisation of production in the weaving industry of Manipur.
II. To study the cultural meaning and perception of weaving among the women weavers.
III. To study the role of weaving as a mechanism for livelihood and of survival across different categories of women weavers.

Methods of Data Collection

Considering the three categories involved in the study, the study used in-depth interviews, group discussions, narratives and some case studies as the main data collection tools. Semi-structured interview guide was used during the interview as a suggestive reference which allowed the researchers considerable flexibility.

Data Analysis

The raw data collected from the field is analysed and presented into two sections. In the first section, the organisation of production in weaving industry among the three categories involved in this study is explained and highlighted followed with the quantitative portion of the data like name, age, educational qualification, marital status of the respondent, years of involvement in the occupation, hours of working, income, etc. For presenting the quantitative data from the field, all the variables are analysed using the statistical package, SPSS. In the second section, the descriptive part of the raw data is sequentially put after identifying the broad themes and sub-themes which emerged out of the data collected from the field. Sometimes, the authors felt necessary to club together one category with another, for the purpose of comparison or drawing out similar points. The themes and sub-themes in this section have been explained and elaborated with the help of narratives, case studies and descriptions gathered from the women weavers in the field.

Theoretical Underpinning

While discussing women's labour and their contribution to the process of development, we intend to draw our attention to women's secondary status. Quite often, women's labour has been left uncounted due to several reasons, however, in this study; we would focus on the socio-cultural aspects surrounding the lives of the women such as the inter-relationship between women's work participation and their low position in the market economy base on gender. To quote Agarwal, equality of women is the basic condition of development of the nation (Agarwal, 2002).

It is evident in the body of literature that an egalitarian society existed somewhere prior to the settled agriculture where the disparity between men and women were almost negligible. The evolution and emergence of private property led to the over throw of many rights including that of women's rights to own property. This was the period which was believed to be the transition from 'hetaerism' to 'monogamy' and from 'mother right' to 'father right' among the Greeks according to Bachofen (Bachofen, 1861 cited in Engels, 1988). It eventually led to the division of labour between men and women in the family and society.

The division of labour gave rise to the male dominance over women as their right. The advent of private property made the disappearance of equal social significance and led to the dichotomy of men's productive work outside home and women's household work. With industrial capitalism, production by men had become exclusively social, outside the household and meant for exchange which left women's work as private (Sacks, 1974). Although not completely in disagreement with Engels concerns on development of private property and control of women's sexuality characterised by the rise of capitalism, Hartmann points out that the control of sexuality or men's power over women might have come much before capitalism. She went ahead and argues that men's direct control of women was translated into indirect impersonal system of control, mediated by social institutions (Hartmann, 1976).

Such indirect control of women and labour power could be well linked to the understanding of socialisation process where varied forms of norms and values are attached to women. Several social theories including that of Hegel considered society as a dynamic entity. The evolution of the modern social thought emerged in response to the French revolution of 1789 which asserted individual freedom and rights (Morrison, 1995).

The idea of an individual as a free social agent in the process of social change which is so much closely tied up with the process of production and the medium of exchange through '*market*' emerged mainly during the industrial revolution in England. With the industrial revolution of late 18th century in England, the human relations in the society had achieved a completely new shape, like human labour, consumption pattern, family structure, social structure and the idea of individualism. By this time, rural economy was replaced with the growth of urban economies and as a result the towns played a bigger role in capitalist development (Hooker, 1996).

The introduction of machines had enabled the capitalist to make not only the ownership or property of the means of production but also the real power and control over the labor process (Navarro, 1986). Machines replaced manual labour which led to the rise of cheap and unskilled labour like women, children and unskilled peasant migrant workers in place of adult male skilled artisans. As Marx said, "the work of women and children was the first cry of the capitalist application of machinery" (cited in Navarro, 1986). Further, Marx and Engels had explained the conditions in which the workers (many of them women and children) had to bear working in the crowded factories for many long hours (seventeen and more hours a day). Women's role in the early phase of industrial revolution still remained significant as the whole household sought for work outside their homes accepting the miserable working conditions (cited in Navarro, 1986).

The condition of the working class in England started deteriorating notably with the advent of industrial capitalism. The workers were neither able to retain health nor live long. Such untimely death was described by Engels as "*Social Murder*". And the cause of death remained natural as articulated by the state and the industrialists (Engels, 2001). Similar situation was observed in Andhra Pradesh, India much later in 1991 among the weavers where deaths due to the larger macro-economic factors were claimed to be natural deaths by the government (Srinivasulu, 1994). The workers had no choice but to work for their survival. Work in general generates income from which a worker has to meet his needs and expectations. In such a picture, a worker is rather viewed or understood as a wage earner or consumer and is defined in the spheres of exchange, distribution, and consumption not in the world of production (Navarro, 1986).

Among other implications brought along with this great transformation in the social relations, the gender division of labour was sharply laid out. Women and children were forced to engage in a non-conducive environment with meager wages to sustain their livelihoods. The emergence of subordination of women is associated with the advent of private property that led to the domestication of women's work. This was followed by the organised capitalist society or class societies with a clear dichotomy between public and private spheres.

It becomes significant to examine the reasons behind the restrictions drawn towards women's right to exercise as a free individual in general and in particular of women in India where women holding main production position are still denied social rights or status. Women's exploitation and oppression have been justified by focusing on the need to maintain and promote social cohesion and stability including the family as a social institution. It was argued that this will bring an overall improvement in the quality of life but we see a very different picture in the current scenario. While examining the intra-household stratification, gender stratification appears to be the prime factor for the differential power between men and women. Regarding any discussion on women's status, the predominant focus has been to assess their roles in relation to men. Mazumdar highlights two dimensions regarding women's status. They are:

"(a) the extent of actual control enjoyed by women over their own lives, and

(b) the extent to which they have access to decision-making processes and are effective in positions of power and authority (Mazumdar, 1978)".

Analysis of power relations mostly starts from the women's access to the decision-making process within the family. This level of analysis is the lowest level yet very crucial in understanding the human relations in general and women's status in particular. Where there is cooperation among the members in particular women inclusion in decision-making, there ought to be less inequality and less discrimination among men and women in the household.

One major contribution of feminist scholars has been to draw our attention to the importance of power followed by control that determines the subordinate position of women in society. In concrete terms, this notion of power or control manifests in the patriarchal ideology which exists in all societies (Nanda and Mangalagiri, 1985). The power to control women by men has become socially sanctioned and mediated through various social institutions. In a study conducted by Kibria (1995) among women garment workers in Bangladesh, it was found that the belief of men's obligation to protect women socially and economically was strongly reflected among the respondents. In a rigid patriarchal family set-up, it becomes difficult for a woman to exercise her rights over her income earned.

It has been observed that a substantial number of women especially in developing countries are absorbed by the global production process resulting from the policy on trade liberalisation. The expansion of female employment has been predominantly concentrated within the 'informal' sector of economy. Debate on gender and its relation to employment has gained importance because of the increasing number of women becoming breadwinners along with their non-negotiable domestic roles (Afshar and Barrientos, 1999).

This was the time when there was growing global economic inequality both among countries and also within countries (Afshar and Barrientos, 1999). The recognition of the value and characteristics of the informal sector appeared in the 1970s and 1980s and finally took the center stage in the 1990s. By then, the sector has been highlighted as an opportunity rather than a failure at the time of stagnating growth and rising unemployment (Afshar and Barrientos, *ibid.*).

The emergence of the term informal sector was captured in a study conducted by Keith Hart (1971) in Ghana among the migrant population in search of job in urban settings. It was found that large sections of the population were engaged in self-employed activities as a means for their survival and livelihood for new entrants to the urban labour force who were unable to obtain employment in the formal sector (Mehta, 1995). Another reason for the involvement in self-employment by these labourers' is their lack of skills and experience required for the jobs in the formal sector (Papola, 1994). The sector plays an important role especially in the developing world in particular with the increasing number of women in the labour force participation.

The informal sector of economy captures the large share of the global workforce which is outside the realm of full time, stable and protected employment. This is very significant while examining the changing trend of employment opportunities in the market. It is also an important sector particularly in developing countries and informal employment comprises 65 percent in Asia. It was estimated in Asia that the organised sector grew at 2 percent per year through 1980s whereas the urban informal sector managed 4 percent growth and more, providing between 40 to 60 percent of employment (ILO's 1992 World Labour Report, quoted in Jain, D. 2005). In all the developing countries, informal employment is generally a larger source of employment for women than formal employment and generally a larger source of employment for women than for men. There are 60 percent or more women workers in informal employment (outside agriculture) in the developing world (Chen *et al.*, 2006). Women were preferred as workers in many of the fast growing sectors of production and export. With respect to India, as mentioned in Samita Sen's work on 'gender and class', very little attention was given to the question of gender. Women who did work in industrial units were subsumed within the category of 'class'. To a large extent, women's productive role has been ignored for a long time. The fact is that women were a critical segment of the industrial labour force since the inception of the industrial development (Sen, 2004). An economic development of a country could be accelerated by enhancing or focusing on the status, position and living condition of women because women play a vital role in the socio-economic development of the country. The feminisation of employment has been presented in two ways: number of women entering the workforce and secondly in terms of the quality of the employment, which is usually poorly paid, physically demanding, and dirty (Jain, 2005).

Feminisation and the Process of Globalisation and Liberalisation

The trend of increasing number of female labour force in the market economy has led to new definitions and studies on feminisation of labour as reflected in many academic as well as non-academic writings. It is observed that feminisation of labour occurs at a time when paid work is becoming increasingly informal (Kabeer, 2008). Existing studies and literatures have revealed that with the restructuring of the market economy globally, particularly in Third World countries, the majority of the new workers are women. According to the ILO statistics, global employment almost doubled between 1965 and 1995. In this, the bulk of expansion was in the developing countries and more than half of the new recruits were women (Hensman, 2004). However, the conditions of working for both men and women were far away from any labour standards. Most of these workers continue to work under such dreadful conditions only because this is the only way in which they and their families can survive. Therefore, it is the question of survival and livelihood of the workers.

With the New Economic Policy (NEP) adopted by the Indian government in 1991, the emphasis has been focused on the free market, export promotion and globalisation. An export-oriented growth strategy has been the prime importance and on the other hand, there has been a radical reduction in the role of the state in the economy and more importantly in the social sectors (health, education, transport and communication). Most of these sectors are being privatised and therefore, the core of accessing these sectors has also increased. It is evident that the process of globalisation will further marginalise women at the level of production and consumption which ultimately will widen gender disparities (Ramanamma, 1999). Apart from these, women face discrimination on two fronts:

"Firstly, pre-market discrimination, that is lack of access to resources like education, training, experience and so forth which could and would develop capital for further enhancement and secondly, to post-market discrimination like differential wages for similar work (Tripathy, 2003)".

Women's issues gained more importance in the nineties, with liberalisation and privatisation of the economy when the old concept of '*growth with social justice*' was replaced with the new concept of '*development with empowerment*' (Mohanty, 2001 cited in Naorem, 2007). Empowerment and inclusion are complementary terms. One act from below and another from above which provide environment to enable individuals to build their capabilities. However, we need to ask the question whose empowerment and inclusion we are discussing about? Sen (1990) throws light on the importance of discussing gender issues in developmental analysis by reminding that male and female have divergent predicaments.

In order to avoid any misunderstanding in terms of both causation and consequences, gender should be taken into account as an important component in any social issue. Gender inequality persists very distinctly in our society whether developed or developing or less developed countries in different degrees. In the Indian context, the inequality between male and female reflects itself in adverse social indicators. Kabeer acknowledges that gender inequalities are multi-dimensional in nature. Among other things, one of the important aspects towards empowerment as it has been argued by Kabeer is the individual's inert sense of self which would then plausibly enhance the capability to exercise his or her own choice (Kabeer, 2005). To empower means either to strengthen an individual's belief in self-efficacy or to weaken one's belief in personal powerlessness (Conger and Kanungo, 1988).

It is also important to note that women should be able to bring out their inert sense of self-acceptance and self-respect which extend, in turn, to respect for and acceptance of others as equals. This is nothing but power which is evolved from within. Women must be convinced of their innate right to equality, dignity, and justice (Sen, 2006). Gender inequality and female deprivation have been characterised as India's most serious social failures as noted by Dreze and Sen (Dreze and Sen, 2002). Gender inequality predominantly exists in Manipur society which has negative implications for women's life. Considering earning as the direct account of contribution, it would be significant to discuss women's earning. Turning to women's earning, the notion of perceived contribution draws attention. With this theoretical background, we would now present the notable facts from the field.

Findings from the Field

The three categories involved in this study have been discussed above. As also mentioned earlier, the data would be arranged in two sections. Firstly, the quantitative portion of the data will be discussed followed with the qualitative aspects concerning the lives of women weavers. Women who are economically active (21-40 years) showed the highest number in the occupation of weaving among the Cat. I women weavers. With age, there is less number of women in the occupation. When we look into their education, a large number of them could only attain till the secondary level of education which probably reflects the financial condition of these families. Majority of women respondents revealed that they joined the occupation out of economic compulsion to meet the basic needs of the family (78.2 percent which is 86 women out of 110).

There is a close relationship between the available support system to the women weavers and the amount of income they could earn as for majority of them weaving is the main source of income and livelihood. Majority of the respondents learnt the art of weaving either from their mothers or sisters. None of them reported of gaining knowledge of weaving from any training program by the government.

Like in Cat. I, quite similarly the largest proportion of women in this Cat. II is economically active and also could only reach till secondary level of education. The socio-economic conditions of the weavers in this category are low and many of them are the main income earners in their respective families. Due to the economic compulsion, these women are drawn into weaving at an early age and leaving their education to make their living and their livelihoods. We observed that in Cat. II one woman had learnt the art of weaving from the handloom department in Imphal West district of Manipur. Except this case, we did not come across any other women who have learnt the art from a government set up.

It is very interesting to observe a slightly different picture as evident from the data of the women weavers in Cat. III. The highest number of weavers is found among the age group of 41-50 along with women in their economically active stage. One of the reasons for this could be that a large number of women in this group are getting loans from the organisation following the principle of micro-credit financing with an aim of empowering women through credit facility. They (elderly women) influence the young women in their own households to join their earning and seek credit facility in order to improve their income which they see as a positive way to improve their livelihoods. Even in this category, none reported of gaining any benefits from the government.

Commonalities and Differences Across the Categories

Except a few numbers of weavers in the whole respondents included in the study, most weavers are managing their family maintenance through their earnings. The knowledge or skill of weaving was acquired commonly from the mothers or sisters in the family. The opportunity to upgrade their skills in weaving was minimal which shows the negligence of the state government responsibility towards their assigned duties especially designed for weavers in total. None of the respondents had the knowledge of any of the government schemes and also so far not availed any provisions. Above all, they did not even have weaver cards though some of them reported of being submitted their passport photographs along with Rs. 40 to some of the unknown survey groups.

Majority of the respondents are secondary level of education which appeared and reported to be one major factor in not knowing whom to ask and where to query. Weaving is reported to be the main source of livelihood to majority of the respondents in the study. Their main concern in day to day life is to get two meals a day and families with other supplementary earning members would plan for small savings. Importance of education has been overshadowed by the need to meet the basic needs of the family. Concern to save some portion of their earnings for the marriage was expressed by the young single women respondents which led them to form and join marup[3] (local saving system) of different kinds.

With this, the authors would hereby bring forth the qualitative aspects of the data from the field. To begin, we try and relate the art of weaving and its relationship with the women folks in the society. It was found that there was a strong cultural meaning attached to weaving in earlier generations (roughly two generations prior to the present generation involved in the study) which could also be due to then nature of production relations. The production relations here are limited to the relationship between the process of production and its relation with the changing market system within the state and also outside the state. Earlier, the production was mainly used for consumption purposes whereas at present the sector has become more commercialised and weaving has become a main source of livelihood to many families in the state along with consumption of the products. In brief, regarding the changing pattern of weaving from the past to present time, weaving means a means to meet the ends to majority of the families in this study.

Some women of the study say *"to be financially independent is the most crucial step therefore we want our daughters to learn the art of weaving apart from the cultural meaning attached to weaving in Manipur. We will definitely teach them when they grow up."* It is evident that the main reason for majority women to take up this occupation is due to financial problems.

Visibility of Earning and Women's Autonomy

Rationing the Income Earned

Almost all women in this study replied that their contribution is being recognised in their own families. Considering this fact, these women are helped by the male members neither in their production process nor in managing the large household activities. To quote, women in Cat. I seek or get support exclusively from female members in their work both productive as well as household activities, except two women respondents who reported of being helped by their husbands (two women out of 110 women respondents in Cat. I).

Another point women brought out was that they could take part in the decision-making process in the family. Again, it was more of male-dominated decision-making process. None of the respondents excluding widows, women without parents reported of taking the main decision of the family. When further asked, their response was 'decisions should be taken by men because *"samaj"* (society) will not accept or respect decisions taken by women in the families and it is not good for the family'. They never try to question on their right to make their own choice in life. The negative implications of this are manifested in the form of restriction towards women's freedom to move freely, early withdrawal from the school to support the family expenditure, low self-esteem to handle life situations, limitation in exploring different opportunities in life, ignoring ill-health, etc.

However, all women respondents (Cat. I, II and III) have mentioned that economic independence is the utmost step in a woman's life. It is understood that women knew the extreme form of exploitation of being completely dependent economically though they could not express or exercise their rights. In a way, they are conditioned to the subjugated status.

Perceived Contribution

An important area to be focused is on women's perceived contribution which could be an effective tool in bargaining or negotiating with other members in the household over their interest. Contributions are of two kinds-one of direct contribution which means income to sustain the family expenditure and another could be of non-economic contribution for example household activities including almost everything starting with domestic chores to endless jobs. As mention, we can conclude by saying that women in this context of the study are involved in both kinds of contributions. In regard to this, a woman who makes others feel her value of contribution would definitely draw more power in the bargaining or negotiating process over the conflict situation in the decision-making process in the family as compared to the one who puts lesser value to her contribution.

Some women in Cat. I reported that they were able to gain recognition of their contribution both monetary as well as the household duties of being a woman in our society. However, they could not completely overrule other male members in the family and also could not take part in the decision-making process of the family. Thus, we cannot consider such responses as positive in bridging the gender gap and unequal power relation within the family. From the women's responses (Cat. II) in terms of their income contribution, it was observed that they could make others value their substantial input towards the welfare of the family. However, this really could not convert into power to bargain their perceived interest.

The recognition of women's income contribution towards the maintenance of the family expenditure was seen in the form of husband's actual help in the process of production in two cases in Cat. III which was exceptional. And this involved only a nominal act of a husband arranging a bulb so that his wife could weave after dinner and the other husband helped her in preparing bobbins for her weaving. Though they made a substantial contribution to the survival and livelihood of the family, majority of them could not bargain much over their interest and also the mainstay of the decision making laid with the men in the family. Some of them reported of domestic violence despite their contributions both productive and domestic chores perceived to be the women's duty in the society.

Income and Women's Social Status

Income confers power in general understanding however it is contradictory when one talks about income earned by a woman engaged in an unorganised sector of the economy. Most women involved in the unorganised sector of economy in particular weaving attached less value to their income earned. This is mainly because their income earned could not make a great difference in their standard of living apart from meeting the basic needs of the family. According to them, "we can't really count on our income earned from this petty work. We just continue with the work because there is no other option available to us for our survival and livelihood. From our income, we can't dream of big things in life. We just roll on life for the sake of living."

Involvement in Decision-making Process

It is very important for us to examine these many women respondents' role in the decision-making process of the family. In the Indian society, almost all women hardly make any voice in the main decision-making process except their role in managing the expenditures on food, their children's small demands like buying toffees, clothes, etc. Examining category-wise, it was found that only four women in Cat. I (four out of 110 women respondents) took the main decisions in their families. The reasons for their capability to do so vary from case to case. In the first case, both parents are physically very weak at present and they are no more earning so this woman makes the major share of the income of the family and manages the whole expenditure. Thus, she takes the main decision of the family. In the second case, she was living with a drug addict husband therefore she had to be the main decision maker in her family. In the third and fourth cases, both were widows and also living separately from their parents-in-law so they were taking the decisions of their own families.

There were only two women in Cat. II and both of them had lost their parents. Moreover, they both were the main income earners in the family. Women in Cat. III had to bargain with their male members for their interests despite their substantial contribution towards the family's income. The unequal power between men and women strongly persist in Meitei community and such a structure is reinforced in the socialisation process which led to discrimination based on gender among the siblings in the family.

Gender Discrimination

Considering the social structure prevailing in Manipur especially among the Meitei community with its strong patriarchy we felt it is relevant to examine the expected discrimination based on gender in the social context as well as within the household. The researchers made an attempt to capture the perceived discrimination among the respondents in the study. The responses showed that a strong sense of gender discrimination among the siblings was prevalent which was the contradictory view expressed by the women respondents. They did not agree that they were being discriminated. This indicates that women accept the 'legitimacy of the unequal order' (Sen, 1990, cited by Kabeer, 2000) and adapted to the system without any feeling of abnormality.

It is significant to highlight the non-existence of women's right over the agricultural land; pulling young girls into the occupation by the mothers or elderly women in the family to support the family expenditure; non-support of the male members in the household work; a sense of less caring towards young girls as compared to the young boys in the family in terms of offering food, providing the best available choice, giving leisure time to boys and male members by letting them to do what they wish to and; finally most women had to work to support the family. All these manifestations are nothing but discrimination based on gender in a strong patriarchal set-up among the Meiteis.

Manipur appeared to be one of the states in eastern India with high level of women's empowerment in terms of women's freedom of movement, active participation in economic domain in the market, access to cash, participation in household decision-making, etc. It is possible that women in the state might be relatively free from strict social obligations that exist in other regions in the nation. However, women in the state do face different levels of ill effects of patriarchy.

Agarwal's extensive work on land rights and its implication for women's bargaining power contribute immensely in understanding the complexity of unequal power relation between men and women in the society and also within the patriarchal family. She points out that without independent resources irrespective of the socio-economic condition of either parental or marital families, women can be economically vulnerable in case of marital breakdown or widowhood (Agarwal, 2008). This is evident in the case of Thambal, a widow is facing the same vulnerability as mentioned by Aggarwal. To quote from Thambal's case study (attached in the annexure I),

> "I am so worried about life without my husband. I have to manage the daily expenditure and also my daughter is growing up. I do not have a single piece of arable land. It is so expensive to buy a kilo of rice in the market and also the other basic needs including vegetables, ngari (fermented fish), etc. I am scare of falling ill as I do not have any savings to face additional expenditures. What I have with me is just the knowledge of weaving."

It is evident in the study that majority of women weavers who weave in their own homestead and their income do not get a centre-stage in the intra-household power dynamics. Eventually they do not take part in the main decision-making process in the family. They sacrifice their own wishes and desire either through the natural process of socialisation or imposed to them by other members in the household. They generally are attuned to fulfil the welfare of the family by involving themselves in earning which is weaving in this context with minimal benefits in some cases especially among the single women and almost without any benefits among the married weavers. None of these women could freely move in the public place without prior permission from the male heads of the household especially from their husbands among the married women weavers despite being the main income earners in their own respective families.

If we examine and focus critically the life of these women workers, who have strong economic role as contributors, one could categorise this as another form of exploitation in their lives, mediated through socio-cultural factors (Batliwala, 1994). These socio-cultural factors are reinforced again and again by the male dominated opinions and also through the process of socialisation. Obviously, the conditions in which an individual live and die, are influenced and shaped by the political, social and economic forces (Commission on Social Determinants of Health, 2008). However, it is important to address them if the 'welfare' traditions have to be kept alive.

Conclusion

Despite their value added services to the family, the mainstay of the family still lies in the hands of the male members in the household except a few exceptional cases such as widows, destitute women, women with weak parents, women without parents, etc. The socio-cultural underpinnings play a major role in the lives of these women which act as constraint in achieving a level of empowerment. It simply indicates that the negative aspects of patriarchal ideology for instance gender discrimination, son preference, male dominance over women, unequal power relationship between men and women, restriction on women's movement so on and so forth within the family and also in the society do exist in Manipur.

The understanding of empowerment does not seem to be striking in the context of the study where women are denied their basic rights, for example, the right to take their own decisions, land right, freedom of movement, etc. Though the constitution guarantees equal rights to men and women in the society. The study shows that it might be very difficult for the women to bring any change in the existing social structure which is extremely rigid. Often, these women have not been benefited by their work participation and the income earned. Failing to get benefits from their income earned or control over their income has negative repercussions on the lives of the women. It is time to consider such an understanding in order to formulate a broader plan in which women workers have to be made inclusive partners in any labour welfare measures.

NOTES AND REFERENCES

1. The organisation was established in 1st March 1983 and registered under the Society Registration Act XXI of 1860 in the year 1984. The focus of the organisation was on the income generation and social upliftment of the women and girls in the rural areas in Manipur. Several trades are under its coverage ranging from embroidery; cane, bamboo, kauna and allied crafts to handloom weaving. In the field of handloom weaving, training-*cum*-production centre was set-up in Moidangpok in which a work shed was built by the organisation.
2. Organisation for Rural Improvement (ORI) was established in 2003 and registered under the Manipur Societies Registration Act, 1989. The organisation is based in Nambol Phoijing Chingmang, Near Oil Pump, Bishnupur District. The thrust area is on improving the living standards of the rural poor undertaking all types of rural development activities. It caters its services through its micro-credit programme under its project "Rural Economic Empowerment Project" (REEP). In the annual report of 2007-08 of the organisation, it was mentioned that the organisation had assisted credit facility to 2279 clients in 101 centres on an average loan of Rs. 10,000 per member. Its functioning is designed with the ethos of Grameen Bank SHG. At present, the organisation is getting loan assistant from North-Eastern Development Finance Corporation Ltd. (NEDFi). The organisation conducts surveys from time to time and documented properly. The researcher could get helpful information from the data collected by the organisation apart from the field interaction with the women weavers.
3. Marup is a form of monetary or property saving system practiced in Manipur since time immemorial. It is a system in which individuals tender some fixed amount and the collected is distributed to the participating individual in a cyclical manner. Marup system has a symbolic meaning and a functional meaning too. Symbolically it is a form of gift exchange system where the participating individuals always belong to the same class and status. Also it signifies a bond or economic and personal relationship among the participating individuals. Functionally marup also serves the purpose for fulfilling the participating member's financial ends and means during shortages of needs. The same description has been written in a paper presented in a National Seminar—"Social Research on North-East India: Issues and Challenges" and the topic of the paper is "Changing the Economic Role of Women Remains a Myth: Women in Manipur" presented jointly by me and my colleague in February 2010 in JNU.

References

Afshar, Haleh and Barrientos, Stephanie (1999), "Introduction—Women, Globalisation and Fragmentation", in Afshar, Haleh & Barrientos, Stephanie (ed.) *Women, Globalisation and Fragmentation in the Developing World*, London: Macmillan Press Ltd.

Agarwal, Bina (2008), "Why Do Women Need Independent Rights in Land?", in John, Mary, E. (ed.) *Women's Studies in India*, India: Penguin Books.

Agarwal, Meenu (2002), "Women in Unorganised Sector—Challenges for the 21st Century", in Singh, J.L. *et al.* (ed) *Women in Unorganised Sector—Problems and Prospects*, New Delhi: Sunrise Publications.

Batliwala, Srilatha (1994), "The Meaning of Women's Empowerment—New Concepts from Action", in Sen, Gita; Germain, Adrienne and Chen, Lincoln, C. (eds.) *Population Policies Reconsidered – Health, Empowerment, and Rights*, Boston: Harvard School of Public Health.

Biswas, Saswati (2008), "The Gender Concerns in North-East India and Relevance of Social Movements", in Ray, Asok, Kumar and Ray, Basudeb, Dutta (ed.) *Women Emancipation—Focus North-East India*, New Delhi: OM Publications.

Chen, Martha, Vanek, Joann and Hentz James (2006), "Informality, Gender and Poverty—A Global Picture", *Economic and Political Weekly*, May 27, 2131-39.

Conger, Jay A. and Kanungo, Rabindra N. (1988), "The Empowerment Process: Integrating Theory and Practice", *The Academy of Management Review*, July 13(3), 471-82.

CSDH (2008), Closing the Gap in a Generation—Health equity through action on the social determinants of health, Final Report of the Commission on Social Determinants of Health. Geneva: World Health Organisation.

Donahoe, Debra, Anne (1999), "Measuring Women's Work in Developing Countries", *Population and Development Review*, September, 25(3) 543-76.

Dreze, Jean and Sen, Amartya (2002), *India—Development and Participation*, New Delhi: Oxford University Press.

Engels, Frederick (1988), "Engels on the Origin and Evolution of the Family", *Population and Development Review*, Dec., 14(4) 705-29.

_____ (2001), The Condition of the Working Class in England, in Purdy, M. and Banks, D. (ed.) *The Sociology and Politics of Health*, London: Routledge.

Hartmann, Heidi (1976), 'Capitalism, Patriarchy, and Job Segregation by Sex'. *Signs*, Spring, 1(3), 137-69.

Hensman, Rohini (2004), "Globalisation, Women and Work", *Economic and Political Weekly*, March 6, 1030-34.

Hooker, R. (1996), The European Enlightenment—The Industrial Revolution Online Web: www.wsu.edu/~dee/ENLIGHT/SCIREV.HTM, access on 20 March 2008.

Jain, Devaki (2005), *Women, Development, and the UN—A Sixty Year Quest for Equality and Justice*, Bloomington: Indiana University Press.

Kabeer, Naila (2000), *Power to Choose—Bangladesh Women Workers and Labour Market Decisions*, New Delhi: Vistaar Publications.

___ (2005), "Gender Equality and Women's Empowerment: A Critical analysis of the Third Millennium Development Goals", *Gender and Development*, March, 13(1), pp. 13-24.

____ (2008), *Mainstreaming Gender in Social Protection for the Informal Economy*, London: Commonwealth Secretariat.

Kibria, Nazli (1995), "Culture, Social Class, and Income Control in the Lives of Women Garment Workers in Bangladesh," *Gender and Society*, June, 9(3), pp. 289-309.

Mazumdar, Vina (1978), Towards Equality? Status of Women in India, in Phadnis, U. and Malani, I. (ed.) *Women of the World—Illusion and Reality*, New Delhi: Vikas Publishing House Pvt. Ltd.

Mehta, M. (1995), Urban Informal Sector—An Indian Sketch, in Mathew, P.M. (ed.) *Informal Sector in India—Critical Perspectives*, New Delhi: Khama Publishers.

Morrison, Ken (1995), *Marx, Durkheim, Weber: Formations of Modern Social Thought*, London: Sage Publications.

Naorem, Arunibala (2007), "Contextualizing Empowerment: A Study of Meitei Women involved in pottery work in Thongjao, Manipur", *Journal of Health and Development*, July-Dec., 3 (3&4) pp.103-14.

Nanda, Bikram and Mangalagiri, Anjana (1985), Patriarchal Ideology and Women's Oppression, in Kaushik, Susheela (ed.) *Women's Oppression: Patterns and Perspectives*, New Delhi: Shakti Books.

Navarro, V. (1986), *Crisis, Health, and Medicine—A Social Critique*, New York: Tavistock Publications.

Papola, T.S. (1994), Informal Sector—Concept and Policy, in Rao, M.K. (ed.) *Growth of Urban Informal Sector and Economic Development*, Delhi: Kanishka Publishers Distributors.

Ramanamma, A. (1999), Globalisation, Women and Economic Development in Sethi, M. (ed.) *Globalisation, Culture and Women's Development*, Jaipur: Rawat Publications.

Sacks, Karen (1974), Engels Revisited: Women, the organisation of production, and private property, in Rosaldo, Z., M. and Lamphere, L. (ed.) *Women, Culture, and Society*, California: Stanford University Press.

Sen, Amartya (1990), Gender and Cooperative Conflicts, in Tinker, Irene (ed.) *Persistent Inequalities—Women and World Development*, New York: Oxford University Press.

______ (2006), *Development as Freedom*, New Delhi: Oxford.

Sen, Samita (2004), *Gender and Class Women in Indian Industry, 1920-90.* Online web: www.indialabourarchives.org, access on 23 March, 2008.

Srinivasulu, K. (1994), "Handloom Weavers' Struggle for Survival", *Economic and Political Weekly*, Sept. 3, 29(36) pp. 2331-33.

Sharma, Manorama (2008). '*The Changing Context of Gender Relations In North-East India: Showcasting Assam and Mizoram*', Unpublished Paper, Professor in Department of History, NEHU, Shillong, Personal Communication.

Tripathy, S.N. (2003), Introduction, in Tripathy, S.N., *Women in Informal Sector*, New Delhi: Discovery Publishing House.

Women, Conflict and Peace: An Experience from North-East India

Barasa Deka and Anubhab Sarmah

In the recent past one of the most debated issues has been the issue of women's empowerment both in academia and otherwise. As women's empowerment has been debated in such a great length that there is need to understand whether women are empowered or not empowered enough to become agents of change and enjoy equal rights in various spheres of life. When we talk about women's empowerment in the context of India, there is need of realising that the issue of empowerment is fundamentally related with the issue of status of women.

There has been a lot of debate, discussion and research work undertaken to study and analyse the status of Indian women in the changing socio-economic and political context. As a result, there are various contradictory positions regarding the status of women in India, which cannot be seen without addressing certain other issues. Any discussion on women's issue brings to the light the issue of gender equality in context of women's right and invariably leads to the question that whether they are treated as equal citizens or not. The idea of citizenship entails equal rights to the members of a political community, which has also been guaranteed in the various provisions of Indian Constitution including Article 15 of the Constitution.

Thus, concession of equal rights is a constitutional guarantee. But after a few decades of Indian independence these provisions of the constitution and the realities seems to present before us a disturbing picture. There has been a history of silence in the discourse of rights, equality, justice and freedom for women. Even after constitutional guarantee it has been argued that the whole idea of citizenship is 'gendered'.

To talk about the status of women in Indian society is no easy task, as 'Indian women' is not a homogenous category. Indian woman is caught into various other identities in relation to her caste, class, religion, ethnicity, etc. The public-private dichotomy in Indian context, where public space has been the monopoly of men and women are confined to the private sphere has been instrumental for Indian women's long struggle for gender equality. Thus, it is established that Indian women do not enjoy equal status with men. So it can be argued that the status of women has changed in the changing time with Indian women's struggle for gender equality. This struggle was in the backdrop of Indian socio-economic and political context and the age old values prevalent in Indian society advocating gender inequality. This struggle is a continuous one, and in Indian society the dream achieving gender equality is far from being realised. The patriarchal structures and the values legitimising gender inequality has raised various questions regarding the availability of public space for women in our society or how well they are able to capitalise this space in order to become agents of change and empower themselves. It has also been argued that in certain cases women are forced to the public space which has traditionally been the domain of men.

In the backdrop of status of women in Indian context, this paper tries to analyse the status of women in North-East India. The North-Eastern region of Indian Union is a rich blend of divergent cultural and social groups. It is a multiethnic, multilingual and multicultural region which can be termed as a 'mini India'. Historically North-East India has been the shelter of the tribal and non-tribal population. It is strategically a very important region as it is connected to the rest of India with a small tract of land and shares international border with some foreign countries. There has been much fancy about the status of women of this region and the assumption that women enjoy a higher degree of mobility and public space that presents a picture of gender equality. This myth has been presented to hide the deep-rooted patriarchal structures of the societies of North-East India.

At this particular stage when we mention about the women in North-East India, there is an attempt locate them in comparison with their counterparts in other parts of the country. The rationale behind taking up the case of women in North-East India is because women in this region is placed in a conflict situation where intra-state conflicts in terms of ethnic assertions and their militant manifestations have kept the region in a state of turmoil. Thus North-East India presents before us a peculiar kind of state of affair.

It has been asserted time and again that women in North-East India enjoy a relative degree of autonomy and mobility in comparison to their counterparts in rest of India, because of the structure of social formation, norms and culture. It is also due to the relative absence of age old social evils of Indian society like casteism, dowry, and child marriage that women enjoy a degree of autonomy in economic and social sphere. So it is assumed that women of this region are more empowered. But this is just one side of the coin. Women of this region are in no better position than the rest of India and gender equality is just a myth. Women of this region suffers from patriarchal domination in all spheres of life, its degree may vary. For instance, although the casteism is absent among the tribal societies evils like "witch hunting" is still prevalent amongst certain tribes which have resulted in physical and mental torture of women. Virginius Xaxa argues that the very practices that are regarded as indicative of higher social status in one kind of setting turn out to be in-built depressor in other settings (Xaxa, 2008). Though tribal society is assumed to be egalitarian in nature but patriarchy is widely prevalent. Moreover, despite of the absence of communal violence in North-Eastern part of India, ethnic violence is very much in action. The ethnic conflicts have plunged the women into a pathetic position. Separatist and autonomy struggles in this part of the country have made the conditions of women fragile. They are the vulnerable victims of conflict. Infact women are subjected to the patriarchal dominance because violent conflicts are predominantly controlled by men.

The North-East India and its politics is confronted with the complexities of the situation and peculiarity of the problems which have kept the region in a constant state of crisis and turmoil. The history and geography of the region has been detrimental in shaping its politics and also has definite impact on the process of integration of the region with the rest of India. In fact within the region these factors along with the political realities have worked as an impediment in proper communication of the people of hills and the plain. Thus, it has become increasingly difficult to generalise the problems of this region and other areas.

Udayon Misra has rightly argued that the entire north east region is today caught in a vicious circle. Assertions of identity often leading to insurgent movement have invariably had their roots in economic deprivation and these in turn have acted as major impediment for development. Therefore from whichever angle one tries to perceive it, the issue related to the development of the north-eastern region of the country are inextricably related to the different ethnic movements and in several cases, their militant manifestations. The situation in north-east has been made more complex by the revivalist ideas and the exclusionist mindset which have come to characterise most of these identity/autonomy movements (Misra, 2006).

If one tries to trace the main cause/causes of identity assertion and demand of autonomy, in North-East India, it will lead to many interrelated issues and problems rooted in the particular context. Ethnicity has been the most pervasive factor responsible for the conflict situation in North-East India. Ethnicisation of politics has given rise of various modes of assertions starting from the creation of separate political units to secession. Although there has been a lot of initiative in the recent past to initiate peace talks both from the state and civil society and also willingness on part of the rebel forces to come to the mainstream, it will not be exaggeration to argue that North-East India is still in a state of war.

In this backdrop of situation, some of the questions that necessarily come to our mind which needs very serious consideration are what happens to women in such a situation? Why women are the easy victims of conflict? Is it because women are thought to be weaker sex? Or is it a sign of so-called timid "masculinity" in this patriarchal society to make women their easy prey? or is this because women do not retaliate against such violence? It is now well established fact that in contemporary conflicts most of victims are civilians but majority of civilian victims are women and children. In this case North-East is not an exception. Women remained to be vulnerable at home and in the society. Violence against women is a common phenomenon whether during conflict or in peace.

As women are caught into this kind of conflict situation specially perpetrated by the intra-state actors, what kind of victimhood and suffering they undergo and how do they take initiative to overcome this situation is the major thrust of this paper. This paper attempts to discuss the role of women in conflict situation and their initiative to bring peace. Thus this is an attempt to see their journey from victimhood to agency. This paper also tries to argue that this agency in terms of giving them a public space to negotiate peace is no way a guarantee of gender equality in the societies of North-East India. This paper tries to argue that concession of public space to women in North-East India is far from they being empowered.

It is worth mentioning here that history has very little records of the experience of women in conflict and their initiative to make peace. History has been conspicuously silent in highlighting women's experience in conflict situation and many of the success stories of peace building by women have gone untold. In case of North-East India the victimhood of women due to conflict situation has been caused mostly by intra-state conflict. Thus, Navnita Chadha Behera rightly argued that, there is a shift in the discourse of conflict from inter-state to intra-state (Behera, 2006). Thus the ethnic assertions and militant manifestation of these assertions have kept the women in a constant state of fear and trauma, where women are made to suffer because of the atrocities of both the state actor and rebel group.

The states of Assam, Nagaland, Manipur has witnessed immense ethnic conflict in the recent past. Identity politics has become the most pervasive factor of the politics of North-East India. Identity assertion has not only remained confined to ethnic movements, but has led to violent conflict and ethnic cleansing. But what has gone unnoticed it the gender perspective of identity politics. Butalia (2006) argues that it is now widely accepted that while women seldom create or initiate conflict, they—along with children and the aged are often its chief victims and sufferers. It is more prominent in places like Kashmir and North-East India. It is worth-noticing that woman's sufferings and victimhood due to various conflicts has gone unnoticed and unacknowledged until recent past.

The impact of conflict on women leads to adverse situation for women where they not only have to lose their husbands and sons by constantly lives under physical and psychological conditions created by stress and trauma. The situation of women caught in conflict has another dimension. It has been argued that conflict situation has pushed women to a kind of public space. It has given them the negotiating space which they never encountered in the pre-conflict situation. But the question that arises here is this space empowering enough? Do women get a better deal in the post-conflict reconstruction in terms of decision-making power, inspite of their role as peace-makers in conflict situation?

In case of Assam the rise of Assam Movement in the 80's led to the way of formation of the outfit United Liberation Front of Assam (ULFA). The attempt of the Indian state to curb its violent activities has revealed that Assamese women were victimised by the security personals and there are instance of women being raped, sexually abused on the mere suspicion of having relation with the militants. The other side of the story is even more glaring when women were abused and sexually used by the members of the militant group fighting for the so called freedom of their nation. Thus there are number of instances of women being victimised in the other states of North-East by both state and the rebel actors, for example, the plight of Naga and Manipuri women due to the continuous conflict situation.

But the attempt of the paper is not only to highlight the victimhood of women. Women in North-East is traditionally playing the role of peacemaking, although it was not been focused or given due importance in the pages of history. The peace initiatives of women has also given them a public space and glorified their roles especially as a 'mother'. Women are often seen as a mute spectator of their own exploitation. Though women are seen as the worst victims of various types of conflict, it has to be emphasised that at times they are the best preventer of conflicts. They are regarded as the manifestation of peace-keeping or peacemaking elements. A woman in peace is not a new concept. Infact there are numerous events from the pages of forgotten history where women played their role as a peace builder. As such the first women's peace society was established in United Kingdom in 1820. At international level there have been numerous instances of women playing active agents of peace-making. During the Cold war period women's peace group manifested itself as an active peace agent to win the Nuclear Test Ban Treaty in the early 1960's and disengaging United States from Vietnam War in 1970's. Similarly, women playing leading role in the movement against Nuclear war during 1980's was also commendable.

In South Asian politics, women's activism in peace process is immense. Women's organisations like Women in Security, Conflict Management and Peace (WISCOMP) and Women's Initiative for Peace in South Asia (WIPSA) facilitated sustained dialogue between women group in the two countries of India and Pakistan during the turmoil period of Indo-Pak conflict. These women groups endeavoured to foster peace and cooperation between the two countries when official relation was not cordial. In Liberia the peaceful and active demonstration of Women's Mass Action for Peace (WMA) helped peace talk between the Rebels and the government. Therefore, women's role in peace could be justified from the fact that from time to time women have proved themselves be pathfinder of peace (Dutta, 2008).

The idea of women being related to nature and mother, whose duty is to care and nurture, despite of facing cruel consequences of human being has facilitated the belief that they are peaceful in nature. The glorification of motherhood has made them manifestation of peace-making. Though, this notion of women being seen as nature has been criticised as 'gendered' and effort to make them a 'weaker sex' but it could be seen from the time immemorial that women have been capitalising this weakness into their greatest strength. From the last few decades it could be seen that women has emerged as the active agents of peace in the conflicting situations.

Motherhood, which is considered to be a gendered concept, in recent years, has gained so much of metaphorical importance that it has been responsible for inspiring many peace movements throughout the world. The so-called "maternal fame" which implies women's activism on the metaphor of motherhood, has now gained importance and relevance. In this context a brief reference could be made to the Mothers front which played a pivotal role in carrying forward the peace agenda in Sri Lanka against the back drop of ethnic violence in 1980's (Das, 2008).

The active participation of women to conceptualise the paradigm of peace and security could be well revealed from the south Asian context. The cases from South Asian countries including India and India's North-East in particular clearly visualises the fact that women are the path makers of peace. The 3rd world countries of South Asia are a conflict prone area. Amongst the high numbers of civilian casualties in contemporary conflicts, a large proportion is women and children. In the conflicting situation, what is more tragic is that women are particularly subject to violence such as rape, forced prostitution, displacement and so on. Such violence is not just an accident of war but often a systematic military strategy. Such a pathetic situation of women in conflict situations has challenged the myth that "men are protectors of women and children" or "men fight war to protect women and children" (Owens, 1997).

This raising conflict not only made women suffer indiscriminate pain but at the same time posed them a new responsibility of making agenda of peace for the protection of their self and society. But women's activism in peace is restricted to non-political, more specifically to domestic roles only. However, it could be seen that during the time of active conflict situation and violence, women tends to play a role of natural peace-builders for discourses on reconciliation and healing. Contemporary women's peace movements have provided a new conceptual framework of security. Today, women's centrality in peace building and conflict, peace and security discourses is clearly visible despite of the fact that women's participation in the peace table are often ignored. Women's peace activism tended to become a manifest example whether in ethnic conflict in Sri-Lanka, in Afghanistan or in identity conflict in North-East India to prevent the outbreak of conflict or as an agent of post-conflict reconstruction.

Emergence of certain radical mothers association has given a new impetus to this peacemaking role of women. For instance, the "*shed no more blood*" campaign by the Naga Mother's Association has brought the possibility of dialogue in the conflict prone Nagaland. Reference could also be made to the protest made by the mothers and grandmothers in Dailekh district in Nepal against Maoist forcible recruitment of one child per family. Similarly, there are numerous cases like the courageous protest by Meira Paibis in Manipur, Kashmir Mother's Front in Kashmir and alike.

It was against the backdrop of continuous conflicts and violence against them that women of North-East came to retaliate such violence. They began to demonstrate that they are not vulnerable any more by showing their active participation in the process of conflict resolution. As women are denied formal political power, in turn they grouped themselves with the feeling of "sisterhood" into strong agent of social transformation to fight injustice against women.

The Naga Mothers Association has been playing the role of peace agent and negotiator in Nagaland and they are able to make remarkable space of action. Infact the peace movement in Nagaland is dominated by the mother association with sheer impressive support. The association came into existence in 14 February 1984, with a preamble that stated, "Naga mothers of Nagaland shall express the need of conscientising citizens towards more responsible living and human development through the voluntary organisation of the Naga Mother's Association" (Banerjee, 2008).

The organisation was established with an aim to encourage human development through education and to eradicate social evils and to work towards peace and progress. The NMA has gained its political relevance and came to play its role with the state machinery along with the other mainstream organisations like Naga Student's Federation and the Naga *Hohos,* the apex body of all Naga tribes. The role of NMA could be traced from its achievement in the formation of the Peace Team in October 1994 to confront the decaying political scenario in Nagaland. Infact the NMA is the only women's group in south Asia that has participated in the cease fire negotiation when it mediated between GOI and NSCN-IM in 1997. The association also opposed the imposition of AFSPA of 1958 in Nagaland.

It should not be mistaken that NMA is the only women organisation in Nagaland, along with the larger NMA there are couples of small women's organisation for peace. The most significant references are *Watsu Mongdung* amongst the Ao women and *Tangkhul Shanao Long (TSL)* which worked in Ukhrul village. In the recent times these three organisations, namely, NMA, Watsu Mongdung and TSL have emerged as the active propagator of peace in Nagaland. These organisations campaigned and facilitated cease-fire in 59 years' conflict prone Nagaland.

In Manipur, the genesis of women's peace movement could be traced from their mythical and historical women's activism. Manipuri women trace their descendence from legendary women such as ***Laisna***, who presided over the **Patcha**, or the women's court, that dealt with women related crimes in 33 AD. Women also remembers and praises the brave military deeds of legendary women like ***Linthoingambi*** of Ningthou Khomba, who was known to have saved her palace from attacks by the enemy (Banerjee, 2008). Manipur have also witnessed women-led uprisings known as ***Nupi lal***, which were against the British. During mid-1970's Manipuri women mobilised themselves into what was popularly known as Night Patrollers. The night patrollers were mainly a group of women who mobilised public opinion in favour of prohibition of liquor. It later converted into a massive anti-liquor movement under the name of Nashabandis.

Meira Paibis movement in Manipur is a land mark event that symbolised the women's activism in peace. It was initially an organised association which undertook a wide range of voluntary task to protect their communities against perceived social evils such as drug abuse and alcoholism. However, this movement did not remain confined to the anti-liquor movement, but the turbulent period in 1980's in Manipur transformed it into a greater movement for peace and security as a result of which Meira Paibis came into being. The period of 1980' witnessed the increase of state repression in Manipur which in a way led to the rise of various separatist groups resulting in severe conflict between the separatist forces and Indian Paramilitary Forces. Mostly women had to bear the brunt of these conflicts in terms of losing their husbands, sons, and fathers and witness the breakup of families.

Moreover the implication of AFSPA in Manipur led to indiscriminate torture to the civilians, mainly the women leading to rape, extrajudicial killing, enforced disappearances, and sexual molestation. It was during such a period of turbulence that the women of Manipur raised a massive protest against human rights violation and unjustifiable torture by the police in the name of security. Thus, Meira Paibis is a movement of women to defend the basic human rights of the people and has emerged as a powerful force of peace movement in Manipur.

Meira Paibis have demonstrated itself with some of the powerful expressions of protest against the atrocities of state coercive forces. One of the most powerful protest was against the state authority was when a group of Meira Paibis staged a nude protest outside the 17th Assam Rifle Battalion, holding up banners that said, "Indian Army Rape Us". This was in the backdrop of the rape and murder of Thangjam Manorama, a 32 years lady, by the Assam Rifles personnel. This incident not only signifies the state repression and insecurity of people in Manipur, but how women body is victimised in such a conflict situation. Women body has been made the site of all sort of conflicts and identity politics in North-East India, where women loses the control over her own body and is monopolised by others. One of such events that signify the valiant role of womanhood in peacemaking glorifies itself from the protest made by Irom Sharmila. In November 2000, Sharmila, resolved fast unto death, as a protest to repeal the draconian AFSPA in Manipur which was responsible for unprecedented torture of the civilians by the state forces. The protest was against the abuse and misuse of powers under ASFPA to kill any person on mere suspicion with impunity.

In the contemporary perspective the conception of peace needs to be redefined. Today peace not merely implies absence of violent conflict but it is a creative process of building sustainable society, living a contended life. In Manipur markets also play very important role in giving women a kind of mobility and help them in building opinion and resolve for bringing peace in their society. In this context the example of ***Khwairamband bazar*** more popularly known as ***Ima keithel*** can be cited which provides an important illustration of role of women in peacekeeping. ***Khwairamband bazar*** is not merely an ordinary market place of economic activity, but also a centre for social and political discussion among the women. The markets have served as the platform of women's politicisation in Manipur. The mutual exchange of ideas and commonality of interest as traders have accommodated the women with a sense of collective action.

It is interesting to note that within North-East, the amount of mobility and public space enjoyed by women vary in a significant way. While the North-Eastern states of Nagaland and Manipur have showed positive pictures of women's power the states like Assam show a reverse image of women's participation in peace. Paula Banerjee observes that the failure of Assamese women to transit to formal spaces of political power has marginalised them. She contrasts how Women's activism in Nagaland has been supported by the state and the Naga Ho council whereas in Assam, Matri Manch type peace initiatives are blocked (Banerjee, 2008). This is also related to the tribal non-tribal division of the population in Assam. In traditional non-tribal Assamese society women are basically confined to the household activities as the public-private dichotomy is still very much in existence, whereas the tribal Assamese women appears to have more mobility. However, it would be a grave mistake to underestimate the role of women in Assam merely on the basis of traditional social framework. Infact the women of Assam in the last few decades have proved themselves as active peace-maker. In this context reference could be made to radical writer like Indira Goswami's effort to negotiate peace between the government and the militant group of ULFA.

The experience of women's peace-making role in North-East India clearly glorifies the fact that during conflict, women have capitalised themselves as active peace actors. Kofi Annan, the then Secretary General of U.N stated, "Women who know the price of conflict well, are also better equipped than men to prevent or resolve it. For generations, women have served as peace educators, both in their families and in their societies. They have proved instrumental in building bridges rather than wall" (Dutta, 2008). But the tragic fact is that the sweat and toil of women movement is not fully recognised. The peace building activities of women are merely considered as volunteered, charitable or social even though they have political impacts. This could be seen from the fact that the protest of Irom Sharmila still did not get active support of the government and the people even after her decade of fast, while on the other hand the five days fast of Anna Hazare has shakened the whole nation. Why is this happening? Is it because that Irom Sharmila is a woman? Such facts will always raise the debated question that why voice of women is always suppressed? As U.N report states, "women make an important but often unrecognised contribution as peace educators in the families and in the society" (Dutta, 2008). Moreover, once the conflict is over women are expected to bounce back to the domestic activism. The peace building role gets transformed into "stretched roles" of women as a housekeeper, nurturer and caregiver. As rightly stated by Anuradha Dutta, in many places all over the world women are expected to go back to the "kitchen" once the conflict is over (Manchanda, 2011).

The above counted roles of women in peace building in North-East India are among those few that are told and shared. But countless remained buried under the forgotten history. Rita Manchanda points out that history provides no chronicle of women's experience of organised political violence, ignoring as inconsequential the differentiated way violence impacted on their lives, forging survival strategies, resistance and peace building; and how it effected a social transformation in gender roles (Manchanda, 2011). Thus, it was rightly viewed by Rita Manchanda, no women, no 'democratic' peace (Manchanda, 2011).

Thus in conclusion, it can be argued that the conception that women of the region are free, liberated and privilege to enjoy a relatively high status is highly contestable. It will be not out of place to argue that the condition of women here is equally degraded if not worse than the rest of the India. In fact there has been deliberate exclusion of women from the political power or the power of decision-making. The patriarchal set-up the societies have very strategically made a space for women to play their public role as mothers, daughters and sisters and their role has been used by the male leadership for gaining more ground in the ethnic politics.

There are apparent reasons which made women to assume the role of peace makers in these societies. Women are witness to children being left traumatised, the husband and sons going underground and the youth taking to alcohol and drug. The brunt of all these problems have been borne by women as mothers and they are left with no other options but to break their exclusivity and try to put their society back in track.

The socio-economic mobility of women and their role in peace making process is not considered as politics as women do not get the decision-making authority. The role of peace making had given impetus for the creation of different women's organisations. But these organisations are thus considered as civil society organisations only. Patriarchy has manufactured consent from both male leadership and women's organisation to propagate the thought that these organisations are apolitical both in their individual as well as in their organisational efforts. This has internalised the idea that the domain of politics where major decisions are taken are exclusively for men and women should concentrate on softer issues. Thus, the space of peace-making is a very strategic space to create a public visibility for women, where women were convinced that politics is not their domain.

References

Banerjee, Paula (eds.) (2008), *Women in Peace Politics*, New Delhi: Sage Publication India Ltd.

Baylis, Steve, *et al.* (eds.) (1997), *The Globalisation of World Politics: An Introduction to International Relations,* New York: OUP.

Behera, Navanita Chadha (eds.) (2006), *Gender, Conflict and Migration*, New Delhi: Sage Publication India Pvt. Ltd.

Butalia, Urvashi (eds.) (2002), *Speaking Peace: Women's voices from Kashmir*, New Delhi: Kali for Women.

Das, Samir Kumar (2008), "Ethnicity and Democracy Meet When Mothers Protest" in Paula Banerjee (ed.) *Women in Peace Politics,* New Delhi: Sage Publication India Ltd., p. 57.

Desai, Neera and Usha Thakkar (2011), *Women in Indian Society*, New Delhi: National Book Trust India.

Dutta, Anuradha and Ratna Bhuyan (eds.) (2008), *Women and Peace: Chapter from North-East India*, New Delhi: Akansha Publication House.

Jain, Devaki (1980), *Women's Quest for Power: Five Indian Case Studies*, New Delhi: Vikas Publishing House.

John, Mary E. (eds.) (2008), *Women's Studies in India*, New Delhi: Penguin Books India: New Delhi.

Manchanda, Rita (2011), "No Women, No Democratic Peace" Presented in IIAS Seminar on Challenge to Democracy In South Asia, 15-16 January, 2011, New Delhi.

Manchanda, Rita (2005), "Women's Agency in Peace Building: Gender Relation in Post-Conflict Reconstruction," *Economics and Political Weekly*, 29 October, 2005.

Manchanda, Rita (eds.) (2011), *Women, War and Peace in South Asia: Beyond Victimhood to Agency*, New Delhi: Sage Publication.

Misra, Udayon (2006), "Ethnicity, Territoriality and Autonomy in India's North-East: From Fragmentary Politics to an Inclusive Social Space" in David R. Syiemlich, *et al.*, (eds.) *Challenges to Development in North-East India,* New Delhi: Regency Publications, 2006, p. 1.

Owens, Baylis, Smith (eds.) (1997), *The Globalisation of World Politics: An Introduction to International Relations,* New York, p. 268.

Roy, Asok Kumar and Rajendra Prasad Athparia (eds.) (2006), *Women and Changing Power Structure in North-East India*, New Delhi: Om Publication.

Xaxa, Virginius (2008), "Women, Gender in the Study of Tribes in India" in John, Mary E. (ed.) *Women's Studies in India,* New Delhi: Penguin Books India, p. 47.

Racial Discrimination Against Women from North-East India: Need of Corrective Measures

Jasdeep Singh Toor, Ranvir Singh and Bhagwant Singh

Introduction

The universal declaration of human rights, (1948) under the aegis of United Nations Organisation (UNO), ensures the equality of honour and treatment to all, irrespective to one's caste, class, race, decent, religion, sex and ethno-cultural distinctiveness's (Devetak *et al.*, 2007). Article 55 of the U.N. pledges to promote "universal respect for, and observance of, human rights and fundamental freedoms for all without distinction as to race, sex, language and religion" (Kapoor, 2004).

Similarly, the Constitution of India works as an impartial and vigilant guardian to the basic human rights of its citizen. The incorporation of fundamental rights in the Part III of Indian Constitution not only ensure the right to equality, liberty, Right to life but also works as an effective custodian of religious, cultural and educational rights of the minorities communities of India (Bakshi, 2005).

In addition, Supreme Court of India, High Courts of Indian states and various institutional arrangements such as National Human Rights Commission, State Human Rights Commissions, and Statutory Commissions for Minorities and Tribal Rights are honestly and sincerely providing their respective physical, financial and technical assistance to the fulfilment of said objective. The presence of a large web of quality educational and research institutions also works to create awareness about the essential human rights of the citizen of India.

Inspite of all these preventive and curative measures, the condition of human rights is not good enough to receive global acclamation and accreditation. The violation of the rights of the subaltern groups, especially, the position of rights of women, is not up to the international standards. The condition is even more alarming with the people of North-East in general and women in particular. The increasing incidents of racial discriminations, sexual harassment and other criminal activities against the women of North-East have a very serious ramification to the rich and diverse cultural harmony of the country. Racial discrimination against the people of North-East is also a stigma to the world's largest democracy and the precursor of human rights under liberal democratic institutional establishments.

North-East: A Distinctive Socio-cultural and Geographic Setting

North-East presents a very unique and distinctive history and socio-cultural ambiance. North-East India comprises of eight contiguous states, Assam, Arunachal Pradesh, Manipur, Meghalaya, Mizoram, Nagaland, Tripura and Sikkim holds 7.6 percent of land area and 3.6 percent of the total population of India. The entire North-East region inhabits around 70 major population groups and sub-groups, speaking approximately 400 languages and dialects (Nepram, 2002).

Racial Discrimination against Women

Discrimination on the ground of race, religion, region, ethnicity, colour and gender is not new to the human relationships. History is full of examples when a specific group of people reigned and subjugated the marginalised sections of the society. The discrimination against women, non-citizen and slaves in the ancient and earliest laboratories of democracies, the Greeks, in both theory and practice demonstrates that, the roots of racial discrimination are old and deep. Even the first political scientist, Aristotle, considered inequality as natural and legalised the institution of the slavery for the essential maintenance of the socio-economic and political affairs of the ancient Greek City States (Wayper, 1964).

The racial holocaust continues to exploit the subaltern groups in the society till the advent of reformism and renaissance in 17th and 18th

century Europe. The democratisation of political institutions and diffusion of modern education systems worked as a catalyst to galvanise the universal values such as, liberty, equality and fraternity (the central tenet of French Revolution. Similarly, the civil war, (1865-69) in United States of America won the decisive victory to the African-American that stand inalienably glorified in the form of Barak Obama, the President of the most powerful State on the earth. Moreover, the process of decolonisation and establishment of United Nations Organisation and thereafter its global efforts to wipe-out the racial discrimination in all its forms successfully culminated in the end of apartheid in South Africa (Ishay, 2004).

Similarly, India progressed ahead with its successful democratic experiments to ensure, at least in theory, an inclusive, equitable and non-discriminatory developmental paradigm in the country. India has diverse, ethnic, cultural, religion and social practices and has been successful in harmonising and synthesising this diversity over the long extended historical process. India, being one of the most heterogeneous countries in the world, has been successful to create harmony and in more phrasal term, to ensure 'unity in diversity'. Though, there has been certain incidence of discrimination against some poor and marginalised sections of the society in India.

As discussed earlier, North-East presents a very distinctive cultural contrast as compared to the mainland India. The process of globalisation and economic interdependence and the absence of developmental exposures, difficult geographical terrain, insurgency and security crisis are primarily attribution to the migration of North-East people to the other parts of the country.

The problem of racial discrimination starts when people from North-East are treated as strangers in their own country. Yarom Sho Ngalung, a member of Naga Students' Union of Delhi, revealed how they are treated a foreigner in their own country as he said, "People in Delhi often refer to North-Eastern people as 'Nepali'. They do not know that Indians from the North-East come from a different racial stock. They also do not know that there are many different tribes in each of the seven states. They assume that people from China, Nepal, Tibet, and the North-East are all the same" (Chandra, NESCH). Discrimination against the people of North-East in general and women in particular has not only been a stigma to the honour and essential human rights of the people but a terrible scourge to the unity and integrity of the nation.

Indeed, the people of North-East are discriminately treated as a stranger in their own country. The Chief Minister of Mizoram, Lal Thanhawla revealed the similar truth at an international seminar in Singapore on June 26, 2009 when he said, "I am a victim of racism. In India, people ask me if I am an Indian. They ask me if I am from Nepal or elsewhere. They forget that the North-East is part of India" (Borpujari, 2010). The women are the worst victims of raciest remarks especially when they arrive to big metropolitan cities to fulfil their educational and financial pursuits. Women have to suffer from snide comments and are even physically harassed and assaulted in many parts of the country.

Sexual discrimination against North-East women is quite common in metropolitan cities in India. National Capital Delhi is infamously a lending destination where cases of rape and other physical assaults against North-East women have increased alarmingly over past decade. The statistics presented by the National Crime Record Bureau, 2005 revealed that Delhi recorded maximum number of crimes against women with an incident of rape in every 29 minutes, molestation every 15 minutes and sexual harassment every 53 minutes. Similarly, out of 1,00,000 people living at Delhi, 41 percent of cases belongs from sexual harassment against women. The growing number of sexual assaults and racial discrimination against the women of North-East in big metropolitan cities like Delhi, Mumbai, Bangalore, etc. are not only the gross violation of human rights but is a great hurdle to the cultural harmony and the unity of the nation (Joshi, 2009).

Moreover, a study conducted by North-East Support Centre and Helpline (NESCH) revealed the gravity of racial discrimination against the people from North-East India. The study revealed that seventy-eight out of one hundred people living in national capital Delhi are racially insulted and humiliated. Women are the worst victims, followed by human trafficking and violence against the people from North-East community (*The Hindu*, 2011). Similarly, an NGO (Jagori) based survey study revealed that there were around 70 percent of cases against the harassment of women on roads as 60 percent men and 71 percent common witnesses confirmed the harassment against women in the year 2009. The following table demonstrates the gravity of racial discrimination experienced by the people from North-East India.

Table 22.1 demonstrates how different cases of racial discrimination appeared against the people from North-East over the period 2005 to 2010. The year 2009 experienced the treatment with the people of North-East with thirty-nine cases of racial discrimination in a single year. However, there was a positive recovery in the year 2010 when only six cases of discrimination occurred. The study also demonstrates that most of the cases are concerned to the discrimination and harassment against women as twenty cases of molestation, three cases of rape and six cases of girl beating were experienced over the given time period.

Table 22.1: Cases of Racial Discrimination against North-East People from the Period 2005-10

Nature of Cases	*2005-08*	*2009*	*2010*	*Total*	*FIR*	*No FIR*
Molestation	15	8	2	25	13	12
Rape	2	1	0	3	3	0
Beating Girls	2	3	1	6	4	2
Beating Boys	0	20	2	22	4	16
Murder	1	3	0	4	4	0
Attempt Rape	1	0	0	1	0	1
Misbehaved	2	1	0	3	0	3
Non-Payment	4	2	0	6	0	6
Rent Non-Refund	1	1	0	2	0	2
Media	1	0	0	1	0	1
Missing Person	0	0	1	1	1	0
Total	29	39	6	74	29	43
Percentage	39.20	52.70	8.10	100	39.19	60.81

Source: Chandra, M. (2010), "Social Profiling: Root Cause to Racial Discrimination Faced by North-Easterners in National Capital", New Delhi.

Moreover, the so-called 'Chinkis' word has emerged as the symbol of racial slur that adds only to the embarrassment and humiliation of the innocent North-East women. Inspite of being an integral part of the Republic of India and the symbol of rich mainstream cultural diversity, the women of North-East feels alienated and marginalised in their own country (Subba and Ghosh, 2003).

In addition, the condition of women is not quite good in their own native states. Though, the women in the North-East enjoys greater autonomy, liberty and visibility in their respective society. For instance, a research on 23 districts in Assam reported 10,423 registered cases of violence against women (The North-East Network, 2004).

Need of Corrective Measures

The entire North-East adds charm and versatility to the rich and diversified cultural culture of India. India is globally applauded for its sheer cultural harmony, tolerance and liberal ideas and ethos. India is home to all the major religions prevailed on the earth. India holds Hindu, Muslim, Sikh, Christians and Jews on secular foundation. The successful functioning of the world's largest democracy on the line of secularism, cultural harmony and tolerance exudes the richness of country's socio-economic as well as political principles and practices. India serves as a unique example of 'unity in diversity' in the world.

However, this diversity receives stiff challenges when the inhuman cases of racial discriminations become evident with people of North-East India. Such discriminations not only infringe the basic human rights of victims but are serious challenges to the unity and integrity of the nation at large. It is therefore imperative to take corrective, curative and preventive measures. Education is fundamental to the revolutionary changes in the society. The cult of racial superiority and cultural arrogance flourishes only in the atmosphere of ignorance and illiteracy. Therefore, the spread of education through public-private institutionalisation and mass media could imbibe a spirit of tolerance and cultural harmony among the people of different cultural sects.

More importantly, the crisis of 'Self' always emerges in the veil of ignorance, illiteracy and poverty. The crisis of identity is always relative as sub-ethnic identity and mainstream culture. The marginalised group continues to stay submissive and even tormented unless it achieves relative socio-economic identity and breakthrough *vis-a-vis* the mainstream cultural prevalence. Undoubtedly, the historic, cultural and physical uniqueness of the North-East people as compared to mainland ambiance remained a major cause of cultural polarisation between the sub-ethnic identity and mainstream cultural parlance. The distinctive facial and physical texture of the North-East people is considerably distinctive to the rest of the nation. This distinctiveness serves as a unique contrast and curiously (may not by intentionally) becomes a victim of racial sneering.

The remedy lies in making a strong and enlightened 'Self'. The people of North-East need more financial incentives to improve their economic fate. The people of North-East are badly afflicted by the insurgency crisis and economic abjectness. The poor state of infrastructure and difficult geographical structure are the major push and pull factor compelling them to migrate to the big metropolitan cities and remain the soft target of racial abuse not more to their physical ambiance but due to their abject poverty. It could be a subject to serious research that most of the victims of racial discrimination are those of the poor than the wealthy and educated north-easterners. It is, therefore, imperative to effectively penetrate developmental activates in the entire

North-East India. The increased economic profile and employment opportunities would prevent migration of these people for jobs. The survey study conducted by the NESCH also rated the absence of educational exposure and lack of employment opportunities as the leading causes of 'push factor' to the metropolitan cities (*The Hindu*, 2011).

Furthermore, there is a need to strengthen the legal and statutory mechanism to effectively encounter the growing crimes and racial discriminations against the people of North-East. The culprits must be given exemplary punishment through speedy legal process. The cooperation from security personnel is an essential pre-requisite. Eliminate all possibilities of discrimination against people of North-East.

Moreover, the centre and the ministry of Development of North-Eastern Region (DONER) could issue comprehensive guidelines for the effective enforcement of policy directives and statutory mechanism to eliminate the possibilities of further racial discrimination, physical and mental harassment and human trafficking afflicting the people from the North-East India.

More importantly, the role of civil society could bring more concrete results in creating awareness toward a more harmonious society for all people, irrespective of their religion, race, colour, culture and biological sex. Civil society and women organisations could serve as an ideological weapon against the racial discrimination and other criminal activates experienced by the people of North-East. Similarly, it could work as important input to sensitise the public and private institutions to take stringent actions against the criminals and ensure proper security of the People of North-East in general and women in particular.

Concluding Remarks

India is globally recognised and revered for its 'unity in diversity' as the county presents a panoramic and vivid cultural harmony and synthesis. The rich cultural heritage fitted firmly with the value of cultural synthesis, communal harmony and respect to all people irrespective to one's race, religion and region attributes to the success and progress of India as a successful democracy, burgeoning economy and social harmony. Only a politically participant, economically inclusive and socially vibrant nation can set example for the perfect and harmonious living on the earth. India, since independence, has been striving for a nation where all citizens would enjoy their basic human rights and live a life of plenty and perfection.

However, like all societies, India has also its challenges and limitations. India is home to 1.21 billion people, the second largest in the world. The increased population and shrinking natural resources have attributed to the demand-supply imbalance in the recent years. The inability to ensure quality of opportunities in terms of education, employment and resource distribution, in general, has attributed to regional disparities and inequality of capabilities. The fault line of most of the social problems starts from the access to resources and the distribution of capabilities to its citizens.

The discrimination against the people of North-East in general and the women in particular, is more attributed to the developmental vulnerability than an ethno-cultural speciality and distinctiveness. As mentioned earlier, the cases of racial discrimination are primarily targeted on those who migrated from their home states to metropolitan cities like Delhi, Mumbai and Bangalore. The people of North-East are harassed because of their abject economic conditions and their inability to generate their own indigenous resources. Therefore, financial revitalisation of these people is the first step to stop 'push and pull factors' as most of the racial discrimination is experienced among the women who have migrated from their native places to the big cities for their livelihood.

Similarly, the construction of a safety architecture works as a preventive measure to ensure the security and safety of the women of North-East India. There should be a greater accountability and transparency in part of police administration in dealing the gravity of criminal cases against the people of North-East. The victims should be ensured justice while culprits should be allotted exemplary punishment.

Finally, a cognitive revolution serves as more effective and long lasting solution. There is a need to change the mind set and perceptional misunderstanding against the people of North-East India. People must know that diversity is the law of nature and it is the moral duty of every rational being to respect this diversity of nature and live in peace, harmony and goodwill.

References

Bakshi, P.M. (2005), *The Constitution of India*, New Delhi: Universal Law Publishing Company.

Borpujari, U. (2010), *Deccan Herald*, 27 June 2010, Online Web URL: http://www.deccanherald.com accessed on 15 December 15, 2011.

Chandra, M. North-East Support Centre and Helpline, Online Web URL: www.nehelpline.net Accessed on 16 December 2011.

Chandra, M. (2010), "Social Profiling: Root Cause to Racial Discrimination Faced by North-Easterners in National Capital", A Term Paper Presented in a Seminar on Sexual Abuse, Social Discrimination and Economic Exploitation organised by Vaiphei Christian Fellowship, Delhi at Murnika, July 24, 2010, New Delhi.

Devetak Richard *et al.* (eds.) (2007), *An Introduction to International Relations: Australian Perspective,* New York: Cambridge University Press.

Ishay, M.R. (2004), *History of Human* Rights: From Ancient Times to the Globalisation Era, Berkeley: University of California Press.

Joshi (2009), North-eastern Women at Risk in India's Capital City, *Women's Future Service.*

Kapoor, S.K. (2004), *International Law and Human Rights,* Allahabad: Central Law Agency.

Nepram, B. (2002), *South Asia's Fractured Frontier,* New Delhi: Mittal Publications.

Subba, T.B. and Ghosh, G.C. (2003), *The Anthropology of North-East India: A Text Book,* New Delhi: Orient Longman.

The Hindu (2011), "Discrimination against People from North-East Rising in Delhi", 12 March, New Delhi.

The North-East Network (2004), "Violence against Women in North-East India: An Inquiry", National Commission for Women, New Delhi.

Wayper, C.L. (1964), *Political Thought,* London: Hutchinson.

Index

INDUSTRIAL RELATIONS
Theory and Practice

INDUSTRIAL RELATIONS

THEORY AND PRACTICE

BIPIN KUMAR

Associate Professor and Head, Department of Economics,
R.R.S. College, Mokama (Patna)
Magadh University, Bodh Gaya, Bihar

REGAL PUBLICATIONS

New Delhi-110027

INDUSTRIAL RELATIONS
Theory and Practice

ISBN 978-81-8484-212-8

Typeset by
S.S. COMPOSERS
3190, Mohindra Park, Shakur Basti, Delhi-110034.

Printed in India at
MAYUR ENTERPRISES
WZ Plot No. 3, Gujjar Market, Tihar Village, New Delhi-110018.

Published by
REGAL PUBLICATIONS
F-159, Rajouri Garden, New Delhi-110027.
Phone: +91-11-45546396
E-mail: regalbookspub@yahoo.com

Dedicated to the Memory of my Father
Late Mahendra Prasad Singh

Contents

Preface

The problems of industrial relations are the basic elements in the economic and social life of any country and as such, likely interest in it has persisted from the very dawn of history of modern times.

Industrial relations play a crucial role in establishing and maintaining industrial democracy. The maintenance of industrial peace and the smooth functioning of industrial relations are one of the basic requirements of public welfare, the industrial relations are a product of the forces of evolution and are dynamic and as such they have changed are changing and will presumably continue to change under the impact of changing social and economic influences. In the field of industrial relations, the social distance between employers and their employees began to widen because employers took little or no part personally in the work of their factories. Hundreds of workmen were and also today are individually unknown to them. As such, relationship became impersonal and indirect. These changes in early years of the industrial revolution have continued even today. Industrial relations in Indian perspectives are challengeable. Many factors have been influencing the industrial revolutions that need to be focused.

Keeping this view, the book primarily attempts to the emerging issues of industrial relations, labour-management cooperation, trade unions and management.

Industrial peace which is prerequisite for the industrialization, through which the goal of a socialist welfare state is achieved by accelerating the production of goods and services, achieving the higher rate of employment, making price stability and social justice and for achieving these factors a conductive environment of industrial relations is vital. The theories of industrial relations have been propounded and principles have been developed through trial and ever method, with an effort to find out the best possible method for quick and satisfactory settlement of industrial disputes.

In its whole life of nearly 100 years only a few strikes have taken place. There have been long periods of industrial peace. Industrial peace had been maintained even prior of enactment of the industrial relations laws. Such a situation draws attention of the experts and students of the industrial relations as to why industrial relations in the Tata Iron and Steel is smooth? Why this private sector steel plant has been able to infuse industrial peace? What is the industrial relations policy of the TISCO management? How industrial disputes are settled? To what extent the degree of labour-management cooperation exists? How far "Closer association of employees with management" scheme has achieved its goal? These are some of the important questions that crop up in the minds of persons interested with industrial relations.

This present book has given a vivid picture of TISCO particularly the industrial relations that has been adopted as prime policy by TISCO.

The present book has been brought to fruition through the help of following distinguished scholars who willingly formed support system which was always available to me : Professor (Dr.) Tapan Kumar Shandilya, Vice-Chancellor, Veer Kunwar University, Ara (Bihar), Dr. Amit Kumar Thakur, General Secretary, Indian Economic Association, Dr. Mithilesh Kumar Sinha, Department of Economics, Nagaland University, Nagaland and Shashi Bhushan Kumar.

I acknowledge the love and affection of my mother Shrimati Indira Devi who relently rendered me throughout the writing of book and my wife Shrimati Suman Rani with my beloved sons Divyanshu Bhardwaj and Priyanshu Bhardwaj.

BIPIN KUMAR

PART A

INDUSTRIAL RELATIONS IN INDIA: ISSUES AND POLICIES

Introduction

The field of industrial relations is
readymade method and solutions cannot be
outside. Each community must find and appl
relevant to its own circumstances that will en
social groups engaged in industry to go in for wi
and purposeful action. The modern industr
involves a high degree of inter-dependence. Wi
of modern technology and scientific methods o
processes of production have become complicat
it is not possible for an individual to work in iso
industry. An engineer, for example, even wit
technical knowledge and brilliance will not be a
much in production unless he is able to work
others, are able to work with him and he
subordinates take interest in the work and take
him. It becomes essential, therefore, to understa
of human relations in management, if we wa
involved workers, good industrial relations and
production. Industrial peace helps in the wealth
and this was realised quite early. Consolidatio
impulses calls for creating space for it in the le
arena, too. Economic democracy, at any rate a me
the form of relevant institutions and pract

Introduction

The field of industrial relations is the one, where readymade method and solutions cannot be imported from outside. Each community must find and apply the principles relevant to its own circumstances that will enthuse men and social groups engaged in industry to go in for willing cooperation and purposeful action. The modern industrial organisation involves a high degree of inter-dependence. With the application of modern technology and scientific methods of production, the processes of production have become complicated and complex. It is not possible for any individual to work in isolation in modern industry. An engineer, for example, even with his specialised technical knowledge and brilliance will not be able to contribute much in production unless he is able to work with others and others are able to work with him and he can make his subordinates take interest in the work and take them along with him. It becomes essential, therefore, to understand the problems of human relations in management, if we want efficient and involved workers, good industrial relations and more and better production. Industrial peace helps in the wealth creation process, and this was realised quite early. Consolidation of democratic impulses calls for creating space for it in the leading economic arena, too. Economic democracy, at any rate a modicum of it, in the form of relevant institutions and practices appeared appropriate. In the labour market it involved a framework of sharing a blend of economic and political power across contending interest groups.

Industrial relations play a crucial role in establishing and maintaining industrial democracy. In the pre-Independence days, workers were 'hired and fired'. The principle of demand and supply governed industrial relations, and the employer was in a commanding position while conditions of employment and wages were very poor. But in post-Independent India, many labour laws are enacted to protect the interests of industrial workers. Industrial relations have become highly regulated. There are several labour laws which have to be complied with and therefore Indian industrial relations are legalistic in nature. On the other hand, the government has also made efforts, in addition to the attempts made by managements and unions in several cases, to promote bipartite collective bargaining.

EVOLUTION OF INDUSTRIAL RELATIONS

The origin of industrial relations lies in the employer-employee relationship. The moment workers are divorced from any ownership of the instruments, materials and means of production, they become wage earners depending for their livelihood upon wages alone. The people—who "own the instruments and materials of production become their employers and own the product. In the beginning of the modern industrial society; the economic system, consisted of a large number of small competitive businesses and industrial establishments, each employing a small number of workers. The relationship between an employer and his employees was informal, personal and intimate, but with the growth of the giant-sized joint-stock companies and business corporations, each employing in many cases thousands of workers, the relationship between the employer and his employees is no longer intimate and informal. Formal institutions have grown upto regulate this relationship. Such factors as the intervention of the State, the growth of trade unions and their federations, employers' associations, the growth of sciences of personnel management, industrial psychology and industrial sociology have all tended to influence the spirit and the course of the relationship between employers and employees.

These factors have changed the nature of the employer-employee relationship and have converted this private relationship into a relationship of public importance affecting the welfare of the community as a whole. One can no longer talk of the employer-employee relationship as the private concern of the employer and his employees only. The maintenance of industrial peace and the smooth functioning of industrial relations are one of the basic requirements of public welfare. The trade unions and their federations of today as well as the large business corporations separately command an aggregate of power which can be used both for the welfare as well as for the disruption of society. The struggle between these two wings of industrial relations fighting for the sharing of the joint products of labour and capital is not a scene which one can view with equanimity. The result is that the problems of industrial relations, such as strikes and lock-outs, industrial discipline, hiring and firing, promotion and transfer, payment of wages, bonus and fringe-benefits have become essentially acute and demand understanding and constructive solutions.

Concept of Industrial Relations

The term 'Industrial Relations' has been variously defined by different writers to suit their own needs and circumstances and the degree of industrialisation in each country. It is sometimes used as an all-inclusive term and sometimes as a term restricted to collective relations. In the restricted sense, the term 'Industrial Relations' is used to connote only collective relations between trade unions and employers. This usage is illustrated by the following extract from an I.L.O. Meeting of Experts on 'Industrial and Human Relations' held in July 1956 at Geneva.

"Labour-management relations include all the relations between workers and management or employers and between workers' organisations or representatives and representatives of employers or their associations or federations........ a deficiency in the conduct or spirit of either personal relationship, which we may call human relations, or of group or collective relationships, sometimes referred to as industrial relations, can each have a detrimental effect on labour-management relations. In the all inclusive sense, industrial relations can be defined as all the relationship between management and employees in the community. In this sense, the field of industrial relations covers relations between individuals such as the individual employer and employee, and between organised groups such as trade unions and employers. It also covers unorganised or informal relations and organised or formal relations. In an all inclusive and broad sense, the term also "includes the relations between the various unions, between the State and unions as well and those between the employers and the Government.

Prof. Yoder, while considering the term 'industrial relations' in its broad sense, defines the term as inclusive of "all the relationships that grow out of the fact of the employment. Prof. Lester explains the dimension of the term 'industrial relations' in the following fine words:

> "The term 'industrial relations' includes not only the dealing between labour organisations and industrial management but also all aspects of labour............ including wages, productivity, employment security, management's employment practices, union policies and governmental action on labour matters."

In view of the broad dimension of the industrial relations just observed, it can be conveniently said that industrial relations system, in its broad sense, comprises three groups of actors of hierarchies:

(i) workers and their organisations,
(ii) managers and their organisatins, and
(iii) governmental agencies concerned with the work place and work community.

The first two hierarchies are directly related to each other in that the managers have responsibilities at varying levels to issue instructions (manage), and the workers at each corresponding level have the duty to such instructions (work). The specialised government agencies as actors may have functions in some industrial relation systems so broad and decisive as to override the hierarchies of managers and workers on almost all matters. In other industrial relations systems the role of the specialised governmental agencies, at least for many purposes, may be so minor or constricted as to permit consideration of the direct relationships between the two hierarchies without reference to governmental agencies, while in still other systems the worker hierarchy or even the managerial hierarchy may be assigned a relatively narrow role. But in every industrial relation system these are the three actors."

'Industrial relations' is thus a broad term which includes individual relations in the industry, i.e., relations between employers and work people at the plant level as well as collective relations, i.e. relations between employers or their organisations and trade unions at various levels, and also the role of the State in regulating these relations.

Two Dominant Aspects of Industrial Relations

There are two important, aspects of the industrial relations' scene in a modern industrial society—

(1) Cooperation, and
(2) Conflict.

(1) Cooperation

Modern industrial production is based upon cooperation between labour and capital. Here labour stands for the workers who man the factories, mines, and other industrial establishments or services. Capital stands for the owners of business enterprises who supply the capital and own the final products. The cooperation between the two is one of the basic requirements for the functioning of modern industries and the growth of industrialization. This needs no further elaboration as it is clear that large factories and other business establishments cannot run successfully unless there is close cooperation between labour and capital. The very fact that the present industrial organization and the economic structure has been able to turn out a quantity of goods and services unprecedented in the history of mankind is an index of the extent of cooperation between the two. Cooperation is the normal feature of industrial relations.

However, this cooperation flows from the pursuit of self-interests both by the owners of capital and the owners of the labour power, i.e. workers. The owners of economic enterprises offer employment, wages and other amenities of life to the workers. The workers in their turn offer their services. Thus, there is a fair degree of give and take and serving of mutual interests which is at the base of cooperation between them. But this cooperation is of a minimal degree and is nothing more than the mere coming together of the labour and capital or the union and the management, and is devoid of any voluntary choice of, and regard for, the other as a partner. It flows from the necessity that some sort of working relationship has to be reached in order that the factory operations, on which both are dependent, may continue. Thus, it is a necessitous and functional cooperation, in the absence of which, neither of the parties can satisfy its interests.

(2) Conflict

The second aspect of the system of industrial relations obtaining today is the existence of conflict. Conflict, like cooperation, is inherent in the industrial relations set-up of today. It becomes apparent when industrial disputes resulting in strikes and lock-outs become frequent. The prevailing industrial unrest, the frequency of work-stoppages resulting either from strikes or lock-outs, and the slowing down of production are the occasional expressions of the ever-present and latent conflict between workers and the management. The daily newspapers give enough indication of the existence of industrial conflict.' The maintenance of an elaborate machinery by the State for the prevention and settlement of industrial disputes flowing from industrial conflict is an indication of its extent and depth.

In the case of physical health we rarely pay any attention to it so long, as we are healthy; similarly, so long as industrial peace prevails and production of goods and services continues uninterrupted, there is little talk of cooperation between labour and management, but any work-stoppage caused by strikes or lock-outs is hotly discussed and debated, solutions are suggested and remedies adopted. Thus, it is clear that the industrial relations' picture consists of two dominant aspects:

(a) Cooperation, and
(b) Conflict, both of which need further discussion and elaboration.

Nature of Industrial Conflict

Industrial conflict is human conflict. It is just one aspect of the general conflict inherent in the capitalist society based upon the pursuit of self-interest in the economic life by every individual and the group to Which lie belongs. If an economic and social order is based upon the open acceptance of the principle that each individual' is the best judge of his self-interest and he should be free to pursue this interest, conflict becomes inherent in that order. The industrial conflict between labour and capital is one manifestation of this all pervasive conflict in the capitalist society. The coming together of workers motivated by their urge of obtaining the highest possible wages and the owners of capital motivated by profit maximization, is the basic cause of industrial conflict in the capitalist economic system. The products of the joint efforts of labour and capital, i.e. the output or the proceeds of an enterprise being limited at a particular time, if more goes to labour in the form of higher wages and other amenities of life, less is available for profits to the owners of capital resources. Thus, at a particular moment of time, file satisfaction of the interests of labour conflicts with the pursuit of the interests of capital and the two groups become antagonistic to each other.

It is realized that this conflict is like the conflict between any buyer and seller. The seller seeks to sell at the highest possible price that lie can extract and the buyer seeks to pay the lowest possible price. The workers are the sellers of the commodity their labour power, and the employers buy this commodity. Even though the ILO may declare that "labour is not a commodity to be sold and purchased", it continues to be so. Naturally, the determination of the price of labour including the other terms and conditions of employment becomes the chief source of conflict between the employer and his employees.

Further, it has to be appreciated that the conflict is not personal, but results from the capitalist system itself. In a competitive market situation the constant drive for cost reduction is needed for the mere survival of a business enterprise., The employer attempts to economies on wages also because they constitute an important elements in the cost of production. But what is cost to the employer is the main source of income to the workers who, therefore, seek to maximise their wages and industrial conflict is the result.

It is not that the employer is cruel and enjoys the sight of misery, disease, squalor and want among his workers. The point is that he cannot afford to be liberal and altruistic. He is himself a victim of the system.

Moreover, labour power is fundamentally different from any other commodity. Not only that, labour power is a function of time and is, therefore, most perishable but also that it cannot be separated from the labourer. The labourer sells his labour power, but retains it in his person. A seller is the least concerned with what happens to the commodity after he has sold it. But a labourer is very much concerned with the way the employer uses the labour power; with the temperature under which it is used, the speed with which it is worked and the tension and the pressure that its use creates, i.e. the conditions under which work is performed are of utmost importance to the life and happiness of the labourer and do become a source of conflict, no less important than wages.

Thus, conflict of interests is found not only in the spheres of wages and profits alone, rather it bedevils the totality of relation ship arising out of the coming together of labour and capital in the capitalist form of economic organisation. The profit maximisation goal of management may demand changes in the types of goods produced, installation of new machineries, adoption of newer methods of production involving loss of hard-earned skills, transfers, retrenchment and compulsory retirement of workers. On the other hand, the workers expect and demand stability in their income, security of employment, protection of skills and improvement in their status.

Profit maximization may also require authoritarian administration of the enterprise, closer supervision of workers, maintenance of strict discipline and complete obedience to the rules of the enterprise. On the contrary, workers may demand a share to the management of the enterprise, a voice in the formulation of the standing orders and scope for self-expression and a respect for the dignity of their individuality. Hence, it is not only the sparing of the fruits of the industry that generates conflict: the very fact of how production is to be carried on and how costs are to be shared also becomes a major source of conflict between labour and capital.

Industrial Disputes

Conflict as one of the features of industrial relations is a general concept. When it acquires a concrete and specific manifestation, it becomes an industrial dispute, i.e. industrial conflict is general whereas industrial dispute is specific. Industrial disputes may be said to be disagreement or controversy between management and labour with respect to wages, working conditions, union recognition or other employment matters. Such a dispute may include, controversies between rival unions regarding jurisdiction also. There can be as many industrial disputes as there are points of contact between management and labour or one industrial dispute may cover many issues of conflict. When issues of conflict are submitted to the management for negotiation, they take the form of industrial disputes.

Therefore, the specific causes of industrial conflict may be treated as causes of industrial disputes also.

Specific Causes of Industrial Disputes

In the background of the general comments it would facilitate understanding if the causes of industrial disputes or industrial conflict were more definitely categorised and specified. A brief illustrative check-list of the specific causes of industrial disputes is given below:

(I) Economic

(A) Division of the fruits of the industry:
- (a) Wage structure and demands for higher wages;
- (b) Methods of job-evaluation;
- (c) Deductions from wages;
- (d) Incentives; and
- (e) Fringe benefits.

(B) Methods of production and physical working conditions:
- (a) Working conditions;
- (b) Machinery;
- (c) Layouts; and
- (d) Changes in products.

(C) Terms of employment

Hours of work, shift working, promotion, demotion, layoff, retrenchment, dismissal, job-security, etc.

(2) Institutional:
  (a) Recognition of the union;
  (b) Membership of the union;
  (c) Subjects of collective bargaining;
  (d) Bargaining unit;
  (e) Union security; and
  (f) Unfair practices.

(3) Psychological:
  (a) Clash of personalities;
  (b) Behavioral maladjustments;
  (c) Demands for recognition of workers' personality;
  (d) Authoritarian administration; and
  (e) Lack of scope for, self-expression and participation; and
  (f) Undue emphasis on discipline.

(4) Denial of legal and contractual rights
  (a) Non-implementation of labour laws and regulations, standing orders, adjudication-awards; and
  (b) Violation of collective agreements, wage boards' recommendations; customary rights, etc.

This check-list of the specific causes of industrial disputes is merely illustrative. The points of contact between the employer and his employees are so numerous that no exhaustive list can be prepared. Besides, the check-list contains the main causes of industrial disputes but does not indicate their relative importance as causative factors. If industrial disputes were to be classified...on the basis of causes and their relative importance it would be found that their relative importance would vary from country to country and in the same country from time to time. In one country, at one time, wages may constitute to be the single main source of industrial disputes, whereas at a different time or in a different country, the relative importance of wages may decline and some other issues may become more important. In which country and at what time, which issue will become predominant will depend upon the importance the workers attach to their problems within the prevailing economic and political climate. It is well-known that in the earlier stages of industrial development wages were the most important cause of industrial conflict. As the wage level rises, hours of work and other working conditions may gain in importance as causative factors. In times of unionization, issues relating to recognition of unions and union security may figure more often in the industrial disputes. During times of depression and slackening of businesses, retrenchment and lay-off will become prominent. Thus, as industrial conflict and industrial disputes are the results of clashes in the goals and aspirations of the workers and the employers, the variations in the causes of industrial disputes will indicate the changes in the pattern of workers goals and aspirations. A study of the classification given above indicates that some of the sources of conflict and individual and others collective in character. For example, the issue of non-payment of wages or the denial of leave may relate to an individual workman but the demand for a general wage increase or the recognition of the union is a matter which always concerns a group of workmen.

Interests and Rights Disputes

Another way of looking at industrial disputes could be to classify them on the American pattern wherein disputes are categorized uncles two heads:

(i) disputes concerning interests; and
(ii) disputes concerning rights.

There can be disputes regarding creation of specific rights and there can also be disputes regarding the implementation of these rights. The former disputes are said to be disputes regarding interests and the latter disputes regarding rights. An illustration would be useful to explain these concepts. A dispute concerning a general wage increase or the acceptance of seniority as the basis of promotion may be said to be a dispute regarding interests. The resolution of this dispute may create certain rights, i.e. right to a higher wage, or right to promotion on the basis of seniority. Later on, if the employer refuses to make payment according to the terms of agreement or the adjudication award or refuses to make promotion in a specific case on the basis of seniority, disputes regarding implementation of the rights will arise. Therefore, they can be said to be disputes regarding rights.

Under the Indian context, disputes regarding the implementation of labour laws and regulations, standing orders, arbitration awards, collective agreements and settlements, wage boards' recommendations and administrative orders of the government will fall under the second category of disputes concerning rights. These disputes in American parlance are called grievances. The American unions and managements are not prepared to submit to arbitration their disputes regarding interests, but often resort to arbitration as the last stage in settling disputes regarding rights. In the J.S.A., a trade union would be rarely prepared to submit its demand for a wage increase to arbitration, but once an agreement has been signed, the union may perfectly be willing to submit to arbitration disputes flowing from the implementation or the interpretation of the agreement.

Results of Industrial Conflict

It requires not a very imaginative mind to realise the' consequences of a situation full of conflicts. It is surprising that the existing set-up of industrial relations, whose roots lie in an all-pervasive conflict, functions at all. It is clear that such conflicts have adverse effects on industrial production, efficiency, costs; quality, human satisfaction, discipline, technological and economic progress and finally on the welfare of the society. Even in the absence of open strifes resulting in strikes and lock-outs, where production machinery comes to a halt and the costs and losses are apparent, the corrosive effect of industrial conflict is much too widespread and deep to be neglected. A discontented labour force, nursing in its heart mute grievances and resentments, cannot be efficient and will not possess a high degree of industrial morale. Under such conditions absenteeism and labour turnover increase, plant discipline breaks down, both the quality and quantity of production suffer and costs mount upto the detriment of all concerned—workers, employers and consumers. In the end, the accumulation of these individual and collective resentments and dissatisfactions finds expression in violent strikes and lock-outs. Then, the realization comes that something is vitally wrong with the relation between the workmen and the employer and that preventive and curative measures have to be urgently needed.

Strike-A Method of Settling Industrial Disputes

In spite of the elaborate machineries that employers, employees and the State have evolved everywhere to bring about a peaceful settlement of industrial disputes, strikes and lock-outs have not been completely eliminated. Analysts continue to identify the causes of strikes, and attempts at refining the methods and machineries for the peaceful settlement of industrial disputes still persist.

Strikes and lock-outs are one of the methods adopted by workers and employers respectively to settle their differences. When the workers fail to secure a redressal of their grievances and fulfilment of their demands by peaceful negotiations with the employer, they try to force the employer to come to a settlement by temporarily withdrawing their services in the form of a strike. They may succeed or fail in their attempt to do so, but for the time being, the issue that gave rise to the dispute is settled either in the favour of the workers or in the favour of the employer. The strike has been and is the main weapon in the armory of labour to achieve its goals. Likewise, the employers resort to lock-outs. According to the view presented here, strikes and lock-outs are not to be identified with industrial disputes. They are not disputes in themselves; they are just one way of settling disputes' for the time being.

Labour reform is a very sensitive subject in the Indian context, given the ground realities of poverty, illiteracy, disease, deprivation, exploitation, low per-capita income, etc. It cannot be discussed purely in the context of organised labour as is the case today. The need of the day is to enlarge the scope of labour reform to cover both organised and unorganised sectors so that their benefits reach everybody. The labour force is an important and indispensable resource in today's age of technological revolution and economic liberalisation. As such the reform must have a human face.

Consequent upon the adoption of the policy of economic liberalisation, privatisation and globalisation the arm of state shifted in favour of the employers as against the employees in the earlier period. This led to a sharp decline in man-days lost due to strikes. The new policies have impacted adversely on the labour unions. As workers remained subdued in the liberalisation period, the employers did not declare lock-outs. There was no need. In October 1999, the government constituted the Second National Commission on Labour on the recommendation of the Indian Labour Conference. The social and labour effects of the new policies are very serious. New investments are taking place, but job creation is quite less. Labour is being pushed from the organised to the unorganised sector. There is increase in casual and contract labour. In this milieu, the role and functions of trade union need to be reviewed. The trade union may disappear from the scene altogether and even the subject of IR may soon be irrelevant.

The rapid growth of industrialization in many parts of the world over the past quarter of a century have been contributed largely by lower labour costs and more flexible labour supply. This reflects the relative lack of protective regulations, weak system of collective bargaining, lack of working-class traditions and expectations, and reduced role of unions. 'Market' as an institution now has over-powered the old 'protective' institutions and society is tending to move from 'status' to 'contract' and in the sphere of labour-management relations is giving primacy to managerial prerogatives and rationality.

The structure of industrial relations in the post-war period was drawn from the spirit of Welfare State. Hence, labour market, presumed by most post-war policy-makers, was one based on the vast majority of the men being in secure, full time wage employment with women being 'economically inactive' or in jobs as 'secondary workers' (Lewis, 1992, Sainsbury, 1954). Within employment and the labour market, the growing forms of labour control were bureaucratic and paternalistic in nature. However, as early as 1929, Slichter, a founder figure of modern industrial relation, saw the dangers of this approach and its effect on industrial relations (see Slichter, 1929). Under Welfare Capitalism, therefore, much of the paternalistic approach was taken over by or extended to state itself. The unions and state played the roles of protectors of labour interest. Industrial relations now were governed by statutory pro-collective regulations,' backed by voice regulations through unions and employers' associations, mainly through tripartism. Not only was centralised or sectoral collective bargaining favoured and trade union confederations and employers organisations regarded as legitimate part of governance, but statutory regulations promoted collective institutions and procedures (Standing, 1999).

In the wake of growing impact of globalisation, state and firms both claim that they need to reduce fiscal and labour costs, particularly indirect labour costs associated with employment, job, and work insecurity. Hence, there is a trade-off between 'flexibility' and 'security' (Standing, 1999). Employers want and are pursuing different kinds of flexibility leading to various types of insecurity on the part of workers in traditional sense. In the new framework of industrialization the unions and state find themselves to play a 'soft' role and make balance between flexibility and security. There have been various examples of countries' practising balance between 'labour market' security on the one hand and 'employment' or job' security, on the other, in order to achieve higher rate of economic growth in a conducive industrial relations situation. Any industrial relations analysis, hence, should accept this as reality and then seek ways that would induce conducive industrial relations in an era of growing labour flexibility.

The present structure of Indian Industrial relations draws its spirit from the concept of welfare state. Around the time of independence several labour laws were enacted to protect the labour from exploitation. Labour policy was directed initially in maintaining harmony for ensuring the realisation of the objectives of economic planning (Venkata Ratnam, 1996). To deal with industrial conflict four types of institutions were created viz.—

(i) interventionist labour laws,
(ii) industrial democracy,
(iii) code of conduct (moral as well as disciplinary), and
(iv) consultation machinery (collective bargaining through bipartism or tripartism).

Among all these state intervention has played the dominant role, complemented by the other three (Shyam Sunder, 1998). Whenever conflict arose between employer and employee, state came in between to sort out the problems. In the process, state introduced an array of regulations, particularly in favour of workers, which continuously added to the market rigidities (Sarath, 1992). This also added to the higher adjustment cost to the employers and consequently low demand for labour in Indian Industries (Fallon and Lucas, 1991, Mathur, 1982 and 1992).

Hence, the laws of job protection itself impeded the job creation. Moreover, on several occasions industrial conflicts took violent form resulting in gheraos, lock-outs, and even deaths. Given the intensity of industrial unrest and resultant violence, it is doubtful whether India has a unified industrial relation system (Venkata Ratnam, 1996).

In the wake of New Economic Policy (NEP) government is deregulating Indian industries in order to compete with multinationals. There was a gradual retreat of state from the arena of industrial relations (IR) (Bhattacherjee, 2000). On the collective bargaining front, there is ascendancy in managerial rights (Venkata Ratnam, 1991 and 1992). New technologies, structural and other adjustments seem to have made unions position much more vulnerable today than any time in the past. The growing flexibility in Indian industries has left the unions with little memberships and little things to do.

Accordingly, workers are resorting to more covert form of protest instead of calling strikes with the help of union. This has been true even in the states where ruling political parties are guided by left ideology and are understood to be more committed to the cause of workers' welfare. In fact, "the changing composition of the labour force and the increased labour force flexibility have tended to lower unionisation, since intermittent and marginal labour force participants are less inclined to join or stay in unions" (Standing, 1999). In the same way Virmani (1995) notes that "collective bargaining has failed us, therefore, we must give up collective bargaining." Firms are restructuring without unions' involvement by adopting various strategies.

The institutional framework of the industrial relations system (IRS) was primarily designed to deal with industrial conflict. Four institutions were created to deal with industrial conflict, viz.. interventionist labour laws, tripartite and federal consultative institutions, industrial democracy, and moral codes. State intervention was the dominant feature of the institutional framework, complemented by the other three institutions. The legal framework of the system was primarily defined by three labour Acts, namely, Trade Unions' Act, 1926 (amended recently), Industrial Employment and (Standing Orders) Act, 1946, and the Industrial Disputes Act, 1947. Of the three, the ID Act is the most crucial piece of legislation. This Act—

(a) Provides for (compulsory) conciliation and compulsory adjudication of industrial disputes and strikes,

(b) Determines the procedural rules for industrial action,

(c) Prohibits industrial actions not conforming to the rules framed,

(d) Determines the rules for changing terms and conditions of employment,

(e) Decides the rules for labour separation and closure of establishments, and

(f) Provides for the establishment of works committees.

The important objectives of the Act are to preempt and prevent the incidence of industrial disputes, ensure that disputes do no result in workstoppages and settle them expeditiously if they do. For a good measure, voluntary methods of resolution of disputers like collective bargaining and voluntary arbitration were also encouraged. They were, the government tirelessly pointed out , in fact complementary to compulsory adjudication and in the long run should replace the latter. State intervention was sought to be complemented by consultative machinery (both bipartite and tripartite) at all levels. What the formal system did not legislate (like recognition of trade unions) was sought to be achieved through the moral codes, viz., the Codes of Conduct and Discipline. The institutional framework of the IRS is comprehensive and was designed to contain, if no: "eradicate" industrial conflict.

The institutional framework of the system was found to be "inefficient" (Shyam Sundar, 1999). At the same time both trade unions and employers demanded changes in the legal framework for different reasons. The government under pressure from international lending institutions and foreign and domestic capital sought to bring about labour reforms in the 1990s. Labour reforms were held to be a necessary complement to economic reforms carried out earlier. Of the several components of labour reforms, two have caused great agitation in the minds of workers; they are, privatization and changes in labour laws. The principal labour law reform measures relate to removal of restrictive clauses in the law on retrenchment, lay-off, closure, determination of terms and conditions of employment, and free use of contract labour. The public sector reform programme includes two important measures: privatize in a significant manner even profit-making public sector undertakings and reduce the employee strength in the governmental sector. All these measures are seen to principally result in two harmful consequences to labour: loss of jobs and unemployment and weakening of trade unions and of bargaining power of workers. These reforms are seen to destroy the precious labour rights won after years of hard struggle. On the other hand, the trade unions have suggested a number of reform measures from their perspective like removal of bonus ceilings, effective implementation of labour laws, radical revision of minimum wages, etc. which have fallen on deaf ears of the government. The pressure on the government to introduce these labour reforms is great and the resistance from the workers and trade unions is equally powerful. The scene is set for conflicts. The government established a number of committees and task forces and commission (the Second National Commission on Labour (SNCL) headed by Ravindra Verma) to recommend measures to reform labour laws and thus create a conducive social climate of opinion to ease the introduction of reform measures at a later date. On the other hand, it has pointed out that reform measures have been stealthily inserted in the system and by backdoor (Bardhan, 2002) and that formalization is only a ritual left. For example, the government 'looks the other way' when employers indulge in acts such as prolonged lock-outs (indeed closures), easing out of workers with or without adequate compensation, sub-contracting and so on (Bardhan, 2002, pp.127-8). However, these clandestine measures lack credibility and strain labour-management relations (via litigation) so long the rules not endorsing these remain on the statute book. Foreign capital demands formal repeal of these rules. Formal labour reforms are said to be inevitable. Efforts to introduce them create tensions and conflicts.

References

Lewis, J. (1992), "Gender and the Development of Gender Regimes", *Journal of European Social Policy*, Vol. 2, No. 3.

Sainsbury, D. (1954), "Dual Welfare and Sex Seggregation of Access to Social

Benefits, Income Maintenance Policies in the UK, the US, the Netherlands, and Sweden", *Journal of Social Policy*, Vol. 22, No. 1.

Slichter, S.H. (1929), "The Current Labour Policies of American Industries", *Quarterly Journal of Economics*, Vol. XLII, No. 3, May.

Standing, Guy (1991), "Structural Adjustment and Labour Market Policies Towards Social Adjustment?", in G. Standing and V. Tokman (eds.) Towards Social Adjustment Labour Market Issues in Structural Adjustment, ILO, Geneva.

Venkata Ratnam (1996), Welfare and Moneyfare: Collective Bargaining and Social Security, A Project of UNDP and Centre for Development Studies. (Memio).

Shyam Sunder (1998), "Industrial Conflict in Tamilnadu 1960-80", Ph.D. Thesis, Mumbai University, Mumbai.

D. Jarath, D. (1992), Employment and Unionism in Indian Industry, Friedrick Ebert Foundation, New Delhi.

Fallon, Petter R. and Robert E.B. Lucas (1991), "The Impact of Job Security Regulations in India and Zimbabwe", *World Bank Economic Review*, Vol. 5, No. 3.

Mathur, A.N. (1989), Industrial Restructuring and Union Power; Micro-Economic Dimensions of Economic Restructuring and Industrial Relations in India, ILO-ARTEP, New Delhi.

_________ (1992), Employment Security and Industrial Restructuring in India: Separating Facts from Folklore, The Exit Policy Controversy, IIM, Calcutta.

Bhattacherjee, D. (2000), "Globalising Economy, Localising Labour", *Economic and Political Weekly*, Vol. XXXV, No. 42, October.

Venkata Ratnam (1991), Unusual Collective Agreements, Global Business Press, New Delhi.

Virmani, B.R. (1995), New Perspective on Industrial Relations, Friedrich Eburt Stiftung, New Delhi.

Shyam Sundar, K.R. (1999), "Indutrial Conflict and the Institutional Framework of the Industrial Relations System in India", *Management and Change*, Vol. 3, No. 1, pp. 53-88.

Bardhan, Pranav (2002), "The Political Economy of Reform in India", In Mohan, Rakesh (ed.). Facets of the Indian Economy, New Delhi, pp. 123, 135.

Industrial Relations: Emerging Trends

Governmental intervention was visualised only as a balancing device, as it were. There were choices in this field, and India did make its own choice in furtherance of its larger nation-building exercise with variation at different stages. Unparalleled in history, "India tried to achieve rapid industrialisation while maintaining political democracy including powerful trade union rights" (Mukherjee, 2002).

Indian industrial relations strategy and the instruments for its implementation were developed with a view to supporting strife-free growth and wealth creation. It even worked that way, at least in the organised secondary sector of the economy. Seemingly the national agenda has remained the same, though not necessarily its path and priorities. Discontinuous changes, triggered by domestic crisis as well as external pressure, and that too recently at a rapid pace, disturbed the established tenuous balance.

The problems of industrial relations are the basic elements in the economic and social life of any country, and as such lively interest in it has persisted from the very dawn of history of modern times. In recent years they (industrial relations) have commanded growing attention not only among industrialists and workpeople but among governments and the public also as a topic of primary concern. "The reasons for such growing interest are not difficult to discover. A large proportion of the population of any civilized country either works for an employer or depends upon employees to get work done. For them the relationships which exist between employees and employers are vital, for they are the people who are immediately concerned. As for the others—those who live on independent incomes, those who perform professional services, those who engage in trade, all those who neither work for an employer nor rely upon hired help—their role is far more intimate than that of mere spectators. Whether as consumers, as purveyors of professional services, or as members of an amorphous and interdependent society, such individuals stand to gain or lose as industrial relations improve or deteriorate."

In view of the above mentioned observations, the importance of harmonious industrial relations for the success of modern industries need not be over-emphasized. As such, the establishment and maintenance of satisfactory industrial relations is one of the main social and political tasks today because the impact of industry upon man and society is significant. Now-a-days labour conflicts may not only cripple significant sections of the economy but also imperil the significant sections of the economy but also imperil the health and safety of the people and even halt the functioning of the government temporarily. No manager, therefore, can afford to neglect the manpower of the enterprise and industrial relations.

I. Revolution and Changing Pattern of Industrial Relations

Industrial relations about which modern societies worry so much today are as old as industry is. As such, they will always remain a significant feature of industrial life. Industrial relations are the result of historical forces. They emerge from the evolutionary process that creates social, economic and political institutions, and the problems of industrial relations are affected by these institutions. "As such their origins are found in the net work of human relations woven in the development of civilizations."

Industrial relations are a product of the forces of evolution. Industrial relations are dynamic, and as such, they have changed, are changing and will presumably continue to change under the impact of changing social and economic influences. It is, therefore, necessary to glance at the antecedents of modern industrialism in order to appreciate the true character of the contemporary problems of industrial relations and to appraise actually the present status of the wage-earning class.

2. Antecedents of Modern Industrialism and the Industrial Relations

In the primitive stage of hunting and fishing, man's wants were very limited and he was largely dependent upon the free gifts of the nature. No formal system of production, distribution and exchange was necessary. There was not much division of labour and specialisation of tasks. The institution of slavery began to emerge, but the idea of private property was also imperceptible. "Because there was no distinct labour class, no labour problem arose."

In the pastoral age also there was no great personal accumulation of wealth though private property existed in a somewhat limited degree. Though a conflict of economic interests developed from frequent disputes over the economic ownership of pasture land, yet society was not sharply divided into class of rich and poor. To some extent, however, "there was division of labour within the tribe, but it cannot be said that a distinct differentiation of employer and employee classes existed. Problem of industrial relations could not, therefore, arise.

Under the manorial system, which dominated all over the world between 11th and 16th centuries, definite economic classes existed. Land owned by lords or manors were cultivated by serfs upon an established service basis. Serfs were more or less similar to those of slaves, but definitely a bit superior to slaves. Under the slavery, slaves were engaged in most ignominious occupation and the treatment meted out to them was more or less inhuman. "Except for slavery to death frequently had presented little choice to slave. On the contrary, serf acquired certain limited right which accorded him a measure of freedom and self-respect, but was still subservient to his lord. His freedom was more apparent than real. A class of independent farmers, known as 'free tenants,' also existed side by side, which held an improved position over serfdom. In course of time, a class of agricultural workers labouring for wages also emerged.

In nutshell, "slavery, serfdom, and the wage system thus

existed side by side; distinct economic classes developed; and conflict of interests became pronounced."

From the limited specialisation of function among slaves and serfs, the status of free artisans developed, who were wage-earners. But "their status differed essentially from that of modern employees, for they were not free to charge any wage they might like."

In the Middle Ages, therefore, "the most common type of employee-employer relationship was that in which employers were masters and employees were essentially slave. Masses of slaves and serfs were regarded as unfortunate who were fallen from grace and born to life time servitude................ The slave was a chattel, the personal property of his master." There was no organisation or union which labourer or employee could join comparable with the Chamber of Commerce, town council type of organisation to which the employers had no trade and who did not possess the talents of the trademan did not lead a very secure existence. During this period Government was not a divergent influence in the matters of industrial relations. Later, political organisation and conquests of the periods supported the authority of property-owners who utilised labour in the manner as they pleased. Thus, Government was also a party to the extreme exploitation of labour during this period. Under such circumstances, the employees were sick with demoralised feelings, frustrations and dissatisfactions, and were restive with hidden resentment against the master-employers.

The period characterised by the existence of serfs, slaves, and a few artisans is generally described as the "Agricultural Period." With passing years, increasing numbers of artisans achieved a status of independence and were thus able to sell their services for wages. Specialisation of productive processes was increased; independent craftsman consequently came into picture, and era of Handicrafts System developed. Craftsman found their economic positions strengthened in the new environment, and began to form Craft Guilds which persisted in one form or another until well into the eighteenth century.

Basically, craft guilds were associations of masters-craftsmen who were in business for themselves. These craftsmen often were employers as well. Craft Guilds had master-craftsmen (the entrepreneurs of the system), journeymen (its wage earner), and apprentices. Journeymen held a superior position to apprentice. Upon the expiration of the term, the apprentice became a Journeyman or full workman. Wage, hours and other conditions of employment were determined by guild regulations. Journeymen and apprentices worked together with craftmen, generally in the latter's home. "The origins of modern trade union benefits for deaths, disability, and unemployment may be traced to the practices of the guilds. Despite the development of guild organisation, no class of permanent wage-earners comparable to that in modern industry was to be found in the guild system. Employment relations of the craft guild system are worthy of special attention. "Under the craft system industrial relations were intimate and congenial—a marked contrast to the strained relations that so often exist in the modern industry under capitalism. A noted historian beautifully characterises the employment relation under the Handicraft System as follows:

> "Drawn from the same social status, united by a sense of common interests, masters and men in the early days of industrial development could toil side by side, in willing cooperation, undivided by the antagonism of capital and labour............... There were no permanent classes of employers and employees, the one rigidly divided from the other by an almost impassable barrier of wealth and social status.

With the intimacy dominating industrial relations, moreover, misunderstandings were less likely to occur than under the impersonal relations of the modern workshop. Under the circumstances, the problems of industrial relations as such did not exist.

Internal divisions and external changes in the distribution of industry gradually began to weaken the guild organisation, and "the guild system saw the shift of industrial production from the homes of self-sufficient, self-contained farmily units to town-located shops. The older system is customarily called 'domestic production'........ while production under the guilds held sway, we note, the emergence of a different type, a capitalistic form, which ultimately made an industrial capitalism possible. It is known as the cottage, or 'putting-out' system. It came into being in the fifteenth century when the Yeomen guilds became prevalent."

Formation of yeomenary guilds—association of journeymen for the specific purpose of bargaining with employees—was a new development in the field of industrial relations. These guilds may be designated as the legitimate ancestors of modern labour organisations. "Eventually they were recognised by the craft guilds (employers' associations) and were accepted into these guilds but in a subordinate position. It is inconceivable that an employers' association should accept into its organisation a union of workers. This amalgamation took place ... only after the journeymen agreed to drop their labour union characteristics and assumed the guise of small independent shop producers."

Employers' associations were tolerated because they were dedicated to this purpose. Employees' organisations were not tolerated, for they were dedicated to realising wages and otherwise attempting to improve the lot of the workers—a line of action which was considered to be against public policy.

Thus, a bold step to form employees' organisations was foiled by the employers, Workers' status could not improve. More and stricter regulations were framed to check anti-capitalist tendencies of the working class. The importance of the employee in an era of expanding industrial activity was recognised, but the policy of ruling class was that under no circumstances should the law recognise the right of workers, either individually or collectively to use their bargaining power in bettering themselves as employees. The result was deterioration in the quality of industrial relations.

3. Modern Industrialisation and Industrial Relations

Modern industrialisation is everywhere primarily a product of the 19th century. But its foundations are set deep in the great epochal mechanical inventions of the 18th century, and it cannot be divorced completely from the industrial antecedents of earlier times. The little more than a hundred years between 1730 and 1840 witnessed the inception of changes that swept aside methods of production and distribution prevailing for hundreds of years. These changes are commonly referred to as the industrial revolution. Important among the changes, were;

first, there was a shift in emphasis from agriculture to industry; next, there was change in the emphasis on production; another feature was the rapid replacement of "putting out system" of cottage production by "factory system."

Unprecedented development of factory system required large doses of capital as well as group of workers employed for regular hours. Functions of labour and capital were separated, and as such, the industrial society was sharply divided into well defined and more or less permanent economic classes—'capitalists-employers' and definite 'wage earners-employees'. Capitalists furnished the necessary capital for the organisation and expansion of industry, while labour sold his labour power for a specified time for more or less definite wages to the employer-capitalist. The dependence of labour upon capital was almost complete.

Development of factory system introduced revolutionary changes in the management of manpower, and made the management of human resources more complicated. Relative positions of capital and labour in the scheme of production was completely changed. No longer could the worker acquire ownership and control of means of production as he had been able to do under the domestic system and earlier guild regime. So, "the chances of rising were very very small." Doomed to a subordinate position, economically and socially, the labour could never quite reconcile himself to his lot." The state was powerless, under the aegis of 'laissez faire,' to protect the workers because legal interference with industrial relations, then, was though to be as unnecessary as it was futile. "The workmen were in the hands of a power that was obliged by the law of its being to secure them all the comforts and freedom of which they were capable." Condition of the employees were worse than in any previous period. Wages were shockingly low, and any effort for getting the wages increased, was blocked by the employers. Children, sometimes as young as six, were chained to either machines or were worked fifteen or sixteen hours a day, and curelty to apprenticed children was common. Moral conditions were at a low ebb. Mills and workshops were small, hot, damp, and unhealthful. A workday of twelve, thirteen or fourteen hours in general, was not unusual. Employment was less regular or account of seasonal and periodical depressions.

The radical changes in organisation and operation of industry ushered in by the Industrial Revolution, emergence of economic classes—employers and employees, deteriorating conditions of the workers, indifferent attitude of the state towards the improvement of employees, lot, etc. were doubtless responsible for many of the human problems including that of Industrial Relations. In the field of industrial relations, the social distance between employers and their employees began to widen because employers took little or no part personally in the work of their factories. Hundreds of workmen were, and also today are, individually unknown to them. As such, relationships became impersonal and indirect. These changes in early years of the Industrial Revolution have continued even today.

As Messers Scott, Clothier and Spriegel have also observed that although mankind as a whole was benefited greatly by the Industrial Revolution, "misunderstanding began to undermine the sympathy and cooperation that had previously existed between employer and employee, whereas, in the home and shop, discontent and friction seldom existed as a result of misunderstanding, a gulf now began to develop between the employer and his workers. Where the workers in a single group previously numbered a handful, they now began to number hundreds and thousands. Previously, the employer enjoyed the friendship of his associates at the bench; it now became possible for him to know them only casually, if at all to know their weaknesses and strengths, their family fortunes, their follies and their hobbies." As a consequence, "the old relations between masters and men disappeared, and a new 'cash nexus' was substituted for the human tie" and there came into being an attitude on the part of management towards the workers that has become known as the "Commodity Conceptions of Labour."

The commodity concept "implies the rights of the employer to purchase labour power in the cheapest market and to keep the price low regardless of its effect upon the workers as a human being in a civilised community. It also implies that the workers have not the right to combine for the purpose of manipulating the labour market for their own advantages." The price of the labour was determined by the supply and demand as was usually done in case of commodities.

The 'commodity theory' overlooked the fact that employer

bought and sold, not the actual labour, but the product of this labour produced. The value of labour was determined, according to the observers, by the goods it brought forth and was thought in these terms. With this end in mind, it is not difficult to see how readily "The employer could regard his employees largely as operating organism, or machines, capable of certain amount of output."

Industrial relations during the period of the currency of 'commodity' and 'machinery' concepts of labour were impersonal and most embittered. Workers were regarded as non-volitioned beings having no feelings, emotions, and aspirations. Industrial relations during this period have been characterised by hostility, suspicion, mutual distrust, violence and subversive activities. Sensitively minded reformers soon perceived the incongruity of the rapid accumulations of wealth and the simultaneous decaying of human well-being and happiness among the employees. It was, in this context, that something was lacking in the relationship between management and workers, and this led to the beginning of the 'humanistic concept of labour.'

The central idea in the 'humanistic concept of labour' is that labour is not a commodity, not a mere inanimate element in the processes of manufacture or just a calculable economic quantity which, like any other commodity, enters into the expense of production. The worker, as an embodiment of labour power, must, therefore, be elevated from the plane of lifeless raw materials and inanimate machines to the pedestal of precious beings. This concept accords to labour the dignity it deserves, and its importance essential to equitable treatment. This doctrine held that all men are equal, in the sense that they have many of the same impulses and reactions, and are not essentially different from human beings in any other station of life. It held that industry had a moral obligation not only to permit its workers to enjoy certain 'inalienable' rights as human beings but to encourage and help them to make as much of themselves as possible. In short, "this doctrine stated that business has its at least four obligations—to their stockholders, to their customers, to their public and to the employees."

Acceptance of the 'humanistic conception of labour' led the employers to realise that there was a direct relation between the welfare of the workers and their productivity, and as such employers began to introduce and promote the welfare measures. At this stage the employer without a welfare movement was considered backward. But, at the same time, these welfare efforts by employers became the points of attack by labour organisations. "The employer who was most active in the welfare movement was often harrassed by the greatest labour turbulence. Employers obsessed with the welfare idea became increasingly paternalistic; yet it became evident that doing something for the welfare of their employees not only failed to solve management's problems but often introduced new and especially disturbing factors."

The increasing strength and growing militancy of trade unions on the one hand and the pressing need to maintain the tempo of production to take full advantage of the opportunities created by the First World War made the employers think in terms of changing their attitude towards labour. The success of the Russian Revolution also influenced tremendously the attitude of the employers towards their employees. The formation of the International Labour Organisation in 1919 put pressures upon the Governments as well as the employers to change their attitude towards the employees. The state also now came into picture as a party to the industrial relation. Attitude of the employers towards the trade unions and the necessity for collective bargaining as a means for the settlement of disputes also changed radically and now "it is well-established that employers in the older countries have generally accommodated themselves to unionism and collective bargaining, once regarded as a subversive and insurrectionary, the union is now accepted as a permanent and perhaps even a welcome part of the enterprise." Underdeveloped countries trying to industrialise rapidly realised the usefulness of trade unions for eliminating improvident and emotional gestures of workers, and for channelising their energy for more constructive purposes also came to be gradually realised by a large number of employers who ultimately accepted them (trade unions) as an integral part of productive mechanism. Now, "trade unions are being regarded as integral part of productive mechanism both in the centrally planned and market economies. In the less developed countries they function as a buffer between organised workers on the one hand and employers on the other, with potentialities of becoming a powerful instrument of economic development.

The changes in the attitude of employers towards unions did not stop at the point of recognition by them of their place and usefulness. Building amicable relations with unions became the primary duty of management.

4. State and the Industrial Relations

State's interference in the field of industrial relations was witnessed in the second half of the 19th century with the extension of social legislation to numerous phases of industrial life. The movement has continued till now. State's intervention in the industrial relations began to gain momentum when workers came to gain voting right, which shifted the balance of politics in their favour. As such the government could no longer ignore the claims of the majority of its electorate. The result was the rise of socialism and the growth of welfare state. Ultimately, the state came to play in active role in the industry as a model employer in relation to public enterprises, economic planner, protector of labour, and supervisor of industrial relations. Thus, promotion and prevention of industrial peace became the most important concern of state in all countries.

To attain the objective of sound industrial relations, states have taken in the first instance a number of protective and ameliorative measures, like guaranteeing workers the right of freedom of association and helping them in the formation of effective unions, planned programmes for reducing unemployment, introduction of a net work of social security measures, and establishment of an organised system of employment exchanges, etc. to remove economic disabilities of workers, and secondly, they (states) directly restricted the property rights of employers and prescribed minimum wages and conditions of employment whenever they thought necessary to prevent exploitation of labour.

As a custodian of good industrial relations, the state has set-up a network of machinery for the prevention and settlement of industrial disputes. Intervention or participation by the state is undertaken to promote the health, safety and welfare of work people, to define the legal relations between the employers and work people and the legal status and functions of employer's organisations and trade unions to facilitate the settlement of disputes, to provide regulations of wastes and working conditions when it is not done effectively by the parties themselves and to take a direct part in industrial relations as the employer of persons in public services and in nationalised industries. In many countries, the state also maintains consultative relations with employer organisations and trade unions on question of economic, industrial and social policy which affect their interests."

Although these measures have gone a long way in preventing severe exploitation of labour by regulating service and working conditions, yet they have failed to harmonise industrial relations, and thus, conflict of interest still continues. In fact, industrial relations are personal relations and cannot be regulated by legislations. It is basically human problem and can only be solved by developing in conflicting groups a sense of mutual confidence, dependence and respect. The outgrowth of this realisation was 'industrial democracy' or 'the citizenship conception of labour'.

"Although relations between employee and employer and employer have changed radically in the last forty years, the element of opposition between various groups and between employer and employee is still a subject of live interest. And it is hoped that industrial democracy will be effective in neutralising conflict in working life."

This concept envisages that just as citizens of democratic countries automatically have certain inherent rights and a voice in determining and exercising these rights, so are workers, as citizens of the industry in which they are employed, entitled to a right to have a voice in determining the rules and regulations under which they work. Schemes of joint consultation and workers' participation in management are the forms in which industrial democracy has developed on the industrial horizon. True industrial democracy, however, is more than that form of organisation whereby employers and employees meet jointly for discussion of difficulties; thus giving the employee an adequate voice in determining his working conditions. Such measures are expected to provide channels for regular exchange of ideas between management and employees to enable employers to understand and appreciate their work life, to demonstrate more clearly to all those engaged in the organisation of the areas in which management and employees have common interest, and to satisfy the urge of self-expression and develop the personality of the worker.

5. Trusteeship Concept of Industrial Relations

Society is indebted to Mahatma Gandhi who gave a new direction to the concept of industrial relations in the 20th century. He felt very much aggrieved on account of the exploitation of working classes at the hands of those who possessed much more wealth than needed by them. The Mahatma decried such tendencies. He was of the view that "everything belonged to God and was from God. Therefore, it was for His people as a whole, not for a particular individual." He said, "earn your crores by all means. But understand that your wealth is not yours; it belongs to the people. Take what you require for your legitimate needs, and use the remainder for society." Therefore, according to him, when an individual had more than his proportionate portion, he became a trustee of that portion for God's people. If this principle is followed by everyone in the society, "then there would be no exploitation and no reserves as in Australia and other countries for white men and their posterity." He wanted every person in the society to have the right to have an honourable livelihood but definitely not better than that enjoyed by millions of others.

The aforesaid feelings of the Mahatma have close relevance with the industry also. Industrialist class has to serve the larger interest of the community in addition to that of its own. Expressing the similar views in the Maharashtra Merchant's Conference, Sholapur, Late Sri G.D. Birla, an eminent industrialist of India, asked the delegates—

> "If you analyse the functions of the Vaishya (businessmen) of the ancient times, we find that he was assigned the duty of production and distribution not for personal gain but for common good. All the wealth that he amassed, he held as a trustee for the nation. Capitalists, if they are to fulfil their real function, must exist not as exploiters but as servants of society."

Just as an individual, as the Mahatma said, holds the excess of his wealth as a trustee for God's people, similarly, an industrialist should hold excess amount of profit as a trustee for the benefit of the workers so that exploitation of the latter is averted. If this 'Concept of Trusteeship', as the Mahatma called it, is accepted it will help definitely in improving industrial relations. This will help in the realisation of a state of equality on the earth.

Following is the Practical Trusteeship Formula as given by Mahatma Gandhi:

1. "Trusteeship provides a means of transforming the present capitalist order of society into an eglitarian one. It gives no quarter to capitalism, but gives the present owning class a chance of reforming itself. It is based on the faith that human nature is never beyond redemption.
2. It does not recognise any right of private ownership of property except in as much as it may be permitted by society for its own welfare.
3. It does not exclude legislative regulation of the ownership and use of wealth.
4. Thus, under state regulated trusteeship, an individual will not be free to hold or use his wealth for self-satisfaction or in disregard of the interest of society.
5. Just as it is proposed to fix a decent minimum living wage, even so a limit should be fixed for the maximum income that would be allowed to any person in society. The difference between such minimum and maximum incomes should be reasonable, equitable and variable from time to time so much so that the tendency would be towards obliteration of the difference.
6. Under the Gandhian economic order the character of production will be determined by social necessity and not by personal whim or greed."

The whole responsibility of developing a sense of trusteeship does not depend upon the employers alone, but upon the workers also who are also the true agents of the trust. Workers should consider themselves as trustees of the employers. It has rightly been observed by Sri Moni Ghosh:

> "The realisation of their (workers) strength combined with adherence to non-violence would enable them to co-operate with capital and turn it to proper use. They will not regard it (union) as a conflicting interest, they will not regard the mill and machinery as belonging to the exploiting agents and grinding them down, but as their own instrument for production and will therefore protect them as well as they would own their property... the trusteeship theory is not unilateral and does not in the least put employee on superiority of the trustees. It is perfectly a mutual affair and each believes that his own interest is best safeguarded by the voluntary acceptance of trusteeship, the sense of conflict will go."

From the primitive age down to the present time industrial relations have, therefore, passed through different phases of their evolution. Labour, from a slave, has now come to be recognized as a dignified and equally effective agent in the productive mechanism of industry, which itself is recognized as a co-operative enterprise. Trade Unions, which were previously looked as an enemy of industry and employer, have now come to stay as a responsible body in the industry. Trade unions today largely influence the industrial relations in any country. It is these organizations which have been taken into confidence for the regulation of industries. State has played and is playing a progressive and dynamic role to bring employers and employees closer by means of social and labour legislations, and has emerged as a protector of workers and a custodian of industrial relations.

Indian Industrial Relations in Perspective

History is a great teacher, and its ex-post analysis facilitates the understanding of the trends and the pattern as well as the forces behind it. From the colonial to the pre-1991 reform era, there has been major transformation in this field. At each distinct stake-holder within the contested terrain of labour market and industrial relations has made its strategic choice. The prevailing economic, social and political contexts, exerted their influence in such choice making.

Colonial India witnessed two sources of marginally pro-labour initiatives. First, labour consciousness was in its nascent stage of formation, and its institutionalisation was only sporadic. But dismal conditions of work, suffering and exploitation of workers and their repressed feelings did not remain unnoticed. The Royal Commission on Labour and subsequent other ones recorded vivid details. Also, there was the need to protect the interest of the British textile industry against the comparative labour cost advantage of the Indian textile products (Mukherjee, 2002, pp. 402-03). The strategy of colonial governance required steps to contain the sources of possible labour discontent as well. Despite "guided underdevelopment" in general (Chandra, 1992) and "stunted industrialisation" in particular, the size of the industrial workforce was large. With the British support, India acquired a permanent berth on the governing body of the International Labour Organisation. This had its own corresponding obligations on labour issues.

The second source had its roots in the strategy of corporate paternalism initiated and promoted by the indigeneous bourgeoisie. It was engaged in leading the process of industrialisation, often in competition with the British interest. To guard its turf on the labour front, it thought of welfare programmes. The 'third force' of labour welfare officers appeared on the scene. The network of Schools of Social and Labour Welfare provided personnel for this with only rudimentary capabilities. The process of structuring the industrial workforce was thus initiated. The Indian capitalist class was fully aware that disparity and deprivation might lead to "social cleavage and disharmony" and could strengthen the forces of the left (Birla quoted in Mukherjee, 2002, pp. 402-03). Apart from this, stabilizing the workers in industrial urban setting was a major task. Soft interventions with welfare measures at micro-levels designed to promote a body of docile and receptive workforce followed. Closer to the Second World War, the provisions of the Defence of India Act constituted a decisive intervention in industrial relations. Pursuit of war needed uninterrupted operations of the factories and the supply lines. Labour consciousness and trade union formation had moved ahead in the meantime. During freedom struggle it had made significant stride with political support. Signs of protest, covert and overt, emerged. An active state in labour market became the necessary strategic choice replacing the earlier gradual, minimal and somewhat tokenist steps.

Post-Independence Period

India decided to move on to the path of directed and planned development with accelerated industrialisation as its vehicle, among others. Within the familiar development model, the large pool of surplus rural agriculture labour was to serve as the feedstock for the modern industrial workforce. Its size grew, it was located in strategic sector, and it received urban exposure. With the support from the trade unions, it was in a position to articulate its protest. Given the divergence of interest, and the likely intensity of protest in the context of political and ideological rivalry, unrest became enevitable. Its "structuring" had to be, therefore, managed carefully.

This needed fresh choice by the leading stakeholder, now the national government, with its own political ideology. Three components of this strategic transformation could be noted. First, there was the enactment of crucial labour laws providing the framework for directing labour protest on a structured legal path. Provisions for—

(a) Trade union protection and its rights (rather old),
(b) Collective bargaining with scope for industrial action,
(c) Conciliation and arbitration, and
(d) Compulsory adjudication with a quasi-judicial flavour came in place.

Accordingly a set of fora like the Indian Labour Conference, the Standing Labour Committee with its counterparts in the states were activised and made more functional. Uniform labour policy, supporting legislations and the administrative machinery alongwith some voluntary efforts became a priority. Other tripartite bodies like the Industrial Wage Boards, the National Productivity Council, the Workers' Education Board, the Apprenticeship Council, etc. belong to in the same category. Even the bipartite institutions like the statutory Works Committee and the voluntary Joint Management Councils, Workers'

Participation in Management, etc. were set-up to prevent protest as far as possible well before the dispute resolution stage. Right for industrial action, though implicitly allowed, was consciously discouraged. For the government employees, the institutions of the Pay Commission, the Joint Consultative Machinery, and the compulsory adjudication were created keeping in view the 'essential' nature of their services. The right to organise and strike for them was not thought of. The relevant ILO Conventions No. 87 and 98 remain unratified even today.

Keeping in view the confrontationalist posture from the rival left ideology led by All India Trade Union Congress, a significant step to carve out a friendly and supportive trade union movement in the form of the Indian National Trade Union Congress followed. Political forces have their own momentum, and the trade union movement became a hunting ground for allies by the rival political forces. In the process it splintered, and has since remained divided. In fact, inter-union rivalry itself brought in a plethora of a new class of disputes and industrial unrest.

The structural alliance between the organised labour and the political party in power or in opposition, brought in a new compact. Pan Indian dominance of one political party in government also served in the early decades as a major moderating influence in sorting out contentious labour issues. With thc statutory power of—

(a) Trade union registration,
(b) Formulation of disputed issues, and their referral for conciliation and adjudication, and
(c) Discretion in administrative choice in declaring any service/activity essential, etc.

The state acquired fully interventionistic character. Socialist and welfare persuasion encouraged a series of protective measures as well as labour welfare and non-wage benefits, including statutory minimum wage and profit bonus. Incorporating the provisions in the Industrial Disputes Act, 1948, requiring prior permission in case of closure, retrenchment and lay-off, etc. consolidated the write of the government in labour matters. A marked pro-labour twist in labour policy became evident. A powerful countervailing force of activist state and vigorous unionism emerged. Power equation in labour-management relations changed radically. Unilateral power initially enjoyed and often even misused some by employers, gave way to a shared power situation in labour market in the organised sector. Power and money issues have always dominated among the causes of dispute, apart from indiscipline.

The Indian industrial relations machinery succeeded in containing and stabilising labour unrest. Disputes were resolved largely by conciliation, including a large number of them settled at the bipartite level itself. Adjudication at different levels functioned and the usual judicial machinery also intervened quite substantially. Workers received job security, wage and benefits gains. At national level, industry-wide bipartite and tripartite agreements dominated the scene. Wage cost and the incidence of mandays lost remained moderately contained.

A part of the Indian economy was well "embedded in society." The state promoted the 'mechanism of redistribution', and it 'enjoyed an era of stability'. State socialism and welfare state capitalism made labour the 'fulcrum of development strategy' (Standing, 2002). A process of "decommodification of labour" by raising wage as well as social income followed. Employers made some concessions, and workers got job security. It is important to realise that the strategic calculation and foresight of the Indian capitalist class remained supportive of this framework which was led by government initiative.

This apparent smooth functioning of the system had its critics too on the following counts:

(a) The trade union movement, an important democratic institution, due to political division could not bring to bean its full strength in its contribution. In fact, it converted itself into "a host of frozen non-competiting groups" (Bardhan, 1992, p. 351). It even faced deceleration in its growth and consolidation;

(b) An alleged small class of 'labour aristocracy' with better levels of wages and benefits, job security, and social security developed. Inequity across labour segments exerted pressure on the system.

Priviledged ones struggled to preserve the *status quo,* while the deprived ones suffered without voice and attention. Suffering in the unorganised sector of—

(i) The working poor,
(ii) The unemployed,
(iii) The unskilled, and
(iv) The other weaker sections intensified;

(c) The creative linkage between compensation and productivity got ruptured due to a 'cost plus' pricing and protected market;

(d) Resistance to technological changes and its currency, as well as to the dynamic restructuring through mergers, acquisitions, closures, etc. became pervasive;

(e) The richness of man-management got drained out of the system;

(f) Excess manning levels, obsolete jobs and skills, and unproductive work practices and norms took toll of competitive efficiency;

(g) Public enterprises with budgetary support, administered price regime, and the 'model employers' syndrome got complacement;

(h) Political and bureaucratic interference reduced the space for their sound decisions on labour-management issues;

(i) Capacity licensing, tariff protection, cost plus pricing, etc., dampened the entrepreneurial capabilities even in the private sector;

(j) Time and cost overrun in products and services and costly compromise in quality, led to erosion of competitive efficiency all round; and

(k) Permissive provision for easy registration of a trade union and lack of firm guideline on its recognition in legal terms have continued. Even the process of determining the bargaining agent is still missing, and the bipartite agreements are yet not legally binding, despite the recommendations of the first National Commission on Labour.

The industrial relations machinery got further battered by the new political and social forces. Under conditions of organised sector job scarcity and social divisiveness, demand for protected 'niche' in the share of job market based on caste acquired momentum, and it has continued. Political capacity to mediate between the state and the society got eroded in a fractured polity. Maturation of labour consciousness and consolidation of its orgnaised strength received severe jolt. The "purposive collective action on economic arrangement" could not be effective. It could be, as it was observed, the result of "uncoordinated modernisation" (Jalan, 1992) and this has its parallel in the post-1991 phase, too.

The Post-1991 Reform Era: Challenges of New Strategic Choice

TABLE 2.1

Certain Changes in the Context

Sl. No.	*Familiar*	*Changed*
1.	State sponsored and state mediated development.	Market led and private enterprise dominated
2.	Protected domestic market.	Competitive market
3.	Budgetary and directed institutional resource allocation	Competitive capital market-led resource allocation
4.	Subsidies and administered price regime	Rational pricing, including user charges
5.	Welfare State active in labour market	Neutral investment-friendly state posture
6.	Systematic de-casualisation of jobs	Fast re-casualisation and contractualisation of jobs
7.	Largely government funded social security and welfare programmes for a small group	Crisis of sustainability of social security welfare programmes, and pressure for security measure for all
8.	Stable governing structure and policy regime	Crisis of governance and fear of instability
9.	Stable, though obsolete, labour intensive technology and system	Micro-electronics-led new generation capital and skill intensive technology
10.	Dominant status of manufacturing	Threat of de-industrialisation and spurt in service sector

Source: *The Indian Journal of Labour Economics*, Vol. 46, No. 4, Oct.-Dec. 2003, p. 641.

The 1991 reform in India was basically a panic response to the crisis. Necessary adequate preparatory steps, as in some other countries, were not taken. Stagnating economy, decomposed and confrontational polity and the explosive social setting called for fresh strategic transformation, including in the labour market and employment relations. Setting up of the Second National Commission on Labour was the result. It was partly to find some fresh answers and partly to buy time for a confused government torn between investment-friendly and labour-friendly choices. Some major shift in the context, however, are evident as shown in Table 2.1.

Separately as well as collectively and above changes have brought about a radically new setting. The governing elite and the leaders of both industry as well as trade unions today face a new challenge of a strategic choice making.

Generation of new knowledge and global implications of business operations are necessary aspects of the new economy. Capital, labour, raw materials, management, information, technology and markets are organized on a global scale, either directly or through a network of linkages between economic agents. These developments have fundamentally questioned the basic premises on which industry was working in most parts of the world before. But perhaps a greater area of concern all around is the fate of the industrial relations (IR) frameworks that have been rooted in different types of protectionism in various parts of the world so far. The most direct impact of the changed scene is the increased vulnerability of the workers' interest in the labour-management power dynamics. It reflects considerable shifts in the assumptions of these relations. It is not a case of simple shift in power from labour to employers especially because mortality of organisations in the new economic scenario is also on the rise. Power is taking place at several levels, both covert and overt. This shift has its casual roots in the changes in various contexts of industrial working in the new economy.

The Tenth Five Year Plan

Notwithstanding its objective of high rate of growth, the Tenth Five Year Plan Document notes: "growth process alone will not be able to provide adequate work opportunities for the emerging workforce, let alone reduce to backlog of unemployment. Further, it recognises the need for "transforming an agrarian economy into a modern multi-dimensional economic power house and an egalitarian society." Creating a modern economic power house, and an egalitarian society through "consultation", as suggested by this Plan, would bring in the relevance of peaceful and participative employment relations as well. The gravity and the magnitude of this challenge do get a mention in the Plan.

"It is inevitable that such a rapid social, economic and

technological and political for a strategy to manage and contain' it 'within limits' that 'preserves the social fabric and permits the nation's transformation." (Planning Commission, 2003).

The era of liberalisation, privatisation and globalisation has brought turbulence world over. Liberalisation has no doubt promoted growth, and added job opportunities. But with global economic integration, social divergences and disparities have accelerated. Within the 'convergence vs. divergence' debate in the industrial relations, it is the latter, pushed by differing national contexts, that is getting the better of the former. Inter-regional disparity in growth and factor endowment within the country has encouraged that trend sharply in India, too. Poverty and labour intensive regions of India have registered slowest rates of growth. Even inter-regional migration has not helped much. It is important to realise that in the organised sector until recently moderate technical changes and stable production structure and secure jobs have dominated. This facilitated some welcome balance among contending interest groups. Labour-management relations appeared stablised, and arrangement of dispute prevention and resolution worked.

The market led growth strategy, however, is pushing for labour market flexibility. A switch from a "protective and pro-collective regulations" to a decentralised employment relations is the suggested path to move on. This raises problems, and the scope for conflicts grows. In this milieu, the contentious debate between neo-classicals and neo-liberals, particularly the state *vs.* market, remains unabated (Thakur, 1969). The empirical data of the post-market era add further sharpness in this debate. Have we entered the era of:

(a) 'profit over people', and
(b) 'disappearing governments'?

Analyses of these issues (*The Economist*, 2001) in labour market context shows certain hard trends.

Overall employment in developed countries did not rise. Among the newly created jobs, the higher paying ones dominate, while the low paying ones have lagged behind. Higher and average wages moved up, but bottom wage fell further down. This has intensified inequity. Trade, technology and immigrations have been identified as major in-equalising factors. Deunionisation has led to further erosion of the real value of even minimum wage. Wherever available, good education and training served as an 'empowering factor' through endowed human capital formation, subject to accessibility for the needy. Some gained jobs, others even improved upon the existing ones. But since losers were not the gainers in this change, gains and pains of change got inequitably shared.

In the developing countries, dominated by the informal sector, the situation is different. Most workers lack legal protection, they have no rights at work and in fact not even voice. Even the union representation for the majority is missing. For those in the organised sector also, the wheel is turning to their disadvantage with rapid informalisation of job, worsening working conditions and work practices, and lagging compensation.

Technological upgradation, restructuring of enterprises, contracting out of work and job, and coercive voluntary retirement schemes are leading to right sizing or downsizing. Competitive efficiency and secure job do not have human-friendly trade-off, as it turns out.

Outsourcing of products (from China, etc.) and services (from India, etc.) is a new and fast growing development affecting global labour market linkages. Footloose financial capital moves across national boundaries in search of relative cost advantage. In fact outsourcing is now a vehicle in acquiring competitive advantage. The receiving countries get stepped up investment, receive technology transfer, experience export push and additional job gains. But the new jobs and their rewards are not comparable in quality to the earlier organised sector ones. (Ghosh, 2002). In the developed countries, trade unions and political pressure like in the USA, the UK, Australia, etc. are in a protectionist posture. Political and economic forces are on a collision course, and its ripples extend over to the industrial relations, if one remembers the events in Seattle. Also, technological advances may not allow this relative gains to the lower labour cost-locations for long.

What about the Indian experience, in particular? During the nineties, the Gross Domestic Product grew and new job opportunities were also created. But net additions in jobs fell far short of increases in labour force (Chandrasekhar and Ghosh, 2002). The Labour force supply was pushed further up by downsizing, VRS, technological upgradation, restructuring and the like. The overall quality of new jobs was far inferior in terms of security, continuity, compensations and working conditions. Disinvestment, privatisation and fall in government employment all added to this labour market turbulence. Disparity across formal and informal sectors was further intensified. The fate of the working poor, the aged, the uneducated and the unskilled worsened substantially. Forces of inequity compared to those of equity and empowerment like access to education, training and retraining, social security and welfare turned more powerful. The "Decent work deficit" in the ILO scheme of things became manifest. Voice, representation, employment and income security all suffered setback. Relative power divide in the labour market turned in favour of employers.

Second National Commission on Labour

In the first place, the Commission was primarily set-up to look into the problems of labour in the informal sector. It has, however, among other things, accepted liberalisation, privatisation and even approved the relevance of contract labour and contracting out of work for competitive efficiency. But, it has also suggested necessary safeguards in wage and other benefits. Closures, lay off and retrenchments, in the view of Commission, are valid on economic grounds of flexibility and efficiency. The need for prior permission has, however, been recommended by it despite appreciating the case for flexibility. But it has advocated for a time bound rejection or acceptance by the appropriate government, rather than clever indefinite delays.

Significantly, the Commission has advised "abundant-caution in abolishing the job security." Assessment of trade off between the gains of flexibility *vs.* social acceptance/rejection of the institution of contract employment has been emphasised. This is an explosive issue by any reckoning. Further, it has recommended largely a labour-friendly solution to the crisis of high incidence of industrial sickness across regions and sectors. Suffering in sick units in intensifying, while solûtions, let along labour-friendly ones, are eluding; Indian working class is facing multitude of insecurities, as is the working class the world over (see Standing, 1999). Tensions between labour and management and between labour and state are mounting. Workers are suffering, employers are quiet, while the government is repeating only platitudes.

The National Commission has recognised the value of some fundamental rights at work:

(a) Right to work of own choice;
(b) Right to social security;
(c) Right to redress grievances;
(d) Right to organise trade union and collective bargaining; and
(e) Right to humane conditions at work.

In the industrial relations framework:

(a) three-tier system of dispute resolution,
(b) tripartite and bipartie interaction for dispute resolution, and
(c) scope for the third party presence have ·been envisaged by the Commission, including Lok Adalat for speedy settlements.

One major issue, which may turn out to be contentious, is the denial of civil court jurisdiction in labour dispute. On the whole, the balancing exercise of the Commission would face the dilemma of desirability *vs*. feasibility. In the meantime, the major stake-holders have already expressed their disapproval of its recommendations. The government is engaged in an elaborate and extended exercise in steering consensus. But the proceedings of the latest Indian Labour Conference, 2003 shows the obstacles in this regard. Efforts, it however appears, would continue, and a degree of realism may follow on the part of all social partners. But it will take time and skillful steering as we move on.

As a cushion to the shocks of the job market, and more as a facilitator to progress on labour market flexibility, a comprehensive social security provisions for all workers received strong approval of the Second National Commission on Labour. The government has been actively engaged in formulating a suitable social safety system. Content, coverage, administrative set-up and funding are the critical components. A substantially reduced state subsidy, multitierism in the benefits and partial privatisation are the emerging features. The Employees Provident Fund Organisation, the Employees State Insurance Scheme, the Insurance Regulatory Authority of India and the proposed Pension Authority are the indicated agencies for implementing the scheme. Private agencies and Mutual Funds are also likely to be brought into the picture. None of these unfortunately have a reputation of efficient functioning. Also, the social partners are yet to give their consent. In fact, the latest social security scheme for the first set of nearly 50 lakh workers in the unorganised sector is shuttling between the Union Cabinet and the Union Ministry of Labour. The pressure for adequate coverage for all, the funding constraints and the challenge of competent administration would continue to raise the sustainability question mark. A major industrial relations issue is just opening up in this process. But there is scope for optimism in this regard though.

Fifth Pay Commission and Industrial Relations

Government employees at different levels constitute a major and visible segment of the Indian labour market. How the government deals with its employees in terms of—

(a) Compensation, and
(b) Employer-employee relations sends powerful signals and provides a benchmark for the rest.

Post-Fifth Pay Commission, the central government employees received—

(a) 40 per cent across the board increase in emoluments, and
(b) Pension benefit at 50 per cent of the last pay with cost of living linkage for dearness allowance.

But against the 3 per cent annual attrition, new employment is now a mere 1 per cent for the eventual goal of optimum manning. All these had its cascading effect down the line. State Governments are facing the fiscal pressure as well as industrial relations crisis. The Supreme Court had to intervene in the case of one state level public sector employees. But the pace of implementation of its verdict is poor.

A new trend of recent judicial activism has added a new sharpness in this regard. The recent Supreme Court judgment declaring that the right to strike has "no legal, moral or equitable basis" has come as a big shock, Banning of 'bandh' by the Kerala High Court and prohibiting the processions during day time by the Calcutta High Court are reducing the public space for workers in general and civil employees in particular for articulating their concerns. Does it amount to 'democratic deficit,' more so when the relevant ILO conventions remain unratified? National debate has just started, but the government is ambivalent, and trade unions dampened and confused. The Supreme Court is likely to re-consider this issue, it appears.

Key Factors Influence New Industrial Relations

Globalisation can be understood in the context of several major international events which have directly affected the organisation of business as also the existence and strength of trade unions. Some of these developments can be discussed as under:

1. Emergence of Chaotic Competition

The chaotic competition is one of the most obvious results of the globalisation philosophy, which is guiding nearly all business policies. Employer mortality is on the rise due to the acuteness of resultant competition. This has led to formation of strategic alliances between major players in manufacturing and service industries world over. Thus, mergers, acquisitions and takeovers are taking place at rapid pace so as to secure strategic competitive advantage of oligopolistic situations in the market. Competitive pressures also lead to attempts to switch operations to green-field sites (new locations) to minimize costs. Being wholly new, these sites also offer management a high degree of discretion, choice, flexibility and opportunity to introduce innovative work practices. Employers find it much easier to influence individual and collective behaviour of employees at such sites, aimed to eventually provide a competitive advantage to the employer.

Interestingly, in high-wage developed world, firms cope

with pressures of international competition by differentiating their products rather than by lowering wages. This results in high wage and high value-added manufacturing in those locations. Such a strategy puts greater premium on employees' skills, cooperation and involvement. Employers thus invest in their more efficacious management, which itself in a way helps promoting fairness in employment relations. But labour in developing countries has become more vulnerable to the competitiveness exigencies caused by the new economic realities than is the case with workers in the developed world. That is how, these realities are the principal determinants of the contemporary IR in India.

2. Privatisation

Since public sector employees are believed to be restrictive in demonstrating initiative and commitment in their working, its role in economic development is being minimized, eventually giving way to privatisation. For example, in the Indian context, it is now accepted as an unchallenged truth that "over-regulation, protection, self reliance and policies of import substitution led to the neglect of quality, cost, delivery/supply schedules and customer orientation" (Venkata Ratnam and Verma, 1998, p. 16). The adoption of these policies resulted in India becoming a high cost, low productivity economy; which makes it more imperative to adopt the rationality of globalisation. Privatisation of the public sector, however, involves complex social and economic implications. Perhaps, the main blow that it gives is to the opinion-making class which justifies labour rights. This class is found more amongst the public sector employees, who can seek a fairer compromise with the power of managerial prerogatives of employers. This is due to the sheer reason of a sense of job security that they enjoy; this is essential for exercise of any countervailing power. This factor surely facilitates at a moral level the strength and organisational capability of workers in the private sector also. Further, privatisation may also lead to re-engineering and retrenchment. Especially in developing countries where unemployment is already a menacing problem, this becomes a cause of grave social concern. Again, the potential of societal unrest resulting from public sector employees becoming unemployed is higher for the similar reasons, which helps in getting greater attention of the state agencies. Private sector employers invest heavily in deunionisation activities. They convertly resort to unfair labour practices (ULPs) to weaken and break unions, though attempting to uphold legal facades. Research involving the practice of IR in private sector in the Indian context reveals such stories of labour disorganisation process (Saini, 2003), thus revealing greater vulnerability of labour in this sector.

3. Technological Changes

In the present high tech industrial society the adoption of new technology becomes one of the strategic considerations of organisations. Greater demand for sophisticated and state-of-the-art technology becomes widespread. It leads to resort to new developments in management of human resources due to considerations of retrenchment, flexitime and teleworking. New technology may also increase the need for organisational flexibility. In developing countries, trade unions have actively or hesitantly shown opposition to the adoption of new technology for fear of its adverse impact on employee solidarily. For, they fear loss of employment and also control over work processes. However, recent literature reports that with the passage of time there is a change in their thinking in this regard (Mamkoottam, 2003).

Issues in Service Sector and Knowledge Economy

Nearly half the GDP is being contributed today by the service sector. It is certainly dominated by low performing government segment, but it has also a highly vibrant part with very efficient performance levels. Software (IT), pharmaceutical, financial services, telecommunications, civil aviation, business-process-outsourcing and call centres, research and development, tourism and hospitality, healthcare and hospitals are surging ahead. New generation retailing is coming up. These are expected to serve as new "locomotive for growth."

Certain aspects from the industrial relations perspective need to be noted in this regard. Firstly, this sector is education and skill intensive. Secondly, it is not employment-friendly—it contributes half the GDP, but accounts for only one fifth of jobs. Thirdly, it is open to sudden shocks as the experiences of dot.com bust and crises in tourism related activities for unpredictable reasons like terrorism, epidemic and civil strife, etc., would indicate.

An interesting part relates to the "differentiating intellectual asset" characterising this sector. Corporate success and sustained competitive efficiency are led by its "intellectual asset" of the knowledge workers. However, "Tension between capital and talent have escalated since 1990's", "because the nature of the economy has changed." (*Harvard Business Review*, 2003). The talent class cashes on the knowledge it creates." They expect "slices of the pie they have helped to create." However, tension between talent and capital as well as talent and labour is a potent source of trouble ahead. Unlike in the manufacturing, the divergence of interest is between financier and entrepreneur, on the one hand, and the intellectual and human skills providers, on the other. Even the nature of the service market is more sensitive because of proximity of the customers and the clients. Stock options, and contract employment have not served well, at any rate the IT sector. High turnover, early burnouts, monotony and irregular working houses are the uneasy systoms. Rising turnover, demand for regular salary scales and greater trust are unfolding as some cases indicate (Jhaveri, 2003) Labour consciousness and its institutionalisation and the forms of articulation are still to acquire firm characteristics. But the challenge of yet another strategie innovation is not far away, it would appear.

Areas of Uneasiness

1. Viability of the institution of the welfare state is now in question. Pressure for an investment-friendly strategy is shaping new orientation in labour regulation. From the familiar "protective of workers" and "pro collective and socially redistributive" to "deregulation" and "labour flexibility" in support of market led growth is a radical transformation.

   Weak, inefficient and often the allegedly corrupt regulatory framework has yet to moderate the excesses of the market. Only effective "rules and the referee" can deliver full positive gains of a market economy. India has a long way to go on both of these parameters at this stage.

2. The earlier generation of private capitalists, faced with fear of—
   (a) foreign capital, and
   (b) leftist ideology, supported and learnt to live with the activist state and the pluralistic institutions in labour market.

   But today the phenomenon of ruthlessness, as the relative high incidence of lock-outs, closures, coercive VRS, retrenchments and harassment through protected legal action indicate, is very much visible. There is a suspected "state capture" where efforts of firms to shape and influence underlying "rules of the game" (Jhaveri, 2003) are on the rise. With the dominance of "profit over people" and the bottom-line, and shareholders concerns over those of other stakeholders, like workers and consumer interests, severe inequity, instability as well as new forms of interest based confrontation could only be delayed but possibly not denied. How to pre-empt such a possibility?

3. The grasp of a much needed workable social insurance so far has remained elusive. The phenomena of receding governments and reducing social obligation, flow from the weakening of the institution of benign welfare state. Even the Pope felt persuaded to observe:

   "The rapid advance towards the globalisation of the economic and financial system also illustrates the urgent need to establish who is responsible for maintaining the global common goods and exercise of economic and social rights. The free market by itself cannot do it, because there are many human needs that have no place in the market"(Quoted by Standing, 2002, p. 9).

   Clearly, in this moral stand by the Pope, there is the

echo of the ILO's struggle for "decent work" which intends to blend economic and social efficiency. The economy needs to be "re-embedded" with some form of "redistribution" in favour of the weak and the deprived exposed to economic and social exclusion.

4. B.R. Ambedkar drew our attention to the contradiction of equality in political life in the midst of inequality in economic and social life, quite early. The continuation of this phenomenon has led to an "uneasy equilibrium" (Dreze and Sen, 2003). How to—
   (a) Re-empower the labour market with stronger and inclusive representation;
   (b) Provide effective voice to the weak and the voiceless for engaging the employers and the state for better terms of employment; and
   (c) Expand and enrich the agenda for bargaining and non-bargaining interactions and the like. These posers are waiting for answers. Vague and only desirable thoughts alone, as are being widely articulated, are unlikely to help.
5. Rich economic and political democracy requires scope for
   (a) facility,
   (b) Involvement, and
   (c) Equity (Venkata Ratnam, 2003). Among others, familiar forms and structure of industrial relations need to be extended for this to the informal and the knowledge sectors and to the proposed Special Economic Zones of the economy. Even within the organised sector there is macro-micro mismatch apart from pervasive institutional obsolescence.

Involvement, on the other hand, needs a track and an agenda for informed engagement among contending interest groups and social partners. These issues are waiting to be revisited with seriousness.

Equity, however in labour market, has always been a serious issue. A non-interventionist State, an assertive financial entrepreneurial power, and the fragmented workforce cannot bring about the desired state. Technology and market forces further add to the iniquitous trend. Even the judiciary has lately turned the other way, as it were, Outlook may look gloomy, therefore.

Some Encouraging Evidences

Examples of new initiatives are emerging, though. Global financial institutions are conceding the mistakes of their strategy and are now accepting the value of strategic state interventions. A new alliance of campus voices, underclass articulation, committed NGOs, and other civic society initiatives is in early stage of evolution (Venkata Ratnam, 2003). A forum for the unorganised workers has emerged in India too. The setting up of the National Centre of Labour by NGO and labour activists is the beginning of a consolidation into an organisation. The scope for alliances among trade unions, NGOs and panchayat raj institutions with the help of like minded persons in each one of these is there. Established institutions and experienced players are re-learning themselves. Negotiated changes have taken place in several cases in India, and elsewhere. The workers Councils in Germany are widening their agenda. Even a tripartite alliance for jobs was experimented there, which was unsuccessful. The Social Charter of the European Union and the proceedings of the Asian Labour Ministers' Conference alluded towards new direction.

Historical trend, and the desirable one, has been to foster the formalisation of the informal sector and its labour-management relations. But the reverse trend is accelerating. Therefore, bringing operating efficiency in the informal economy with better technology, financial support and market access is necessary. Workers empowerment through better education, training and some social security are critical. Only 5 per cent workers in the age group, 19-21 years with vocational training, and the high incidence of illiteracy do not provide the basis for encouraging outlook.

Changing Work Organisation, Flexibility Exigencies and Contractualisation Syndrome

Large-scale changes are noticeable in work organisation.

One of the much-talked about management concepts is business process re-engineering (BPR). Hammer and Champy (1993), the originators of the term BPR, write: "Reengineering is the search for new models of organizing work. Reengineering is the new beginning." Re-engineering is aimed to increase productivity and flexibility of the organisation; it also emphasizes multi-trade and flexible job. In order to fully utilize the labour capacity, workers are trained in several skills. Various traditionally popular jobs, especially white-collar ones, are now becoming redundant and are giving way to new roles based on reengineering. Despite complexities involved in re-engineering dynamics, research reveals increasing labour-management cooperation in industrial restructuring and trends towards negotiated flexibility at the enterprise level (Venkata Ratnam, 2003).

Mass-production systems based on Taylorism and Fordism have ruled the industrial world in the pre-globalisation world. They emphasize division of labour and specialisation. Customisation is now becoming the rule, giving way to what is referred to as Toyotaism or flexible specialisation. This concept is based on the principle of lean and mean production adjustable as per the needs of the customer. Since customer is the king in the globalisation era, product differentiation by employers has substantially increased, resulting into lean customized production that forms part of Toyotaism. Lean production also necessitates employers' ability to engage contingent or peripheral labour force as per their business exigencies so as to help them remain flexible. While core workers are permanently needed in the organisation for giving a kind of stability, periphery workers consisting of *ad-hoc*, casual, part-time, temporary and contract workers, are replaceable. They fulfil the contingent business needs as and when new demands are made on the organisation. Labour flexibility has become more important today than ever before. Performance-related pay system, flexitime, and telecommunicating are also aspects of facilitating flexibility in work organisation.

The flexibility management needs of business are often accompanied by adoption of unfair procedures. In India, for example, this has led, among others, to a serious problem of lack of implementation by employers of minimum standards of employment in case of vulnerable sections of labour. Despite the existence of Contract Labour (Regulation and Abolition Act), 1970 (CLA), which makes it very difficult to employ contract labour in permanent operations, a large number of employers are resorting to employment of contract labour in several of their operations. They are doing so on a permanent basis and not just to meet any contingencies as intended by the CLA. the justification given by employers for this is the need for flexibility to cope with the onslaught of greater competition.

Emergence of New Actors in IR

The traditional notions of bipartism or tripartism of yester-years are giving way to IR becoming a more composite issue. Trade unions and collective bargaining institutions are under pressure so as to take care of all aspects concerning variegated people at work (Kochan *et al.*, 1986); thus tending to make IR as a multi-lateral power game. Consumers and general public are beginning to pay a significant role in these matters. Increasing concern is being shown to issues such as child labour, women's problems, environmental concerns, health and safety of employees and workers in the informal sector. There is pressure for inclusion of issues such as social clause, social exclusion, social protection, social security and social action to deal with all types of discrimination (Venkata Ratnam, 2001). The notions on which this changed thinking is based include; faith in maintaining a power balance between social partners, integrality, trust, and community interest. This can also be seen as a method of mustering societal opinion in favour of the new policies by their ideologues. Thus, there are attempts towards evolving new concepts of income security, job security and social security.

The quest for industrial peace has been the main objective behind the continued efforts of the Government, the employers and the workers. The three parties have realized that only industrial peace could help in fulfilment of their interests. The realization of this fact has been though late, after a considerable period of strike, strain and conflict. In this scene of industrial relations, the two parties, capital and labour, carry different group attitudes and conducts towards one another. Functioning within the industrial framework, their attitude and conduct differ because they are supplied by two independent groups. The capital claims the right of property and labour claims the right of humanity. These two clashing principles head to existence of divergent interests and rights.

The relationship between capital and labour started from the day they co-operated with each other though for fulfilment of their own interests. The capital provided by the employer needed labour for production and profit. On the other hand, labour needed employment for livelihood. Thus, from the day the employer provided employment and the labour got employment—the relationship emerged, which therefore Dale Yoder accepts that "industrial relations that grow out of and is associated with employment relationships." The two groups, persuing different aims, came in contact with each other and started co-operating for satisfaction of their conflicting interests. Therefore, cooperation started out of their necessity and so it is called as "necessitous relationship." W.G. Summer has called it as a "state of antagonistic cooperation." This means that the two groups co-operate with each other and at the same time they fight for their interests. Thus, the relationship has two natures-relationship of cooperation and relationship of conflict. Originally, the relationship of cooperation started but soon it turned into relationship of conflict.

The relationship between the employer and the labour is relationship of action and inter-action, pleasant and unpleasant, live and let live other. This relationship is more than that of husband and wife—which cannot be severed for all time. There can be divorce between a husband and wife, who can live rest of the life without other. But capital and labour cannot divorce each other. There may be differences and breakdown of relationship but only for a short period. The employer and the employee have to work together for all time, however, bitter the differences and disputes may be. There may be casual short differences but they must patch up differences. The industrial relation is an art, the art of living together for purpose of increased production, satisfaction of group interests, for welfare of society and for establishment of industrial peace and industrial democracy. The emergence of differences leading to conflict is unfortunate but differences are understandable. At times conflict becomes inevitable because two groups carry conflicting aspirations. It is how the eg1fforts are made to reconcile their differences and evolve a pattern creating mutual understanding, mutual good-will and mutual satisfaction.

The problems of industrial relations are many, complex and highly sensitive. The maintenance of contract of service, settlement of common issues in accordance with law and the role played by the top management as a coordinator between the two groups are basic essentials of cordial relationship between the management and the labour. Preservation of the interests of the national economy by increased productivity and the satisfaction to the management and the labour are also conditions of cordial industrial relations.

References

Mukherji, Aditya (2002), Imperialism, Nationalism and the Making of the Indian Capitalist Class, 1920-47, Sage, New Delhi.

Nayyar Baldev Raj, (2003), "Economic Globalisation and its Advance, From Shallow to Deep Integration", *Economic and Political Weekly*, November 8, pp. 4780-82.

Chandra, Bipin, (1992), "The Colonial Legacy", in Jalan, Bimal (ed.).

Standing, Guy (2002), "Human Security and Social Protection", in Ghosh and Chandrasekhar (eds.).

Bardhan, Pranab, (1992), "A Political Economic Perspective in Development", in Jalan, Bimal (ed.).

Jalan, Bimal (ed.) (1992), "The Indian Economy: Problems and Prospects", Viking, New Delhi.

Thakur, C.P. and Munson, Fred. C. (1969), Industrial Relations in Printing Industry, Shri Ram Centre for Industrial Relations, New Delhi.

The Economist (2001), "Survey of Globalisaiton", September 29.

Ghosh, Jayati, (2002), "Exporting Jobs or Watching Them Disappear", in Ghosh and Chandrasekhar (eds.).

Ghosh, Jayati and Chandrasekhar, C.P. (2002), The Market That Failed, Left Word, New Delhi.

Venkata Ratnam, C.S. (2003), Negotiated Change: Collective Bargaining. Liberalisation and Restructuring in India, Response (A Division of Sage Publications), New Delhi.

_______(2001), Globalisation and Labour-Management Relations: Dynamics of Change, Response (A Division of Sage) Publications, New Delhi.

Saini, Debi, S. and Pawan Budhwar (2003), "HRM in India", in Pawan Budhwar (ed.), Human Resource Management in Asia-Pacific Countries, Routledge, London.

Dreze, Jean, and Sen, Amartya, Development and Participation, Oxford University Press, New Delhi.

Mamkottam, K. (2003), Labour and Change: Essays on Globalisation, Technological Change and Labour in India, Response (A Division of Sage), New Delhi.

Harward Business Review (2003), "Capital *vs.* Talent", July.

Jhaveri, Narendra, (2003), "India's Growth Chase", *Economic and Political Weekly*, pp. 4336-50.

Hammer, M. and J. Champy (1993), Reengineering the Corporation: A Manifesto for Business Revolution, Nicholas Brearley, London.

Kochan, T., H. Katz and R. Mckersie (1986), The Transformation of American Industrial Relations, Basic Books, New York.

Yodder, Dale (1957), "Personnel Management and Industrial Relations, Prentice Hall, INC, New York.

3

Labour-Management Cooperation

The modern 'Industrial Relations' (IR) scene has two important aspects:

(a) Cooperation, and
(b) Conflict

The present chapter discusses the problems of cooperation. The cooperation between labour and capital is the basic requirement for the successful functioning of modern capitalist enterprises is a statement needing little further elucidation; this cooperation is available only at a minimal degree is also a statement that can hardly be controverted. Chamberlain calls this sort of relationship conjunction, i.e. a state of relationship under which the parties, instead of offering their best, offer the least in the absence of which the relationship will break. The workers attempt to produce only that much which can keep them in employment. Under the existing institutional arrangements, special efforts have to be made to induce them to put forth their best efforts for productive purposes. In the case of self-employment, under which a person 'owns' his own tools, premises, raw materials and also the final products, he always seeks to work at his best. Even where he does not own the tools, i.e. capital and obtains them on hire, he still exerts his best. But the moment capital becomes separated and is treated as an independent factor of production, the problem of motivating the worker becomes acute. How to generate under the existing capitalist form of economic organisations, the energy, sincerity and enthusiasm which the workers display when they work on their own account? It is the search for the answer to this question that has led to the acceptance, formation and implementation of many schemes for promoting cooperation between labour and management in almost all industrially advanced capitalist countries. What was assumed till now to exist automatically is sought to be promoted today, deliberately and consciously. Stich terms as "labour-management consultation", "labour-management cooperation" and "participation of labour in managernent" have bccomc words of common parlance and no book on industrial relations' is thought to be complete without a reference to them.

Labour-Management Cooperation and Its Goals

The term "labour-management cooperation" refers to thejoint efforts of labour and capital to find out solutions and remedies of problems common to both. In contrast to collective bat gaining, which, involves of joint decision-making in the matters of admittedly divergent interests, cooperation represents joint decision-making in matters of admittedly common interests. Thus, before such cooperation can take place, each of the parties has to be convinced that in'some defined areas, interests are in fact common; that by cooperation'with the other in the decision-making process in this area, each would be promoting its own interests; and that by such cooperation, it will not become, a tool of the other.

Means of Increasing Productivity

It is said that the area of the most common 'mutual interests where labour and management may cooperate consciously to the advantage of both consists of promoting efficiency and producti vity, eliminating wastes, reducing cost, and improving the quality of the product. In a word, the area of common interests lies in increasing the size of the cake so that each of the parties may have a larger piece as its share. Dividing the cake may be a source of conflict but increasing its size represents a common interest. But here again, a number of questions arise. What is the guarantee that labour will get its share of the increased size of the cake? What will happen when increasing the size involves retrenchment, speed-up and increase-in the work-load?

It is on such issues that many schemes of labour-management cooperation have foundered. If, however, methods satisfactory to the workers for sharing the increased productivity can be devised either on the basis of collective bargaining or legislation, labour may willingly gooperate with the management in promoting the eefficiency of the enterprise. Thus, a satisfactory collective bargaining relationship is a condition precedent to the formulation ohe schemes of cooperation. It is collective bargaining that sets the terms on which cooperation takes place in the field of common interests, guaranteeing each its proper share in the fruits of cooperation. From what has been said here of cooperation as a joint decisions-making process, it is clear that it implies giving to workers and the unions a voice in the operation of the business enterprises. The field of decision-making which was reserved hitherto for the legal owners of business enterprises or their representatives is now either partially or wholly, thrown open to the workers also in order to enlist their cooperation to promote the economic health of the enterprise. Therefore, labour-management cooperation "becomes a means to achieve higher productivity which is said to be a matter of common interest.

Promoting Industrial Democracy

Labour-management cooperation is also advocated as a means o promote industrial democracy. It is said that workers should have a voice in the administration of the enterprise to which they belong. Industrial enterprises which furnish the material needs of the workers will also start giving non-material human satisfactions if workers acquire a say in the determination of the conditions—

(1) The expression "the enterprise to which they belong" sums LIP the paradox of the situation. If the expression "the enterprise which belongs to then" could, be used instead, the need for ensuring a voice

to the workers would not have arisen because the workers could automatically become the administrators of the enterprise. The crux of the problem is that the workers are asked to cooperate in promoting the efliciency and health of an rnte, prise which does not belong to them, and one should not be surprised if they raise a question, "What for?" ownera should have full freedom to manage their enterprises hindered by any outside control in order that the risk may be minimised success assured. Any interference with their right is likely to cause dislocation.

(2) The maintenance and development of industrial efficiency lemands that the managers should be able to take quick decision in the ever-changing market conditions. Any delay which may be entailed because of a long cumbersome consultative procedure in decision-making may lead to serious economic losses. Therefore, the, owners of enterprises should have the necessary power to make quick adaptations and take quick decisions as and when so demanded. Thus, the exercise of the absolute power by the owners owners is thought to be a necessary condition for the maintenance of the economic health of the enterprise. It is said that the management of a large-scale business enterprise is necessarily authoritarian in character which does not lend itself to democratic control. There has to be a hierarchical organisation with the decision-making power vesting at the top in the selected few, and compliance and obedience from the bottom.

(3) Finally, it is said that management of industrial enterprises today has become a highly skilled and technical job. The skill of managing enterprises comes only through long experience and training which, under the present social system, only a few, can afford. Therefore, the owners of business enterprises or their legal, represcrrtatives, who are in the best position to receive that training and hick-up that experience, should possess full freedom to

control and manage their property. It will not be in the interest of ecoinomic efficiency if persons without training and experience are given the right to share the decision-making power.

It is on the basis of the foregoing arguments that the absolute power of the owners of business enterprises is exercised and justified. Essentially, the power to manage flows from the right to own property. Therefore, management's rights are basically property rights. However, graduully, the workers and the trade unions have not only challenged these management rights but have also succeeded in restricting them and in participating in the managerial decisions.The managements have been forced to share one right after another with the workers, but this is a forced sharing rather than a voluntary process. It is on such issues that many schemes of labour-management cooperation have foundered. If, however, methods satisfactory to the workers for sharing the increased productivity can be devised either on the basis of collective bargaining or legislation, labour may willingly cooperate with the management in promoting the efficiency of the enterprise. Thus, a satisfactory collective bargaining relationship is a condition precedent to the formulation of the schemes of cooperation. It is collective bargaining that sets the terms on which cooperation takes place in the field of common interests, guaranteeing each its proper share in the fruits of cooperation. From what has been said here of cooperation as a joint decisions-making process, it is clear that it implies giving to workers and the unions a voice in the operation of the business enterprises. The field of decision-making which was reserved hitherto for the legal owners of business enterprises or their representatives is now either partially or wholly, thrown open to the workers also in order to enlist their cooperation to promote the economic health of the enterprise. Therefore, labour-management cooperation becomes a means to achieve higher productivity which is said to be a matter of common interest.

The significance of labour-management cooperation, which may vary from simple consultation to workers' participation in management, can best be realised by contrasting it with the traditional form of control and management of industrial enterprises. Under capitalism, the laws relating to private property vest the power of control and management in its owners or their representatives. The absolute right of the owners to control and manage property is restricted by law in exceptional cases where public interest is involved and that too to a very limited extent. The owners of business enterprises have been traditionally exercising the powers to management their employees and to unilaterally decide all questions relating to their hiring and firing, promotion, demotion, transfer or lay-off; the owners have also been deciding the methods and techniques of production, the nature and quantum of products, fixation of prices, and all other matters in respect of the administration of the enterprise. The advent of trade unionism and the institution of collective bargaining has encroached upon these traditional rights and powers but the basic principle still persists.

Labour-Management Problems

The practical economic questions which all the time haunt the minds of planners, enterprisers and manpower at the present time may be conceived as compounded in various manners out of three central problems. D.H. Robertson had laid down three problems as:

(a) Problem of Production,
(b) Problem of Distribution, and
(c) Problem of Government or Control.

He has emphasised more on last problem saying:

"how, if at all, can we ensure that the men and women engaged in industry shall not become mere instruments of production or mere passive receptacles of its fruits, but shall retain, in their relation to the economic circumstances of their life, the character of self-directing human beings?"

The problem of control of industry basically depends upon the structure of the economic organisation of a country. The whole effort aims at increasing production of goods and services for greatest welfare of the society. In order to achieve this aim, as D.H. Robertson says:

> "how the limited natural resources of the community, its limited flow of savings, its limited equipment of human brains and hands, is to be allocated between the infinity of different uses in which they are capable of yielding a harvest of enjoyment."

The social philosophy has gone under a change with changing needs, ideas, assurances and aspirations. The modern democratic socialist society aims at reducing inequalities in different work of life and ensuring a minimum desirable standard of living through democratic and principal means. This can be achieved by creating democratic atmosphere at the place of production. This can be achieved by creating democratic atmosphere at the place of production. This demands a change in style of control of the management. Participation is an important manifestation of power which pervades our dynamic social phenomena and it frequently envisaged both the cause and consequent of social change. Worker's participation is an important means of obtaining control of industrial organisation by workers bringing a social change. The participation of workers with the management is an essential condition of the factory system of production. It has established a relationship based on the needs of the parties. The capitalist wants profit out of capital invested and labour wants job for livelihood and high price for labour. The wants of both these parties necessitate cooperation with each other. As the capitalist earns profit only when he cooperates with labour so labour can have livelihood only when he cooperates with capitalist in getting job. Therefore, the factory system has established a relationship based on necessitous cooperation. So long they desire to get their necessitous needs fulfilled they must have to cooperate with each other.

From the early stage of individual cooperation between labour and capital the stage of group cooperation has come in existence. Dennis H. Robertson in his book, "The Control of Industry" has contained his prediction that:

> "... working-class effort must continue along the well-established lines of negative or inhibitory control, while

preparing itself, by organisation and education, for the assumption of positive powers of government at some future date."

He further said that the managerial decision must be "workable" but experiences of capitalist economy show that the decisions have been mostly unworkable leading to misunderstanding, confusion and conflict. He advised that such a situation could be saved if those who are firiven to make it had been "partners to the decision in the first instance." Efforts have been made in this direction to get workers associated with the management at various levels.

Cooperation between labour and management is the first condition for continued production of goods and services, but it has become more vital for a planned economy. The idea behind it is the establishment of industrial harmony and industrial peace. The idea behind it is not only the absence of conflict rather to increase the degree of cooperation. But the level of cooperation is minimum called as "Conjunction" by N.W. Chamberlain. Thus, there is problem of increasing the degree of cooperation at various levels. This can be achieved not only by raising wage rates or by making better living and working conditions but by filling up sense of deprivation resulted from loss of independence. This can be compensated by realisation of partnership in an enterprise. The realisation of this partnership is not only a matter of money reward. It is an question of human dignity. It is a question of psychological satisfaction. This differentiates the worker from machine. Success of planned economy through increased productivity and efficiency of labour for greater welfare of society is the crux of the whole world. Higher productivity and efficiency can be achieved more by social and morale values than financial. The responsibility for optimising productivity falls squarely on the shoulders of the workers and the management. Mere wage increase will no longer suffice, what is needed is a human engineering approach to solution of human relationship problems by a system of participative management at all start on the basis of equality and mutual respect for specific and rightful role of both labour and management in industry. To achieve this, one has to dispense with our traditional and autocratic attitude towards labour. Labour should no longer be regarded as "commodity value" that is to be brought in maximum use, replaced periodically and discarded when damaged or worn out. It is the human factor which will determine the final productivity of the enterprise. Our modern industrial organisational structure with its emphasis on specialisation leaves little opportunity for creative personnel expression or assumption of personnel responsibility.

Our industrial management today had been evolved into a complex art of social behaviour. It is the practice of cooperation between the human resources of the industry right from the top managing man to the rank and file of workers. So the key to the future of good industrial relations and harmonious atmosphere for optimum production and efficiency lies in the growth and development of industrial democracy and in finding a realistic basis for cooperation. N.W. Chamberlain has put it as:

> "An industry consists of two distinct parties that is the management and the labour, therefore, each party is dependent on the other, and can-as a matter of fact... achieve its objective more effectively if it wins the support of the other."

The concept behind labour and management cooperation lies in real treatment of worker as a partner and not as a machine or a commodity or a factor of production. He must be given human treatment. He must get opportunity for bearing responsibility at the work place. He must get opportunity to show his creative power. He likes to be consulted on common problems. The ego satisfaction of a man surpasses all other considerations. This is the clue for the success of industrial relations system in modern world.

The modern philosophy of human relations demands a change of heart on the part of both sides. The management, must accept it in right spirit setting aside the old theory based on "Right of Property" to conducts his own business in his own way. They must not be affraid of loosing their right of ownership. It should be accepted as a method for establishing industrial peace, increasing productivity and production. On other hand labour must be prepared to extend hands of cooperation for good of all. Labour-management cooperation should not be treated as a step toward nationalisation of industry. It should be accepted as a process for cooperating in the present managerial system fulfiling their economic and human needs. Naturally, this demands change of heart as called by Mahatma Gandhi in his 'Principle of Trusteeship'.

The basic purposes behind labour-management cooperation are:

(1) Increasing productivity and production, and
(2) Establishing industrial democracy and human respect.

The two purposes are interlinked with due human element. Naturally, this demands fundamentally a change of outlook towards industrial relations. The traditional concept of treating labour as a cog in the big complex of production must be replaced by a sense of partnership. This human factor has become an effective tool of modern management system. Labour participation in management has been interpreted in many ways by different authors. M.S. Vitles has observed that "workers participation in decision-making democratic atmosphere serves to raise the levels of employee motivation and morale. Another author, R. Likert has stated that "participation means ego involvement on the part of the workers and that it could make the maximum use of the lated abilities of the worker." N.R. Seth is of the opinion that "labour participation in management is a means towards the goal of industrial harmony and productivity under the ideology of liberalism and equalitarianism." K.C. Alexander has seen it in a different way. According to him "Workers' participation in management is the sharing of a portion of management power with worker." According to him workers participation in management is the achievement of greater organisational health and effectiveness. A. Saraoji has remarked that the people who are managed in have some say about decision which affect them. Thus, one finds that one has interpreted it in ego satisfaction, other has seen it as a means for establishing industrial harmony and some other have seen as sharing of managerial power.

Though the problem of labour-management cooperation goes back to the modern productive system but this problem first became apparent and get due attention during the first world war period. The outbreak of the world war necessitated undisturbed production of war materials. The Government felt the need of associating workers with management in industry to increase output and efficiency of labour during the war period. Though, there had been isolated instances of this development but it received great stimulous from the out burst of demand for pure workers control during the revolutionary period of 1917-1920. It was during the war period this experiment was made though on workers' pressure. The war needs were also factors pressuring the Government and industry for opening a new chapter in the managerial system of industrial organisations, first in U.K. For the survival of the country it became essential for managements and workers to cooperate with each other. This gave the idea of joint consultation. The British Government set-up an enquiry committee known as Whiteley Council for conducting enquiry into the question of industrial democracy. The Whitley Council in its report of 1916 recommended for the establishment of Joint Consultative Body at three levels, at the factory, the District and the National level. This is known as Whitley Council but in industry it is known as Works Council. The Works Council established in many factories in U.K. Developed after the war on voluntary basis. The functions of Works Council were mostly concerned with the elimination of waste, better utilisation of tool, machine and materials, training of workers, accident prevention, prevention of friction and misunderstanding and the welfare measures. It worked as a medium of communication and a means of settlement of grievances. Whatever the early shortcomings might be, that was the beginning of a new era in industrial management.

In Germany the Works Councils were established in the same period. It was supported by a constitution of 1919 and later it became an integral part of the organisation of industry by specific statute of 1920. The labour-management cooperation was first established in formal manner during the first world war period in the world. A new experiment in industrial relations with better emphasis on human approach in industry was the gift of outbreak of the first world war and allied economic problems. The economic problems forced the Government and the managements of industries to find out solutions for removing misunderstandings and developing mutual understanding and mutual cooperation for the good of the country, the company and the workers. The problems of production and productivity are most vital perils, can be overcome only through united efforts which alone can be lasting and progressive. The achievements of first world war in the field of human relations can easily be applied during peace period for the betterment of all.

The adoption of the principle of democracy, first in the field of politics, has become common demand of the time. Industrial democracy can only, in the present time, find out solution of many economic and industrial problems. It is wise to read the nerves of the time and to change accordingly setting aside old traditional pattern of management.

The Owners' Absolute Right to Manage

To owners' absolute right to manage economic enterprises is justified on a number of grounds including the following:

(1) The golden rule of capitalism that "risk and control go together" provides the most important justification. According to this rule, the owners of business enterprises subject their capital resources to unforseen risks; the business venture may succeed and bring profits or it may fail causing bankruptcy. Therefore, the owners should have full freedom to management their enterprises unhindered by any outside control in order that the risk may be minimised and success assured. Any interference with their right is likely to cause dislocation.

(2) The maintenance and development of industrial efficiency demands that the managers should be able to take quick decision in the ever changing market conditions. Any delay which may be entailed because of a long cumbersome consultative procedure in decision-making may lead to serious economic losses. Therefore, the owners of enterprises should have the necessary power to make quick adaptations and take quick decisions as and when so demanded. Thus, the exercise of the absolute power by the owners is though to be a

necessary condition for the maintenance of the economic health of the enterprise. It is said that the management of a large-scale business enterprise is necessarily authoritarian in character which does not lend itself to democratic control. There has to be a hierarchical organisation with the decision-making power vesting at the top in the selected few, and compliance and obedience from the bottom.

(3) Finally, it is said that management of industrial enterprises today has become a highly skilled and technical job. The skill of managing enterprises comes only through long experience and training which, under the present social system, only a few can afford. Therefore, the owners of business enterprises or their legal representatives, who are in the best position to receive that training and pick-up that experience, should possess full freedom to control and manage their property. It will not be in the interest of economic efficiency if persons without training and experience are given the right to share the decision-making power.

It is on the basis of the foregoing arguments that the absolute power of the owners of business enterprises is exercised and justified. Essentially, the power to manage flows from the right to own property. Therefore, management's rights are basically property-rights. However, gradually, the workers and the trade unions have not only challenged these management rights but have also succeeded in restricting them and in participating in the managerial decisions. The managements have been forced to share one right after another with the workers, but this is a forced sharing rather than a voluntary process.

Workers and unions have argued that the success or failure of a business enterprise is too closely linked with their own fate to be left under the absolute control of the owners. In the event of its failure, the owner may lose his capital only, which may or may not mean his starvation, but the workers lose their jobs, their bread and their hard-learnt experience and skill. Therefore, they ask, "Who is more interested in the success of the enterprise, the workers or the owners?" The workers accept that managing an enterprise is a skilled job but the owner is not automatically a skilled manager. In the larger industrial undertakings of today, the real managers are not the owners. There is an industrial bureaucracy consisting of experts of various kinds which manages the undertakings today. If the owners, by virtue of their property rights, have the power to control this bureaucracy, the workers, by virtue of their property rights, have the power to control this bureaucracy, the workers, the virtue of their right to jobs, should also have a voice in exercising this control.

Another line of argument advanced by workers and their unions is that the right to manage an industrial enterprise does not imply the right to manage men an industrial enterprise does not imply the right to manage men also whose cooperation is essential for the success of an enterprise. They take the argument to a higher ethical plane and contend that control and management of men must be based on their consent. The unilateral determination of the terms and conditions of employment by the owners means an imposition. Workers are human beings and as such they should have the right to participate in the determination of the terms and conditions of employment. Thus, there is no case for the owner's absolute right to manage his enterprise in the interests of his profits only. If the goals of the management are so modified as to include the interests of the workers, the case for workers' participation in the decision-making process is further strengthened.

Forms of Labour-Management Cooperation

Labour-management cooperation may take various forms and may be of different degrees. To mention a few, labour-management cooperation may take any of the following forms:

(1) Information sharing;
(2) Problem sharing;
(3) Joint consultation; and
(4) Workers' participation in management.

(1) Information Sharing

Under this type of cooperation, the employer agrees or undertakes to keep the employees informed about business conditions and the general prospects of the company and about changes in the methods of production before they are put into effect. This practice of keeping the employees and their union informed of the economic position of the enterprise help the union in formulating its policies and the workers in their attitude-formation. It is quite legitimate to infer that, once the workers receive prior information of the changes in the methods of production and the economic difficulties of the enterprise, they would put forward their own ideas and suggestions which could receive a due consideration by the employer.

(2) Problem Sharing

The second form of labour-management cooperation may relate to problem sharing. An employer faced with some problems may consult the workers and their union and seek their help in solving them. This sort of cooperation is specific and related to particular issues. However, the experience thus gained may result in a more formalised and regular structuring of consultation and advice. The relationship between the Amalgamated Clothing Workers of America and the clothing factories is an illustration of this type of experience. When some clothing manufacturers finding themselves in economic difficulties called for the union cooperation, the union and the various managements jointly succeeded in resolving the economic difficulties and thereby laid the foundation of a more widespread cooperation between the union and the clothing industry.

(3) Joint Consultation

Whereas the first two forms of labour-management cooperation may be of a temporary nature designed to get out of occasional difficulties, there may be formal and regular consultation between a management and the workers represented by their union on all or some common issues as decided upon beforehand. It means consultation of the workers by the management before any decisions are made so that the workers' point of view could also be taken into account by the decision-making authority. This consultation also provides the management an occasion to explain its own aims and problems. The management retains its prerogative to manage, i.e. the exclusive right to take decisions. It also thereby has the clear and undivided responsibility for the results of its actions. When consulted, the workers and their unions may offer their suggestions and give their view-points, but cannot insist that their view-points be accepted. Consultation in this form does not imply joint decision-making. The acceptance by the management of the workers' ideas and claims depends entirely on their merits as understood by the management.

However, it should be mentioned here that in the process of consultation, the workers and their union acquire a definite status. It will be a rash and imprudent management which will summarily reject the opinions and view-points presented by strong and well-organised unions. What appears to be a mere consultation may acquire a binding character in course of time.

(4) Workers' Participation in Management

The final form of labour-management cooperation may provide for workers' participation in management. Under this form, the process of decision-making becomes really joint and bipartite. Both the union and the management have a say in decision-making and they also undertake responsibilities for the results of their action. Workers' participation in management, in many cases, may imply a representation of the workers on the Board of Directors of a company or it may simply mean the establishment of joint councils consisting of the representatives of the workers and the management. These councils are vested with the power to take final decisions on matters entrusted to them either on the basis of bargaining or legislation.

The workers' participation in management as a form of labour-management cooperation is quite different from the participation of the union through collective bargaining in the managerial decision-making process. The emergence of collective bargaining has enabled workers and unions to share the decision-making power of the management in many areas of the administration of an enterprise. Wages, working conditions, hours of work, hiring, dismissal, promotion, demotion, lay-off, retrenchment, job evaluation, fringe benefits, health, safety and welfare, and many other related matters are being decided on the basis of collective bargaining today. Management's prerogatives in these areas no longer exist and what was formerly decided unilaterally by the management is now the subject matter of a bipartite decision. Further, whatever management's prerogatives exist have an uncertain future. As the scope of collective bargaining widens, management's prerogatives shrink. But workers' participation in management as a form of labour-management cooperation is different from participation on the basis of collective bargaining, not only because the subject matter of the former is different from that of the latter, but also because of the spirit which lies behind labour-management cooperation. In labour-management cooperation, the guiding motive is the improvement of efficiency and production, generally speaking, with a spirit of cordiality and good will. The sanction behind participation through collective bargaining is the relative coercive powers of the parties concerned; whereas the sanction behind workers' participation as a form of labour-management cooperation is the spirit of goodwill and reason.

The foregoing discussion gives an indication of the variety of forms and extent of labour-management cooperation. As cooperation is a voluntary movement, its forms depend upon the extent of the willingness to cooperate amongst the parties concerned and the needs of the particular industrial establishments, industries and the nation as a whole at a particular time. Cooperation cannot be exacted under legislative powers and, therefore, it cannot be put into straight, uniform and standardised jackets, though attempts have been made to develop cooperation on the basis of legislation. Every establishment, every industry and every nation chooses its own form of labour-management cooperation. Hence, experiments in the field of labour-management cooperation differ from country to country. Even within the same country, its forms and levels are not the same for all plants or industries.

Labour-management cooperation in India is primarily a government sponsored movement. As early as 1947, the Industrial Truce Resolution adopted at the Industries Conference held at Delhi, recommended inter alia the formation of Unit Production Committees in industrial establishments for promoting the efficiency of workers and improving production. The Central Government, under the Industrial Policy Resolution of the 6th April, 1948, also professed the setting up of bipartite Production Committees consisting of representatives of employers and workers. After a further discussion of the matter at the first meeting of the Central Advisory Committee on Labour held at Lucknow in November, 1948, the Central Government prepared a model constitution for the establishment of Unit Production Committees as well as for enabling the existing Works Committees to function as Production Committees. Under the model constitution, the functions of these Committees were to consult and advise on matters relating to production problems in so far as they pertained to specific problems of production in which labour had a direct interest.

In particular, the functions of the Committee included:

(a) A better upkeep and care of machinery, tools instruments, etc.;
(b) Efficient use of the maximum number of production hours;
(c) Elimination of defective work and waste; and
(d) Efficient use of safety precautions and devices.

The Committees were to consist of representatives of management, and representatives of workers who were not to be less than those of the management. The representatives of the workers were to be elected from amongst the workers employed in the undertaking or factory. These Committees were prohibited from dealing with the problems of planning, development and production in their wider sense and functions which were purely managerial. They were further precluded from dealing with such issues as were normally taken by the trade unions.

Joint Management Councils

Nothing very definite came out of the recommendations referred to above and the need for the establishment of such Committees continued to be felt. It was also realised that a very limited association of workers with the management of industrial undertakings purely from the point of view of increasing production, would not enthuse the workers. Thus, the Second Five Year Plan recommended the setting up, in the first instance, of Councils of Management consisting of representatives of management, technicians and workers in the larger industrial undertakings. These Councils of Management were supposed to enjoy wider functions and powers than those of the Unit Production Committees.

In pursuance of the recommendations of the Second Five Year Plan, the Government of India sent abroad a study group to study the extent and methods of workers' participation in vogue in Great Britain, Sweden, France, Belgium, Germany and Yugoslavia. The Report of the study group was considered by the Indian Labour Conference at its 15th session held in 1957. The Conference, while accepting the recommendations of the study group, set-up a sub-committee of representatives of employers, workers and government to work out the details of a scheme of workers' participation in management. The sub-committee laid down the following criteria for the selection of undertakings for introducing schemes of workers' participation in management:

(a) The undertaking should have a well established, strong trade union functioning;
(b) There should be a readiness with the parties viz. employer, workers and the union, to try out the experiment in a spirit of will cooperation;
(c) The size of the undertaking (in terms of employment) should be at least 500 workers;
(d) The employer in the private sector should be a member of one or the other leading employers' organisation, so should the trade union be related to one of the central federations; and
(e) The undertaking should have had a fair record of industrial relations.

In order to work out further details a seminar on labour-management cooperation was held at New Delhi in January 31, and February 1, 1958. The seminar made recommendations with regard to:

(a) size of the Joint Council;
(b) methods of selection of workers' and management's representatives;
(c) office-bearers of Joint Councils;
(d) constitution of sub-committees;
(e) schedule for the meetings of Joint Councils;
(f) minimum qualifications pertaining to education, etc;

(g) liaison between Joint Councils and Ministry of Labour and Employment;
(h) guidance from panels of experts;
(i) training programmes in units experimenting with workers' participation in management;
(j) dissemination of informations to workers;
(k) informal meetings;
(l) relationship between Joint Councils and Works Committees; and
(m) responsibilities of the Council.

Out of the deliberations of the seminar also emerged a draft of a model agreement regarding establishment of Councils of Management. The model agreement is intended to guide management and unions seeking to set-up Councils of Management.

Composition and Functions of Joint Councils of Management

The recommendations of the seminar on Labour-Management Cooperation and the Draft Model Agreement give a complete procedural picture of the Joint Councils of Management.

Composition

Under the recommendations of the seminar, the Joint Councils, to be effective and manageable, are to consist of equal number of representatives of management and employees not exceeding twelve in all, but not less than six in small undertakings. The employees' representatives are to be nominated by a representative union, if any, where there is a law providing for the registration of the representative union. In case there are no representative unions but there is only one union well established, that union should nominate employees' representatives. Where there are two or more well-established and effective unions, the Joint Councils will be formed when the unions themselves agree as to the manner in which representation should be given to employees. The trade unions, if they so feel, can nominate non-employee members to the extent of not more than 25% of their quota. However, if the employers have no objection, the number of such members can be raised to two.

Functions

The functions of the Joint Management Councils are laid down in the Draft Model Agreement. Its preamble stresses the appreciation of the fact that an increasing measure of association of employees with the management would be desirable and would help in:

(a) promoting increased productivity for the general benefit of the enterprise, the employees and the country;
(b) giving employees a better understanding of their roles and their importance in the working of the industry and in the process of production; and
(c) satisfying the urge for self-expression.

Section 4 of the agreement lays down that it would be the endeavour of the Councils:

(i) to improve the working and living conditions of the employees,
(ii) to improve the productivity,
(iii) to encourage suggestions from the employees,
(iv) to assist in the administration of laws and agreements,
(v) to serve generally as an authentic channel of communication between the management and the employees, and
(vi) to create in the employees a live sense of participation.

So far as the specific status and functions of the Councils are concerned, they are consultative, information-sharing and administrative.

Consultative Functions

The Councils should be consulted by the management on matters like:

(i) general administration of standing orders and their amendments, when needed;

(ii) introduction of new methods of production and manufacture involving reemployment of men and machinery; and
(iii) closure, reduction in or cessation of operations.

Information Receiving and Suggestion-making Functions

The Councils would also have the right to receive information, discuss and give suggestions regarding the following matters:

(i) general economic situation in the concern;
(ii) organisation and general running of the undertaking;
(iii) the state of the market, production and sales programme;
(iv) circumstances affecting the economic position of the undertaking;
(v) methods of manufacture and work;
(vi) the annual balance sheet and profit and loss statement and connected documents and explanation;
(vii) long-term plans for expansion, redeployment, etc; and
(viii) such other matters as may be agreed to.

Administrative Functions

The Councils would be entrusted with responsibility in respect of the following:

(i) administration of welfare measures;
(ii) supervision of safety measures;
(iii) operation of vocational training and apprenticeship schemes;
(iv) preparation of schedules of working hours and breaks and of holidays;
(v) payment of rewards for valuable suggestions received from employees; and
(vi) any other matter as may be agreed to by the Joint Council.

In order to maintain a clear-cut distinction and avoid overlapping and confusion between the roles of the trade union and those of the Councils, the Draft Agreement provides that all matters such as wages, bonus, and allowances, which are subjects for collective bargaining, be excluded from the scope for the Councils. Individual grievances are also excluded. In short, creation of new rights as between workers and management in outside the jurisdiction of these Councils.

The second national seminar held in 1960, after reviewing the working of the Joint Management Councils for two years of their existence, reiterated their usefulness. The Third Five Year Plan also expected a good deal from these Councils and considered workers' participation in management essential for "the peaceful evolution of the economic system on a democratic basis." the Plan further hoped that such participation would throw up, in course of time, "management cadres out of the working class itself," and would help "to promote social mobility which is an important ingredients of a socialist system." The Plan, therefore, recommended the establishment of Joint Management Councils in all undertakings found suitable for the purpose so that the scheme might ultimately become a normal feature of the industrial system. The Indian Labour Conference also adopted resolutions from time to time to encourage the formation of these Councils.

In order to facilitate the implementation of the policy statements, the Government of India made some promotional efforts up a panel of names from the organisations of employers and workers at various centres with a view to advising Joint Management Councils in the event of difficulties. Besides, it also set-up a tripartite committee on labour-management cooperation to advice on all matters connected with the implementation of the scheme. A special cell for the purpose was set-up in the Ministry of Labour and Employment. Many State Governments, on their part, entrusted the promotion of the scheme to special officers. Gradually, Joint Management Councils came to be set-up in both public and private sectors.

A glance at the number of undertakings having Joint Management Councils, available reports on their working, and pronouncements made by the employers and trade union leaders here and there will clearly show that these Councils, contrary to the expectations of the promoters of the scheme, have not made much headway. There was a great fanfare, show and publicity when JMCs were set-up in the initial periods. However, as time passed, the scheme could not receive a willing acceptance even by those who had supported it earlier. The National Commission on Labour in its report of 1969 also came to the conclusion "...the fact remains that the JMCs have not been a resounding success at any place either from the point of view of the employers or labour. If they had been, one or the other party would have worked for popularising it further."

Apart from the general handicaps underlying any such scheme of labour-management cooperation in the country to be discussed adoption of JMCs and their smooth functioning. Some of the specific handicaps are listed below:

(1) Although representatives of the central organisations of employers and workers supported the scheme at national conferences and committees, they have shown inadequate interest in making their affiliates enthusiastic about it.

(2) Employers already having an effective system of consultation in their establishments find a Joint Management Council in its present form superfluous.

(3) Many employers and trade unions are averse to having a multiplicity of joint bodies.

(4) In undertakings characterised by uncordial industrial relations, and absence of works committees or other joint bodies, grievance procedure or a recognised union, it is futile to expect the formation or smooth functioning of JMCs.

(5) Many trade union leaders think that JMCs divert the attention of workers from other important issues such as wages, bonus and allowances, etc. and thus they are not enthusiastic about the success of the scheme.

It is further difficult to predict with any amount of precision the future of JMCs in India. The National Commission on Labour is, however, of the view that "when the system of union recognition becomes an accepted practice, both managements and unions will themselves gravitate towards greater cooperation, in areas they consider to be of mutual advantage and set-up a JMC." There appears to be some force in the prediction of the National Commission on Labour that the system of compulsory recognition of trade unions will eventually accelerate the process of collective bargaining, and when collective bargaining is firmly established, the schemes of labour-management cooperation will have opportunities to succeed.

Joint Councils in Government Service

A proposal to set-up a type of machinery on the pattern of Whitley Councils for Government Departments was recommended by the Second Pay Commission which also recommended provision for compulsory arbitration. After accepting the recommendations in principle, the Government of India took action to set-up a machinery for joint consultation and arbitration in consultation with the representatives of the employees. The object of the scheme was "promoting harmonious relations and for securing the greatest measure of cooperation between the government in its capacity as employer and the general body of its employees in matters of common concern and with the object further of increasing the efficiency of public service." The success of similar schemes in railways, posts and telegraphs and defence establishments also provided an impetus. A voluntary scheme was eventually drawn and put into operation in October 1966. The main features of the scheme are given below.

Coverage

The scheme coves all regular civil employees of the Central Government other than those: (a) in Classes I and II (except Central Secretariat Services and coparable services in the headquarter's organisation of the Government); (b) persons in industrial establishments employed mainly in managerial or administrative capacity; and (c) those who being employed in supervisory capacity draw salary in scales going beyond Rs. 575 per mensem, employees in Union Territories and Police Personnel.

Structure

The Scheme provides for the formation of a National Council, Department Councils, Regional and Office Councils. Each Council consists of nominees of the government who form the official side, and representatives of the unions or associations of employees recognised for the purpose. Accordingly, the National Council came to be set-up, which held its first meeting on December 5, 1966. Departmental Councils have been established in almost all the Ministries and Departments. In some Ministries or Departments, Regional and Office Councils have also been formed.

Functions

The scope of the Councils include all matters relating to conditions of service and work, welfare of the employees, and improvement of efficiency and standards of work. However, so far as the questions of recruitment, promotion and discipline are concerned, consultation is to be confined to matters of general principles only. The schemes further provide for limited compulsory arbitration on pay and allowances, weekly hours of work, and leave of a class or grade of employees. The arbitration award in binding unless rejected by the Parliament.

The National Council deals with matters affecting Central Government employees generally and those relating to two or more Departments not grouped together in a single Departmental Council. A Departmental Council generally deals with such matters which affect the employees in the Department concerned. The National Council has so far taken decisions on such matters as leave travel concenssion, house rent and incidental allowance, merger of dearness allowance in basic pay, hospital leave, and reversion of pre-emergency working hours. Similarly, Departmental Councils have taken decisions on subjects of immediate concern to the employees in the Departments concerned.

It was only after two years of the existence of these Councils that a number of unions and associations of employees gave a call for a general strike in September 1968 on the Government's refusal to refer to arbitration the question of the need-based minimum wage and related issues, thinking that they were not arbitrable. In consequence, the Essential Services

Maintenance Ordinance was promulgated on September 13, 1968 which declared Government Services as "essential services" and prohibited strikes in them. The Ordinance was replaced by an Act of the same name enacted late in the year. It appears today that the schemes of joint consultation in government services are going to meet the same fate as the scheme of Joint Management Councils in industrial undertakings. The real test of any such schemes lies in their capacity to solve the basic issues dividing the employer and the workers. It is here that the Councils tend to fail at crucial moments.

Joint Councils in Railways, Posts and Telegraphs and Defence Establishments

Joint consultative machineries combining in them functions of "cooperation, consultation, discussion and negotiation" have been in operation in Indian Railways, Posts and Telegraphs and Defence establishments even prior to the establishment of Joint Councils in pursuance of the recommendations of the Second Pay Commission. In practice, however, the main function of the joint machineries in these industries has been that of negotiating for resolving differences or disputes.

Railways

In the Indian Railways, a Permanent Negotiating Machinery (PNM) was set up in 1952 with the consent of both the All-India Railwaymen's Federation and the Indian National Railway Workers' Federation. The main objective behind the establishment of the PNM was "maintaining contact with labour and resolving disputes and differences which may arise between them and the Administration." The PNM has a three-tier structure, i.e.

(a) At the Railway level—the recognised unions have access to the District/Divisional Officers and subsequently to Officers at the Headquarter of the Railway concerned;

(b) At the next tier, matters not settled at the District/ Divisional level are taken up by the respective federations with the Railway Board; and

(c) Lastly, if agreement is not reached between the

federation and the Railway Board and the matters are of sufficient importance, reference may be made to an adhoc Tribunal composed of representatives of the Railway Administration and workers, presided over by an impartial Chairman.

Posts and Telegraphs

In the Posts and Telegraphs Department there are standing arrangements under which employees' demands and difficulties are discussed periodically at the Divisional and Circle levels. Matters not settled at these levels are taken up by the Central Union to the Posts and Telegraphs Board.

Defence Establishments

A Joint Negotiating Machinery was set-up by the Ministry of Defence in 1954 with a view to promoting settlement of disputes between the administration and civilian employees in Defence establishments. This scheme has also a three-tier set-up. the three levels are:

(a) The unit/factory/depot leve;
(b) The level of DGOF/Naval Headquarter/Air Headquarters/Command Headquarters/DTD; and
(c) The Ministry of Defence level.

Labour-Management Cooperation Schemes in Particular Industrial Units

Here, it is necessary to discuss briefly the efforts of some managements and unions in the private sector who initiated labour-management cooperation schemes even prior to the efforts at the governmental level. These schemes have been the outcome of comprehensive collective agreements reached between the management and labour.

Labour-Management Cooperation in TISCO

By their supplemental agreement of January 8, 1956, the Tata Iron and Steel Company Ltd. and the Tata Workers Union agreed to set-up the following joint councils in order to provide for a closer association of employees with the management:

(i) Joint Departmental Councils;
(ii) Joint Works Council for the plant as a whole;
(iii) Joint Town Council; and
(iv) Joint Consultative Council of Management at the topmost level.

The Company and the Union agreed that the representatives of employees to these councils were, in the first instance, to be nominated by the union, but steps were to be taken, gradually, to introduce the principle of election by a secret ballot. The representatives of the management were to be nominated by the management.

The Three-tier Structure of Joint Councils

The agreement has framed a three-tier structure of joint councils. At the base the Joint Department Councils (J.D.C.) have been established on for each department for normal work force in the works or a combined for two or more smaller departments. Above them at the intermediate level is the Joint Works Council (JWC) for the entire works, and parallel to its Joint Town and Medical Council (JTMC) for dealing with matters relating to town, education, health and medical services. At the top level is the Joint Consultative Council of Management (JCCM).

The Joint Councils aim at helping (a) in promoting increased productivity for the general benefit of the enterprise, the employees and the country, (b) in giving employees a better understanding of their role and importance in the working of the industry and in the process of production, and (c) in satisfying the urge for self-expression.

Joint Departmental Councils (JDC)

The Joint Departmental Council has been established at the departmental level. The size of the council, depending on the size of the department, consists of two to ten representatives of the management and an equal number of representatives of the employees. The representatives are nominated by the respective sides for a period of two years. The chairman belongs to the management side the Vice-Chairman from the union side. The council meets once a month.

(a) To study operational results and current and long-term departmental production problems.

(b) To advise on steps necessary at departmental level to promote and rationalise production; improve methods, layout and processes, improve productivity and discipline, eliminate waste, effect economies with a view to lowering costs; eliminate defective work and improve the quality of products; improve the up-keep and care of machinery tools and instruments, promote efficient use of safety precautions and devices, promote employees' welfare and activities like sports/picnics, encourage suggestions, improve working conditions and better functioning of the department.

(c) To implement the recommendations or decisions of Joint Consultation Council of Management of the Joint Works Council approved by management.

(d) To refer any matter to the Joint Works Council for their consideration of advice.

Joint Works Council (JWC)

Thee has been a Joint Works Council consisting of twelve representatives of management and an equal number of representatives of employees. The representatives of the management are nominated by the management. The representatives of employees, including a fair representation of employees within the sphere of the Supervisory Unit of the union, are nominated by the union from among the employees of the company, exclusive of those covered by the Joint Town Council except that one of such representatives is an officer of the union, who is not an employee of the company. The chairman is designated by the management from among the representatives of management on the council. The council holds its meetings normally once a month. The term of office of the members is two years, except that half of the original members of the council retires at the end of first year.

The functions of the Joint Works Council are as follows:

(a) To study operational results and current and long-term production problems of the works as a whole.

(b) To advise an steps necessary to promote and rationalise production, improve methods, layout and processes, improve productivity and discipline, eliminate waste, effect economies with a view to lowering costs, eliminate defective work and improve the quality of products, improve the up-keep and care of machinery tools and instruments, promote efficient use of safety precautions and devices, promote employees' welfare and activities like sports/picnics, encourage suggestions, improve working conditions and better functioning of the works as a whole.

(c) To plan and supervise the works of the following committees within the framework of duly approved budgets and company rules and procedures:
   (a) Central Canteen Managing Committee,
   (b) Welfare Committee,
   (c) General Safety Committee,
   (d) Safety Appliances Committee, and
   (e) Suggestion Box Committee.

(d) To follow-up the implementation through the appropriate Joint Departmental Councils of its recommendations or decisions approved by Management,

(e) To refer any matter to the Joint Consultative Council of Management for their consideration or advice, and

(f) To advise on any matter referred to it by the Joint Departmental Councils or by the Joint Consultative Council of Management or by Management.

The General Safety Committee, which at present consists of twelve management representatives, has been reconstituted to provide for eight management representatives including the chairman, and four representatives of employees.

The composition of the present Welfare Committee, which consisted of nine management representatives, now consists of five representatives of management, including the chairman and five representatives of employees.

The composition of the Central Canteen Management

Committee, the Safety Appliances Committee and the Suggestion Box Committee are the same as at present.

The representatives of management including the chairman of the Central Canteen Managing Committee, the Welfare Committee, the General Safety Committee, the Safety Appliances Committee, and the Suggestion Box Committee are nominated by the management and those of employees by the union.

The General Safety Committee, the Central Canteen Managing Committee and the Welfare Committee have been reconstituted. The Safety Appliances Committee and the Suggestion Box Committee function as sub-committees of the Joint Work Council.

Joint Town Council

Joint Town Council consisting of six representatives of management and six representatives of employees has been established. The representatives of the management are nominated by the management. The representatives of the employees, including a fair representation of employees within the sphere of the Supervisory unit of the union, are nominated by the union from among the employees of the company in the Town, Medical and Health Departments, including the Education Departments, except that one of such representatives is an officer of the union, who is not an employee of the company. The chairman is designated by the management from among its representatives and the Vice-Chairman by the union from among the representatives of employees of the council. The council meets normally once a month. The term of office of the members is two years except that half of the original members of the council retires at the end of first year.

The functions of the Joint Town Council are as follows:

(a) To advise on steps necessary to promote, rationalise and improve output and methods of work, reduce costs, improve quality, effect economies, reduce waste and ensure improved working conditions and better functioning of the organisation as a whole,

(b) To advise on social welfare activities in the town within the frame-work of duly approved budgets and company rules and procedures,

(c) To follow-up implementation of its recommendations or decisions approved by management, and

(d) To refer any matter to the Joint Consultative Council of Management for their consideration or advice.

Joint Consultative Council of Management (JCCM)

A Joint Consultative Council of Management exists consisting of eight representatives of management and an equal number of representatives of employees, in addition to a chairman. The representatives of the company and the chairman are nominated by the company. The representatives of the employees, including a fair representation of employees within the sphere of the Supervisory Unit of the union, are nominated by the union from among the employees of the company, except that not more than two of such representatives may be officers of the union who are not employees of the company. The council normally meets once a quarter at Jamshedpur or Bombay. The term of office of the members is two years except that half of the original members of the council retires at the end of the first year.

The functions of the Joint Consultation Council of Management are as follows:

(a) To advise management on all matters concerning the working of the industry in the fields of production and welfare.

(b) To advise management in regard to economic and financial matters placed by management before the council, provided that the council may discuss questions dealing with general economic and financial matters concerning the company which do not deal with questions effecting the relations of the company with its shareholders or managerial staff or concerning taxes or other matters of confidential nature.

(c) The consider the advise on any matter referred to it by the Joint Works Councils or the Joint Town and Medical Council.

(d) To follow-up the implementation through the Joint

Works Council or the Joint Town and Medical Council of any recommendations made by it and approved by the Company.

The agreement between the TISCO and Tata Workers' Union providing for the closer association of workers with management is the most detailed of all such agreements in the country. As the TISCO is the largest single employer in the private sector employing nearly 40,000 workers, it is natural that in such a large organisation, relations become more formalised and standardised.

The arrangement of joint councils is hierarchical with the Joint Departmental Council at the bottom and the Joint Consultative Council of Management at the top-informations and recommendations flowing in both directions.

The joint councils are essentially advisory in nature; their functions being to advise management, and the company has reserved to itself the right to accept or reject the recommendations and suggestions of the joint councils. However, it should be noted that it is not the formal constitution and functions of the councils but the spirit in which they work that ultimately determines their effectives in guiding the management. In practice, most decisions of the councils are enforced by the management.

Labour-Management Cooperation in the Indian Aluminum Company

By their agreement of the 31st August, 1956, the Indian Aluminum Company Ltd. Belur Works and the Indian Aluminum Belur Works Employees' Union decided to set-up a joint consultation machinery. The parties, realising that the solution of problems and settlement of disputes and grievances can be best achieved by joint consultation which also contributes towards better understanding and relations, agreed to set-up five joint committees as:

(1) Joint Personnel Relations Committee;
(2) Joint Production Committee;
(3) Joint Job Evaluation Committee;
(4) Joint Standards Committee; and
(5) Joint Canteen Committee.

Composition and Functions of Committees

The first three of these committees consist of equal number of members nominated by the Company and the union. For the last two the principle of equality of representation is not mentioned. They are to consist of competent representatives nominated by the company and the union. These committees are consultative and advisory in character and have no executive authority. They study and discuss problems and advise the management accordingly.

Handicaps in the Growth of Labour-Management Cooperation Schemes in India

The fundamental difficulties of labour-management cooperation are inherent in the concept itself. There is a fundamental conflict of interests between the workers and the owners of business enterprises. Labour-management cooperation is sought to be used as a method of getting around that conflict. It is futile to expect that employers and the trade unions who wage a battle around the bargaining table would sink their differences and become partners in a common enterprise on another table. Employers are interested in labour-management cooperation as a method of increasing production. Workers are interested in labour-management cooperation because they think it to be method of gaining control supplement to collective bargaining, i.e. from the workers' view point it is an instrument of furthering industrial democracy. But who can say that furtherance of industrial democracy would lead to better production and efficiency? Whereas, industrial democracy is of secondary importance to the employer, it is of primary value to the workers. The conflict of goals bedevils the working of labour-management cooperation schemes at every step.

The second difficulty in the way of the successful operation of labour-management cooperation in India is the multiplicity of unions and lack of close contacts between trade union leaders, on the one side, and the rank and file, on the other. If labour-management cooperation schemes are to succeed, it is the genuine representatives of the workers who ought to represent the employees of the concern. Where there is a multiplicity of unions and only the formally registered representative union gets the right to nominate the workers' representatives, labour-management cooperation is destined to fail. It is known to all students of industrial relations and trade unionism in India that unions, which are designated as representative unions on the basis of their membership, may not always be really representative. Besides, the representatives nominated by the unions may not have close contacts with the ordinary workers. It is the strong unions which are sure of their strength and certain of their security that can cooperate with the management. The best way to achieve labour-management cooperation is to help the growth of strong and stable unions not artificially boosted and propped up with membership verification and State support. Weak unions can neither cooperate nor fight. Therefore, the first step that ought to be taken in the interests of labour-management cooperation is the acceptance of the principle of direct elections both for the purpose of finding out the representative union as well as the representatives on the Joint Management Councils. To deny the workers their right to elect their representatives on the ground that the workers are likely to be swayed away by wild promises is to deny their maturity to participate in the Joint Management Councils or other joint bodies. If the same workers can be expected to exercise their franchise in intelligent and appreciative manner in the general elections, they can also be entrusted with the task of choosing their representatives in the field of labour-management cooperation, which is much closer to them.

The third difficulty relates to the sharing of the gains of the labour-management cooperation. Workers are assured in a vague manner that they would gain if production increases as a result of labour-management cooperation; but vague promises cannot be expected to enthuse the workers. Therefore, the principles and the procedures of distribution of the gains should be worked out in details before labour-management cooperation schemes are launched. This will give a definite assurance and commitment to the workers that they would not have to fight round the bargaining table for a share in the gains of labour-management cooperation. One appropriate test for a favourable atmosphere for the working of labour-management cooperation schemes is the prior agreement between the union and the management regarding the principles and procedures mentioned above. If the union and management cannot reach an agreement with regard to them, it is a clear indication that schemes of labour-management cooperation would not succeed.

Fourthly, the idea of labour-management cooperation in India does not appear to be the result of an inner urge on the part of the workers and management. There is a greater realisation in the governmental circles of the utility of labour-management cooperation than among employers and workers. That is why it is the government which is more anxious for the establishment of the schemes of labour-management cooperation than the parties which have to work them out. In many cases, the inducement takes the form of imposition. Under such conditions, labour-management cooperation schemes cannot be expected to succeed.

Finally, the difficulties of language, lack of proper orientation of the representative of both labour and management, absence of cooperation and support from the ranks of middle management are present everywhere. Nevertheless, with more experience, these difficulties may be overcome by and by. Launching of labour-management cooperation should not wait till these difficulties are overcome. It is the working itself that will lead to their solution.

However, any sort of mental reservations either on the part of management or labour in regard to labour-management cooperation is likely to prove a source of its death. It is difficult, no doubt, may be well nigh impossible, for managements and workers in a capitalist society to shed their reservations completely. To think that labour-management cooperation can create a common purpose in industry is to expect too much out of it; may be, in times of national emergencies such as created by wars, labour-management cooperation schemes might succeed as is demonstrated by the history of joint consultation in Great Britain.

Origin of Participative Management in India

The origin of participative management in India can be traced back to 1910, when the humanistic employer in cotton textile industry started holding informal meetings. War times problems forced the management to invite for discussions on immediate problems of increasing production for meeting the war needs. The immediate problems were:

(i) Undisturbed production of textile,
(ii) Increasing production of textile, and
(iii) Utilising the experiences of textilemen.

During the first world war period textilemen were invited for informal talks. That showed the willingness on the part of the employers of the cotton textile industry, the only developed industry in India by then, to have joint consultation for the benefit of all. The fruitful experiences of joint consultation during the first world war period helped in strengthening this relationship in future.

The TISCO, the first steel plant of India, was the first industrial organisation to introduce formal joint consultation machinery in 1919 by setting up a Works Committee. The Works Committee consisting of workers and management representatives had discussed many common issues. The establishment of formal joint consultation machinery in TISCO was an improvement over the cotton textile industry's informal joint consultation. This proved that right from the beginning the Tata Steel had adopted human approach as the corner stone of industrial management philosophy.

The Joint Consultation Machinery within a year of its establishment gained social recognition in 1920, when it was decided by workers and employer organisations to settle disputes by mutual discussions, failing which they were to be resolved by arbitration. The successful experiments in cotton textile industry in Ahmedabad, Bombay and Madras and iron steel industry at Jamshedpur opened a new chapter in industrial relations at an initial stage, when many had not thought of.

Since then many joint committee with various names came in India in 1920, but their functioning was not satisfactory. This issue was discussed at length by the Royal Commission on Labour in India. The Commission had expressed dissatisfaction on the working of these committees. However, it showed great hopes in future and recommended for the establishment of Works Committees at the plant levels for consultation and settlement of disputes. But the world depression of 1929 and thereafter with serious impacts on industrial relations did not allow these committees to serve any meaningful purpose. Till 1937 the recommendations of the commission could not infused any spirit of cooperation.

The establishment of the first Congress Government in 1937 gave a new hope to the workers but its failure within a couple of years shattered all hopes. The outbreak of the second world war again created national emergency, suspending all industrial labour laws. The war again created market scarcity of goods and services. It demanded full labour cooperation in maintaining supply line. The demand for increased industrial production of goods and services, increased productivity and production and better utilisation of workers cooperation came in forefront. This trend was set first during the first world war. Fruitful experiences of first time motivated the Government of taking help of labour on industrial basis. Consequently, the first tripartite conference was called in 1942 inviting representatives of the Government, the managements and the workers. This tripartite conference at national level was a big step ahead in the principle of industrial relations. It set a trend for joint consultation at different levels in course of time.

The war experiences helped in framing a new set of industrial relations law. The Industrial Disputes Act, 1947 incorporated provision for the establishment of Works Committee in any industrial establishment employing one hundred or more workmen, consisting of representatives of workmen and their company. The Works Committee under the law has been assigned the duty "to promote measures for securing and preserving amity and good relations, between the employers and workmen and, to that end, to comment upon matters of their common interest or concern and endeavour to compose any material differences of opinion in respect of such matters."

It was the first legislative measure for promoting good relations between the employers and workmen in India. It hoped to provide a platform where both parties could meet, discuss and resolve problems of the common interests. Such an opportunity would infuse spirit of cooperation by removing misunderstanding. The legislative measure was framed with a right spirit and in right direction. The number of Works Committees set-up in India rose from 1142 in 1951 to 2574 in 1959-60. The Works Committees had shown satisfactory progress in the beginning. It was appreciated much in first plan but the experiences were not uniform everywhere. Soon there had been allegations and counter allegations from both sides. Reviewing the working of the Works Committees in India, the Indian Institute of Personnel Management has remarked that in practice it rarely worked out as intended. It has remarked:

> "Some blamed the legislators for not defining more closely the objects and functions of the Works Committee, but the fact remains that one cannot compel people by law to cooperate. They can be forced to sit together, but that does not produce joint consultation if the spirit is not there behind the legal machinery. Management, with a few exceptions, were skeptical of the value of joint consultation; the trade unions were frankly suspicious."

The Indian Institute of Personnel Management has accepted that Works Committee's experiment had been failure. However in some places it has functioned well. The system has worked well where both the sides were convinced of its value and are willing to listen on other side in each case. The institute observed that:

> "Works Committees, however, have generally been more successful where they have confined themselves to the sphere of working conditions, welfare amenities and social activities and have avoided discussion of any subject which is normally a matter for negotiation between management and organised Labour."

In spite of its failure, whatever little success has been achieved is the source of encouragement to this new experiment. There might have been many courses for its failure somewhere but those failures should not be discouraging.

The Indian Institute of Personnel Management had assessed that the Works Committees wherever successful have followed a common pattern, as remarked in the following lines:

> "At first the committee was little more than a grievance committee an opportunity for airing individual grievances and complaints—and the attitude of the members a mixture of aggressiveness and false dignity. Managers were on the defensive and inclined to oppose

every suggestion that was made and to consider attendance at the works committee a waste of time. To get beyond this stage required patience and perseverance on the part of the Personnel Officer, who was usually joint secretary of the Committee. He found he had to educate management representatives as well as workers' representatives, is the real objects of the committee and the right attitude to adopt. Sometimes it was extremely difficult to obtain any constructive suggestions from the workers' representatives, and managements found that to encourage the right approach they had themselves to propose improvements for instance better amenities and have them discussed and endorsed by the works committee in order to have some positive results to show to the employees as a whole."

The Government's decision to set-up and encourage Joint Production Committees, a second step in this new system of industrial relations, through means of persuasion was also a right step but the industrial environment was not ripe for such a quick experiment in India on western pattern.

A little success, whatever India had, showed the seed for future growth. The legislative step under Industrial Disputes Act, 1947, encouragement for the establishment of Joint Production Committee and the first five year plan envisaging faster economic growth laid down bright future for a joint consultation machinery in India. The Government, the industrial organisations and the trade unions were separately and jointly discussing the various problems confronting joint consultation. The Indian Institute of Personnel Management in its 8th Annual Conference had reviewed the joint consultation machinery and laid down the following prerequisites for the success of joint consultation—

(i) Works Committees should be recommendatory in function,

(ii) Some provision should be made to include supervisory levels in these consultatives bodies;

(iii) Information about the work done in a consultative body should be widely disseminated and steps should be taken to ensure that the supervisory levels are not short circuited;

(iv) Subjects discussed in joint consultative bodies should not encroach, in any way, on such spheres as are normally the subject of management union negotiations;

(v) It is desirable that workers' representatives in consultative bodies should be employees of the organisation concerned; and

(vi) Measures like making it compulsory that the chair manship of a joint consultative committee should go to an employees' representative and a management representative alternately should be avoided.

It was also a matter of discussion at the All India Labour Welfare Officers Conference, Nagpur in December 1955. The conference had accepted the principle of associating the workers in the administration of industries, though it also felt that the time was not still ripe for full participation and that the whole process had best been gradual, the idea was put forward in a concrete form in the industrial policy resolution of the 30th April, 1956.

It was stated there in that "in a socialist democracy, labour is a partner in the common task of development and should participate in it with enthusiam... There should be joint consultation and workers and technicians should, wherever possible, be associated progressively, with management." The idea received official recognition when a specific recommendation in this connection was made in the Second Five Year Plan as one of the progressive measures of labour policy. The plan stated:

> "For the successful implementation of the plan increased association of labour with management is necessary. Such a measure would help in (a) promoting increased productivity for the general benefit of the enterprise, the employees and the community, (b) giving employees a better understanding of their role in the working of industry and of the prices of production, and (c) satisfying the workers' wage for self-expression, thus, leading to industrial peace, better relations and increased

cooperation. This could be achieved by providing for councils of management consisting of representatives of management, technicians and workers. It should be the responsibility of the management to supply such a council of management a fair and correct statement of all relevant information which would enable the council to function effectively. A council of management should be entitled to discuss various matters pertaining to the establishment and to recommend steps for its better working. The matter which falls within the purview of collective bargaining should, however, be excluded from the scope of discussion in the council. To begin with the proposal should be tried out in large establishments in organised industries. The pace of advance should be regulated and any extension of the scheme, should be in the light of the experience gained.

The idea of Joint Management Council was still a new one and required thorough study before it could be adopted widely in Indian conditions. Hence, subsequent to the publication of the Second Five Year Plan, the Government of India sent a tripartite study group to Europe to study the working of the joint consultation and labour participation in those countries and to submit its finding on a suitable scheme for India.

The Report of the Study Group was considered at the 15th Indian Labour conference held at New Delhi in July 1957. The Conference accepted most of the recommendations of the study group. The only departure was in respect of premissive legislation. Since the employers were willing to introduce schemes of workers' participation in selected industrial units on a voluntary basis. The Conference felt that no legislative measures be adopted for a period of two years. If, however, this experiment did not succeed, steps might be taken to bring in legislation.

The Sub-committee, tripartite in nature, set-up on August, 6 1757 considering the details regarding the scheme of labour-management cooperation had laid down the following criterias.

(1) The undertaking should have a well established, strong trade union functioning.

(2) There should be readiness in the parties, viz,

employers, workers and the union to tryout the experiment in a spirit of willing cooperation.

(3) The size of the undertaking (in terms of employment) should be atleast 500 workers (Shri Kulkarni suggested that a few units with less than 500 workers might be tried in the pilot stage to make it easier to watch the impediments and ractify them. It was agreed that three or four such units might be taken up in addition to those contained in agreed list).

(4) The employer in the private sector be a member of one or the other of leading employers' organisations should the trade union be related to one of the central federations.

(5) The undertaking should have a fair record of industrial relations.

20-Point Economic Programme and Participative Management

For more effective and speedy economic development in the country, the 20-point economic programme was adopted. Under this programme the scheme for workers' association in industry was announced on October 30, 1975, which provides for setting up Shop Councils and Joint Councils in industries.

Shop Councils

The main features of the scheme of participative management through Shop Councils may be as follows:

(i) In every industrial unit employing 500 or more workmen, the employer constitutes a Shop Council for each department or shop or one council for more than one department or shop, considering the number of workmen employed in different departments or shops.

(ii) (a) Each council consists of an equal number of representatives of employers and workers; (b) the employers' representatives are nominated by the management and must consist of persons from the unit concerned, (c) all the representatives of workmen are from amongst the workers actually engaged in the department or the shop concerned.

(iii) The employer decides in consultation with the recognised union or the various registered trade unions, or with workers as the case may be, in the manner best suited to local conditions, the number of shop councils and departments to be attached to each council of the undertaking or the establishments;

(iv) The number of members of each council is determined by the employer in consultation with the recognised union, registered unions or workers in the manner best suited to local conditions obtaining in the unit, the total number of members may not generally exceed 12;

(v) All decisions of a Shop Council are on the basis of consensus and not by a process of voting, provided that either party may refer the unsettled matters to the Joint Council for consideration;

(vi) Every decision of a Shop Council is implemented by the parties concerned within a period of one month unless otherwise stated in the decision itself and compliance report shall be submitted to the council;

(vii) Such decisions of a Shop Council which have a bearing on another shop, or the undertakings or establishment as a whole are referred to the joint council for consideration and decision;

(viii) A Shop Council once formed, functions for a period of two years. Any member nominated or elected to the council in the mid-term to fill a casual vacancy shall continue to be a member of the council for the unexpired portion of the term of the council;

(ix) The council meets as frequently as is necessary and at least once in a month; and

(x) The Chairman of the Shop Council is a nominee of the management, the worker members of the council shall elect a Vice-Chairman from amongst themselves.

Functions of Shop Councils

The shop councils in the interest of increasing production, productivity and overall efficiency of the shop/department attend to the following matters:

(i) Assist management in achieving monthly/yearly production targets;
(ii) Improvement of production, productivity and efficiency, including elimination of wastage and optimum utilisation of machine capacity and manpower;
(iii) Specifically identify areas of low productivity and take necessary corrective steps at shop level to eliminate relevant contributing factors;
(iv) To study absenteeism in the shops/departments and recommend step to reduce them;
(v) Safety measures;
(vi) Assist in maintaining general discipline in the shop/ departments;
(vii) Physical conditions of working, such as, lighting, ventilation, noise, dust, etc. and reduction of fatigue;
(viii) Welfare and health measures to be adopted for efficient running of the shop/department; and
(ix) Ensure proper flow of adequate two way communications between the management and the workers, particularly on matters relating to production figures, production schedules and progress in achieving the targets.

Joint Councils

In every industrial unit employing 500 or more workers, there is a joint council for the whole unit. The main features of the scheme of joint council are as follows:

(i) Only such persons who are actually engaged in the unit can be members of the joint council;
(ii) The council functions for a period of two years;
(iii) The chief executive of the unit is the chairman of the joint council, there is a vice-chairman who is nominated by worker-members of the council;
(iv) The joint council appoints one of the members of the council as its secretary. Necessary facilities for the efficient discharge of function by the secretary are provided within the premises of the undertaking/ establishment;

(v) The term of the council, once formed is for a period of two years, if, however, a member is nominated in the mid-term of the council to fill a casual vacancy, the member nominated in such vacancy continue in office for the remaining period of the term of the council;

(vi) The joint council meets at least once in a quarter; and

(vii) Every decision of the joint council are taken be on the basis of consensus and not by a process of voting and are binding on employers and workmen and are implemented within one month unless otherwise stated in the decision itself.

Functions of Joint Council

The Joint Council looks after the matters relating to:

(i) Optimum production, efficiency and fixation of productivity norms of man and machine for the unit as a whole;

(ii) Functions of shop council which have a bearing on another shop or the unit as a whole;

(iii) Matters emanating from shop councils which remain unresolved;

(iv) Matters concerning the unit or the plant as a whole, in respect of matters relating to work planning and achieving production targets; more specifically, tasks assigned to a shop council at the shop department levels but relevant to the unit as a whole will be taken up by the joint councils;

(v) The development of skills of workmen and adequate facilities for training;

(vi) The preparation of schedules of working hours and of holidays;

(vii) Awarding of rewards for valuable and creative suggestions received from workers;

(viii) Optimum use of raw materials and quality of finished products; and

(ix) General health, welfare and safety measures for the unit or the plant.

Composition

There is a considerable diversity in the situation prevailing from unit to unit in different industries. Even departmental undertakings and public enterprises under the same ministry of the Government of India, have had to adopt different system depending upon the local conditions and their individual needs. Keeping this diversity in view, no uniform pattern is being laid down for the constitution of Shops Councils and Joint Councils, particularly relating to the representation of workers. The management in consultation with workers should evolve the most suitable pattern of representation so as to ensure that the representation of the workers results in effective meaningful and broad-based participation of workers.

Communication

For any scheme of workers participation to succeed, there must be an effective two-day communication and exchange of information between the management and the workmen. It is only then the workers would have a better appreciation of the problems and difficulties of the undertaking and of its overall functioning. With this end in view, each unit should devise a suitable system of communication within the undertaking.

Works Committee

The Work Committee as prescribed under the Industrial Disputes Act shall continue to function as it at present.

Appropriate Government

The scheme not being statutory, the concept of "appropriate government" as in the I.D. Act is not relevant. However, the Central and State Governments have an important role in promoting the healthy and speedy implementation of the scheme in as large a number of units as possible. While the initiative for the introduction of the scheme will mainly be with undertakings concerned, all matters relating to the operation of the scheme will be death with by the Central Government in the case of the public sector/departmental units of the Central Government.

Government are aware that it is only providing for such arrangements for workers' participation particularly at the shop floor and unit level that the involvement of workers in the effective functioning of the unit and in improving production and productivity can be ensured. Government would, therefore, appeal to all the managements and workmen and trade unions concerned to take speedy and effective measures for the early adoption of the scheme in their units and for its continued healthy functioning.

With high hope the scheme for workers participation in management was framed at tripartite level. By then the internal industrial environment had become more favourable. The managements had became more enlightened. The workers had become more conscious, educated and responsible. The Government had become eager for giving a trial of such a scheme on voluntary basis. The development of understanding at national level between the parties was an indicator of favourable climate in the country.

The new scheme for workers' participation in industry has been given wide experiment both in public and private sectors. By now the two parties have realised the importance of this new scheme. The industrial environment has become gradually favourable for success of a scheme. The workers have become conscious and are acquiring knowledge and ability to discharge this new role. Setting aside the traditional outlook, the managements have shown the willingness to give a fair trial to this new scheme. This scheme has brought a new hope in the human relations for reaping good harvest for all.

Association of Work and Management

The Scheme Comments on

After prolong negotiation an agreement was arrived at on January 8, 1956 between the Tata Steel management and Tata Workers Union. Agreement covers many aspects of collective bargaining. On the present issue, the agreements clause No. 15 stated that "an increasing measure of closer association of workers with management in the working of the industry was desirable because it would help

(a) In promoting increased productivity for the general benefit of the enterprise, the employees and the country,

(b) In giving employees a better understanding of their role and importance in the working of the industry and in the process of production, and

(c) In satisfying the urge for self-expression."

The preamble of the agreement clearly laid down that the purpose of the agreement was to establish and maintain orderly and cordial relations between the company and the union so as to promote the interests of the employees covered by this agreement and efficient operation of the company's business. The parties realised the importance and need of maintaining such good and cooperative labour-management relations for the effective and timely implementation of the scheme of modernisation and expansion programme involving a capital expenditure of about Rs.110 crores.

Three tier structure of Joint Councils opened a new chapter in the history of industrial relations, particularly association of employees with management, not only in the TISCO or the Iron and Steel Industry but in the whole country. The agreement was hailed by all sections of the society like the Government, the management, the workers, the press and the public. At the time of signing August 1956 agreement J.R.D. Tata had accepted that:

> "Our task in devising means for a closer association between employees and the management was made easier by the fact that over the years, we have already established machinery for joint consultation on many subjects. The steps we are now taking is a further advance, and a big one, in the same direction."

He further added that:

> "If life is to be breathed into the Scheme, there must be on both sides a spirit of friendly cooperation in which individual or sectarian interests make way for the interests of the community as a whole."

A similar opinion was expressed by Michel John, the then President of the T.W.U., when he said that if the agreement succeeded then "Tatas and the Union would have set an example of having done the best for the industry, the workers and the country."

> "The agreement would provide opportunities to the workers to acquire knowledge and skill so essential for managing industries and when India achieved her goal of socialist pattern of society, they would be well prepared to play a full and effective part in running the country's industries."

Indian Worker, the weekly journal of the I.N.T.U.C. to which the TWU is affiliated, in its editorial column had lauded in the following words:

> "The recently concluded agreement between the Tata Workers' Union and the Tata Iron and Steel Company is a landmark not only in the history of the Union, but also in the history of trade unionism in India. ...In our view the agreement is a pointer to the social change which is taking place in India. It gives concrete shape to the concept of workers' participation in management of industries, thereby implementing the resolution on the subject adopted at the Eighth Annual Conference of the INTUC at Surat."

The Hindustan Times, a Delhi newspaper, welcoming this agreement as of great historical importance contained:

> "President of the Tata Workers' Union, has hailed this development as a major advance towards a socialist pattern of society... the privilege of giving the lead, however, has gone to private enterprise and the course of the experiment at Jamshedpur will have a lot to teach not only to private employers but also to managers of the nationalised undertakings."

The comment of the *Hindustan Times* was really an assessment full of appreciation of the private enterprise which has acted as a pioneer in this field of human relations and industrial democracy. If other industrial establishments could follow the footsteps of TISCO definitely the industrial relations environment in India would provide congenial atmosphere for speedy economic growth. The National Press described the agreement as "industrial history." Thus, the agreement set-up a new stage for greater and closer cooperation between labour and management in future.

To ensure effective functioning of these councils the management provides relevant information, data and statistics. It has established joint consultation section under the charge of a Manager. This section serves as liaison between the various Departmental Councils and Joint Councils and coordinates their activities.

The Government of India came forward with a new industrial relations policy designed under Industrial Disputes Act, 1947. The Industrial Disputes Act, 1947 brought statutory obligation on the employers to establish Works committee. It was the first major step towards the establishment of industrial democracy in India. The Works Committee provided a platform for discussions between the representatives of the workers and the management on common matters. In accordance with this legislative provision the Tata Steel management reconstituted these two committees in 1948. Five Works committees were set-up, each of them covering departments having similar operation and production problems. Grievance procedure was also placed in the organisation where by reference to the committee was included.

In the field of employees association with management in TISCO, one more step was added in 1950, when the Trade Test Specification Committee was set-up. This committee was entrusted with the task of specification of the trade tests, which is important for appointment, job-classification and wage structure. The committee consists of two management representatives and two union representatives besides the chairman. This again opened a new chapter in the history of association of employees with the management in TISCO.

The successful functioning of these joint committees acted as morale booster for the progressive managerial personnel of Tata Steel. In order to prepare a detail scheme of joint consultation machinery, a British expert was engaged in 1952. The British expert suggested the setting up of joint consultative machinery.

This shows that the Tata Steel management was eager for adopting a more constructive policy for utilising the experiences of its employees, for taking workers in confidence and for giving psychological satisfaction. Three years later, a top official of the company was sent to West Germany attending an international conference on joint consultation and later to study the various patterns of employees association with management in a number of European countries, such as West Germany, Belgium, Sweden and Yugoslavia. On the basis of his report and after an intensive study of all aspects of the matter, the Tata Steel was well set to formulate its plan for a machinery for closer association of employees with management in keeping with its traditions and suited to its needs.

During the decade 1946-56, in the Tata Steel altogether 24 joint committees were formed for dealing with grievances, wages rates, minimum qualifications and employees services. During the same period in order to have greater employees association with the operational performance of the production departments, there had been formation of six Advisory Development and Production Committees, having equal number of representatives from the management and the union. These committees discussed all problems having a bearing on production and recommended suitable corrective measures to the management.

The establishment of six Advisory Development and Production Committees had certain special features to its credit. Firstly, these committees consisted of equal number of representatives of both sides having equal status. Secondly, it was the first time that union came in picture for sending representatives. Thirdly, these committees were advisory in nature but it concerned with production and other development of the company. Thus, the expanding scope of the committee was of greater importance as probably for the first time it crossed the early limitation of employees services. And lastly, it was matter of appreciation that these committees had recommended many corrective measures for improvement of production, both in quantity and quality. Thus, these special features of the joint committees laid down ground for better understanding and industrial relations in the course.

References

Allan Flanders and H.A. Clegg, *op. cit.*, p. 354.

Government of India, Report of the National Commission on Labour, 1969, p. 345, par. 24.14.

Government of India, Report of the Second Pay Commission, 1959, p. 551.

Ibid., par. 24.13.

Ibid., par. 24.15.

Rastogi, J.L., *op. cit.*, p. 9.

T.E. Chester and Gardner Foresight, "Concept of Joint Consultation in Great Britain", *Indian Journal of Labour Economics*, Vol. II, Nos. 2-3, July-October 1959, pp. 141-42.

The typical example being South Metropolitan Gas Company.

U.K. Industrial Relations Handbook, 1961, p. 23.

Chamberlin, W. Neil (1951), "Collective Bargaining", Mc Graw Hill, New York.

INTUC: Eight Annual Conference at Surat.

Robertson, D.H., "The Control of Industry."

The Hindustan Times, New Delhi.

Trade Unions and Management

Trade unions have become an integral and powerful factor in the contemporary system of producing and distributing goods and services. Wherever modern industrialization has touched, trade unions have followed. They are exercising a strong influence on the methods of production of goods and services, their distribution, the allocation of economic resources, the volume of employment and unemployment, the character of rights and privileges, politics and policies of governments, the attitude of millions of persons, the status and standing of large masses of the population and the very "nature of economic and social organisations. Under such conditions, their role has evoked deep and wide controversies." For a developing economy such as ours, trade unions and their policies are of special significance. Therefore, in order to assess their role and prospects, it is essential to go into the origin and development of the trade union movement and to analyse the factors that have helped the trade unions become a mighty torrential movement from very small and moderate beginnings.

Definition

Numerous authors and books have discussed the origin, growth, structure and functions of trade unions without formulating a formal definition of a trade union. Of all the definitions of a trade union, one by the Webbs—is the most outstanding and oft-quoted. The Webbs say, "A Trade Union, as we understand the term, is a continuous association of wage-earners for the purpose of maintaining or improving the conditions- of their working lives." Dankert thus formulates what he calls a comprehensive general definition, "A Trade Union is a continuing organization of employees established for the purpose of protecting or improving, through collective action, the economic and social status of its members."

A comparison of these two definitions shows that Dankert has not been able to improve upon the Webbs' definition in any significant manner, except that the expression "wage-earners" has been substituted by the term "employees" and Dankert has added the expression "collective action" as the trade union method, whereas the, Webbs are silent in this regard. As there are numerous differences in the structure, objectives, methods, types and conditions of membership of the organizations going by the common name of "trade union", it is difficult to evolve a definition which will cover all unions in all their distinguishing features. Ultimately, a union is "what it does" or unionism is "what it is."

It is needless to go into the controversies raised by the Webbs' definition or other definitions, for, however a 'trade union' is defined; the functions of trade unions have become too well-established to be mistaken and no particular definition is necessary in order to recognize and specify the main features of a trade union. Different definitions simply seek to emphasize those particular aspects and functions of trade unions which different authors may have in their view. As the discussion on the objectives of, and the methods adopted by trade unions for the achievement of their goals progresses, various definitions will unfold themselves.

GENESIS AND GROWTH OF TRADE UNIONS

Genesis of the TUs can be traced back to the industrial revolution itself. The miserable conditions prevailing at work and home at the time have been brought out vividly in various writings (Cole, 1962a; Engels, 2002; Hobsbawm, 1988; Kuczynski, 1975; Morton, 1974). Workers began to organise as early as the 18th century and their movements gained momentum by the beginning of the 19th century as they realised that the only way to fight against the conditions like the one described below—a description of the wage payment at a textile factory in Germany around the 1840s—was to organise

> "The suffering faces of these wretches, the silent agony in their features which cried vengeance louder than the yelling of a revolutionary mob, the joy of one who hurried home with wages intact, the sobs of another who suddenly saw himself cheated of half his earnings, the rasping voice of the foreman who waved a stick threateningly if anyone was impertinent enough to rear his head indignantly like a crushed worm, the swearing of the clerks who called for peace and quiet lest they miscalculate a single farthing, the grinning book-keeper who, in his brutal, lewd way, gloated with delight over the whole proceedings, and finally the chink of money, of sordid metal, which was the reason for the enactment of this whole performance. Really, the factory counting house on this day, as on every Saturday, presented a spectacle which could not be grosser, more vulgar or more hideous if one found it in a brothel, a robbers' lair or a gambling den" (Kuczynski, 1975, p. 76).

Factory labour consisted of "the scum of every class and every occupation" (Marglin, 1974). Around the same time, Marx (1978a, p. 234) quotes a 12-year-old child, worker in the potteries of Staffordshire, England:

> "I turn jigger, and run moulds. I come at 6. Sometimes I come at 4. I worked alt night last night, till 6 o'clock this morning. I have not been in bed since the night before last. There were eight or nine other boys working last night. All but one have come this morning. I get 3 shilling and six pence. I do not get any more for working at night. I worked two nights last week."

Workers were quick to realise that they were 'doubly unfree'—capitalist could exercise an arbitrary authority at work; moreover, they had no choice but to sell their labour power in order to survive (Bagchi, 2002). By the middle of the 19th century 'profession' of 'proletarian' had spread far and wide to tens of millions of workers as Blanqui observed for France in 1832 (Kuczynski, 1975). Gradually, the proletariat internalised their 'profession' across industrialising nations. In the words of railway 'navvies' of Germany as Wilhem Wolff put it (see Kuczynski, 1975, p. 215).

> "If we are ill and weak, we may lie down and chew potatoes—if there are any—or die on a dung-heap for all the rich man cares. But there is one advantage in all this for us. We have flocked together in our thousands, we have come to know one another, and in the whole long business of give and take, most of us have become more sensible.... (W)e are the real supporters of the wealthy, we need only to be unwilling to work, and they will be compelled to beg us for their bread and butter or starve, unless they are willing to work themselves."

Workers gradually realised that organising themselves was the only way to deter the double onslaught of wage-cutting by the owners and replacement by machines. The following quote of Tonny Ramsay, a pioneer of trade unionism among the Durham miners in the middle of the 19th century, captures the sentiment (Morton, 1974, p. 44):

> "Lads unite and better your condition. When eggs are scarce, eggs are dear; When men are scarce, men are dear."

The primary assumption of early TU organisations was that the workers were an indispensable component for production process, and therefore, negotiations and fruitful bargaining was possible by virtue of a possible disruption, or in extreme circumstances, even stoppage of work through mobilisation of workers. In fact, the first influential unions were formed by highly skilled workers coming from craft traditions (Sirianni, 1982). Cole (1962c) concludes that the TUs were formed to protect "standards of living or the dignity of their crafts." Nineteenth century was full of expectations from trade unions and labour organisations. Marx and Engels hoped that they would create political consciousness amongst the working classes for a revolutionary movement. They envisioned of the proletarian movement as "the self-conscious independent movement of the immense majority" (Marx and Engels, 1977). Engels remarked that, "as schools of war (against capitalism), the unions are unexcelled" (Engels, 2002). Marx hoped that the TU activity would lead to worker solidarity beyond the structural context of the capitalist order and facilitate forging of class consciousness (Clements, 1978). Geneva Congress of the First International expressed the hope that the unions would "promote the abolition of the very system of wage labour" (Lozovsky, 1975). Even Lenin, who in *What is to be Done?* denied the possibility of development of workers' consciousness through TU struggles, was more hopeful about them both before and after this writing (Hyman, 1971). In 1899, Lenin (1960, p. 317) emphasised: "(S)ocialists call strikes 'a school of war', a school in which the workers learn to make war on their enemies for which the liberation of the whole people, of all who labour, from the yoke of government officials and from the yoke of capital."

However, the trade unions could not live upto these expectations and some of the hopes pinned on them were belied even during the lifetimes of early proponents, like Marx and Engels. They realised the tension between the potential for radical practice of the TUs on the one side and getting co-opted as a capitalist institution on the other (Hyman, 1987). In 1858, Engels lamented: "(T)he English proletariat is becoming more and more bourgeois ..." (Morton, 1974). While addressing the General Council of the International Working Men's Association in 1865, Marx (1978b, p. 55) observed:

> "Instead of the conservative motto, 'a fair day's wage for a fair day's work!' they (working classes) ought to inscribe on their banner the revolutionary watchword 'abolition of the wages system!'"

The primary reason for the conservativism of the TUs can be attributed to the increasing superfluity of the workers themselves in the production process belying the premise of a labour organisation. Marx, in his first volume of Capital, propounds a brilliant analysis of how more 'efficient' forms of production lead to extreme waste of human labour (see Engels, 1978, p. 66): "(M)achinery becomes the most powerful weapon in the war of capital against the working class; that the instruments of labour constantly tear the means of subsistence out of the hands of the labourer; that the very product of the worker is turned into an instrument for his subjugation. ...That machinery, the most powerful instrument for shortening labour time, becomes the most unfailing means for placing every moment of the labourer's time and that of his family at the disposal of the capitalist for the purpose of expanding the value of his capital."

In sum, one cannot emphasise strongly enough that the trade unions have played a historic role in the institutionalisation of labour rights across the world. In fact, the TUs had a key role in creating the parliamentary democracy based on universal adult suffrage, the idea of which can be probably traced back to the Chartist movement. Thompson (1980) stresses that militant working class movement was a primary force behind the institution of free and popular press, cheaply available to the working class, in the 19th century England. Thus, the English working class was 'made' approximately over a century after the onset of industrial revolution. By the time of the Second World War, trade unions as institutions, and some minimum political and economic rights for workers, were legally recognised almost across the three worlds, though there were differences amongst them. As Amin (2000) says, capital had to make historical compromises because of its weakened position *vis-a-vis* labour in the post World War II scenario. Hobsbawm (1964) observed that labour movement was an organisation of selfdefence, of protests, and of revolution. Yet paradoxically, as labour rights got institutionalised in the form of trade unions across the world by the middle of the 20" century, the scope of unionism receded from revolution to protest and finally to defend the privileges already gained by the unionised strata of the working classes. From means of compromise, unions themselves became the end of the compromise!

Authors and students of the trade union movement may differ with regard to the proper functions, objectives, role and methods of trade unions, but they are all agreed that the trade union movement is the result of the modern industrialization. Though attempts have been made to trace the ancestry of the trade unions to the medieval period and even to earlier ages, they have not succeeded in any convincing manner.

Institutions grow to meet the needs of a particular time and place. Trade unions have grown in response to the peculiar needs and problems which the wage earners have had to face in the course of industrialization under the capitalist economic system. What are the features of the process of industrialization that have necessitated the origin of trade unions.

1. Separation between Capital and Labour

England of the second half of the eighteenth century is the first home of trade unions it was during this period that the economic system of England was undergoing rapid changes. An economic order, commonly known as the capitalist economic system, emerged. New industries based on iron and coal came into existence; they underwent rapid technological changes; and large-scale production replaced the small workshops of the past. In the preindustrial society, the worker producer owned his tools, provided his own raw materials, worked in his own home, owned the final product mostly for his own consumption and occasionally for sale in the market. The worker was his own master, his own capitalist and his own seller. 'But under the new economic system, demanding a large accumulation of capital and congregation of a large number of workmen-at one place, capital and labour—came to be supplied by two different sets of persons'.

The capitalist mode of industrialisation has involved a separation between the ownership of capital and labour, both of which are necessary for the production of goods and services. As a matter of fact, the moderti factory system was preceded by the creation of a class of landless labourers the proletariat which had no other means of livelihood except the use of its labour power. Similarly, a class of owners of capital grew which used its capital for earning profits. A class of people came to the labour, market to sell its labour power—the only source of its livelihood, and became the sellers of labour. The other class, with large aggregates of capital at its disposal, came to the labour market to buy labour power and to put it to productive use. As buyers, they were interested in paying the lowest possible price and, as suppliers of labour, the labourers were interested in securing the highest possible price. Thus, the two classes with divergent and conflicting interests came together giving rise to a conflicting relationship. The capitalist econoraic order is based upon the notion that the pursuit of his self-interest by every individual leads to the establishment of an economic and social order which serves best the interests of all concerned. The capitalist economic system is an order of all pervading conflict of interests.

The owners of capital and the entrepreneurs are motivated by the goals of profit maximisation. This drive of profit-making led to excesses in the early phases of industtial revolution which initiated the process of industrialisation. Excessive hours of work, insanitary working and living conditions, overcrowding, the employment of young children, inflicting of corporal punishment for the maintenance of industrial discipline, competitive debasement of wages and unemployment—were the main features of industrialisation under early capitalism. Wherever industrialisation went under the capitalist framework, these processes were repeated. Widespread poverty and misery resulted from the working of an unbridled competitive economy. In vain did the workers try to protect their economic interests and status by submitting petitions to kings, courts and parliaments invoking the implementation of protective regulations of the medieval period.

2. *Philosophy of* laissez faire

The dominant philosophy of *laissez faire* and economic liberalism prevented the State from coming to the rescue of the suffering mass of industrial workers. In the eyes of law, the workers and the employers were equal and had equal claims to the protection afforded by it. Their relationship was supposed to be based upon freedom of contract, freely and voluntarily entered into. The disgruntled, dissatisfied and oppressed workers were supposed to be freepersons; they were free to choose their employers, occupations and place of work and they were free not to work under terms and conditions which they did not like. The terms and conditions of employment were further supposed to be determined by bargaining between the individual workman and his employer on the basis of equality: Under these prevailing notions and doctrines, the State remained silent and, through a policy of non-intervention in the economic life of the community, further hightened the degree of exploitation, misery and suffering of the working class. Even the rudimentary protections that the craftsmen enjoyed in the medieval times disappeared under the impact of rising capitalism.

3. Lack of Bargaining Power on the Part of Workers

Whatever might have been the position and the status of the industrial workers in the eyes of law, in reality, the individual workman, deprived of any independent means of livelihood and being the seller of the most perishable commodity, was no match for his employer either in the bargaining skill or in the knowledge of the trade and market conditions or in economic resources and waiting power. The freedoms of the labour market were illusory and non-existent. It was the competition between a pigmy and giant that, as a matter of fact, determined the terms and conditions of employment in favour of the latter. It was the employer who unilaterally determined the wage rates, the hours of work and other conditions of employment without any semblance of bargaining. The workers had either to accept the job on the terms and conditions offered by the employers or to give it up, remain unemployed and starve. The individual workman was dispensable to the employer. The mass of the 'reserve army' of the unemployed was always knocking at the factory gates looking for employment to take the place of the workmen who dared defy the employer. It is logical and natural that the workers accepted the former. To have a job was always better than to have none.

4. Individual Dispensability but Collective Indispensability

However, under these deteriorating conditions and all-enveloping darkness, there was one ray of light and hope for the working class. The individual workman was dispensable to the employer but workmen, collectively, were indispensable to him. The employer could easily and always get rid of the services of a few workmen and replace them by others, but he could not dispense with the services of all his workmen and readily replace them. Though it took a long time to come, it must have been a great moment in the history of the working class when this realisation came. It is also true that this realisation has not come to many workers of many countries even today. But when it came, it heralded the dawn of a new day after a long and dreary night, of mute submission to the economic needs of the employers, to their whims and vagaries and to the so-called natural laws of the economic system.

Emergence of Trade Unionism

It was under these conditions that the workers' organizations employer, faced with common problems and common tasks, deve***loped*** common sentiments. They developed group interpretations and reactions to the external environment, social and economic situations and tried to organise themselves into associations which could meet the employers on the basis of equality. Thus, "labour's organizations and concerted efforts, owe their inception and growth to one of the most basic of the problems of social life, the struggle for possession of material things, and to some of the most powerful of human motivations."

There were many hurdles to be crossed before the inchoate labour organizations could develop into full-fledged stable trade unions. There were internal dissentions, persistent and determined opposition from the employers, merciless persecution and suppression by the State and full-throated condemnation of trade unionism by the advocates of free competition and *laissez faire*. The incipient labour organisations, which had their birth during the last quarter of the 18th century in England and much later in other countries, survived the many pronged attacks against them and succeeded in overcoming formidable obstacles. They, finally passing through many vicissitudes of fortune, have come to occupy an integral and prominent place in the economic and social life of today. This shows the inherent strength of the working class and the utility of such organizations in meeting the changing needs of time.

The foregoing few pages give a brief outline of the processes of economic, social and political changes that led to the emergence of the trade union movement. Of these processes of change, the State's attitude of utter indifference and connivance at the sufferings and privations of the working masses arising from the capitalist system of production stands out most prominent. It was this indifference that induced and forced the workers to rely on their own strength of unity, combination and concerted efforts when they felt helpless and desperate in the face of, deepening capitalist exploitation.

One may. say that machine is the cause and the labour movement is the result; "another may say that the trace union appears as a group interpretation of the social situation in which workers find themselves, and as a remedial programme in the form of aims, policies and methods;' still another may say that trade unionism arises from the job consciousness and scarcity of job opportunities." Nonetheless, it may also be contended that labour organizations, perhaps, would not have emerged-but for the attitude of the State which exhibited, in, the early-periods of modern industrialisation, a callous disregard to the sufferings and the needs of the toiling masses.... If the State had shown even a modicum of responsibility for the protection and welfare of the working class which it is doing in many cases at present, labour organizations, perhaps, would not have come into existence and if they had, they would have taken a course, pursued policies and adopted methods, different from those existing today.

Legal and Other Handicaps of Early Trade Unions

When the growing sufferings and disabilities of workers arising from the ruthless exploitation by the capitalist employers, the gradual disappearance of the customary and traditional protective legal sanctions and the indifference of the State forced the workers to organise, the State, not being content with an attitude of indifference, came down hard on the trade unions. "Combinations of workmen to better their conditions were declared illegal as early as the fourteenth century, and every century thereafter, the law put down such combinations to the harshness with which attempts were made to suppress the trade unions after the advent of the factory system was unprecedented. In England, France, in Germany and in the United States, combinations of workmen per se were declared illegal. The judges punished the members. of trade unions and participants in strikes with imprisonment and fines. Trade unions were treated as criminal conspiracies, functioning in restraint of trade, violating freedom of contract, and inducing workmen to break their contracts with the employers.

The British Parliament enacted the Combination Acts, 1799 and 1800 prohibiting the workmen from combining and declaring any such combinations illegal. It would not be out of place to quote here from a judgment of 1816 sentencing, nine Stockport hatters to two years' imprisonment for conspiracy. The Judge, Sir William Garrow, in a judgment, remarked, "In this happy country where the law puts the meanest subject on a level with the highest personages of the realm, all are alike protected, and there can be no need to associate.... A person, who like Mr. Jackson has employed from 100 to 130 hands, common gratitude would teach us to look upon him as a benefactor to the community." It would not serve any purpose to fill in pages with quotations from numerous judgments, but one or two more quotations would illustrate the point sought to be made here. In the U.S.A. also, the courts, while interpreting the common law and its application to labour organisations applied to them the same doctrine of criminal conspiracy and restraint of trader In the Philadelphia Cordwainers Case of 1806, the court, with untroubled simplicity, declared that "a combination .of workmen to raise their wages may be considered from a two-fold point of view; one is to benefit themselves, the other in to injure those who do not join their society. The rule of law condemns both." This was not, a rare judgment in the U.S.A.; the viewpoint was reiterated with or without modifications in many judgments. In India as late as 1921 in the Buckingham and Carnatic Mills case, the Madras Labour Union led, by Wadia was indicted as a criminal conspiracy and damages were awarded against the union.

In spite of these efforts at suppression, trade unions continued to grow, sometimes working underground and sometimes openly, and the land of law failed to break the resistance of the workers to the excesses of capitalist factory system. They continued to defy the laws prohibiting the combination of workmen; trade union organisations multiplied and trade unionism spread. Under incessant pressures from the workers and their organisations, the law and the attitude of the courts gradually came to be modified. The history of the trade union movement everywhere is a history of blood, tears and toil. That is why Millis and Montgomery, while commenting on the British policy and law relating to labour organisations remark,

"British policy and law relating to labour combinations have undergone an interesting development from stout opposition and attempts at outright suppression to limited acceptance and toleration, then to general acceptance and comparatively few restrictions." This trend in the British policy and law relating to labour organisations is common to all capitalist countries. Trade unions in all these countries have passed through these three stages:

(a) outright suppression,
(b) limited acceptance and toleration, and
(c) general acceptance and recognition.

However, trade unions in the world today are not at the same stage of development everywhere. In some countries, especially in those 'under colonial rule and dictatorships, trade unions are struggling hard to cross the first stage; in the underdeveloped countries recently freed from colonial yoke, they are in the second stage; and in the full-fledged industrially advanced capitalist democracies, they are in the third stage. In the communist countries, trade unions occupy an altogether different position and status where they represent the workers freed from exploitation and where they do not have exploiting employers to fight.

Objectives of Trade Unions

A discussion of the objectives of trade union movement cannot be better begun than by a quotation from Samuel Gompers—the founder President of the American Federation of Labour to quote him, "Trade unions .... were born of the necessity of workers to protect and defend themselves from encroachment, injustice and wrong .... To protect the workers in their inalienable right to higher and better life; to protect them, not only as equals before the law, but also in their rights to the product of their labor; to protect their lives, their limbs, their health, their homes, their firesides, their liberties as men, as workers, as citizens; to overcome and conquer prejudice and antagonism; to secure them the right to life, and the opportunity to maintain that life; the right to be full sharers in the abundance which is the result of their brain and brawn, and the civilization of which they are the founders and the mainstay." Trade unions are essentially an organisation for the protection and promotion of the interests of their members in particular mud workers in general, as opposed to these of the employers. Tine primary function of trade unions is to protect the workers against the excesses committed by the employers and to meet other needs of the workers-economic and political.

The aims, philosophies, theories and social and economic programme of the trade union movement are all related to one supreme goal, i.e. the protection and promotion of the interests of the working class. All other objectives flow from this supreme goal. However, as this goal is sought to be achieved by multitudes of trade unions working under vastly different concrete economic, political and industrial environments, different forms of trade union organizations, different subsidiary short-term goals and different methods have emerged. These variations have to be viewed in the light of the needs of the particular situation, changing times and different levels of workers' consciousness. The long-term. goal of securing recognition to the workers' importance, their role and position in society and promoting their multilateral interests can be achieved only through short-term expediencies and subsidiary objectives. Therefore, different programmes of actions have evolved in a dynamic manner to keep abreast of the changing times. It has become custom try to differentiate between trade unions with respect to heir objective, methods, policies and programmes of actions, but one should not lose sight of the fact that all these differences are united by the ultimate common goal and are but one expression of the fact that methods and policies, in order to be successful, must be adjusted to the needs of real situations.

This generic goal of protection and promoting workers' interests consists of such specific objectives as;

(a) improved economic status;
(b) shorter working day;
(c) betterment of working and living conditions;
(d) income security, e.g. pension, provident fund, compensation for work-injuries and unemployment, obtaining job security such as protection against layoff, retrenchment and victimization, etc.;

(e) better health, safely and welfare standards;
(f) respect for the personality of the workers, humane treatment from supervisors and others;
(g) a greater voice in industrial administration and management by the establishment of industrial democracy; and
(h) improving political status.

It should be noted here that the listing of these objectives is not in order of priority nor does it indicate the relative emphasis given to them. The same union over a period of time may shift the emphasis from one objective to the other. The early unions everywhere emphasized the wage issue; much more than any others. Later on, the hours of work and still later, the income security aspects came to occupy greater prominence. Which objective will come to occupy a higher priority for which unions and when is a function of time and place?

It is pertinent here, while discussing the fundamental objectives of the trade union movement, to refer to the ideas of Perlman According to him, the trade unions have a home grown philosophy based on 'workers' experience and psychology. Trade unions, growing out of the workers day-to-day experience, have the only objective of protecting the jobs of the workers and securing day-to-day improvements in the 'working and living conditions.' Such trade unions are neither concerned with the fundamental reconstruction of the economic system nor with the various politicalisms and ideologies. It is the outside intellectuals, whether they are Marxists, Efficiency Experts or Ethical who, according, to Perlman, seek to impose political ideologies on the trade union movement. It is partly true that trade unions, left to themselves, would devote their attention to workers' sectional and temporary advantages. Being voluntary associations, trade unions are under constant pressure of the immediate and proximate needs of their members, and distant and long-term objectives may not have the same urgency.

But it is also equally true that trade unions may develop interests in political ideologies and issues on their own as they learn out of their experience and find that temporary palliatives provide no permanent cure. When the air is thick with political discussions and different view-points are under circulation regarding the nature and functions of the economic systems, it is not unnatural for many of the trade unions to get influenced by them. Thus, political ideologies and objectives may grow out of the day-to-day activities of trade unions without being imposed from outside intellectuals.

Even in the U.S.A., where the dominant trade unions express their faith in the essentials of the free enterprise system and disclaim any attachment to socialist ideals, advocates of capitalism aprrehend that the trade unions' support of capitalism would-be temporary. Walter Gordon Merritt, while surveying. the ultimate destiny of the American labour movement expresses this apprehension when he says, "A real test may come when the economic forces inherent, in the free enterprise system compel the union leader to return with an empty game bag, either because of a depression or because the system can not increase labor costs." Will labor then be satisfied to continue to accept the benefits that free enterprise has left to offer, or will new leaders, understanding the art of damagoguery and mindful of the emotions that have been nourished in the hearts of union members, possess the field with dreams of a promised land. In this context attachment to socialist ideas becomes as much a part of home-grown philosophy of labor as attachment to jobs and job-security, and political ideologies' cease to be foreign to trade-unions. It is in this context again that Merritt, while talking of the ultimate goal of unionism, quotes Gompers with apprehension, who, when questioned about the ultimate goal of unionism, said, "What does labor want? It wants the earth and the fullness thereof."

Further, it should be emphasized that changes in the economic system, whether demanded by trade unions or advocated by outside intellectuals, are not ends in themselves. They are thought to be a means for securing the permanent interests of the working class which is the supreme goal of the trade union movement as a whole. A particular trade union may not be concerned with the working class as such, but the trade union movement is.

The trade union movement in many countries and some trade unions in all countries have developed political ideologies which advocate replacement of the capitalist economic system by socialism. The legitimacy of such an ultimate political objective is questioned by many. It is in regard to the political objective of changing the capitalist economic system and replacing it by socialism that controversies are raging everywhere. It is contended that the objective of changing an economic system should really be sought by political parties competent to develop and propagate political ideologies. Trade unions as such should involve themselves in only the day-to-day working conditions of their members. Any involvement on the part of the trade unions with the fundamental political objectives of bringing about changes in the economic system its it whole would exercise a divisive influence on the tank-and-file. To the advocacies of this view-point, nursing or fighting for a political ideology is not a legitimate function or objective of a trade union. While they support the workers' right as citizens to become members of political parties standing for socialism and in that capacity to work for the overthrow of capitalism and the establishment of a socialist order, they deny that trade unions should be actively associated with movements for fundamental changes in the economic system.

On the other hand, Socialists and Marxists argue that in the struggle for the establishment of socialism, trade unions cannot and should not remain neutral. Being the primary organs of the working class whose deliverance lies in socialism, trade unions should actively engage in political education of the members in favour of socialism.

Methods of Trade Unions

How do the trade union movement and trade unions seek to achieve their goals as discussed above? There is no method and means which trade unions in their long history have not used to achieve their goals and objectives. When they were illegal, they defied the law either, openly or surreptitiously; they resorted to illegal strikes and even to physical violence when the needs so demanded. When they came to be recognised, they tried to influence the course of legislation to get it modified to make their position secure and protect the interests of their members. They developed organisations for mutual help, protection and insurance to meet specific needs. The classic description of trade union methods by the Webbs as consisting of mutual insurance, collective. bargaining and legal enactment, still holds good, but what the Webbs call legal enactment is only a part of the broader political action, which the trade unions undertake for the achievement of their goals. Each of these methods, i.e.

(1) mutual insurance,
(2) collective bargaining, and
(3) political action needs further elaboration.

1. Mutual Insurance

From their very inception, trade unions have been spending u part of their income in providing insurance and other welfare benefits for improving the conditions of their members, promoting good will among then and maintaining solidarity within the organisation. The nature and extent of the benefits provided has gradually expanded during the course of years. The effectiveness of this method is directly dependent upon the income—of trade unions. Where trade unions are rich, they are in a better position to provide insurance or other benefits to their members. On the other hand, it is futile to expect much from the poor trade unions which are all the time worried about their finances. The funds for mutual insurance may come from membership subscriptions, special levies and donations.

The British trade unions have a strong tradition of adopting mutual insurance for the benefit of there members. Even prior to 1880's, many trade unions in Great Britain provided insurance to their members against such risks as sickness, accident, disablement, old age, death and also against unemployment. However, the nature and scale of benefits provided varied considerably, depending on the financial position of trade unions and the extent of incidence of particular, risks. It were principally the craft unions which took to mutual insurance. An appreciable number of trade unions functioned as Friendly Societies and many of them voluntarily registered themselves with the Registrar of Friendly Societies. Of the friendly benefits, the most generally provided was funeral benefit. The funeral benefit, in addition to covering funeral expenses, also covered a grant to the widow of the deceased member, his young children and parents. In some cases, sickness and accident benefits were combined. Many trade unions also provided for medicine and medical attendance. Accident benefit might be in lump sum or in the form of periodic payments during incapacity. Only a few trade unions could provide for superannuation benefit. Unemployment benefit could consist of an out-of-work allowance, the tramp benefit and emigration benefit. Tramp benefit was paid in the form of daily or weekly allowance to members travelling in search of work.

Although from 1880's, the British trade unions started laying a greater importance to collective bargaining and subsequently to political action also, mutual insurance has continued to be emphasized by many trade unions, particularly the craft ones. However, mutual insurance as a trade union method has increasingly been overshadowed by the provision of social security and welfare measures introduced at the instance of the State. Now that a comprehensive system of national insurance, supplementary benefits and health services has been established in Great Britain, the trade unions there do not have to worry much over the provision of friendly benefits for their members. Nonetheless, many trade unions still supplement the benefits available under the State schemes. Besides, the British trade unions have also come to spend a substantial amount over many new items, which were not or only scantly covered under their earlier activities. In this regard, particular mention may be made of workers' education, recreational and educational activities, housing, banking, cooperatives and payments during strikes, etc.

The American trade unions have also a similar tradition of providing, out of their funds, benefits to meet the economic uncertainties to which their members are exposed. Likewise, they -have also developed educational and cultural facilities, banking, housing and similar ventures.

The Indian trade unions have lagged, far behind their counter parts in Great Britain and the U.S.A. in taking recourse to mutual insurance primarily because of their poor financial 'position. Only a few trade unions in India have been able to develop certain welfare activities, not to speak of mutual insurance against the more common risks of life. The Textile Labour Association Ahmedabad and the Madras Labour Union deserve to be mentioned here for their welfare activities.

In general, it were the early trade unions, particularly the craft .ones, that emphasized mutual insurance for improving the lot of their members. At that stage, they were unable to adopt the method of collective bargaining owing to the legal handicaps and openly hostile attitude of the employers. At the same time, they were not in a position to engaged in-political activities for securing protective labour legislation or other measures at the instance of the State. However, inmost capitalist countries, once trade unions obtained legal recognition, they started giving more importance to collective bargaining. In 'these' countries, collective bargaining has now become the most outstanding of the methods adopted by the trade unions. Besides, in many countries trade unions have succeeded in improving the lot of their members by political action, which includes exerting pressures for protective labour legislation and welfare amenities and establishing political parties of the working class. In spite of the gradual shift in emphasis, the method of mutual insurance has come to stay along with the methods of collective bargaining and political action.

2. *Collective Bargaining*

Another method used by trade unions for improving the conditions of their members is collective bargaining. Under this method, their representatives bargain with the employer over the terms and conditions of employment and enter into agreement with him. The agreement thus arrived at between the representatives of a trade union and the employer is known as a collective agreement.

The method of collective bargaining came to be emphasised after the trade unions secured recognition under law and became free from the criminal and civil disabilities which they had to suffer in their early stage. At that stage, collective action on the hart of workers for improving conditions of employment could he illegal under the doctrine of restraint of trade and individual workmen could be indicted on the charge of breach of contract. Under such conditions the workers could bargain with the employer only individually. The decision of the worker to accept or realise the conditions offered by the employer was made with reference to his own strength or weakness as a bargainer. However, when the trade unions came to be entrenched on a sound fooling, it was collective bargaining, more than any other method, that witnessed the widest adoption.

The method has now assumed great significance in the trade union programme of action in almost all the capitalist countries.

Evolution of collective bargaining has, however, not been uniform everywhere. Considerable variations can be seen in the" process of collective bargaining, its area, subject matters covered, nature of collective agreements and legal provisions having a bearing on the method. Many of these variations may be explained in terms of variations in the nature and extent of trade union growth, but there are other influencing factors also. In coilairies where, trade unions are in a highly developed stage, as in the U.S.A. and Great Britain, collective bargaining is extensively used.

The bargaining units vary greatly in size or make-up. In many cases, trade unions enter into collective agreements with the employers at the local level, i.e. at the factory; mine or the shop level. Even within a factory or other industrial establishments, different craft unions may bargain separately with the employer. In other cases, a combination of trade unions, whether craft, industrial or general, operating in a particular region may bargain at the regional level with one employer or a group of employers. Similarly, collective bargaining may also take place at the industry or national level. With the formation of trade unions at the industry or national level, there has been a strong trend toward industry or nation wide collective bargaining. In many cases, bargaining takes place with a single employer, but in many others, employers also unite or cooperate for bargaining purposes. During recent years, there has been a marked growth of multiunit bargaining.

A wide variety of subjects has come to be included in collective agreements. As a matter of fact, collective agreements may relate to any kind of employment conditions. Some of the items most frequently covered under collective agreements include: wages, hours of work, physical working conditions, apprenticeship, incentive payments, welfare amenities, promotion, bonus, gratuity, superannuation and economic benefit plans. Even in cases where many of the employment conditions are regulated by law, the trade unions often bargain with the employers for securing more improved standards than what are prescribed under the law. A collective agreement may deal with a single issue or may cover a wide range of subjects.

One important consequence of collective bargaining for the determination of terms and conditions of employment has been that trade unions are enabled thereby to participate in the decision-making process regarding wages; hours of work, working conditions, etc. These issues were unilaterally decided by the employer, but with the advent of collective bargaining, they have become subjects of bilateral negotiations. What was hitherto treated as the management's prerogatives has come to be controlled and regulated by collective bargaining. Thus, collective bargaining has succeeded in introducing an element of industrial democracy in the field of industrial and labour-management.

In general, the trade unions and employers engage in collective bargaining voluntarily. However, in some cases, they are under the legal obligation to do so. Thus, in the U.S.A., both the trade unions and employers are obligated under the Labour-Management Relations Act, 1947 to bargain with each other. Refusal to bargain either on the part of, the trade union or the, employer is an unfair labour practice forbidden under the Act. Besides, in many countries, certain issues having a bearing on collective bargaining have come to be regulated by law e.g. determination of the representative character of a trade union and its recognition for the purpose of bargaining, certification of collective agreements, control of certain unfair practices, and union security clauses, etc. These legal limitations are, for the most part, intended to ensure a healthy growth of collective bargaining rather than to impair, it. The trade unions and the employers continue to enjoy considerable freedom at every stage of bargaining.

Collective agreements may be written or unwritten. Whether written or unwritten, they may be looked upon as legislative acts which set forth rules governing employment relationship for a given period of time. These laws are, however, private in nature. In many cases, they are of a greater importance to the workers than many of the labour laws passed by legislature. Like the general laws, collective agreements also involve the question of interpretation which is usually solved by the provision of a grievance machinery.

Traditionally, collective agreements had been looked upon as, private agreements not enforceable in a court of law, i.e. law did not look upon them as civil contracts which, in case of a party backing out of the obligations of the contracts, could be legally enforced.

The main sanction behind a collective agreement is supposed to be the economic strength of the parties. In case of reluctance of a party to abide by and fulfil its commitments under the agreement, the other party can resort to economic pressures to force the other to meet its obligations. The same economic pressure, which is at the back of the signing of the collective agreement, is also the main instrument for its implementation.

However, many countries are not prepared to allow the parties: the freedom to resort to economic warfare in order to secure the implementation of a collective agreement, though the same countries are prepared to permit the right to engage in economically coercive measures in order to arrive at an agreement. Collective agreements now cover the terms and conditions of employment of such a large number of workers spread over all kinds of industries and employments that to permit the parties to resort to strike and lock-out for securing the implementation of the collective agreements is patently wasteful, uneconomic and unnecessary. Therefore, a trend has developed to treat collective agreements as solemn contracts to be enforced by courts of law. in case a party so desires, i.e. collective agreements tend to cease to be private agreements and become agreements with social and public consequences. The Labour-Management Relations Act, 1947 of the U.S.A. has inserted a provision-making collective agreements enforceable in a court of law. Similarly, the British Industrial Relations Act, 1971, has also made collective agreements enforceable by a court of law at the instance of either of the parties. Collective agreements have secured a limited degree of enforceability in India also. Under the Industrial Disputes Act, 1947, if a collective agreement is registered with the appropriate government, it becomes a settlement and the violation of the settlement becomes a penal offence under the Act. Nonetheless, collective agreements are still not treated as contracts enforceable in a court or law under any other civil law in India today.

A notable feature of collective bargaining in some countries, particularly those having planned economies, is that, instead of remaining confined to bilateral negotiations between the trade unions and the employers, it has come to take into consideration the interests of the community also. In such countries, many important, issues having a bearing on employment conditions are decided by tripartite forums consisting of representatives. of the trade unions, employers and the public.

This description 'of the role of collective bargaining as a method used by the trade unions to attain some of their goals should have made it clear that the freedom of collective bargaining implies the right to strike in the case of a union and lock-out in the case of an, employer in the event of the failure of negotiations. Collective bargaining involves mutual negotiations and failure of negotiations may lead to the use of coercive measures such as strike, picketing, boycott and lock-out, etc. There are many persons who support collective bargaining as a method of settling industrial disputes under the impression that this ensures their peaceful and prompt settlement, but they forget that settlement of disputes by free mutual discussions and collective bargaining in eludes the right of the parties to resort to economic pressure in case they think it necessary. The right to strike is an integral part of collective bargaining. Any restriction on the right to strike weakens the process of collective bargaining. In the words of Taylor, "No one should have any doubt about the unlikelihood that collective bargaining can be maintained in the absence of right to strike and lock-out."

3. Political Aaction/Legal Enactment

In many countries trade unions engage in political action for securing better working and living conditions for the workers. The main features of trade unions' political action are; exerting pressure for protective or other prolabour legislations and welfare amenities at the instance of the State setting-up of labour parties or developing allegiance to one political party or the other; and securing, control over industry. Unlike mutual insurance and collective bargaining, which are designed to benefit only the trade union members of employees of a particular plant, industry, craft or a group of them, political action is intended to benefit the working class in general. The trade union practices with respect to political action also vary widely.

Exerting pressure for securing protective or other prolabour legislations has been the most extensively used of the political actions. In the early stages of their growth, when the various legal disabilities prevented the unions from engaging in collective bargaining with their employers, there was a strong pressure for protective labour laws for regulating such conditions of employment as hours of work, rest period, weekly rest, safety, employment of children and women, compensation against work-injuries, protection of wages, etc. The series of protective labour lws that came to be adopted in Great Britain during the 19th century was essentially the outcome of the efforts of organized labour. In U.S.A. also, the early trade unions demanded protective labour laws, particularly relating to hours of work and secured the same. Pressures for new labour legislations und improvement over the existing ones are still made by trade unions in many parts of the world. Similarly, the trade unions also seek to obtain welfare amenities under laws of the State. In many countries, trade unions have been able to secure such statutory welfare amenities as housing, recreational and educational facilities, medical and health facilities, etc.

In some countries, the trade unions have also formed their independent labour parties or have come into relationship with other political parties of their choice. In Great Britain, the TUC established the Independent Labour Party. Similar labour parties have come into existence in many other countries, particularly those which have recently become independent. It is expected that the labour parties, on coming into power, will take effective measures for the improvement of the conditions of the working class. In India, the trade unions have formed their national centres having, allegiance to one political party or the other. Thus, the INTIUC has a close relationship with the Indian National Congress, the AITI it with the Communist Party and the HMS with the Socialist Party. In the past, the American trade unions had a pragmatic approach towards political action. Their main political programme to organize the values of trade union members in such it manner as to reward the 'friends' and punish the enemies i.e to vote for a pro-labour candidate in the Presidential elections and to try for the defeat of the one who was not pro-labour. However, the American trade unions are now fast discarding their orthodox attitude towards politics and are increasingly emphasizing political action for the benefit of the workers.

All over the world, trade unions are developing political wings and political links both for the purpose of securing reforms within the capitalist economic structure and for a fundamental reconstruction of the economic system by peaceful means, if possible, and by violence, if necessary. The links between the trade unions, on one side, and the guild socialists, syndica lists, socialists and communists on the other, are well-known. The State control and ownership of the means of production has all along been one of the important planks of trade unions in many countries.

There are unions which believe in the essentials of capitalism, free competition and free enterprise and seek to promote and protect workers' interests within this economic framework. There are others which think that, so long as the capitalist system survives, there is no permanent remedy to the workers' ills. They believe that the workers may secure temporary relief but the fundamental' process of exploitation is an integral part of the capitalist economic order. However, such unions, even while working for the ultimate replacement of capitalism by a different economic order, do not neglect the day-to-day interests of the workers. They take part in everyday struggle, engage in collective bargaining, secure improvements in working and living conditions of workers but, at the same time, realise the limitations of these short-term gains.

Some may rely on the use of their own economic power such as collective bargaining others may rely on the power of the State to secure protection and favourable labour legislation. Of the unions which have the ultimate goal of replacing the capitalist economic system, there are some which believe in the gradual transformation of the capitalist system and its ultimate replacement by securing political power through parliamentary methods, and others which believe in the overthrow of capitalism through general strikes and revolutions.

This classification is not unreal in view of the complex situations faced by different unions in different countries and is illustrated by the history of trade union movements in different countries. There have been and are unions which are extremely violent and have resorted to extra-legal methods to secure their goals. On the other hand, there are many others which attempt to secure workers' interests and rights through peaceful and non-violent means. There are unions which have at different times believed in capitalism, have grown skeptical of the efficacy of capitalism and have later on become openly hostile to it. The methods the trade unions adopt , to achieve their objective of promoting the interests of their- members, in particular, and the working class, in general, are conditioned, to some extent, by their attitude to the economic systems in which they operate.

Legitimacy of the Methods

The history of the trade union movement in different countries does not point out in an unequivocal manner the trade unions' methods and goals which may be called 'legitimate' and others, which may be said to be 'illegitimate'. There was a time when the trade unions in the U.S.A. distrusted the government and did not have any faith in labour legislation. At that time they sought to rely primarily on collective bargaining and building up their own economic strength. Today, the American trade unions are no less reliant on labour laws than on collective bargaining. Similarly, there was a time when involvement in politics was decried by leading trade unions and trade unionists. Today, the AFL-CIO is as much concerned with the political education of its members as with strengthening the instrument of collective bargaining.

Again, the unions in the U.S.A. may primarily put their faith in collective bargaining, but trade unions in India, especially those affiliated to the INTUC, believe in compulsory adjudication and rely on their political strength. The trade unions of the syndicalist type believed in the efficacy of the weapon of general strike for overthrowing capitalism, whereas the trade unions under guild-socialism believed in replacing private ownership by workers' ownership of industries by peaceful methods.

Practically everywhere there are trade unions in existence today, which openly profess the replacement of capitalism by socialist order as one of their objectives. The aims and objectives of the AITUC include: the establishment of a socialist State in India and socialization and nationalization of the means of production, distribution and exchange, as far as possible: The methods of the AITUC include legislation, education, propaganda, mass meetings, negotiations, demonstrations and in the last resort; strikes. Similarly, the aims and objects of the UTUC include: the establishment of a socialist society, the establishment of workers' and peasants' State. In India and the nationalisation of the means of production, distribution and exchange.

Under this diversity of objectives and methods of trade unions, which ones can be said to be legitimate and which others, 'illegitimate'? There is no objective standard by which one can judge the legitimate functions and methods of trade unions in general. Trade unionism is essentially a pragmatic movement which constantly reshapes its organisational structure, reformulates. its policies and objectives and re-examines and evaluates its methods, keeping all the time in its view the welfare of the working class as its goal.

The particular goals and methods of trade unions generally are conditioned by the following factors:

(1) the degree of group and class consciousness among workers;
(2) the nature of political organisation of the. particular society;
(3) the nature of economic organisation of the society and its stage of economic development; and
(4) the nature and type of trade union leadership.

Trade Union Activities

The foregoing analysis of the generic trade union methods can be better understood if they are further analysed in terms of the specific activities in which they result. These activities may be summarised as follows:

(1) Economic activities:
Under this head come all those activities which result in exercisd of the economic pressure on the employer, e.g. engaging in collective, bargaining, demonstration, strike, boycott, picketing, etc.
(2) Political Activities:
    (a) Carrying on political education of the workers.
    (b) Obtaining political power and influence,

through developing political parties of their own, and extending help to candidates of other political parties who are sympathetic to the cause of labour.

(c) Carrying on lobbying activities for influencing the course of labour and other legislation.

(d) Participating in, and representing the workers on, institutions and bodies.

(e) Developing militancy and revolutionary urge amongst workers, etc.

(3) Social activities:

(a) Initiating and developing workers' education scheme.

(b) Organising welfare and recreational activities such as mutual insurance, providing monetary and other help during period of strikes and economic distress.

(c) Running cooperatives.

(d) Providing housing facilities.

(e) Participating in community development and cousa a unity protection activities.

(4) International activities:

(a) Participating in the organisation and activities ILO.

(b) Participating in the international federations of trade unions such as the WFTU, the ICFTU and the International Trade Union Secretariats for the purpose. of building working class unity and solidarity.

(c) Sending monetary and other help to workers of other countries during periods of strikes and natural disasters.

Determinants of the Rate of Trade Union Growth

The analysis of the factors leading to the origin of trade unionism has emphasised such factors as:

(a) the separation between ownership of capital and labour,

(b) the emergence of the factory system and the

economic distress and hardships resulting therefrom, increasing the workers' dissatisfaction with their working and living conditions,

(c) the growth of group attitude and class sentiments among workers as a result of their congregation at particular places working in common groups and facing common problems, and

(d) realisation of the fact of individual dispensability and collective indispensability of the workers to the employers.

These factors provide a general explanation of the origin of trade unionism, but there will be specific factors working in different countries which will assist in or delay the origin and growth of trade unions. That is why trade unionism has appeared at different times in different countries. Further, the rate of growth of trade unions has not been uniform everywhere or, over the course of time, in the same country. There have been periods in the history of every country when the number of trade unions and their membership have increased by leaps and bounds, whereas during other periods, they have fast declined and, still at other times, they have either remained stable or have recorded a very slow growth. How can one explain this rapid increase, relative stability and fast decline at frequent intervals? It is the task of this section to examine and evaluate the factors that condition the rate of union growth.

Many American writers, e.g. John T. Dunlop, Joseph Shister, Irving Bernstein and Julius Rezler have sought to analyse the factors determining the rate of trade union growth in the U.S.A., and on the basis of their study, they have tried to develop a general framework which may be applicable to the rate of trade union growth in other countries also. A review of the relevant literature shows that the following factors constitute the important determinants of the rate of trade union growth:

(1) Industrial commitment of labour force;
(2) Changes in the composition of labour force;
(3) Variations in the business activity;
(4) Change in technology;
(5) Trade union leadership;

(6) Structure of union organisation;
(7) Union security provisions in collective agreements and laws;
(8) Attitude of employers toward unionism;
(9) The political climate and legal framework;
(10) Role of political parties;
(11) The value system and public opinion; and
(12) Proximity influence.

The factors noted above exert conflicting as well as complementary influences on the rate of union growth and unionisation. Besides, they may not have the same influence everywhere. For example, the role of political parties may be important in India and countries similarly situated, but not in the U.S.A. Likewise, variations in economic activities may tend to exercise an influence favourable to trade union growth, but the legal framework may operate in the opposite direction. Thus, union growth is the resultant of the operation of a number of diverse factors mentioned above, some of which may have an accelerating and others a retarding influence. It is the totality of these influences which ultimately determines the rate of union growth.

(1) Industrial Commitment of Labour Force

The degree of unionisation and union growth is greatly influenced by the industrial commitment of the labour force. The crystallisation of the working class wholly dependent upon industrial employment and wages as the source of its livelihood and without any expectation of rising above the working class status is an important contributing factor. The Indian experience is typical in this regard. So long as the individual workers in India maintained their connection with agriculture in the villages and continued to be migratory in character, the rate of unionisation was slow. Workers who look upon industrial employment as a temporary stop-gap arrangement will not create a fertile soil for the germination and growth of tráde unionist. Similarly, one of the important facto accounting for the slow growth of organisation among American workers during early years of industrialisation—was the availability of abundant opportunities far individual advancement. During those days, many Americans looked upon their wage-earning status as a temporary event. They expected to become self-employed or even an employer by hard-work and saving habits. In a period or in situations in which individual employees expect to become foremen and ten owners of their own business, permanent and stable organisation is virtually impossible.

(2) Changes in the Composition of Labour Force

This factor is closely related to the industrial commitment of the labour force discussed above. If the proportion of skilled workers in the total labour force increases, unionisation becomes easier. Experience has shown that the skilled workmen took to unionisation first. Similarly, if employment expands fast' in industries susceptible to unionisation, the rate of union growth becomes faster. It is difficult to organise women and children. In a labour force in which women and children constitute a Significant proportion; unionisation would be slow.

(3) Variations in the Business Activity

History records that the number and membership of trade unions increase during cyclical upswings in business activity and fall during the downward swing. It is well known that during periods of war also, when economic activities expand, employment increases, and cost of living rises while wages lag behind, there is a relatively greater swing toward unionisation. Here again, the Indian experience is relevant. It was the First World War that gave birth to unionisation and again trade unions recorded an unprecedented growth in membership during the Second World War. Thus, the membership of registered trade unions increased to approximately 9 lakh in 1944-45 from nearly 4 lakh recorded in 1938, whereas, during a corresponding period of seven years, i.e. 1931 to 1938, the membership of registered trade unions had increased from 2 lakhs to about 4 lakhs only.

(4) Change in Technology

Changes in technology imply changes in products, methods of production, skill and composition of labour force. As the technology advances, different sectors of economy become closely interdependent and quicker means of communication and transport develop. Further, technological changes may lead to disilporalice of many traditional jobs; skills become obsolete 'creating both job and income insecurities'. The need for developing and strengthening organisations becomes mote urgent and pressing. Thus, periods of rapid technological change are also periods of rapid trade union growth.

(5) Trade Union Leadership

It is usual to describe economic and, social forces as the sole determinants of union growth, but the character and nature of trade union leadership also has a powerful influencing role. No doubt, the economic and social factors create the necessary conditions for union growth, but it is for the leaders to. exploit them. A militant and aggressive leadership wedded to the cause of labour may not only fully exploit the favourable factors but can also overcome conditions and impediments adverse to trade union growth. Leaders have the role of acting as the catalytic agent. The appearance of certain types of leaders lends a vigour to the union growth, which would have remained dormant, otherwise. The history of labour movement abounds in examples of such leaders who have molded the course of labour movement to a very appreciable extent. Names of such leaders as Mahatma Gandhi, N.M. Joshi, S.A. Dange, V.V. Giri and a host of others are known to all students of trade unionism in India.

(6) Structure of Union Organization

The structure of union organization also influences trade union growth, though not in a decisive manner. Unions based upon crafts and skill generally are less interested in the organization of the mass of unskilled workers. So long as the craft structure of trade unionism exists, the pace of union growth cannot be accelerated. There may be leaders of trade unions who are more interested in the maintenance of the monopoly of power arising out of the compact and strategic nature of the craft and the skills they control. Particularly, with the advent of mass-production industries and the numerical predominance of semi-skilled labour force, craft as a base of unionization may have a regarding influence. It is in this context. That the role of industrial unions in accelerating the pace of union growth has for be visualized. The structure of the trade union movement has to adapt itself to the changing need of the labour force, otherwise, it would become archaic and hamper the pace of growth.

(7) Union Security Provisions in Collective Agreements and Laws

It has become customary these days for collective agreements to contain union security provisions for the closed shop, union shop, agency shop, and maintenance of membership shop, etc. It is the institutional interest of the unions that demands insertion of union security clauses having the effect, of making union membership more or less compulsory on workmen. The workers become union members automatically without any additional efforts on the part of their unions. The more widespread such agreements are, the union membership is more likely to expand automatically along with the expansion of employment.

(8) Attitude of Employers toward Unionism

Since its very inception; trade unionism has faced stiff opposition from the employers. Everywhere in the past, the employers ***left no*** stone unturned to suppress trade unionism and punish the trade unionists. Utilised all legal and political avenues, economic pressures and administrative devices to prevent the growth of trade unions and the unionisation of their employees. Later on, the employers were forced to modify their stand and today they have come to tolerate trade unions. It is true that trade unions have grown in the face of this stiff opposition from the employers. However, if the employers become moderate in their opposition, the pace of unionisation is accelerated. Unionising the workmen is like climbing a hill; steeper the seight, slower is the progress; stiffer the employer's opposition, slower is the pace of unionisation.

(9) The Political Climate and the Legal Framework

The political climate and the legal framework of the country obtaining at a particular time exercise a decisive influence over the pattern and the rate of union growth. The hostile political atmosphere that the early trade unions had to face in all the capitalist countries is a story that need not be repeated here. It was this political climate and the adverse legal institutions, that prevented the seeds of trade unions from taking roots in the early days of industrialisation. A dictatorship of the Fascist or the Nazi type generally seeks to eliminate trade unions and to subvert them During the 1930's in Italy and Germany under Mussolini and Hitler, the trade unions were the first to receive the blows of their attack on democratic institutions. Where political climate is generally conservative and the employers' influence is much too predominant, circumstances are not at all propitious for the growth of trade unions.

On the contrary, a sympathetic political administration can do a lot to further the growth and the influence of trade unions. A review of the history of trade unions in Great Britain will show clearly the influence of political climate on the growth of trade unions. A Liberal or Labour Government, by its practices and policies, tended to help the trade unions, whereas, a Conservative administration had a restrictive influence. Similarly, the series of legislation enacted during the 1930's in the U.S.A. are an illustration of how a government can promote the growth of trade unions. With his sympathetic appreciation of the problems of the working class and the role of trade unions in the political and economic life of the community, Roosevelt initiated a number of legislative and administrative measures which gave a boost to the organising activities of the American trade unions. The National Industrial Recovery Act, 1933, the NIR codes worked out the reunder, and the National Labor Relations Act, 1935 (also known as the Wagner Act) helped the growth of trade unions by guaranteeing to workers, the right of collective bargaining and preventing employers from interfering in any manner with the organizations of workers. A feeling that the government is supporting the organising efforts of the union dispels fear from amongst the workers and encourages them to organise. Similarly, in India, the establishment of a national government after independence created a favourable climate for the growth of trade unions and since then Indian trade unions have recorded a phenomenal growth both in terms of numbers and membership, and influence.

The state of political climate as discussed above is reflected in the legal framework obtaining at a particular time. It has been shown earlier how laws, codes and administrative practices of governments in almost every country mercilessly sought to suppress the trade unions in their formative years. Subsequently, however, laws favorable to workers guaranteeing them the right to organize, and declaring illegal antiunion practices of employers have been enacted in all democratic countries. The legal framework existing in India prior to the enactment of the Indian Trade Unions Act, 1926 definitely exercised a retarding influence on trade union growth. The contribution of the Indian Trade Unions Act, 1926 to the growth and spread of trade unionism in India, through the protection it afforded to the members and officers of registered trade unions, cannot be minimised. Thus, it is seen that the nature of the legal framework consisting of laws and court decisions can accelerate or retard the growth of trade unions.

(10) Role of Political Parties

Political parties, through their ideologies, contribute to the changing political climate and the legal framework. In order to maintain their influence and power, where power depends on the outcome of elections based upon universal, adult franchise, some political parties tend to develop political programme and action sympathetic to labour and trade unions. Political parties have been founded with the specific goal of promoting the cause of labour. In many countries, labour, socialist and communist parties compete with each other in organising the workers into trade unions. With the advent of the communist parties in the field of politics, this competition has become all the more acute. The communist ideology believes that the working class constitutes the progressive and revolutionary section of the capitalist society. The communist parties; therefore, concentrate on the working class, organize the workers into trade unions and ceaselessly attempt to build the class solidarity for the purpose of establishing a communist working society.

In the colonial countries, struggling for independence, the political parties, in the vanguard of the struggle for freedom, seek to organize the workers for the purpose of enlisting their support and sympathy for the cause of national liberation. Thus, trade union movements under such conditions become a part of a broad national movement for political independence. It is this fact that accounts fear both the speedy growth of trade unions and their domination by political parties in countries which have just attained independence or are struggling for the same.

In the industrially advanced countries of the word, though the early trade unions grew unaided by political parties, latter on either the trade unions founded their own political parties other embraced the cause of labour and trade unionism. In these countries, trade unions and the progressive political parties have developed a system of mutual interdependence. But in the economically backward societies, the left-wing political parties will continue to play on effective and dominant role in the trade union growth. One may adversely look upon injection of politics in the field of trade unionism by political parties, tail one cannot overlook their contribution to the spread, and growth of trade unions. The Indian experience typifies the role of political parties in accelerating the growth of trade unions.

(11) The Value System and Public Opinion

In societies where dominant value system puts a premium oil on indivisualism, or attributes the hardship and sufferings of life to supernatural forces or the ordains of God not changeable by the efforts of man, trade unionism faces an uphill task. It was this emphasis on individualism and individual competition that hampered the growth of trade unions in the early days of the newly emerging capitalist system in the countries of the west. The enemies of the trade union movement could easily quote passages from books on economic proving the futility of trade unions in raising wages or improving working conditions and also showing the done to the economic progress by trade unions.

The dominant academic and intellectual circles wrote and argued against trade unionism and accordingly shaped public opinion. In societies, suits the Indian dominated by a hierarchical social system and authoritarian family pattern and firmly believing in the doctrine of Karma, starting protest movements against poverty, exploitation and economic inequality presents formidable difficulties. So long as people believe that poverty and sufferings in the present life are lie punishments for misdeeds of their previous birth and have, therefore to be suffered, they would rarely raise it voice against the economic institutions that are really responsible for their troubles.

Trade unionism being essentially a protest movement, teaches the workers to protest against the authority and tyranny of the employer. It takes a long time for the workers to be convinced dial their sufferings are not the results of punishments inflicted by God, rather they are the man-made results of the working of economic forces, which can be moulded and controlled by conscious human efforts. In the early days of Indian industrial growth, it was difficult to induce the workers drawn from villages where Zamnindars, landlords and the priestly class exercised and enjoyed completed control over the economic and social life, to think of challenging the might of the employers. Gradually, the mood changed. As democratic ideals spread and the traditional strongholds of authority and power vanish, a climate more favourable to unionisation will be created.

Apart from the role of this value system in retarding or helping the growth of trade unions, the prevailing public opinion, not necessarily related to the value, system also has an influencing role. If the prevailing public opinion takes unkindly to the activities of the trade unions, they will suffer in terms of their growth as well as their influence. Public opinion influences the policy and programme of governments, of political parties, as well as the outcome of particular strikes. That is why both the unions and the employers seek to mould the public opinion to their view-point. Trade unions have developed programmes of educating not only the members and other workers but also to educate the non-workers as regards the beneficial effects of trade unionism.

(12) Proximity Influence

Unionization grows due to what may be called demonstration or proximity effects. News relating to gains secured by unions spread like a wild fire and workers in the plants and factories will close proximities are likely to be stirred and they may start organizing and making similar demands. Developments in the means communication of ideas accelerate this in larger cities, if organizations succeed in big plants, even smaller plants are also likely to follow suit. It is this proximity influence which operates as an important contributing factor in bigger cities. The spread of trade unionism from the manual to the white-collar workers is also partly the result of the demonstration effects.

The foregoing presents a summary of the factors that influence the pace of the growth of trade unionism under specific conditions. These determinants of trade union growth are to be distinguished from the basic economic and political factors that create the necessary conditions for the origin of the trade union movement. The basic economic and political conditions discussed in the beginning of this chapter and the determinants of the pace of growth taken together explain the origin and development of trade unionism.

Trade unions are unique organisations in many ways. They are formed mainly for protecting the interests of workers or employees against those who would harm them. These could be the employers, the state or any agency identified as such. In this sense, trade unions can be viewed as opposition organisations. Most trade unions broadly centre around this basic objective. Secondly, trade unions are a product of industrialisation. They were born out of the Industrial Revolution and as such had no connections with any pre-industrial form of social organisation. Thirdly, the most important feature of trade unions is that theory did not play much part in their initial formation. In other words, there are no theoretical roots to the origins of trade unions. Their growth was a spontaneous, healthy process, which grew out of the needs of the common people (Flanders, 1970, p. 1). The result is not a neat and tidy pattern but something which is complex and overlapping. Hence, in order to understand the nature of trade unions one has to go back to their origins. In this paper, we will deal with the features of trade unions in India and in doing so we will start with the origin and growth of trade unions and then discuss the problem of trade unionism in the country.

Trade unions had their origins in England and they were a result of the Industrial Revolution. In the early stages, they were formed to regulate competition among the workers. The Industrial Revolution had improverished the village artisans as the goods they produced were replaced by mass produced goods made in factories. These people were forced to flock to the industrial townships in different parts of the country. They were desperate for work and provided cheap labour for factory owners. The factories were damp, unhealthy places with little light or ventilation. The hours of work were long. Men, women and children worked for over 16 hours every day in order to get a wage that would cover their minimum requirements. The wages prevalent and children were used for cleaning the machines or carrying goods from under the machines as they were small and could easily crawl under the machines.

Low wages and appalling conditions of work prevailed mainly because the number of unemployed was large. There was constant competition between the low paid workers and unemployed job-seekers. If a worker was unwilling to work for a particular wage. The employer could find several others who would be willing to work for even less. This competition for jobs depressed the wage rates and provided total power to the employers. Friedrich Engels (1973, p. 115) wrote in 1848 that this was the "worst side of the present state of things in its effects upon the workers, the sharpest weapon against the proletariat in the hands of the bourgeoisie." Workers tried to overcome this competition by forming associations. They did so in the face of stiff opposition from the employers. In fact, trade unions were a result of these spontaneous attempts of the workers to end competition.

Engels explains that at first, these associations carried out their activities underground, as they were not given legal status. They were able to organise a few strikes. These were ruthlessly crushed by the state. The main form of expressing their grievances was through acts of sabotage or by beating up managers. The prevalent conditions meant that these associations had to function in secrecy and as Engels notes, it was this secrecy that prevented these associations from spreading among all sections of the working class. Thus, these efforts at organisation remained isolated instances that depended more on violence than on the mass action of the working class.

It was only in 1824 when the British Parliament granted the right to free association through the Freedom of Association Act that trade unions could finally take-off. As a result, "These combinations were soon spread all over England and attained great power."(*ibid.*, p. 252). The unity achieved through trade unions gave workers a feeling of confidence resulting from collective action. It also resulted in better awareness among them. Trade unions strove to remove competition among the workers and changed the conflict between individuals within the class to the conflict between classes. The working class gradually realised that the only way of improving their conditions of existence was through confrontation with their employers rather than fighting among themselves for jobs. The workers realised that the supremacy of their employers lay in their being disunited. This is one of the most important contributions of trade unions.

Thus, Trade Unions are among the major and most influential social institutions in modern societies. They act as agents of labour, and organise large number of workers into a single entity. As collective organisations of workers, they overcome the structural weakness of workers *vis-a-vis* employers in labour markets. There is long standing debate on the role of trade unions, but there is no dispute over the fact that wherever they exist they have major influence on the wages and other conditions of work. They monitor employers' compliance with government regulations; limit their behaviour which are arbitrary, exploitative, and retaliatory; reduce work place discrimination; and ensure greater wage equality among its members. They not only negotiate wages and fringe benefits for their members, but also effect productivity, equality and workers' involvement at workplace. They also affect conditions of work of non-union workers through spillover effect. Finally, unions by acting as pressure groups contribute to the passage of labour legislations for employment protection and occupational safety and health. In sum, as expressed by Freeman and Medoff (1984), they "alter nearly every measurable aspect of operation of work places and enterprises."

Trade unions exist in all parts of the world, but what a union is and what it does varies from country to country. Globalisation with opening up of countries' borders for trade and investments has increased the need for comparative study of unionisation across countries. Such studies are important not only for the managers and union officials, but also for the policy-makers. The rights of workers to organise and levels of unionisation are now central issues in the global debate on linkages between trade and labour standards. The two indicators frequently used in the comparative studies are union membership and union density. Union membership calculated as the number of union members is a prime measure of union power and an indicator of collective action of workers (Shorter and Tilly, 1974; Korpi, 1983). It fulfils in important role as we derive from it measures of absolute and relative size of unions. The comparisons of unionisation across countries or regions are in terms of degree of 'completeness' or penetration of unions in labour markets. The more nearly complete a society in unionisation, the greater is the union power. Union density defined as the percentage of union members in wage earners is the most widely used comparative indicator to measure union influence across labour markets (Freeman and Medoff, 1984). Over time, across countries, and across industries these two indicators—union membership and union density—offer pictures of union power and influence.

There are many studies for estimation of union membership and union density for the developed countries (Visser, 1989; Ebbinghaus *et al.*, 2001), but there are few such studies for developing countries. In India, there is no comprehensive study dedicated to computation of the two indicators. Some studies in industrial relations refer to union density as low as 2 per cent of the total labour force (Venkatratnam, 1977; Kuruvilla, 1996). The International Labour Organisation (ILO) documents union density to be 5.4 per cent of the wage earners (ILO, 1997). Such low level of unionisation is often cited as reasons for exploitation of workers, but in reality it is hard to believe that in India unions represent such a negligible percentage of workers. These estimates are grossly inaccurate as they are based on incomplete data published in the Indian Labour Yearbook. This paper identifies the problems in computation of union membership and union density in the country and estimates the two indicators following the procedure followed in the developed countries. The results show that union density is above 30 per cent of the wage employed workers. The rigorously scrutinized estimates of the two indicators in this paper certainly present a more accurate picture of unionisation in India.

The organised and the unorganised sectors of the labour force in India can be distinguished from each other on the basis of the labour market and legal rights of the workers. The labour market in the unorganised sector is largely unstructured and unregulated for the workers. In legal terms too, the unorganised sector hardly offers any protection to its workers. Given the number of unskilled job-seekers in this sector, the situation results in low wages and lack of bargaining power for the workers. The labour market in the organised sector, in comparison to the unorganised sector, is more structured and regulated. In addition, workers in this sector have better skills. The workers are more protected due to the operation of laws regulating their work and employment conditions. These basic differences between the organised and the unorganised sectors also underline the wide gap between the working and living conditions of abourers in the two sectors.

The bulk of the labour force is engaged in the unorganised sector. The 1991 Census noted that the total working population in the country was 317 million, of which 290.2 million (92 per cent) was in the unorganised sector while only 26.8 million (8 per cent) was in the organised sector. The earnings of the workers in the two sectors differed considerably. Although the organised sector employed only 8 per cent of the total labour force, the workers collectively earned around 33 per cent of the country's total wages and incomes (Davala, 1995).

The organised sector comprises mainly workers who get regular wages or salaries and have greater security of employment. Their services cannot be terminated at the whims of their employers. Their working time is regulated and they get benefits of social security. It is significant that the major group of employers in this sector are in the public sector and the government. Around 70 per cent of the work force in the organised sector is employed in these agencies (Papola, 1994, p. 68).

The more recent statistics on employment show that the informal sector has increased considerably in size. The report of the 55th Round of the National Sample Survey (1999-2000) shows that 397 million persons were employed in the informal sector. This figure increases to 458 million in the 61st Round (2004-05). Employment in the formal sector has remained static at around 35 million during the same period. The informal sector constitutes 93 per cent of the total workforce (NCEUS, 2007, p. 4).

The unorganised sector comprises two types of workers, namely, self employed and casual wage earners. The self-employed are those who earn paltry incomes through their own assets. In the urban sector, these would include petty vendors, rag-pickers, artisans, domestic servants, and so on. In the rural sector, small and marginal farmers would be included. The entire employment in agriculture, 75 per cent of the employment in the manufacturing in sector, 36 per cent of the employment in the construction sector and 50 per cent of the employment in the transport sector, are in the unorganised sector (Papola, 1994).

Besides the basic features of informal employment such as insecure work without protection or social security, another feature is that a very small proportion of this workforce is unionsed. This could be the main cause of their helpless condition. The trade union verification drive of 1986 showed that only 1 per cent of the membership of the seven recognised trade union federations was from the informal sector (Davala, 1995, Introduction). The later verification of 2002 shows that the proportion of informal sector workers in trade union federations has increased considerably but it is still not significant. In fact, the federations that have done well in terms of an increase in membership are those that have attempted to organise the informal sector workers. One significant case is that of the All India Trade Union Conference (AITUC), which has risen from fifth position in 1986 to the third position in 2002 because of its membership of workers in the informal sector. However, there is no doubt that these efforts are not enough; many more initiatives in this direction are still required.

Any study of trade unions needs to take into consideration the structures and functions of unions. This knowledge is essential as it helps us to understand the scope and limitations of unions and how they are linked and influenced by external institutions. Looking at differences in membership structure, there are three types of unions:

(a) crafts unions, which organise workers engaged in a single occupation;
(b) industrial unions, which organise workers on the basis of an industry rather than craft; and
(c) labour unions that have all workers regardless of craft or industrial division as their members.

The dominant organisational form of the Indian labour movement is the industrial union such as unions in textile, jute, plantations and engineering industry. There are, however, a few craft unions like airline pilots associations, artists unions and journalists unions. The industrial unions are typical in old industries; however, many new units have unions limited to a single firm or factory.

On the basis of geographical coverage, trade unions in Indian may be classified as local unions, state federations and national federations. The national and state level labour unions generally operate as umbrella unions and have unions of all varieties of industries affiliated to them. Excepting a few, most of them are affiliated to political parties. Typically, the plant level unions are fundamental units of organisation and it is to these units that the members belong in the first instance. Plant-level unions can be independent unions or affiliated to some political or non-political federations. Unions are also classified as internal unions or external unions; external unions have external leaders in their executive committees, but it is not so in internal unions. Some firms have workers' committees that do not have the legal status of unions, but perform all functions of unions. Even though plant-level unions are fundamental units of union organisations, their legal status varies across industries. In old industries, typically industrial unions are the building blocks of the labour movement, with a constitution, an office, membership, and an identity under the Act signified by a registration number (Ramaswamy, 2000). In relatively newer industries, the legal existence of a union is at the plant level as they are registered under the Act.

Trade unions also differ in their functions and accordingly are classified into different types. First, some unions like the independent unions and craft unions are business unions that are essentially trade conscious, rather than class conscious. They express viewpoints and interests of workers in a craft or industry rather than those of the working class as a whole. Second, some unions are idealistic in their viewpoints. They may be trade conscious, or broadly class conscious, and at times think in the interest of society as a whole. Third, some unions are the revolutionary type and extremely radical, both in viewpoint and in action. They are distinctly class conscious rather than trade conscious. Of the revolutionary type, the socialist unions believe in the ideology of a socialistic state and its ultimate means is in invoking political action. Fourth, some unions, regardless of ethical and legal codes or the effect upon those outside their membership, are ruthless in pursuing their objectives by whatever

TABLE 4.1

Membership of Central Trade Unions, 1980-02 (Millions)

Union/Year	*1980*	*1989*	*2002*
INTUC	3.51	2.69	3.95
BMS	1.88	3.12	6.22
HMS	1.84	1.48	3.34
UTUC(LS)	1.23	0.84	1.37
UTUC	0.61	0.58	0.61
NLO	0.41	0.14	0
TUCC	0.27	0.23	0.73
NFITU	0.53	0.53	0.60
AITUC	1.06	0.94	3.44
CITU	1.03	1.78	2.68
Others*			1.94
Total	12.39	12.33	24.88

Note: *Others include LPF (0.61 million members), AICCTU (0.64 million members), and SEWA (0.69 million members).

Source: Ministry of Labour, Verification of Membership of Central Trade Unions.

means seem most appropriate at that time. Finally, some trade unions always act directly against their employers (Hoxie, 1920). In the Indian context, as in other countries, individual unions may not perfectly fit into any of the typical types, but there is no doubt that there exist different types of unions.

In India, the differences in the functions of unions are also seen in their affiliation to the state or national federations. The apex of the Indian labour movement comprises a number of central organisations that affiliate individual unions. There are a few non-political federations, but most union federations are explicitly political. The political parties control them and supply them with the upper crust of their leadership (Ramaswamy, 2000). Every central trade union claims to have a unique ideology, though in practice it is not easy to discern much difference between them. The INTUC is inspired by the Gandhian philosophy, with principles of non-violence and emphasis on cooperation between employers and employees. The AITUC is the older of the two communist centres, but it is the CITU, which symbolises radical Marxism in the Indian labour movement. The HMS with its commitments to socialist ideology lies between the soft line of the INTUC and the radicalism of the communists. The BMS claims to be an independent and non-political union, but in practice it has close links to the Bharatiya Janata Party (Ramaswamy, 2000). The membership of major central trade unions in 1980, 1989 and 2002 is presented in Table 4.1. The central trade union organisations differ in their influence in different sectors and some of them put more efforts in organising workers in the informal sector. Table 4.2 presents union membership of central trade unions in the formal and informal sectors.

TABLE 4.2

Membership of Major Central Trade Unions, 2002 (in '000)

	Organised Sector		*Unorganised Sector*				*Total*
			Non-Agriculture		*Agriculture*		
BMS	2842	(46)	2037	(33)	1336	(21)	6216
INTUC	2337	(59)	672	(17)	945	(24)	3954
CITU	946	(35)	1622	(61)	111	(4)	2678
AITUC	894	(35)	1078	(31)	1470	(43)	3442
HMS	1816	(26)	866	(26)	656	(20)	3338
UTUC(LS)	324	(54)	303	(22)	746	(54)	1373
Others	712	(24)	789	(20)	2381	(61)	3883
Total	9872	(18)	7368	(30)	7645	(31)	24885

Note: Figures in brackets are per cent in total membership.
Source: Verification of Membership of Central Trade Unions, 2002.

In India, the Trade Union Act, 1926 recognises workers' right to organise and engage in trade union activities and provides for registration of trade unions. Once a union is registered, it is formally considered a union. The registration status is, therefore, a popular criterion for identification of unions, but it is not a necessary condition. In India, many workers' organisations are not registered under the Act, but they perform all functions of unions. The government employees' organisations, for example, are not registered under the Act because of restrictions in their service rules. Their associations are not unions under the Act, but on many occasions they have organised strikes and actively bargained with the government for benefits of their members. In the government sector, the railway workers, however, enjoy all trade union rights at par with the other industrial workers and can get their organisations registered under the Act. Another example of unregistered organisations is 'Krishak Sabha', which is an organisation of agricultural labours and small-farmers affiliated to CPI(M).

1. Union Membership and Union Density

The two indicators frequently used to union influence and union power are union membership and union density (Shorter and Tilly, 1974; Korpi, 1983). Union membership gives a count of total number of union members in a country or industrial sector. Union density, which is the ratio of actual to potential members, is used to compare levels of unionisation across industrial sectors, across countries and over time. The knowledge of the two indicators is important not only for the policy-makers entrusted with the formulation of industrial and labour policies, but also important for union leaders and managers to understand their bargaining positions. It is also important for international comparison of union influence. More particularly, comparison of unionisation in developing countries has recently become an important subject in discussions on linking trade with labour rights. It is argued that the low level of unionisation in developing countries is leading to exploitation of workers and hence there is need to strengthen labour rights. It is argued that the low level of unionisation in developing countries is leading to exploitation of workers and hence there is need to strengthen labour rights. In India, the low level of unionisation in most estimates is because of inaccurate estimates of union membership and union density that are based on incomplete data.

In India, the published estimates on union membership and union density indicate very low levels of unionisation. The ILO in its World Employment Report, 1997-98 documents trade union density in India to be 5.4 per cent of salary and wage-earners. Some researchers even compute union density as low as 2 per cent of total labour force (Venkata Ratnam, 1997; Kurnvilla, 1996). They indicate extremely low levels of unionisation in India compared to other countries, but it is hard for union leaders, managers, and labour officials to believe that unions in India represent such a negligible percentage of workers.

In fact, plant-level evidence in several studies indicates a high level of union activity in the formal sector (Table 4.3). The low estimates are because of inaccurate data on union membership published in the Indian Labour Yearbook, which do not include reports from all states in India and include only membership of unions submitting returns. The inaccurate estimates have led to poor understanding of union strength in the country. In this paper, the estimates include membership data of all the states and membership of all registered unions irrespective of whether they submit returns or not. The results are far different from what is published in the Indian Labour Yearbook. The estimate for 2002, for example, shows presence of 56.7 million union members in the country in place of 6.3 million reported in the Indian Labour Yearbook.

TABLE 4.3

Unionisation in Large Firms

State	*Sector*	*Year*	*Union density (%)*	*Source*
West Bengal	Tea Plantations	1991	96	Bhowmik (1992)
West Bengal	Jute	1990	100	Sen (1992)
West Bengal	Coal	1990	100	Sen (1992)
West Bengal	Engineering	1990	90	Sen (1992)
All India	Ports and docks	1990	100	Vaidya and Arora (1992)
Andhra Pradesh	Automobiles	1990	71	Guptan (1992)
Andhra Pradesh	Engineering	1990	97	Guptan (1992)
Andhra Pradesh	Electronics	1990	71	Guptan (1992)
Uttar Pradesh	Glass Industry	1993	72	Raghubanshi (1993)
Maharashtra	Chemical and Pharmaceuticals	1991	80	Davala (1992)

Source: Verification of Membership of Central Trade Unions, 2002.

Union density is defined as the ratio of union members to potential union members. There are some measurement issues in computation of union density. First, there is a dilemma about choice of potential members. The possible choices are:

(a) wage and salaried workers;
(b) workers in non-agricultural sector;

(c) wage and salaried workers in non-agricultural sector; and

(d) workers in the formal sector.

Depending on what aspect of industrial relations one is interested in, one can use the different choices and compute union density. For example, if one is interested in union influence on government's policy, the most appropriate indicator is gross union density calculated as a percentage of union members to the total workforce. Similarly, if a manager is interested in knowing the probability of unionisation in a unit, the most important is the union density measured as a percentage of formal sector workers. Of the different choices, the most popular is the unionisation among the wage-employed workers. It is most widely used as a comparative indicator for measuring impact of trade unions on firms and labour markets in the developed countries (Freeman and Medoff, 1984; Ebbinghaus *et al.*, 2001). Computation of union density needs to follow a standard procedure so that the estimates can be used to compare unionisation across countries and over time. Unfortunately, the available estimates in India do not follow this standard approach. This paper computes union membership after making necessary corrections for incomplete data and then follows the procedure followed in developed countries to compute union density. The results show union density as 31 per cent of wage employed workers in 2002, which is much higher than the estimates published by ILO and other studies referred to above.

2. Multiplicity of Unions and Small Size of Unions

Data on union membership and union density serve as a useful starting point for study of cross-national tends in industrial relations, but to understand industrial relations practices and arrangements one needs to consider issues and factors beyond unionisation rates. The Trade Unions Act, 1926 stipulates that any group of seven workers or more can register itself as a trade union and it allows registration of multiple unions in a firm or industry. Further, it does not stipulate a means of determining which union is representative of workers and thus any number of unions can claim to represent workers in a given workplace. In brief, the Act does not have any provision for recognition of trade unions. The Act thereby creates an opportunity structure for the co-existence of multiple unions in a single firm or industry. It allows 'union entrepreneurs' to form a union and deliver its services to workers for a price. Partly because of the liberal provisions in the Act on formation of unions, many workplaces in India have multiple unions and most unions are very small. The Act provides for some protection of workers from their employers, but by allowing presence of multiple unions it also curtails the strength of unionised labour. Multiple unions within a workplace are not as powerful in their relations with management as a single union would be. This is partly because they are often more interest in scoring against each other primarily because of their ties with political parties. Fragmentation of unionised labour is often cited as the primary reason for the weak voice of organised labour in India (Rudolph and Rudolph, 1987).

In India, most rade unions have links to some political party or the other. There are some independent unions, but most unions are linked to union federations that are either wings of political parties or at least affiliated to political parties in some way or the other. The ties between union federations and different political parties have frequently resulted in polarisation of union federations. This is partly because political parties often use union federations as weapons of political rivalry. This political link has prevented emergence of an apex organisation that may represent a significant majority of unionised labour. Thus, whereas the AFL-CIO in the US, the DGB in Germany and TUC in the UK are each empowered by a majority of union members in their countries, none of India's federations/confederations are empowered in this way. The ties between unionised labour and political parties, however, have not necessarily been all bad for the unionised labour. Union federations have sometimes used affiliated political parties in the governments to receive various kinds of protections. However, this dependency also leaves unions vulnerable to withdrawal of such protection.

Indian trade unions are small in comparison to unions in developed countries. The Indian Labour Yearbook reports the average size of unions for different years based on samples of unions submitting returns. It was 790 during 1991-2000 and it varied from state to state. The data, however, do not give size distribution of unions. A scrutiny of union size in West Bengal in 1998 indicates extremely skewed size distribution. The average size of unions was 1490 and more than 85 per cent of the unions had less than 500 members. This clearly indicates that most unions are very small and there are only a few large unions. The size distribution of unions is somewhat similar to those seen in the UK in the 1950s and is similar to the size distribution of firms (Hart and Brown, 1957). This is not surprising because unions grow in the same way as firms do some expand, some shrink and die, some swallow others; new ones are created and big ones are formed by amalgamations. In most developed countries, the number of unions has fallen over time with increasing merger activity and growing concentration. In India, however, we do not find similar changes. On the contrary, the fragmentation of political parties over time has led to increased fragmentation of unions and the fragments have become smaller over the years.

3. Unionisation Across Sectors and Across States

Universally, there are wide variations in trade union activities across sectors and across employments. The differences are in terms of union density, intensity and strengths of unions. There are similar variations in India. The levels of unionisation are higher in manufacturing, transport, or public administration than in agriculture, trade, or financial services. Unionisation is high in mining, railways, storage and communication; and in some Sectors it is almost total (Seth, 1993). It is higher among blue-collar or factory workers than among white-collar workers or clerical staff. While most formal-sector firms have high levels of unionisation, the majority of workers in the informal sector and agriculture are without any union power. The more formalised a sector is the higher in its unionisation rate. This is seen both in the data published in the Indian Labour Yearbook (1992) and in the results of Verification of Membership of Central Trade Union Organisations. As in other countries, union density in India is higher in the public sector than in the private sector (Venkata Ratnam, 1997). Unionsation is higher in large firms than in small firms. This is partly because the possibility of initiating and retaining collective bargaining is better in large firms. Unionisation also varies among different types of workers.

It is lower among contract or casual workers than permanent workers. Further, unionisation for casual and contract workers very across industrial sectors and depending on whether they work for the public sector or private sector.

TABLE 4.4

Unionisation in Large Firms

Sector	*Membership as % of workers*	*Sector*	*Membership as % of workers*
Agriculture	4.3	Iron and Steel	28.2
Tea plantation	48.1	Textile	23.2
Minining and quarry	79.9	Electricity, gas, ower	54.5
Coal mining	100.00	Transport	30.6
Construction	17.0	Roadways	14.0
Manufacturing	15.4	Railways	100.0
Chemical	9.2	Services	4.0
Sugar	32.8	Financial Institution	8.6
All workers	8.0	Hotels and restaurant	3.3

Source: Verification of Membership of Central Trade Unions, 2002, published in January 2008; NSSO Data on Wage-Employment, 2003, 59th Round).

In India, there is considerable difference in trade union activity across states. The membership of Central Trade Union organisations and union densitites in some major states are shown in the Table 4.4. It clearly shows varions in trade union activity across states. In some states like West Bengal and Kerala, workers are more organised than in other parts of the country. The differences are to be seen in conjunction with structural differences of unions across states. Structurally, unions in Gujarat are mostly organised at the enterprises or unit level and not affiliated to any state federation or central organisations (an exception is the textile industry). In contrast, West Bengal has many trade union federations (jute, textile, engineering, plantation) and most unions are affiliated to them. Unionisation in the informal sector also varies across states; for example, it is higher in West Bengal than in Gujarat.

New Trade Union Strategies

While organising workers in the informal sector, the

traditional strategies may not work. In the formal sector, organising workers is largely centred around their pay and working conditions. Trade unions are also engaged in the control over the labour process. These processes, however, may hold true for sections of the informal sector as well, where there are employers. Thus, workers in small scale factories (who number over 28 million) could be unionised in a similar manner. However, insecurity of employment of these workers would act as strong deterrents to traditional methods of unionising. If trade unions press too strongly for increasing wages or improving working conditions, there is every likelihood of the employer closing down the factory and moving elsewhere with new workers. The most successful cases of unionising such workers can be found in small industries in Kolkata. The Centre of Indian Trade Unions (CITU) has unionised workers in small industries but the union has the backing of the state government, which is a big help. In other cases, such help may not be possible. The major section of the working class in informal employment is self-employed. Moreover, women form a significant part of this section. How does one unionise when there is no clear employer? We can use some examples of such instances that are quite different from the way traditional trade unions in the formal sector operate. Ela Bhatt, in her autobiography (Bhatt, 2006) has discussed this issue when she started organising garment workers. Her objective of unionising the women was to gain better rates from the agents who bought the garments and from the government for providing financial support to them. However, she soon found that these women were not necessarily interested in organising against someone. They were interested in organising for themselves as this solidarity gave them greater confidence to face challenges. These experiences of Ela Bhatt helped her in shaping the trade union known as the Self-Employed Women's Association (SEWA), today the largest trade union of women in the country.

4. Growth and Decline of Trade Unions

In developed countries, there has been progressive decline in union membership, union density, and union popularity in the last three decades. The decline is evident in the time series data of the two indicators for industrialised countries; they show that the declines started in late 1960s and early 1970s. In the newly industrialising countries, union declines started in the 1980s and 1990s (Table 4.5). In Maxico, labour unions made significant inroads in the seventies, but with economic restructuring in the in the eighties they started to loose their power. In Korea and Tiawan, unions started to grow in the 1980s and in initial years of 1990s, but then they started to decline (World Labour Report, 1997-98). In India, the union membership and union density data do not show similar declining trend in union coverage, but there are clear indications of decline in union power since early nineties (ILO, 1997; Kuruvilla *et al.*, 2002).

In India, the absence of reliable union membership data does not allow us to evaluate changes in union membership and union density over the years with considerable accuracy. The main source of data of union membership is those published in the Indian Labour Yearbook. Unfortunately, it only gives membership data of unions that have submitted returns and does not include membership of all unions. An assumption here is that the unions that do not submit their return do not exist, but this is hardly a valid assumption. In practice, majority of the registered unions in India do not submit their returns regularly. Further, the published data do not include data of all the states and some of the major states are always missing. This paper computes union membership by using primary data of number of registered unions and average size of unions in different years. In this method of computation, one may object that some of the registered unions may not exist. This is, however, somewhat compensated as some associations of workers that performs all functions of unions but do not get them registered as unions. Examples of this include associations of government employees, organisations of agricultural workers affiliated to CPI (M), and some independent unions like workers' committees. The estimates of union membership and union density (measured as a percentage of union membership among wage-employed workers) and their changes over time are presented in Table 4.6. It clearly shows that both the indicators have steadily increased over the years.

The changes in union membership and union density in India do not indicate decline of the two indicators similar to those seen in the developed countries. There are, however, enough indications of decline of union power in the post-reform years. The state-level data on registration of new unions indicate decline in registration of new unions in the post-reform era. Further, most new unions are in the informal sector. Union membership has increased in the informal sector, but it has declined in the formal sector. The shift of unionisation to the informal sector has a major implication, as unions in the informal sector are not as strong as the unions in the formal sector. Another indication is that in the post-reform period, there has been growth of non-union firms, and increasingly firms are adopting strategies to remain non-union. In some firms employers are adopting union avoidance strategies. For example, some employers are promoting workers into administrative/supervisory ranks to take them outside the purview of the Industrial Disputes Act. The loss of job in the public sector through VRS and closures or privatisation of inefficient and 'sick' public sector units has also contributed to decline in union power and union membership in the organised sector. All these have led to decline in union power.

TABLE 4.5

Unionisation in Large Firms

Country	*1950*	*1960*	*1970*	*1980*	*1990*	*1995*	*2000*	*2003*
USA	29	30	28.3	22.8	15.6	14.9	13.5	12.4
Japan	50	NA	34.5	30.3	24.7	24.0	22.2	19.7
Australia	52	50	43.4	46.4	42.7	35.2	24.7	22.9
France	32	19	21.5	17.6	10.2	9.1	9.1	8.3
Germany	35	36	33.0	34.3	30.8	28.9	28.1	22.6
UK	41	42	44.6	44.1	33.5	32.9	29.5	29.7
Denmark	50	58	60.2	76.3	72.5	74.7	75.8	70.4
Sweden	67	71	66.2	78.0	82.9	91.1	81.0	78.0
Italy			33.4	44.1	33.5	44.1	35.4	33.7

Notes: (a) Trade Union Density as % of wage-employed workers.
(b) The Union densities of Japan, Germany and the UK in 2000 are for 1999 (Visser, 2006).

Source: World Labour Report, 1993; Hirsch and Macpherson, 2000; Visser, 2006.

The available data on union membership do not indicate decline of trade unions in India in the post-reform period, but the changes in the economic and social contexts give a clear picture of changes in union influence. In the pre-liberalisation period, unions developed in an environment that protected both industry and labour and this led to progressive growth in union membership and union density. The new economic policy removed many of the protections and has led to decline in union power. There has not been any major change in labour legislation, but economic liberalisation has put pressure on the Indian industrial relations institutions to change and has affected the behaviours of unions (Kuruvilla, 1996). With the withdrawal of industrial licensing in the post-liberalisation period, the states are now actively lobbying and hence competing for both national and international capital investment and adopting industry-friendly policies. This has weakened labour's tie with the political parties and government support has shifted towards employer's side (Kuruvilla, 1996). With the shift in the balance of power in favour of the employers, they are now more aggressive in dealing with the unions and workers. In various locations, they are adopting practices that help them to avoid unionisation or curtail union power.

The decline of union power is also evident in the increase in income inequality and in growing variations in employment practices. In advanced industrialised countries, increases in earnings inequality in the 1980s and 1990s coincided with the decline in union density and union power. The changes also accompanied growing variations in employment relation practices (Katz and Darbishire, 2000). In developed countries, since the 1970s, non-union employment has grown rapidly through expansion of non-union subsidiaries, sub-contracting, outsourcing, opening of non-union green-field plants, and union de-certification. There has been decentralisation of bargaining and more issues are now decided at the firm level than at the industry level. In addition, wages are now more closely linked to performance and skill that vary widely across individuals. In India, there have been similarly changes. The distribution of per-capita expenditure shows increases in inequality in the post-reform period compared to those in the pre-reform period (Dev and Ravi, 2007). There is no aggregate data on distribution of wages for formal sector workers, but available piecemeal evidence shows growing wage inequality in the formal sector in

Table 4.6

Unionisation in Large Firms

Year	All Workers	Wage Employed	No. of	Union submitted Returns			Union membership (in mn)	Union density (%)
				No. of unions	Membership (mn)	Average membership per union		
1951	140.0	54.6	4623	2556	2.00	781	3.61	6.6
1961	160.2	63.6	11614	7087	3.98	561	6.52	10.2
1971	180.4	70.4	22484	9029	5.47	606	13.63	19.4
1974	198.3	78.5	28648	9800	5.72	632	19.41	24.7
1975	204.2	81.8	29438	10324	6.06	634	20.10	24.6
1976	210.2	85.1	29350	9778	6.09	666	20.20	23.7
1977	216.2	88.4	30810	9003	5.55	670	21.37	24.2
1978	222.1	91.7	32361	8727	5.77	711	22.62	24.7
1979	228.1	95.1	34430	10021	6.92	746	24.25	25.5
1980	234.0	98.4	36507	4432	3.51	841	25.91	26.3
1981	240.0	101.7	37539	6682	5.01	808	26.85	26.4
1982	247.8	106.3	38313	5044	2.82	595	27.60	26.0
1983	255.6	110.9	38935	6844	5.01	792	28.26	25.5
1984	263.4	115.5	42609	6451	4.71	798	31.16	27.0
1985	271.2	120.1	45067	7815	5.83	823	33.20	27.7
1986	279.0	124.6	45830	11365	7.37	720	34.01	27.3
1987	286.8	129.2	49329	11063	7.21	719	36.87	28.5
1988	294.6	133.8	50048	8730	6.33	810	37.67	28.2
1989	302.4	138.4	52210	9758	8.21	953	39.58	28.6
1990	310.2	143.0	52016	8828	6.18	795	39.71	27.8
1991	318.0	147.6	53535	8418	6.10	725	41.16	27.9
1992	326.5	150.9	55680	9165	5.75	627	43.10	28.6
1993	335.0	154.3	55784	6806	3.13	460	43.48	28.2
1994	343.6	157.6	56872	6277	4.10	652	44.63	28.3
1995	352.1	160.9	57952	8122	6.54	801	45.79	28.5
1996	360.6	164.2	58988	7242	5.60	773	46.92	28.6
1997	369.1	167.6	60660	8872	7.41	835	48.58	29.0
1998	377.6	170.9	61992	7403	7.25	979	49.98	29.2
1999	386.2	174.2	64817	8152	6.41	786	52.60	30.2
2000	394.7	177.6	66056	7253	5.42	747	53.96	30.4
2001	403.2	180.9	66624	6531	5.87	900	54.77	30.3
2002	409.6	183.1	68544	7812	6.97	893	56.72	31.0

Note: Membership as percentage of wage employed workers.
Source: Indian Labour Yearbook; NSSO data for various years.

the post-reform period with increasing wage gaps between managers and workers, and also among blue collar workers. Increase in wage inequality in the formal sector is also evident in the fact that in overall changes in inequality, the increase is higher in urban sector. The increase in income inequality, increasing variations in wages, decentralisation of bargaining, and growing variations in employment practices in India also point towards decline of unions.

There is not only the growth of union membership and union density over the years, but also decline of union power in the post-reform years. The paper has confined to growth and decline in union membership and union density, but equally important issues are the changes in the structures and functions of unions. Over the years the shares of different types of unions have changed in India, but it is difficult to capture such changes in statistical terms. It is easy to identify whether an enterprise in unionised or not, but the shades of union presence is often difficult to identify. Another unanswered question is how union density has changed in different industrial sectors? All these need further investigation. The framework presented in the paper can be used for such study. It can be also used for comparison of unionisation across developing countries with similar legislation for union registration.

Trade unionism in India is passing through a critical phase and facing unprecedented challenges in a liberalised, privatised, and global economy. Labour is being pushed from the organised sector to the unorganized sector leading to an increase in casual and contract labour. Downsizing, organisational restructuring, labour laws, political instability, the apathetic attitude of government, and gap in knowledge and skill-base are the major factors responsible for this state of affairs. Thus, trade unions have to rethink their position and adopt such strategies, which would help them to act as responsible partners in the organisation.

Trade unions are losing their membership and their influence is declining as labour has shifted to the unorganised sector. These workers are not protected by unions, and no sincere efforts have been made to organise them. Plant-based independent unions have increased. without affiliating themselves to any central-level federations, and have concentrated on plant level issues such as productivity-based wage settlements. This has weakened the power of unions. Many sick public sector units, unable to compete in an open market system, have compelled trade unions to adopt 'concession bargaining' for their existence and survival. The lack of mature leadership and inter-union rivalry continue to be the pertinent issues. Employers are bypassing unions as they find them obstructing the production process. They have started sub-contracting, outsourcing, and signing individual contracts. The government has not been able to provide a method for union recognition and choosing the sole bargaining agent. The law has so far been unable to take the unorganised sector in its stride. At this crucial juncture, the trade unions' role and functions need to be reviewed and redefined so that they can cope with the restructuring process.

In an era of economic restructuring where management is trying to sideline the union and the trade union is also struggling to maintain its *status quo*, the attitude of management towards the union can be crosschecked with the attitude of the union towards management for evolving better labour-management relations. It could help sick units to revive, and the smooth-running units to flourish and achieve a competitive edge. The attitude of workers towards the union and *vice versa* can be studied in order to identify the dominating factors which motivate them to join unions or not. The strategy of the trade union can also be examined to find out how they can satisfy the individual needs of the workers. The literature showed a contradiction over the relationship between job-satisfaction and union-participation and it could be examined whether higher job-satisfaction leads to more participation in union activities. Union strategies and their impact on productivity can be studied to counter the proposition that trade unions have an adverse impact on the productivity of the organisation. Research can also be conducted to know how trade unions influence job satisfaction, wages and benefits, workers' participation in management, absenteeism, industrial disputes, employee-turnover and overall economic growth of the organisation. Further, research can also be conducted to define the role of trade unions as to whether unions should adopt a path of cooperation or confrontation for their development. There is a strong need to evolve such strategies which can help unions to retain their influence and the power of collective bargaining.

Given the weaknesses, inadequacy and vulnerability of unions as discussed above, should the unions pack up and quit and fulfil the prophecy of the 'dying union' analysts? The alternatives before the unions are either that they muddle through the current turmoil and play the survival game or accept an increasing collaboration with employers in their plans for participative management and human resource development (HRD) with the prospect of being treated as responsible partners. They can change their main focus from the protection of the interests of poor workers to the welfare and social well-being of the workers in general, and enhance job-opportunities by taking over sick or dying enterprises to develop the workers' sector of industry. Trade union leaders should change their attitude towards management and behave as professional leaders. They should adopt revival strategies to gain their original mandate and play an effective role in the new economic environment.

CRISIS OF TRADE UNIONISM

Some of the serious limitations of the trade union movement were pointed out in the early 20th century itself. They only became further prominent and the crisis precipitated as the historical concessions that capital had to make *vis-a-vis* labour, like welfare state, were revoked after the fall of the 'second world' towards the end of the previous century. In spite of the formation of the Soviet Union, serious practitioners of the labour movement had long ago cautioned that there was every danger that the trade union movement might end up being part of the capitalist system rather than a means to destabilise it. As institutions, TUs do not challenge the class based capitalist order, they merely express it (Anderson, 1978). While talking about the Turin Workers' Council, Gramsci (1977) observed that the trade unions were product of political liberty as part of the bourgeois democracy. But "they do not supersede the bourgeois state." The following comments by him (1975, p. 224) succinctly sum up the problem:

> "Trade unionism has shown itself to be no more than another form of capitalist society, not a potential

suppression of it. It organises the workers not as producers but as wage earners, that is as products of the capitalist system of private property, as sellers of the commodity of labour. Trade unionism invites the workers on the basis of the tool they use in their labour and the material they must transform; in other words, it invites them on the basis of the forms imposed upon them by the capitalist systems, the system of economic individualism."

1. Problem of Economism

Labour market, and, for that matter, all the markets veil the true nature of the capitalist system. Hence, it is inadequate to think of furthering class struggle only as a market struggle (Yates, 1999). It has been clearly recognised at least from the time of Lenin that only furthering economic demands of the working classes will not necessarily take forward the political consciousness of the workers, and was understood as the problem of 'economism' (Lenin, 1978). He argued that the essence of economism was the reformist tendency of the TUs as their primary activity boiled down to seek better terms for the commodity sale of labour power (Clements, 1978). In fact, critiques have pointed out that trade unions have become a cause, among others, for the differentiation of the working classes (Gapasin and Yates, 1997; Yates, 1997). All that they are able to do is redistribute the national income in favour of the unionised work force, but the total share of the working classes in general does not change (Herding, 1972). Others have brought out the contradictions of 'corporatist status' of TUs as they become dependent on the state for their existence instead of members, resulting in goal displacement (Hyman and Fryer, 1978; Offe and Wiesenthal, 2002). Mann (1973) contends that institutionalisation of industrial conflict has reduced it to 'aggressive economism and defensive control'. Yates (1997) contends that the success of the labour-movement amongst the white males in the US has led to 'modes of thinking' that "precluded critical thought and radical action." Gapasin and Yates (1997) go even further and suggest that the unions today exist only to protect and service what their own members have already won. Gorz (1967, p. 26) asserts that unions as an economic movement can at best be placed at the tail end of the consumer society.

> "...(T)hey place the workers as a class on the tail end of the "consumer society" and its ideology; they do not challenge the model of that society, but only the share of the wealth which the society accords to the salaried consumer. They consciously bring into question neither the workers condition at the place of work, nor the subordination of consumption to production..."

As the goals of the TUs become limited and incorporated within the existing order, the means to achieve them inevitably get restricted. Union leadership may encourage 'private bargains' than risk wider solidarity (Herding, 1972). 'Compromise' and accommodation becomes an end in itself, a part of TU consciousness. Moreover, this 'conservatism'—the tendency to maintain the *status quo* and protect the gains of the minority elite-is not too far away from a reactionary agenda, especially when it loses a forward looking progressive ideology. In fact, Adler (1978) went one step ahead and attributed responsibility for diffusion of conservative ideology amongst working classes to the TU movement in fascist Germany.

2. Lack of Democracy

The second most important criticism of the TU movement has been with regard to its bureaucratic propensity and/cr oligarchic tendencies. Setting out with the grand ambition of an egalitarian system, TUs soon reflect almost with faultless loyally the existing hierarchic order. Though Michels' (1966) primary focus in his controversial assessment of inevitability of oligarchy was on political parties, he insisted that, "in the trade union movement, the authoritative character of the leaders and their tendency to rule democratic organisations on oligarchic lines are even more pronounced than in the political organisations." In Wright Mills's (1948) famous phrase, TUs end up being "managers of discontent" at best. The bureaucracy and the hierarchy within the TUs diffuse any possibility for autonomous political action and spontaneity of workers. For instance, it has been repeatedly observed that often the militant actions of the workers came up spontaneously at the decisive moments of crisis when workers as a collective decided to disregard their leadership and were able to forge an impromptu and rooted leadership from within. Mann (1973) quotes from Gorz's analysis of the TUs in France of the 1960s to bring the contradiction between spontaneity of masses and their efficient organisations, between the revolutionary consciousness and compromising institutions. Gramsci (1968, p. 35) also observed:

> "The workers feel that the complex of 'their' organisation, the TU, has become such an enormous apparatus that it now obeys laws internal to its structure and its complicated functions but foreign to the masses... They feel that their will for power is not adequately expressed, in a clear and precise sense, in the present institutional hierarchy..."

Moreover, as pointed out above, probably the increasingly narrow conception of the trade union movement, as primarily a vehicle for economic advancement, leaves little scope for participation by members. Lipset (1960, p. 226) makes the following perceptive observation: "Participation in any organization appears to be related to the number and saliency of the functions, which it performs for its members and the extent to which they require personal involvement. In most cases, trade unions perform only one major function for their members-collective bargaining, which can be handled by a more or less efficient union administration without requiring any membership participation, except during major conflicts. In such unions, we would not expect continuous participation by more than the handful of members who are involved in administration."

The objectives of the TUs have become one-dimensional and often are confined to raising tactical issues. Under theses circumstances, the union leadership is required to remain in continuous negotiations with the management and in communication with the state to raise economic demands and protect workers' legal rights. Such activities, by their very nature, need middle class sophistication; also, they are of immediate nature, which makes it difficult to have participative decision-making. Expediency demands political action and not participation; in any case, often the only expression of participation in TUs may get restricted to raising hands or a voice vote. Democracy in its day-to-day manifestation requires some slack and institutionalisation of alternate culture (Varman and Chakrabarti, forthcoming) that may not be possible in an organisation that is perpetually in an agitation mode combined with service-client relationship, as exists between leaders and the workers (Moody, 1997). Probably, unions do not have either the means or inclination to develop staff and leaders as 'educators', as suggested by Sciacchitano (2000), in order to support democracy within such organisations.

Actually, organisation goals guided by economism (as in TUs) and a hierarchical organisation structure with power concentrated at the top reinforce each other. Further, the primacy of economic goals fits in squarely with the agenda of the dominant system. The point one is trying to make is that, given the present economic system, furthering economic prosperity is the widely shared aim in most organisations including in TUs. After the historical phase of struggle towards establishing or rather legalising of trade unions that had involved a wide cross section of workers, it has been generally accepted that economic goals can be most effectively pursued by a small set of individuals at the top. Only addressing more abstract notions that are often in the social, political and cultural domain may require wider participation of the collective. Even amongst the industrialised nations, democracy has been able to find roots in the unions only when there is specific context like low status differential among members or strong 'locals' to begin with (Lipset, 1960). Analysing the British TUs in the first quarter of the previous century, Trotsky (1969) observed that the TU bureaucracy had turned all their 'accumulated authority' "against the socialist revolution and even against any attempts of the workers to resist the attacks of capital and reaction." In traditional societies, with less developed bourgeois values, the leadership and worker relationship can be even more hierarchic. This turns out to be quite convenient for the management as they can negotiate with the middle class leadership and the two can jointly impose their will over the workers (see Bahl, 1995 for instance). A respected leader of the working class movement in one of the oldest and most important industries in India—the jute industry of Bengal, made the following observation (see Chakraburty, 1966, p. 54):

> "Ever since he can remember, the jute worker has understood by 'union' nothing more than an office situated outside the mill and some union 'babus' whose job is to write occasional petitions and hold gate, bustee, or mass meetings."

3. Globalisation and Trade Unions

By the 1980s, the capital-labour equilibrium forged after the two world wars and the creation of 'second' and 'third' world crumbled, first due to post-OPEC economic crisis and later because of fall of the Eastern Europe. Since then, it has been moving fast backward for the labouring classes and the labour movement. With the ever growing automation and the weakening bargaining position, labour as a political force, at least *prima facie*, has been on the defensive. Memberships of trade unions have declined precipitously across the world and labour rights and trade unions have become dispensable in times of peripatetic capital and contingent workforce amongst the elite and even the middle classes. In fact, in the past two decades, trade union as an institution has lost the legitimacy it had accumulated over a period of time, not only among the upper classes, but also perhaps with the working classes all over the world.

As has been mentioned earlier, the premise behind trade union movement is that the employer needs the workers as much, if not more, as the workers need the employment. In effect, workers, by organising themselves, can strike a bargain by threatening to stop the work and force the employers to negotiate with them. However, the economic context has changed dramatically over the past decades. We would like to point out two primary issues for the need to open the debate on the premise itself:

(i) End of Work

While the labour movement has been busy in organising for the immediate gains, and protect and preserve them, capital has been devising ways to do away with the labour. Unemployment has taken menacing proportions by the beginning of the twenty-first century. Capital is continuously in search of either reducing work by replacing humans with machines and/or intensifying the process further through management methods like reengineering and restructuring (Rifkin, 1996). Though such large scale unemployment and underemployment itself may be a source of deepening contradiction between supply and demand—the basis of capitalist system (Marx, 1978a) and therefore a serious crisis of capitalism—it is also a source of a difficult predicament for the TUs as well. Even if there is no end of work, there is 'informalisation' of work at a large scale and 'traditional' TU movement has become practically ineffective because employers threaten closure, mechanisation, outsourcing, or some combination of the three (Thomas, 1995). For instance, in India, not more than 1 per cent of the labour force is covered by collective wage agreements at present (Bhowmik, 1998). And yet as the world is turning 'job less', it is definitely not 'work less' or worker less. Working classes are still generating enormous surplus and finding innovative means to eke out their living across the globe. Point is that the TUs in general have found it almost impossible to cope with this changed situation. They have not been able to respond to this 'informalisation' and sub-contracting of work. In India, mainstream unions, even in the organisations where they had or still have strong presence, have failed to bring non-permanent, contract or casual workers within their fold. Regular forms of bargaining do not work in this case, as there is no stable, 'employment contract'. As a Vice-President of AT&T observed (Henwood, 1996, p. 9) 'Jobs' are being replaced by 'projects' and field of work, giving rise to a society that is increasingly 'jobless but not work less'.

(ii) Peripatetic Capital

Globalisation has been restricted only to capital and its keepers, while labour's mobility, especially in the lower strata, if anything, has reduced. Capital is continuously on the move in search of more and more profits. It can move to comparatively less unionised areas within an economy, switch over to faster growing, more profitable industry segments, or convert itself into speculative finance capital or simply move to 'less' developed economies, where the going wage rates are significantly lower. As Bagchi (2002, pp. 233-34) asserts:

> ".......Capitalism all the time tends to reproduce duality between advancing and declining sectors, and privileged and under privileged workers, by continually and unpredictably changing the structure of production, and making the workers with no other asset than labour power compete among themselves for jobs and better deals...... Capitalism..... seeks to reduce labour power every where to commodity sold in auction markets without any legal or TU protection."

Traditional trade unions have been generally unable to deal with these new features of capitalism. We have appreciated this through our association with the TU movement in one of the old industrial centres in India, which was known for its militancy. Kanpur became an important textile centre of the country in the second half of the 19th century and by the end of the Second World War, had more than 150 factories and more than a lakh workers. There were 12 integrated textile mills employing around 50 thousand workers. As the mills faced crisis and imminent closure after the war because of a complex set of policy, managerial and technological reasons, they were taken over by the government (Chakrabarti, 1995). These mills specialised in large-scale army demands. Instead of a genuine attempt to adapt the available facilities with the existing demand and simultaneously initiate process for appropriate innovations and techniques, the government let the mills make enormous losses due to non-production and piled up stocks. Finally, in the wake of restructuring of the Indian economy in the 1990s, the government has simply stopped production in the state-owned textile mills. But unfortunately, all that the trade unions have fought for in the last three decades of government ownership including a decade in which the mills had completely stopped production, was increase in wages and bonus—the demand has never really included a concern for the future of the mills which logically is intricately related with the future of the workers, not even to restart the production. Finally, it has reached the present desperate situation, when workers are not getting their wages for several months (at the time of this writing). At present, neither the present owner—the state, nor any private party is forthcoming to run the mills in their existing condition where workers' rights can also be protected. Even in the remote possibility of a private operator taking up the management of the mills, it is going to be a serious blow to the present employees and significant numbers may loose their job. Our assessment is that because of deep-seated economism amongst the unionised workers and complete lack of democracy in the functioning of TUs in Kanpur, working classes have neither been able to cope with globalisation nor set any further progressive agenda. Even in the industrial capital of the country, Bombay, during the recession of the 1960s, the left dominated TU movement found that its traditional means of seeking redressal, like mass rallies and work stoppage, became ineffective and stage was set for the rightward shift of the movement and finally its degeneration into intimidation and violence (Bhowmik, 1998).

PROLETARIAN STRUGGLE: POSSIBILITIES

So far, we have identified four limitations of the trade unions, which are relevant in the present context:

(i) TUs are primarily an instrument for furthering the economic interests of the workers, and thus have gradually become part of the present order, decoupled from the issues of social transformation and emancipation of the working classes.

(ii) TU bureaucracy and its 'efficient' functioning towards these economic interests have become an end in itself making these organisations as hierarchic as the system that they were formed to fight against.

(iii) The present order has been systematically attempting to replace labour by capital, that too at an accelerated pace in the past decades, leaving TUs in shambles.

(iv) To compound all this, in the present times of globalisation, capital has been successfully moving away from high wage-unionised areas in search of higher profits.

Nevertheless, perhaps the fundamental shortcoming of the global TU movement historically has been their inadequacy in questioning the capitalist organisation of work. Marglin (1974) convincingly argues that the social function of hierarchical work organization is not technical efficiency but accumulation. He elaborates that the capitalist division of labour and factory system is an institution to guarantee an essential role for the entrepreneurs in the production process, and substitute the capitalist control for the workers' control over the work process and quality of output.

He further brings out how Soviet style socialism, which attempted to bring about a comprehensively different form of society, ended up in borrowing the fundamental principles of work organisation from capitalism.

We are of the opinion that the most significant shortcoming of the TU practice has been the missing domain of an alternate cultural practice (Gorz, 1967). According to Gramsci (1988), the working class must organise itself culturally as it has tried to organise itself economically and politically. TUs have failed to bring a vision of new society into their daily practice. Justifying this by claiming that 'party' is supposed to fulfil that role as propounded in 'What is to be Done? ' clearly will not do now that working classes have the Soviet experience of the previous century. We all know that this kind of division of labour finally ended up in a new ruling class consisting of a small elite of 'experts' (Bettelheim, 1976; Siriani, 1982). From these experiences, we have also learnt that the "state power was more limited" than what it was anticipated to be" (Wallerstein, 2002). The unique proposition that the 'socialist consciousness' should be introduced from outside the 'economic struggle', that is the TU movement (Lenin, 1978), by middle class intellectuals through party is not tenable in a protracted process aimed at a fundamental transformation. Any change process and the institutions thereof ought to address a combination of political and economic issues and cannot afford to lose either ends. Delegating separate institutions for political and economic ends creates an unbridgeable gap between the two-often hierarchic and reduces the effort to a caricature of the vision aimed for. Socialist vision, if it remains the preserve of a few outside experts during the course of struggle for transformation, then as the Soviet experience suggests, the vision becomes so much more elusive for a common worker after the 'revolution'. Hence, the need to bring the socialist vision close to the daily practice of every individual worker and forge institutions that are capable of doing this. As Gorz (1967, p. 99) emphasises:

> "If ....mediations between the overall goal and everyday action are lacking, then in the absence of intermediate goals capable of making the ultimate goal and the road toward it concrete, socialism will remain an abstract idea, an idea in the name of which dogmatic extremists will reject all structural reforms that indeed are not yet socialism in themselves, while underlying, under the cover of revolutionary phraseology, in fruitless, visionless, and primitive rear guard actions."

In the same vein, possibilities of a new culture cannot be simply left to a catchall 'revolution'. This would be a recipe to fall back repeatedly into economism. If one believes that a socialist society is possible, then that belief has to be brought into daily struggle and practice. Striving for democracy has to be part of the genetic code of every working class institution. Point is to bring in actuality or at least strive to do so, the 'freedom' that Marx (1986) talks about into the realm of a possibility:

> "Freedom in the field of material condition cannot consist of anything else but the fact that socialized men, associated producers, regulate their interchange with nature rationally, bring it under their common control instead of being ruled by it as by some blind power; that they accomplish their task with the least expenditure of energy and under conditions most adequate to their human nature and most worthy of it."

All the same, we must accept upfront that we have no straightforward 'solutions' to offer for the problems presented above. Yet, probably there is no other way than seeking and forging practice, which is close to our vision and inclusive of all its dimensions—economic, political as well as cultural. In this regard, we would like to bring three 'variations' of working class practice into discussion. All these have been undertaken in the past, and yet they have not become part of the mainstream

TU practice. We feel that we have to not only rediscover from history and past practice, but also innovatively reinvent too in order to find possible directions for a better future. These are more in the spirit of directions rather than formed 'solutions' to specific problems or even complete alternatives to TUs. In other words, we suggest that working class practice can move in at least the following three directions in order to overcome some of the limitations as discussed above.

1. Control of Work

In a factory system, worker lost control over the work process, besides losing control over the product (Marglin, 1974). A basic feature in the conception of any socialist society is selfgovernance, control over one's own destiny. Any such idea of self-governance must begin with some minimum control over work and workplace individually and collectively by workers. Such demands have been part of the labour movement in various forms continuously across the world—workers' participation, workers' control, factory committees, factory councils, shop stewards movement, etc. At many places, there have been significant gains as well, notably in Yugoslavia, Germany and Scandinavia in the second half of the 20th century. At times there have been occupation of factories by workers: Turin, Italy after the First World War, 1919-29; Popular Front in France, 1936-38 or Peronista unions in Argentina in 1964, but in none of the cases workers could sustain it (Anderson, 1978), primarily because of the missing sustained support from the larger system. Yet, at most other places and times, demand for work and shop floor control have not been part of the TU movement and in fact, often TUs have been hostile to any such initiative and looked at it with suspicion, as an alternate centre of power at the shop floor. For instance, shop stewards movement during the time of the First World War England faced stiff resistance from the established TUs (Hinton, 1973). In an incisive study, Siriani (1982, p. 331) makes the following assessment about the factory committees—"probably the most democratically responsive organs that the Russian workers ever had", in immediately post-revolution Soviet Russia:

"Ironically, the labour movement that would face the

most challenging tasks of workers control was the one least prepared to do so ideologically."

Nevertheless, the demand for shop floor control can be part of the democratic resurgence of the TUs by bringing self-governance to the workplace. Such measures can become instrumental in bringing 'socialist discipline' to the workplace based on autonomy and spontaneity, by going beyond mere legality (Gramsci, 1988). It is understandable that topdown unions and union leaders are suspicious of shop-floor control by workers. Even the best of accounts of worker control in the regime of the TUs suggest that shop-floor workers could muster control only by defying their leadership through their own initiative and spontaneity (Beynon, 1975). Further, such 'control' generally manifested only in resistance to the claustrophobic supervision, through sabotage and subversion at the workplace. But there is every need to initiate bottom-up organising and demand for workers' control at the workplace can be a basic component of any such movement (Cole, 1962c; Hyman and Fryer, 1978). There is a possibility of mass participation to 'gain a measure of self-respect' in this case, while only a select few can participate in the TU activity (Gramsci, 1988). Evidence suggests that such bottom-up organisations may be better placed to tide over the present crisis. For instance, Hancke (1993) in a survey of TU membership in Europe in 1960-90 shows that unions with strong locals lost few members or actually gained some, while union without strong local structures saw union density drop by between one-quarter and one-third. Perhaps the most significant point in favour of seeking workers' control at the shop-floor is that democratic functioning cannot be compartmentalised in various facets of work life—we cannot have a democratic TU, while the same set of individuals work under an authoritarian regime at the shop floor. As Siriani (1982, p. 6) emphasises:

> "If the democratic gains of socialist transformation are to be consolidated and extended, they cannot be interdicted from the realm of everyday life in which people produce and reproduce themselves simultaneously with goods and services for social consumption. Relations of domination in the work-place inevitably tend to pervade

other areas of social life and ultimately threaten to undermine the democratic foundations of the polity at large."

2. Worker Ownership of Capital

If the experiences of state ownership of capital in the previous century have any lessons for socialism, it is that there is need to seek new forms of worker control over capital. Moreover, not all such experiments need to wait until the revolution happens. If the workers have all the skills to run a factory, then they may as well hire capital and even some specific missing skills (Perrow, 1992). This can be especially relevant for the labour-intensive production, and there are plenty of such work sites, including a large part of service sector, across the globe.

Cooperatives (as an organisational form) developed as part of the proletarian movement simultaneously along with the trade union movement. In England, Robert Owen's cooperative experiments at New Lanark preceded his leadership role with the Grand Consolidated Trade Union in the first half of the 19th century (Cole, 1962a). Even in the early days, reservations were voiced about cooperatives being 'reformist' in nature, and for instance, attempts to differentiate between producers' cooperatives from consumers' cooperatives were made by the First International (Cole, 1962b). However, by the twentieth century, especially after the Bolshevik revolution, TUs became the institution of choice for mass working class politics and cooperatives became almost synonymous with 'reformism'.

Yet, there are plenty of possibilities in experiments like Mondragon, where a complex of more than a hundred workers owned cooperatives has become the flagship of industrial development in the Basque region of Spain (Whyte and Whyte, 1988). Even for some of the immediate problems that we have posed earlier, cooperatives appear to offer some promise. For instance, in Argentina in 2002, around 150 abandoned factories were taken over by the workers and they have been able to run many of them successfully (Lindsday, 2002). The occupation and taking over of the factories can be an appropriate answer to capital flight. While finance capital can move by punching keyboard, physical spaces and facilities are not amenable to such convenient flight, which generates fresh possibilities for political and cultural struggle (Podur, 2003).

Without worrying about how the core of capitalism, represented by the gigantic global corporations, can be transformed, let us begin with the periphery, let us look for worker and community ownership in low-tech, worker-intensive, abandoned, located away from the metropolitan centres, capital as potential targets for worker ownership. Such ownership can entail not only control over a factory by workers, but also open possibilities for redefinition of cycles of work and leisure (Thompson, 1967), bringing fresh promise for organising. It may give impetus to 'rekindling of socialist imagination' (Panitch and Gindin, 2000). As a worker at one of the occupied Argentine factory said (Podur, 2003, p. 63):

> "But since they abandoned us we've learned a lot. We've learned that we can run the place, we can produce, manage, sell, work and have good relations among ourselves."

3. Bringing Community In

The worst fallout of TU economism has been complete filtering out of family and community from the TUs, at least in the routine functioning. This has been further compounded by the fact that, historically, primary TU constituency has been highly skilled, male workers. Even if women, community or neighbourhood were included, they were part of TUs only in those decisive moments of struggles and crisis, after which they were again back to their place and the TU activity repeatedly became the preserve of a small elite amongst the workers. To the extent that TUs can overcome their gender bias, they will be able to bring community in through organising informal workers, seeking capital from the community or forging new kinds of struggle that go beyond workplace, especially in today's times of privatisation of public utilities and receding state responsibilities. For instance, in the Argentine movement of factory takeover by workers mentioned above, there is wide ranging community participation in the process of take-overs and then running the organisations and/or providing them support, though asamblias-community based organisations, as they are called (Podur, 2003). On similar lines, community can be brought in through labour exchanges, where labour can be mutually exchanged without bringing in money, the instances of which go back to the early nineteenth century (for instance in Birmingham, see Thompson, 1980), but there are plenty of recent examples as well (Rifkin, 1996). Skill rights, that is, rights to protect skills or to acquire skills rather than protecting jobs can also help in decoupling worker rights from the workplace and bring them more towards the community (Perrow, 1992).

In the end, one cannot overemphasize that there is every need to seek new forms in order to expand the scope of working class struggles, given the present crisis. The important point is that socialism cannot be reduced merely to centralised state control of production. Further, merely pointing out that all of the forms above have a danger of getting embroiled in economism will not take us any further. We are neither suggesting to limit our horizon only to the workplace nor alluding that trade unionism by itself can bring socialist transformation like syndicalism (Anderson, 1978). We are not suggesting limiting ourselves only to organisational experimentation either (Trotsky, 1969). It is true that the working classes are building up their struggles against tremendous odds, especially in the societies which have suffered colonialism (Bagchi, 2002; Sarkar, 1998) or suffering worst forms of imperialist plunder, like in present Iraq and Afghanistan. Besides, the danger of economism and hierarchy are always present in a fast degenerating capitalist order. In fact, precisely for this reason, there is need to experiment in order to bring socialist vision into daily practice. Without thrusting middle class aspirations (Nair, 1998), working classes need to undertake emancipatory praxis, which is democratic and advances cultural practice (Siriani, 1982). Such praxis must be capable of improving not only the immediate but also further the long-term struggle. Hence it must be able to forge institutions that have the capacity to find expressions not only for the immediate interests of the working classes, but also the latent socialist consciousness (Mann, 1973; Thompson, 1980). We submit that in the directions that we have proposed above, there are possibilities for initiating collective processes and wholesome engagement of the working classes (Pateman, 1970). Of course, an underlying assumption here is that such latent consciousness cannot wait only to explode at 'appropriate'-revolutionary-moments as per Lenin (1978) and Hobsbawm (1964). These aspirations, to be master of one's own destiny, to cooperate and work towards a new world, must find immediate expression, without in any way reducing the urgency that the present order must go. There is clearly a long-haul ahead of us, wishing it away is not going to help, nor simply waiting for the 'party' to bring revolution is going to further our cause. If "socialism is not established on a day", as Gramsci (1988) proposed, and if it has to be "controlled by the majority of citizens", then the process must begin now.

We reiterate that socialism in the present context means experimenting with new forms for working class organising, such that their capacity to engage the elite and the state is furthered and yet, at the same time, they can retain the dream and the possibility of a future society. The dream, not merely as a faith or an utopian vision, but as a microcosm of the larger vision, as something realizable very much within the domain of the present (Panitch and Gindin, 2000). To conclude in Levins' optimistic note (1996, p. 20), there is urgent need for rooted but innovative proletarian practice (in close conjunction with theory building:

> "Any action that pushes back the boundaries of the permissible, that legitimises thinking and questions the unquestionable, that strengthens our own capacity to analyse and organise and that lightens the ties that unite us for the long haul, that invents ways for broadening burdens of racism and sexism and homophobia and hierarchical posturing within our own movements, is revolutionary practice."

Losing Power due to Membership Loss?

The trade "union decline is a world-wide phenomenon." They also have argued that although "union influence remains strong in a number of nations and especially northern Europe, most have witnessed a fall in union membership, on which this influence ultimately depends." In support of their claim about union decline, they have adduced statistics on trade union density which show that union densities have fallen in different degrees in most of their sample countries in the 1990s (in India however union density shows a slight increase from a figure of 18.2 in 1980 to 18.9 in 1993). In the same way Kuruvilla *et al.* (2002) based on union density data in a number of selected countries in Asia including India during the period 1980-97 have argued that there has been "a steady decline in union density in the 1990s in all countries" (Table 4.7 below provides data on union density in India separately). Not only that, in China, Taiwan, India and the Philippines, "union decline has occurred even as the percentage of employment in industry has been increasing"

TABLE 4.7

Trade Union Density in India, 1974-99 (%)

Year	*Union density*	*Year*	*Union density*
1974	16.55	1987	19.60
1975	16.64	1988	19.79
1976	16.82	1989	19.57
1977	16.98	1990	19.40
1978	17.16	1991	L9.2.
1979	17.60	1992	19.07
1980	18.17	1993	18.91
1981	18.00	1994	NA
1982	18.32	1995	NA
1983	18.54	1996	NA
1984	18.81	1997	NA
1985	19.09	1998	NA
1986	19.36	1999	

Source: Various issues of Indian Labour Yearbook, Labour Bureau, Govt. of India

Talking specifically about India, they have argued that although "reliability of official union density data is suspect, data from a variety of different sources show the beginnings of a decline in the 1990s" (*ibid.*, p. 433). Thus, they quote Bhattacharjee (2001) who "shows decline in unions submitting annual 'returns' to the central government." Similarly, they quote Das (2000) who shows that "the rate of union growth has declined sharply -in the state of West Bengal" in the 1990s. Thus, during "the nine years (1982-90) in the pre-liberalisation period, 4380 new unions with a total membership of 629,151 were registered" in the state of West Bengal but in the "nine years following liberalisation (1991-99) the number was 2686, with 240,624 new members. Thus, the rate of new formation has also decreased in the 1990s" (*ibid.*, p. 433). On the other hand, using a new measure of 'union influence', which "is a proxy for labour union's ability to represent their potential membership as well as their influence in the socio-economic sphere" (measured by level and coverage of bargaining), they find India to be very low on union influence and argue that this "new measure of union influence does not capture the case of India well." In fact, even though "Indian union density is not that high and its union influence score is extremely low", "Indian unions perhaps have the most supportive institutional environment in Asia (based on the logic of industrial peace and the logic of employment-income protection), and have the opportunities to increase their strength, given the steady growth in employment in the industrial sector" (*ibid.*, p. 444). However, as they argue, economic "liberalisation in 1990 brought about a sea change in industrial relations practices." "On the one hand, employers, faced with increased competition, have become more aggressive in their labour relations. In several key industries and firms, union membership has declined as employers have reduced manpower through voluntary retirements, as well as increasing sub-contracting. On the other hand, there is an increasing schism between the unions and their traditional allies, the political parties" (*ibid.*, p. 444) because of changes in India's economic policy in the 1990s which are based on the logic of competition. They conclude by saying that "Although we do not have clear national data showing union decline, data from individual states show clear evidence of decline."

It is true, as Bhattacharjee (2001) shows (see Table 2), unions submitting returns have declined over the years. But the fact is that this trend did not begin in the 1990s. It started long back, i.e. in 1966 and acquired a pronounced character in the 1980s which became further pronounced in the 1990s. On the other hand, the declining trend of union registration in West Bengal and consequent fall in union membership in the state during the 1990s which Das reports may not be the result of lack of propensity of employees to join unions as of difficulty to register unions under a regime that has been trying desperately especially since the late 1980s to project West Bengal as an investor-friendly state and to attract new investment in the state by taking different measures including measures to bring order and stability in the field of industrial relations.

Again, if one compares the trend of figures of claimed union membership with that of the figures of unions submitting returns, then one fords important differences between these two trends (see Table 4.8). Thus, unlike the trend of unions submitting returns, the trend of claimed union membership shows an increasing trend from 1961 to 1978. Thus from 3.98 million members in 1961-62 it rose to 6.20 million in 1978. Thereafter it

TABLE 4.8

Number of Registered Unions, Union Submitting Returns and Claimed Unions Membership

(in Millions)

Years	*Unions registered (no.)*	*Unions sub. returns (no.)*	*Claimed members (in millions)*
1961-62	11614	7087 (61.02%)	3.98
1963-64	11954	7250 (60.50%)	3.98
1966	14686	7244 (49.32)	4.40
1968	16716	885k (52.95)	5.12
1970	20879	8537 (40.89)	5.12
1972	23628	9074 (38.40)	5.34
1974	28648	9800 (34.21)	6.19
1976	29350	9778 (33.32)	6.51
1978	32361	7727 (23.88)	6.20
1980	36507	4432 (12.14)	3.73
1982	38343	5044 (13.15)	3.00
1984	42609	6451 (15.14)	5.15
1986	45030	11365 (25.24)	8.19
1988	50048	8730 (17.44)	7.07
1990	52016	8445 (16.24)	7.02
1991	53574	8418 (15.71)	6.10
1993	55784	6806 (12.20)	3 13
1994	56872	6277 (11.04)	4.09
1995	57952	8162 (14.08)	6.53
1996(P)	58805	7309 (14.43)	5.61

Source: Various issues of Indian Labour Yearbook, Labour Bureau, Govt. of India.

registered a significant fall in 1980 when it touched the figure of 3.73 million. In 1982 it fell further to 3.00 million. But union membership again rose to 5.15 million in 1984.From there it jumped to a high of 8.19 million in 1986. During 1988 and 1990 it maintained an average membership of 7 million. Thereafter it shows a fluctuating trend which does not allow us to draw any firm conclusion regarding the decline of unions in India in the 1990s. On the other hand, growth of registered unions throughout the period 1961 to 1996 have shown an increasing trend though in the 1990s the rate of growth of unions seems to have slowed down somewhat compared to the one at which unions grew in the 1980s. Thus, the three sets of data as presented in Table 4.2 do not seem to show any relationship to one another.

On the other hand, there is another set of evidence which shows that trade union membership grew at a much faster rate during the period 1980-89 than the one indicated by claimed union membership figures (see Table 4.9). Thus, membership of Central Trade Union Organisations (CTUOs) practically doubled during the period 1980-89—from 5.917 million in 1980 to 12.33 million in 1989. In fact, "not only the memberships of CTUOs increased in these years (1960 to 1989) but the number of CTUOs has also grown almost three times" (Srivastava, 2001, p. 465). Since these figures are based on verification by the central government, they appear to be more réliable than the membership figures which are based on the claims of unions. The data in respect of verified membership of central trade unions however are not available beyond 1989 and therefore we are not in a position to throw any light on its trend during the 1990s.

All this in fact raise the question of reliability of data on claimed union membership on which union density figures are based (see Srivastava, 2001). Consequently, it is difficult to draw the conclusion that union membership has declined in India in the 1990s (see also Mamkootam, 2000). It is however true that thousands of workers have in recent years been thrown out of their employment either voluntarily or involuntarily particularly in the organised manufacturing sector which must have eroded the membership size of unions working among them. But it is quite possible that these losses have been made up by growth of union membership in other sectors of the economy. Thus as one study (Srivastava, 2001) shows none of the CTUOs—BMS, HMS,

TABLE 4.9

Central Trade Union Organisatons and their Verified Membership

(in Millions)

Sl. No.	*Name*	*1960*	*1963*	*1966*	*1968*	1980	*1989*
1.	BMS	0.286	0.330	0.437	0.464	1.210	3.117
2.	INTUC	1.050	1.268	1.418	1.326	2.230	2692
3.	CITU	—	—	—	—	0.127	1.775
4.	HMS	—	—	—	—	0.763	1.481
5.	AITUC	0.508	0.501	0.434	0.635	0.345	0.939
6.	UTUC(LS)	—	—	—	—	0.621	0.843
7.	UTUC	0.110	0.108	0.093	0.126	0.166	0.585
8.	NFITU	—	—	—	—	0.084	0.5 30
9.	TUCC	—	—	—	—	0.123	0230
10.	NLO	—	—	—	—	0.247	0.139
11.	HMKP	—	—	—	—	—	0.004
12.	IFTU	—	—	—	—	—	(only 428)
	Total Membership	1.957	2.207	2.382	2.551	5.917	12.334

Source: Srivastava (2001).

AITUC and CITU—agrees with the view that trade union membership is declining in India. Some of them believe that membership losses in the manufacturing sector may have been compensated by growth in membership in the service sector and in the unorganised sector.

Yet the fact remains, as will be seen below, trade union power and influence has been declining in India especially since the mid-70s and this certainly cannot be explained in terms of loss of union membership. In fact whether one goes by the verified membership of the central, unions or by the membership as claimed by the unions (excepting the years 1980 and 1982 when the claimed membership figures came down to 3.73 million and 3.00 million respectively), one will find that trade union membership trend has been an increasing one more or less upto 1989-90. Moreover, trade union density has never been very high in India. Finally one should not assume, as will be seen later, that those who take membership of a union are necessarily involved in its activities or support it actually. In fact, as will be seen later, large majority of employees look upon trade unions in purely instrumental terms and take union membership for fulfiling different personal objectives. Consequently if one is not satisfied with one union one may move on to a rival union which promises to fulfil his objectives which incidentally is one reason for which inter-union rivalry is very high in India. This would in fact explain why often a union which obtains recognition on the basis of membership verification or check-off system looses elections organised to constitute works committees or similar such bodies in the company (this happened for example, in the Durgapur Steel Plant in the 1960s and the BHEL, Haridwar in the 1970s). On the other hand, minority unions often enjoy considerable power in the company.

We will argue that decline in union power in India that has been taking place since the mid-70s and which has taken a very pronounced character in the 1990s should be understood not in terms of loss of union membership but in terms of generic weaknesses from which unions in India suffer from and the changes in the economic and political environment in which they operated especially till the early 1970s or so which have contributed to their loss of power. In fact trade unions as an institution have always been weak in India. Yet they enjoyed considerable power both at the national and bargaining levels (especially in the public sector) especially till the early 1970s or so because of their linkage with political parties and the support they received from them and the government in power. Not only the institutional framework of industrial relations that the government created after the independence was very favourable for labour and unions in that it protected them at the workplace but the government also intervened to a great extent in labour-management disputes in their favour. But with the beginning of crisis that has gripped the Indian economy since the mid-60s and which has deepened over the years, this political support has increasingly tilted in favour of the employers. Consequently trade union power in India has begun to fall. In fact, any discussion of not only of the loss of union power but also of revival of union power must take these issues into consideration.

Trade union power and influence in India has begun falling since the mid-70s though it has acquired a pronounced character especially after 1991 when the second phase of economic reforms began. The explanation for the same, as the above analysis brings out clearly, should not be sought in the fall in union membership in the 1990s as some writers have tended to do. This is because trade union density has never been high in India. Moreover, it is also difficult to prove whether trade union density has really fallen or not in India in the 1990s. Furthermore, trade union power has begun to fall much earlier, i.e. in the mid-70s. The fact is that trade unions are inherently weak in India for different reasons. Yet they have enjoyed considerable power and influence at both the national and bargaining levels particularly in the public sector especially till the early 1970s or so because of their linkage with political parties and the support they received from the government in power. Since the mid-70s with the deepening of economic crisis in the country this political support has increasingly shifted in favour of the employers which in fact would explain the decline in union power in India. Review of actions taken by the unions so far does not however lead to any optimism regarding revival of union power in India in the foreseeable future.

References

Sidney and Beatrice Webbs, "The Histroy of Trande Unionism", p. 1.

Clyde E. Dankert, "On Temporary Unionism", p. 1.

R.F. Hoxie as coated in *Ibid.*, p. 3.

Cole, G.D.H. (1962a), A History of Socialist Thought, Vol. 1, Macmillan, London.

______(1962b), A History of Socialist Thought, Vol. 2, Marxism and Anarchism, 1850-90, Macmillan, London.

______(1962c), An Introduction to Trade Unionism, George Allen and Unwin, Third Impression, London.

Engels, F. (1978), Engels, F. (1978), *Socialism: Utopian and Scientific*, Progress Publishers, First Printing 1954.

Hobsbawm, Eric (1988), The Age of Revolution, Cardinal, London, First Published 1962.

Kuczynski, Jurgen (1975), The Rise of the Working Class, McGraw Hill, New York.

Mortan, A.L. (1974), A Peoples' History of England, International Publishers, 4th Impression, New York.

Marglin, S.A. (1974), "What Do Boses Do?—the Origins and functions of Hierarchy in Capitalist Production", *Review of Radical Political Economics*, Vol. 6, pp. 60-112.

Marx, Karl (1978a), *Capital*, Vol. 1, Progress Publishers, First Published 1954, Moscow.

——(1978b), *Wages, Price and Profit*, Progress Publishers, Moscow, First Published in 1947.

Bagchi, A.K. (2002), *Capital and Labour Redefined: India and the Third World*, Tulika, New Delhi, pp. 233-34.

Sirianni, Cannen (1982), Workers' Control and Socialist Democracy: The Soviet Experience, Verso, London.

Marx, K. and Engels, F. (1977), *Manifesto of the Communist Party*, Progress Publishers, 2nd revised edition, reproduction of the translation made by Samuel Moore in 1888, Moscow.

Clements, Laurie (1978), "Reference Groups and Trade Union Consciousness", in Clarke, Tom and Clements, Lawrie (eds.), *Trade Unions under Capitalism*, Humanities Press, New Jersey, pp. 309-32.

Lozovsky, A. (1975), *Marx and the Trade Unions*, Radical Book Club, 2nd print in India, Calcutta.

Hyman, Richard (1971), *Marxism and the Sociology of Trade Unions*, Pluto Press.

Lenin, V.I. (1960), *Collected Works*, Vol. IV, Progress Publishers, Moscow.

Thompson, E.P. (1980), The Making of the English Working Class, Penguin, London.

Amin, Samir (2000), "The Political Economy of the Twentieth Century", *Monthly Review*, Vol. 52, No. 2, pp. 1-17.

Harris, A. Millis and Royal E. Mongtomery, *The Economics of Labour*, Vol. III, Organized Labour, p. 3.

Frank, Jannenbaum, "The Labour Movement", p. 29.

George, W. Jaylor, "Government Regulation of Industrial Relations", p. 20.

Joh, T. Dunlop, "The Development of Labour Orgnisation", pp. 163-96.

Joseph, Shister, "The Logic of Union Growith", *Journal of Political Economy*

Irving, Bernstein, "The Growth of American Unions", *American Economics Review*, June (1954).

Julius, Rezler, "Union Growth Reconsidered" (M/S).

Shorter, E. and Tilly, C. (1974), Strikes in France, 1830-1968, Cambridge University Press, Cambridge.

Korpi, W. (1983), The Democratic Class Struggle, Routledge and Kegan, London.

Freeman, R. and Medoff, J. (1984), What Do Unions Do?, Basic Books, New York.

Sheth, N.R. (1993), "Our Trade Unions: An Overview", *Economic and Political Weekly*, Vol. 28, No. 6, pp. 231-36.

Visser, Jelle (1989), European Trade Unions in Figures, Kluwer Law and Taxation Publishers, Boston.

Kuruvilla, Sarosh (1996), "Industrialization Strategies and National Industrial Relations Policy in Southeast Asia: Singapore, Malaysia, Philippines, and India", *Industrial and Labour Relations Review*, Vol. 49, No. 4, pp. 635-57.

Venkata Ratnam, C.S. (1977), Industrial Relations in Indian States, Industrial

Relations Research Association and Global Business Press, New Delhi.

ILO (1997), World Labour Report, 1997-98: Industrial Relations, Democracy, and Social Stability, International Labour Organisation, Geneva.

Davala, Sarath E.A. (1992), Employment and Unionisation in Indian Industry, Friedrich Ebert Stiftung, New Delhi.

Papola, T.S. (1994), "Employment, Growth and Social Protection of Labour in India", in P. Sinha, C.S. Venkatratnam and G. Botterweek (eds.), Labour and Unions in a Period of Transition, Friedrich Ebert Stiftung, Delhi.

NCEUS (2007), Report on Condition of Work and Promotion of Livelihoods in the Unorganised Sector, National Commission on Enterprises in the Unorganised Sector, www.nceus.gov.in.

Ramaswamy, E.A. (2000), Managing Human Resources: A Contemporary Text, Oxford University Press, New York.

Hoxie, Robert F. (1920), Trade Unionism in the United States, D. Appleton and Company, New York.

Ibid.., p. 7.

Rudolph, Lloyd and Rudolph, Susanne (1987), In Pursuit of Lakshmi: The Political Economy of the Indian State, The University of Chicago Press, Chicago.

Sheth, N.R. (1993), "Our Trade Unions: An Overview", *Economic and Political Weekly*, Vol. 28, No. 6, pp. 231-36.

Dev, Mahendra S. and Ravi, C. (2007), "Poverty and Inequality: All India and States, 1983-2005", *Economic and Political Weekly*, 10 Feb. 2007, pp. 519-20.

Katz, Harry C. and Darbishire, Owen, (2000), Converging Divergences: Worldwide Changes in Employment System, Comell University Press, Ithaca.

Anderson, Perry (1978), "The Limits and Possibilities of Trade Union Action", in Clarke, Tom and Clements, Lawrie (eds.), *Trade Unions Under Capitalism*, Humanities Press, New Jersey, pp. 333-50.

Gramsci, Antonio (1977), "The Turin Workers' Council" (trans. From L' Ordine Nuovo, 1919-20), in Robin Blackburr, *Revolution and Class Struggle: A Reader in Marxist Politics*, Glasgow, pp. 307-409.

Yates, Michael D. (1999), "Braverman and the Class Struggle", *Monthly Review*, Vol. 50, No. 8, pp. 2-11.

Lenin, V.I. (1978), *What is to be Done?*, Progress Publishers, First Published in 1947, Moscow.

Gapasin, Fernando and Yates. Michael (1997), "Organising the Unorganised: Will Promises become Practices?", *Monthly Review*, Vol. 49, No. 3, pp. 46-62.

Hyman, R. and Fryer, R.H. (1978), "Trade Unions: Sociology and Political Economy", in Clarke, Tom and Clements, Lawrie (eds.), *Trade Unions under Capitalism*, Humanities Press, New Jersey, pp. 152-74.

Offe, Claus and Wiesenthal, Helmet (2002), "Two Logics of Collective Action", in John Kelly (ed.), *Industrial Relations*, Vol. II, Routledge, London.

Gorz, Andre (1967), *Strategy for Labour: A Radical Proposal*, Beacon, Boston.

Adler, Max (1978), "Metamorphosis of the Working Class" in Bottomore, Thomas B. and Goode, Patrick (eds.), *Austro Marxism,* Oxford University Press.

Michaes, R.W.E. (1966), *Political Parties,* Free Press, First Published in 1915, NY.

Mann, Michael (1973), *Consciousness and Action among the Western Working Class,* Macmillan.

Lipset, S.M. (1960), "The Political Process in Trade Unions: A Theoretical Statement", in W. Galenson and S.M. Lipset (eds.), *Labour and Trade Unionism,* Wiley, New York.

Moody, Kim (1997), "American Labour: A Movement Again?", *Monthly Review,* Vol. 49, No. 3, pp. 63-79.

Sciacchitano, Katherine (2000), "Unions, Organising and Democracy: Living in One's Time, Building for the Future", Dissent, Spring, pp. 75-81.

Trotsky, Leon (1969), "The Trade Unions in Britain", in Leon Trotsky on the Trade Unions, Pathfinder Press, pp. 53-57.

Bahl, Vinay (1995), *The Making of the Indian Working Class,* Sage, New Delhi.

Henwood, Doug (1996), "Post What?", *Monthly Review,* Vol. 48, No. 4, pp. 1-11.

Gramsci, Antonio (1968), "Soviets in Italy", *New Left Review,* Vol. 51.

Wallerstein, Immanuel (2002), "New Revolts Against The System", *New Left Review,* 18, Nov.-Dec.

Bettelheim, Charles (1976), Class Struggles in the USSR, *Monthly Review Press,* New York.

Sirianni, Cannen (1982), Workers Control and Socialist Democracy: The Soviet Experience, Verso, London.

Beyron, H. (1975), *Working for Ford,* E.P. Publishing, Wakefield.

Hancke, Bob (1993), "Trade Union Membership in Europe, 1960-90", *British Journal of Industrial Relations,* 31, No. 4, pp. 593-613.

Perrow, Charles (1992), "Organisation Theorists in a Society of Organisations", *International Sociology,* Vol. 7, No. 3, pp. 371-80.

Whyte, W.F., and Whyte, K.K. (1988), Making Mondragon: The Growth and Dynamics of Worker Co-operative Complex, ILR Press, Ithaca, NY.

Podur, Justin (2003), "Beyond Disillusionment", *Frontline,* Vol. 20, No. 5, March 1-14, pp. 62-63.

Panitch, Leo and Gindin, Sam (2000), "Transcending Pessimism: Rekindling Socialist Imagination", in Panitch, Leo and Leys, Colin (eds.), *Socialist Register,* K.P. Bagchi, Calcutta, pp. 1-30.

Pateman, Carole (1970), *Participation and Democratic Theory,* Cambridge University Press, London.

Thompson, E.P. (1980), The Making of the English Working Class, Penguin, London.

Gramsci Antonio (1988), *An Antonio Gramsci Reader,* in David Frogacs (ed.), Shocken Books, New York.

Industrial Relations: Policy and Measurements

Industrial relations were not satisfactory prior to the introduction of economic reforms. Strikes were common and conflicts between labour and management were perpetual problems leading to clashes and confrontation, both in public and private sectors. Trade unions represented vested interest rather than the welfare of the workers mainly due to political dominance over them. Sometimes strikes and other coercive methods were adopted by the leaders to satisfy their self-interest and also to oppose the management, though of course, these were also motivated by other factors like genuine grievances of the working class and exploitative methods of the management. This led to an unhealthy industrial relations scenario in the country as a whole resulting in colossal wastage of manpower and adverse impact on the productive system. With the adoption of economic reforms in 1991 the number of strikes, and workers involved and mandays lost have declined consistently but this is not indicative of harmonious industrial relations. Retrenchment, lay-off, closure of industries and their sickness poses a threat to job security and hence they are forced to accept the terms and conditions dictated by the management, which is sometimes justified but sometimes is an outcome of militant attitude. This is evident from the fact that the number of mandays lost due to lock-outs is far greater than the losses due to strike. This situation is detrimental to the industrial health of the economy.

Attitudinal change and transformation in the work culture and organisation of unions are inevitable if further deterioration in the situation is to be prevented. Consultation in place of conflict and cooperation in place of confrontation should be the guiding both for the workers and management and the government should endeavour to achieve this objective by introducing suitable legislations and appropriate policy measures. Consequent upon the adoption of the policy of economic liberalisation, privatisation and globalisation the arm of state shifted in favour of the employers as against the employees in the earlier period. This led to a sharp decline in mandays lost due to strikes. The new policies have impacted adversely on the labour unions. As workers remained subdued in the liberalisation period, the employers did not declare lock-outs. There was no need. In October 1999, the government constituted the Second National Commission on Labour on the recommendation of the Indian Labour Conference. The social and labour effects of the new policies are very serious. New investments are taking place, but job creation is quite less. Labour is being pushed from the organised to the unorganised sector. There is increase in casual and contract labour. In this milieu, the role and functions of trade union need to be reviewed. The trade union may disappear from the scene altogether and even the subject of IR may soon be irrelevant.

In the deregulated and liberalised economy, the day-to-day industrial relations matters are best left to the parties themselves in substantial measure, with a more nationalized and well-administered labour legislation in place. Also, there is need to set-up an independent or a tripartite professional body to conduct an objective inquiry into major or controversial industrial relations policy matters and industrial disputes which have a wide impact. Earlier similar efforts were made under the Code of Discipline and also by the National Arbitration Promotion Board. There is a need now to revive social practices that were abandoned earlier for the wrong reasons.

In the last decade, profound changes in the political and economic environment have impacted negatively on the position and influence of trade unions. These changes have eroded stable employment relationship, the traditional basis for union strength. They have led to demands for deregulated labour markets, and for changing the balance and content of industrial relations system in the economy.

Presently, globalisation of market, technological changes and changes in public and political attitudes influence the industrial relations system. Globalisation has led to intensified competitive pressures in product market, accelerated mobility of capital, and increased segmentation in labour market. Technological changes make it possible to reshape production through new forms of industrial organisation, including sub-contracting and the spatial coordination of production system. The government has always played an important and significant role in shaping the pattern of industrial relations. One significant aspect of its role is to evolve norms through tripartite forums to act as guidelines for shaping IR. State intervention has primarily aimed at ensuring industrial peace by preventing industrial disputes and settling them when they do arise.

The trade union activity was at its peak upto 1970s resulting in maximum labour militancy. This period also experienced growth in white collar unionism in sectors like banking, insurance and other service organisations. Trade Unions which could reach the commanding heights by 1970s suddenly found losing ground in 1980s. In all probability the time is for them to stop their activities and take a hard look at reality and prepare themselves for adopting strategies which would give them a new identity. Employees who joined organizations after 1970s are markedly different from their counterparts who joined earlier. They have different ideological values and commitments. These 'new value employees' seek more satisfaction from their work and are amenable to more micro level participation. Further, an increasing number of women employees, young workers, part time and contractual workers have changed the nature of workplace drastically, which requires finding new ways of handling them. A number of organisations are trying to distinguish between core and peripheral work so that some work can be outsourced. Out sourcing, sub-contracting, flexible workplace like home office arrangements are going to change the traditional way of working, the workplace and even the nature of working relationship.

There is a growing trend in restructuring organisations with severe implications for organised sector and shop floor workers such as greater job insecurity, lesser employability, reduced bargaining power, work pressure and compulsion to adapt to newer work practices. These exercises have significant influences on employment relations. The search for alternative models in this milieu is definitely going to give a new form and identity to the traditional IR System.

INDUSTRIAL RELATIONS: POLICY OF THE GOVERNMENT

India's industrial relations policy has had the following two basic objectives:

(i) Prevention and peaceful settlement of disputes, and
(ii) Promotion of good industrial relations via labour-management cooperation.

The Legal Arrangement: Industrial Disputes Act, 1947

A major step towards accomplishing the first objective was taken in 1947 itself with the passing of the Industrial Disputes Act, 1947. The object was to pre-empt industrial tensions, provide a mechanism for the settlement of disputes and set-up the necessary infrastructure. The act provides for the settlement of industrial disputes through conciliation, arbitration or adjudication. It lays down the preconditions for the legality of strikes and lock-outs. Provision is also made for payment of compensation for lay-off and retrenchment. The Act has been amended several times (most substantive amendments being in 1982).

Conciliation and Adjudication

The Act empowers the government to appoint conciliation officers for bringing about settlement of disputes through conciliation. If attempts at conciliation fail, the government can refer the disputes for adjudication if the parties to the dispute jointly or separately apply for it or if the dispute relates to some public utility service and there is a notice of strike or lock-out. 'Disputes' which have not occurred but are apprehended, can also be referred for adjudication. For purposes of adjudication, there is a three-tier system consisting of Labour Courts, Industrial Tribunals, and National Tribunals. The Labour Court deals with disputes on minor matters such as the propriety or legality of an employer's order regarding discharge or dismissal of workmen, etc. The Industrial Tribunal adjudicates on more important matters such as wages and allowances, hours of work, leave and holidays, etc. National Tribunals tackle questions of national importance and those that affect establishments situated in more than one State. The parties can, by agreement, refer a dispute for arbitration before it has been referred to a Labour Court or an Industrial Tribunal or a National Tribunal for adjudication. The Industrial Tribunals-*cum*-Labour Courts have been set-upto adjudicate in the central sphere. Of these, three are at Dhanbad, two at Mumbai and one each at Kolkata, Jabalpur, Delhi, Chandigarh and Kanpur. The States have their own tribunals and labour courts. The Tribunal-*cum*-Labour Court at Kolkata and one of the Industrial Tribunal-*cum*-Labour Courts at Mambai are functioning a National Tribunal.

Lay-off, Retrenchment and Closure

The special provisions relating to lay-off, retrenchment and closure are applicable to establishments employing 100 or more workmen on an average per working day. The Act also provides for protection in the shape of retrenchment compensation and notice to the workmen who have completed 240 days continuous service in the establishment in the proceeding 12 months before effecting retrenchment, closure, etc.

Work Committees

The Industrial Disputes Act, 1947, provided for the setting up of a Work Committee consisting of representatives of management and employees in every undertaking employing 100 or more employees. The duty of the Work Committees was defined as promoting measures for securing and preserving amity and good relations between the management and the employees.

Settlement of Grievance

The amendment in 1982 introduced a new chapter providing for the setting up of Grievance Settlement Authority

(GSA). The GSA is concerned with the settlement of all individual disputes in an establishment coming within its purview. An important feature of this machinery is that no reference to a Tribunal/Labour Court is to be made by the appropriate government till such time the dispute is heard by this authority and its decision becomes unacceptable to any of the parties to the dispute.

Unfair-Labour Practice

Another chapter introduced by the amendment in 1982 related to unfair labour practices on the part of the employer and workman as well as penalty thereof. The chapter says that no employer or workman or a trade union whether registered under the Trade Union Act, 1926 or not is to commit any unfair practice. Any person who commits such a practice is punishable with imprisonment or with fine or both. The amendment empowered the Registrar to verify the membership of any union and to cancel the registration of any union which 'calls' or 'participates in' an illegal strike.

The Voluntary Arrangement: Code of Discipline and Industrial Truce Resolution

Code of Discipline

A Code of Discipline was adopted in 1958 by all the central organisations of employers and workers aimed at preventing and settling industrial disputes on a voluntary basis. The Code lays down that there should be no strike without notice, no unilateral action should be taken in connection with any industrial matter; no deliberate damage should be done to plant or machinery, acts of violence, intimidation, coercion or instigation should not be resorted to; there should be no recourse to go-slow tactics and normal work should not be disturbed; in case of disputes, the existing machinery should be utilised with the utmost expedition; the employers should recognize the majority union in the establishment and frame a grievance procedure; the management should take prompt action for the settlement of grievances and should implement the awards and agreements speedily, etc.

Industrial Truce Resolution, 1962

The Code of Discipline was strengthened by an Industrial Truce Resolution adopted in November 1962 by the central organisations of employers and workers. It laid down that there would be no interruption or slowing down of production; on the other hand, production will be maximized and defense effort promoted in all possible ways. A standing committee was set in August 1963 to review the working of the Truce Resolution. This has since been merged with the Central Implementation Evaluation Committee.

Other Measures

Regulation Wages

The payment of wages is governed by the Payment of Wages Act, 1936, and Minimum Wages Act, 1948, as amended from time to time. The Payment of Wages Act, 1936 has been enacted with a view to ensure that wages payable to employed persons covered by the Act are disbursed by the employers within the prescribed time limit and that no deductions other than those authorised by law were made. At present, the Act covers only those workers whose wages are below Rs.1,600 per month. A bill to raise this limit to Rs. 6,500 per month was introduced in the Parliament in May 2002 and now comments/concurrence of various ministries/departments are being obtained.

The Minimum Wages Act, 1948 provides for fixation, review, revisions, and enforcement of minimum wages by the Central Government and the State governments in respect of scheduled employments in their respective jurisdiction. There are 45 scheduled employments in the Central sphere whereas the number of these employments in the States' sphere is 1,424. To protect the wages against inflation, the government introduced Variable Dearness Allowance (VDA), which is linked to Consumer Price Index. The VDA is revised every six months. So far, 24 States/Union Territories have already adopted VDA as a part of minimum wage. In the absence of a uniform national minimum wage, the concept of a national floor-level wage was mooled by the Central Government in 1996 based on the recommendations of the National Commission on Rural Labour in 1991 and subsequent increase in the price level. It was last revised to Rs. 66 per day from February 1, 2004.

Industrial Employment Standing Orders

Model rules were framed by the government under the Industrial Employment (Standing Orders) Act, 1948, for adoption by the industrial establishments employing 1,000 or more workers to ensure industrial peace. Amendments to the Act were made in 1961 and 1963. The Central Government by notification on May 19, 1982, extended the Act to all industrial establishments under the control of the government for which it is the appropriate government and all mines, wherein 50 or more but less than 100 workers are employed.

Equal Remuneration for Equal Work

The Equal Remuneration Act, 1976, provides for payment of equal remuneration to men and women workers for "the same work or a work of similar nature" and for the prevention of discrimination against women in matters of employment. The provisions of the Act have been extended to all employments.

Labour Legislation

Labour legislation is considered as "a most dynamic institution. From a simple restraint on child labour in 1881, labour legislation in India has become an important agency of the State for regulation of working and living conditions of workers as indicated by the rising number and variety of Labour Acts. The rapid development of labour legislation is an integral part of modern social organisation."

V.V. Giri has classified labour legislation in India under the following broad heads:

1. Laws relating to weaker sections:
   - (i) Children, and
   - (ii) Women.
2. Laws relating to specific industries:
   - (i) Factories and Workshops,
   - (ii) Mines and minerals,
   - (iii) Plantations,
   - (iv) Transport,
   - (v) Shops and commercial establishments,
   - (vi) Labour welfare, and
   - (vii) Forced or bonded labour.

3. Laws relating to specific matters:
   (i) Wages,
   (ii) Bonus,
   (iii) Social security,
   (iv) Labour welfare, and
   (v) Forced or bonded labour.
4. Laws relating to:
   (i) Trade unions, and
   (ii) Industrial relations.

Laws Relating to Weaker Sections

The important legislations covering employment of children relate to minimum age of employment, health certification, working hours, employment on hazardous machines, etc. The Factories Act, 1948; The Mines Act, 1952; the Plantation Labour Act, 1951; the Employment of Children Act, 1938; and the Shops and Establishment Acts of various States have determined the minimum age of employment. To ensure that children employed in factories are physically fit, the Factories Act provides that children upto the age of 18 cannot be employed unless they produce a Health Certificate which is considered to be valid for one year only. The Factories Act, the Mines Act, the Plantation Labour Act, and the Shops and Establishment Acts of various States have also prescribed the maximum hours of work for children. The significance of this legislative provision is that it prevents employers from employing children for long hours which is harmful at their tender age.

The legislative provision for protecting the interests of women workers have been made primarily in the framework of the ILO conventions on—

(1) Maternity Protection, 1919;
(2) Night Work, 1919; and
(3) Underground government.

However, also took into consideration the Indian situation while enacting various laws when either intend to safeguard interests of women workers or promote their welfare. From the point of view of women workers, maternity benefits are of great importance. In India, these benefits are provided under the

Maternity Benefit Act, 1961, and the Employees' State Insurance Act, 1948. The other legislative provisions for women relate to provision for creches, separate rest rooms and toilets and restrictions on lifting of weights and employing them in hazardous occupations.

Laws Relating to Specific Industries

The Factories Act, 1948 which provides for licensing, registration and inspection of factories also protects the interests of workers. It ensures better conditions of work, regulates conditions of employment and provides for certain labour welfare measures. The Industrial Employment (Standing) Orders Act, 1946 defines the rights and obligations of both employers and workers in respect of recruitment, discharge, holidays, leave, disciplinary action, etc. The purpose of these legislative provisions is to minimise the scope for disputes between management and workers in industrial undertaking. The Factories Act also provides for the framing of standing orders in all industrial establishments, including factories, mines, plantations, railways and docks employing 100 or more workers.

The Indian Mines (Amendment) Act, 1959; the Coal Mines (Conversation and Safety) Act, 1952; the Iron Ore Mines Labour Welfare Cess Act, 1961; the Coal Mines Labour Fund Act, 1947; and the Coal Mines Provident Fund and Bonus Schemes Act, 1948 are important labour legislations in the field of mining activity. The Indian Mines Act restricts the employment of workers in a mine when its owner does not comply with the notice of the Mines Inspectorate to rectify some such defect in the mine which may be hazardous to human life. The Coal Mines (Conversation and Safety) Act authorises the Central Government to take such measures which it may consider necessary for the safety of workers in coal mines. Other Acts in the field of mines relate to certain social security benefits to labour.

The Plantation Labour Act, 1951 applies to tea, coffee, rubber and cinchona plantations. The State Governments may, however, apply it to other plantations also. The Act regulates the conditions of work of plantation workers and provides for certain welfare measures beneficial to them.

The State Governments have enacted legislations on shops and other commercial establishments. These Acts cover workers employed in shops, commercial establishments, restaurants, cinema theatres, etc. They generally contain provisions in respect of hours of work, rest intervals, weekly holidays and overtime rates.

There are separate laws for regulating the working and service conditions of workers employed in different transport systems. The important legislations in this field are the Indian Railways Act, 1930; the Motor Vehicles Act, 1939; the Motor Transport Workers' Act, 1961; the Indian Merchant Shipping Act, 1923; the Indian Dock Labourers Act, 1934; and the Dock Workers' (Regulation and Employment) Act, 1948.

Construction work is an unorganised activity. There is no specific legislation to regulate the working and service conditions of construction labour. However, certain provisions of the Minimum Wages Act, 1948; the Workmen's Compensation Act, 1923; the Contract Labour (Regulation and Abolition) Act; 1970 and Standing Instructions relating to casual labour are applicable to construction labour. The limitation of these legislative measures is that they do not provide for the safety at work.

Contract Labour is generally employed for casual or irregular work. The Contract (Labour Regulation and Abolition) Act, 1970 which is implemented both by the Centre and the States has abolished contract labour system in perennial economic operations. However, for casual and irregular economic operations, the Act seeks to regulate contract labour system as it is not possible to abolish the system. The Act applies to all contractors who employ 20 or more workers and the industrial establishments in which 20 or more workers are employed.

The Working Journalists and other Newspaper Employees (Conditions of Service) and Miscellaneous Provisions Act 1955 regulates the service conditions of working journalists and other workers employed in newspaper establishments. In this Act, it has also been provided that the provisions of the Industrial Disputes Act with certain modifications are applicable to working journalists.

Laws Relating to Specific Matters

Specific matters which are important from workers' point of view are wages, bonus, social security, welfare and abolition of forced labour. There are two important legislations in respect of wages. These are Payment of Wages Act, 1936, and the Minimum Wages Act, 1948. The Payment of Wages Act, 1936 has provisions whereby it is ensured that industrial workers are paid their wages at regular intervals and employers do not make any unauthorised deductions from their wages. The Minimum Wages Act, 1948 has empowered the appropriate governments to fix the minimum wage rate payable to workers employed in Scheduled industrial operations.

The Payment of Bonus Act, 1965 regards bonus as a deferred wage and thus imposes a statutory liability on employers to pay it to their employees. The Payment of Bonus Act Applies to every factory covered under the Factories Act and every other establishment in which 20 or more workers are employed on any day during a year.

The important social security legislations in India are the Workmen's Compensation, Act, 1923; the Maternity Benefit Act, 1961; the Employees' State Insurance Act, 1948; the Employees' Provident Fund Act, 1952 and the Payment of Gratuity Act, 1972. These have been discussed in detail in the next section on 'Social Security in India'.

The important legislations which provide for labour welfare are the Factories Act, 1948; the Mines Act, 1952; the Plantation Labour Act, 1951; the Merchant Shipping Act, 1958; the Motor Transport Workers' Act, 1961 and the Coal Mines Labour Welfare Fund Act, 1947. If one goes by the provisions of these Acts, then the welfare facilities to be provided to the workers by the employers of industrial units and other establishments may appear to be quite extensive. However, these facilities can be broadly classified under the following heads;

(i) shelters, rest rooms and lunch rooms,
(ii) canteen,
(iii) facilities for sitting,
(iv) washing facilities,
(v) facilities for storing and drying clothes,
(vi) first-aid appliances,
(vii) creche,
(viii) housing,
(ix) educational facilities; and
(x) appointment of a welfare officer.

Bonded Labour System was abolished all over the country from 1976 through the Bonded Labour System (Abolition) Act, 1976. The Act envisaged release of all bonded labourers and discharged them completely from their debt obligations. Under the Act, responsibility for identification, release and rehabilitation of bonded labourers is entirely with State governments.

Laws Relating to Trade Unions and Industrial Relations

Interests of the employers and the workers are often in conflict. Workers thus organise themselves into a trade union with the objective of improving their bargaining power and protecting their interests. However, frequent industrial disputes adversely affect industrial activity and, therefore, the government invariably strives for peace. To minimise industrial disputes it enacts various labour legislations. To enhance labour welfare, it also enacts social security legislations.

According to V.V. Giri, "trade unions are voluntary organisations of workers formed to promote and protect their interests by collective action." The important functions of trade unions are listed by the National Commission on Labour as follows:

1. To secure fair wages for workers.
2. To safeguard employment and improve conditions of service.
3. To improve opportunities for promotion and training.
4. To improve working and living conditions.
5. To provide for educational, cultural and recreational facilities.
6. To cooperate in and facilitate technological advance by broadening the understanding of workers of its underlying issues.
7. To promote identify of interests of the workers with their industry.
8. To offer responsive cooperation in improving levels of production and productivity discipline and high standard of quality.
9. To promote individual and collective welfare.

Trade Unions

- Trade Union Movement in India.
- Obstacles to Trade Union Movement in India.
- Suggestions for Strengthening Trade Unions in India.

Industrial Disputes

- Magnitude of Industrial Disputes Causes of Industrial Disputes.

Industrial Relations: Policy of the Government

- *The Legal Arrangement*: Industrial Disputes Act, 1947.
- *The Voluntary Arrangement*: Code of Discipline and Industrial Truce Resolution.
- Other Measures.

Labour Legislation

- Laws Relating to Weaker Sections.
- Laws Relating to Specific Industries.
- Laws Relating to Specific Matters.
- Laws Relating to Trade Unions and Industrial Relations.

Social Security in India

Social Security Legislations in India

- Workmen's Compensation Act, 1923.
- Maternity Benefit Act, 1961.
- Employees' State Insurance Act, 1948.
- Employees' Provident Fund and Miscellaneous Provisions Act, 1952.
- Employees' Deposit Linked Insurance Scheme, 1976.
- The Payment of Gratuity Act, 1972.
- Employees' Pension Scheme, 1995.
- A Critical Review of Social Security Measures in India.

Trade Union Movement in India

In India, the beginning of modern industries was made in the mid-nineteenth century and with that the working class emerged. However, the organised trade union movement did not begin until the First World War. The first trade union was organised by V.P. Wadia in 1918. In the next two years 12 strikes were organised on a nation-wide scale in which about 4,50,000 workers participated. Movement on this scale developed tremendous confidence in trade unions among the workers. However, limitations of local unions were clear. Therefore, on October 31, 1920 an all India organisation was set-up to which any labour union could be affiliated. This organisation was the All India Trade Union Congress (AITUC). Its character was affiliating and any labour union could joint it. To begin with, AITUC was a broad-based organisation and people having allegiance to different ideologies were associated with it. In the earlier phase the AITUC was under the control of the rightists. However, in 1927 the communists succeeded in gaining majority. The liberals were unable to reconcile to this situation. The programme of the communists was not acceptable to them. Therefore, in 1929 they disaffiliated all the labour unions under their influence from the AITUC. A new central union named the Indian Trade Union Federation was organised under the leadership of N.M. Joshi to which most of the disaffiliated unions from the AITUC were affiliated. This gave tremendous setback to the labour movement in India.

Having realised the damage the split in the labour movement had done to the cause of workers, some labour leaders made efforts for unit which, however, did not succeed. In this phase the National Federation of Labour was organised. In 1932 the Indian Trade Union Federation and the National Federation of Labour were merged and the new organisation was named the National Trade Union Federation. In 1937, attempts were made to unite the All India Trade Union Congress and the National Trade Union Federation. As a result of these efforts unity in the working class movement could be achieved and the National Trade Union Federation was merged into the All India Trade Union Congress. However, this unity in the labour movement did not last long. On the question of the role of Indian workers in the World War II major differences developed. After the War was over the Congress workers were in minority in the AITUC. Having failed in establishing their supremacy over the AITUC they left it and in 1946 established the Indian National Trade Union Congress (INTUC). There was further split in the labour movement in India when in 1948 socialists established the Hind Mazdoor Sabha (HMS). In 1949 another all India trade union, named the United Trade Union Congress (UTUC) was organised. It had left orientation and was led by K.T. Shah and Mrinal Kanti Bose. Hence within two years of the Independence, the labour movement in India got divided along political lines.

The AITUC was the biggest and the strongest trade union in 1947. However, after the INTUC and HMS were organised, its hold on workers was very much reduced. The AITUC, nonetheless, continued to grow in terms of the number of unions affiliated and membership until 1970. In 1970, the Communist Party of India (Marxist) established the Centre of Indian Trade Unions (CITU). Hence, they got all the labour unions under their influence disaffiliated from the AITUC. This naturally gave a severe jolt to the AITUC. During the past fifty-five years the INTUC has grown both in terms of the number of unions affiliated and the membership. Presently, it is the biggest trade union in the country. With the emergence of several new trade union organisations claiming all India character and large membership, the government decided to undertake verification of membership on December 31, 1977 and December 31, 1979 of unions affiliated to central trade union organisations, namely,

(i) the Indian National Trade Union Congress (INTUC),
(ii) the All Indian Trade Union Congress (AITUC),
(iii) the Hind Mazdoor Sabha (HMS),
(iv) the United Trade Union Congress (UTUC),
(v) the Centre of Indian Trade Unions (CITU),
(vi) the Bharatiya Mazdoor Sangh (BMS),
(vii) the United Trade Union Congress-Lenin Sarini (UTUC-LS),
(viii) the National Labour Organisation (NLO),
(ix) the Trade Union Coordination Centre (TUCC), and
(x) the National Front of Indian Trade Unions (NFITU).

Reliable and upto date data on the number of trade unions

in India and their membership are not available. This is due to the reason that it is not obligatory on the part of trade unions to secure registration under the Indian Trade Unions Act. Even among registered trade unions, the response of the unions submitting annual returns is generally less than 50 per cent. Data regarding unregistered unions are not available. However, whatever data on registered trade unions are available point to the fact that the number of registered unions has declined in the post-liberalisation period. Thus, the number of registered workers' unions declined from 52,773 in 1991 to 41,136 in 2000 (over the same period, the number of workers' unions submitting returns declined from 8,351 to 7,231). However, the membership rose somewhat from 60,94,000 in 1991 to 63,94,000 in 2000.

The Trade Unions Act was passed in 1926. It provides for registration of trade unions of employers and workers and in certain respects, defines the law relating to registered trade unions. It confers legal and corporate status on registered trade unions. The Trade Unions Act, 1926 has been amended and following amendments have been enforced from January 9, 2002

1. not trade union of workmen shall be registered unless at least 10 per cent or 100, whichever is less, of workmen are members of the union;
2. in no case shall a union be registered without a minimum strength of seven members;
3. a provision for filing an appeal before the Industrial Tribunal/Labour Court in case of non-registration/ restoration of registration has been provided; and
4. all office-bearers of a registered trade union, except not more than one-third of the total number of office-bearers or five, whichever is less, shall be persons actually engaged or employed in the establishment or industry with which the trade union is connected.

It is noteworthy that in the absence of a strong trade union movement neither is it possible to safeguard the interests of the workers, nor one can hope to end the exploitation of workers. Hence, there must be an improvement in the condition of the trade unions in India. The following suggestions are generally made for this purpose.

1. The Need for Unity

An essential condition to strengthen labour movement in this country is that there should be greater unity among the various trade unions. At present there are several all India trade unions. This, in fact, reflects the weakness of the trade union movement in India. If the trade union movement is to be strengthened, then there should be just one central organisation of workers and V.V. Giri's suggestion—one industry one trade union should be accepted and implemented.

2. Need for National Integration

Workers must not be divided on the basis of caste, religion, language and region, if a strong trade union movement is to be built in this country. The employers dislike unity among the workers. Hence they often sow the seeds of dissensions on the basis of language, religion, caste, etc. Workers must be protected from these tendencies. They should be educated that in spite of the regional, linguistic, religious and caste diversities, they belong to the same class and the unity among them is to be maintained at all costs.

3. Increased Membership

Strength of a trade union depends on its membership. Therefore, the attempt of trade union leaders should be that every worker joins the trade union. Often the relatively well-off workers, particularly if they have no grievance against the employer, fail to understand their class interest and thus show indifference to the activities of the trade unions. Some workers do not join trade unions because of the lack of concern towards the activities of the latter. In fact, class consciousness has to be created among workers and this will enthuse them to join the trade unions.

4. Improvement in the Financial Position

Financial position of most of the trade unions is not sound. This is often the result of their low membership. Moreover, many members of labour unions do not pay subscription on a regular basis. This situation demands improvement. Workers whose financial position is weak should be made class conscious and should be convinced that regular payment of subscription by them to the trade union is as much important as any other expenditure incurred by them.

5. Paid Employees

Trade unions should employ paid workers to look after their office work. Those of the members of the unions who volunteer their services for this work fail to do it over a long period. It has been observed that soon their interest dampens and then they fail to discharge their responsibilities in a sincere manner. Hence, it is always advisable that the trade unions employ paid workers to do office work.

6. Strike Fund

Perhaps the most powerful weapon in the arsenal of workers is strike. It is through the weapon that trade unions pressurise the employers and thus succeed in realising their demands. The strike certainly inflicts losses on the employers, at the same time it causes tremendous hardships to the workers. Saving of most workers are meagre. Therefore, in cases of prolonged strikes workers and their families face starvation. This often breaks the will power of the workers and, as a result, strike fails. Hence, trade unions must create strike funds by collecting small contributions from the members on a regular basis. These resources can be used by the trade unions to assist the members, if the strike is prolonged.

7. Creation of Welfare Funds

So far trade unions in India have neglected welfare work. Hence their connections with the workers are not stable. Many workers often come to know of the existence of the union when a struggle is launched against the employer for realising certain demands. This approach is not correct. The trade unions should make arrangements for medical facilities to workers and their families, provide adult education and sources of entertainment. For these purposes welfare funds should be created.

8. Creation of Favourable Public Opinion

In a democratic political system, no class can hope to be successful in its struggle without public opinion being in its favour. Therefore, trade unions should undertake publicity work to explain their policy and demands. Their attempt should be to enlist the support of other sections of the society in favour of their demands. The mobilisation of public opinion in this manner often brings pressure on the employers and creates conditions for the intervention of the government in a decisive manner which is definitely helpful to the workers in a prolonged struggle.

The Industrial Disputes Act, 1947 strives to pre-empt industrial tensions and provides a mechanism of conciliation, arbitration or adjudication for the settlement of industrial disputes. The Act specifies all those cases in which a strike or a lock-out will be illegal. It also lays down conditions necessary for the legality of strikes and lock-outs. The Act provides for payment of compensation for lay-off and retrenchment of workers. There is also a provision in the Act for the setting up of a Work Committee consisting of the representatives of workers and management in an undertaking for preserving good relations between the management and employees.

The industrial sector frequently faces disputes and struggles on account of the fact that the interests of the employers and the employees are often at variance. While the former are interested in reducing wages and increasing the hours of work, the latter are interested in increasing wages and bettering the conditions of work. Industrial disputes often lead to 'strikes' and 'lock-outs.' Strikes are resorted to by the workers to safeguard their interests, while lock-outs are resorted to by the capitalists pressurize the workers and compel them to tow their lines. Accordingly, both of these activities form a part of industrial disputes and lead to struggles disturbing the peace and tranquility of the industrial sector. This affects industrial activity adversely leading to under-fulfilment of targets laid down in the plans. It is on account of this reason that all plan documents in India have emphasized the necessity of preserving industrial peace. The First Five Year Plan, while recognizing the right of the workers to strike, emphasized that "the stress of the administration as well as the efforts of parties should, however, be one avoidance of disputes and on securing internal settlement."

The progress of industrialization has been accompanied by increases in industrial disputes in India. This is a natural outcome of the conditions prevailing in the country. In addition to the fact that the base of industrial structure has considerable broadened and diversified over the years (opening new fields of industrial activity and thus, by implication, increasing the scope and area of industrial conflicts and confrontations), steep price increases and rising costs of living have compelled the workers to resort to strikes to maintain their real wages at least at constant levels.

The total number of work stoppages in 1951 was 1,071 involving 6.91 lakh workers and resulting in a total loss of 38.2 lakh mandays. The number of work stoppages, workers involved and total mandays lost increased considerably over the planning period. The number of work stoppages rose to the high figure of 2,938 in 1974 with the number of workers involved in the strikes rising to 28.55 lakh and the number of mandays lost to 402.6 lakh. The imposition of the Emergency in 1975 and suppressive measures that followed it, resulted in a steep decline in industrial disputes. However, restoration of normal conditions released the 'pent up' unrest among the workers and the years 1977 and 1978 saw a substantial increase in industrial disputes. In January 1982, the textile workers of Mumbai went on a prolonged general strike which resulted in a substantial loss of mandays. During 1989-90, the total mandays lost due to strikes and lock-outs was 30.77 million. As stated earlier, the phase of liberalisation since 1991 has seen considerable restructuring of businesses in India in such a way that the strength of workers' unions has been eroded significantly. As a result, the number of industrial disputes declined steeply from 1,810 in 1991 to only 674 in 2001 and further to 552 in 2003. What is more significant is the fact that strikes have decreased at a much faster rate than lock-outs. From 540 strikes in 1999, the number of strikes fell to only 225 in 2003 and the number of mandays last due to strikes fell from 10.62 million to just 3.20 million over these four years. As against this, the number of lock-outs fell from 387 in 1999 to 297 in 2003. However, mandays lost due to lock-outs increased from 16.16 million to 27.04 million over these four years. This shows the weakening of labour movement and strengthening of the position of employers.

As noted earlier in this chapter, industrial disputes are natural in the industrial sector since the interests of the employers and the workers are diametrically opposite. While the former aim at maximization of profits, the of work, leave, privileges, victimization of employees, etc. are quite common in all countries. The two most important causes of industrial disputes in India have been the issue of 'wages and allowances' and 'personnel and retrenchment'. In fact, the issue of 'wages and allowances' alone accounted for about 30 per cent of industrial disputes for a considerable period of planning. In the post-liberalisation decade (1991-2001), 'wages and allowances' accounted for 25 per cent of industrial disputes. Another 17.5 per cent of disputes were due to the issue of 'personnel and retrenchment'. This is a natural outcome of the situation that has prevailed in the country during the period of planning. In addition to the fact that wages of industrial workers are very low in this country, the rising price spiral has made it more and more difficult for them to keep their real wages at a constant level. Naturally the workers were forced to resort to strikes. However, despite all their struggle, the industrial workers did not succeed much in forcing a rise in the level of their real income. For example, while the average per capita annual earnings of factory workers rose from Rs.12,208 in 1991 to only Rs.15,784 in 1999, the consumer price index number for industrial workers rose from 212 in 1991 (base 1982 = 100) to 424 in 1999 (i.e. double the index number in 1991). This implies that the real wages of industrial workers actually declined over the post-reform decade. It would be revealing to note that the real earnings of factory workers (base 1960=100) which were 99.2 in 1952, stood at 98.7 in 1965 and 100.2 in 1971 (and this despite the fact that average productivity of factory workers and increased at the rate of 4 per cent per annum since 1952). This means that over a period of two decades the industrial workers were just able to manage constancy in their real earnings even after resorting to strikes on this issue about one-third times of the total strikes. Therefore, people who rebuke workers for irresponsible behaviour are totally misguided in their approach to the whole problem. Had steps been taken to ensure an automatic adjustment process in the wages and prices, the total number of disputes would have been much less.

In addition to 'wages and allowances' and 'personnel and retrenchment', another important cause of industrial disputes has been the issue of bonus. The government has not been following a consistent policy on this issue also. It appointed the

Bonus Commission in December 1961 under the chairmanship on M.R. Mehar to study to entire issue of bonus. The Commission laid down that bonus was the share of the employees in the prosperity of the unit in which they were employed. It recommended a minimum bonus of 4 per cent of annual earning of Rs. 40 whichever was higher. Consequent upon the recommendations of the Mehar Committee, the government enacted the Payment of Bonus Act in 1965. This Act was to apply to all factories employing 20 or more workers and bonus was to be payable to an employee earning wages upto Rs. 1,600 per month. The recommendation regarding minimum bonus was accepted implying that bonus was to be 4 per cent of annual earnings or Rs. 40 whichever was higher. The workers were not satisfied with the award and considered 4 per cent as too low. Accordingly the government appointed a Bonus Review Committee in 1972 with B.D. Madan as chairman. The Committee recommended minimum and maximum bonus of 8.33 per cent and 20 per cent respectively. In addition, it extended the benefit of bonus to employees earning less than Rs. 2,000 per month as against the then prevailing limit of Rs. 1,600 per month. The net of coverage was widened in another important respect also. Whereas hitherto only public sector undertakings competing with the private sector undertakings paid bonus, it was made obligatory for the non-competitive public sector undertakings as well to pay the minimum increased bonus of 8.33 per cent. Consequent upon the recommendation of this Committee, the government raised the minimum bonus from 4 per cent to 8.33 per cent. However, during Emergency the government scaled down the minimum bonus to 4 per cent. The lifting of the Emergency in 1977 brought the suppressed resentment of the workers into the open and there were large scale strikes on the issue of bonus. As a result, the government had to raise the minimum bonus to 8.33 per cent. The eligibility limit for payment of bonus was raised from Rs. 1,600 to Rs. 2,500 by an amendment to the Payment of Bonus Act in 1985. This eligibility was raised further to Rs. 3,500 by another amendment to the Act in August 1995. The payment is subject to the stipulation that the bonus in respect of employees drawing wages between Rs. 2,500 to Rs. 3,500 per month would be calculated as if their salary or wage in Rs. 2,500 per month.

Social Security and Industrial Relation

A coverage of the programmes under social security would be clear from the following definition put forward by Lord William Beveridge, "The term 'social security' is used to denote the security of an income to take the place of earnings when they are interrupted by unemployment, sickness or accident, to provide for retirement through age, to provide for loss of support by the death of another person, and to meet an exceptional expenditure, such as those connected with birth, death and marriage."

Social security measures involve:

(i) Providing cash payments to persons and families of a specified class whose income from earning has been reduced drastically or ceased temporarily or permanently.

(ii) Providing medical benefits and medical care to persons in the specified class in the event of sickness, maternity, etc.

(iii) Providing cash payments in the form of stipends, pensions, etc. to the dependants of an employee in the event of his death.

Social security measures are usually divided into the following two categories: (i) social insurance, and (ii) social assistance. Social insurance schemes are usually financed through contribution by the employees, employers and the State. The benefits to insured persons are linked to their contributions. Social assistance schemes seek to provide assistance to the poor and needy persons. They are not linked to the contributions made by the persons and are financed from the general revenues of the State.

The important social security legislations in India are discussed below.

Workmen's Compensation Act, 1923

A beginning in social security in India was made in 1923 when Workmen's Compensation Act was passed. The Act covers only workmen in factories and provides for the payment of compensation to them and their families in the case of industrial accidents and of certain occupational diseases arising out of and in the course of employment and resulting in death or disablement. The Act is very wide in coverage and covers many diverse industries including mines, factories, transport, plantations, construction activities, electricity generation, etc. but certain specified categories (like members of the armed forces) are excluded. The government can include any class of persons employed in any other hazardous occupation. However, the Act does not apply to those industries or factories where Employees' State Insurance Act, 1948, is in operation. Prior to Amendment Act of 1984 the term "workman" covered only persons employed on wages not exceeding Rs. 1,000 p.m. However, the WC (Amendment) Act, 1984, has done away with the salary restriction and thus any person who is employed in any capacity stipulated in Schedule II will be included in the definition irrespective of the wages drawn by him. Minimum rate of compensation for permanent disablement and death have been fixed at Rs. 90,000 and Rs. 80,000 respectively. Maximum amount for death and permanent total disablement can go upto Rs. 4.56 lakh and Rs. 5.48 lakh respectively depending on wages of workmen.

Maternity Benefit Act, 1961

The Maternity Benefit Act, 1961, regulates the employment of women in certain establishments for certain period before and after child birth (six weeks before and six weeks after confinement) and provides for maternity and other benefits. The Act also provides that no pregnant women shall, on request being made by her, be required by her employer to do any arduous work one month before her expected delivery. The Act applies to mines, factories, circus industry and plantations, including any such establishments belonging to government, except the employees who are covered under the employees' State Insurance Act, 1948. It can be extended to other establishments by the State governments. There is no wage limit for coverage under the Act.

Employees' State Insurance Act, 1948

The most important step in the field of social security was taken in 1948 when the employees' State Insurance (ESI) Act was passed. The Act is applicable to non-seasonal factories using power and employing 10 or more persons and non-power using factories employing 20 or more persons. The Act is being gradually extended by the State Governments to new classes of establishments, namely, shops, hotels, restaurants, cinemas including preview theatres, road motor transport undertakings and newspaper establishments. The Act covers employees drawing wages not exceeding Rs. 7,500 per month with effect from April 1, 2004. Persons of armed forces are not covered in the ESI scheme. As on December 31, 2003, the total number of employees covered under the scheme was about 78 lakh.

Benefits Under ESI

The ESIC has its own fund known as the ESI Fund. It is utilised for payment of cash benefit to the insured persons, provision for medical benefits under the scheme, establishment of hospitals, dispensaries, etc.

The ESI Act provides the following six major types of benefits to the insured persons—medical benefit, disablement benefit, maternity benefit, dependants' benefit and the funeral benefit. As far as medical benefit is concerned, it involves free and complete medical care to all insured persons and their families. The person seeking such medical benefit gets free hospitalization, free medical treatment and attendance, free consultation and dispension, etc. During indoor medical treatment, food is supplied free of cost. As on December 31, 2003 there were 142 ESI hospitals and 43 annexes with 26,849 beds and 1,447 dispensaries under the scheme.

The scheme of sickness benefit provides for periodical cash payments to an insured person in the event of his certified sickness. The benefit is payable for a maximum period of 12 weeks (six weeks before and six weeks after the date of confinement). Disablement benefit is payable to an employee who suffers an injury resulting into disablement, whether permanent or temporary or who suffers from an occupational disease. The worker is paid for the period for which he is unable to work but if the period is less than three days, no benefit is paid. In the case of permanent disablement, the payment is made for life time and its rate is determined in proportion to the degree of disability as decided by the medical board. Dependants' benefit is paid to the dependants of the employee in the event of an employment injury resulting in the death of the employee. The dependants include the widow, minor children and parents of the deceased. Funeral benefit comprises the payment towards the expenditure on the funeral of the deceased insured person and is payable to the eldest surviving member of his family.

Employees' Provident Fund Act and Miscellaneous Provisions Act, 1952

Retirement benefits are available to the employees under the Employees' Provident Funds and Miscellaneous Provisions Act, 1952. The object of this Act is to make:

(1) some provisions for the future of the industrial worker after he retires,
(2) to provide for the dependants in the case of the employee's death, and
(3) to cultivate the spirit of saving among the employees.

The Act covers 180 industries/classes of establishments employing 20 or more persons all over India, except Jammu and Kashmir.

Refund and Claims

Under the scheme, a subscriber can withdraw the full amount in the fund in the following cases:

(i) retirement from active service after attaining the retirement age;
(ii) retirement on account of permanent and total incapacity;
(iii) migration from India for permanent settlement abroad; and
(iv) termination of service in the course of mass retrenchment.

Full amount of employer's contribution with interest is payable only when the subscriber has remained a member of the scheme for at least 15 years. If a subscriber remains member for less than 15 years, only a part of the accumulation of employer's share is payable to him. However, in all cases, he will always get back his own contribution to the Fund.

The scheme also provides for payment of non-refundable advances in certain contingencies like illness of family members, house building, purchasing shares of the Consumers' Cooperative Credit Housing Societies, marriage of the member himself or of this dependant, damage to property due to some grave calamity, etc.

Employees' Deposit Linked Insurance Scheme, 1976

The Employees' Deposit Linked Insurance Scheme was introduced for the members of the Employees' Provident Fund and the exempted Provident Fund with effect from August 1, 1976. A special feature of this scheme is that the members are not required to contribute to the Insurance Fund; only the employers and the government are required to make contributions. On the death of a member, the person entitled to receive the provident fund accumulations would be paid an additional amount equal to the average balance in the provident fund account of the deceased during the proceeding twelve months. The maximum amount of benefit payable, under the scheme, is Rs. 60,000.

The Payment of Gratuity Act, 1972

Gratuity is defined as a lumpsum payment made to a worker or to his heirs by the company on termination of his service due to retirement, retrenchment, invalidity or death. The Payment of Gratuity Act, 1972, is applicable to factories, mines, oil fields, plantations, ports, railways, motor-transport undertakings, companies, shops and other establishments. The Act provides for payment of gratuity at the rate of 15 days wages for each completed year of service subject to a maximum of Rs. 3.50 lakh. In the case of seasonal establishment, gratuity is payable at the rate of seven days' wage for each season. The Act does not affect the right of an employee to receive better terms of gratuity under any award or agreement or contract with the employer.

Employees' Pension Scheme, 1995

This scheme was introduced for the industrial workers with effect from November 16, 1995. Under the Scheme, pension at the rate of 50 per cent pay is payable to the employees on retirement/superannuation on completion of 33 years' contributory service. A minimum 10 years' service is required for entitlement to pension. Depending upon the salary and service of the employee at the time of death the scheme also provides for grant of family pension ranging from Rs. 450 per month to Rs. 2,500 per month. In addition, children-pension at the rate of 25 per cent of widow pension subject to a minimum of Rs. 115 per child is also payable upto children. The scheme is financed by diverting the employer's share of provident fund representing 8.33 per cent of the monthly wage to the pension fund. In addition, the Central government also contributes to the scheme at the rate of 1.16 per cent of wage. The upper limit has been raised from Rs. 5,000 to Rs. 6,500 with effect from June 1, 2001.

A Critical Review of Social Security Measures in India

As would be clear from the brief review of social security legislation in India, the government has undertaken various steps in the post-Independence period to provide social security to employees. However, we have only made a start so far and much needs to be done as would be clear from the following discussion:

1. Insufficient Coverage

The most important criticism of the social security measures undertaken by the government is their totally insufficient coverage. A majority of the people continue to remain outside the ambit of social assistance and social insurance schemes. For example, as per the survey carried out by the National Sample Survey Organisation in 1999-2000, the total employment in both organised and unorganised sectors in the country was of the order of 39.7 crore, i.e., around 2.8 crore in the organised sector and the balance 36.9 crore (about 92.0 per cent) in the unorganised sector. No social security scheme worth the name is available for the workers in the unorganised sector. Particularly miserable has been the condition of 23.7 crore workers employed in the agricultural sector (of the total 36.9 crore workers employed in the unorganised sector) who have irregular employment and no land or property to fall back upon. Even in the organised sector, only persons working in establishments employing more than 20 persons are covered under most of the social security schemes.

In addition to workers employed in organised and unorganised sectors, they are a large number of 'unemployable people'—old and sick people, persons suffering from various disabilities, etc. No social security measures worth the name have been undertaken for this class of people. However, in recent times, the government is trying to provide some semblance of social security to these people by introducing old-age pension schemes and health insurance schemes (for example, the four public sector general insurance companies launched a community-based 'Universal Health Insurance Scheme' in July 2003). For old persons an 'Integrated Programme for Older People's is being implemented which includes setting up of old-age homes, day care centres and introducing mobile medicare units.

2. *No Unemployment Insurance*

In many developed countries, there is provision for unemployment insurance. Benefits under such schemes are available to those individuals who are able to work and are available for work (as evidenced by registration at a public employment office). Such insurance enables the individual to meet his minimum subsistence requirement during the period he is seeking employment. However, because of the immense economic costs of this scheme, most of the underdeveloped countries (including India) have found it difficult to implement it. What we have in our country is a provision for retrenchment and lay-off compensation which does not even touch a fringe of the problem. Unless something is done to provide unemployment insurance, economic security cannot be achieved and in the absence of economic security, social security will also remain a dream.

3. *Overlapping of Schemes*

India does not have an integrated scheme of social security. On account of this reason, there is considerable overlapping of schemes and similar benefits are being disbursed under various schemes. This results in wastage of effort and money. Though the idea of integrating the various schemes has been mooted at various seminars and discussions, nothing concrete has been done in this direction so far with the result that different schemes of practically the same nature continue to be administered by different agencies.

4. Inadequate Facilities in Relation to the Needs of Beneficiaries

The social security schemes are woefully inadequate in relation to the demand for them by the beneficiaries. For example, the medical and dispensing facilities available under the ESI schemes are very insufficient. The number of dispensaries and hospitals is much less than desired. Even the dispensaries and hospitals that exist are understaffed. The beneficiaries are put to a lot of trouble and botheration. There is overcrowding in the dispensaries and hospitals and their staff finds it difficult to cope with the demand on this service. Naturally they get irritated and their behaviour towards patients is anything but cordial.

The critical review of the social security schemes in India suggests that their is a need to widen their coverage so that a majority of the people who continue to be outside their ambit are brought within it. There is also a need to bring about a qualitative improvement in the services provided, introduce unemployment insurance and bring about an integration amongst the various social security schemes.

Workers' Participation in Management in India

Works Committees

The Industrial Disputes Act, 1947 took the first step in Independent India toward workers' participation in management when it provided for the setting of a Working Committee, consisting of representatives of management and employees in every undertaking employing 100 or more workers "to promote measures for securing and preserving amity and good relations between the employer and the workmen." The usefulness of Works Committees as a machinery for joint consultation was stressed by the successive five year plans. Because of the legal requirement and the encouragement given by the government, a number of Works Committees were set-up by different industries. However, the pace of progress was slow, halting and uneven in different parts of the country. Many criticisms were also levied against these Works Committees as their working was often found to be ineffective. Their ineffectiveness was due to the reasons that they were statutory and the persons on these Committees did not evince much interest in their functioning.

Joint Management Councils

Joint Management Councils (JMCs) owe their origins to the observations made in the Industrial Policy Resolution of 1956 and later incorporated in the labour policy statement of the Second Five Year Plan. Following the statement of the Second Plan, a scheme for setting up JMCs was pushed through in the 15th Session of the Indian Labour Conference held in 1957 in 1958. In 1958, a scheme of JMCs was envisaged and such councils were set-up in 23 units. The Third Plan proposed the progressive extension of JMCs to new industries and units so that, in the course of a few years, they could become a normal feature of the industrial system. The objectives of the JMCs were as follows:

(i) to provide for mutual consultations between employers and workers over many important issues which affect industrial relations;

(ii) to promote cordial relations between management and workers;

(iii) to promote labour welfare and provide better facilities to the workers;

(iv) to help the workers in understanding the responsibilities of management; and

(v) to create an environment conducive to increase in industrial productivity.

Scheme for Workers' Participation in Industry at Shop Floor and Plant Level

The 20 point economic programme of the government adopted during the period of Emergency in 1975 introduced a scheme for workers' participation in industries particularly at the top floor level and in production programmes. The scheme was initially made applicable to those industries which had 500 or more workers on their rolls. The scheme provided for shop councils at the shop/departmental levels and Joint Councils at the enterprise level.

Shop Councils

The Scheme laid down that in every industrial unit employing 500 or more workers, the employer would constitute a shop council for each department or shop, or one council for more than one department or shop, considering the number of workman employed in different departments or shops. Each council was to consist of an equal number of representatives of employer and workers. The employer's representatives were to be nominated by the management and had to be from amongst the persons of the unit concerned. Similarly, all the representatives of workmen had to be from amongst the workers actually engaged in the department or the shop concerned. It was provided that the number of members of each council may be determined by the employer in consultation with the recognised unit but should not, in general, exceed twelve. A shop council, once formed, was to function for a period of two years and was to meet at least once in a month.

The main functions of the shop councils were defined as under:

(i) to assist management in achieving monthly/yearly target;
(ii) to help in improving production, productivity and efficiency and eliminate wastage;
(iii) to identify areas of low productivity and take necessary corrective steps;
(iv) to study absenteeism and recommend steps to reduce it;
(v) to assist in maintaining general discipline in the shop/department;
(vi) to adopt welfare and health measures, improve physical conditions of working and undertake safety measures; and
(vii) to ensure adequate two-way communication between management and labour.

Joint Council

The scheme provided for the setting-up of a Joint Council in every industrial unit employing 500 or more workers. The main features of the Joint Council were to be as follows:

(i) only such persons who are actually engaged in the unit were to be members of the Joint Council;
(ii) the Council was to function for a period of two years;
(iii) the chief executive of the unit was to be the chairman of the Joint Council;
(iv) the Vice-Chairman of the Council was to be nominated by workers-members of the Council;
(v) the Joint Council was to appoint one of the members of the council as its Secretary;
(vi) the term of the Council was to be two years and it was laid down that it would meet at least once in a quarter; and
(vii) every decision of the Joint Council was to be on the basis of consensus and had to be implemented within one month unless otherwise stated in the decision itself.

The Joint Council was to deal with matters relating to:

(i) optimum production, productivity and efficiency;
(ii) functions of a shop council which have a bearing on another shop or the unit as a whole;
(iii) matters emanating from shop councils which remain unresolved;
(iv) matters concerning the unit or the plant as a whole (for instance, tasks assigned to a shop council at the shop/department levels but relevant to the unit as a whole);
(v) the development of skills of workmen and adequate facilities for training;
(vi) the preparation of schedules of working hours and of holidays;
(vii) awarding of rewards for valuable and creative suggestions received from workers;
(viii) optimum use of raw materials;
(ix) quality of finished products; and
(x) general health, welfare and safety measures.

In the light of some experience gained in the working of

the scheme of 1975, the government introduced another scheme in January 1997 for workers' participation in management in commercial and service organisations having large scale public dealings and employing at least 100 persons. The scheme was made applicable to organisations like hospitals, posts and telegraph offices, railway stations/booking offices, road transport corporations, State electricity boards, banks, insurance, educational institutions, etc.

Committee on Workers' Participation in Management and Equity

The working of 1975 scheme was discussed at a Tripartite Labour Conference held on 6-7 May, 1977. On the recommendations of the conference, a Committee on Workers' Participation in Management and Equity was appointed under the chairmanship of the Union Minister of Labour, Ravinder Verma, in December 1977. The Committee consisted of 21 members representing central organisations of trade unions and employers, some of the States and professional institutes of management. The Committee was asked to deliberate and make recommendations on the following issues:

1. recognising the need for the participation of workers at different levels of management in industrial establishments/undertakings, to consider and recommend an outline of a comprehensive scheme for such participation keeping in view the interests of the economy, efficient management and workers;
2. whether there should be a statutory scheme for participation in management which should replace the existing statutory Works' Committee and any other similar committee functioning in a plant/unit;
3. whether the proposed scheme should cover, in addition to management at shop and plant levels, the higher levels of management also, for example, the board of directors;
4. to what extent, and in what manner, can the concept of trusteeship in industry be given a practical shape in the proposed scheme of workers' participation; and

5. whether and to what extent and in what manner participation by workers in equity holdings of industrial establishments/undertakings should be encouraged or provided for.

The Committee submitted its Report in March 1981. The majority of the members favoured the adoption of a three-tier system of participation, namely, at the corporate level, plant level and shop-floor level. The Committee laid down the detailed functions of the councils at the shop level, plant level and the corporate/board level. The participation envisaged at these levels included full sharing of information to enable joint decision-making and, in certain areas, joint administration. It also envisaged collective formation of policies and norms. A monitoring agency at the Centre and State levels was also suggested to monitor the implementation of the scheme of workers' participation.

Scheme for Workers' Participation in Public Sector Undertakings, 1983

On the basis of the recommendations of the above-mentioned Committee on Workers' Participation in Management and Equity, the government introduced a new and comprehensive scheme for workers' participation in the management of Central public sector enterprises vide resolution dated December 30, 1983. The scheme was introduced in all Central public sector enterprises except those which are given specific exemption and the departmental undertakings. The State governments/Union territories were requested to introduce the scheme in their own public sector enterprises and the private sector was also encouraged to implement the scheme. As far as the Central public sector undertakings are concerned, the scheme was to be operated both, at the shop-floor and the plant levels. The list of functions of these participative forums was made more elaborate and comprehensive in the new scheme. For example, it was stated that at the shop-floor level, the participative forum will look into a wide range of functions like production and storage facilities in the shop, material economy, operational problems, wastage controls, safety problems, monthly targets and production schedules, cost reduction measures, welfare measures related to the shop, etc. The functions of the participative forum at the plant level were divided into the following categories;

(i) operational areas,
(ii) economic and financial areas,
(iii) personnel matters,
(iv) welfare areas, and
(v) environmental areas.

Operational areas included functions relating to enhancing production and productivity levels, review of monthly targets and schedules, materials supply and its shortfall, review of working of the shop level bodies, etc. Economic and financial areas included functions relating to profit and loss statements and balance sheets, review of operating finances, labour and management costs, etc. Personnel matters included administration of social security schemes, special problems of women workers, initiation and supervision of workers' training programmes, etc. Welfare measures included implementation of welfare schemes, medical facilities, safety measures, housing, sports and games, canteen facilities, etc. Environmental areas included extension activities and community development projects, and pollution control.

The Participation of Workers in Management Bill, 1990

The Government of India introduced a Bill 'The Participation of Workers in Management Bill, 1990' in the Parliament in 1990 "to make provision of workers in the management of undertakings, establishments or other organisations engaged in any industry and to provide for matters connected therewith or incidental thereto." The Bill noted that while the Constitution was amended in 1976 and Article 43A was inserted in Directive Principles of State Policy stating that "the State shall take steps by suitable legislation, or in any other way to ensure the participation of workers in the management of the undertakings, establishments or other organisations engaged in any industry", most of the schemes pertaining to programmes of workers in management have been non-statutory with the result that they have been unable to provide an effective framework for a meaningful participation of workers in management at all levels. The Bill, therefore, sought a statutory status for the participation schemes. It intended to:

(i) provide for specific and meaningful participation of workers in management at shop floor level, establishment level and board of management level in industrial establishments;
(ii) provide for formulation of one or more schemes to specify detailed criteria, such as, the manner of representation of workmen and other workers on the Board of Management, Shop Floor Council and Establishment Council, procedure to be followed in the discharge of the functions by a council, etc.;
(iii) provide for the principle of secret ballot for determining the representation of workmen on the shop floor and management level councils and of workmen and other workers on the board of management; and
(iv) provide for rules to specify the power which an Inspector may exercise, the number of members of the Monitoring Committee and the manner in which they will be chosen, etc.

The Bill provided for the setting up of Shop Floor Council at the shop floor level and Establishment Council at the establishment level. These councils were to consist of equal number of representatives of the employer and the workmen. The functions of the Shop Floor councils and the Establishment Councils were approximately the same as considered above in the case of the 1983 comprehensive scheme for workers' participation in public sector undertakings. The Bill also provided for representatives of the workers on the Board of Management. Persons to represent the workmen on the Board of Management were to be elected from amongst the workmen of the industrial establishment by secret ballot, or nominated by the registered Trade Union, in accordance with the Scheme. Every representative of the workers was given all the powers and entitled to discharge all the functions of a member of the Board of Management and was entitled to vote. The Board of

Management had powers to review the functioning of the Shop-Floor Councils and the Establishment Council.

The Bill also provided for the setting up of a Monitoring Committee (constituted of equal number of members representing the appropriate government, the workers and the employers) to review and advise the government upon matters arising out of the administration of the provisions of the Bill, any Scheme or any rules made thereunder.

However, the Bill could not get the necessary clearance from the parliament and did not become an Act. The schemes pertaining to workers' participation in management in India have not able to accomplish much. Even in the case of Central public sector undertakings, only 91 enterprises have introduced the scheme on employees' participation in management at shop floor/plant level. There has been no board level participation from the workers' representatives. The Works Committees and the Joint Management Councils also failed in their objectives. In their evidence before the National Commission on Labour, the State Governments pointed out that the Works' Committee had failed to deliver the goods as the representatives of these Committees did not envince much interest in their functioning, there was vagueness regarding their exact scope and functions, the nature of recommendations was advisory in character, inter-union rivalries did not allow a common workers' perspective to emerge, the attitude of employers was unhelpful, etc. The National Commission on Labour also found that there was not much supprot for Joint Management Councils in their existing forms. These Councils had proved to be ineffective and their functioning was unsatisfactory. In those enterprises where Works Committees were functional, JMCs were found to be superfluous. Even when JMCs were formed, the managements did not take their opinions seriously while actually evolving policies. Even in matters concerning the welfare of workers, the role of the Councils was merely consultative and the final decisions rested with the management. Matters relating to personnel, economic and technological aspects were rarely discussed. Because of this 'peripheral role', the concerned parties lost interest in these joint bodies. Consequently, more emphasis is placed in India on collective.

It may be said that managements should pay attention to

resolve the issues instead of using threat tactics to reduce the frequency of strikes. For the time being these strategies of management are able to bring down the frequency of strikes, but it can only suppress their feelings. Moreover, such attempts to suppress their demands without removing the underlying causes of unrest, may merely divert the conflict into other forms such as absenteeism, restriction of output, sabotage, turnover, refusal to work overtime, slow downs, etc., which are more harmful and difficult to combat. A congenial environment needed for work cannot be achieved by following these devices. It can only be achieved after fulfiling their legitimate demands. Management must be inclined towards industrial harmony, i.e. the existence of understanding, cooperation, and a sense of partnership between the employers and employees rather than the so called industrial peace, which is somewhat restrictive and negative.

There is a need for a drastic overhaul of the industrial relations procedures and machinery in the country. The existing one is essentially limited to conflict resolution rather than maintenance of harmony. The focus needs to shift from curative to preventive and proactive approaches.

The grievance redressal mechanism should be equipped to deal with disputes arising from the interpretation and/or implementation of an existing collective agreement or of existing conditions of employment arising from personal complaints about the abuses, if any, due to exercise of management prerogatives. Even in the public sector, there is a change in emphasis from it being it a 'model employer' to being a 'model performer'. These and similar changes warrant a new attitude and orientation towards union-management relations in the future.

CHANGES IN LABOUR LAW/POLICY AT STATE LEVEL

During the post-liberalisation period, the Central government has dilly-dallied on labour reform fearing political risks. Given the pressure for wooing investment and generating new jobs, some state governments, however, have announced far-reaching changes.

I. Recognition of Bargaining Agent

In India, the Trade Unions Act, 1926, which is a Central

legislation, provides for registration, not recognition. Unions generally press for collective bargaining rights and shun any legislation on recognitionr. Some state governments (for instance, Maharashtra, Gujarat and Rajastan) have provided for certain criteria through state-level labour laws. For years, Andhra Pradesh has been using the secret ballot as a method of trade union recognition. Between 1991 and 1996, two state governments—Orissa and West Bengal—introduced, for the first time in the country, secret ballots through a tripartite social dialogue at the state level for the purpose of trade union recognition. The Kerala legislature also passed similar legislation which is awaiting the accent of the President before the new law on secret ballots in that state comes into operation.

The problem with secret ballots, however, is that it does not resolve all the contentious issues. For example:

(a) The complexities associated with the campaigning and conduct of elections.
(b) Would the tenure of recognition be coterminus with the currency of a subsisting collective agreement?
(c) What would be the role and rights of unrecognised union(s)?
(d) What happens in states that choose to give individuals the right to raise industrial disputes on any aspect, including those aspects which are a part of union-management agreement?
(e) The inability or indifference to deal with situations which produce different results in membership verification even as secret ballot results in the concerned enterprises continue to be valid.

While secret ballots in Orissa have thrown up quite a few surprises due to an anti-incumbency negative vote, West Bengal is yet to make the secret ballot a preferred way of choosing a collective bargaining agent. Orissa has been holding secret ballots but West Bengal has chosen to defer secret ballots except when the parties at the enterprise level want it.

2. Simplified Labour Inspection

From June 1991 to September 2000, some state

governments simplified labour inspection (see Box 1). In Uttar Pradesh, a labour inspector can carry out an inspection only after the prior consent of an officer of the rank of labour commissioner or district magistrate.

Rajasthan has reduced the scope of labour inspection, simplified forms and exempted several establishments from the purview of labour inspection. The system of separate inspection under industrial labour laws has been done away with. Instead, there is going to be only a common inspection of industry in accordance with a checklist prepared for the purpose. The number of inspections under labour laws have been reduced to 5 per cent of the establishments in the small-scale and tiny sectors and 10 per cent in other sectors selected on a random basis.

Box I

TRADE UNION RECOGNITION RULES IN SELECT INDIAN STATES

Orissa: *In pursuance of the Industrial Policy Resolution of Orissa, 1992, and as per the unanimous resolution of the State Implementation and Evaluation Committee, The Verification of Membership and Recognition of Trade Union Rules, 1994, were brought into force with effect from 1 November 1994. The special features of these rules include:*

(a) Where only one union is functioning at least for a period of one year after registration, it will be recognised as the sole bargaining agent.

(b) The union which secures the maximum number of votes, but not less than 30 per cent of the total number of votes polled, shall be entitled to be recognised. In the event of two or more unions getting an equal number of votes, the union having the longer period of existence after registration shall be declared duly voted by the employees.

(c) In the event of none of them securing 30 per cent votes, the labour commissioner shall constitute a 'negotiating committee' for the industry based on the number of votes polled by each union in the verification process, subject to the condition that each union shall have at least one member on the negotiation committee. The total membership of the committee shall not exceed nine.

(d) In order to qualify to be represented in the negotiation committee, a union must have secured a minimum of 10 per cent of the total number of votes polled.

Maharashtra: Under the BIR Act, 1946, registered unions are classified as follows:

(a) Representative union with at least 25 per cent membership in an industry in a local area

(b) Qualified union with at least 5 per cent membership in an industry in a local area.

(c) Primary union in an undertaking with at least 15 per cent membership and complying with the conditions laid down in respect of the approved union.

To reduce inter-union rivalry, a code of discipline was adopted at the 16th Indian labour conference and a procedure for verification of strength was laid down, which must be followed by unions for getting recognition. Where there are several unions in an industry, the one with the largest membership will be recognised as the representative union.

The BIR Act, 1946, was initially made applicable to the textile, sugar and transport industries and cooperative banks. It was extended to some other industries like engineering throughout the state via the Bombay Industrial Relations (Extension and Amendment) Act, 1964.

Rajasthan (proposed rules): To be eligible for registration, a union should have at least 15 per cent of its workforce employed in the unit of an industry. When two or more unions fulfil the above condition, the union having the largest membership of workers employed in the unit of the industry shall be registered.

Small-scale industrial units are now required to send only one return and display one common notice covering all labour laws. The state government has special powers to prohibit strikes or lock-outs in general or in connection with any industrial dispute if, in the opinion of the state government, it is necessary for securing public safety or convenience or maintenance of public order of supplies and services essential to the life of the community or for maintaining industrial peace.

In 2000, Andhra Pradesh, too, has simplified, the number and contents of the forms under the A.P. Factories Rules and issued the revised formats on CDROM.

3. New Thrust In Labour Policy

The Kerala government announced a labour policy as a part of its new industrial policy in 1994, which contained, among others, the following provisions:

The entrepreneur will have the full right over hiring of labour and shall not be WMbimed by any claims from the sons of the soil displaced persons from acquired laid construction/ contract labour and dependants of employees.

All restrictive labour practices, including intimidation, *gherao* and *dharna inside the* factory, harassment of managers and their families and extortion of any kind including *attimari will* be treated as criminal offences and dealt with accordingly.

The management will have the prerogative to deploy workers in any section of the unit as part of a multicraft approach.

Disciplinary action against individual workmen will be taken in accordance with the procedure provided in the Industrial Disputes Act.

Unions will be recognised for participation in labour-management negotiations only if they have a minimum membership of 15 per cent of the total number of employees. The government will bring about a comprehensive legislation for this purpose.

The government will encourage long-term agreements. Long-term enhancement in wages will be linked to productivity. The possibility of long-term bonus settlement will also be explored.

The government will do all that is in its power to avoid work-stoppages during the first five years of a project. Even after the first five years, any dispute that might arise, involving stoppage of work and lowering of production, is to be discouraged.

In all new enterprises with an investment of Rs. 300 million or more, an officer of the labour department of appropriate status and with adequate power will be exclusively appointed at the cost of the government for the first five years to ensure that labour disputes do not lead to any stoppage of work.

The viability of an industrial unit depends, to a considerable extent, on whether construction activity can be completed within the scheduled time and at the estimated cost. Work stoppages, whether due to labour disputes or non-fulfilment of obligations by contractors will not be tolerated.

Industrial relations committees will be constituted in all existing and potential industries. These committees, it is hoped, will ultimately create an atmosphere of complete understanding, between labour and management in all industrial areas.

Existing institutional machinery will be strengthened and innovations introduced to ensure that disputes are resolved quickly and without any disruption of productive activity. A joint cell of the labour department will be constituted to study what changes need to be made in laws, rules and regulations and in the administrative and institutional arrangement to achieve these objectives.

Many of these policy procurements remain on paper, more so, when the Left Front alliance replaced the Congress as the ruling party in the state.

4. Permissions for Closure, Retrenchment or Lay-off

Under Chapter V-B of the Industrial Disputes Act, 1947, prior permission of the appropriate government is required for closure, retrenchments and lay-off. The general feeling in India is that the government usually refuses permission for closures, retrenchments and lay-offs. But it is not quite so. As seen from Table 5.1 the Central government has been more liberal in granting permission than any state government. Information on the subject is not available from all the states, including some of the industrially important states like Maharashtra and West Bengal. The situation varies from state to state. In Tamil Nadu, during 1991-95, 38 per cent of the applications for closure/

retrenchment/lay-off were considered in favour of employers, 53 per cent in favour of workers and in the remaining 11 per cent a decision was kept in abeyance. Evidently, of course, there were more permissions for lay-offs, than for retrenchment. West Bengal, a state ruled by the Marxist party for over two decades, was among states more cautious in granting permission for lay-off or retrenchment or closure. But this is the state where, for several years, 95 per cent of the mandays lost due to industrial strife were on account of lock-outs, and only 5 per cent due to strikes.

TABLE 5.I

State/UT	*Closures*				*Retrenchment*				*Lay-off*			
	A	*B*	*C*	*D*	*A*	*B*	*C*	*D*	*A*	*B*	*C*	*D*
Andhra Pradesh	17	1	8	8	3	—	3	—	22	5	15	2
Assam	—	—	—	—	4	—	4	—	2	—	2	—
Goa	—	—	—	—	1	—	I	—	2	—	2	—
Gujarat	6	6	—	—	21	5	12	4	23	2	14	7
Manipur	—	—	—	—	1	1	—	—	3	1	1	1
Nagaland	—	—	—	—	1	—	—	I	—	—	—	—
Orissa		—	—	—	—	—	—	—	I	I	—	—
Punjab		—	—	—	4	—	2	2	4	—	2	2
Tamil Nadu	22	0	11	5	2	1	1	—	2	—	2	—
A and N Island	1	—	—	1	21	7	14	—	56	25	28	3
Daman and Diu	—	—	—	—	—	—	—	—	—	—	—	—
Delhi	2	—	2	—	—	—	—	—	—	—	—	—
Pondicherry	1	—	I	—	—	—	—	—	—	—	—	—
Rajasthan	1	—	I	—	3	1	2	—	—	—	-.	—
State Sphere	50	13	23	14	61	15	39	. 7	115	34	66	15
Central Sphere	21	16	5	15	39	18	21	IS	4	15	4	—
Grand Total	71	29	28	14	100	33	60	7	119	34	70	1 5

Note: Information in respect of remaining slates/union territories is awaited;] —=Nil; A=No. of applications received; B=No. of cases in which permission was granted; C=No. of cases in which permission was not granted; D=Under process/withdrawal court case.

Source: Government of India (1996), *Annual Report, 1995-96*, Ministry of Labour, New Delhi, p. 28.

5. Wages

The role of the state in fixing minimum wages is a hotly debated issue in the context of global competition. There is no uniform wage policy for all sectors of the economy. Wage costs as a percentage of turnover vary from less than 2 per cent in certain petrochemical firms to over 100 per cent in sick units. In many firms in different sectors they are usually well below 20 per cent. In fact, they vary widely even in a single company. For instance in Coal India, wage costs are less than 15 per cent in new, open-cast mines in Mahanadi Coalfields and 60 per cent in old, sick, underground mines in Eastern Coalfields and Bharat Coking Coal Limited. The average labour cost for Coal India as a whole is less than 30 per cent.

Although the Minimum Wages Act, 1948 is a Central legislation, state governments (and the Central government where it is the 'appropriate government') are responsible for the constitution of tripartite minimum wages advisory bodies to recommend minimum wages. Often state governments tend to be populist, and unilaterally declare hikes in wages because they are sure that unions will back them in ratification and hence opposition if any from employers can be easily overcome. Minimum wages in India vary widely across states (Table 5.2) and within a state across sectors. For instance, as of October 1998, in Maharashtra alone, minimum wages for unskilled workers vary from Rs. 42.46 to over Rs. 85.92. In Kerala range between Rs. 30 to Rs. 157.81. The range in Delhi, where the range of minimum and maximum wages at minimim wages level is Nil (Rs. 90.30).

Adherence to wage board recommendations is also not uniform throughout the country. Wage boards have become unpopular for a variety of reasons. Currently, there is only one wage board working as against nearly 20 in the 1970s. The recommendations of the Bachawat Wage Board in the mid-1980s were not implemented by 910 out of 1563 newspaper establishments even till a decade later. In the meanwhile, another wage board was set-up in 1995 which submitted its report in 1999. Over two-fifths of the newspaper establishments which did not implement the recommendations were located in West Bengal and Bihar. In West Bengal, 15 of 420 establishments implemented fully or partially the Bachawat award, while in

TABLE 5.2

State-wise Details of Minimum Wages (as on 1999)

Central/State Government/Union Territory	No. of employments for which minimum wages have been fixed/revised@	Range of minimum wages per day (in Rs. Minimum/Maximum as on 1.10.98	
I. Central Government	44	46.22	84.12
II. State			
1. Andhra Pradesh	60	27.00	63.19
2. Arunachal Pradesh	25	35.60	37.60
3. Assam	62	32.80	55.80
4. Bihar	74	38.61	125.00
5. Goa	23	21.00	125.00
6. Gujarat	49	58.80	79.20
7. Haryana	56	70.12	73.12
8. Himachal Pradesh	24	26.00	45.75
9. Jammu and Kashmir	18	30.00	30.00
10. Karnatka	59	26.00	45.75
11. Kerala	40	30.0()	157.81
12. Madhya Pradesh	36	49.46	56.46
13. Maharashtra	62	42.46	85.92
14. Manipur	5	44.65	49.50
15. Meghalaya	22	35.00	35.00
16. Mizoram	3	45.00	45.00
17. Nagaland	36	25.00	25.00
18. Orissa	83	42.50	42.50
19. Punjab	60	54.07	60.96
20. Rajasthan	38	32.00	44.00
21. Sikkim*	—	—	—
22. Tamil Nadu	60	22.40	82.72
23. Tripura	11	17.70	36.00
24. Uttar Pradesh	65	42.02	64.21
25. West Bengal	45	36.55	79.99
III. Union Terriotries			
26. Anadaman and Nacobar lalands	5	44.00	86.77
27. Chandigarh	44	52.09	71.93
28. Dadra and Nagar Haveli	43	38.00	44.00
29. Daman and Diu	72	50.00	60.00
30. Delhi	29	90.30	90.30
31. Lakshadweep	9	41.46	41.46
32. Pondicherry	4	19.25	65.00

Note: @ Excludes employments where wages were fixed on piece-rate basis: Minimum War yet to be extended and enforced.

Source: Government of India (Ministry of Labour), *Annual Report.* 1999-2000, p. 55

Bihar, 112 of 245 establishments implemented (fully or partially) it. Although over one-third of the newspaper establishments in the country are located in these two states, the percentage of establishments complying with the wage board recommendations is abysmally poor in these states.

The Central government monitors about 18 of 68 Central legislations on the various aspects of labour. More than half the states do not submit even statutory returns to the Labour Bureau, like the number of unions registered in their respective states and the number of workers enrolled in these unions. The data on mandays lost and accidents and the impact of both is also only cursory. Hence, the facts contained in the usually dated annual publication of the Labour Bureau invariably fail to present a true and fair picture of the labour scene in the states.

References

"Compulsory Adjudication Syndrome in India: Some Implications for Workplace Relations", in Debi S. Saini (ed.) Labour Law Work and Development: Essays in Honour of P. Gopa Krishnan, Westvill, New Delhi.

"Productivity Agreements and Industrial Relations in India", *Management and Change*, Vol. 3, No. 2.

AITUC (2001), Recent Wage Agreements, All India Trade Union Congress (AITUC), New Delhi.

Bengal Chambers of Commerce (BCC) (1998), Productivity on the Rise in West Bengal, BCC, Calcutta.

Business India (1998), "Clutching at Straws", *Business India*, March 9-22.

D'Art, Daryl and Thomas Turner (2003), "Union recognition in Ireland: One step forward or two steps back?", *Industrial Relations Journal*, Vol. 34, No. 3.

Dreze, Jean, and Sen, Amartya (2003), Development and Participation, Oxford University Press, New Delhi.

Globaiisation and Labour-Management Relations: Dynamics of Change, Response (A Division of Sage) Publications, New Delhi.

Harvard Business Review (2003), "Capital *Vs.* Talent", July.

Hyman, Richard (1999), "Imagined Solidarities: Can Trade Unions Resist Globalisation?", in Leisink (ed.).

Jhaveri, Narendra (2003), "India's Growth Chase", *Economic and Political Weekly*, pp. 4336-350.

Kamoche, Ken (2000), Sociological Paradigms and Human Resources: An African Context, Ashgate Publishing Limited, Aldershot (U.K.).

Kochan, T. and M. Weinstein (1994), "Recent Developments in U.S. Industrial Relations," *British Journal of Industrial Relations*, Vol. 32, pp. 483-84.

Kochan, T., H. Katz and R. Mckersie (1986), The Transformation of American Industrial Relations, Basic Books, New York.

Lambert, Rob (1999), "Australia's Historic Industrial Relations Transition", in Leisink (ed.).

Mabey, Christopher, Denise Skinner and Timothy Clark (eds.), Experiencing Human Resource Management, Sage, London.

Mamkoottam, K. (2003), Labour and Change: Essays on Globalisation, Technological Change and Labour in India, Response (A Division of Sage), New Delhi.

Mathur, A.N. (1991), Industrial Restructuring and Union Power, ILO-ARTEP, New Delhi.

Mishra, L. (2001), Economy and Labour, Manak Publications Pvt. Ltd., New Delhi.

Mukherjee, Aditya (2002), Imperialism, Nationalism and the Making of the Indian Capitalist Class, 1920-47, Sage, New Delhi.

Nayyar, Baldev Raj (2003), "Economic Globalisation and its Advance, From Shallow to Deep Integration", *Economic and Political Weekly*, November 8, pp. 4780-782.

New Perspectives in Human Resource Management, Rouledge, London.

Ramaswamy, E.A. (2000), Managing Human Resources: A Contemporary Text, Oxford University Press, New Delhi.

Saini, Debi S. and Sami A. Khan (eds.) (2000), Human Resource Management: Perspectives for the New Era, Response Books (A Division of Sage), New Delhi.

Saini, Debi. S. and Pawan Budhwar (2003), "HRM in India", in Pawan Budhwar (ed.), Human Resource Management in Asia-Pacific Countries, Routledge, London (Forthcoming).

Shyam Sunder, K.R. (2003), "Trade Unions and New Strategies for Organising Labour: New Wine in Old Bottle?", *The Indian Journal of Labour Economics*, Vol. 46, No. 2.

Thakur, C.P. and Munson, Fred. C. (1969), Industrial Relations in Printing Industry, Shri Ram Centre for Industrial Relations, New Delhi.

The Economic Times (2003), "See No Evil, Hear No Evil," November 14. (Quotes Forbes on Hiring illegal immigrants on the sly through layers of contract by Wal-Mart and other retailers in the U.S.A.)

US Department of Labour (1994), Fact Finding Report—Commission on the Future of Worker-Management Relations (also called John T. Dunlop Commission Report), Washington, D.C., USA.

Venkata Ratnam C.S. and Anil Varma (ed.) (1998), Challenge of Change—Industrial Relations in Indian Industry, Allied, New Delhi.

Venkata Ratnam, C.S. (2003), Negotiated Change: Collective Bargaining, Liberalisation and Restructuring in India, Response (A Division of Sage Publications), New Delhi.

Venkata Ratnam, C.S. (2003), "Negotiating Flexibility", in Negotiated Change, Response Books, New Delhi.

Freeman, R.B. (1992), Labour Market Institutions and Policies: Help or Hindrance, proceedings of the World Bank Annual Conference on

Development Economics, supplement to the *World Bank Economic Review and World Bank Research Observer*, World Bank, Washington, D.C., pp. 117-56.

International Labour Organisation (1991), *Report of the Director General to the 78th Session*, ILO, Geneva. Government of India (1996a), *Agenda: 33rd Session of the Standing Labour Committee*, September 13, Ministry of Labour, New Delhi.

———(1996b), *Agenda: 33rd Session of the Indian Labour Conference*, Ministry of Labour, New Delhi, October 23-25.

———(1996c), *Annual Report, 1995-96*, Ministry of Labour (also 1998-99 report), New Delhi.

———(1996d), *Report of the Working Group on Labour Policy: Ninth Five Year Plan (1997-2002)*, Ministry of Labour, New Delhi.

Nair, K.R. (1996), "Kerala", in Venkata Ratnam, C.S. (2000.), *Economic Changes and Industrial Relations in Indian States*, Global Business Press, New Delhi.

Observer Research Foundation (1996), *Economic Reforms: The Role of the States and the Future of Centre-State Relations*, New Delhi.

Papola, T.S. and G. Rodgefs (eds.) (1992), *Labour Institutions and Economic Development in India*, International Institute for Labour Studies, Geneva.

Venkata Ratnam, C.S. (1996), *Welfare to Moneyfare: A Study of Social Security Clauses in Collective Bargaining*, A study sponsored by UNDP and the Centre for Development Studies, International Management Institute, New Delhi.

World Bank (1995), *World Development Report—Workers in an Integrated World*, World Bank and Oxford University Press.

Summary and Conclusion

Economic growth within a democratic polity, tempered with the spirit of equity and social justice, has been the national agenda since independence. Support to growth endeavours required enthusiastic cooperation from all power holders and interest groups. Industrial peace helps in the wealth creation process, and this was realised quite early. Consolidation of democratic impulses calls for creating space for it in the leading economic arena, too. Economic democracy, at any rate a modicum of it, in the form of relevant institutions and practices appeared appropriate. In the labour market it involved a framework of sharing a blend of economic and political power across contending interest groups. Governmental intervention was visualised only as a balancing device, as it were. There were choices in this field, and India did make its own choice in furtherance of its larger nation-building exercise with variation at different stages. Unparalleled in history, "India tried to achieve rapid industrialisation while maintaining political democracy including powerful trade union rights" (Mukherjee, 2002).

Indian industrial relations strategy and the instruments for its implementation were developed with a view to supporting strife-free growth and wealth creation. It even worked that way, at least in the organised secondary sector of the economy. Seemingly the national agenda has remained the same, though not necessarily its path and priorities. Discontinuous changes, triggered by domestic crisis as well as external pressure, and that too recently at a rapid pace, disturbed the established tenuous balance. Globalisation can be understood in the context of several major international events which have directly affected the organisation of business as also the existence and strength of trade unions. Some of these developments can be discussed as under:

1. Emergence of Chaotic Competition

The chaotic competition is one of the most obvious results of the globalisation philosophy, which is guiding nearly all business policies. Employer mortality is on the rise due to the acuteness of resultant competition. This has led to formation of strategic alliances between major players in manufacturing and service industries world over. Thus, mergers, acquisitions and takeovers are taking place at rapid pace so as to secure strategic competitive advantage of oligopolistic situations in the market. Competitive pressures also lead to attempts to switch operations to green-field sites (new locations) to minimize costs. Being wholly new, these sites also offer management a high degree of discretion, choice, flexibility and opportunity to introduce innovative work practices. Employers find it much easier to influence individual and collective behaviour of employees at such sites, aimed to eventually provide a competitive advantage to the employer.

Interestingly, in high-wage developed world, firms cope with pressures of international competition by differentiating their products rather than by lowering wages. This results in high-wage and high-value-added manufacturing in those locations. Such a strategy puts greater premium on employees' skills, cooperation and involvement. Employers thus invest in their more efficacious management, which itself in a way helps promoting fairness in employment relations. But labour in developing countries has become more vulnerable to the competitiveness exigencies caused by the new economic realities than is the case with workers in the developed world. That is how, these realities are the principal determinants of the contemporary IR in India.

2. Privatisation

Since public sector employees are believed to be restrictive in demonstrating initiative and commitment in their working, its role in economic development is being minimized, eventually giving way to privatisation. For example, in the Indian context, it is now accepted as an unchallenged truth that "over-regulation, protection, self-reliance and policies of import substitution led to the neglect of quality, cost, delivery/supply schedules and customer orientation" (Venkata Ratnam and Verma, 1998, p. 16). The adoption of these policies resulted in India becoming a high cost, low productivity economy; which makes it more imperative to adopt the rationality of globalisation. Privatisation of the public sector, however, involves complex social and economic implications. Perhaps, the main blow that it gives is to the opinion-making class which justifies labour rights. This class is found more amongst the public sector employees, who can seek a fairer compromise with the power of managerial prerogatives of employers. This is due to the sheer reason of a sense of job security that they enjoy; this is essential for exercise of any countervailing power. This factor surely facilitates at a moral level the strength and organisational capability of workers in the private sector also. Further, privatisation may also lead to re-engineering and retrenchment. Especially in developing countries where unemployment is already a menacing problem, this becomes a cause of grave social concern. Again, the potential of societal unrest resulting from public sector employees becoming unemployed is higher for the similar reasons, which helps in getting greater attention of the state agencies. Private sector employers invest heavily in deunionisation activities. They covertly resort to unfair labour practices (LJLPs) to weaken and break unions, though attempting to uphold legal facades. Research involving the practice of IR in private sector in the Indian context reveals such stories of labour disorganisation process (Saini, 2003), thus revealing greater vulnerability of labour in this sector.

3. Technological Changes

In the present high-tech industrial society the adoption of new technology becomes one of the strategic considerations of organisations. Greater demand for sophisticated and state-of-the-art technology becomes widespread. It leads to resort to new developments in management of human resources due to considerations of retrenchment, flexitime and teleworking. New technology may also increase the need for organisational flexibility. In developing countries, trade unions have actively or hesitantly shown opposition to the adoption of new technology for fear of its adverse impact on employee solidarity. For, they fear loss of employment and also control over work processes. However, recent literature reports that with the passage of time there is a change in their thinking in this regard (Mamkoottam, 2003).

4. Changing Work Organisation, Flexibility Exigencies and Contractualisation Syndrome

Large-scale changes are noticeable in work organisation. One of the much-talked-about management concepts is business process re-engineering (BPR). Hammer and Champy (1993), the originators of the term BPR, write: "Reengineering is the search for new models of organizing work. Reengineering is the new beginning." Re-engineering is aimed to increase productivity and flexibility of the organisation; it also emphasizes multi-trade and, flexible job. In order to fully utilize the labour capacity, workers are trained in several skills. Various traditionally popular jobs, especially white-collar ones, are now becoming redundant and are giving way to new roles based on reengineering. Despite complexities involved in reengineering dynamics, research reveals increasing labour-management cooperation in industrial restructuring and trends towards negotiated flexibility at the enterprise level (Venkata Ratnam, 2003).

Mass-production systems based on Taylorism and Fordism have ruled the industrial world in the pre-globalisation world. They emphasize division of labour and specialisation. Customisation is now becoming the rule, giving way to what is referred to as Toyotaism or flexible specialisation. This concept is based on the principle of lean and mean production adjustable as per the needs of the customer. Since customer is the king in the globalisation era, product differentiation by employers has substantially increased, resulting into lean customized production that forms part of Toyotaism.

Lean production also necessitates employers' ability to

engage contingent or peripheral labour force as per their business exigencies so as to help them remain flexible. While core workers are permanently needed in the organisation for giving a kind of stability, periphery workers consisting of *ad hoc*, casual, part-time, temporary and contract workers, are replaceable. They fulfil the contingent business needs as and when new demands are made on the organisation. Labour flexibility has become more important today than ever before. Performance-related pay system, flexitime, and telecommuting are also aspects of facilitating flexibility in work organisation.

The flexibility management needs of business are often accompanied by adoption of unfair procedures. In India, for example, this has led, among others, to a serious problem of lack of implementation by employers of minimum standards of employment in case of vulnerable sections of labour. Despite the existence of Contract Labour (Regulation and Abolition Act) 1970 (CLA), which makes it very difficult to employ contract labour in permanent operations, a large number of employers are resorting to employment of contract labour in several of their operations. They are doing so on a permanent basis and not just to meet any contingencies as intended by the CLA. The justification given by employers for this is the need for flexibility to cope with the onslaught of greater competition.

5. Emergence of New Actors in IR

The traditional notions of bipartism or tripartism of yester-years are giving way to IR becoming a more composite issue. Trade unions and collective bargaining institutions are under pressure so as to take care of all aspects concerning variegated people at work (Kochan *et al.*, 1986); thus tending to make IR as a multi-lateral power game. Consumers and general public are beginning to play a significant role in these matters. Increasing concern is being shown to issues such as child labour, women's problems, environmental concerns, health and safety of employees and workers in the informal sector. There is pressure for inclusion of issues such as social clause, social exclusion, social protection, social security and social action to deal with all types of discrimination (Venkata Ratnam, 2001). The notions on which this changed thinking is based include: faith in maintaining a power balance between social partners, integrality, trust, and community interest. This can also be seen as a method of mustering societal opinion in favour of the new policies by their ideologues. Thus, there are attempts towards evolving new concepts of income security, job security and social security.

The socialism in a Gramscian sense, is "a never-ending development towards the realm of freedom that is organised and controlled by (the) majority of citizens, that is proletariat" (1988, p. 52). A brief background to the process of our personal quest for seeking alternative forms of institutions for challenging the present order is probably called for. Though we attempt to make generalised observations about TU movement in the present writing, our understanding is based on the vantage point of being 'partisan' observers of working class practice in an old industrial centre of India, which is known for its militant working class movement. However, after almost a hundred years of glorious resistance, now the city is referred to as 'industrially dead' and the movement is in shambles. We are partisan observers in the sense that though we have primarily been on the sidelines, we have been friends of the movement now for some years, and in that sense, we have definite biases. To that extent, we do not make any claims to 'absolute' standards of objectivity. Moreover, this is an exercise in self-criticism, very much from within the movement (see Appendix for a brief note on the TU movement in the city). The idea here is not to blame the victims themselves for their conditions (Bagchi, 2002), but to situate them in their historical context (Sarkar, 1998) and yet seek the possibilities in the realm of the future. As Luxemburg (1918, quoted in Hyman, 1971, p. 43) declared:

> "The battle for socialism can only be carried on by the masses, directly against capitalism, in every factory, by every proletarian against his particular employer ...... Socialism cannot be made by order, not even by the best and most capable Socialist govt. It must be made by the masses, through every proletarian individual."

In the following sections, we trace the genesis of the TUs in the 18th century, its growth and limitations in the 19th century and the crisis of unions in the previous century. In the final section, we look beyond for addressing the present challenges to socialist practice in the face of globalisation.

By the 1980s, the capital-labour equilibrium forged after the two world wars and the creation of 'second' and 'third' world crumbled, first due to post-OPEC economic crisis and later because of fall of the Eastern Europe. Since then, it has been moving fast backward for the labouring classes and the labour movement. With the ever growing automation and the weakening bargaining position, labour as a political force, at least *prima facie*, has been on the defensive. Memberships of trade unions have declined precipitously across the world and labour rights and trade unions have become dispensable in times of peripatetic capital and contingent workforce amongst the elite and even the middle classes. In fact, in the past two decades, trade union as an institution has lost the legitimacy it had accumulated over a period of time, not only among the upper classes, but also perhaps with the working classes all over the world.

It has been mentioned earlier, the premise behind trade union movement is that the employer needs the workers as much, if not more, as the workers need the employment. In effect, workers, by organising themselves, can strike a bargain by threatening to stop the work and force the employers to negotiate with them. However, the economic context has changed dramatically over the past decades. We would like to point out two primary issues for the need to open the debate on the premise itself:

(i) End of Work

While the labour movement has been busy in organising for the immediate gains, and protect and preserve them, capital has been devising ways to do away with the labour. Unemployment has taken menacing proportions by the beginning of the twenty-first century. Capital is continuously in search of either reducing work by replacing humans with machines and/ or intensifying the process further through management methods like reengineering and restructuring (Rifkin, 1996). Though such large scale unemployment and underemployment itself may be a source of deepening contradiction between supply and demand—the basis of capitalist system (Marx, 1978a) and therefore a serious crisis of capitalism—it is also a source of a difficult predicament for the TUs as well. Even if there is no end of work, there is 'informalisation' of work at a large scale and 'traditional' TU movement has become practically ineffective because employers threaten closure, mechanisation, outsourcing, or some combination of the three (Thomas, 1995). For instance, in India, not more than 1 per cent of the labour force is covered by collective wage agreements at present (Bhowmik, 1998). And yet as the world is turning 'job less', it is definitely not 'work less' or worker less. Working classes are still generating enormous surplus and finding innovative means to eke out their living across the globe. Point is that the TUs in general have found it almost impossible to cope with this changed situation. They have not been able to respond to this 'informalisation' and sub-contracting of work. In India, mainstream unions, even in the organisations where they had or still have strong presence, have failed to bring non-permanent, contract or casual workers within their fold. Regular forms of bargaining do not work in this case, as there is no stable, 'employment contract'. As a Vice-President of AT&T observed (Henwood, 1996, p. 9) 'Jobs' are being replaced by 'projects' and field of work, giving rise to a society that is increasingly 'jobless but not work less'.

(ii) Peripatetic Capital

Globalisation has been restricted only to capital and its keepers, while labour's mobility, especially in the lower strata, if anything, has reduced. Capital is continuously on the move in search of more and more profits. It can move to comparatively less unionised areas within an economy, switch over to faster growing, more profitable industry segments, or convert itself into speculative finance capital or simply move to 'less' developed economies, where the going wage rates are significantly lower. As Bagchi (2002, pp. 233-34) asserts:

> ".......Capitalism all the time tends to reproduce duality between advancing and declining sectors, and privileged and under privileged workers, by continually and unpredictably changing the structure of production, and making the workers with no other asset than labour power compete among themselves for jobs and better deals ...... (C)apitalism.... seeks to reduce labour power every where to commodity sold in auction markets without any legal or TU protection."

Traditional trade unions have been generally unable to deal with these new features of capitalism. We have appreciated this through our association with the TU movement in one of the old industrial centres in India, which was known for its militancy. Kanpur became an important textile centre of the country in the second half of the 19th century and by the end of the Second World War, had more than 150 factories and more than a lakh workers. There were 12 integrated textile mills employing around 50 thousand workers. As the mills faced crisis and imminent closure after the war because of a complex set of policy, managerial and technological reasons, they were taken over by the government (Chakrabarti, 1995). These mills specialised in large-scale army demands. Instead of a genuine attempt to adapt the available facilities with the existing demand and simultaneously initiate process for appropriate innovations and techniques, the government let the mills make enormous losses due to non-production and piled up stocks. Finally, in the wake of restructuring of the Indian economy in the 1990s, the government has simply stopped production in the state-owned textile mills. But unfortunately, all that the trade unions have fought for in the last three decades of government ownership including a decade in which the mills had completely stopped production, was increase in wages and bonus—the demand has never really included a concern for the future of the mills which logically is intricately related with the future of the workers, not even to restart the production. Finally, it has reached the present desperate situation, when workers are not getting their wages for several months (at the time of this writing). At present, neither the present owner—the state, nor any private party is forthcoming to run the mills in their existing condition where workers' rights can also be protected. Even in the remote possibility of a private operator taking up the management of the mills, it is going to be a serious blow to the present employees and significant numbers may loose their job. Our assessment is that because of deep-seated economism amongst the unionised workers and complete lack of democracy in the functioning of TUs in Kanpur, working classes have neither been able to cope with globalisation nor set any further progressive agenda. Even in the industrial capital of the country, Bombay, during the recession of the 1960s, the left dominated TU movement found that its traditional means of seeking redressal, like mass rallies and work stoppage, became ineffective and stage was set for the rightward shift of the movement and finally its degeneration into intimidation and violence (Bhowmik, 1998).

It may be said that managements should pay attention to resolve the issues instead of using threat tactics to reduce the frequency of strikes. For the time being these strategies of management are able to bring down the frequency of strikes, but it can only suppress their feelings. Moreover, such attempts to suppress their demands without removing the underlying causes of unrest, may merely divert the conflict into other forms such as absenteeism, restriction of output, sabotage, turnover, refusal to work overtime, slow downs, etc., which are more harmful and difficult to combat. A congenial environment needed for work cannot be achieved by following these devices. It can only be achieved after fulfiling their legitimate demands. Management must be inclined towards industrial harmony, i.e. the existence of understanding, cooperation, and a sense of partnership between the employers and employees rather than the so called industrial peace, which is somewhat restrictive and negative.

Keeping in view the compulsions of globalisation exigencies, India needs to make its labour law framework realistic. There is a need to suitably amend the IDA provisions related to retrenchment and lay-off in Chapter V-B and section 9-A so as to facilitate a realistic introduction of change in employee service conditions. The framework of laws like the CLA also needs to be re-examined so as to focus on ensuring adherence to minimum standards of employment rather than total denial of employment of contact labour. The IR law discourse should focus on salvaging unionism and strict enforcement of minimum labour standards. The plight of contact labour is pitiable not because of the absence of labour law framework but due to the lack of willingness on the part of the state and its agencies to enforce them. If the labour laws are reasonable and practicable, their implementation will be easier. We need to think of evolving a system where collaborative efforts are needed for stopping the dehumanisation of work by employers in collusion with state agencies. Not just the trade unions but the NGOs, self-help groups and even consumer organisations too have to play an important role. For example, in the Western world they have been able to pressurize multinationals like Nike, Reebok, Levi Strauss to observe labour codes, to respect the right to organize, to ban child labour and to ensure payment of minimum wages (Leisink, 1999, p. 22).

The globalisation syndrome places trade unions in a tight spot. To cope with the situation they have to redefine their structures and role. It is being advocated that there may develop a new style of global social movement unionism (Lambert, 1999). In this regard, it is also argued that in order to retain bargaining power, unions have no choice but to "put consumers' interests first, company's interest second and their members' interest third", Venkata Ratnam (2003, p. 246). They have to engage themselves in internal dialogue and elaborating worker-oriented meanings of concepts such as "flexibility, security and opportunity" that are being shown to workers as methods of promoting the trickle down (Hyman, 1999). Unions also need to understand the changed realities for employers. The decline in unionism in USA is steep due to their continued hostility towards employers in the new economy (Mamkoottam, 2003, p. 145). In India since unions are oligarchic, hierarchical and highly politicized, adjustment to their new role is going to be a complex process. To be effective in the new, economy, they have to learn to work more as network organisation to cope with the new challenges, making use of new modes of information and communication. In fact, considerable thought process is needed in terms of viable suggestions to the three social partners to adapt themselves to the new realities. Building an enlightened society is to remain supplementary to any model of economic working. This essentially requires reconciling the goals of adapting to the changing global business environment and salvaging unionism as a countervailing force.

TOWARDS A NEW FRAMEWORK

The task of creating a new industrial relations framework is difficult, and of course full of imponderables. Some building blocks of a new framework could, however, be identified. These are as follows:

1. The legislative process of repeals, amendments and

new enactment need to be pushed ahead further. Fewer good laws and more effective enforcement and compliance must be in place, in the first place.

2. New experiments in different states like Andhra Pradesh, Kerala, West Bengal, Rajasthan are taking place. Apparently, they are departing from the historical uniform national pattern. The coalition era, with a weak centre, is facilitating the deviations. As experiences gather, some common trends would emerge and the scope for healthy re-convergence would arise.
3. Voices to encourage the "gainers" of the market era to share more with the "losers" is being heard, and this could gather momentum in India and elsewhere, too. It will have enormous moderating influence on the climate of industrial relations.
4. An extended social security for all workers, in a phased manner, is a serious agenda. All investments in this regard would enrich the industrial relations interactions, apart from meeting the long felt need in the country.
5. Work first, and decent work later is a dangerous palliative. This needs to be resisted strongly. Yet the prolonged presence of the informal sector is a strong possibility. Therefore, its productivity with support from—
   (a) better technology,
   (b) improved skills,
   (c) easy access to capital, and
   (d) market linkage must improve for the benefit of good employer-employee relations.
6. Progress on free cross-boarder economic migration of natural persons would bring balance in the distribution of human factor endowment. Labour shortage economies would mainly gain, while the labour surplus transitional economies would get needed relief. Connivance of the state in labour shortage mature economies, illegal migration for cheap labour, enclave settlements for immigrant guest workers, and liberal quota for professional

workers are evidences of market forces asserting over political and social barriers. A relative balance in labour supply and demand within and between economies will be beneficial to all. Successful social engineering at a global scale is the need of the hour. The rounds of the World Trade Organisation (WTO) negotiations could cover these issues.

7. Accelerated growth is desperately needed. A labour intensive but efficiency promoting technology would help. Both global and national market place needs regulatory institutions led by competent and Committed professionals. A national climate for receptivity to change the vested interest-led present set-upto its socially acceptable replacement is building up. Deliberations of the Second National Commission on labour and subsequent national debate have helped. A final package with—
   (a) a revised arrangement for the organised sector,
   (b) a strong beginning for strengthening the informal sector,
   (c) the necessary legislative reforms, and
   (d) a social security and welfare package of credible and sustainable kind, must soon emerge.
8. A rigid national uniformity is now behind us. Moderated diversity with strong centrality of linkages should be encouraged Trade unions and civic society institutions need concerted action with benign assistance from forward looking employers and the remaining state power (Shyam Sunder, 2003) In the new market place, risks of common injury should unite all interest groups. Stakes are high in creatively holding together and looking ahead with hope. There is scope as well as space to promote the interest of all with an optimum blend of strategy and agenda to be tapped. Some uneasy trade-off inevitably is a part of a workable next package.

Some light bearing, if not immediately fruit bearing, exercise among man-management professionals, policy-makers, and social partners should help. The growing intellectual and political unease on the "winner take all" situation should help somewhat. From "champions of the impossible rather than the slaves of the possible that evolution draws its creative force", said Barbara Wooton (quoted in Standing, 2002). This should serve as the basis for cautious optimism. The current crisis has opened up "space for significant strategic choices by the actors." With known constraints, the key actors need wider support in regaining their control on the functioning of the labour market and industrial relations system. Re-visiting the theoretical and conceptual parts, have to wait until the transitional churning settles down. In the meantime, the painful reality of obsolescence of both the theories and practice would, in all likelihood, continue.

PART B

INDUSTRIAL RELATIONS IN TISCO: A CASE STUDY

Introduction

Tata Steel, established in 1907, is the largest Private Sector Steel Company in India with a total installed capacity of 3.5 Million Tonne Per Annum (mtpa) crude steel production. The operations of the Company are spread all over India. Steel manufacturing unit is located at Jamshedpur in the State of Jharkhand and other manufacturing and mining activities are situated in the States of Jharkhand and Orissa at eight locations. Tata Steel exports its products to Japan, USA, Middle-East and South-East Asian countries.

Tata Iron and Steel Company Ltd. (TISCO) is the iron and steel production company associated with the Tata group of some 80 different industrial and other business enterprises in India, founded by members of the Tata family. TISCO operates as India's largest integrated steel works in the private sector with a market share of nearly 13 percent and is the second largest steel company in the entire industry. Its products and services include hot and cold rolled coils and sheets, tubes, construction bars, forging quality steel, rods, structurals, strips and bearings, steel plant and material handling equipment, ferro alloys and other minerals, software for process controls, and cargo handling services. Through its subsidiaries, TISCO also offers tinplate, wires, rolls, refractories, and project management services. Consistent with the vision and values of founder Jamsetji Tata,

Tata Steel strives to strengthen India's industrial base through the effective utilization of staff and materials. The means envisaged to achieve this are high technology and productivity, consistent with modern management practices. Tata Steel recognizes that while honesty and integrity are the essential ingredients of a strong and stable enterprise, profitability provides the main spark for economic activity.

Today, the World Steel Dynamics has identified it as the number one steel company amongst world steel makers. World Steel Dynamics, in its recent assessment, has rated the Company as the third most competitive steel plant in the world for the year 2002, behind Posco, South Korea and Bao Steel, China. The story of TISCO is the story of one family or, more accurately, one man whose vision and determination to give India a modern industrial economy helped provide a platform for the country's independence half a century after his death. At the same time, he helped create what was by 1970 India's biggest non-public enterprise. Jamsetji Nusserwanji Tata was born into a well-to-do family of Bombay Parsees in 1839. The Parsees, a religious minority group, had carved a niche for themselves in business, in this case in the economy of Victorian India, which was dominated by British interests and was being developed as a client imperial economy. Tata's father was a successful merchant with interests in the cotton trade to Britain. Tata joined the family business after an education at Elphinstone College in Bombay and was sent to Lancashire, England, in 1864 to represent the firm there. This was to be the first of many travels in Europe, North America, and the Far and Middle-East during which he formulated his ideas on the best strategy to realize his own ambitions for success in business and to contribute to the economic development of India.

Global Scenario of Steel Industry

The global economy experienced robust growth in 2005, despite significant concerns about the impact of higher world oil prices. World GDP is estimated to have increased by 3.2% in the calendar year 2005, down from 3.8% in 2004. In 2005, World Crude Steel output at 1129.4 million metric tonnes was 5.9% more than the previous year. The global steel industry suffered from structural deficiencies of large unutilised capacity, high degree of fragmentation and cyclical ups and downs of demand and prices. With consolidation in the industry gathering pace, this is now changing, albeit slowly. However, the industry is still fragmented, with the top ten steel producers controlling less than 30% of the world's steel output. China remained the world's largest crude steel producer in 2005 (349.4 million metric tonnes) followed by Japan (112.47 million metric tonnes) and USA (93.89 million metric tonnes). India occupied the 8th position (38.08 million metric tonnes). The International Iron and Steel Institute (IISI) in its forecast for 2006 has confirmed the trend of recent years of an increase in steel use in-line with general economic growth and with the fastest growth occurring in the countries with the highest GDP growth such as India and China. Apparent world-wide steel demand is forecast to grow to between 1,040 and 1,053 million tonnes in 2006 from a total of 972 million tonnes in 2004. This is a growth of 4-5% over the two year period. However, according to IISI the cost of raw materials and energy would continue to represent a major challenge for the world steel industry.

The surge of industrialisation in China and its emergence as a growing economic power has transformed the world steel scenario. While the more matured economies of the West and Japan have seen little change in their per capita consumption of steel, China's consumption of steel has been growing at over 20% in the last five years and it has become the most dominant factor in the world steel market so much so that in last five years the global steel production has increased by more than 30% (280 mt) and the bulk of that increase has been contributed by China (222 mt). Globally, the average capacity utilisation of steel has increased significantly during the year. Global crude steel production grew by 5.6%. The apparent steel demand is estimated to have risen by 2.7% to 998 million tonnes in the calendar year 2005. The bulk of the increase in steel demand was contributed by China. China accounted for 30% of global steel demand and 31% of crude steel production in 2005.

During the year, most of the steel raw material shortages witnessed in earlier years have been eased out especially in the area of coking coal, coke and ocean freight which had an impact on the steel prices.

Indian Scenario of Steel Industry

The industrial sector registered a strong growth during the year, primarily due to the growth of the manufacturing sector of 9%, compared to 8.69% in the previous year. During the year under review, domestic steel production and apparent steel consumption increased by 5.1% and 7.1% respectively, over the previous year. Demand in the domestic market was strong, with double digit growth in the automobiles, capital goods and consumer durable segments. Exports volume increased by 18% as compared to the previous year. Domestic steel prices moved in tandem with the international prices showing a downward trend as compared to the previous year. Most agree that the Chinese role has been prominent in decline in steel prices. November 2005 saw the release of National Steel Policy – the first Vision document for the Indian Iron and Steel Industry. The policy aims at hiking steel production to 110 million tonnes by 2019-20. The long-term goal is that India should become self-reliant and globally competitive in the steel sector in terms of cost, quality and product mix.

The calendar year 2002 was characterised by a recovery in steel demand in the international markets, particularly with the increased consumption in China and the rest of Asia. Consequently, there was a significant increase in steel prices. At the same time, quantitative restrictions and/or additional tariffs on steel imports were introduced by the U.S. and a few other countries, in an effort to protect their domestic steel industries. The world steel community is now engaged in discussions to bring about a better balance between demand and supply, by eliminating inefficient capacities around the world.

The steel market had a marked turnaround during the year. World crude steel production of 65 countries, constituting about 98% of the global steel production, showed an increase of over 6% at 887 mil. tonnes in Calendar Year 2002, compared to 834 mil. tonnes in 2001. Amongst the major steel producing nations, China outpaced the rest with an increase of 20%. Steel consumption is estimated to have risen from 780 mil. tonnes in 2001 to 829 mil. tonnes in 2002. The strong Chinese demand as well as the regional imbalances arising from import restrictions provided an impetus for the strong run-up in international steel prices, despite increased global production. The prices of commercial quality, commonly traded, hot rolled coils rose by about 40% in Europe, from the low levels at the end of the previous financial year. The steel cycles are becoming increasingly sharp and unpredictable. While, last year, a better year for the industry had been projected, the dramatic turnaround in steel prices that was actually witnessed surpassed the expectations of the entire industry.

China is expected to continue to dominate the global steel trade. It has emerged as the single most important market, and its ability to sustain its rapid growth will have a fundamental impact on the global supply of steel and prices. The International Iron and Steel Institute (IISI) is cautiously optimistic that the world consumption of steel will grow by 4.6% in 2003. The international community will also watch with keen interest the ongoing efforts to shut down inefficient capacities in various countries. India, last year, had one of its worst droughts of the past two decades, as the monsoon failed after several years. However, to the credit of the economy, it showed great resilience in withstanding this shock and did not permit this natural calamity to adversely affect the other sectors of the economy. Had it not been for the shrinkage in agricultural output, the economy would have seen one of its best performances in recent years. The GDP is estimated to have grown at about 5.1%, as compared to 5.6% in the previous year, pulled down by a sharp contraction in the Agriculture sector, which registered a negative growth of 1% as compared to a healthy growth rate of 5.7% in the previous year. The Manufacturing and Services sectors recovered smartly from last year's recession. Industrial production grew by 5.7% compared to 2.7% in the previous year. The Indian steel industry was driven by a significant pick-up in most user segments. The capital goods segment, which had actually contracted in the previous year, grew significantly. The automobile industry too displayed strength, doubling its growth rate. Consumer durables were, however, adversely impacted due to a fall in rural disposable incomes. While Manufacturing and Services did well, the exception was Agriculture, which tends to have a knock-on effect on the industrial sector. The recovery of global markets rubbed-off on domestic demand and prices firmed up, particularly for flats. The increase in prices was sustained right through the year, albeit from the very low base of the previous year. Trade actions by several countries distorted the market equilibrium and resulted in the peculiar phenomenon of their domestic prices being substantially higher than the international prices. Indian steel exports are estimated to have risen by 35% over the previous year, with the U.S. and China being the primary markets. Exports of hot rolled coils from India to the U.S. were adversely affected by continuing anti-dumping duties. However, shipments of CR galvanised, which were outside the purview of punitive actions, surged as the exporters found a ready and lucrative market in the U.S. With most of the end user segments showing improved growth, demand for steel picked up during the year. Domestic production was higher by 8% at 28.9 mil. tonnes (2001-02: 26.7 mil. tonnes). Apparent domestic consumption rose by 6% during the year at 26.8 mil. tonnes (2001-02: 25.3 mil. tonnes). Flat and Long products are estimated to have grown by 6.5% and 5.6% respectively.

Transforming Vision into Reality

Tata Steel, India's first steel plant was set-up almost a hundred years ago. This pioneering spirit endures. Today, Tata Steel is one of Asia's largest integrated steel plants. Anticipating the trends of the future, we have charted a growth route to achieve our Vision 2007. To transform this Vision into reality we have, year after year, repositioned paradigms, redefined benchmarks and revisited our core competence. This has accelerated the continuous change and improvement that we are endeavouring to bring about in our operations, in our work culture and in our efficiencies. This is our real achievement. One that will enable us to sustain what we have aspired for and build further upon it. So that we continue to be an EVA+ company and create greater stakeholder value.

A faster economic growth for the development of the society, particularly for common people, has been the goal of a socialist welfare society. This goal demands a better role of the private and public sectors for augmenting production of goods and services. In a mixed economy, like India, under economic planning, the key industries occupy a significant position in the field of production. Key and heavy industries have been put recently under the public sector. The private sector has been playing an active role from the very beginning. The recent developments in the field of production have certain impacts on industrial relations, which economy had never experienced earlier. The private sector, though is receiving importance next to the public sector, is yet playing important role in the national economy of the country. This applies more in the field of industrial relations where it has developed concepts and practices worth appreciable. Any term of industrial relations has a close link with the past development, particularly in the private sector, because the public sector was not in existence by then.

The desire for industrial peace is a world phenomenon. It is a prerequisite for the growth of the economy, the higher rate of employment, price stability and social justice. Since the establishment of industries and emergence of industrial disputes attempts have been made for early settlement of industrial disputes with a view to establish and maintain industrial peace. The theories of industrial relations have been propounded and principles have been developed, through trial and error method, with an effort to find out the best possible method for quick and satisfactory settlement of industrial disputes. Iron and steel industry occupies key place in our economic development. In India the Tata Iron and Steel Company is the oldest steel plant with a long history of peaceful and harmonious industrial relations.

Industrial Peace in Tata Iron and Steel Company

In its whole life of nearly 100 years only a few strikes have taken place. There have been long periods of industrial peace. Industrial peace had been maintained even prior of enactment of the industrial relations laws. Such a situation draws attention of the experts and students of the industrial relations as to why industrial relations in the Tata Iron and Steel is smooth? Why this private sector steel plant has been able to infuse industrial peace? What is the industrial relations policy of the TISCO management? How industrial disputes are settled? To what extent the degree of labour-management cooperation exists? How far "Closer association of employees with management" scheme has achieved its goal? These are some of the important questions that crop up in the minds of persons interested with industrial relations.

All these questions can be answered after examining

thoroughly the policies and practices of industrial relations of the TISCO, amended and adjusted from time to time, in order to suit the changing industrial environment and industrial requirements. This naturally diverts attention towards the philosophies propounded by the founder of the company, Jamsetji Naussarvanji Tata and his successors Dorabji Tata, Naval H. Tata, J.R.D. Tata and followed by a bunch of top managerial personnel. The basic philosophy of Tata is guided by the humanitarian approach of the founder Jamsetji, who always stressed on human relations and humanitarian approach in industry. The Tata's tradition dealing with labour is based on human attitude as Jamsetji stated:

> "We do not claim to be more unselfish, more generous or more philanthropic than other people. But we think we started on sound and straight forward business principles, considering the interests of the shareholders our own, and the health and welfare of the employees the sure foundation of our prosperity."

The human relations approach of Jamsetji was followed by Dorabji Tata, who propounded a more clear-cut policy of industrial relations. He stated in 1917 that

> "The welfare of the labouring classes must be one of the first cares of every employer. Any betterment of their conditions must proceed more from the employers downward rather than be forced up by demands from below, since labour, contended, is not only an asset and advantage to the employer, but serves to raise the standard of industry and labour in the country."

Dorabji Tata was of the view that betterment of the conditions of labour should come from the employers voluntarily rather than the demand forced upon them by the employees. In other words, opportunity should not be given to the employees to express dissatisfaction, organise agitation and submit demands backed by the strong force and power. He gave clear hint that industrial relations policy of the company should always endure to adopt suitable methods for settlement of common issues.

Efforts must be made for betterment of service conditions and establishment of industrial peace. The thread of industrial relations was strengthened by the attitude and philosophy of Naval H. Tata, who has been strong force and symbol of the labour policy of the house of Tata. He had accepted that:

> "... differences leading to conflicts are unfortunate. But they are understandable. Conflict is sometimes inevitable, because the labour-management relationship is based on, what the sociologists call, 'antagonistic cooperation'. It may sound paradoxical but is nevertheless true that the interests of industry and labour can almost simultaneously be in harmony and at variance with each other."

The quest for industrial peace has been the common meeting point of all the three parties. It will not come from the top or from outside. It is something which must be generated from within. Emphasizing on this point, Naval H. Tata observed clearly that

> "However strong our passion for peace and harmony in industry may be, peace is not likely to descend on us from heavens by mere exhortations and prayers. Serious efforts will have to be made by all concerned to keep the path of industrial peace free from misunderstandings, misrepresentations and undue interference from third parties."

Lamenting on the problems of industrial relations in order to retrieve it from a jungle of discord to give some semblance of sanity and peace, he prepared a blue print in order to help in preparation of a programme from establishing industrial peace. In his blue print he emphasised on adoption of collective bargaining as a method for settlement of industrial disputes. Repeatedly he stated that

> "I shall never tier of repeating what I have been saying from time to time; more of bipartite agreements and less of adjudicated awards, more of voluntary codes and less

of labour laws, more of self-reliance on the part of employers and workers and less eagerness on the part of Government to interfere may, in course of time, put us on the path of enduring industrial peace which we need so badly to make our best contribution to the national economy.

The industrial relations policy of Tata has been further reshaped by J.R.D. Tata when he observed in 1955 that

"To create good working conditions, to pay the best wages in the industry, to promote welfare and provide decent housing, is not enough. The ultimate aim of good personnel and industrial relations programme should be to find a solution to the problem of better relations between the management and labour, or between labour and capital, which will be potentially the greatest reward we can have in the long-run. Such a happy relation can be obtained only by creating a sense of confidence on the part of the ranks of the labour that (a) they have a stake in the industry, and (b) they are something more than mere cogs in the machines or mere tools of Management and that their dreams, their feelings and their human problems, are part of the company's problem and Management's problem—a feeling that they have some voice, if not in policy, in some of the processes of Management."

The industrial relations policy and a turning point with the acceptance of the new policy "Closer association of employees with management" in 1956, which had been in operation since 1946. This new policy based on humanitarian approach aims at establishing more harmonious industrial relations with higher possible degree of cooperation. On such a progressive industrial relations policy the TISCO has celebrated the thirty years of industrial peace. Talking about the industrial relations situation of the country and TISCO, J.R.D. Tata had remarked that—

"Why is it that all these years, when there has been industrial unrest all over the country, we should continue to remain peaceful in Jamshedpur. I think there are two main reasons. One is a sincere and respected system of consultation that we have established at three levels, at the shop-floor level, the division level and at top management level. I think this is perhaps what has been mostly responsible for our successful industrial relation in this company. The other reason is the support we extend to our own employees – the educational facilities for their children, the medical facilities, housing and other amenities. A large number of our workers are second and third, and in some cases, even fourth generation employees of Tata Steel."

The TISCO claims to have better industrial relations policy compared to other industrial establishments in India, both public and private sectors. R.S. Pande, the then Managing Director of Tata Steel, in 1973 had accepted that—

"One encouraging sign in recent years has been the strengthening of the forces of bipartism. One outstanding example of the effectiveness of bipartite machinery is the Joint Negotiating Committee for the Steel Industry where representatives of employers and workers, belonging to various shades of public opinion, sit at a table and try to thrash out their common problems. That bipartite talks are the best for securing industrial peace is a fact which can hardly be disputed."

He had further claimed to have a record of long industrial peace attributing to the Tatas policy of participative management in the following words:

"If Tata Steel has enjoyed complete industrial peace over all these years when the country, on an average, loses about 20 million mandays every year, it can, to a great extent, be attributable to the principles of participative management followed under a successful three-tier system of closer employee association with management."

The claim of the Tata management to be pioneer in industrial relations is something which cannot be accepted unless examined closely the principles propounded and practices implemented. There are many achievements, no doubt, on the part of TISCO which claims as a pioneer in industrial relations but there are events which have raised questions for reconsidering the practicability of the whole policy of industrial relations. The TISCO was first amongst a few to recognise a union, first to negotiate with the union, one amongst a few to sign an agreement, first to provide an hours a day as working period in 1912 first to provide medical aid in 1915, set-up Welfare Department for providing welfare measures, granted leave with pay in 1920 and set-up shops committee in 1919.

In spite of long record of industrial peace the TISCO had been rocked by two strikes, one in 1958 and other in 1981. The first strike was unprecedented in the history of TISCO and Jamshedpur because that had thrown the whole factory on the verge of explosion. The strike had given a jerk to the industrial relations policy demanding amendment and modification to suit the changing industrial environment. The strike, in spite of its failure, had given many lessons to the two parties. It forced the management to realise in the words of R.S. Pande that—

> "... recognition of a union alone may not produce the necessary climate for healthy and stable industrial peace particularly when there are more than one union. Thus, a new pattern of industrial relations, which has been emerging of late, is some managements' readiness to talk to both recognised and unrecognised union under certain situations. Though this phenomenon is not widespread, the beginning of the acceptance of this principle at some places strikes a new note in the pattern of industrial relations."

The unrecognised union, Jamshedpur Mazdoor Union, a militant organisation had succeeded in awakening the moderate labour leaders and the TISCO management as not to over look a section of employees organised by an unrecognised union. It also raised the basic question as to what role an unrecognized union can play in maintenance of industrial peace? Should it be consulted by the management in day-to-day affairs? What status should be given to an unrecognised union? These basic questions have called for adoption of a new pattern of industrial relations policy. Naturally, this call for new pattern of industrial relations has outdated the old industrial relations policy of TISCO.

The second strike known as contract labour strike of 1981 again came as a challenge to the claim of the TISCO to have a long record of industrial peace. It is a matter of paradox that this strike occurred just after a few years of celebration of industrial peace. This strike was again unparallel for Jamshedpur because the other industrial establishments such as TISCO, the Indian Tube Co., Tin Plate Company and the T.R.F. had agreed to absorb contract labour whereas TISCO alone remain adament violating the provisions of the contract Labour (Regulation and Abolition) Act, 1970. The importance of the strike lies with the fact that the TISCO employees above 10,000 contract labour, which forms nearly one-fifth of the total labour force both regular temporary and contract labour. Such a policy of the TISCO management to violate the law of the country particularly by the company, which claims better and progressive labour policy, is condemnable. Though the strike has failed but the basic issues still exist. This further demands readjustment of the policy for maintaining its record of longer industrial peace and industrial harmony.

The three key pillars of the international financial markets are confidence, capital and liquidity and these three are somewhat interrelated. Until September 2008, all these three pillars were on a high and therefore, businesses across the various sectors were performing in a robust manner. However, the confidence in the financial system was shaken with successive crises across various banks in the US and Europe. This then resulted in a significant erosion of capital in the banking industry in the developed world which eventually spiraled into an unprecedented global financial crisis. This phenomenon brought about a sharp decline in consumption of steel as it did in other products, affecting the steel demand across the globe.

Consequently, global liquidity was choked and the manufacturing sectors including the consumers of the steel industry were severely affected. It is estimated that during the second half of the year, the steel demand declined by around 20% globally over the same period last year.

The Group has responded in time and with great speed

executing several initiatives to counter the slowdown. Our actions have been geography specific and well planned. In India, we have responded by increasing production post-commissioning of the 1.8 mtpa programme and focussing on performance improvement to neutralize the effect of reduced realisations, whereas in South-East Asia, the focus is on working capital management and cost reduction. In Europe we have cut production by idling blast furnaces at three sites in order to align production with demand as a part of the "Weathering the Storm" initiative which resulted in cash savings of £712 million (US$1.02 billion) in the second half of the financial year 2008-09. Further, these efforts have been supplemented by a strategic restructuring initiative launched as "Fit for Future" programme which when completed, will result in improvement of the operating profit of around £200 million annually. In all our sites across the Group, the journey of 'Continuous Improvement' stays on course, covering the entire range of manufacturing and mining processes.

The strategic levers of the Group have remained the same over the last few years. The current global economic scenario has only rephrased some of these strategies in terms of timing and speed. The four levers are:

(a) Making our European operations competitive by hastening the speed of the "Weathering the Storm" and "Fit for the Future" programme.
(b) Quick completion of our expansion plans in India. The 3 mtpa project will be commissioned by 2011 and will add significant value to the Group. Further expansion in India through the Greenfield project in Orissa and Chhattisgarh are ongoing and their commencing will depend on ground realities and iron ore allocation.
(c) Investment in raw material assets to provide better raw material security especially to our European operations.
(d) Vigorous pursuit of continuous improvement across all our operations.

The global recovery that started in the second half of 2009-

10 continued in most markets in 2010-11. However, the recovery was not uniform as the emerging markets grew faster than the developed markets, which still face headwinds due to fi scal imbalances in some geographies. The sustainability of the global recovery depends on how the developed markets manage their public debt, boost private economic activity and generate employment. The emerging economies face the risk of very high inflationary conditions due to high commodity prices and food inflation. This is prompting the central banks to tighten monetary policies which in turn may affect growth significantly. The emerging market countries including India, need to continue their economic reforms to attract capital investments, which in turn would facilitate growth and employment.

Although India registered 0.9% GDP growth in FY 11, it is now faced with high-core inflation due to rising commodity prices and food inflation. This is forcing the Reserve Bank of India to tighten its monetary policy even at the cost of slower growth. The growth data in the EU zone reveals significant differences at the country level. Recovery in Germany and most of the Northern European countries remains well on track, whereas growth in the peripheral countries has been hampered by several factors such as export competition and weak domestic demand, exacerbated by cuts in government spending. Euro-area growth is sustained by strong investment and is largely export led, which will remain its key driver, helped by exchange rates and specialised products. The UK, in contrast, remains a fragile market and lags behind some of its European peers. The construction activity remains below pre-crisis levels in Europe. While the forward indicators point to modest growth in the coming quarters, the outlook for this sector remains sober due to weak recovery in private construction and cuts in public expenditure. Real steel consumption in the EU zone is expected to rise by 4% but will still be below the pre-crisis levels. Steel inventories in Europe remain relatively low both in tonnage as well as months of consumption and the level of imports is currently below historic levels, as stock replenishments are done in small quantities while avoiding longer lead times. While the global economy is certainly in a better shape than a year ago, the risk of sustaining the recovery is high and it really depends on the national governments to prudently steer the fiscal management and take policy decisions to facilitate growth and employment.

The prime objective of this Part is to provide holistic review of TISCO in terms of production performance, managerial performance and human relations.

References

TISCO, Man-Management in Tata Steel, P. Introductory page.
Lala, R.M.: 'The Creation of Wealth', p. 125.
______, 'The Creation of Wealth', p. 119.
Tata Steel, Annual Reports (2000-01).
Tata Steel, Annual Report (2001-02).
Tata Steel, Annual Report (2002-03).
Tata Steel, Annual Report (2003-04).
Tata Steel, Annual Report (2004-05).
Tata Steel, Annual Report (2005-06).
Tata Steel, Annual Report (2006-07).

Historical Overview of TISCO

THE FOUNDER JAMSETJI

Jamshetji Nusserwanji Tata (1839-1904):

Sir Jamshetji Nusserwanji Tata was born on 3rd March, 1839 into a family descended from Parsi priests in Navsari, Gujarat, a centre for age-old Parsi culture. He was educated at Elphinstone College, Bombay. Sir Jamshetji Nusserwanji Tata was a successful merchant and textile mill owner. In 1882, at the age of 43, Jamshetji Nusserwanji Tata read a report by a German geologist, Ritter Von Schwartz on the availability of Iron Ore in Chanda District in the Central Provinces, which gave him the idea of giving India a Steel plant. He was a born entrepreneur, a born risktaker, a man with vast foresight. Starting his business carrier as a supplier, soon he became owner of a textile mill at Bombay. He shifted his work place from Bombay to Nagpur, cotton growing area and opened a textile mill in 1877. The mill flourished in a short span of time. A local Marwari banker had remarked that "Tata had not put gold into the ground but in earth and taken out gold."

Jamsetji was a man of destiny. Every day of his life was spent for the growth of modern India. R.M. Lala in his book, "The Creation of Wealth", has fairly written that:

"When he surveyed the untilled industrial field of India

> he perceived the benefits it could gain through science and technology. Not only did he grasp the full significance of industrial revolution of India, but his clear mind spelt out the three basic in gradients to attain it. Steel was the mother of heavy industry. Hydro-electric power was the cheapest energy to be generated. And technical education coupled with research was essential for industrial advance."

The successful venture in textile industry showed Jamsetji's mind, entrepreneurship and high management skill. He then choose the unknown path to give India steel and hydro-electric power on a big scale. By 1902 he planned everything in mind and enfused lifeblood in establishment of steel plant. It was in 1902 when a more helpful attitude appeared, Jamsetji immediately sought expert advice from the United State for locating the natural resources available in India for the steel industry. The Sahlin and Company, leading consultants of that time on Metallurgical plant construction, on the advice of Kennedy, sent consulting engineer Charles Page Perin. By April 1903 C.M. Weld, who was Perin's assistant, had began search for iron ore in India. Before the search he came to a conclusion, those far-seeing eyes that had seen vision of an industrialised India were closed in eternal sleep. Jamsetji N. Tata died on May 19, 1904. But Dorabji and Rotanji Jamsetji Tata, his sons and Ratanji Dadabhai Tata, his cousin, continued the work.

Jamsetji, one of the founders of modern India, was an industrialist, philanthropist and a philosopher. He realised that mere political freedom without economic and industrial growth to support and defend it would be an illusion which could not bring about the real economic, social and moral upliftment of the country. Drawing the picture of the first steel city of India, Jamsetji Tata wrote to his son Dorabji in 1902:

> "Be sure to lay wide streets planted with shady trees, every other of a quick growing variety. Be sure that there is plenty of space for lawns and gardens. Reserve large areas for football, hockey and parks. Earmark areas for Hindu Temples, Mohammaden Mosques and Christian Churches."

That shows his foresightedness, large heartedness and practicability of the social life. He took every step in building not only the steel factory but also a neat and clean modern society, preserving religious sentiments and providing all welfare amenities for a better living and working conditions.

The Pioneers

Sir Dorabji Tata (1859-1933)

J.N. Tata had exhorted to his sons to pursue and develop his life's work, his elder son, Dorab Tata carried out the bequest with scrupulous zeal and distinction. Thus even though it was Jamshetji Tata who had envisioned the mammoth project, it was in fact Dorab Tata who actually brought the ventures to existence and fruition. He was the first Chairman of the gigantic Tata. He had a deep interest in people. The great labour strike in 1920 in Jamshedpur ended in a day due to his intervention it demonstrated India could have no better employer of labour than Sir Dorab.

Bharat Ratan Jehangir

His was a life which often shaped history. Pioneering civil aviation on the sub-continent, funding Dr. Homi Bhabha's ambition to catapult India into the nuclear age, initiating the family planning movement much before it became the official policy and bankrolling the efforts to record and preserve for posterity the country's priceless folk arts which were in danger of obliteration. J.R.D. Tata was indeed a legend in his time.

Born in Paris on July 29, 1904, Jehangir Ratanji Dadabhoy Tata was the second child of Mr. Ratanji Dadabhoy Tata and his French wife Sooni. The young Tata spent his early years in Hardelot, a beach in France, where his interest in flying was sparked off. He had varied interests, desired to become a scholar at Cambridge, had a passion for fast cars, and served in a regiment called Le Saphis (The Sepoys) with the French army in 1924.

In 1925, Mr. Tata arrived at Bombay House to work under Mr. John Peterson, the director-in-charge of Tata Steel. In 1938 when Sir Nowroji Saklatvala, the Chairman of Tata Sons expired, Mr. Tata was catapulted to head the country's largest industrial empire. He was barely thirty four! And he guided the destiny of India's largest Industrial house for well over half a century.

In 1939 Tata Chemicals started its struggle towards pioneering a self-reliant, basic inorganic chemical industry for India, in the face of repeated crises. Just before India's Independence, Tata Steel promoted the Tata Engineering and Locomotive Company (TELCO) in 1945 with an objective to produce locomotives 'for the Indian Railways. Today, TELCO has emerged as India's largest Commercial Vehicle producer. JRD's passion for flying was fulfilled with the formation of the Tata Aviation Service in 1932. The first flight of Indian Civil Aviation took-off at Drigh Road airfield in Karachi on October 15, 1932, with Mr. Tata at the controls flying the Puss Moth solo to Ahmedabad and on to Bombay. In its first year of operations, the Tata Aviation Service, achieved cent percent punctuality and chalked up a profit of Rs. 10,000.

Arrival of the inaugural mail flight from Karachi to Bombay: (from left) Nusserwanji Guzder, Homi Bharucha, J.R.D. Tata, Nevill Vincent and two officials of the postal service.

The Leopard Moth in which J.R.D made a commemorative flight in 1962, on the 30th anniversary of the first mail flight from Karachi to Bombay. Alongside is an Air-India Boeing 707. On every flight which Mr. Tata flew, he made key observations and suggestions to emphasize on the quality of service. Even though, over the years, Air India International had struck a high note for Indian Aviation, the domestic airline scenario was in a mess. The government decided in 1953 to nationalize the entire airline business and invited Mr. Tata to chair the enterprise. He devoted a disproportionate time with Air-India while his group companies were all run by efficient chief executives he had personally recruited.

Air Chief Marshal Arjun Singh with J.R.D at the latter's investiture as Honorary Air Commodore.

J.R.D. at the controls of a Vampire jet.

In 1978, Mr. Tata's services in Air-India were terminated by Mr. Morarji Desai, India's Prime Minister. This was a body blow for JRD and compared the experience to losing a child he had nurtured for years.

J.R.D. with the Leopard Moth in 1982 on the 50th anniversary of the inaugural mail flight.

Despite enormous pressures on his time, Mr. Tata took the role of a citizen very seriously and never failed to be of service to the nation. The concept of establishing Asia's first Cancer hospital in Bombay was implemented under Mr. Tata's purview in 1941. The Tata Memorial Hospital was the first large contribution of India to the international fight against cancer. Citizen Tata's greatest gift to the scientific establishment came in 1945 when he gave the founding grant to Dr. Homi Bhabha to set-up the Tata Institute of Fundamental Research. This Institute has proved to be, in Dr. Homi Bhabha's words "the cradle of our atomic energy program".

Mr. Tata was among the first Indians to be drawn to the cause of population control when he realised the drag unchecked population growth could have on the country's developmental efforts. It was in 1951 when he came across statistics which revealed that the country had crossed the mark of 350 million people, Mr. Tata sounded out Prime Minister Mr. Pandit Nehru on the issue and the latter ignored it. JRD didn't wait for the government to act, but part funded Mrs. Avabai Wadia's efforts in starting the Family Planning Association of India. In 1970, he started the Family Planning Foundation jointly with the Ford foundation and was instrumental in conditioning the thinking of an entire generation, treating the issue as one of essential transformation of the society. For his crusading endeavours in the field, Mr. Tata was bestowed the United Nations Population Award in 1992.

The President of India, Mr. R. Venkataraman conferring the Bharat Ratna.

For his enormous contributions to India, Mr. Tata was awarded the country's highest civilian honour, the Bharat Ratna, in 1992, one of the rare instances when the award was granted during the person's lifetime. And with his death on November 29, 1993, India lost one of its pioneering sons. The Indian Parliament, in an unusual gesture for a private citizen, was adjourned in his memory and the state of Maharashtra declared three days of public mourning.

Ratan Naval Tata

Ratan Tata

Born	December 28, 1937 (Age 70) Surat, India
Residence	Mumbai, India
Nationality	India
Ethnicity	Parsi
Citizenship	India
Education	Architecture and Structural Engineering
Occupation	Chairman of Tata Group
Employer	Self-Employed, Tata Group
Home town	Mumbai, India
Net worth	▲ $50.6 billion USD (2008)
Religious beliefs	Zoroastrianism
Spouse(s)	Never married
Children	None

Ratan Tata

Ratan Naval Tata (born December 28, 1937, in Surat) is the present Chairman of the Tata Group, India's largest conglomerate founded by Jamsetji Tata and consolidated and expanded by later generations of his family.

Early life

Tata was born into the wealthy and famous Tata family of Mumbai. He was born to Soonoo and Naval Hormusji Tata, a Gujarati-speaking Parsi family. Ratan is the great grandson of Tata group founder Jamsetji Tata. Ratan's childhood was troubled, his parents separating in the mid-1940s, when he was about seven and his younger brother Jimmy was five. His mother moved out and both Ratan and his brother were raised by their grandmother Lady Navajbai. He was schooled at the Campion School, Mumbai and graduated from Cornell University in 1962 with a degree in Architecture and Structural Engineering.

Early career

Ratan joined the Tata Group in December 1962, after turning down a job with IBM on the advice of JRD Tata. He was first sent to Jamshedpur to work at Tata Steel. He worked on the floor along with other blue-collar employees, shoveling limestone and handling the blast furnaces. Ratan Tata, a shy man, rarely features in the society glossies, has lived for years in a book-crammed, dog-filled bachelor flat in Mumbai's Colaba district.

JRD Tata with his successor Ratan Tata.

Career

In 1971, Ratan was appointed the Director-in-Charge of The National Radio and Electronics Company Limited (Nelco), a company that was in dire financial difficulty. Ratan suggested that the company invest in developing high-technology products, rather than in consumer electronics. J.R.D. was reluctant due to the historical financial performance of Nelco which had never even paid regular dividends. Further, Nelco had 2% market share in the consumer electronics market and a loss margin of 40% of sales when Ratan took over. Nonetheless, J.R.D. followed Ratan's suggestions.

From 1972 to 1975, Nelco eventually grew to have a market share of 20%, and recovered its losses. In 1975 however, India's Prime Minister Indira Gandhi declared a state of emergency, which led to an economic recession. This was followed by union problems in 1977, so even after demand improved, production did not keep up. Finally, the Tatas confronted the unions and, following a strike, a lock-out was imposed for seven months. Ratan continued to believe in the fundamental soundness of Nelco, but the venture did not survive. In 1977, Ratan was entrusted with Empress Mills, a textile mill controlled by the Tatas. When he took charge of the company, it was one of the few sick units in the Tata group. Ratan managed to turn it around and even declared a dividend. However, competition from less labour-intensive enterprises had made a number of companies unviable, including those like the Empress which had large labour contingents and had spent too little on modernisation. On Ratan's insistence, some investment was made, but it did not suffice. As the market for coarse and medium cotton cloth (which was all that the Empress produced) turned adverse, the Empress began to accumulate heavier losses. Bombay House, the Tata headquarters, was unwilling to divert funds from other group companies into an undertaking which would need to be nursed for a long time. So, some Tata directors, chiefly Nani Palkhivala, took the line that the Tatas should liquidate the mill, which was finally closed down in 1986. Ratan was severely disappointed with the decision, and in a later interview with the Hindustan Times would claim that the Empress had needed just Rs. 50 lakhs to turn it around. In 1981, Ratan was named director of Tata Industries, the Group's other holding company, where he became responsible for transforming it into the Group's strategy think-tank and a promoter of new ventures in high-technology businesses.

In 1991, he took over as group chairman from J.R.D. Tata, pushing out the old guard and ushering in younger managers. Since then, he has been instrumental in reshaping the fortunes of the Tata Group, which today has the largest market capitalization of any business houses on the Indian Stock Market.

Under Ratan's guidance, Tata Consultancy Services went public and Tata Motors was listed on the New York Stock Exchange. In 1998, Tata Motors introduced his brainchild, the Tata Indica.

On January 31, 2007, under the chairmanship of Ratan Tata, Tata Sons successfully acquired Corus Group, an Anglo-Dutch steel and aluminium producer. With the acquisition, Ratan Tata became a celebrated personality in Indian corporate business culture. The merger created the fifth largest steel producing entity in the world.

On March 26, 2008, Tata Motors, under Ratan Tata, bought Jaguar and Land Rover from Ford Motor Company. The two iconic British brands, Jaguar and Land Rover, were acquired for £1.15 billion ($2.3 billion).

Ratan Tata's dream was to manufacture a car costing Rs. 100,000 (1998: approx. US$2,200; today US$2,528). He realized his dream by launching the car in New Delhi Auto Expo on January 10, 2008. Three models of the Tata Nano were announced, and Ratan Tata delivered on his commitment to developing a

Ratan Tata's dream fulfilled, His Tata Nano Car 2008.

car costing only 1 lakh rupees, adding that "a promise is a promise," referring to his earlier promise to deliver this car at the said cost. Recently when his plant for Nano production was obstructed by Mamta Banerjee, his decision of going out of West Bengal was warmly welcomed.

On October 7, 2008, After a controversial stay in West Bengal, Ratan Tata and his men on Tuesday shifted their Rs 1-lakh car Nano project to Sanand near Ahmedabad at an investment of Rs. 2,000 crore (Rs. 20 billion), declaring that efforts will be made to roll out the world's cheapest car from a make-shift plant to meet the deadline. Praising Modi for speedy allocation of about 1,100 acres (1.5 km^2) of centrally located land, Ratan Tata said that the company had a great deal of urgency in having a new location and was driven by the reputation of the state. He successfully made a secret deal with Narendra Modi who agreed to give him a soft loan to the tune of approximately $10 billion to make the car in Gujarat.

Awards and Recognition

On the occasion of India's 58th Republic Day on 26 January 2000, Ratan Tata was honoured with the Padma Bhushan, the third highest decoration that may be awarded to a civilian. On 26 January 2008 he was awarded the Padma Vibhushan, the second highest civilian decoration. He was one of the recipients of the NASSCOM Global Leadership Awards-2008 given away at a ceremony on February 14, 2008 in Mumbai. Ratan Tata accepted the Carnegie Medal of Philanthropy in 2007 on behalf of the Tata family.

Ratan Tata serves in senior capacities in various organisations in India and he is a member of the Prime Minister's Council on Trade and Industry. In March 2006 Tata was honoured by Cornell University as the 26th Robert S. Hatfield Fellow in Economic Education, considered the highest honor the university awards to distinguished individuals from the corporate sector.

Ratan Tata's foreign affiliations include membership of the international advisory boards of the Mitsubishi Corporation, the American International Group, JP Morgan Chase and Booz Allen Hamilton. He is also a member of the board of trustees of the RAND Corporation, University of Southern California and of his alma mater, Cornell University. He also serves as a board member on the Republic of South Africa's International Investment Council and is an Asia-Pacific advisory committee member for the New York Stock Exchange. Tata is on the board of governors of the East-West Center, the advisory board of RAND's Center for Asia Pacific Policy and serves on the programme board of the Bill and Melinda Gates Foundation's India AIDS initiative. In February 2004, Ratan Tata was conferred the title of honorary economic advisor to Hangzhou city in the Zhejiang province of China.

He recently received an honorary doctorate from the London School of Economics and was listed among the 25 most powerful people in business named by Fortune magazine in November 2007. In May 2008 Mr. Tata made it to the Time magazine's 2008 list of the World's 100 most influential people. Tata was hailed for unveiling his tiny Rs. one lakh car 'Nano'.

On 29th August 2008, the Government of Singapore conferred honorary citizenship on Ratan Tata, in recognition of his abiding business relationship with the island nation and his contribution to the growth of high-tech sectors in Singapore. Ratan Tata is the first Indian to receive this honour.

A history of positive response

Over the past 100 years Tata Steel has witnessed many global crises. Every time the company has responded positively and proactively, enabling it not merely to overcome each crisis but to grow through the experience. India's Swadeshi Movement began in the early 1900s. It encouraged the boycotting of imported goods in order to stimulate the demand for products made in

India. As a part of the Indian Independence Movement, it was a successful economic strategy to improve economic conditions in India through the principles of self-sufficiency as well as to prove that Indians had what it takes to produce for themselves, administer themselves and be self-reliant. The market also needed a boost that would encourage Indian trade and enterprise. The Movement gave tremendous impetus to the Indian industry, opening the way for the manufacture of swadeshi salt, sugar and other products.

From the mid-1880s, Tata commissioned a series of surveys in India's coal-producing areas, such as Bihar and Orissa in the northeast of the subcontinent, to locate iron ore within easy reach of coal deposits and water, both essential elements in steel production. He visited the United States to seek the advice of the world's foremost metallurgical consultant, Julian Kennedy, and went to Birmingham, Alabama, to study the coking process in action. In England in 1900, he discussed his plans with the secretary of state for India, Lord George Hamilton. In India, the way had been opened for private enterprise with the introduction of a more liberalized mineral concession policy in 1899. With Julian Kennedy's help, American specialists were brought in and began surveying in 1903. After a series of disappointments, rich iron ore deposits were identified in the dense jungle in Bihar at the confluence of two rivers near Sakchi three years after Jamsetji Tata's death in 1904.

The Swadeshi Movement (1905–1908)

BIRTH OF TATA STEEL

The Swadeshi Movement encouraged Jamsetji Tata to set-up Asia's first ever privately-owned integrated iron and steel plant. His interest in iron making was triggered in 1882 when he came across an official report on the Chanda district which identified large deposits of high-quality iron ore but also noted a lack of suitable coal in the region. His idea of endowing his country with its own iron and steel industry gained support within the government and in 1907, when the Swadeshi Movement was at its height, the Tata Iron and Steel Company Ltd. was incorporated.

The Tatas raised the finance to build the steel plant within India—a significant milestone in Indian economic history. They proved a point to the then British government that an Indian company had the vision and the wherewithal to build an industry from the ground up and had the know-how to apply international standards to meet local needs. The setting up of the Tata Iron and Steel Company Ltd. gave Indian industry a voice paving the way for many a future enterprise.

World War I (1914 –1918)

World War I began as a local European war on 28th July, 1914 and eventually became a global conflict spanning four years and involving 32 nations, before finally ending on 11th November, 1918. It caused unprecedented carnage and devastation across the world. During the war no fewer than 26 vessels carrying Tata Steel material were sunk. The war effort took almost 80% of Tata Steel's production.

Tata Steel Responds

During World War I there was a requirement for substantial amounts of steel to oppose the German aggression. Through innovative efforts like stopping the manufacture of highly profitable ferro-manganese in favour of using its blast furnaces to convert pig iron into the steel that the war effort required, Tata Steel supplied 1,500 miles of rail and 300,000 tonnes of steel material at concessional rates for the military campaigns. The plant was geared to meet the priority needs of the government. It worked on a 24-hour schedule, and sold its products to the government at a fraction of the price prevailing in the open market. Two more open hearth furnaces, each of 60 tonnes capacity, were added to make more steel. The British acknowledged at the end of the war that the allied victory would not have been possible without the 1,500 miles of railway track supplied by Tata Steel.

In 1919, in recognition of the Company's contribution to the war effort, Lord Chelmsford renamed Sakchi as Jamshedpur and Kalimati Railway Station as Tatanagar. It was also during this time that the Company decided to expand its capacity.

The Great Depression (Late 1920s – early 1940s)

The Great Depression, which originated in the US with the Wall Street Crash of October 1929, was a worldwide economic downturn that had a disastrous effect on virtually every country. It was the most severe economic depression of the 20th century, wiping out the value of equities, wrecking the international currency system and causing world commodity prices to collapse. International trade plunged by half to two-thirds, as did personal income tax revenues, prices and profits. Construction came to a virtual halt in many countries. Facing plummeting demand and rocketing unemployment, areas dependent on basic industries such as farming, mining and logging suffered the most. In the UK the Great Depression brought to a head the mounting discontent of the British steel industry's financial backers, some of which had already effectively taken control of many family-owned companies.

Tata Steel Responds

Early in World War I Tata Steel had embarked on an expansion of the Works and this was followed by a larger expansion programme in 1917 to raise its steel production to 500,000 tonnes. The value of this expansion programme was not fully appreciated until the world was reeling under the pressure of the Great Depression. The Tatas survived the Depression and supplied nearly three quarters of the country's steel requirements at that time.

Formation of the British Iron and Steel Federation

Co-ordinated by the Bank of England and boosted by a devaluation of the Sterling, which helped exports and hindered imports, a series of measures were adopted in the early 1930s to cure the industry's chronic ailments. In 1934 the British Iron and Steel Federation (BISF) was formed. Under its leader, Sir Andrew Duncan, the BISF espoused a policy of rationalized regional steel making. It left investment decisions to individual firms but retained a strong influence over policy matters, as well as control over the industry's relations with the government. This industry structure remained largely intact until the second nationalization of the UK's steel industry in 1967 (the first was in 1949). The result was a swift improvement in business performance as living standards finally began to rise.

BIRTH OF KONINKLIJKE NEDERLANDSCHE HOOGOVENS

In September 1918 Koninklijke Nederlandsche Hoogovens en Staalfabrieken was founded as a private-sector initiative. Inspite of the uncertain future, at the end of the War, a group of 23 men comprising bankers, industrialists, merchants and politicians founded the company under the leadership of the visionary Henry Wenckebach. In 1924 iron making started up in

IJmuiden, using cutting-edge coke making and blast furnace technology. Skilled labour was attracted from all around Europe.

By 1929, as the Depression took hold, the company was operating its two blast furnaces at full capacity, selling all the pig iron output, as well as all the furnaces' by-products. However, a couple of loss-making years in the pre-Depression period made it financially impossible to realise the dream of expanding downstream into the melting and rolling of steel.

In 1931 Hoogovens made a profit and, with exports of 225,000 tonnes of pig iron, was the most important merchant iron supplier in the world. By carefully building up a dedicated worldwide customer base, establishing low-cost/high-quality integrated iron-making operations and fully exploiting the opportunities to sell by-products, the new company had acquired the ingredients which would ensure its survival through the years of the Great Depression.

Beginning with the German invasion of Poland on 1st September, 1939, World War II was the largest armed conflict in history, spanning the entire world and involving more countries than any other war. It involved the great powers, organised into two opposing military alliances—the Allies and the Axis. In a state of "total war", the countries directed their entire economic, industrial, and scientific capabilities towards the war effort, erasing the distinction between civilian and military resources. Over seventy million people, the majority of whom were civilians, were killed, making it the deadliest conflict in human history.

Tata Steel Responds

During the years of World War II, Tata Steel again made a major contribution in supplying the materials necessary for war. The Company pledged its entire output to the war effort. The war also greatly challenged the ingenuity of Tata Steel's scientists and in the course of the next five years the Company produced 110 varieties of steel, despite the fact that there were hardly any worthwhile facilities available anywhere in the country except in the plant. In 1941, Tata Steel put up a wheel, tyre and axle plant to meet the requirements of the railways; in 1942 a mill to manufacture 1,000 tonnes per month of armour plates for defence carriers was added; a benzol recovery plant for producing toluene, needed for the manufacture of explosives, was put up in 1943. Tata Steel's major achievement was armour-plating for cars. After experimenting with different compositions of steel, the Company came out with 'The Tatanagar', a light armoured vehicle that was used extensively during the war.

Hoogovens Responds

Not long after the war started and following the initial German western offensive, Hoogovens came under the supervision of the occupying army. Throughout the war years the Dutch management was faced with the challenge of steering the company through air-strikes, the constant threat that the occupier would force Hoogovens personnel to go to work in Germany, as well as German efforts to take over the company completely. The war took its toll and the main priority in the post-war period was to repair the damage caused and to secure scarce resources and spare parts in order to re-start operations. The heavy plate mill, which had been dismantled and shipped to Germany during the war, was also returned to IJmuiden.

In a country impoverished by the war, without financial resources, with a huge demand for steel and a government committed to rebuilding, Hoogovens faced many challenges. Although the government stressed the importance of providing materials for the home market, Hoogovens was convinced it should maintain its international outlook and was inspired by its new semi-continuous wide hot strip mill technology, which originated in the US and was obtained under the American Marshall Aid recovery programme after lengthy negotiations.

Soon after India won her hard fought battle for independence in 1947, the country was hit by the Partition and its after-effects. In the next couple of years the government had the task of nation-building to make India self-sufficient. Serious efforts began to boost industry and commerce and build a stable economy.

Tata Steel Responds

The Tatas were ready to take part in the Herculean task of nation-building. The badly needed steel for the new Five-year Plans came from the Tata factory—steel for the Howrah Bridge in Kolkata. Having a long-term international vision, opting for completely new technologies, quick decision-making and fostering social cohesion among its workforce, all these things allowed Hoogovens to emerge successfully from the post-war period, the Bhakra Nangal project, the Damodar Valley Corporation and many more important projects.

Tata Steel played a key role in the recreation of post-independence India. Initiatives such as Leave with Pay, the Workers' Provident Fund Scheme, the Workmens' Accident Compensation Scheme, Maternity Benefits, Eight-Hour Working Days, Free Medical Aid, Retirement Gratuity and Profit Sharing Bonus were introduced by Tata Steel long before they were enforced by law.

POST-WAR REBUILDING OF THE UK STEEL INDUSTRY (1946-67)

At the end of World War II it seemed unlikely that the UK steel industry was about to enter a long period of growth, given the fact that the post-World War I boom had been short. Despite being criticized for profiteering, UK steel makers had worked tirelessly, contributing 97% of their output to the War and related purposes. However, since the War had provided no opportunity to focus on capital expenditure or on consolidation, there were fears that the industry might sink or stagnate.

BIRTH OF BRITISH STEEL

Initially, under the auspices of the Iron and Steel Control (set-up during the war under the Ministry of Supply) and based on the recommendations of the 1945 Franks Report, a development plan for the steel industry was drawn up. Over the next two decades four more five-year plans were published, at the end of which the condition of the British steel industry had immensely improved. A succession of ambitious investment programmes were undertaken to build new blast furnaces and modern rolling mills (in particular hot strip mills). Production grew to keep pace with demand and reached a peak of 27 million tonnes of crude steel in 1965. However, problems caused by fragmented ownership continued until a solution was provided in 1967 by way of nationalisation under the Iron and Steel Act, 1967. As a consequence, the British Steel Corporation was formed, which incorporated 90% of UK steel making.

ECONOMIC DEVELOPMENT OF SINGAPORE (1960s)

The 1960s was a time of economic uncertainty in Singapore. Infrastructure was poor and the existing industrial facilities were mainly for domestic consumption. There were few exports and very little foreign investment. In addition, Singapore was also battling unemployment and labour unrest after the withdrawal

of British troops. The need of the hour was to give the country's economy a boost, accelerate industrial development and create jobs.

BIRTH OF NATSTEEL

National Iron and Steel Mills Ltd. (NISM) was incorporated on 12th August, 1961 to manufacture, export and trade in iron and steel products for the construction industry in Singapore, Malaysia and the adjoining region. Tasked to support Singapore's nation-building efforts, NISM's products were used in most construction projects, such as HDB flats, MRT lines and Changi Airport. In 1990, NISM changed its name to NatSteel. By the beginning of the 21st century NatSteel had established a strategic footprint in the growing economies of the Asia Pacific and had built a premium brand name that was widely respected for its quality and production know-how. Since its inception NatSteel has nurtured an ethic of positive response to challenge, a tradition it continues as part of the Tata Steel Group.

ECONOMIC MALAISE AND THE OIL CRISES (1967-88)

During the late 1960s and the early 1970s UK steel demand dropped for the first time since the war. The oil shocks of 1974 and especially 1979 exacerbated the downturn in UK steel consumption, with output dropping in 1980 to less than 12 million tonnes. Britain was not alone in suffering the effects of the economic turbulence. Regulation of the steel industry had transferred to Brussels in 1973, when Britain joined the tariff-free Common Market. In 1980 the European Commission declared the steel industry to be in "manifest crisis", introducing production quotas, delivery ceilings, and state aid in return for capacity cuts.

British Steel Responds

British Steel entered the 1980s suffering from surplus capacity and chronic over manning that had caused employment to rise to 38% of total costs. In 1980, the industry suffered a lengthy steel workers' strike. However, British Steel's workforce had shrunk to 53,000 by 1988 from 250,000 in 1967. Furthermore, it had reversed ten years of heavy losses from the mid-1970s. By the late 1980s it was making a healthy profit and was hailed as one of the world's most efficient steel-makers. In 1987, the government decided that it had made an impressive turnaround in performance and had a sufficiently healthy outlook for privatisation to take place. The sale of British Steel was a pioneering transaction that sparked-off a mass migration from state to private ownership.

STEEL DENATIONALISES AND CONSOLIDATES (1988 ONWARDS)

The 1990s were, in general, good years for British Steel plc, despite the continuing cyclicality of the industry that could still produce loss-making years. By and large shareholders had opportunities to prosper and the privately-owned company continued to modernize and rationalise, so much so that at times the company was held up as a model for the rest of the world's steel-makers. Meanwhile, the national players in a still-fragmented European and global industry were unable to cope with economic troughs and maintain the heavy capital expenditure the steel industry required. There arose an increasingly obvious need for the industry as a whole to free itself of state aid and to consolidate, which was recognised by the European Commission's shift in policy towards accepting "one-time last-time" state aid in exchange for removal of state ownership together with rationalisation and support for cross-border mergers.

Formation of Corus

In 1999 British Steel plc and Koninklijke Hoogovens N.V. merged to form Corus in the largest European steel industry merger to date. Together they formed Europe's second largest steel maker and the world's fourth largest. In the first few years of the new millennium the global steel demand balance oscillated wildly and by 2003 Corus was in severe difficulty. The company adopted a programme of strategic reforms called "Restoring Success", which aimed at going beyond a mere adaptation to new market conditions. This 3-year programme restructured the Group's UK operations to give a focus on three core sites: Scunthorpe, Port Talbot and Rotherham. One of the key decisions was the closure of the hot end at Lanwern. By 2005 Corus had returned to profit and restored value to shareholders.

ECONOMIC LIBERALISATION IN INDIA (1991 ONWARDS)

The economic liberalisation reforms did away with the Licence Raj. In 1991, after being bailed out of bankruptcy by the International Monetary Fund, the government of P.V. Narasimha Rao initiated several breakthrough reforms, including opening up international trade and investment, deregulation, initiation of privatisation, etc. This period was hailed as a breath of fresh air after the tight and rigid control of the licensing policy that was earlier prevalent in the country. India has been on a fast track of economic growth ever since.

Tata Steel Responds

The 1991-92 government policy was a momentous change from the earlier trade controls and restrictions and brought with it a new era of growth for the country. The iron and steel industry became one of the foremost sectors to be opened under the New Economic Policy. Substantial private investment flowed in, with the consequent changes heralding a new beginning for the interplay of free market enterprise in this vital sector. Embracing these new liberalisation measures, Tata Steel, under the guidance and leadership of its senior officers, embarked on a series of modernization and restructuring initiatives which helped it grow from strength to strength. The full impact of economic liberalisation, which meant that steel could be easily imported, was felt in 1993-94. The Company set targets to reduce costs of production and raise the level of net realisation. This was a turning point for the Company, which was judged Number 1 in the league table of world-class steel companies by World Steel Dynamics in the year 2001. The Company also began work in earnest on Phase III of its multi-thousand crore modernization programme and, after the fifth phase of modernisation, was awarded ISO-9000 certification. The Six Sigma programme was introduced thereafter. In addition, as a measure to upgrade quality, a model of the US's Malcolm Baldrige Awards was adopted under the banner of the JRDQV Awards. Tata Steel Limited (India) is today one of the lowest cost producers of steel in the world.

COLLAPSE OF THE SOVIET UNION (1992)

The disarray in the post-Soviet era created a flood of steel imports from East European countries. In 1992 the situation worsened due to a softening business cycle and the devaluation of the US Dollar. All these elements led to plummeting prices.

Hoogovens Responds

Inspired by Nippon Steel's Nagoya plant, a master plan was launched in 1990 which aimed at repositioning Hoogovens into the group of 'Best in Europe' by 1995. This plan covered a wide range of aspects such as organisation, education, complete customer focus and operational excellence. The basis for this improved competitiveness was a drastic reduction in cost-base by gradually reducing the number of personnel and by increasing output. Alarming financial results in early 1992 forced the company to accelerate the master plan. Through the joint efforts of its personnel, trade unions, shareholders and a large group of very loyal customers in Europe and the US , the company was able to counter the threat within two years. The efforts paid-off in the late 1990s, when Hoogovens in IJmuiden was declared the best plant in Europe for financial performance.

The 2001 Financial Challenge

2001 was a dramatic year. The 9/11 disaster and the burst of the dot.com bubble sent strong negative messages rippling through the economy. Many American companies sought refuge which afforded them protection against possible bankruptcy. There was a concurrent impact on exports to the US, which affected steel-makers elsewhere.

Corus IJmuiden Responds

As a response to this business environment, on 5th March

2002 the US administration announced that under Section 201 of the US Trade Act it would impose a three-year safeguard duty on steel imports, which in practice meant tariffs of upto 30% on steel supplied from IJmuiden into the US. With over half a million tonnes of high-quality steel products supplied from the Netherlands to a stable group of US customers, this presented a major threat to IJmuiden's market position. The first response was to assure US customers that Corus IJmuiden would do everything to keep them supplied. Already well-versed in legal battles with the US administration, IJmuiden stepped up its efforts. The basis of this confrontation revolved around the fact that much of the material that IJmuiden supplied simply could not be produced by US mills because of its specific physical properties and qualities. Politicians, ambassadors, US governors and the American customers played vital roles in keeping the trade channel open.

In order to continue dedicated services to its US customers, which in most cases had a history as far back as the 1960s, the plant in IJmuiden was able to secure a minimum lifeline to meet its customers' delivery needs. This included securing emergency supplies from other plants, in some cases. In May 2003 the US president withdrew the Section 201 tariffs. A history of providing unique products along with the united defense against the trade restrictions served to reinforce the very valuable bond between US customers and Corus in IJmuiden.

First Iron and Steel Plant

Jamsetji's dream helped a batch of engineers to select a sight, located on the confluence of two rivers—kharkai and Subernrekha, and on the sloping lap of hard hilly tracks of the Dalama range. An adivasi village, Sakchi, was selected for giving a practical picture of the dream of Jamsetji N. Tata. It was linked with a small railway station then known as kalimati under Bengal-Nagpur Railway. After three years of the death of Jamsetji his dream started taking shape in the heart of the Chhotanagpur Jungle, full of natural respurces and beautiful God gifted hilly track. The Tata Iron and Steel Company Limited was registered on August 27, 1907. The construction works started in 1907. Within four years of the steel works, first ingot rolled out on February 16, 1912. Thus, the day, February 16, 1912 can be written in gold for expediting the fast growth of industrialisation in India. The normal capacity of production of TISCO was started by 1916. In the early stages, the company had to face numerous problems. The coal was not of uniform quality. Designs of furnances were found unstatisfactory. Communication was slow. Labour was untrained. There was no post of technicians or scientists at home. Threat from dumping of foreign steel was haunting.

The country was helped much by this newly established steel plant in India during first world war period. During that emergency period, when import had become difficult, the government would have faced much difficult in meeting increased demand for iron and steel. Even after end of war the demand for more iron and steel for reconstruction of devastated economy was there. To cope up with the increasing demand a seven years expansion scheme was launched in 1917, which on completion helped to double the output. The expansion scheme works one after another have been taken in hand since then.

The high chimney of the TISCO went far and wide in changing the whole picture of that jungle area. Many ancilliary industries came up around it. In place of huts big buildings began to come up. The calm and quiet area turned into industrial areas, full of lives. Sakchi became the centre of attraction not only for industrialists but for the whole society. The dream of Jamsetji N. Tata, his aspirations and directions, had been guiding the planners to build up a model industrial centre. The small railway station, Kalimati, turned into one of the busiest railway station. 'Kalimati' has now become 'Steelmati' in real sense. Out of 'Kalimati' now iron steel rods are coming which are famous in whole world for their quality.

Sakchi became the centre of gravity. The then Viceroy, Lord Chelmsford, visited that industrial centre in 1919. In the honour of the founder of the Steel Plant Jamsetji N. Tata it was renamed as Jamshedpur. The Kalimati railway station was also renamed as Tata Nagar. Thus, Jamshedpur and Tata Nagar, the two words, are the first and last parts of the name of the founder. Jamsetji will be remembered so long Jamshedpur and Tata Nagar will remain in existence.

Landmarks of Tata Steel

1882—At the age of 43, Jamshetji Nusserwanji Tata read a report by a German geologist, Ritter Von Schwartz on the availability of Iron Ore in Chanda District in the Central Provinces, which gave him the idea of giving India a Steel plant.

1900—November 14—Jamshetji was in England seeing the Secretary of State for India, Lord George Hamilton and sparked his imagination on building a steel plant in India.

1904—February 24—P.N. Bose, an Indian Geologist who discovered the lofty Gorumahinsani Hills with its input storehouse of iron-ore, informs J.N. Tata about his findings.

Dorab Tata, C. M. Weld arrived in Durg and found Dhalli and Rajhara hills had the finest ore in the world. But did not find a steady supply of water.

1907—C.M. Weld and Srinivasa Rao discovered the village of Sakchi at the confluence of two rivers, Subarnarekha and Kharkai and the Railway Station of Kalimati.

August 26—The Tata Iron and Steel Company was floated.

Tatas plunged into the Indian market and issued their Prospectus to raise Rs.1.5 crores as Ordinary Shares, Rs. 75 lakhs in Preference shares and Rs. 7 lakhs in deferred shares. 8000 Indian investors subscribed within three weeks for a total of Rs. 2.32 crore.

1908—Construction of the works begins at Sakchi. The first stake is driven on February 27th.

1911—December 2— First cast of Pig-iron produced on December 2nd.

'A' Blast Furnance went into operation.

1912—First Steel made on 16th February. The Bar Mill commences rolling in October. Eight-hour working day introduced.

1913-14—Hospital and the first school opened.

1915—Free Medical Aid introduced.

Ferro-manganese made for the first time in India.

1916-17—Welfare Department established. Mining and Prospecting Department organized.

Launches Greater Extension Scheme to raise capacity to 450,000 tons and diversity production.
Schooling facilities for child.

1919—Visit of Lord Chelmsford to rename Sakchi as Jamshedpur and Kalimati Railway Station as Tatanagar.
Formation of Works' Committee for handling complaints concerning service conditions and grievances.

1920—Leave with pay, Workers' Provident Fund Scheme, Workmen' Accident Compensation Scheme introduced.
Jamshedpur Labour Association formed. The Principle of Joint consultation introduced for the first time in India.

1921—Jamshedpur Technical Institute of Tata Steel opened with 23 students on the roll.

1923—The Tinplate Company of India commenced manufacture.

1928-29—Scheme of Maternity benefits introduced.
Subhas Chandra Bose, President, Jamshedpur Labour Association signed an agreement with N.B. Saklatvala.

1931-32—First Founders' Day celebrated in Jamshedpur.

1934—Profit-sharing Bonus granted first time in India.

1937—Research and Control Laboratory opened.
Retiring Gratuity introduced.

1938—J.R D. Tata succeeds Sir N.B. Saklatvala as the Chairman of the Company.
Sir Jehangir Ghandy takes over as the first Indian General Manager.
Dr. Rajendra Prasad and Pandit Jawaharlal Nehru gave awards on labour dispute. Bihar Labour Enquiry Committee under the Chairmanship of Dr. Rajendra Prasad visit Jamshedpur.

1941—Manufacture of special steels for war purpose developed.
A Benzol plant and the Wheel Tyre and Axle Plant the first of its kind in the country went into operation.

1942-43—Armour plates and various alloy steels produced.

1947—Personnel Department, first of its kind in India, was started.

1951-52—Tata Steel launches a Modernisation and Expansion Programme.
Production linked incentive bonus scheme introduced.

1956—Agreement between management and Tata Workers' Union signed in January.

1958—The Golden Jubilee celebrations presided over by Jawaharlal Nehru.

Ferro-Manganese plant commences production at Joda, in April.

Jubilee Park dedicated to the nation.

1965—The Steel Ministry agrees to expansion to 4-Million Ingot tonnes with a Strip Mill.

1968—Tata Yodogawa Limited, a new company to undertake the manufacture of steel mill rolls was incorporated.

1978-79—Five year Rural Development programme for upliftment of the villagers around Jamshedpur taken up.

1980—First Social Audit Committee Report submitted.

1982-83—Basic Oxygen Furnance Shop—LDI inaugurated.

1984-85—JRD Tata becomes Chairman Emeritus after guiding Tata Steel as Chairman for 46 years.

Russi Mody takes over as new Chairman.

Merger of the Indian tube company with Tata Steel.

1987-88—Human Resources Department restructured.

1989—Pension Scheme introduced.

1992-93—Mr. Ratan N. Tata takes over as the Chairman.

Dr. J.J. Irani becomes Managing Director.

The new One-million ton capacity "G" Blast Furnance was commissioned.

1993-94—JRD Tata passes away in Geneva on 29th November 1993 at the age of 89.

Several divisions of the Company received ISO-9000 certification.

The centre-piece of the Company's Modernisation Programme, viz. the one million tonne per annum Hot Strip Mill was commissioned.

The first Slab Caster in operation.

Cement Division with units at Sonadih and Jojobera starts production.

1994-95—The third phase of the Modernisation Programme completed.

Employees' Family Benefit Scheme introduced.

1995-96—The aggregate production of cement from the company's plant at Sonadih and Jojobera crossed the 1 million tonne mark.

With the playing of the foundation stone by the Prime Minister of India, Mr. P.V. Narasimha Rao, Tata Steel has set the ball rolling for its new 10 million tonnes integrated steel plant at Gopalpur in Orissa.

1996-97—The Company sold the 67.5 MW Power Plant, under construction at Jojobera, put under its earlier Modernisation Programme—Phase III, to Tata Electric Companies for a total consideration of Rs. 300 crore.

Received Prime Minister's trophy for the Best Integrated Steel Plant for the year 1995-96.

Dr. J.J. Irani was conferred an Honorary Knighthood by the Queen of Great Britain.

2000—Mr. Ratan N. Tata conferred 'Padam Bhushan'.

Inauguration of the Cold Rolling Mill Complex.

2001—Jamshedpur Amusement Park set-up.

Mr. B. Muthuraman became Managing Director.

2002—Conferred the Prime Minister's Trophy for the Best integrated steel plant for 2000-01 for the third consecutive year and four times in all.

Launch of Vision-2007.

2003—ASPIRE and one million tonne expansion launched.

Completion of 75 years of Industrial Harmony at Tata Steel.

2004—Acquired Indian Steel Wire Products, Jamshedpur.

His Excellency, Dr. A.P.J. Abdul Kalam, the President of India visited Tata Steel to commemorate 75 years of Industrial Harmony at Tata Steel.

Jamshedpur Utilities and Services Company Limited (JUSCO) formed.

2005—MoU for 5 million tonne steel plant at Chhattisgarh.

MoU for 12 million tonne steel plant at Jharkhand.

Renewal of Land Lease.

Joint Venture with Blue Scope Steel Ltd., Australia for quoted steel manufacturing facility.

2006—"World's Best Steel Maker Declared by the world steel Dynamics (WSD) for the 3rd time.

The Board of Directors of Tata Steel Limited Approved the offer to acquire entire issue of Share Capital of Corus Group of Companies.

As a result of effective functioning of TISCO, it has achieve a tremendous physical and financial achievement that can be shown in the Tables 8.1, and 8.2 respectively.

Table 8.1
Production Statistics

('000 Tonnes)

Year	*Iron Ore*	*Coal*	*Iron*	*Crude Steel*	*Rolled/ Forged Bars & Structurals*	*Plates*	*Sheets*	*Hot Rolled Cols/ Srips*	*Cold Rolled Cols*	*Rail-ways Mate-rials*	*Semi-Finish-ed for Sale*	*Total Sale-able Steel*
1956-57	1999	1528	1169	1088	220	64	161	35	—	106	226	812
1957-58	2074	1488	1109	1122	210	72	161	71	—	103	182	799
1958-59	2198	1590	1149	1166	212	71	134	103	—	77	302	899
1959-60	2551	1705	1591	1555	298	89	134	164	—	88	454	1237
1960-61	2275	1714	1586	1622	369	85	132	161	—	112	404	1263
1961-62	2104	1700	1645	1643	449	77	134	173	—	114	371	1318
1962-63	2616	2047	1764	1799	472	90	149	178	—	131	393	1413
1963-64	2963	2173	1809	1892	534	96	154	162	—	127	434	1507
1964-65	3125	2264	1895	1956	548	101	164	197	—	133	425	1568
1965-66	3232	2175	1917	1979	555	96	196	181	—	128	440	1568
1966-67	3009	2088	1926	2001	568	104	152	177	—	114	465	1568
1967-68	2728	1974	1798	1933	518	111	155	138	—	118	494	1534
1968-69	2821	2108	1715	1816	510	110	163	186	—	125	371	1465
1969-70	2564	2172	1624	1708	479	104	159	179	—	120	399	1440
1970-71	2402	1959	1664	1716	512	101	164	160	—	78	340	1375
1971-72	2844	1940	1631	1709	497	106	184	185	—	85	330	1387
1972-73	3231	1997	1681	1690	530	99	175	187	—	55	412	1458
1973-74	2922	2134	1435	1514	482	93	131	169	—	22	303	1200
1974-75	2940	2209	1668	1732	562	103	166	179	—	38	413	1461
1975-76	2965	2181	1652	1787	547	111	164	173	—	46	445	1486
1976-77	3138	2135	1754	1908	522	112	146	178	—	48	544	1550
1977-78	2972	2239	1762	1968	510	107	129	165	—	56	634	1801
1978-79	2808	2134	1672	1866	493	103	132	180	—	53	555	1516
1979-80	2549	2065	1516	1781	409	73	122	154	—	34	656	1448
1980-81	2698	2196	1648	1875	381	82	121	148	—	28	777	1537
1981-82	2991	2327	1774	1962	525	99	151	149	—	22	660	1606
1982-83	3224	2671	1793	1957	501	103	137	119	—	11	750	1621
1983-84	3137	3335	1746	1973	488	107	129	138	—	20	744	1626
1984-85	3454	3582	1804	2049	512	122	139	168	—	19	754	1714
1985-86	3184	3739	1752	2094	484	108	134	169	—	18	859	1702
1986-87	3305	3796	1940	2250	436	93	122	152	—	13	1091	1861
1987-88	3237	3793	2018	2275	591	99	127	155	—	13	929	1862
1988-89	3569	3793	2238	2313	637	93	131	166	—	13	904	1900
1989-90	3726	3754	2268	2323	553	91	117	166	—	17	1033	1913
1990-91	3509	3725	2320	2294	558	88	118	153	—	14	1013	1901
1991-92	3996	3848	2400	2415	599	92	123	170	—	9	1045	1978
1992-93	4126	3739	2435	2477	575	78	122	163	—	7	1179	2084
1993-94	4201	3922	2596	2487	561	—	124	281	—	6	1182	2117
1994-95	4798	4156	2928	2788	620	—	137	613	—	2	1074	2391
1995-96	5161	4897	3241	3019	629	—	133	1070	—	—	869	2660
1996-97	5766	5294	3440	3106	666	—	114	1228	—	—	811	2783
1997-98	5984	5228	3513	3220	634		60	1210	—	—	1105	2971
1998-99	6056	5137	3626	3264	622	—	—	1653	—	—	835	3051
1999-00	6456	5155	3888	3434	615	—	—	2057	—	—	615	3262
2000-01	6989	5282	3929	3566	569	—	—	1858	356	—	647	3413
2001-02	7305	5636	4041	3749	680	—	—	1656	734	—	566	3596
2002-03	7985	5915	4437	4098	705	—	—	1563	1110	—	563	3975
2003-04	8445	5842	4466	4224	694	—	—	1578	1262	—	555	4076
2004-05	9803	6375	4347	4104	706	—	—	1354	1445	—	604	4074
2005-06	10834	6521	5177	4731	821	—	—	1556	1495	—	679	4551
2009-07	9776	7041	5552	5046	1230	—	—	1670	1523	—	506	4929
2007-08	10022	7209	5507	5014	1241	—	—	1697	1534	—	386	4858
2008-09	10417	7282	6254	5646	1350	—	—	1745	1447	—	833	5375
2009-10	12044	7210	7231	6564	1432	—	—	2023	1563	—	1421	6439
2010-11	**13087**	**7024**	**7503**	**6855**	**1486**	—	—	**2127**	**1544**	—	**1534**	**6691**

wotes: Figures of total saleable steel are adjusted for:

(a) From 1965-86 and onwards—steel transferred to and product at the Company's Tubes Division.

(b) Total saleable steel for 2003-04 includes production of the erstwhile Tata SSL Ltd., pursuant to its merger with the Company.

Source: Annual Report (2010-11) TISCO.

TABLE 8.2
Financial Statistics

(₹ *crores*)

Year	*Capital*	*Reserve and Surplus*	*Borrow-ings*	*Gross Block*[*]	*Net Block*	*Invest-ments*	*Gross Reve-nue*	*Expen-diture*[*]	*Depre-ciation*	*Profit before Taxes*	*Taxes*	*Profit after Taxes*	*Net Trans-fer to Reserves*	*Divi-dends*
1956-57	25.94	20.20	21.53	93.45	54.79	5.38	44.14	32.69	2.47	8.98	3.42	5.56	3.70	1.93
1957-58	30.66	24.50	60.19	147.06	106.04	5.41	48.25	38.47	3.91	5.88	0.90	4.98	2.92	2.41
1958-59	3.072	26.15	83.78	171.79	124.78	5.94	56.12	47.12	5.53	2.87	0.17	2.70	0.57	2.47
1959-60	3.072	26.15	83.78	171.79	124.78	5.94	56.12	47.12	5.53	2.87	—	2.70	0.57	2.47
1960-61	38.97	27.67	69.04	185.52	116.76	8.85	87.08	68.27	13.92	6.09	—	6.09	1.44	4.65
1961-62	38.97	27.97	64.08	190.23	109.06	8.87	62.48	73.24	13.15	6.09	—	6.09	1.44	4.65
1962-63	38.97	4.027*	54.62	195.88	103.32	8.85	103.44	81.22	11.66	10.56	0.80	9.76	4.86	4.89
1963-64	38.97	47.41*	47.27	200.38	100.15	9.86	115.20	90.76	7.97	16.47	4.75	11.72	6.45	5.25
1964-65	38.97	50.94*	43.74	204.45	94.52	10.62	126.91	102.06	10.14	14.71	6.15	8.56	3.30	5.25
1965-66	38.97	56.35*	34.87	211.87	92.27	11.66	134.00	106.86	10.40	16.74	7.10	9.64	4.40	5.25
1966-67	50.00	48.44*	51.47	239.03	107.36	11.26	130.78	107.32	11.49	11.97	4.40	7.57	2.32	5.27
1967-68	50.00	50.23*	50.23	251.56	109.07	11.29	137.67	117.21	12.12	8.94	2.45	5.80	0.82	5.27
1968-69	50.00	51.82*	44.05	258.08	103.62	12.28	142.87	120.11	12.94	9.82	3.60	6.22	0.95	5.27
1969-70	50.00	52.71*	37.73	268.31	101.51	12.22	151.21	126.69	13.19	11.33	5.20	6.13	0.86	5.27
1970-71	50.00	55.58*	36.10	287.86	106.02	12.21	158.51	128.29	16.10	14.12	6.70	7.42	2.15	5.27
1971-72	50.00	56.92*	48.03	305.78	109.98	12.22	171.95	143.91	16.07	11.97	5.80	6.17	0.90	5.27
1972-73	50.00	58.46*	48.03	329.74	118.36	12.24	210.22	187.19	17.51	5.52	—	5.52	0.25	5.27
1973-74	50.00	63.16*	49.49	346.18	121.31	12.17	197.95	167.10	16.63	14.32	4.45	9.77	6.48	3.29**
1974-75	50.00	75.55*	63.45	306.57	127.30	11.01	279.72	236.63	15.11	27.98	12.80	15.18	10.07	5.11**
1975-76	50.00	77.97	88.30	395.84	142.34	11.09	287.63	258.78	16.20	12.67	3.25	9.42	4.59	4.83
1976-77	62.86	71.17	94.36	417.99	149.57	11.14	332.84	297.51	17.28	18.05	6.00	12.05	6.06	5.99
1977-78	62.86	73.60	87.68	87.68	438.51	156.02	11.17	361.30	335.18	18.25	7.87	0.10	7.77	1.27
1978-79	62.86	80.26	77.74	464.30	165.11	11.45	380.85	335.83	20.12	24.90	7.35	17.55	10.53	7.02
1979-80	62.86	88.11	84.22	499.70	184.51	12.05	454.94	407.04	22.97	24.93	9.00	15.93	8.14	7.79
1980-81	62.86	10.6.01	104.65	550.48	216.76	14.01	520.86	445.10	23.70	52.06	25.60	26.46	17.90	8.56
1981-82	83.44	120.60	233.74	650.14	304.05	14.04	70469	599.83	27.21	77.65	30.00	47.65	34.56	13.09†
1982-83	83.44	152.80	310.34	789.76	420.31	20.40	798.16	729.52	23.77	44.87	—	44.87	31.78	13.09
1983-84	72.02+	160.61	380.62	843.64	453.46	20.22	889.54	826.39	43.14	20.01	—	20.01	7.77	12.24
1984-85	72.02	230.24	398.52	911.55	451.55	103.12	1105.02	938.33	69.95@	96.74	12.00	84.74	69.62	15.12
1985-86	82.74	334.19	47.43	1115.76	577.41	144.54	1285.51	1078.55	49.28	157.68	50.00	107.68	90.88	20.00
1986-87	82.63	401.05	517.83	1299.84	708.09	130.12	1416.39	1259.27	57.60	99.52	50.00	107.68	90.88	20.60
1987-88	136.01	476.33	476.65	1525.46	861.88	163.52	1526.78	1340.65	73.98	112.15	20.00	92.15	65.81	29.34
1988-89	156.09	645.53	611.64	1753.13	998.71	234.44	1861.77	1587.74	93.69	180.34	26.00	154.34	108.17	46.17
1989-90	229.43	1103.11	954.11	2062.76	1200.09	795.32	2135.57	1840.95	118.79	175.83	27.30	148.53	97.94	50.59
1990-91	229.89	1194.22	1183.75	2703.29	1713.79	571.88	2330.83	1955.67	137.03	238.13	78.00	160.13	88.79	71.34
1991-92	230.12	1315.36	2051.30	4026.16	2878.19	248.77	2869.70	2426.65	164.89	278.16	6400	214.16	133.61	80.55
1992-93	278.45	1707.94	3039.55	5463.13	4107.64	170.06	3423.33	3094.84	215.37	127.12	—	127.12	62.30	64.82
1993-94	335.21	2189.53	3428.59	6539.94	4924.39	261.62	3822.64	3464.10	177.70	180.84	—	180.84	84.29	96.55
1994-95	336.87	2351.17	3561.24	6962.89	5213.48	220.65	4649.06	4120.01	247.93	281.12	—	281.12	162.88	118.24
1995-96	367.23	3375.17	3842.17	7408.48	5393.56	410.94	5879.96	5016.58	297.61	565.79	—	565.79	408.82	158.97
1996-97	367.38	3606.64	4082.65	7850.82	5526.40	664.90	6409.43	5540.39	326.83	542.21	73.00	469.21	286.98	182.23#
1997-98	367.56	3697.32	4579.14	8948.52	6300.04	653.45	6546.58	5810.02	343.23	363.33	41.25	322.08	160.10	161.98#
1998-99	367.97	3796.45	4938.93	10032.17	7058.58	585.44	6335.60	5638.19	382.18	315.23	33.00	282.23	118.94	163.29#
1999-00	517.97	4040.43	4907.23	10668.33	7426.38	803.10	6943.33	6040.20	426.54	476.59	54.00	422.59	250.69	171.90#
2000-01	507.97	4380.46	4672.22	11285.17	7538.09	846.92	7810.05	6715.36	492.25	602.44	49.00	553.44	335.83	217.61#
2001-02	367.97	3077.99	4705.48	11742.44	7543.70	912.74	7682.70	6906.95	524.75	251.00	46.10	204.90	55.51	149.39#
2002-03	369.18	2816.84	4225..61	12393.79	7543.80	1194.55	9843.66	8028.68	555.48	1262.50	250.19	1012.31	679.30	333.01#
2003-04	367.18	4146.68	3382.21	13269.47	7857.85	2194.12	12069.62	8778.55	625.11	2665.96	919.74	1746.22	1329.97	416.25#
2004-05	553.67	6506.25	2739.70	14957.73	9112.24	2432.65	16053.48	10137.42	618.78	5297.28	1823.12	3474.16	2652.79	821.37#
2005-06	553.67	9201.63	2516.15	16470.71	9865.05	4089.96	17398.98	11383.92	775.10	5239.96	1733.58	3506.38	2685.95	820.43#
2009-07	727.73	13368.42	9645.33	18426.52	11040.56	6106.18	20196.24	13115.30	819.29	6261.65	2039.50	4222.15	3117.82	1105.33#
2007-08	6203.30	21097.43	18021.69	20746.57	12623.56	4103.19	22526.80	14625.83	834.61	7066.36	2379.33	4687.03	3293.48	1393.55#
2008-09	6203.45	23972.81	26946.18	23444.22	14482.22	42371.78	27152.00	18862.99	973.40	7315.61	2113.84	5201.74	3709.24	1492.50#
2009-10	887.41	36074.39	25239.20	26043.59	16006.03	44979.67	27611.59	19314.11	1083.18	7214.30	2167.50	5046.80	4168.35	878.45#
2010-11	**2637.61**	**45807.02**	**28301.14**	**29689.34**	**18774.48**	**46564.94**	**32692.81**	**21769.77**	**1146.19**	**9776.85**	**2911.16**	**6865.69**	**5553.38**	**1307.77#**

- * Inclusive of Dividends subsequently paid from Reserves arid Surplus.
- ** Payable as per the Companies (Temporary Restrictions on Dividends) Act, 1974.
- † Including an additional Jubilee Dividend of ₹ 2 per share.
- \+ Excluding Preference Shares which have been cancelled with effect from 1-4-1992 and Non-Convertible Bonds issued in lieu thereof.
- @ Including ₹ 15.05 crores additional depreciation for 1983-84.
- \# Including tax on dividends.
- ∗ Gross Block is net of impairment, if any.
- ★ Expenditure includes excise duty recovered on sales.

Source: Annual Report (2010-11) TISCO.

REFERENCES

Lala, R.M., 'The Creation of Wealth', p. 125.
Tata Steel, Annual Report (2005-06).
Tata Steel, Annual Report (2006-07).
Tata Steel, Annual Report (2007-08).
Tata Steel, Annual Report (2008-09).
Tata Steel, Annual Report (2009-10).
Tata Steel, Annual Report (2010-11).

9

Organizational Management of TISCO

Top Administrative Set-up

The head office of the management is situated at Bombay. At the top of the administrative organisation in the TISCO is the Chairman of the Board of the Directors. The Board of the Directors is the highest policy-making body for the organisation. The role of the directors in the organisation is not functional. The chairman is assisted by the Vice-Chairman-*cum*-Managing Director. The Chief responsibility for executing the policy and programme goes to the Managing Director, who is assisted by two Deputy Managing Directors. R.H. Modi is then Chairman-*cum*-Managing Director, alongwith two Deputy Managing Directors (one for Jamshedpur and another for Calcutta) the Special Advisor to V.C., the Director of Accounts, the Director of Internal Audit and the Director of Industrial Relations also directly inform to the Managing Director.

Vice-President (Administration and Collieries)

The Vice-President (Administration and Collieries) looks after administrative side. He is assisted by the General Manager (Administration), the Director of Town Services, the Director of Medical Services and the Director of Collieries. On the technical side he is assisted by the Senior Technical Advisor, the Director of Accountants, the Director of Industrial Relations, the Director of Staff Services, and the Director of Collieries.

Vice-President (Operation)

The Vice-President (Operation) looks after two wings, the operation wing and the engineering wing. In the operation wing he is assisted by the General Manager (Operation), the General Superintendent, the Director of Scientific Services, the Director of Township and many Divisional Managers. For the engineering wing, he is assisted by the General Manager (Engineering), the Director of Projects, the Director of Administration Complex, the General Manager (Spl. Project), the Director of Budgets and many Divisional Managers.

Vice-President (Commercial)

The Vice-President (Commercial) is assisted by the Director of Commercial, the Director of O.M.O. and the Chief Marketing Manager.

Deputy Managing Director (Jamshedpur)

The Deputy Managing Director (Jamshedpur) is assisted by personnels, namely the General Manager (Operation), the General Manager (Town, Medical and Health), the General Manager (Engg.), the Directors of Projects, the Directors of Staff and Training, the Director of Security Services, the Chief Personnel Managing (General), the Divisional Manager (Employment), the Divisional Manager (Data Processing) and the Manager (Aviation Services).

Deputy Managing Director (Calcutta)

The Deputy Managing Director (Calcutta) is assisted by five personnels, namely, the Director of Raw Material, the Manager (Shipping and Cleaning), the Resident Representative (Bihar), the Resident Representative (Orissa) and the Director of Marketing.

The Director of Raw Material is assisted by the Director of Collieries (Jharia), the Director of Collieries (West Bokaro) and the Director of Ore, Mines and Quaries.

The organisational chart of the TISCO management has been presented below:

The Tata Iron and Steel Company Limited, Jamshedpur

Organisation Chart

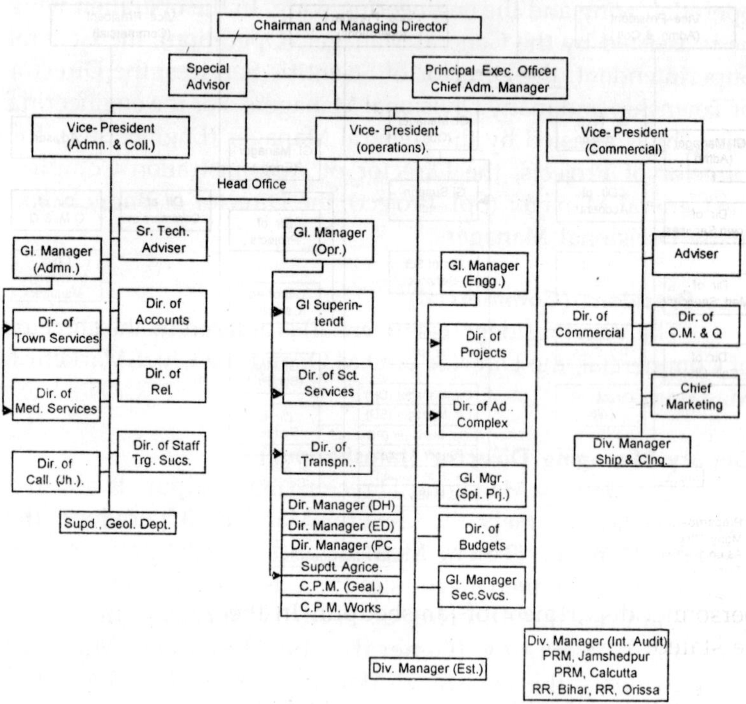

THE TATA IRON AND STEEL COMPANY LIMITED, JAMSHEDPUR

Personnels Management and Industrial Relations Department of TISCO

The Need of Personnel Department

The vast structure of personnel and industrial relations department at present in the TISCO own its origin on the initiative of the Chairman of the Steel Company, J.R.D. Tata. In 1943 the Chairman proposed for the creation of a full-fledged

The Tata Iron and Steel Company Limited, Jaamshedpur

Organisation Chart

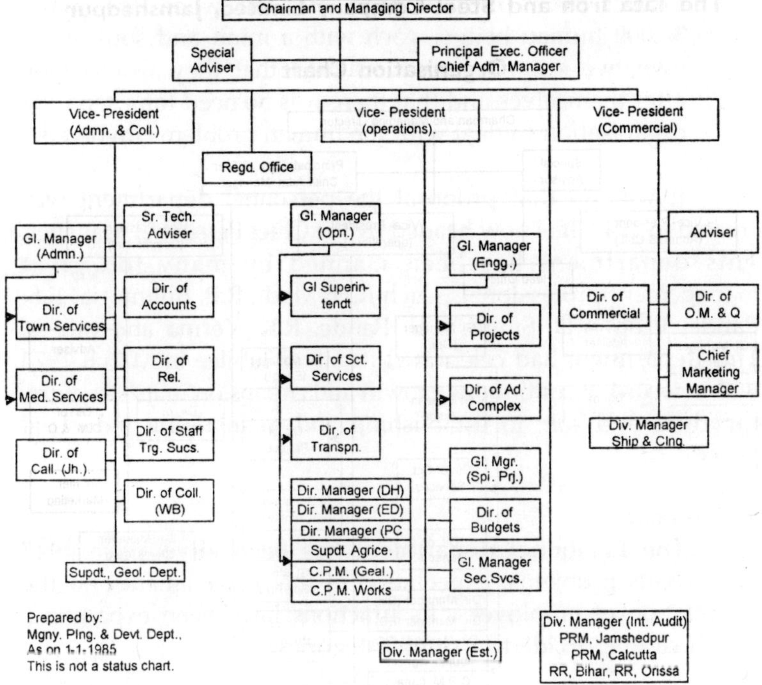

personnel department of Jamshedpur. In the basic project note he stated:

> "Of the three main concerns of industrial management, viz. Machines, materials and men, the last one is certainly the most complex and different. Yet, while we have spent enormous amount of money, energy and thought in coping with the first two problems, we have done practically nothing to equip ourselves properly for the highly complex, at least equally important, task of dealing with 30,000 to 40,000 men."

He further stated:

> "If our operations required the employment say 36,000

machine tools, we would undoubtedly have special staff or department to look after them, to keep them in repair, replace them when necessary, maintain their efficiency, protect them from damage, etc. But when employing 30,000 human beings, each with a mind and soul of his own, we seem to have assumed that they would look after themselves and that there was no need for a separate organisation to deal with the human problems involved."

It was on that proposal the personnel department was created in 1947. It is now headed by the Chief Personnel Manager. This department has been manned by many top great management professionals, such R.H. Modi, R.P. Billimoria, R.S. Pande, Prof. A.D. Singh, S.N. Pande, R.K. Verma and others. This department had celebrated its silver Jubilee in March 1973 with a record of continuous growth and expansion in its structure, functions and role in establishing and maintaining industrial peace.

Its Functions

The Personnel department has been alive since 1947 towards its problems, expectation of the management and the expectation of employees. Its functions have been expanding, which can be divided in three categories:

(i) First, the Personnel Division is entrusted with the task of administering certain programmes. Under this head will come canteen services, technical training, welfare activities, like games and recreation, community development programme in and around Jamshedpur and various types of employee services like indebtedness, processing and supply of ration cards to the employees, etc.

(ii) Another group of activities under the personnel division relate to such functions as are in the nature of centralised and co-ordinated services to be rendered to the entire organisation, long service awards farewell gifts, etc.

(iii) Last, but not the least is the function of rendering functional advice to the line executive on all matters pertaining to man-management and industrial relations. This includes matters like promotion, transfer, disciplinary action, grievance handling, union negotiations, etc.

Its Objectives

The personnel and industrial relations policy of Tata Steel is the product of the basic philosophy of the founder, Jamsetji Nusserwanji Tata. His outlook was humane and paternalistic towards labour force. He had clearly stated:

> "We do not claim to be more unselfship, more generous or more Philanthropic than other people. But we think we started on sound and straight forward business principle, considering the interests of the shareholders our own, and the health and welfare of the employees the sure foundation of our prosperity.

His thinking and philosophy has been appreciated by Prof. A.D. Singh, the then Director of Personnel in these words:

> "his anticipation of modern thinking has been a continuing source of surprise and admiration of future generations. His emphasis on the application of science and modern techniques and methods in industrial management; his generous and yet realistic understanding and acceptance of the needs and rights of the workers at a time when they were frequently exploited in the west as well as in India, his sense of trusteeship and his realisation that to survive and prosper, free enterprise must serve the needs of the society, are all in tune with modern thinking and with the ethical, social standard of the most advanced societies of today."

The statement of objective of the steel company as stated by Prof. A.D. Singh, the then Director of Personnel, which is in line with our Founder's philosophy spells out the management thinking and it clearly affirms the company's aim of discharging its obligations towards its employees by—

(i) Realistic and generous understanding and acceptance of their needs and rights and an enlightened awareness of the social problems of industry,

(ii) by providing adequate wages, good working conditions, job security, an effective machinery for speedy redressal of grievances and suitable opportunities for promotion and self-development,

(iii) treating them as individuals, giving them a sense of self-respect and better understanding of their role in the organisations and satisfying their urge for self-expression through closer association with management.

Creating a sense of belonging though humane and purposeful activities as an integral part of human relations, ensuring their willing cooperation and loyalty.

The existing personnel department has grown and development on the humane philosophy of Jamsetji for proper development, utilisation and management of manpower of the country. It is a difficult task to manage nearly 37,000 labour force so effectively even in this age without retrenchment when the whole world is facing depression in steel industry. The TISCO is one among a few industrial undertakings which has maintained its labour force entact providing full job security.

The philosophy of industrial relations has gone under change. The two faces of industrial relations, conflict and cooperation, exist since beginning. It has not been possible to eliminate industrial conflict from the scene of the industrial life. Attempts have been made to minimise the industrial conflict through various methods. This study aims to find about the method adopted for the settlement of industrial conflict in TISCO. On the other hand, it also aims to study the co-operative aspect of the industrial relations. How the TISCO has practiced since 1946 the policy of participative management? Why in 1956 it negotiated a fresh scheme of "Closer association of employees with management"? How far the scheme has advanced in achievement of real participation of workers with management?

An attempt has been made to present a consolidated picture of industrial relations, the changing policy of the company, the pressures operating from the union and a combination of mutual understanding and mutual adjustment between the two sides and to trace the ingredients of healthy industrial relations in TISCO.

Origin of Participative Management in India

The origin of participative management in India can be traced back to 1910, when the humanistic employer in cotton textile industry started holding informal meetings. War times problems forced the management to invite for discussions on immediate problems of increasing production for meeting the war needs. The immediate problems were:

(i) Undisturbed production of textile,
(ii) Increasing production of textile, and
(iii) Utilising the experiences of textilemen.

During the first world war period textilemen were invited for informal talks. That showed the willingness on the part of the employers of the cotton textile industry, the only developed industry in India by then, to have joint consultation for the benefit of all. The fruitful experiences of joint consultation during the first world war period helped in strengthening this relationship in future.

The TISCO, the first steel plant of India, was the first industrial organisation to introduce formal joint consultation machinery in 1919 by setting up a Works Committee. The Works Committee consisting of workers and management representatives had discussed many common issues. The establishment of formal joint consultation machinery in TISCO was an improvement over the cotton textile industry's informal joint consultation. This proved that right from the beginning the Tata Steel had adopted human approach as the corner stone of industrial management philosophy.

The Joint Consultation Machinery within a year of its establishment gained social recognition in 1920, when it was decided by workers and employer organisations to settle disputes by mutual discussions, failing which they were to be resolved by arbitration. The successful experiments in cotton textile industry in Ahmedabad, Bombay and Madras and iron steel industry at Jamshedpur opened a new chapter in industrial relations at an initial stage, when many had not thought of.

Since then many joint committee with various names came in India in 1920, but their functioning was not satisfactory. This issue was discussed at length by the Royal Commission on Labour in India. The Commission had expressed dissatisfaction on the working of these committees. However, it showed great hopes in future and recommended for the establishment of Works Committees at the plant levels for consultation and settlement of disputes. But the world depression of 1929 and thereafter with serious impacts on industrial relations did not allow these committees to serve any meaningful purpose. Till 1937 the recommendations of the commission could not infused any spirit of cooperation.

The establishment of the first Congress Government in 1937 gave a new hope to the workers but its failure within a couple of years shattered all hopes. The outbreak of the second world war again created national emergency, suspending all industrial labour laws. The war again created market scarcity of goods and services. It demanded full labour cooperation in maintaining supply line. The demand for increased industrial production of goods and services, increased productivity and production and better utilisation of workers' cooperation came in forefront. This trend was set first during the first world war. Fruitful experiences of first time motivated the Government of taking help of labour on industrial basis. Consequently, the first tripartite conference was called in 1942 inviting representatives of the Government, the managements and the workers. This tripartite conference at national level was a big step ahead in the principle of industrial relations. It set a trend for joint consultation at different levels in course of time.

The war experiences helped in framing a new set of industrial relations law. The Industrial Disputes Act, 1947 incorporated provision for the establishment of Works Committee in any industrial establishment employing one hundred or more workmen, consisting of representatives of workmen and their company. The Works Committee under the law has been assigned the duty "to promote measures for securing and preserving amity and good relations, between the employers and workmen and, to that end, to comment upon matters of their common interest or concern and endeavour to compose any material differences of opinion in respect of such matters."

It was the first legislative measure for promoting good relations between the employers and workmen in India. It hoped to provide a platform where both parties could meet, discuss and resolve problems of the common interests. Such an opportunity would infuse spirit of cooperation by removing misunderstanding. The legislative measure was framed with a right spirit and in right direction. The number of Works Committees set-up in India rose from 1142 in 1951 to 2574 in 1959-60. The Works Committees had shown satisfactory progress in the beginning. It was appreciated much in first plan but the experiences were not uniform everywhere. Soon there had been allegations and counter-allegations from both sides. Reviewing the working of the Works Committees in India, the Indian Institute of Personnel Management has remarked that in practice it rarely worked out as intended. It has remarked:

> "Some blamed the legislators for not defining more closely the objects and functions of the Works Committee, but the fact remains that one cannot compel people by law to cooperate. They can be forced to sit together, but that does not produce joint consultation if the spirit is not there behind the legal machinery. Management, with a few exceptions, were skeptical of the value of joint consultation; the trade unions were frankly suspicious."

The Indian Institute of Personnel Management has accepted that Works Committee's experiment had been failure. However, in some places it has functioned well. The system has worked well where both the sides were convinced of its value and are willing to listen on other side in each case. The institute observed that:

> "Works Committees, however, have generally been more successful where they have confined themselves to the sphere of working conditions, welfare amenities and social activities and have avoided discussion of any subject which is normally a matter for negotiation between management and organised Labour."

In spite of its failure, whatever little success has been achieved is the source of encouragement to this new experiment. There might have been many courses for its failure somewhere but those failures should not be discouraging.

The Indian Institute of Personnel Management had assessed that the Works Committees wherever successful have followed a common pattern, as remarked in the following lines:

> "At first the committee was little more than a grievance committee an opportunity for airing individual grievances and complaints and the attitude of the members a mixture of aggressiveness and false dignity. Managers were on the defensive and inclined to oppose every suggestion that was made and to consider attendance at the works committee a waste of time. To get beyond this stage required patience and perseverance on the part of the Personnel Officer, who was usually joint secretary of the Committee. He found he had to educate management representatives as well as workers' representatives, is the real objects of the committee and the right attitude to adopt. Sometimes it was extremely difficult to obtain any constructive suggestions from the workers' representatives, and managements found that to encourage the right approach they had themselves to propose improvements for instance better amenities and have them discussed and endorsed by the works committee in order to have some positive results to show to the employees as a whole."

The Government's decision to set-up and encourage Joint Production Committees, a second step in this new system of industrial relations, through means of persuasion was also a right step but the industrial environment was not ripe for such a quick experiment in India on western pattern.

A little success, whatever India had showed the seed for future growth. The legislative step under Industrial Disputes Act, 1947, encouragement for the establishment of Joint Production Committee and the first five year plan envisaging faster economic growth laid down bright future for a joint consultation machinery in India. The Government, the industrial organisations and the trade unions were separately and jointly discussing the various problems confronting joint consultation. The Indian Institute of Personnel Management in its 8th Annual Conference had reviewed the joint consultation machinery and laid down the following prerequisites for the success of joint consultation:

(i) Works Committees should be recommendatory in function,

(ii) Some provision should be made to include supervisory levels in these consultative bodies;

(iii) Information about the work done in a consultative body should be widely disseminated and steps should be taken to ensure that the supervisory levels are not short circuited;

(iv) Subjects discussed in joint consultative bodies should not encroach, in any way, on such spheres as are normally the subject of management-union negotiations;

(v) It is desirable that workers' representatives in consultative bodies should be employees of the organisation concerned; and

(vi) Measures like making it compulsory that the chairmanship of a joint consultative committee should go to an employees' representative and a management representative alternately should be avoided.

It was also a matter of discussion at the All India Labour Welfare Officers Conference, Nagpur in December 1955. The conference had accepted the principle of associating the workers in the administration of industries, though it also felt that the time was not still ripe for full participation and that the whole process had best been gradual. The idea was put forward in a concrete form in the industrial policy resolution of the 30th April, 1956.

It was stated there in that "in a socialist democracy, labour is a partner in the common task of development and should participate in it with enthusiam... There should be joint consultation and workers and technicians should, wherever possible, be associated progressively, with management." The idea received official recognition when a specific recommendation in this connection was made in the Second Five Year Plan as one of the progressive measures of labour policy. The plan stated:

> "For the successful implementation of the plan increased association of labour with management is necessary. Such a measure would help in:
>
> (a) promoting increased productivity for the general benefit of the enterprise, the employees and the community,
>
> (b) giving employees a better understanding of their role in the working of industry and of the prices of production, and
>
> (c) satisfying the workers' wage for self-expression, thus, leading to industrial peace, better relations and increased cooperation.

This could be achieved by providing for councils of management consisting of representatives of management, technicians and workers. It should be the responsibility of the management to supply such a council of management a fair and correct statement of all relevant information which would enable the council to function effectively. A council of management should be entitled to discuss various matters pertaining to the establishment and to recommend steps for its better working. The matter which falls within the purview of collective bargaining should, however, be excluded from the scope of discussion in the council. To begin with the proposal should be tried out in large establishments in organised industries. The pace of advance should be regulated and any extension of the scheme should be in the light of the experience gained.

The idea of Joint Management Council was still a new one and required thorough study before it could be adopted widely in Indian conditions. Hence, subsequent to the publication of the Second Five Year Plan, the Government of India sent a tripartite study group to Europe to study the working of the joint consultation and labour participation in those countries and to submit its finding on a suitable scheme for India.

The Report of the Study Group was considered at the 15th Indian Labour Conference held at New Delhi in July 1957. The Conference accepted most of the recommendations of the study group. The only departure was in respect of premissive legislation. Since the employers were willing to introduce schemes of workers' participation in selected industrial units on a voluntary basis. The Conference felt that no legislative measures be adopted for a period of two years. If, however, this experiment did not succeed, steps might be taken to bring in legislation.

The Sub-committee, tripartite in nature, set-up on August 6, 1757 considering the details regarding the scheme of labour-management cooperation had laid down the following criterias:

(1) The undertaking should have a well established, strong trade union functioning.

(2) There should be readiness in the parties, viz, employers, workers and the union to tryout the experiment in a spirit of willing cooperation.

(3) The size of the undertaking (in terms of employment) should be atleast 500 workers (Shri Kulkarni suggested that a few units with less than 500 workers might be tried in the pilot stage to make it easier to watch the impediments and ractify them. It was agreed that three or four such units might be taken up in addition to those contained in agreed list).

(4) The employer in the private sector be a member of one or the other of leading employers' organisations should the trade union be related to one of the central federations.

(5) The undertaking should have a fair record of industrial relations.

Labour-Management Cooperation in TISCO

By their supplemental agreement of January 8, 1956, the Tata Iron and Steel Company Ltd. and the Tata Workers' Union agreed to set-up the following joint councils in order to provide for a closer association of employees with the management:

(i) Joint Departmental Councils;

(ii) Joint Works Council for the plant as a whole;

(iii) Joint Town Council; and

(iv) Joint Consultative Council of Management at the topmost level.

The Company and the Union agreed that the representatives of employees to these councils were, in the first instance, to be nominated by the union, but steps were to be taken, gradually, to introduce the principle of election by a secret ballot. The representatives of the management were to be nominated by the management.

Joint Departmental Councils

The agreement provides for the setting up of a Joint Departmental Council in each Department of Works. Such Councils consist of two to ten representatives of management and an equal number of representatives of the works-employees, depending on the size of the department. The representatives of the works employees are nominated by the union from among the employees of the company. The functions of these councils are as follows:

(a) to study operational results and current and long-term departmental problems; to advise on steps necessary at the departmental level; to promote and rationalise production; improve methods, layout and processes; improve productivity and discipline; eliminate waste; affect economies with a view to lowering cost; eliminate defective work and improve the quality of product; improve the upkeep and care of machinery, tools, and instruments; promote efficient use of safety precaution and devices; promote employees' welfare and activities like sports and picnics; encourage suggestions; improve working conditions and better functioning of the department;

(b) to implement the recommendations and decisions of the Joint Consultative Council of Management or the Joint Works' Council as approved by the management; and

(c) to refer any matter to Joint Works Council for their consideration and advice.

Joint Works Council

The agreement provides for the establishment of a Joint

Works Council consisting of twelve representatives of the management and an equal number of representatives of the employees. The representatives of the employees are to be nominated by the union from amongst the employees of the company but exclusive of those covered by the Joint Town Council except that one such representative may be an officer of the Union who is not the employee of the company. The representatives of the management are to be nominated by the management.

The functions of the Joint Works Council are the following:

(a) the same as those of the Joint Departmental Council at the works level;

(b) to plan and supervise the work of the following committees within the framework of duly approved budgets and company rules and procedures;
   (i) Central Canteen Managing Committee;
   (ii) Welfare Committee;
   (iii) General Safety Committee;
   (iv) Safety Appliances Committee; and
   (v) Suggestion Box Committee.

(c) to follow-up the implementation through the appropriate Joint Departmental Councils of its recommendations or decisions approved by the management;

(d) to refer any matter to the Joint Consultative Council of the Management for their consideration or advice; and

(e) to advise on any matter referred to it by the Joint Departmental Councils or by the Joint Consultative Council of Management.

Joint Town Council

The Joint Town Council consists of six representatives of management and an equal number of representatives of employees. The employees' representatives are to be nominated by the Union from among the employees of the Company in the Town, Medical Health Departments including the Education Department, except that one of such representatives may be the officer of the Union who is not an employee of the Company.

Functions

The functions of the Joint Town Council are as follows:

(a) to advise on steps necessary to promote, rationalise and improve output and methods of work, reduce costs, improve quality, effect economies, reduce waste and ensure improved working conditions and better functioning of the organisation as a whole;
(b) to advice on social welfare activities in the town within the framework of duly approved budgets and company rules and procedures;
(c) to follow up the implementation of its recommendations as decisions approved by the management; and
(d) to refer any matter to the Joint Consultative Council of Management for their consideration and advice.

Joint Consultative Council of Management

The Joint Consultative Council of Management consists of eight representatives of management and an equal number of representatives of employees. The representatives of employees are to be nominated by the Union from amongst the employees of the Company except that not more than two of such representatives may be officers of the Union who are not the employees of the company.

The functions of the Joint Consultative Council of management are as follows:

(a) to advise management on all matters concerning the working of the industry in the fields of production and welfare;
(b) to advise management with regard to economic and financial matters placed by management before the council, provided that the council may discuss questions dealing with general economic and financial matters concerning the company which do not deal with questions affecting the relations of the company with share-holders or managerial staff or concerning taxes or other maters of confidential nature;

(c) to consider and advise on any matter referred to it by the Joint Works Council or the Joint Town Council; and

(d) to follow-up the implementation through the Joint Works Council or the Joint Town Council of any recommendations made by it and approved by the company.

The agreement between the TISCO and Tata Workers' Union providing for the closer association of workers with management is the most detailed of all such agreements in the country. As the TISCO is the largest single employer in the private sector employing nearly 40,000 workers, it is natural that in such a large organisation, relations become more formalised and standardised.

The arrangement of joint councils is hierarchical with the Joint Departmental Council at the bottom and the Joint Consultative Council of Management at the top-informations and recommendations flowing in both directions.

The joint councils are essentially advisory in nature; their functions being to advise management, and the company has reserved to itself the right to accept or reject the recommendations and suggestions of the joint councils. However, it should be noted that it is not the formal constitution and functions of the councils but the spirit in which they work that ultimately determines their effectives in guiding the management. In practice, most decisions of the councils are enforced by the management.

References

TISCO, Seminar on "Man Management for Peace", 'Productivity and Progress,' Proceeding of the Seminar, p. 20.

TISCO, 'Man-Management in Tata Steel'.

Lala, R.M., 'The Creation of Wealth', p. 199.

'Second Pay Commission Report' (1959), Govt. of India.

Chester, T.E. and Gardner, foresight (1959), "Concept of Joint consultation in Great Britain", '*Indian Journal of Labor Economics*', Vol. II, Nos. 2-3, July-October, p. 142.

'UK Industrial Relations Handbook' (1961).

'National Commission on Labour' (1969), Government of India Report, p. 345, para 24.14.

Rastogi, J.L. (1958), 'Casselman's Labour Dictionary', "Industrial Relations in Uttar Pradesh, Kitab Printing, Lucknow.

Dunlop, John T. (1958), 'Industrial Relations Systems', Hennry Hott and Company, New York.

Tata Steel, Annual Report (2005-06).

Tata Steel, Annual Report (2006-07).

Singh, A.D., "Welcome Address, Seminar on Man-Management For Peace, Productivity and Progress, p. 5.

Industrial Relations and Human Resource Management

The conflict between labour and capital is so fundamental that it can never be ignored and it is impossible to think of a situation where industrial growth occurs in the absence of an institutional and effective mechanism through which conflict in interests of the two parties are balanced. Exceptions to this statement can be found only in history, of nearly two centuries back, when industrial revolution had just started in Europe but the notion of democratic principles was yet to be crystalised. In the recent history, it would be very difficult to find a country situation where democratic values have been completely ignored and the authoritarian state has suppressed the conflict by ruthless laws and physical force. Fortunately, for whatever historical reasons, the democratic values had taken firm roots in Indian polity even before independence and thus the role of industrial relations in promoting industrial growth and attaining other objectives of planned development was vital. For historical reasons again, formal trade unionism in India was nearly three decades old at the time of independence and the urgency of the task of evolving a suitable framework for industrial relations in independent India was felt very early. It is thus not unusual that nearly one-third of the Presidential addresses included in this volume are concerned with problems of industrial relations and other related issues.

TRADE UNIONS AND INDUSTRIAL RELATIONS

In the very inaugural conference at Lucknow, Shri V.V. Giri (1958) had devoted most of his Presidential address to discuss industrial relations and trade unionism in India. With his vast personal experience in the field, he was quite aware that 'industrial peace does not merely signify the absence of industrial unrest, but the active presence of harmonious and good industrial relations generating amity and goodwill between the partners in an industry'. Such being his perception, it was only expected that he would be averse to the arrangement of arbitration (by the state machinery) in any collective bargaining and would insist on an internal settlement, except on very special circumstances. But unfortunately the statutory provision on compulsory arbitration prevents such an internal settlement, instead of acting as a safeguard against bypassing the process of collective bargaining. However, far more than the legal and administrative provisions, the most important factor standing in the way of improving the industrial relations in India has been the absence of any trust between the trade union and the employer. One of the ways to build that missing trust was to involve the workers in the affairs of the industry through workers' participation in management. In his second Presidential address in the following year Shri V.V. Giri (1959) discussed the prospects of such participation programme in India and specified two main hurdles against the programme—the basic weakness of the trade unions in India in terms of workers' disunity and the employers' indifference. His hope that these difficulties would gradually disappear was, however, belied as would appear from the fate of the programme even three decades later.

Although industrial relations concern mainly two parties, trade unions and employers, it cannot function in isolation from its political, economic and social environment. It is thus only desirable that an evaluation of the industrial relation policies in India is done in the overall context of Indian society and Professor G.P. Sinha (1979 and 1980) attempts the task in his two Presidential addresses in successive years. In his first oration, he characterizes the crisis in industrial relations in India, not in terms of an irresponsible trade union or rigid attitudes of employers, but as a consequence of the industrial relations policy trying to serve simultaneously many contradictory goals, e.g., technological change and progress but no resistance from the workers, economic stability with the freedom of labour and capital to set wages and prices, industrial democracy, i.e. increasing workers' control over management of enterprise without requiring the workers to bear the risk, and the like. Obviously this is too demanding a situation where scope for behaviour modification of the trade unions is extremely limited. A supplementary factor behind the existing crisis in industrial relations in India is the dated perception, particularly of the employers, that the only contribution that healthy relations can make is to avoid stoppage of production process. The associated benefit of improving the production process through higher productivity is generally not thought about by the employers and, to that extent, there is also scope for behaviour modification of the employers towards promoting healthy industrial relations.

In most of the discussions on industrial relations, the focus is generally on the work stoppages caused by strikes and the role of trade unions on causing them. Rather surprisingly, the equally disturbing phenomenon of lock-outs is overlooked. Professor Ruddar Datt (1991) tried to remove this particular gap in the study of industrial relations by analysing the trend of lock-outs in India over the last three decades. In the later half of this period, he observed, the intensity of lock-outs therefore, pleaded for more effective government interventions in this regard 'by strengthening the legal framework so as to prevent the malafide action of the employers'.

Quality of Human Inputs

The question of quality of human inputs requires a framework in which industrial relations is only a part and, within that, collective bargaining even a smaller part. As even those partial issues of collective bargaining and industrial relations were far from settled in Indian industries, the wider issue of quality of human inputs had rarely been given the due attention it deserves in planning process. That this important issue has not been ignored at least by the scholars concerned with the problems of labour is indicated by the discourse of Professor K.C. Saxena (1981) which takes a very practical view of the question and offers a feasible agenda towards improving the quality of human inputs and human relation, in general, in the industrial sector. In a real human relation policy, the human factor is given priority over all other factors of production and the basic objective of that policy is to promote a complete phychological integration of a worker within the industry. The different components of that policy, as identified by him, were role clarification of the workers, fair wage and good working conditions, selection and placement of personnel, training and education, opportunity for advancement, role of supervisory personnel, two-way communication and respect for the personality of subordinates. Viewed in this manner, the task of building proper human relations in Indian industries might be difficult, but not impossible.

The vital role of human factors of production returns as a theme of Presidential address when Professor D.L. Narayana (1983) discusses the problem of low productivity in Indian industries, along with some related issues. He starts his presentation with the concept of human resources and the enormous contribution that it had made in the Japanese growth process. Looking for the reasons why that Japanese phenomenon could not be repeated in India, Professor Narayana comes out with several factors like inefficient administration, too many holidays, wasteful style of time management, liberal socio-political environment and, finally, poor work motivation. Obviously, all these factors do not operate independently and they are highly related with each other, precipitating a work environment where low productivity is an inevitability.

Workers' Participation in Management

Planners in India were quite aware about the utmost necessity of establishing industrial democracy as a prerequisite for industrial growth. The formal expression of that awareness was embodied in Second Five Year Plan document and since then a number of measures were taken to provide an institutional base for the emergence and growth of industrial democracy in the country. Some of these measures were regulatory in nature in the form of legislations on industrial relations and related issues. In contrast, the ambitious scheme of Workers' Participation in Management was a promotive measure which aimed at 'transforming the attitude of both employers and workers for establishing a cooperative culture which may help in building a strong self-confident and self-reliant country with a stable industrial base'. As the concept was new, its operational character had to be evolved over some stages of experimentation, since its beginning in late fifties as a non-statutory scheme. However, upto the mid-seventies, the scheme was generally treated with indifference by both the workers and employers. Thereafter, some of the enterprises have made efforts to run the scheme and, during the eighties, several economists have tried to evaluate its functioning and suggest ways to improve it. One of the most persistent suggestions arising out of such evaluative exercises is to lend further strength to this scheme by incorporating employee ownership as a part of Workers' Participation in Management and Professor D.N. Nanjundappa (1990) argues for the same strategy after making an exhaustive analysis of the scheme, taking into account its legislative base and working experience, particularly since mid-seventies. Although specific details about working of the scheme relate to a single case study, the overall working experience suggests that employee-ownership has generally been resorted to when the companies were in red, 'perhaps to minimise the loss of the private owners, and to evoke sympathy by advancing the case of labour who would be thrown out of employment if the company closes its doors'. But even under such trying circumstances, when the labour opts for owning the industry, they do so with a full sense of responsibility and are prepared to make temporary sacrifices in wages in return for expected higher benefits later on. Obviously such display of sense of responsibility by the workers is more related to their joint ownership than to the fact that it is a crisis situation and it thus strongly indicates the positive results that both employers and workers can obtain if employee-ownership is allowed under normal circumstances.

A second pleading for employee-ownership as an effective strategy of workers' participation in management is made by Professor V.M. Dandekar (1989) along with discussing some important financial implications of the scheme in fair details. He also deplores the tendency that employee-ownership has generally been introduced till now as a last resort to prevent plant closures; but, based on the successful experience of the scheme in United States and Britain (not in western Europe, though), he considers the scheme worth pursuing in India. As regards the financial arrangement, he proposes the utilisation of employee provident fund for employee-ownership home. Using the data of 500 plus large public limited companies in India, he shows that such funds can cover the entire share of those companies and, thus, necessary funds for the scheme is already there. In view of the fact that the income level of the workers in organised sector is not very low, and they may not be entirely averse to take some work, employee-ownership scheme may get accepted in near future, fusing a new role for employers, workers and trade unions.

Confronted with the problem of containing spiralling inflation and blaming the workers and their unions for contributing to the spiralling prices by pushing wages beyond the rate of rise in productivity, many people advocate productivity-indexed wage and bonus payments. In India, the payment of bonus to the industrial employees of the Government of India has been linked to productivity. While clamour is made for productivity-linked wage-increase in the management and official circles, trade unions are equally vociferous in resisting such a linkage, not only because they do not treat the existing distribution of income as sacrosanct, but also because they fear that linking wage and bonus payments to productivity is a device to cheat them of their legitimate claim to a living wage. Though there is so much of talk of the importance of growth. In productivity for speeding up economic growth, there is little analysis of the concrete situation which can facilitate or hinder improvements in productivity. The gains of the 'green revolution' are reflected in the improvement of agricultural productivity in the area of wheat production by way of improved inputs like water, seeds, fertilizer, insecticide, herbicide, etc., but there has not been any reference to the quality of human input, as if it does not have much to contribute. In the industrial field also, new technologies are being introduced and additional capital input of improved quality is being provided to increase production. Larger input can give larger returns but that does not necessarily mean improvement in productivity. In all economic organizations, apart from the quality and the quantity of material input it is recognised on all sides that the quality of the human input is the crucial factor in promoting productivity, consequently in economic growth and development.

The relationship between employer and his employees is a necessitous relationship flowing from the necessity of the worker for a job and the necessity of the employer for labour. Therefore, the worker tends to give the least which is just sufficient enough to protect his job and the employer also seeks to give him the least barely sufficient enough to retain the worker in the firm. It is the relationship of giving the least on both sides that leads to what has been termed 'X' inefficiency mentioned earlier. The capacity to work may be there but they will to work is absent. Chamberlain (1951, p. 445) calls this situation a relationship of 'conjunction' and not of 'cooperation'. This relationship is vividly and dramatically illustrated in the answer to a question which you can put to the workers of any enterprise. Who are you working for? The question is invariably answered as "Working for the TISCO, TELCO, or the BATA"? Therefore, if this be so, should one expect a worker to give his best when he is working for somebody else? Sociologists, social-psychologists, human relationists and management consultants have been toiling and experimenting with and analysing the depths of human motivation in a work situation. They have been trying to find out ways by which this gap could be eliminated altogether, if possible, and reduced in extent so far as feasible. To name a few, A.H. Marlow (1954), Chris Argyris, Frederick Herzber (1959), Douglas McGregor (1960), David C. McClellan (1969), Victor H. Vroom (1964), Kae H. Chung (1969), Rudhard Stollberg, P.N. Singh (1963), K.K. Singh (1967), and others made significant contributions towards the understanding of human behaviour in wage-employment situation. But these studies are so much conditioned by the particular social, economic, political, cultural and religious environment of the particular place and the country and so much limited by the particular technology and methodology of research and experiments that conclusions from one conflict with the conclusions of others. More important than this is the fact that the technology of steel production in Soviet Union may be the same as in the U.S.A. or Germany or Great Britain or Japan, but the managerial practices, particularly personnel management practices, differ exceedingly from country to country. Therefore, technologies of production can be transplanted from one country to another but not the technologies of man-management. The motivations of workers in a socialist country are in no way comparable to the motivations of workers in a capitalist country nor those in semi-feudal, semi-capitalist country like India.

The TISCO management has been alive to the problems of industrial relations right from the very beginning. The desire for a strong industrial peace, happy industrial relations and smooth human relations has always been a guiding point for their better industrial relations policy. The Tata Management has always given due attention towards its employees, individually and collectively, by providing them better working and living conditions, better service conditions and establishing better understanding between them. Dorabji Tata, as early as 1917, had said:

> "The welfare of the labouring classes must be one of the first cares of every employer. Any betterment of their conditions must proceed more from the employers downward rather than be forced up by demands from below, since labour, contented, well housed, well fed and generally well looked after, is not only as asset and advantage to the employer, but serves to raise the standard of industry and ..... labour in the country."

The introduction of works Committee in 1920 by TISCO much ahead than the Government had thought of under Industrial Disputes Act, 1947, was the proof of strong desire for creating an environment for mutual discussions of grievances and other common issues. The essence of such committee was the mutual discussion, mutual settlement, mutual understanding of grievances and other problems. The Company had adopted the policy of mutual negotiations at a time when such practice had been uncommon in India. That was again an evidence of a better industrial relations policy of the TISCO management.

On the occasion of Silver Jubilee of the Personnel Department, held in March 1973, a commemorative volume was published which contains the casual development of industrial relations policy. Naval H. Tata in his article "Industrial Relations" has drawn our attention towards this fact when he said:

> "Howsoever strong our passion for peace and harmony in industry may be, peace is not likely to descend on us from heavens by mere exhortations and prayers. Serious efforts will have to be made by all concerned to keep the path of industrial peace free from misunderstandings, misrepresentations, and undue interference from third parties."

Stressing on the need for serious efforts for maintaining industrial harmony as an objective of the company, he had drawn attention towards "The Pot-holds cut in the path by rough passage of negotiations and/or breaches of agreements, strikes and lock-outs." Being conscious of the unfair practices by the other side he drew attention towards strikes and lock-outs and other practices as usual features of the present industrial life. In such a situation, when trade union has come in to bargain collectively in good faith it must be adopted as a method for settlement of industrial disputes and establishment of industrial democracy. He had clearly underlined the policy of industrial relations of the company in these words:

> "I shall never tire of repeating what I have been saying from time to time: more of bipartite agreements and less of adjudicated awards, more of voluntary codes and less of labour laws, more of self-reliance on the part of employers and workers and less eagerness on the part of Government to interfere may, in course of time, put us on the path of enduring industrial peace which we need so badly to make our best contribution to the national economy."

The industrial relations have to be rescued from the "Jungle of discord" to some "semblance of sanity and peace." Naval H. Tata had taken pains in summerising essential features which could help in establishing healthy industrial relations:

(i) It is a fact that in the absence of an arrangement for

statutory recognition of unions, or voluntary recognition by employers and on moral grounds, collective agreements have made no headway.

(ii) Consequently, there is an unlimited scope (so far unexplored) for greater reliance on collective bargaining thereby replacing avoidable adjudication or any form of undue governmental interference.

(iii) To create appropriate climate for collective bargaining, it becomes necessary to resort to statutory recognition of a sole bargaining agents, where voluntary efforts fail.

(iv) Recognition should be made compulsory under a central law:

(a) for all undertakings employing more than 100 workers;

(b) provided the trade union seeking recognition has atleast 30 percent membership among the workers;

(c) there should be a properly recognised authority under a central legislation like the Industrial. Relations Conference to decide disputes through verification of records. Where the difference in the verified membership is 10 per cent or less, then a secret ballot open to all employees should be taken.

(v) The recognised union should be statutorily given:

(a) exclusive right of sole representation;

(b) exclusive right to enter into collective bargaining;

(c) exclusive right to collect membership subscription within the factory premises including the right of check-off; and

(d) right to nominate representatives on Works/ Grievances Committee and/or Management Committees.

(vi) The minority union should only be allowed the right to represent individual cases of dismissal and discharge before a labour court.

(vii) All collective agreements should be registered with a duly authorised Government agency.

(viii) Collective bargaining can not exist without the right to strike and lock-out after a due process of conciliation and voluntary arbitration.

(ix) Since strike and lock-out are reciprocal weapons, in certain essential industries/services the right to strike and lock-out can be by mutual agreement curtailed or voluntarily forfeited by both sides provided there is an effective alternative of a foolproof grievance procedure culminating into compulsory adjudication. Where Government, as an employer in public services, out of its obligation to the community, cannot lock-out the workers as an industrial employer can do, there is, in effect, no collective bargaining, because one party is armed while the other is not.

(x) Whilst strikes and lock-outs are legal, every strike or lock-out should be preceded by a notice to the other party. In the case of labour such notice can only be given after a strike ballot, open to all members of the union, is taken and provided it is backed by atleast 2/3rd of the members present and voting, Despite such in-built reciprocity between management and labour, it is unfortunate that out Government has a tendency to deprive the employer of the discretion to lock-out by insisting that the employer should give a prior notice to Government which makes a mockery of collective bargaining. Such one-sided approach on the part of Government gives immunity to the worker from the threat of a lock-out, a reciprocal weapon to complete the process of collective bargaining. As a result, numerous strikes take place without strike notices, either through want of a recognised union or just as a wanton measure on the part of the workers. Our Government has unfortunately failed to appreciate that the threat of a strike when countered by a reciprocal threat of a lock-out holds the balance even towards maintenance of industrial peace. Unless such a threat exists for both sides, the very essence of collective bargaining is not fulfilled.

(xi) Unfair labour practices on the part of both employers and workers should be liable to penalties prescribed by law.

(xii) Grievance procedure should be simple, with provision for an appeal to—
  (a) the departmental manager
  (b) a bipartite grievance committee, and
  (c) reference to an arbitrator.

(xiii) By way of convention, no case should be referred to an industrial tribunal unless it involves a bonafide industrial dispute.

(xiv) Similarly, any strike or industrial dispute culminating into organised violence should be out of bounds of an industrial tribunal until the law and order aspect of it is decided under common law and the blame is if apportioned equitably.

The essential pre-requisites for industrial peace underlined by N.H. Tata are determinants of industrial relations policy of the TISCO. These determinants can be applicable in national policy, if there is a desire for the same. The time demands a positive policy and a similar legislative step for underlying conditions and criterias for recognition of union by the management as a sole bargaining agent, rights of the recognised and un-recognised unions, provision of grievance procedure, restrictions on utilisation of the right to strike and lock-out, unfair labour practices and wider use of collective bargaining method. This approach of N.H. Tata shows his foresightedness and sense of determination in industrial relations practices. It is therefore, the TISCO's policy and practices of industrial relations have not only been appreciable rather worth adoptable by other industrial establishments.

The Policy-Streamlined

The industrial relations practices are in tune with the policy of the TISCO. In its whole life of 96 years for the settlement of industrial disputes the adjudication machinery has not been used. Occasion has not come as yet to experiment the method of arbitration. Even the conciliation machinery has been used occasionally. The faith in collective bargaining is so strong that arbitrate on and adjudication have not been adopted in TISCO. This convinces us that industrial relations policy and practices are both in tune with each other reaping the best harvest for years of long periods.

The industrial relations policy and pattern have gone under changes by the middle of the century. A new pattern of industrial relations has emerged under the broad guidance of J.R.D. Tata, N.H. Tata, R.H. Modi, R.P. Billimorta, R.S. Pande and Prof. A.D. Singh, R.S. Pande, the then Managing Director, had clearly accepted that:

> "One encouraging sign in recent years has been the strengthening of the forces of bipartism. One outstanding example of the effectiveness of bipartite machinery is the Joint Negotiating Committee for the Steel Industry where representatives of employers and workers, belonging to various shades of public opinion, sit at a table and try to thrash out their common problems. That bipartite talks are the best for securing industrial peace is a fact which can hardly be disputed."

A new pattern of industrial relations has emerged in the TISCO. The new pattern of industrial relations is based on the experiences of strike of 1958 as R.S. Pande commends:

> "Recogntion of a union alone may not produce the necessary climate for healthy and stable industrial peace particularly when there are more than one union. Thus, a new pattern of industrial relations, which has been emerging of late, is some managements readiness to talk to both recognised and unrecognised unions, under certain situations. Though this phenomenon is not widespread, the beginning of the acceptance of this principle at some places strikes a new note in the pattern of industrial relations."

This new pattern of industrial relations has added a stage in the growth of industrial relations system. There was a time when the management had been negotiating only with the recognised union. The unrecognised union was always kept out of the scene. Even the recognised union had been claiming as the sole bargainer on behalf of all workers. But the industrial relations experiences have forced the managements and the recognised union to give up this old idea. Probably, they have realised that for better industrial relations and longer industrial peace, the unrecognised union-unions should also be invited and made parties to joint settlement. This should help in acceptance of the terms and conditions of negotiations by all workers and in the implementation of the terms of negotiations. If this new pattern of industrial relations is adopted by the management, it would satisfy the unrecognised unions and the members that they too, have been heard and have been given an opportunity in discussing common issues, thus, the human element in industrial relations, a most sensitive feature, could be satisfied by the new pattern which in long-term would prove advantageous by strengthening industrial relations, establishing permanent industrial peace and industrial harmony.

The role of the two parties in industrial relations is important. Their attitudes, aspirations policies and actions play in giving a shape to it. The policy of the management has been underlined by top officials of the TISCO. The other party, the Union, its role is also significant for peaceful industrial relations. The role of the Union and its leaders in maintaining healthy industrial relations and collective bargaining practices has been appreciated by Prof. A.D. Singh, the then Director of Personnel, on the occasion of Silver Jubilee celebration of the Personnel Department in 1973 in the following lines:

> "... the present function arises of the Union... have maintained the balance between the dual role of a trade unions, namely, union as a protest organisation which zealously guards the interests of the workers which it presents, and union as an organisation which is conscious when there are differences between the Management and the Union, it had been our combined effort not to allow an industrial dispute to take the shape of an industrial disorder."

Industrial relations study includes the study of conflicts and cooperation. In this chapter conflicts have been studied, efforts to settle those conflicts and the results thereof have been analysed. The problem of cooperation, efforts for establishing cooperation and the achievements of "Close Association of Employees with Management."

The industrial disputes are of two types:

(a) disputes of interests, and
(b) disputes of right.

The disputes of interests is based on the particular interest of workers, their wishes and aspirations. It is called as 'Demand'. The methods used for settlement of demands are:

(a) collective bargaining (bi-partite),
(b) collective bargaining with conciliation (tri-partite),
(c) Arbitration, and
(d) Adjudication.

The dispute regarding the right arises out of standing order, collective agreements, awards, service rules and regulations, executive orders and labour laws. This is called as "Grievance" for the settlement of which grievance procedure is adopted.

TISCO: Industrial Disputes

The Tata has a long practice of collective bargaining, a practice adopted first in 1920, within a period of one decade of its establishment. By that time trade unionism was in its infant stage at many industrial places. There was even no union in many industrial undertakings. The unions, then in existence, were where the workers were mostly organised and conscious of their rights. There was no law giving legal status to the union. The union was treated as an unlawful combination of workers. In such a stage of industrial relations the managements were enjoying the full sacrosanct prerogatives. They were commanding the uninterrupted right of ownership and right of management. The terms and conditions of service were determined by the management. The workers, individually or collectively, had no voice in determination of the wages and other service conditions. That was the stage of uninterrupted industrial relations or better to be called as *laissez-faire* industrial relations.

The First Example of Settlement

In the TISCO the normal condition was disturbed by a strike in 1920, a spontaneous reaction of workers against the poor service conditions, lower wages and ever increasing cost of living index without adequate compensation. That was a strike without an organised association of workers but the credit goes to workers for immediately attracting attention of many social and labour leaders from far-off, who provided leadership for carrying the load of strike. The leaders were S. Halder and Yogesh Ghosh. Under the able leadership the first association, namely, the Labour Association was set-up in 1920. That newly established Labour Association win whole hearted support of steelmen. The management had to come forward, leaving aside its earlier stand, to talk with the leaders. As a result of the talk the first settlement was arrived at on March 20, 1920 between the management and the association. A close review of demands and terms of agreements highlights the achievements.

Demands	*Terms of Agreement*
[1] Immediate increase in 50% Wages.	[i] Pay rising from 8% to 16% and further increase of 10% to 20%.
[2] Payment of Bonus.	[ii] Provident Fund with company's contribution of one month's Pay.
[3] Improvement in Service conditions.	[iii] Payment of Production Bonus.
[4] Leave with wages.	[iv] Payment of gratuity to the employees.
[5] Compensation for accident.	[v] Two days festival leave annually on full pay.
[6] Prompt payment to the family of deceased employees.	[vi] Two weeks leave on full pay annually to daily rated employees.

The first agreement of the TISCO was important one from many angles. This agreement was the result of February 1920 strike, the strike spontaneous in nature and without any organisation. Secondly, the newly established association successfully conducted strike and negotiated with the management. Thirdly, the management of the TISCO by negotiating and settling demands had shown its progressive character, unparallel in India. Fourthly, the comparative analysis of demands and achievements shows that wages had increased upto 36%, payment of production bonus, provident fund, gratuity, leave with full pay and accumulation of leave were the achievements to the credit of the workers. And lastly, the negotiations with the Labour Association was virtually a case of its recognition as workers' representative, though informally. Thus, the practice of collective bargaining was adopted in the TISCO by 1920, much earlier than enactment of Trade Unions Act, 1926.

The practice of collective bargaining and its adoption in 1920 in the TISCO was also a landmark in the history of industrial relations because even by then Trade Unions Act had not come in existence. The Labour Association, without enjoying legal status, was recognised by the TISCO for all practical purposes. That proves the contention that absence of registration and legal status are no bar for recognition of union by the management. Recognition of union solely depends on the strength of union, its pressure and the policy of the management. It further confirms the notion "the management gets a union the type it likes." If the policy of the management is cooperative, constructive, fair and just—the union reacts in the similar fashion. The TISCO management has shown the whole country its outlined policy with the workers and their association right from 1920 and normal smooth industrial relations resulting therefrom. There are many industrial establishments where, inspite of registered unions and their power, unions have not been recognised by the respective managements.

Recognition of union by the management has been an issue of central legislation. There are, however, a few states like Maharashtra, Gujarat and Madhya Pradesh—where state legislations incorporate provisions regarding recognition of union. But in spite of the presence of statutory obligation on the management—many managements have been taking please in support of non-recognition of union. The TISCO management is one, which had recognised union in 1920 even prior of enactment of Trade Unions Act, 1926 and even in absence of any statutory obligation for the same. Such a spirit of the management of TISCO had opened a new chapter in the history of industrial relations in India, parallel to that of Ahmedabad's T.L.A. the

Ahmedabad and Jamshedpur have been two leading industrial centres adopting new practices, directing new pattern and guiding the country for smooth and peaceful industrial relationship.

A Temporary Setback

The success of 1920 strike and achievements thereafter was morale booster for the workers. That laid down a platform for building a structure of joint negotiation but there had been a temporary break down. A strike started in September 1922 for security of service, better service conditions, etc. was a failure. In reaction to this strike the Labour association was derecognised. There are conflicting ideas where the management had really recognised Labour Association in formal way therefore, recognition had been drawn. However, a committee was set-up with C.R. Das, as Chairman, for conciliating over the issues but that too had failed. It was one the intervention of Mahatma Gandhi and C.F. Andrews, the management again recognised Labour Association and its General Secretary was reinstated in 1925. This shows that the relationship between the management and Association was tagged by a thin thread which could be broken even by a slight jerk. The management did not hesitate in withdrawing the recognition and breaking its normal relationship which had its origin only one and half years, back. It is history of industrial relations everywhere that in absence of the law making obligatory in the part of the management to recognise an association as bargaining representative that the managements have been using this weapons frequently. At a matter of fact in absence of statutory obligation on the management to recognise a union as the sole bargaining agent, the management still enjoys the prerogative to recognise the union even by the close of the 20th century.

Revival of Relationship

Soon after the revival of recognition of Labour Association in 1925 the normal relationship was re-established with better understanding. The management also had realised that it would not ignore the labour organisation for long. But history repeats itself and that again happened in TISCO, when requests, appeals and memoranda failed to move the management towards immediate problems leaving industrial unrest to deepen soon. Consequently, the union resorted to strike in 1928 which lasted for 105 days. Ultimately the dead lock was resolved by a bilateral agreement arrived at on September 11, 1928. Thus, the third agreement adding one more stop in the ladder strengthened the system of collective bargaining in TISCO.

A comparative analysis of demands and terms of agreement would give a clear picture of the comparative bargaining power of parties concerned as presented below.

Comparative Analysis of Demands and Terms of Agreement of 1928

Demands	*Terms of Agreement*
[1] All Sheet Mill and Boilder men to be taken back on the old privileges.	[i] Discharged men of Sheet Mill and Boiler departments were reinstated.
[2] Reduction to be stopped.	[ii] Company had agreed to pay benefit of railway fares for their homes to employees obtained to leave work.
[3] Wages for lock-out and strike periud.	[iii] Maternity benefit to female employees.
[4] General increment of wages.	[iv] Job security and security of income to the surplus staff.
[5] Minimum monthly wage to be Rs. 30 for men and Rs. 20 for women.	[v] Provision of safety Appliacane.
[6] Bonus to be extended.	
[7] Grade and time scale to be fixed for all jobs.	
[8] Departmental grievance to be settled.	
[9] Service and leave rules to be revised.	

The comparative study of demands and terms of agreement indicates various features of importance. Firstly, the discharged men of Sheets Mill and Boilder Department, as demanded, were reinstated and their continuity of service was restored. Secondly, the company had agreed to pay benefit of railway fare for their homes to employees obtained to leave work with full provident fund and gratuity. Thirdly, the management agreed to introduce maternity benefit to female employees. Fourthly, it granted job security and security of income even to the surplus staff. Further safety appliances were to be supplied by the management. Thus, the agreement of 1928 was again important from many considerations because for the first time the union had secured job security and security of income. This agreement was again important because it showed employees and their association's long staying power as strong striking power. It was important for further addition in the list of bargainable issues. Agreement on many important issues without legal obligation was a matter of appreciation and a landmark in the history of industrial relations.

Bunch of Agreements

The practice of collective bargaining was strengthened during the decide (1938-47) when five agreements, one over another, were signed. Singing of a bunch of agreements during that period was itself an indicator of greater recognition of the system of collective bargaining. This was a fact accepted by the company on the eve of Silver Jubilee of Personnel Department when it recorded that

> "A better understanding grew between Union and Management, fostering a desire for cooperation and finding solutions through negotiations across the table. This has not only promoted bi-partite relations, but has also helped the workers to reap the fruits through collective bargaining."

This bunch of agreements was opened by an agreement arrived at in June 1938 between the management and the TWU. The agreement of June 1938 covers terms like additional half a month's wages, reduction of electric charges from 1 anna to ½ anna per unit, electrification of all quarters, completion of 33% of quarters, temporary hands with one year's service be made permanent, consideration on revision of departmental bonus, payment of general production bonus and revision of gratuity rules. This agreement reflects the increasing bargaining power of the TWU as the management had agreed to pay additional half month wages, reduction in electric charges, permanency of temporary hands, revision of departmental bonus and gratuity rules and payment of general production bonus. These were some of the additional gains secured over and above the previous payments, and permanency of temporary hands are indicators of changing comparative bargaining power of parties concerned. Any additional gain was an advancement towards wider scope of collective bargaining and the gradual maturity of the practice.

The war time strains, increasing prices of essential commodities and the economic difficulties, led to signing of an agreement in 1942. The management conceded demand for 10% emergency bonus to be paid to all those on the salary of Rs. 500 and below. The end of the second world war and many pending demands necessitated an early settlement. The management too, realised the need of a fresh settlement on many old issues and a few new issues. Consequently, an agreement was arrived at in 1945 in a cordial atmosphere. This agreement, an important part of bunch of agreements, was important for many reasons. That agreement granted wage increase to lower wage bracket, special bonus of ½ month's wages in addition to profit sharing bonus, increase of food subsidy from Rs. 3-11-0 to Rs. 4-14-0, increased payment of gratuity from 12 years to 15 years, extension to medically fit employees after superannuation for a maximum period of 3 years, 12 days' leave for every year service for unskilled workers, promotion on the criteria of seniority-*cum*-merit reinstatement of discharged employees during strike of 1942 and absorbtion of surplus men of AGRICO in Main Works. This agreement again is important for adding new subject-matters in the list of bargainable issues, such as, criteria of promotion, leave with wages, subsidy of food, bonus and extension of service. Addition in the list of bargainable issues was the proof of developing collective bargaining practice. Any addition in the number of agreements adds to this practice in their mutual understanding between the Management and the TWU.

In the following year, September 1946 a fresh agreement was signed in which the wage structure was revised by a new graded incremental time scale of pay consisting of basic wages, good attendance bonus at the rate of 20% of basic wage, performance bonus at the rate of 40% of basic wage, the revision of profit sharing bonus, formulation of promotion procedure, establishment of permanent Joint Rates Committee with two union representatives and loans for house building and construction of quarter. Here again one finds that collective bargaining had encroached upon certain managerial functions. Negotiation even on promotion procedure, imparting of training for appearing at the trade tests, establishment of permanent Joints Rates Committee were some of the new issues. These new issues bargained were sufficient to pinpoint the further development of mutual understanding and mutual adjustment. Negotiation on procedure, practices and training programme, which were non-economic in nature, added weight because bargaining on managerial functions was a new feature.

The bunch of agreements was closed by a single issue agreement of 1947 in which production and maintenance bonus was revised upward. That decade was really important for the growth of collective bargaining because there had been multi-direction advancement. In this period of scope of collective bargaining crossed from economic to non-economic fields and the nature of collective bargaining, changed from Marketing Theory of Collective Bargaining to Managerial Theory of Collective Bargaining.

Collective Bargaining towards Maturity

Collective bargaining trend of the last decade (1938-47) continued to flourish in following years. It became an usual feature to settle matters through table-talk both informal and formal ways. Normally small issues were settled verbally of which records are not available. Many executive orders really are based on verbal understanding and informal settlements. Apart from those informal verbal settlements there are signed agreements which are records of progress or collective bargaining. The present assessment is based on signed agreements only. If the unsigned settlement of issues would have been available the picture would have been much clear and better. However, the signed agreements available are sufficient indicators of the trend of healthy industrial relations.

During 1948-53 four agreements had been signed. Agreement of 1948 further upward revised wage structure.

Agreement of 1949 raised profit sharing bonus from 22½% to 27½%. The agreement of 1951 gave service bonus at a rate of 1/3rd of the maintenance bonus and bonus at the rate of 66.67% of production and maintenance bonus to lower income groups. Agreement of 1953 again raised profit sharing bonus from 27½% to 30%, introduced incentive bonus scheme and upward revised wages, D.A. and food rebate. These four agreements were mostly economic in nature and therefore, there had not been any expansion in the scope of collective bargaining. But the revision of profit sharing bonus rate twice within a period of four years was an indicator of increased bargaining power of the T.W.U. Introduction of Incentive Bonus scheme through negotiation was only a new addition in this period.

A close review of all agreements has exposed the fact that the TWU had been continuously making its position solid by increasing bargaining power. The mutual settlement of common issues helped in establishing industrial peace so much so that the TISCO thought of celebrating Silver Jubilee of industrial peace and industrial harmony. This achievement was the result of adoption of the practice of collective bargaining.

TISCO: A Change in Trend

Collective bargaining has been viewed as a tug of war between the two parties over their common issues,/shares and power. The union had been attacking on the prerogatives of the management and the management had been preserving its prerogatives desperately. This scene of tug of war had been replaced by a new understanding in 1956 in which the two sides agreed on a new set of terms of agreement accepting the principle of participative management. The principle of Industrial democracy was put before the practice of tug of war for a better industrial relations and industrial peace. Instead of fighting all the same, the two parties resolved to share power through a scheme 'Closer association of employees with management'. Thus, the scene of war turned into a scene of cooperation and peace through the method of collective bargaining. This change in trend has justified that collective bargaining is not only a method for securing a big share of the cake but a method for establishing industrial democracy and industrial peace.

This change in trend became apparent in the first

comprehensive agreement signed in January 1956. The management wanted to modernise the method of productive system. The modernisation and expansion programme involving a capital expenditure of about Rs. 1.10 crore was ready. But this modernisation scheme would not have been smooth sailing without cooperation of steelmen and the TWU because there would have been many cases of manpower adjustment. The management by entering into an agreement with the TWU had shown its progressive and cooperative nature with many gains secured thereafter. It was in this light this comprehensive agreement is a corner stone in the history of growth of collective bargaining and smooth industrial relations.

The agreement of 1956 has many new features to its credit. The management and the union gave assurances to each other granting mutual security. The company assured the TWU as the sole bargaining agent and agreed in principle to union membership security system by collection of union subscriptions through pay roll, i.e. check-off system. The management agreed to provide all reasonable facilities to the office bearers of the union and to elected group representatives for attending meetings and conferences and facilities to union representatives of all the joint committees to attend meetings. In exchange to it the union agreed to recognise the right of the company to take disciplinary action, recognised functions, powers and authorities of the company regarding production, its methods, equipments, products, etc. The union had also recognised the company's right to hire, transfer, promote, number of man required for a particular job, etc. Such mutual assurances by one to other were special features, rarely heard of these agreements.

Another remarkable feature of this agreement was the introduction of "Closer Association of Employees with Management." There had not been such an agreement in India introducing a systematic system of labour-management cooperation in an industrial establishment.

Another feature of this agreement was incorporation of "productivity" clause. Probably first time the union had agreed to cooperate in securing improvement in labour productivity. The parties had also agreed to the established standard force of labour. In exchange to it the company assured "no retrenchment of existing employees" and "guaranteed present earnings to employees."

Appointment of a Joint Committee, with equal number of representatives for job evolution and wage structure, was another height of this agreement. The revision of wages and gratuity for the first time was again based upon mutually finalised job evaluation.

Negotiation. on commercial policy, both for supervisory or non-supervisory posts, and formulation of promotion procedure and clarified the managerial position. Agreement on grievance procedure, Works Committee and maintenance of discipline were not less important. Till then maintenance of discipline had been solely a responsibility of the management. For the first time the union had agreed to share responsibility of maintenance of discipline in the company.

It demands to pause for some time to think over the changing rend in the nature of collective bargaining. In the Marketing Theory of Collective Bargaining the Union's interest rests with the fixation of price of labour and that at a higher point, whatever the difficulties of the management may be. There is a common slogan "मेरी माँगें पूरी हो, चाहे जो मजबूरी हो".

It is the management headache to manage the financial burden of demands. In this agreement, the union readily agreed to share one responsibility of maintenance of discipline. Sharing managerial responsibility, agreed upon through collective bargaining, is definitely a turning point in the nature of collective bargaining from Marketing Theory to Managerial Theory. It does not need to emphasise the importance of industrial discipline in increasing productivity. If the union agrees to work hand in hand for increasing production, well it is a wise step to share jointly the management's responsibility of maintenance of discipline. It was really a matter of appreciation for both sides in generating a constructive cooperative attitude for the good of both.

This was the first agreement signed for a period of three years. The beginning of three years agreement practice and labour-management cooperation movement opened a new chapter in the history of collective bargaining. A mutual assurance to each other and recognition of their rights added more importance to this comprehensive agreement. The bi-partite committee initiated in 1956 became the basis for supplementary agreement drawing mutually a detailed network of Join Councils for increasing the degree, area and nature of cooperation. In the history of industrial relations one may not find such an example where a trend has moved from conflict to cooperation and from collective bargaining to labour-management cooperation. The mutually agreed framework of Joint Council, in absence of any law in the country, was really highest achievement of collective bargaining. The credit goes to progressive TISCO management, the steelmen and the TWU for such a new experiment in India. For evolving a detail scheme of 'Closer association of employees with management' a fresh agreement was signed in September 1956 supplementing the agreement of February 1956. This supplementary agreement voluntarily prepared a network of structure for association of employees with management. This laid down the formal basis for development of mutual cooperation in an effort to minimise frictions whatever may be the result. This agreement was welcomed as a new step in labour-management cooperation. The then Union Labour Minister, Khandu Bhai Desai, had observed of this achievement as:

> "... How the relationship between the Company and the Union was evolved at a point where the parties can come together and discuss questions like greater association of workers with management, a unique experiment in Indian industry."

This agreement was a turning point in the relationship between the management and the TISCO steelmen which has since then become an example for others.

The changing out look and policy of the union was manned by the moderate labour leaders. The union accepted its new role of sharing responsibilities for the good of all. Addressing the workers in 1956 the President of Tata Worker's Union, Michael John, welcomed the agreement of 1956 calling it as a landmark in the history of labour-management cooperation. He called upon the workers and the union that:

> "Trade Union should combine its protective functions with the representative functions in a harmonious blending of labour interest. The agreement is a pointed to the social changes which are taking place in India. It gives

concrete shape to the concept of workers' participation in the management of industries.

The agreement would provide opportunity to the workers to acquire knowledge and skill so essential for managing industries and when India achieved her goal of a socialist pattern of society, they would be well prepared to play a full and effective part in running the country's industries.

Within a couple of years through the process of conciliation a fresh agreement was signed in February 1958 which contained rationalisation of wage structure, revision of wages from 8% to 33%, Consolidation of D.A., food allowance and emergency bonus into slab system and revision of incentive bonus plan. The conciliation machinery of the government of Bihar was always been helpful in providing conciliation for bringing the gap between the two sides. This tri-partite agreement helped in promptly settling many economic issues.

Jerk to Peaceful Industrial Relations

The industrial relations scene is influenced by internal and external environments. The internal environment centres around the attitude and conduct of various groups within the industrial framework. The external environment is influenced by economic, social and political factors. Both internal and external environments influence each other. Therefore, efforts are made to establish and maintain proper industrial environment suitable for industrial peace.

In the second half of 1950, Jamshedpur industrial belt became politically hot with the arrival of Marxists and their revolutionary philosophy which presented rosy picture before the workers. Starting from the coal belt, the communists began to concentrate at Jamshedpur for establishing their hold. Tata Workers' Union was the only union acting as the single spokesman of the steelmen. The T.W.U. had definitely established itself with moderate philosophy but there was absence of close and intimae contact between the leaders and the workers. The absence of close contact between the union officers and the workers provided opportunity and scope for the communist leaders to establish friendship with the workers. This shortcoming of the T.W.U. was utilised by the revolutionary leaders, who in no time established themselves which a flag and a organisation, Jamshedpur Mazdoor Union. The Jamshedpur was rocked by unexpected and unprecedented strong strike combined with violence. The rosy picture drawn by Jamshedpur Mazdoor Union had enough attraction to gain support of a large number of steelmen. It demanded 25% wage increase, revision of P.F., weekly-off day, improvement in working conditions, reinstatement of victimised workers and recognition of Jamshedpur Mazdoor Union.

The strike was unprecedented in history. No one had thought of such a big strike throwing the whole TISCO on the verge of crisis and explosion. Big national labour leaders arrived at Jamshedpur. The Chairman and Directors of the company move towards Jamshedpur. A large number of officers and police were called for maintenance of law and order. The strike became a matter of prestige for both sides. It had challenged to long proclaimed progressive industrial relations policy of the management. The mounting unrest, spread of militant philosophy and the strike of 1958 demanded a fresh approach to the whole policy. That also proved that the top management had become over sure of peace of lasting nature so much that it less cared to be vigilant about under current amongst workers. The recognised union had also become uncared about the real feelings of new generation. They were undermining the communists and their increasing influence. The curtain on their eyes had covered the happenings of the other side allowing it strengthen them. The strikers had shown the strength sufficient to force the management to reconsidered the whole industrial relations policy. Though, the strike failed but it brought many lessons for both sides to review and restructure the whole industrial relations system for better and peaceful relationship. The strike of 1958 gave a jerk to the old industrial relations system which awakened the recognised union and the TISCO management. TWU must read the feelings of non-members in order to act as a real representatives organisation. The management also learnt that it should not hear only the words of recognised union. The unrecognised union should be given due place in the modern system of industrial relations.

In presenting the key-note address by the Managing Director, R.S. Pande, had drawn attention towards changing pattern of industrial relations and challenge of time facing the parties. The role of unrecognised union had been underlined for future industrial relations policy. He did not hesitate in accepting the fact that:

> "Other trade unions also have their role to play, but it should be similar to that of the democratic Opposition which can criticise the policies and programmes of the ruling party if it differs with them, but which cannot claim the right to participate in the meetings of the cabinet."

For a better and stable industrial relations the unrecognised union should not be completely ignored. It represents a section of workers which has own outlook, wishes and aspirations. The Indian industrial relations system and industrial relations law should take lessons from U.S.A. and another countries where unrecognised union has been given secondary status and the society expects a desirable role from it. Could Indian system of industrial relations adopt such practice for a better and Stable system? It not, now and then there may be industrial unrest expressing the dissatisfaction of the members of unrecognised union and the disapproval of the whole industrial relations system. The management has recognised the need of frequent communication at shop-floor level. It was a fact accepted by J.R.D. Tata, the then Chairman of TISCO, in following lines:

> "Thirty years of labour peace at Jamshedpur had perhaps dimmed to some extent the realisation that sound labour relations and enduring cooperation need unremitting vigilance and effort, particularly on the shop floor, as well as the maintenance and constant use of good channels of communication between management, supervisory staff and labour."

The lessons of May 1958 strikes acted as a guideline in remodeling the whole industrial relations system. The management went ahead with the policy of closer association of employees with management in order to re-establish industrial peace and industrial harmony. The new policy has brought desirable result in next fifteen years.

Wage Board

The establishment of Wage Board at industrial level has been a recent trend in India. In the Iron and Steel industry and Central wage Board was established in January 1962 for introduction of uniform wage structure in the whole industry leaving sufficient scope for plantwise adjustment. In persuance of the award of July 1965, a fresh conciliated settlement was arrived at in 1965 which brought some more reliefs to the steelmen. The upward revision of basic wages and D.A., five days' additional casual leave with pay, a paid holiday on 2nd October each year, computation of ½ month pay for purpose of gratuity, free education upto middle stage and improvement in quarter and bustees were covered under the agreement.

Another agreement, following recommendations of October 1970 of the Joint Wage Negotiating Committee for steel industry, was arrived at in November 1970 which further revised wages upward with a minimum benefit of Rs. 67, transport subsidy, additional gratuity, revision of D.A., acting allowance and an *adhoc* payment. The agreement was for a period of four years. The practice of Wage Board and Joint Wage Negotiating Committee has made wage issues a matter of industry wise negotiation. This has diverted the strain from plant to industry. It is a good trend of collective bargaining in establishing uniformity of service conditions, standardising labour cost and controlling plants' competitive power.

In accordance with the decision of the Joint Negotiating Committee of July 30, 1975 and the two charters of demands submitted by the TWU in August 1975, a prolong negotiation took place between the management and the TWU in August 1975. The Deputy Labour Commissioner of the Government of Bihar, through his conciliation efforts and advices, made it possible to arrive at an agreement on August 20, 1975 between the TISCO and the TWU. It is again a comprehensive agreement for a period of four years. This agreement covers economic issues like rationalisation and revision of wage structure, revision of D.A., linking of variable D.A. to the cost of living index, pay in promotion, incentive bonus. Housing and house rent allowance, leave travel concession, special retiring gratuity, transport, worksmen compensation benefit and protection of existing benefits. The non-economic issues of the agreement were supply of essential commodities, community development and bustee improvement, education facilities, abolition of contract labour, technological improvement, standardisation committee, modernisation and labour productivity and industrial peace. Thus, this agreement had raised the minimum wage from Rs. 200 to Rs. 300. The linking of variable D.A. to the cost of living index was a new feature. Leave travel concession, supply of essential commodities, advance for purchase of scooter, motor-cycle, special retiring gratuity for those retired between 1974 and 1975 were new economic gains. Abolition of contract labour was a new feature of this agreement. Community development and bustee improvement were programmes of community development, originally initiated in 1958 were being further expanded. Thus, the necessity of modernisation, technological improvement, increased labour productivity and continuation of standarisation committee were a few important features of the agreement. It showed that the TWU was conscious of its constructive role in the progress of the company. This is really an appreciable stand of the TWU.

Silver Jubilee Celebration of Industrial Peace

For better man management for peace, productivity and progress and the maintenance of healthy industrial relations the Personnel Department was established in 1947. J.R.D. Tata, the then Chairman, had initiated the establishment of the Personnel Department. This department also looks after the industrial relations. The industrial relations policy is based on the humanitarian approach giving proper care towards welfare of its employees. Its basic industrial relations philosophy has been framed under the guidance of the humanitarian approach of the founder, Jamsetji Tata, who had clearly stated that—

> "We do not claim to be more unselfish, more generous or more philanthropic than other people. But we think we started on sound and straight-forward business principles, considering the interests of the shareholders our own, and the health and welfare of the employees the sure foundation of our prosperity."

The humanitarian approach of Jamsetji was followed by Dorabji Tata, who gave much attention in dealing with labour.

The Tata's human approach was not less systematic and scientific than its technical approach. The call of social scientists like Sidney and Beatrice Webb to suggest for proper industrial relations was a matter of appreciation. It was on that line the industrial relations policy has been framed and modified in order to suit with the changing requirements. The TISCO celebrated Silver Jubilee of the Personnel Division in 1973 claiming to have a long history of industrial peace. The celebration was appreciated by various corners of the society. On that occasion then Chairman, J.R.D. Tata had observed:

> "To create good working conditions, to pay the best wages in the industry, to promote welfare and provide decent housing, is not enough. The ultimate aim of good personnel and industrial relations programme should be to find a solution to the problem of better relations between the management and labour, or between labour and capital, which will be potentially the greatest reward we can have in the long-run. Such a happy relation can be obtained only by creating a sense of confidence on the part of the ranks of the labour that (a) they have a stake in the industry, and (b) they are something more than mere cogs in the machines or mere tools of Management and that their dreams, their feelings and their human problems, are part of the Company's problems and Management's problems—a feeling that they have some voice, if not in policy, in some processes of Management."

Recognition of the interests of the rank and file in the management has become a cornerstone of the Tata's Policy. This human approach has helped in yielding the desired goal. The policy of industrial relations was also praised by Michael John, the then President of Tata Workers' Union following lines:

> "Tatas' have the unique privilege of enjoying the reputation of being the pioneers, not only in the Steel Industry but also in other connected fields, a significant one being in the sphere of industrial relations and personnel management, in which they have taken great strides and have thus stolen a march over their

contemporaries both in the private and public sectors in the country thereby setting examples worthy of emulation."

The industrial relations during the past period had different trends, pleasant and unpleasant, ups and downs progresses and reverses. Every year of that period had given something new experience for remodeling their way of functioning for better, healthy sand satisfactory relationship. In spite of the differences coming on the surface, the two parties had gradually learnt to adjust with each other by compromising their divergent interests. The workers were no longer being treated as a cog in the big industrial complex for production rather they were being considered as partners in their joint venture for better production, productivity and greater welfare of all concerned. Reviewing the whole trend of industrial relations in TISCO and the existing situation by 1973, the then Managing Director, R.S. Pande, in his key-note Presidential address on the occasion of Silver Jubilee Seminar on 'Man-Management and Peace, Productivity and Progress' held in March 1973 at Jamshedpur had remarked that—

> "As an active partner, unlike a sleeping partner, the worker has positive contributions to make and he can legitimately claim a share in the gains of collective endeavour, along with the two other partners, namely, shareholders who have invested their money and, what is generally forgotten, the industry itself which must have its share for it very survival and sustenance. There have been conflicting views on the exact share of each partner, and discussion on them should always be rewarding for industrial managers, particularly those in the personnel field. This status of the worker as a partner entails his closer association or his active involvement with the organisation of which he is an integral part, beginning with the shop floor and going upto the top level, for the last 15 years, we in Tata Steel have been working with a three-tier scheme of such closer employee association with management and it has brought encouraging results."

The industrial relations system in TISCO has been stabilized due to fair role of both the parties. The world accepted practice of collective bargaining and association of employees with the management are the two pillars of the industrial relations structure. Carefully, the scope of the two practices have been drawn in order to avoid overlapping. The union has been discharging the responsibility carefully both as a fighting institution and cooperative institution. As a fighting institution it has been preserving and securing better terms and conditions of employment and has a cooperative institution it has been extending fall cooperation in increasing production and productivity, modernisation of plant, improvement of technology and method of production and reducing cost of production. The discharge of double role to the best of its capacity proves the unions progressive policy, procedures, methods and ability of its leaders. The thirty years period of undisturbed industrial relations, except strike of 1958, is the best proof of the healthy and harmonious industrial relations system of TISCO.

Strengthening of Collective Bargaining Practice

The desire for long-term industrial peace initiated the adoption of comprehensive and long-term agreements. Both the parties have learnt that *ad-hoc* agreements do not serve the purpose of establishing healthy industrial relations. That also needs frequent meetings, frequent strife and strain, wastage of time and energy and still leave scope for conflict. Well there can be conflict at any time even in face of comprehensive and long-term agreements but the chances are rare. With all efforts to sit in a cool atmosphere to discuss the problems considering all pros and corns a beginning was made in this direction in 1956. A more comprehensive agreement was signed on November 10, 1970 which covered many issues including the wage structure, production incentive bonus, house rent allowance, production and productivity, etc. It is a matter of satisfaction that wage structure, the more sensitive cause of the industrial conflict, is mutually agreed upon. Agreement of 1958 was being further expanded covering issues like the necessity of modernisation, technological improvement, increased labour productivity and continuation of standardisation committee were a few important features of the agreement. It has shown that the TWU was conscious of its constructive role in the progress of company. This is really an appreciable stand of the TWU.

On the same pattern comprehensive agreements were arrived at in 1979 and 1983. Both these agreements cover broad terms with increased provisions and a few additions. There had been upward revision of pay scales, D.A., and other incentives, house rent allowance, leave travel concessions, gratuity and higher compensation. Security of job to the dependents of deceased employees and preference to dependence in job of retiring employees had been new achievements.

The practice of collective bargaining is advancing towards maturity. The practice of *ad-hoc* agreements has been replaced by comprehensive agreement. The agreements are signed for a term of four years. Discussions on bargaining table are held in cool atmosphere. Facts are considered purely by the bargaining representatives which helps in development of mutual understanding, mutual adjustment of ideas and interests and mutual discussions. The present industrial peace is the fruit of the practice of collective bargaining.

TISCO: A New Industrial Relations Framework

The task of creating a new industrial relations framework is difficult, and of course full of imponderables. Some building blocks of a new framework could, however, be identified. These are as follows:

1. The legislative process of repeals, amendments and new enactment need to be pushed ahead further. Fewer good laws and more effective enforcement and compliance must be in place, in the first place.
2. New experiments in different states like Andhra Pradesh, Kerala, West Bengal, Rajasthan are taking place. Apparently, they are departing from the historical uniform national pattern. The coalition era, with a weak centre, is facilitating the deviations. As experiences would arise.
3. Voices to encourage the "gainers" of the market era to share more with the "losers" is being heard, and this could gather momentum in India and elsewhere, too. It will have enormous moderating influence on the climate of industrial relations.

4. An extended social security for all workers, in a phased manner, is a serious agenda. All investment in this regard would enrich the industrial relations interactions, apart from meeting the long felt need in the country.
5. Work first, and decent work later is a dangerous palliative. This needs to be resisted strongly. Yet the prolonged presence of the informal sector is a strong possibility. Therefore, its productivity with support from—
   (a) better technology,
   (b) improved skills,
   (c) easy access to capital, and
   (d) market linkage must improve for the benefit of good employer-employee relations.
6. Progress on free cross-boarder economic migration of natural persons would bring balance in the distribution of human factor endowment (Nayyar, 2003). Labour shortage economies would mainly gain, while the labour surplus transitional economies would get needed relief. Connivance of the state in labour shortage mature economies, illegal migration for cheap labour, enclave settlements for immigrant guest workers, and liberal quota for professional workers are evidences of market forces asserting over political and social barriers (see *The Economic Times*, 2003). A relative balance in labour supply and demand within and between economies will be beneficial to all. Successful social engineering at a global scale is the need of the hour. The rounds of the World Trade Organisation (WTO) negotiations could cover these issues.
7. Accelerated growth is desperately needed. A labour-intensive but efficiency promoting technology would help. Both global and national market place needs regulatory institutions led by competent and Committed professionals. A national climate for receptivity to change the vested interest-led present set-upto its socially acceptable replacement is

building-up. Deliberations of the Second National Commission on labour and subsequent national debate have helped. A final package with

(a) a revised arrangement for the organised sector,
(b) a strong beginning for strengthening the informal sector,
(c) the necessary legislative reforms and
(d) a social security and welfare package of credible and sustainable kind, must soon emerge.

8. A rigid national uniformity is now behind us. Moderated diversity with strong centrality of linkages should be encouraged Trade Unions and civic society institutions need concerted action with benign assistance from forward looking employers and the remaining state power (Shyam Sunder, 2003). In the new market place, risks of common injury should unite all interest groups. Stakes are high in creatively holding together and looking ahead with hope. There is scope as well as space to promote the interest of all with an optimum blend of strategy and agenda to be tapped. Some uneasy trade-off inevitably is a part of a workable next package.

Some light bearing, if not immediately fruit bearing, exercise among man-management professionals, policy-makers, and social partners should help. The growing intellectual and political unease on the "winner take all" situation should help somewhat. From "champions of the impossible rather than the slaves of the possible that evolution draws its creative force", said Barbara Wooton (quoted in *Standing*, 2002). This should serve as the basis for cautious optimism. The current crisis has opened up "space for significant strategic choices by the actors." With known constraints, the key actors need wider support in regaining their control on the functioning of the labour market and industrial relations system. Re-visiting the theoretical and conceptual parts,. have to wait until the transitional churning settles down. In the meantime, the painful reality of obsolescence of both the theories and practice would, in all likelihood, continue.

The globalisation syndrome places trade unions in a tight

spot. To cope with the situation they have to redefine their structures and role. It is being advocated that there may develop a new style of global social movement unionism (Lambert, 1999). In this regard, it is also argued that in order to retain bargaining power, unions have no choice but to "put consumers' interests first, company's interest second and their members' interest third", Venkata Ratnam (2003, p. 246). They have to engage themselves in internal dialogue and elaborating worker-oriented meanings of concepts such as "flexibility, security and opportunity" that are being shown to workers as methods of promoting the trickle down (Hyman, 1999). Unions also need to understand the changed realities for employers. The decline in unionism in USA is steep due to their continued hostility towards employers in the new economy (Mamkoottam, 2003, p. 145). In India since unions are oligarchic, hierarchical and highly politicized, adjustment to their new role is going to be a complex process. To be effective in the new economy, they have to learn to work more as network organisation to cope with the new challenges, making use of new modes of information and communication. In fact, considerable thought process is needed in terms of viable suggestions to the three social partners to adapt themselves to the new realities. Building an enlightened society is to remain supplementary to any model of economic working. This essentially requires reconciling the goals of adapting to the changing global business environment and salvaging unionism as a countervailing force.

INDUSTRIAL RELATIONS AND HUMAN RESOURCE MANAGEMENT

The continuing right sizing efforts of the Company resulted in a reduction in the men on rolls from 46,234 at the end of the previous year to 43,248 as on 31st March, 2003. During the year, 2,031 employees separated under the employees' separation scheme. A new bonus agreement was signed covering the Company's unionized employees, which ascribes a higher weight to financial performance. Industrial relations remained cordial during the year. The Management acknowledges the contribution of all employees in achieving the record performance.

Given the Company's ambitious growth plans in India and overseas, development of human resources assumes an even more important dimension. To prepare the Company's human resources for future responsibilities in terms of professional skills as well as business skills, several initiatives have been undertaken, such as rotation policy, leadership development programme, sponsored diploma programme and e-learning. Since a decade, the employee strength has been reduced from about 78,000 to around 38,000 presently through separation schemes and normal retirement. The Company is investing in the modernisation of the plant and training of manpower for upgrading their skills.

Industrial relations remained normal at all locations. The men on roll in the Company as on 31st March, 2006 were 38,182 as compared to 39,648 as on 31st March, 2005. The development of human resources is a key strategic challenge in order to prepare people for future responsibilities in terms of professional skills as well as business skills. Company is investing in the modernisation of the plant and training of manpower for upgrading their skills. Further, it is planned to redeploy the surplus manpower to various Greenfield projects being undertaken.

Industrial relations remained normal at all locations. The men on roll in the Company as on 31st March, 2007 were 37,205 as compared to 38,182 as on 31st March, 2006. The development of human resources is a key strategic challenge in order to prepare people for future responsibilities in terms of professional skills as well as business skills. The Company is investing in the modernisation of the plant and training of manpower for upgrading their skills. Further, it is planned to redeploy the surplus manpower to various green field projects being undertaken.

Tata Steel Group recognises people as the primary source of its competitiveness, and continues to focus on people development by leveraging technology and developing a continuously learning human resource base to unleash their potential and fulfil their aspirations. The company is on a growth path along with the domestic steel and mining industry and rise in competition. The human resources team has been continually focusing on the means to achieve the company's goals of meeting such growth targets through external recruitment and right skilling and by improving the capabilities of existing people through people development initiatives. With the expansion plans of Tata Steel at Jamshedpur by another 2.9 mtpa by 2012, there was an increased need of highly skilled and qualified workforce to support construction and quick ramp up of the new technology plants. One of the key challenges, therefore, was to build the capability of its existing workforce to meet the higher level skill requirements. Tata Steel geared upto meet the challenge of growth by recruiting technically qualified persons and maximising utilisation of the existing employees through instituting programs to right skill them and improve the overall skill mix of employees. A focused training and development approach was adopted to achieve this task.

As a result of such focused approach, there has been a significant increase in the percentage of skilled employees and also a simultaneous increase in the workforce. The employees' strength in Indian operations increased to 34,912 as on 31st March, 2011 as against 34,440 as on 31st March, 2010.

Major highlights of the people development process in Tata Steel India during the financial year under review were:

- 70:20:10 framework for Learning and Development was expanded to a much larger number of officers. This approach has greater focus on on-the-job and coaching and mentoring components of leaning.
- In an effort towards building a culture of coaching and mentoring, over 600 officers were trained in several batches of workshops through internal and external faculty.
- Focus on wider coverage for class room training (Percentage of unique officers trained increased from 41% in FY 10 to 70% in FY 11) which included some unique offerings of programs for different customer segments like laterals, lady officers, etc.
- Train maximum possible people on TQM.
- Over and above the normal training for employees, close to about 1000 persons recruited for the 2.9 mtpa expansion have been provided induction training.
- On skill development front, focus has shifted towards more hands on training. Many of the programs were restructured keeping in view the needs of tomorrow.

- Introduction of "Value Education" for the young recruits. To create fun at work environment functions like Technical Exhibition for all cadre trainees, "Parichay" for fresh MTTs, "Varshikotsav" for fresh TAs and "FROLICA" to celebrate mentors day have been organised.

Two initiatives were undertaken principally to improve the HR practices of the company:

- *Employee Connect Program (ECP)*: An Initiative to build employee connect, understand concerns and follow-up action plans. Employees from across levels and Business areas have been met individually on a monthly basis to gauge engagement levels and to understand concerns.
- *Job Rotation and Career Planning (JRCP)*: An Initiative to provide career opportunities for officers through planned movement across functions and also to build functional expertise in the organisation. In FY 2010-11 19% of all Lateral movements were through JRCP and this process is being further strengthened in FY 2011-12.

Tata Steel India reached the milestone of 82 years of industrial harmony and peace. During the financial year 2010-11 industrial relations remained normal at all locations. Market-based new wage series (lower than the existing wage series but higher than the market median) was introduced after arriving at a settlement with the Union during FY 2010-11. All the new recruitments for the expansion units have been done in the new series of wages.

Recruitment

A good recruitment methodology demands that there is continual emphasis on developing and improving this area. To ensure a continued availability of a technically competent bench strength of Engineers and Business Managers for the future, Tata Steel's Management Trainee programme has recruited a large number of trainees from different premier Institutes across India.

As part of an induction process, this group will undergo a one year development programme before being ready to take independent responsibility in different businesses. The focus this year has been to increase the intake of Engineers and Business Managers through the Pre-Placement Offer (PPO) route from the campuses to cater to the next financial year.

The Corus graduate and apprentice recruitment programmes have also been enhanced in the last year and remain a key focus area. In the Netherlands, the Corus brand is rated as a top employer in manufacturing and in the top five amongst all companies in any segment. In the UK, the company is considered among the top 100 graduate recruiters.

Post-recruitment, there is a continued effort at staying in touch with employees to ensure that there is the right culture to engage them in performance improvement. Employee surveys will be continued on a consistent basis through the coming year.

LEVERAGING THE HUMAN CAPITAL

The Tata Steel Group's Vision, having been co-created by its people, speaks of creating value for all its stakeholders. It is a strong belief that this creation of value depends on the professional and personal well-being of its people. In keeping with the demands of the future, it is a strategic priority at the Tata Steel Group to be an employer of choice in every country in which the Group operates. And this requires focussed efforts to recruit, train and retain skills on an ongoing basis.

Building Entrepreneurs

Functioning as a wholly-owned subsidiary of Corus, the aim of UK Steel Enterprise (UKSE) is to improve the economies of those areas of the UK most affected by changes in the steel industry. It offers business information and planning advice, as well as loans and investment for start-ups and expanding businesses. To counter the mothballing of the steelworks at Teesside, UKSE offered a combination of grants and loans for various start-ups.

Building Beyond Borders

This TSTH programme reaches out to the underprivileged elderly and to less fortunate children and youth in the area of education.

Grow Smart with Tata Steel

This project is aimed at encouraging learning and self-development in students from remote areas of India. It also focuses on spreading knowledge through vocational training for adults.

Employee Volunteerism

One of the primary focus areas of Tata Steel, India is to involve employees and encourage them to volunteer their services for Community Development Programmes. A total of 136 employees rendered their voluntary services in 2010 in various projects.

In keeping with its stated policy, education is an area of special emphasis and Tata Steel India has made available several scholarships and programmes to encourage quality education. Among these are the Jyoti Fellowship for financial assistance; the Sakshar Samaj Programme for functional literacy in adults; the Moodie Endowment for financial assistance to students pursuing professional courses; Coaching Programmes; Early Child Education (ECE) Centres and Camp Centres to accelerate education.

Training and Development

Employee Training and Development received a major thrust with larger numbers of employees making use of e-learning facilities available on the Company's Intranet which was facilitated by Computer Literacy training imparted to hundreds of employees in the recent past. Apart from several proprietary e-learning courses, employees are being encouraged to learn on their own using Computer Based Training packages and Multimedia training materials. Safety training received special attention based on the DuPont guidelines. These skill and safety training programmes will continue during the next year covering greater numbers. With a view to further improve the process of identification of skill gaps, there is a plan in place to introduce a technical competency assessment system for all employees in the Company. Simultaneously, it is also proposed to augment the training resources including faculty support which would facilitate upgradation of technical capability of employees.

With the continuing expansion of capacities at the existing

units as well as installation of capacities via green field projects, one of the key challenges is to upgrade the skills and improve the mix of workers and supervisors. The Company continued its endeavours for up-skilling employees through process-based, on-the-job training and diploma courses through premium engineering institutes.

In order to bring in greater focus in Training and Development of Executives the training process has been re-engineered towards Directed Learning in order to align the learning initiatives with the twin strategic imperatives of strengthening the leadership pipeline coupled with emerging needs of growth projects across geographies.

Inclusive Growth

Believing that a happy workforce is a productive workforce, the Tata Steel Group has always extended its support to the extended community in which their workforce lives and operates. Through various programmes that include making available jobs to extended communities, to vocational training that generates employment, Tata Steel has extended its family to beyond its immediate employees. The well-being of employees also extends to nurturing and fostering extra curricular skills that allow a more enriched life. Towards this end, Tata Steel has put into practice many events and programmes that involve the families of employees. Sports days, social events, contests for children, education opportunities, celebrating festivals together are some of the initiatives that have become a way of life at Tata Steel. Such initiatives have proven to create not only an enduring loyalty amongst employees, but also enabled them to have a more fulfiled life.

HEALTH AND SAFETY

Occupational Health

A joint committee comprising of representatives of Union and Management on the basis of occupational health surveillance, recommends to the Management appropriate measures to be taken to ensure a healthy work force. Occupational health department in Tata Steel with all its facilities caters to health checkups of employees. In addition, Public Health Engineering

Department ensures hygiene through regular cleaning of drains, toilets, roads and malaria control measures. An indicator of improvement in environmental standards is the reduction in ocular foreign bodies in workers in last five years by 40%. Following activities are performed under occupation health:

- Check-up for hypertension, diabetes, vision defect, chronic bronchitis, eosinophllia, hearing defects, Pneumoconiosis, Heart diseases.
- Regular spray for vector control in the colonies.
- Health education on AIDS, Child and Mother Care, Drug Addictions and Water Born Diseases carried out.
- Immunization for Hepatitis-B.

During the reporting period Rs. 10.4 million were spent on occupational health activities.

Ergonomic Initiatives

Ergonomics issues are taken up proactively at the project stage. Employees take part in identifying these issues through JDC's, Suggestion scheme, Dialogues and Hot mail scheme. It has been shown in Tables 4.1 and 4.2 respectively.

Every unit of the organization prepares an Annual Safety, Health and Environment Plan integrated with the Annual Operating Plan (AOP). Eight Zonal Committees headed by a Divisional Head monitor the entire Plant Safety. A SHE (Safety Health and Environment) Committee consisting of representatives from Unionised employees and Management representative caters to all aspects of safety, health and environment. Tata Steel appoints "Worker Safety and Environment Inspector" (WSEI) from the unionised cadre in all units selected by the JDCs. All WSEI are trained. Personnel Executives counsel employees to follow safe working practices (4 hours/week). In the reporting year contractor employees were also trained for one full day on safety, health and environment. A General Safety Committee carries out safety surveillance, without on a weekly basis, randomly.

The highlights of the achievements in safety front during the year are presented Table 4.3.

TABLE 10.1

Occupational Health Activities (At Steel Works)

	2000-2001	1999-2000
Health Check Ups		
Department covered	16	8
Employees examined	4584	3693
Other statutory examination	658	598
Health Education		•
Sessions	180	165
Participants	3660	3265
Training for Trainers on Occupational Health – 25 participants from 11 departments.		
Water Quality Analysis for Canteens.		
Health check-up of 1057 contractor employees done for the first time.		

Source: Annual Report (2000-01) TISCO.

TABLE 10.2

Curative and Prevention Services

	2000-2001	1999-2000
Referral to TMH (34% reduction) Numbers	396	599
Blood Grouping (181% increase) Numbers	857	473

Source: Annual Report (2000-01) TISCO.

TABLE 10.3

Achievements

Items	Record Achievement 2000-2001	Previous Best	Year
Total No. of Reportable Accident (Works)	55	60	1999-2000
Lowest No. of Accident in a month (Works)	2 (April'2K) 4 (July '2K)	3 (April'2K) 6 (July '2K)	1999-2000 1998-1999
No. of Man-Days trained in Safety & APS (Works)	7265	6922	1999-2000
Items	**Year 2000-2001**	**Year 1999-2000**	**% Reduction**
Reportable Accidents for employees (Fatal)	55(4)	60 (6)	8
Non Reportable Accidents for employees	48	87	45
Total Accidents(Employees)	103	147	30
Reportable accidents for Contractors (Fatal)	25 (6)	23 (4)	-
Man-days Lost due to employees accident	3979	4927	19
Man-days Lost/Employee/Year	0.207	0.244	15

Source: Annual Report (2000-01), TISCO.

In line with our Corporate Vision to improve the safety and quality of life of employees, your Company has initiated a safety excellence journey under the guidance of DuPont Safety Resources, world-class leader in safety. DuPont has helped to improve the safety performance of many industries across the globe. The safety programme which began at the Steel Works has been rolled across all locations including mines. These initiatives have shown perceptible change in the behavior of employees at and outside the place of work. Gains achieved are irreversible. The Company aspires to become world-class in safety.

As the Tata Steel Group strives to reach greater heights, the Company is focusing on continual improvement in the areas of health and safety across its operations.

Tata Steel is committed to ensuring zero harm to its employees, contractors and the communities in which it operates. This is integral to the Company's business process and is laid down in the Company's health and safety policies, standards and working procedures. Health and safety is a key performance indicator and one of the prime drivers of the Company's corporate vision. One of the key goals of the Group is to achieve a Lost Time Injury Frequency (LTIF) rate target of 0.4, with zero fatalities by 2012. Each of the Group's four regional sectors has a well-established and comprehensive health and safety policy with supporting principles, standards and procedures. In January 2011, a health and safety policy was implemented across the Tata Steel Group with clear objectives for process safety, occupational safety and health. As part of the policy, health and safety is reviewed at all Board meetings of the Company. A Health, Safety and Environment Committee, incorporating senior executives and non-executives from the Board has also been established to carry out more detailed reviews.

In Thailand and China, a programme called Safety Excellence Journey was rolled out during the year at the Group's wire mills, as well as some of Tata Steel's associated companies. NatSteel embarked on a two-year DuPont-guided safety excellence journey in 2009. Measures taken to date include the continuous active involvement of senior management, safety training, establishment of a safety council and formation of risk containment groups to identify and contain high-risk activities.

The Tata Steel Group is committed to ensuring the health and safety of its employees, its plants and its surrounding communities at all its operation sites. The Group constantly endeavours to provide safe and hygienic working conditions for its employees as well as its contract workers. It takes an integrated and systematic approach to managing health and safety, which is encompassed in the Tata Steel Safety Programme and the Corus Health and Safety Management System with a successful delivery reliant on employee engagement and felt leadership. Both the programmes have been developed with the support and expertise of DuPont consultants. Since 2005, with the help of the DuPont Safety Resources organisation, a quantum jump has been achieved in the safety culture of the organisation through the implementation of the 'behavioural safety model'. Potentially fatal situations have been rectified with a focussed 'Fatality Risk Control Programme' (FRCP). Pursuing this initiative will help the Company realise its goal of becoming a fatality free organisation in the near future. For the sustainability of its operations, the "Process Safety and Risk Management" (PSRM) programme has been started for the high hazard operations and processes, in order to ensure freedom from a high consequence, low frequency process incidents. PSRM will be implemented in all facilities by Financial Year (FY-12) 2012.

Tata Steel is also extending support to the community for improving their safety standards with the help of the Safety Awareness For Everyone (SAFE) organisation. School children are being given special training on road and behaviour safety. A safety curriculum has been introduced in the schools in Jamshedpur to generate an awakening within the community. With these initiatives, the Company has been able to reduce the Lost Time Injury Frequency Rate (LTIFR), an accepted measure of safety performance worldwide, to 0.80 for FY 2009 from 1.70 in FY 2008 and is confident of achieving its target of 0.40 LTIFR by 2012.

Health and Safety continues to be one of the prime drivers of the Corporate Vision of your Company. The Tata Steel Group lays significant emphasis on sustainable Health and Safety performance as it has a direct impact on performance. The Company is continuing its 'Safety Excellence Journey' with a philosophy that 'Safety is a Line Management function and all injuries can be prevented'. Health and Safety is reviewed at all Board meetings of Tata Steel with a Health, Safety and Environment Committee established to carry out more detailed reviews. In TSE an integrated and systemic Health and Safety Management System was introduced in 2008 with a governance process for improvement actions at executive level and regular safety tours by the Board and executive members. This system is being evaluated for Group-wide application.

Every initiative at Tata Steel is governed not only with a cost efficient and quality conscious approach but with a special emphasis on safe practices. During the financial year 2009-10 the Indian operations recorded a Lost Time Injury Frequency Rate (LTIFR) of 0.56, a reduction of 31% from 0.80 registered in the financial year 2008-09 while in the UK and European operations the LTIFR reduced by 15% compared to the previous financial year. During the year,

Tata Steel Group operations recorded a LTIFR of 0.95 against 1.31 in FY 2009, a 27% improvement over the last year. However, during the year there were 5 fatalities across the Group which included 3 contractor employees and every effort is being taken by your Company to avoid such unfortunate incidents. The Board expresses its sincere regret at these tragic fatalities. The Group Vision has a target of 0.4 LTIFR with Zero fatality by 2012. With reduction in the LTIFR, TSE is focusing towards measuring total recordable incidents from FY 2010-11. Recordable incidents are work-related incidents which result in harm to a person or persons, other than those which require no more than first aid treatment.

For sustainability of its operations and reducing process hazards by strengthening safety in processes, the Indian operations have initiated implementation of Process Safety and Risk Management (PSRM) in high hazard operations. The prime objective of Process Safety Management is to achieve "Operating excellence through operational discipline." PSRM will be implemented in all facilities by the financial year 2011-12.

The recent expansion campaign in Tata Steel India called for a large content of unskilled contract workforce, to be employed at various project sites. The onus was on Tata Steel to get the jobs executed with least possible injuries. The Company partnered with DuPont for improving the performance of construction activity by instilling the DuPont proven model of construction safety to our contract partners. Recognizing the excellent practices in the field of Construction Safety, in pursuit of an injury free and illness free healthy workplace, World Steel Association awarded Tata Steel with "World Steel Association Safety Excellence Recognition Award 2009."

Community safety is an important feature of the safety excellence journey of Tata Steel. Safety has been introduced as a curriculum in schools from nursery onwards by providing necessary inputs and motivation to the schools of Jamshedpur. This is done with the help of 'SAFE', an NGO run for the improvement of safety in the schools and society.

Health and Safety continues to be a key performance indicator and one of the prime drivers of the Corporate Vision of your Company. The Group Vision is to achieve a target of 0.4 LTIFR with zero fatalities by 2012. Tata Steel's safety and health responsibilities are driven by the belief within our policy which was launched for Tata Steel group from January 2011: "The safety and health of all the people who work in and with the Tata Steel Group is our number one priority." In pursuance of this belief, we are committed to continual efforts to improve health and safety in Tata Steel as we strive for excellence. Health and Safety is reviewed at all Board meetings of your Company with a Health, Safety and Environment committee incorporating senior executives and non-executives from the Board also established to carry out more detailed reviews. The integrated and systemic Health and Safety Management System introduced in Tata Steel Europe in 2008 with a governance process for improvement actions and regular safety tours by the Board and executive members is being evaluated for Tata Steel Group-wide application.

During the financial year 2010-11, the Group recorded a LTIFR of 0.78 improving by 18% against 0.95 in FY 2009-10. Tragically, during the financial year under review there were 10 fatalities across the Group which included 5 contractor employees. The Board expresses its sincere regret at these fatalities and is committed to learning from each of these incidents to prevent any recurrence and also in its implementation of measures to ensure that any fatality potential is identified and controlled in our operations. The safeguarding and promotion of the physical, mental and social well-being of employees of the Group has been enhanced from a number of programmes across the Group. In India, the programme 'Wellness at Workplace' targets the major health risks such as heart disease, diabetes and includes proactive reviewing of individual medical condition and identifying improvements. In

Europe, health promotion is also done on major risks such as cancer, heart disease with an additional focus on minimizing exposure to potential health hazards like noise, vibration and the need to use personal protective equipment.

SECURITY

Tata Steel has full-fledged fire service department consisting of dedicated fire personnel which cater to the need of Steel Works the people of the industrial Township with a population of more than 1.5 million approximately and all the local industries. Trained home guards of Tata Steel along with fire brigade service assist the District Administration as and when required. More than 200 employees volunteer service three to four times a year. Tata Steel is fully associated with the off-site emergency planning of the region. In the year Fire Services of Tata Steel attended 81 fire calls from non-Tisco areas and 158 other service calls like drowning, flooding, etc. The cost borne by Tata Steel to incorporating security and human right is Rs. 4.2 milion approximately.

REFERENCES

Chamberlin, W. Neil, Collective Bargaining, Mc Graw-Hill, New York, 1951, p. 121.

Flanders, Allen, "Bargaining Theory: The Classical Model Reconsidered," Industrial Relations—Contemporary Issues, Edited by B.C. Roberts, Macmillan, London, 1968, p. 25.

Pande, R.S., "Changing Pattern of Industrial Relations", Man-Management in Tata Steel, p. 10.

Singh, A.D., "Welcome Address, Seminar on Man-Management for Peace, Productivity and Progress, p. 5.

Tata, Naval H., "Industrial Relations", Man Management in Tata Steel, p. 1.

Nayyar, Baldev Raj, (2003), "Economic Globalization and its Advance, From Shallow to Deep Integration", *Economic and Political Weekly*, November 8, pp. 4780-82.

Pandey, R.N., "Industrial Relations in Major Industrial Units at Jamshedpur", (Ph.D. Thesis submitted in Bhagalpur University), 1970, p. 18.

The Economic Times (2003), "See No Evil, Hear No Evil," November, 14. (Quotes Forbes on Hiring Illegal immigrants on the sly through layers of contract by Wal-Mart and other retailers in the U.S.A.).

Shyam Sunder, K.R. (2003), "Trade Unions and New Strategies for Organising Labour: New Wine in Old Bottle?", *The Indian Journal of Labour Economics*, Vol. 46, No. 2.

Lambert, Rob (1999), "Australia's Historic Industrial Relations Transition", in Leisink (ed.).

Venkata Ratnam, C.S. (2003), "Negotiating Flexibility", in *Negotiated Change*, Response Books, New Delhi.

Hyman, Richard (1999), "Imagined Solidarities: Can Trade Unions Resist Globalization?", in Leisink (ed.).

Mamkoottam, K. (2003), Labour and Change: Essays on Globalisation, Technological Change and Labour in India, Response (A Division of Sage), New Delhi.

Saini, Debi S. and Sami A. Khan (eds.) (2000), Human Resource Management: Perspectives for the New Era, Response Books (A Division of Sage), New Delhi.

Saini, Debi S. (2003): "Dynamics of New Industrial Relations and Postulates of Industrial Justice", *The Indian Journal of Labour Economics,* Vol. 46, No. 4, Oct.-Dec.

Collective Bargaining in TISCO

CONCEPT OF COLLECTIVE BARGAINING

The term 'Collective Bargaining' was first used by Webbs some sixty years ago in 'Industrial Democracy,' wherein is stated that it will be best understood by a series of examples. That is to say, they did not define it. Since then many changes have taken place in the realm of industrial relations. In the first edition of his work 'Collective Bargaining' in 1951, Chamberlin, while summarising the various theories held about the nature of collective bargaining, observed that "collective bargaining is

(1) A means of contracting for the sale of labour,
(2) A form of industrial government, and
(3) A method of management."

He called them respectively the Marketing, Governmental and Managerial theories of Collective Bargaining. According to him, Marketing Theory of Collective Bargaining is "the process which determines under what terms labour will continue to be supplied to a company by its existing employees, and by those newly-hired as well. But the Governmental Theory of Collective Bargaining acknowledges the contractual character of bargaining relationships. It observes the contract between employers and employees mainly as providing a constitution for industrial self-government. Its main function is to "set-up organs of government, define and limit them, provide agencies for making, executing and interpreting laws for the industry and means for their enforcement. The Managerial Theory stresses "the functional relationship between union and companies they combine in reaching decisions on matters in which both have vital interests."

These theories of collective bargaining serve at least one important purpose, and this purpose is that they reflect the different stages in the historical development of the system of collective bargaining. Flanders, while commenting on these theories of collective bargaining, observed:

> "One might say that, while the first theory draws attention to the trade union acting as a labour cartel in collective bargaining; the second sees it as introducing an autonomous and agreed rule of law into employer-employee relation; and the third stresses its contribution towards making management more democratic in furthering industrial democracy."

In brief, collective bargaining may be defined as a system of negotiation between employers and employees or accredited representatives of either which decides in the form of an agreement the conditions of employment of such employees. It differs from a contract between an individual employer and an individual employee in that it is 'collective'—that is, covers more than one employee—and also because very often the negotiations are not conducted by the employees themselves but by their accredited representatives on their behalf. Therefore, collective bargaining process is a continuing one. Its most spectacular phase is that in which employer and union members meet to thrash out contract terms.

Pre-requisites for the Success of Collective Bargaining

For modern employers, collective bargaining has added a heavy responsibility beyond that of early owners and managers, and is recognised as occupying a position of major importance among the functions of manpower management. Since both employees and employers are directly involved in the process of collective bargaining, a great responsibility lies on both the sides. This process leads to more satisfactory solutions as the parties directly concerned reach agreement based on compromise. However, it is essential that the parties concerned must see that it is successful. In order that collective bargaining is effective and successful, certain conditions must be present. These conditions are:

(i) There must be a change in the attitude on the part of employer as well as labour unions. Collective bargaining should not be considered approach of litigation.
(ii) The most important essential condition is that there should be a truly representative, enlightened and strong union functioning in the organisation. Where there are two or more unions, collective bargaining should start only after a union has been recognised as per rules.
(iii) Employers and employees should enter into bonafide negotiations on the points of difference or demands with a view to reaching an agreement.
(iv) Parties must depend on facts and figures for supporting their respective case.
(v) Unfair labour practices must be avoided by both sides.
(vi) Once an agreement is reached, it must be respected and implemented.

Settlement of Industrial Disputes without State Intervention

There are two ways in which the basic parties to an industrial dispute, i.e. the employer and the employees can settle their disputes. These are:

(1) collective bargaining, and
(2) voluntary arbitration.

1. Collective Bargaining

The emergence and stabilisation of the trade union movement has led to the adoption of collective bargaining as a method of settling differences and disputes between the employer and his employees. Collective bargaining implies the following main steps:

(i) Presentation in a collective manner to the employs their demands and grievances by the employees;
(ii) Discussions and negotiations on the basis of mutual give and take for settling the grievances and fulfiling the demands;
(iii) Signing of a formal agreement or an informal understanding when negotiations result ill mutual satisfaction; and
(iv) In the event of the failure of negotiations, a likely resort to strike or lock-out to force the recalcitrant party to collie to terms.

The four steps mentioned here indicate the step by step conclusion of the process of collective bargaining conducted by the parties without any outside assistance. Sometimes, when collective negotiations reach a deadlock, the parties themselves may call in third persons to help them settle their disputes. Here, the role of the outsider who is a commonly agreed person is to break the deadlock, to assuage feelings, to interpret the view-point of one to the other, and thereby to help the parties arrive at an agreement. But the solution, if ally, comes out of the parties themselves; the presence of the outsider doers not supersede the process of collective bargaining or the freedom of the parties to agree or to disagree. However, bargaining with the help of the third party is called conciliation or mediation. If the negotiations result in a mutually satisfactory position, an agreement may be formally signed or just an informal understanding may be arrived at.

The fast step in the process of collective bargaining is a likely resort to coercive measures, i.e. strikes or lock-outs. Strikes and lock-outs are an integral part of the process of collective bargaining and may be viewed as a method of settling industrial disputes—as war is a method for settling disputes between two or more nations. In the present context of national sovereignty, war is still recognised as a legitimate instrument of settling international disputes, however, disastrous its consequences might be for the humanity as a whole. So, are strikes and lock-outs recognised in many countries as legitimate weapons in the armoury of labour and management, however detrimental their consequences may be to the welfare of the community. Apart from the role of reasonableness or otherwise of the demands and grievances in determining the outcome of collective bargaining, the threat of strikes and lock-outs exercises it potent degree of pressure on the 'parties concerned to' settle their disputes and to come to an agreement. If the threat of a strike were not there, mutual negotiations; would rarely succeed and, therefore, if collective bargaining is to be developed as a method of settling industrial disputes, the right to strike has to exist unimpaired. The solutions arrived at in the process of collective bargaining are ultimately evolved by the parties themselves and are of lasting value. Where collective bargaining has been firmly established, as in the U.S.A. or Great Britain, Sweden, etc., the trade unions and the employers do come to an agreement without very frequent resorts to the trail of economic strength, but in some cases, it is the resort to till trial. That ultimately resolves a disputes.

(2) Voluntary Arbitration

The second way in which the parties can settle disputes without any State intervention is voluntary arbitration. The parties, feeling that mutual negotiations will not succeed, and realising the futility and wastefulness of strikes and lock-outs, pray decide to submit the dispute to a neutral person or a group of persons for arbitration. The neutral person hears the parties and gives his award which may or may not be binding on them. At the time of submitting a dispute to arbitration, the parties may agree in advance to abide by the award of the arbitrator and thus-industrial peace is maintained and the dispute is resolved. Sometimes, however, the parties may agree to submit the dispute to an arbitrator but at the same time reserve their right to accept or reject the award when it comes. Under such a condition, voluntary arbitration loses its binding force. However, even this limited form of voluntary arbitration is not without its utility.

The Gandhian technique of resolving industrial disputes accords a high place to voluntary arbitration. The constitution of the Textile Labour Association, Ahmedabad provides for voluntary arbitration. At Dalmianagar, the Rohtas Workers' Union and the management of the Rohtas Industries Ltd. have on a number of occasions submitted their disputes to voluntary arbitration. Many industrial disputes are settled today through voluntary arbitration.

The Industrial Disputes Act, 1938 and the Industrial Relations Act, 1946 of Bombay recognised voluntary arbitration as a method along with others for the settlement of industrial disputes. The Five Year Plans have constantly emphasised its role. An amendment to the Industrial Disputes Act, 1947 provides for joint reference of disputes to arbitration. The Code of Discipline also reiterated the faith of the parties in voluntary arbitration in the event of the failure of mutual negotiations. The need for according a wider acceptance to voluntary arbitration was further recognised in the 1962 session of the Indian Labour Conference which held, "Whenever conciliation fails arbitration will be the next normal step, except in cases where the employer feels that for some reasons he would prefer adjudication. The Conference, however, said, the reasons for refusal to agree to arbitration must be fully explained by the party concerned in each case and the matter brought up for consideration by the Implementation Machinery concerned.

Again, the Industrial Truce Resolution, 1962 emphasized voluntary arbitration and specified certain items which could be conveniently brought under its purview. These included: complaints pertaining to dismissal, discharge, victimization and retrenchment of individual workmen. Later, a tripartite National Arbitration Board was set-up with a view to reviewing the position, examining the factors inhibiting its wider acceptance and suggesting measures to make it more popular.

In spite of the support and blessings of Mahatma Gandhi and efforts made by the government, voluntary arbitration has not made much headway in the country. Some of the factors which have hampered the adoption of voluntary arbitration as a method of settling industrial disputes in India were highlighted in the evidence before the National Commission on Labour. These included:

"(i) Easy availability of adjudication in case of failure of negotiations;

(ii) Dearth of suitable arbitrators who command the confidence of both parties;

(iii) Absence of recognised unions which could, bind the workers to common agreements;

(iv) Legal obstacles;

(v) The fact that in law no appeal was competent against an arbitraibr's award;

(vi) Absence of a simplified procedure to be followed involuntary arbitration; and

(vii) Cost to the parties, particularly workers."

In the U.S.A., most collective agreements provide for resort to arbitration as a final step in the settlement of grievances, and grievance procedures jointly worked out by the parties usually provide for voluntary arbitration as the last step.

In Great Britain also, many national collective agreements provide for arbitration of unresolved differences relating to application of the agreements during the period of their operation. Very often, the parties, at the time of entering into an agreement, also undertake to accept the decision of the arbitrator as binding. In case where a particular company, enters into an agreement with the union in modification of a national agreement at the industry level, voluntary arbitration may be provided at the company level also.

Settlement of Disputes under the Influence of the State

The peaceful and smooth functioning of industrial relations is of vital, importance to the community. Interruptions in production because of strikes and lock-outs cause untold inconvenience and loss of economic welfare to people in general, especially if the supply of essential goods and services is stopped. The changing nature of strikes and lock-outs involving entire industries has further strengthened the need for intervention by the State in the settlement of industrial disputes. The underdeveloped countries, which have launched upon vast programmes of economic development and have adopted planning, find that they cannot afford frequent interruptions in production. Therefore, there is a growing tendency on the part of the State to intervene and to seek to promote peaceful ways of settling industrial disputes in both the industrially developed and underdeveloped countries.

The most common ways in which the State intervention

takes place are the following:

(1) Compulsory establishment of bipartite committees;
(2) Establishment of compulsory collective bargaining;
(3) Compulsory investigation;
(4) Conciliation and mediation (voluntary and compulsory); and
(5) Compulsory arbitration or adjudication.

(1) Compulsory Establishment of Bipartite Committees

It is well-known to students of industrial psychology and labour economics that, apart from,such issues of conflict as wages and hours of work, bonus, pensions, gratuity, etc., there are many other industrial grievances which, if allowed to accumulate and to fester, grow into big industrial disputes ultimately threatening interruptions in production. Therefore, the State has passed enactment requiring the establishment of bipartite committees consisting of the representatives of workers and their employer at the plant or industrial level. These bipartite committees are given the power to settle differences between the workers and the employers as soon as they appear and thereby they prevent them from growing into big conflagrations. On the basis of the recommendations of the Whitley Committee, Joint Industrial Councils, District Councils and Works committees were set-up in Great Britain for considering matters affecting both labour and capital. Similarly, in India the Industrial Disputes Act, 1947 provide, for the compulsory formation of Works Committees in industrial establishments employing 100 or more persons, if so required by the appropriate government.

The Works Committees consist of representatives of the workers and employers and are charged with the responsibility "to promote measures for securing and preserving amity and good relations between the employer and the workmen and, to that end, to comment upon matters of their common interest or concern and endeavour to compose any material difference of opinion in respect of such matters. The relevant rules framed by the Central Government under this Act lay down the details concerning the size of Works Committees, the selection of workers' representatives, terms of office, facilities for meeting;, etc. The State Governments have framed similar rules requiring the formation of Works Committees in different industrial establishments. Many of these Works Committees are functioning successfully and discharging their functions in a responsible manner. However, most of them have not come to the expectations because of:

(i) The reluctance and hostility of the employer or the trade union concerned,
(ii) Illiteracy and ignorance of the workers, and
(iii) Absence of leadership from the rank-and-file.

Thus, the primary ideas behind the establishment of such bipartite committees are:

(a) Giving encouragement to the parties concerned to settle and compose their differences by themselves in order to avoid the direct intervention of a third agency, and
(b) Facilitating the composition of the differences at their embryonic stages without causing work-stoppages.

While emphasising the importance of Works Committees in the settlement of industrial disputes, the Statements of the Objects and Reasons of the Industrial Disputes Act, 1947 said, "Industrial peace will be most enduring where it is founded on voluntary settlement, and it is hoped that the Works Committees will render recourse to the remaining machinery provided for in the Bill for the settlement of industrial disputes infrequent." In the eyes of the framers of the Act, the Works Committees were to provide the king-pin in the machinery for the settlement of industrial disputes. The Act created a forum for the voluntary settlement of industrial disputes and imposed it on the employers. In a way, the provision for the constitution of Works Committees under the Industrial Disputes Act, 1947 meant the compulsory imposition of voluntarism in the settlement of industrial disputes.

(2) Establishment of Compulsory Collective Bargaining

As the State encourages and requires the establishment of "bipartite committees for the purpose of composing grievances and differences between workers and their employer, it may also think it advisable to encourage and, if necessary, to force workers and employers to enter into formal collective bargaining through their representatives. The idea behind such a policy is to force the parties to seek to settle their differences through mutual negotiations, and discussions before they decide to resort to strikes or lock-outs. Where the parties themselves have set-up a machinery for collective bargaining and negotiation, the imposition of collective bargaining by the State becomes unnecessary. But, if either or both the par ties resist the establishment of collective bargaining and the State feels that collective bargaining helps the peaceful and democratic conduct of industrial relations, it may impose collective bargaining compulsorily. It was in this frame of mind that the Federal Government of the U.S.A. under President Roosevelt enacted the National Labour Relations: Act, 1935 popularly known as the Wagner Act. This Act made the refusal by the employer to bargain. with the representatives of his employees an unfair labour practice and imposed penalties for the same. The Labour-Management Relations Act of 1947, commonly known as the Taft, Hartley Act, made the refusal to bargain either by the employer, or by the trade union an unfair labour 'practice. Thus, in the U.S.A., the employers and the workers both are required by law to bargain collectively, if one of the parties so desires. However, the outcome of collective bargaining is not dictated by the government. Here again, the spirit is to require the parties to solve their dispute by their own efforts before they resort to a trial of strength. In India, there is no such enactment.

(3) Conciliation and Mediation

The third method used by the State for promoting a peaceful settlement of industrial disputes 'is the provision of conciliation and mediation services. There is no essential difference between conciliation and mediation and the two terms are used interchangeably, though some people tend to differentiate between the two on the basis of the degree of the active role played by the third person. To some, the conciliator is more active and more intervening than the mediator who is said to perform a "go messenger" service.

(A) Voluntary Conciliation and Mediation

Under the method of voluntary conciliation and mediation, the State sets-up a conciliation and mediation machinery consisting of personnel trained in the art of conciliating disputes. The services of this machinery are always available to the disputants. Whenever, they feel that the conciliator may help them in resolving their dispute or in breaking a deadlock, they may call up on the services of the conciliation machinery. The State provides the service without imposing any obligation on the disputants to use it. Sometimes, a conciliation service is empowered to be a little more active. The conciliator may inform the parties that—his services are available and also request them to keep him informed of the developments in their negotiations.

The aim of the conciliator is to break the deadlock, if any, explain the stand and the view-points of one party to the other, convey messages and generally keep the negotiations going. Suggestions may come from the conciliator or the mediator, but the parties are free to accept or reject them. It is the parties who ultimately decide the issues. They may come to an agreement, they may not. This sort of conciliation or mediation is not different from voluntary collective bargaining and maybe said to be a mere continuation of the process of collective bargaining.

(B) Compulsory Conciliation and Mediation

In many countries, and in the same country for many disputes and industries, the State does not rest content with the mete creation of a conciliation service and making it available to the parties, leaving them free to make use of it if they so like, The State goes a step further; it imposes an obligation on the parties to submit their dispute to the conciliation service and makes it a duty of the latter to seek to conciliate the dispute. Meanwhile, the State requires the parties to refrain from causing any work-stoppage for the purpose of resolving the dispute so long as the conciliation proceeding is going on.

Generally, there is a time limit for the conciliators and mediators to conclude their efforts at conciliation. There are three main considerations for prohibiting the parties from causing work-stop pages and imposing this time limit. Firstly, it is felt that conciliation will provide a cooling off period during which emotional tensions may subside and a settlement can be arrived at. Secondly, it is felt that the freedom of the parties to settle their disputes even by causing work-stoppages should not be taken away from them for a long period. Thirdly, it is argued that, if conciliation does not achieve an early break-through, it is not very likely to succeed later. If, at the end of the conciliation proceeding, the parties fail to settle their dispute, they are free to go on a strike or a lock-out, but the State may further persuade the parties and use other methods for bringing about a peaceful settlement of disputes. On the other hand, if a settlement is arrived at, an agreement may be signed in the presence of the conciliator and it is declared legally binding on the parties.

Compulsory Arbitration in India

Though a small beginning in this direction was made by the Bombay Industrial Disputes Act of 1938 which provided for the creation of a Court of Industrial Arbitration empowering it to decide cases relating to registration of unions, standing orders and legality of strikes, etc., compulsory arbitration has essentially been a child of the Second World War for the country. As a whole, the exigencies of the war necessitated the adoption of certain emergency measures for preventing strikes and lock-outs in industries. The fullest mobilization of the country's economic and manpower resources and the need for uninterrupted production of goods and services demanded that work-stoppages be prohibited. But the simple prohibition of strikes or lock-outs under the authority of a law without, at the same time, providing for a fair and just settlement of the dispute that caused work-stoppages, would have been of no avail. The workers, driven to desperation on account of rising prices and falling real wages would have violated any law and faced any penalties in order to protect their meagre living standards. Therefore, the prohibition of strikes and lock-outs had to be combined with the provision of compulsory arbitration of disputes in order to convince the workers that their claims had received a fair hearing. Initially, the Bombay Industrial Disputes Act, 1938 was amended in 1941 empowering the Provincial Government to refer industrial disputes to. the Court of Industrial Arbitration if it considered that the dispute would lead to serious outbreak or disorder affecting the industries concerned adversely and cause prolonged hardship to the community.

Later, in January 1942, the Government of India amended the Defence of India Rules by adding Rule 81-A in order to restrain strikes and lock-outs. This Rule empowered the government to prohibit strikes and lock-outs, refer any dispute to adjudication, require employers to observe such terms and conditions of employment as might be specified and enforce the decisions of the adjudication. Later, the Provincial Governments were also vested with similar powers. After the war, the Industrial Disputes Act, 1947 continued the practice of adjudication and now it has become an important feature of the law relating to the settlement of industrial disputes in the country. The Industrial Disputes Act, 1947; as it stands amended upto date, provides for three types of adjudication authorities for the adjudication of industrial disputes, namely, Labour Court, Tribunal and National Tribunal.

The Labour Court and the Tribunal can be established both by the Central and State Governments, but the National Tribunal is set-up only by the Central Government to adjudicate such disputes as involve any question of national importance or are of such a nature that industrial establishment situated in more than one State are likely to be interested in or affected by them. The Labour Court is intended to adjudicate them as relate to the propriety or legality of an order passed by the employer under the standing orders, discharge or dismissal of workmen, legality or otherwise of a strike or lock-out. The Tribunal and the National Tribunal generally deal with such subject matters as wages, bonus, profit-sharing, rationalisation, allowances, hours of work, provident fund, gratuity, etc. Strikes and lock-outs are prohibited during the tendency of the proceedings. before any of the adjudication authorities and two months after the conclusion of slick proceedings and during any period in which an award is in operation in respect of any matter covered by the award.

The use of compulsory arbitration has raised controversies in India and opinions are widely divided as to its utility and efficacy in maintaining industrial peace and securing to the workers their just demands. Nevertheless, there does not appear any early prospect of the rigours of compulsory arbitration being relaxed under the existing economic and political conditions of the country.

COMPULSORY ARBITRATION *VS.* COLLECTIVE BARGAINING

The foregoing comments necessitate a discussion and critical evaluation of compulsory arbitration. It is also necessary to compare it to its only alternative collective bargaining and to find out which one of these is best suited to the needs of the peculiar economic and political situation that prevails in India. The arguments for and against compulsory arbitration can be discussed under two heads:

(a) Arguments relating to its principle; and
(b) Arguments relating to its practice in India.

Arguments for Compulsory Arbitration

In spite of many arguments against compulsory arbitration, it has come to stay in India and there are influential protagonists of it. The supporters of compulsory arbitration assert its superiority over collective bargaining as a method of settling industrial disputes not only in the prevailing Indian conditions but also in principle. This point of view is presented below.

(a) Relating to its Principle

Supporters of compulsory arbitration contend that adjudication, coercive though it may be, is superior to collective bargaining. Collective bargaining settles a dispute on the principle of trial by combat. In the case of collective bargaining, it is not the just cause but the relative strength of the parties that ultimately triumphs. A strong union may take up a weak case and still win and *vice versa* compulsory arbitration, though imperfect, introduces an element of law and justice in the conduct of industrial relations. The judicial standards available to the judges in adjudication of industrial disputes may be imperfect, yet they are far better than the principle of 'might is right' that underlies collective bargaining.

Besides, as the institution of compulsory arbitration grows, so will industrial jurisprudence. The concept of what is just and fair, may be nebulous and, to an extent, crude today, but it will get refined and become more acceptable with the development of compulsory arbitration. This is how any jurisprudence grows and industrial jurisprudence will also follow the same course. Further, it is true, no doubt, that compulsory arbitration is based upon the coercive power of the State, but the institution of collective bargaining is also rooted in the coercive power of the parties themselves. It is any time better to let the coercive power of the community as exercised by the State be the arbiter of the conflicting claims of labour and capital than to let the coercive powers of privately organised groups be the determinant of the outcome of such conflicts. The authority of the State should be used to prevent strong groups and organizations whether they belong to the employers or to the workers from holding the community to ransom. The workers and employers engaged in providing services vital to the community's health and safety are in a position to charge any prices for their services. Here, compulsory arbitration is in a position help the community by imposing such terms and conditions of employment which appear fair to it and thereby keep the cost of production within reasonable limits.

(b) Relating to Prevailing Indian Conditions

The adoption of planning as an instrument of economic growth and the marginal, subsistence standard of living in the country demand that industrial peace be maintained in order to achieve planned targets. The adoption of free collective bargaining with the freedom to resort to strikes and lock-outs would jeopardize the fulfilment of the objective of planning. Industrial peace is the supreme need of the hour. Collective bargaining may be democratic, but it endangers industrial peace. Therefore, compulsory arbitration has to be used for the purpose of resolving industrial disputes.

Further, it is pointed out that compulsory arbitration in India does not suppress collective bargaining rather supplements it. The parties to an industrial dispute are free to settle it peacefully and, only if they fail to come to an agreement, compulsory arbitration comes into play. If the workers and the employers are so anxious to preserve their rights of collective bargaining, they can resolve all the disputes themselves without any threat or hindrance by the government.

So far as the arguments of heavy expenses and delay are concerned, the machinery of compulsory arbitration can be improved and is gradually improving. The government can also be made more responsible and discrete in the exercise of its power to refer disputes to adjudication. In the prevailing state of trade unionism in India, compulsory arbitration has conferred more benefits on workers than a divided trade union movement could have been able to achieve, otherwise compulsory arbitration might have, to some extent, weakened collective bargaining, but has helped the workers in many poorly organised sectors in securing significant gains.

Arguments against Compulsory Arbitration

Opposition to the use of compulsory arbitration for the purpose of settling industrial disputes comes from many sources including trade unions, mostly of the left-wing, students of industrial relations and prominent personalities like V.V. Giri. On the other hand, sentiments in favour of compulsory arbitration are equally widespread.

(a) Relating to its Principle

The main argument against the principle of compulsory arbitration is that it leads to an authoritarian imposition of the terms and conditions of employment and suppresses the possible self-government in industries based upon the democratic freedom of the parties to resolve their disputes through collective bargaining. In a democratic society, industrial democracy, implying collective and joint determination of the terms and conditions, of employment and the settlement of their disputes by the parties themselves without any outside interference, is no less important than political democracy. It is contended that the parties should be free to work out their relations and sort out their problems by mutual discussions and negotiations, if possible, and even by strikes and lock-outs, if necessary. According to this view-point, the use of coercive economic power by one party against the other is preferable to the use of the coercive power of the. State to impose a settlement on the parties. The success of compulsory arbitration depends upon the coercive power of the State which penalises the parties for non-compliance with the provisions of the laws pertaining to compulsory arbitration. Any solution imposed from outside will never provide a lasting solution to the problems of industrial relations. Even if they fight for the time being, the parties will ultimately succeed in working out a lasting. solution of their problems as they have to live together on a permanent basis: If they have to coexist, they will evolve the principles and the arrangements necessary for their co-existence. Compulsory arbitration is a poorer method for this purpose as compared to collective bargaining.

The second argument against compulsory arbitration relates to the absence of standards which can be used by arbitrators to resolve divergent interests and to judge the fairness or otherwise of conflicting claims. For example, in arbitrating claims for higher wages, what are the guides which are available to the arbitrator. What are just wages? What are fair rates of profits? What are just working hours? These are such questions, for the resolution of which, no objective standards are available in the present state of industrial jurisprudence. While the' function of a judge in a civil dispute is that of locating the facts, and applying to them the known law of the land, the arbitrator in an industrial dispute does not have any such laws which can guide. him in resolving differences of opinion relating to economic interests. Whereas the Civil Judge is an interpreter of law, the arbitrator of an industrial dispute becomes a law giver. He performs the function that essentially belongs to the legislature. The arbitration award in industrial disputes becomes highly subjective. It is the psychological bent, mental make up and prejudices of the 'arbitrator that may finally decide the outcome if an arbitration proceeding. Under such conditions, the explanations behind an award are nothing more than a rationalization of the arbitrator' prejudices. It is also argued that judges are essentially conservative in nature and detest making far-reaching departures from the *status duo*. This puts the worker it a disadvantageous position because their interests often lie in challenging the existing economic order and the existing distribution of the fruits of industry.

Thirdly, compulsory arbitration is criticized for its inability to ensure industrial peace the maintenance of which is claimed to be the primary justification for its adoption. It is pointed out that no award can be enforced when the masses of workers are dissatisfied with it and have developed sentiments against its provisions. Ultimately, the arbitrators may abandon their quest for a just basis for arriving at an award and look for such solutions which would be acceptable to the parties and would avoid work-stoppages. In many cases, the quest for a just solution may run counter to the quest for industrial peace. In India, despite the operation of compulsory adjudication for a period of more than 30years, the number of industrial disputes workers involved and mandays lost has not shown a declining trend. On the other hand, a number of strikes have taken place in public utility services and other industries, very often in complete defiance of the penal provisions of the Industrial Disputes Act, 1947 and Essential Services Maintenance Act, 1968.

Finally, compulsory arbitration is said to vitiate industrial relations by creating a litigious atmosphere. Under compulsory arbitration, trade unions may make fantastic demands because they know that these demands will not be required to be backed and secured through the organized strength and solidarity of their members. The blame for the non-fulfilment of the demands call be easily shifted to the courts of arbitration. Similarly, the employers develop the habit of saying 'no' to every demand, thinking that any concessions made earlier would weaken their position before the tribunals to which the disputes would be ultimately carried. Thus, compulsory arbitration creates an extremely artificial atmosphere because both the parties try to evade the real issues; as possible. Compulsory arbitration then lays an excessive stress on legalism which may satisfy the law but may not solve the problem. It is agreed on all sides that, clinical rather than legalistic approach to industrial disputes is more effective in creating healthy industrial relations.

(b) Arguments against Compulsory Arbitration as Practised in India

The main argument relating to compulsory arbitration 'as practised in India at present is that it involves long delays and heavy expenditure which put the trade unions in a comparatively disadvantageous position. The employers, by raising legal quiblings in points of law and by utilising the services of legal experts, succeed in carrying cases upto the Supreme Court of India. This means that starting from the Tribunal and ending up in the Supreme Court, thus, it may take many years before a final legal verdict is available on an industrial dispute. How many unions in this country are in a position to match the resources of the employers in a legal battle? Can the workers wait that long? Can they not in the meantime be driven to desperation and resort to violent methods which could be very well avoided if the solutions came early?

Secondly, compulsory arbitration, as practised in India at present, depends in most cases upon the reference of a dispute to the adjudication authorities by the appropriate government in its discretion. As the government has the discretionary power to refer a dispute or not to refer it to adjudication, the government is in a position to pick and choose. It is alleged by many trade unions, particularly of the left wing, that the exercise of this discretion is influenced by political pressures and, in such references, the INTUC gets a preference. Thus, it is often said that the Industrial Disputes Act, 1947 places an instrument in the hands of the government which ultimately boosts tip the growth of the INTUC unions at the cost of others.

Thirdly, the practice of compulsory arbitration in India has hindered the, growth of a genuine and effective trade union movement. It has consequently weakened collective bargaining by making the workers and their leaders look upto the courts of law rather than to their own strength and organisation for the redressal of grievances and the achievement of their demands. The main task of many trade union leaders is to keep loitering in the corridors of the State Secretariats and to hover round the Minister of Labour to secure the reference of a dispute to adjudication. Many trade unions spring to life at the time of submitting a set of demands for the purposes of getting them referred to an appropriate court and become silent after an award has been delivered. The number ,of registered trade unions has increased since 1947, no doubt, but it cannot be said that the trade union movement has also been proportionately strengthened. It was in this context that V.V. Giri said that compulsory arbitration was his enemy number one.

Preparation of Demands

Demand is the basic essence of collective bargaining. Demands concern with the interests of employees. The interests cover issues arising out of recruitment to retirement. Demand may be of any nature and any dimension. Demand reflects the real wishes and aspirations of the party. Demands may be raised by either party but commonly union raises the demand. Some times the management also demands for changes in service conditions and standing orders.

Collective bargaining processes start with the preparation

of demands. It is the first stage of collective bargaining and the whole show depends upon the list of demands, presented by the party. The question arises who frames the demands? Whether it is framed by a few top officials of the union or by the Executive Committee or by the General Body or by Demand Framing Committee? The preparation of demand is an important job because the demands reflect wishes of the workers. The demands should be genuine and fair as it gives strength and high morale on bargaining table. The whole success and gains depend upon the demands, their nature, their costs and their impact on bargaining power. That shows the importance of the role of persons responsible for framing of demands.

The Tata Workers' Union has laid down the processes of preparation of demands in its constitution and rules. In the TWU the Executive Committee is entrusted with the responsibility of framing demands under the guidance of the President and the General Secretary of the union. The members of the Executive Committee submit demands after consulting their respective constituencies. The demands submitted by the members are included in the agenda of the meeting of the Executive Committee. The Executive Committee discusses the demands submitted by the members and passes demands thereafter. Sometimes the office-bearers of the TWU prepare draft demands, which are placed before the Executive Committee. The Executive Committee after discussions on the draft demands accepts the demands. The demands passed by the Executive Committee require ratification by the general body. On ratification of the demands by the general body, the charter of the demands is prepared by the President and General Secretary for presenting before the management.

The Executive Committee of the TWU consists of 225 members, 213 are directly elected by the members of the general body according to the seats allotted constituency-wise and the rest 12 are office-bearers of the union. The office-bearers consist of the President, one Deputy President, four Vice-Presidents, one General Secretary, four Assistant Secretaries and one Treasurer.

The constituencies for the election of the members of the Executive Committee have been made on department-wise considering the strength of the department. The allotment of seats of the executive members in different departments helps the union leaders in framing demands in the sense that the members of the respective departments know fully the problems of the department and aspirations of the rank and file because they are themselves engaged there in the same nature of work. So it becomes easy for the Executive Committee to collect demands from the bottom level.

The processes of preparation of demands in TISCO are systematic. The draft demands are prepared by the members of the Executive Committee after consulting the rank and file workers. The draft demands are placed before the Executive Committee for further scrutiny. The scrutinized demands are placed before the general body. The check and counter-check of demands at various levels, the consultation of the ordinary workers and the role played by the office-bearers convince that the processes of preparation of demands are democratic and systematic. The preparation of demands has gradually become an ordinary process in TISCO. The early practice of framing demands solely by the President and the General Secretary or by the office-bearers of the union has gone under change. At present the demands are invited from different departments through the departmental representatives. Thus, the rank and file is consulted in the present processes of framing of demands.

Factors Influencing in Preparation of Demands

The formulation of demands is a process that operates in the existing situation. Various pressures, in and out, operate in the situation. The demand formulators function in an atmosphere of pressures from in and out. They have to keep in mind the wishes and aspirations of the workers on the one hand and the economic, political and managerial pressures on the other hand. Therefore, it seems desirable to study in brief the various pressures that operate in this ticklish problem.

To begin with the first pressure comes from the union side. In the union there are ordinary workers and union leaders. The workers' wishes and aspirations, interests and future outlook always pressurise the formulators of the demands. Therefore, the demand formulators act wisely and tactfully by reading nerves of the workers. On the other hand, the union leaders by dint of their personality, long experiences and tactfulness always direct and influence the workers' wishes as well as pressurise the demand formulators. In the TWU the Presidents, Michael John and V.G. Gopal, have always enjoyed the high position influencing to a large extent in formulation of demands.

Secondly, unsettled demands form a major part of fresh demands. Normally, all demands are not settled at a time. Some of them are dropped. Out of dropped demands a few demands come before the demand formulators for inclusion in the fresh list of demands.

Thirdly, the demands accepted elsewhere also become an attractive demands, for example, the achievement of Life Cover Scheme by the TELCO workers became an issue of the charter of demands of the TWU in 1974. This is called as proximity influence.

Fourthly, the political pressure also plays an important role. The basic reason for political pressure comes out of close relationship between the political parties and the trade unions. It is more so in case of India where unions are guided by the political parties even at the time of framing demands.

Fifthly, sometimes the union has to place tactical demands. In course of the talk with the office-bearers of the TWU it was revealed that though the main motive of the tactical demands, for example, the demands framed on leave concessions, house-rent allowance, take-over of the Tata hospital by the Government and nationalisation of TISCO in 1975. The first two demands were real and the last two were tactical demands. The last two demands were included in the charter of demands only as a tactical practice in order to pressurise the management to accept the demands relating to house-rent allowance and leave concession. The union expressed satisfaction over the reduction of hospital charges for non-employees and restoration of some facilities to the employees in regard to the admission of their distant relations. In return the union decided not to pursue their earlier demand for take-over of Tata Hospital by the Government and natinalisation of the TISCO. So such types of tactical demands are adopted backed by the political influences.

Sixthly, the role of the labour leader, his knowledge and experiences count much in demand formulation. The leaders of the TWU have always played active and dominant role in formulation of demands. They formulate demands in such a way that the name could be okeyed by the Executive Committee and be ratified by the general body. They also keep in mind the management's attitude, its financial implication and acceptability of demands by the management. Therefore, they do not prefer to submit exaggerated demands. But they do not follow the policy of minimum unalterable demands. They adopt a middle course with some scope for give and take process.

There are two ways of demand formulation. In one way, the demands are exaggerated. The exaggerated demands adopted with a view to provide sufficient scope for give and take process on the bargaining table. In other way, the demands prepared are fair and genuine, with less or no scope for give and take process. It has been called as 'minimum unalterable demand' by Gandhiji: The TWU following the Gandhian labour philosophy has adopted the principle of fair and minimum demand. It is a correct approach and has greater possibility of successful negotiation.

Seventh, the ever rising cost of living index, the desirability of revision of D.A. slabs, the revision of pay scales, the revision of D.A. rates are some of the issues which fluctuate according to the fluctuating economic conditions. The economic hardship caused, by the rising prices of essential goods without adequate compensation pinches the lower paid employees much. The economic factor has greater force over other factors—pressurising the demand formulators.

Eighth, with the adoption of the practice of Steel Wage Board and desirability of uniformity in basic terms and conditions of employment, the scope of fringe benefits has increased. In recent years more pressures have been operating for inclusion of fringe benefits such as rates of concession, leave travel concession, provision of subsidised food grains, transport facilities, better housing facilities, full medical facilities, health facilities, educational facilities, etc.

Lastly, the growing unemployment situation in the country has created two problems: (i) security of job and security of income of the existing employees, and (ii) guarantee of job to the dependents of the deceased employees and jobs to dependents of the retiring employees. The Union has been striving hard against retrenchment of employees. The questions of security of job and security of income are these days top problems. Further union wants to have security of job for the dependents of the deceased employees on humanitarian ground. Even more interesting interest of the union has become the preference to dependents of the retiring employees in job. Naturally the union acts as preserver of the interests of its members, broadly speaking the employees class, in this age of insecurity of job and income.

There are many pressures that operate in different degrees at different times. The degree of a particular pressure varies from time to time. However, there are certain factors which exist and operate all the time. All these influencing factors are kept in mind by the demand formulators.

Bargaining Representatives

The bargaining representatives are the backbones of the collective bargaining processes. The whole bargaining scene is presented by the representatives of the two sides. Therefore, the scenes of the bargaining processes entirely depend upon how the representatives play their role. Naturally, it is the ability, experiences and tactfulness of the representatives which become important. The success or failure of the bargaining process depends upon actions and counter-actions between the representatives of the two sides. The two sides are represented by their respective representatives. Therefore, it has representative character. They represent a larger section standing behind them.

The Indian industrial relations policy of free and voluntary collective bargaining leaves the issues of bargaining team for the parties to decide. There is no law to control or guide the parties in this respect. It is paradox of our industrial relations policy which wishes to have industrial peace without adopting positive steps for regulating the relationship. It leaves the vital issues untouched, unlike U.S.A. or U.K. or even unlike some of our state Governments like Maharashtra, Gujarat and Madhya Pradesh. In such a situation even by the end of the 20th century the managements are enjoying full prerogatives in respect of recognition of the union, criteria for recognition of union, status and rights of recognised union. The unions have to fight for securing recognition and that leaves much scope for inter-union rivalry and practice of Company Union. However, there are some progressive managements, realising the necessity and benefits of recognition of union, have adopted the practice voluntarily. Therefore, the policy has been called as 'free and voluntary collective bargaining' because collective bargaining necessitates recognition of union first.

In TISCO the task of bargaining team is easy because of simple organizational set-up and progressive industrial relations policy. The management nominates the bargaining representatives. The power to nominate the bargaining representatives is vested with the top officials. The General Manager nominates the representatives on the basis of the issue involved. Generally, the General Manager, the Director of Industrial Relations, the Director of the Personnel, the Manager of Wages and Salary Administration and others participate in the negotiations. Apart from these officials, other technical officials are also nominated according to the demands and issues concerning such sections/departments.

The TISCO workers are represented by the Tata Workers' Union, the recognised union. The supervisory and technical workers are represented by the Supervisors and Technicians Unit of the Tata Workers' Union. The TWU is commanding the support of about 92% of workers and therefore the task of representation is easy. The bargaining representatives are nominated by the Executive Committee of the TWU. Normally, the bargaining team consists of all the office-bearers plus five or six other members, who may be members of the Executive Committee or ordinary members or even outsiders. The President and the General Secretary act as main spokesmen of the bargaining team. In case of any special demand concerning any technical section, a particular plant or a department, the Executive Committee nominates any of the office-bearers of the Executive Committee belonging to that particular section. So in the Tata Workers' Union the method of nomination of the bargaining representatives has been adopted. The workers are quite satisfied by their bargainers. There is no permanent bargaining team. The team is prepared as and when required. In TISCO with the adoption of the practice of signing comprehensive agreement for a period of 4 years the question of selection of permanent bargaining team does not arise.

The President, the head of the bargaining team, is answerable to the Executive Committee. If, 10% of the members of the Executive Committee demand explanation then the President has to give explanation. However, in practice rarely such occasion has come up. The President takes most decisions carefully, so that his decision would be endorsed by the Executive Committee. This shows that the Executive Committee has retained power on actions of the President and the bargaining team.

Scope of Collective Bargaining

The history of collective bargaining is full of scenes of attacks and counter-attacks on the rights of the managements and the claims by the workers. It is a battle field covering managerial, prerogatives based on right of ownership and the right to manage the industry. The management has been advocating the principle of ownership whereas the union has been claiming to have a voice in the managerial processes, where their interests lie. The union advocates the principle of humanity.

The question of bargainable issue is still unsolved. No one can draw a line of demarcation between the issues bargainable and non-bargainable. Theoretically, one may draw a line but that will be valid only for that time and in respect of that particular establishment. Practically, the scope is flexible. It fluctuates along the changing comparative bargaining power of the parties concerned. If the management is strong the scope will be narrow. In case, the union is strong the scope will be wider. The scope of collective bargaining depends upon the comparative bargaining power of the parties concern. In the beginning the management was much stronger than the union but gradually the union has gathered strength and power so much so that it has forced the management to share more managerial prerogatives to a considerable extent. Beginning with the wage rates the scope now covers a fair portion of the managerial functions, which is evident from the various tables presenting a comparative picture of the subject matter covered under agreements between 1920 to 1983. As in India there is no law governing subject matter of collective bargaining it is still underlined. A subject matter of collective bargaining is the subject discussed on collective bargaining table covering all matter relating to working conditions and terms of employment. However, in TISCO the actual scope of collective bargaining is clear from the clauses of agreements signed till 1983.

For convenience of the study the subject matter have been divided into five heads. The first head consists of economic issues such as wage rates, D.A. incentive schemes, bonus. The second head consists of matter of social security such as retirement benefits, provident fund, maternity benefit and other benefits. The third head converse matter like recruitment, training, promotion, and job security. The fourth head covers issues like welfare, health, housing and leave facilities. In the fifth head issues like safety, production, productivity and modernisation have been covered. These five tables present a comparative picture of subject matter, gains secured by the unions, the rights of the management and the union and scope and nature of the agreement.

Duration of Agreement

The duration of agreement is also a test of matured collective bargaining. In early days the duration of validity of agreement had never been bargained. It was always left for the parties concerned to propose a change, but it was always followed by industrial unrest along with strike and lock-out. In order to ensure industrial peace and to avoid industrial unrest, it was first adopted in 1956 when an agreement was signed in the month of January 1956 for a period of three years. This new practice of signing a long-term agreement was a new mile stone towards maturity of collective bargaining practice. The three years period was further extended to four years agreement. This shows the strong desire for a long-term agreement. The adoption of the long-term agreement practice since January 1956 has been maintained. Before the expiry of the agreement the parties start fresh negotiation in order to replace the old agreement by a new agreement with addition amendment and improvement. This agreement is important as both sides have recognised and accepted certain rights of each other in order to facilitate the implementation of modernisation scheme. This has added a big list of bargainable issues. Agreement on modernisation, production and productivity has rarely being heard of as these are quite new areas of bargaining in India.

There are a few new fields for bargaining such as anti-pollution measure, safety and occupational diseases, abolition of contract labour, final settlement on retirement and death and productivity and industrial peace, and longivity increment. This shows that in TISCO the scope of collective bargaining has expanding trend. In every agreement a few new issues have been included in the bargainable list. Old issues are always repeated, revised and improved. The role of collective bargaining in empowering unorganised labour is analysed and a case made for greater cooperation amongst countries with formation of "labour blocks."

Collective bargaining seeks to fulfil three objectives—that of fixing the price of labour services, providing a system of industrial jurisprudence where terms apart from wage are set and lastly, it "represents the extension of the democratic idea into the work community." Article 19 of the Constitution of India, the Trade Unions Act, 1926 and the Industrial Disputes Act, 1947 deal with provisions relating to protection of labour rights and collective bargaining.

Conventional economic theory cites collective bargaining agreements as maintaining artificially high wage rates and creating unemployment. However, countries with highly coordinated collective bargaining have lesser unemployment, wage dispersion and strikes than countries with semi-coordinated collective bargaining.

Globalization leads to decentralised modes of production on a global scale, combining the tools of efficient communication, transportation and sourcing activities. Simultaneously, collective bargaining is gradually seeing a reduction, as pressures of worldwide production possibilities weaken trade union activities. This has been seen in India as well.

Furthermore, to attract foreign investment and promote exports, often recourse is taken to "diluting" labour legislation. There are appalling work conditions in international garment export units. Units in export processing zones have been conferred the title of "public utility status" which limits the "Striking" power of employees.

Inherent is the threat of "a race to the bottom" where countries with similar production forces compete with each other to offer the cheapest labour force to attract bigger contract orders. Only one true winner emerges—the company that out sources its production. Critics of globalisation highlight the misery associated and call for companies to follow best practices when employing labour outside the boundaries of the West.

The challenge lies in integrating the unorganised sector into a formal system of functioning. We argue for the creation of a "labour bloc" where governments of concerned countries could make the effort to commonly decide on a certain set of common labour standard parameters, which would apply across all of them. For example, this could involve making mandatory the adherence to a minimum acceptable level of working conditions in the garment industry, failing which, entry to their markets and workforce would be barred. This region arrangement will involve competing countries, and need not be limited to geographical proximity. In the case of the garment industry a labour bloc could arise where minimum conditions of work for garment production are set.

One could argue that companies could then just shift production. However, issues surrounding corporate social responsibility and international pressure for better working conditions in developing countries would form the first barrier. Corporate social responsibility involves the evolution of a code of conduct of businesses, which will avoid exploitative practices and ensure humane conditions of work. The growing importance attached to social labelling, environmental and health concerns along with the necessity for companies to respond to consumer concerns necessitate corporate social responsible practices.

Secondly, companies that choose to ignore regions with these conditions risk a poor public image by the threat of being labelled "exploitative." It would be in the companies 'best interests' to remain in a region that has collectively agreed to ensure certain minimum standards.

Ensuring a common set of standards though collective bargaining across the participating countries would increase economic stability within these countries as well. Countries would then compete with each other on alternative factors, such as on the basis of infrastructure facilities. This would put pressure on governments to invest in their populations and in both physical and knowledge infrastructure rather than depending on "cheap labour."

It differs from the "social clause" of the World Trade Organisation agreements in that it recognises the inherent difficulties countries face and allows them to themselves reach a pragmatic implementable solution.

Globalisation is often treated with pessimism. However, it is itself a dynamic force and a win-win strategy can come about with better conditions of work, leading to higher efficiency, profitability and competitive edge. Collective bargaining could play a fundamental role with greater cooperation and rising labour standards.

HRM strategies invariably act as de-unionisation devices in almost all parts of the globe. In the post-Reagan USA union membership dropped to below 16 per cent of the total labour force and to 12 per cent of the private sector labour force in 1994; it further dropped to 14 per cent in 1997. Table 11.1 representing one of the most recent union data in the Western world shows decline taking place in union density almost all over in 1997 compared to 1980, except some of the Scandinavian countries. In Scandinavian countries there exists provision for automatic recognition of a union. Also, this has been supported by favourable political climate for union legitimacy in these countries which is responsible for increase in union density. There is tremendous pressure on union membership in the Indian case as well; presently a mere 7 per cent of Indian workers are working in the organized sector and a major portion of them belongs to public sector employees, which is facing the pressure of privatisation. Membership of unions that are submitting returns is still low; as per the latest estimates it is barely 2 per cent of the total workforce in India. Over 47,000 unions in the country have a membership of 6,329,000. As per the estimate of a former labour secretary of the central ministry of labour, the number of members covered by collective agreements in the country is barely one per cent of the total work force.

India has not resolved the question of statutory union recognition despite a 55-year debate on this issue. Recognition is still largely guided by voluntarist procedure and is not justiciable by the quasi-judicial forums, which I believe is also one of the reasons for low density of unions. The protagonists of HRM claim that soft HRM strategies themselves have a great potential of rendering workplace justice; they are also seen as becoming instrumental in a more efficacious realisation of organisational goals. Leading firms in the advanced world, therefore, have carved out such empowerment strategies of managing the human resource as models of workplace justice. This eventually leads to

TABLE 11.1

Trends in Union Growth and Decline, 1980-97

Approach	*Country*	*Union density 1980*	*Union density 1997*	*% change 1980 to 1997*
Voluntarist approach	UK	51	33	-18
	Ireland	60	50	-12
	Australia	50	30	-20
	New Zealand	48	23	-25
Statutory Union Recognition	USA	20+	14	-6
	Canada	38	34	-4
Scandinavian model	Sweden	78	86	+8
	Denmark	79	76	-3
	Finland	69	78	+9
	Norway	55.2	54.8	-0.4

Note: The density figures reported here refer to the employment density of union membership, that is trade union membership as a proportion of employees at work.

Source: D'Art and Turner (2003).

individualisation of IR. The possibility of the use of empowerment strategies of IIRM is, therefore, brighter in such countries, even as some IR scholars have often labelled empowerment devices as part of a "managerial propaganda offensive" (Hyman, 1999, p. 109). At the same time, researches in the Western context have begun to question these claims, and have found that the projected claims of HRM are suspect and the realized aims are those which are hidden.

As reported by the John T. Dunlop Commission Report in the USA there is an increasing tendency on the part of employers towards weakening or busting unions so as to promote organisation flexibility and competitiveness (US Department of Labour, 1994). In developing countries like India too, despite the existence of a comprehensive labour law framework its implementation in the private sector leaves much to be desired (Saini, 1995). Both proactive and reactive methods are being used to dilute union efficacy. This process is visible with much greater intensity after the failure of the Bombay textile strike of 1982 which lasted more than a year, and officially has not been withdrawn even today. After this defeat of labour-management in general has been able to bring about a sea change in the concept of collective bargaining; it is now less and less on industry basis and more on unit basis.

One device used to dilute legal protection to job holders in India is to re-designate their jobs so as to take them out of the ambit of IDA, which is the principal central law for adjudicating interest as well as rights disputes between labour and management. The new designations that are being used include: officers, junior executives, supervisors, etc. Under the Indian labour laws non-workers don't enjoy almost any legal protection against acts of unfair termination nor can they espouse disputes before the disputes' settlement machinery created by the IDA. Interestingly, the nature of work of these employees remains the same as before.

Many employers have comprehensive human relations programmes touching every aspect of workers' lives and their families. This is typically known as the IBM model of union avoidance. This model, of course is known to be a viable alternative model of industrial justice. Tata Steel has also successfully used this type of paternalism in managing change at Jamshedpur, though along with union sustenance. In India, among others, Jindal Aluminium Ltd. in Bangalore has successfully followed IBM type of non-union policies.

As noted above, the incidence of unionism is declining. The number of strikes resorted to is much less than the lock-outs, (*Business India*, 1998; Mishra, 2001; Sen Gupta and Sett, 2000). These developments have also reduced workers' resistance to change to the new HRM initiatives. Still there are some stories of working class success in resisting the individualisation of IR through devices such as HRM in the private sector (Ramaswamy, 2000, p. 219). But as revealed by some of the researches, unions are increasingly cooperating in the change process both in the private and the public sectors.

Though Indian Legislature has not brought about any of the oft-repeated changes to rationalize IR laws so as to be in consonance with the new realities, changes are discernible in the government's attitude at the executive level. Many state governments have announced significant changes in their labour policies, which henceforth appeared sacred cow in favour of workers. State governments are showing greater concern for attracting industrial investment by giving tacit support to: hire and fire policies; forbidding of bandhs as happened in the case of Kerala; and easing of requirements for labour inspection, for example, in Rajasthan. West Bengal government (which is headed by a Marxist Party) has cancelled registration of hundreds of unions for non-submission of returns to the Registrar of Trade Unions, which is contrary to its earlier position. Also, a rising incidence of granting permission for closure and retrenchment (as required under the IDA) is visible in many states including Tamil Nadu.

Some evidence is available on the type of changes that have taken place due to the policies of new IR on the incidence and type of unionism, the type of collective bargaining (CB) and the implications that these changes will have on the shape of IR in India. Some micro-level studies have been carried out by Indian scholars to analyze the post-liberalisation scene of changes in the patter of CB. Among others, these studies include those by Mathur (1991), Mamkoottam (1999), Bengal Chambers of Commerce (1998), and AITUC (2001). However, Venkat Ratnam's (2003) recent study of 234 collective agreements in public and private sectors that were signed in 10 years following the new economic policy gives a clearer larger picture that is emerging in the new IR. It unravels the dynamics of the processes through which the adversarial bargaining of the welfare state era is giving way to cooperative bargaining. It nutshell, he has analyze the impact of negotiated changes on restructuring, modernisation, flexibility and productivity. Among others, his findings include some important shifts taking place in the IR Scene. These shifts are from centralized to decentralized bargaining, collective to individual contracts, conjunctive bargaining to emphasis on productivity bargaining, employee-focused agreements to consumer and community-oriented agreements, and 3 to 5 years agreements to 4 to 5 year agreements. While the salutary signal is that there is greater degree of cooperation between labour and management and thus of industrial peace, but one needs to know more fully the dynamics of dis-empowerment that has undergone in the above situations. Qualitative research needs to be undertaken to unravel a fuller view of the structures and processes that are bringing about the new results. This can facilitative evolution of a more articulate agenda of IR law reform so as to be in consonance with the projected aims of the country's labour policy and international labour standards which India has endorsed formally or impliedly. Overall, however, the signals are discouraging for the survival of the countervailing power in economy and society, even as some scholars opine that HRM ideology and industrial pluralism can fundamentally survive together. But that requires a proactive state involvement towards this end, like something that is being expected of the Labour Government in the UK. For example, the Employment Relations Act, 2000, there provides for statutory procedure for union recognition, which is a shift from the earlier voluntarist procedure and, I believe, will be good for the British working class solidarity.

After its decontrol in 1991, the Indian economy saw strong growth with the steel industry minoring it. The global steel market, however, experienced a sharp downturn in 1999-2002, which also impacted India. This led to a keenness among all global players to consolidate capabilities. Rapid growth once again began in 2003, with the BRIC Countries (Brazil, Russia, India and China) consuming extremely large volumes of steel, China's long-term strategy of quadrupling in GDP by 2020 was perhaps the greatest impetus for this growth. In India, the auto and white goods sectors along with the construction sector spurred domestic demand for steel.

On the basis of the above study covering scope of collective bargaining a few inferences can be drawn. Firstly, collective bargaining in TISCO started as early as 1920. Secondly, its scope has been expanding, it means more and more managerial prerogatives are now shared by both the management and TWU. Thirdly, the bargaining power of the TWU has been strengthening. This is supported by the two facts—enjoying a command of 92% of the employees and securing better terms of agreements. Fourthly, the practice of *ad-hoc* bargaining has been replaced by comprehensive agreements. Fifthly, the duration of agreement has also been enhanced from three years to four years. Lastly, the nature of collective bargaining has changed from Marketing theory to Managerial theory though partially. These features of collective bargaining supports the contention that collective bargaining has become matured in TISCO. The practice of collective bargaining has been used so successfully that not a single dispute has been referred to adjudication or abitration. The non-reférence of industrial dispute to alternative machinery, other than collective bargaining, is proof of strong faith in mutual negotiation.

Industrial relations remained normal at all locations. The men on roll in the company as on 31st March, 2008 were 35,870 as compared to 37,205 as on 31st March, 2007. The development of human resources is a key strategic challenge in order to prepare people for future responsibilities in terms of professional skills as well as business skills. The Company is investing in the modernisation of the plant and training of manpower for upgrading their skills. Further, tells planned to redeploy the surplus manpower to various greenfield projects.

It is clear from above study that the practice of collective bargaining, adopted since 1920, was strengthened during 1940s and 1950s. Scores of agreements were signed between the TISCO management and the representative union, the TWU under the Presidentship of Prof. Abdul Bari. The TISCO steelmen reaped fruits through negotiations across the table. Prof. Bari, who was very critical to the management, proved a man of different personality on negotiation table. Michael John, the successor of Prof. Bari carried same spirit in foregoing ahead. During 1938-1953, there were ten agreements reached between the TISCO and the TWU. Out of these the agreements of 1938, 1945 and 1946 were important. Besides wage revision, bonus, gratuity rules, etc., the remarkable achievements of this period were formation of a permanent Joint Rates Committee composed of two union and two management representatives for review of grades and rates, fixation of promotion procedures and permanency of temporary hands completing one year of service. The achievements, both economic and non-economic, were leading to healthy industrial relations system.

The agreement of 1956 can be called as a landmark in the history of collective bargaining and a big leap in unions gains. It guaranteed mutual security to union and the management. The management reaffirmed its stand to continue to recognise the Tata Workers' Union, provision of check-off, agreed to give reasonal facilities of office-bearers, gave facilities to elected group representatives for attending meetings and conferences and to facilitate the Joint Committees representatives in attending meetings. The other highlight of the agreement was the provision of "Closer association of employees with management." Though TISCO employees had been associated with the management since long, yet framing of the new scheme through negotiation was of special importance. It laid down details of labour-management cooperation, its objectives, and stages of cooperation.

In the field of collective bargaining a new trend was adopted in January 1962 by forming Central Wage Board for Iron and Steel Industry. The Board has become a forum of negotiation at Industry level where broader terms of services and problems are discussed and recommendations are adopted. The successful functioning of the Board had helped in framing a new policy. In 1969, the Union Ministry of Labour appointed the Joint Wage Negotiating Committee for steel industry. These practices have helped in establishing industrial peace in steel industry and more particularly in the TISCO. This has paid rich dividends in promoting trust and confidence between the TISCO and the steelmen. In the last 100 years, therefore, Tata Steel has not only built a steel factory but also created the foundation for a nation. That this legacy of nation-building will be carried forward in evident from the zeal reflected in its Vision.

Jamsetji Tata was intensely patriotic. He believed that political freedom would be a cruel delusion if India did not gain economic freedom. He fought a long and lonely battle to set-up his steel plant, the funds for which came entirely for Indian investors. His vision, however, was not limited to the steel plant alone. He was in the creation of an enterprises the means to an end: economic value creation for its people. He believed the *raison d'etre* for this enterprise was to improve the quality of life of the people of India. While at the business level he and his successors planned for the business and raw material needs of the company, they also simultaneously planned for the development of the steel township, assuring employees, and subsequently ordinary citizens, amenities that even very few cities overseas offered. By 1911, Jamshedpur located in the jungles of Bihar, had electricity, water, sanitation and public health services.

Tata Steel was the first steel company to address human

development. In 1920, the Jamshedpur Labour Union was formed, a precursor of the Tata Workers' Union. Several employee welfare initiatives were introduced, including an eight-hour working day and maternity benefits, well before these were enacted as laws in India. Despite its opposition to British-rule, Tata Steel made significant contributions during World War I by meeting war time needs for steel machinery and railways. World War II also saw Tata Steel's robust presence. Armoured cars called Tatanagars' fitted with bullet proof armour plates and rivets manufactured by Tata Steel were extremely popular and the Company's pride during the War. Later, technical personnel trained at Tata Steel's Shavak Nanavati Technical Institute (SNTI), formed the pool of technicians that fulfilled the country's need for technical manpower. When the Indian government was setting up steel plants in Bhilai, Rourkela and Durgapur, it was Tata Steel that trained their first batch of engineers.

Tata Steel's ability to assess the needs of the future, innovate it to adopted a slow and steady phased modernisation programme during the severely restrictive license raj. The plant underwent a major transformation through capacity expansion, induction of modern technology and capital equipment to become one of the most modern and environmental-friendly works in the world. The Cold Rolling Mill set-up by it in 2000, placed Tata Steel in a commanding position to produce customised steel for consumers in the flat products market. This served the needs for customised steel from the automobile, consumer durables and infrastructure sector.

Beyond business as well, Tata Steel's pioneering initiatives in the area of social uplift of communities and employee welfare make it a role model for using corporate skills and resources in public interest. Beginning with the setting up of a dispensary (today the 1000-bed Tata Main Hospital) for providing medical aid to its employees and citizens of Jamshedpur in 1991, profit-sharing bonus in 1938, creating the Community Development and Social Welfare Department dedicated to urbanisation and community progress in 1951, the Rural Development Society in 1979 and promoting sports amongst employees and aspiring sportspersons and today, through vocational and employability training, Tata Steel has touched lives of people in every possible way. The skilled personnel and infrastructure available in this model industrial township has promoted several multinational companies (Timken, Lafarge and Cummins) and small scale industries in Adityapur Industrial Area Development Authority (AIADA) to set-up operation in Jamshedpur. They enjoy the best industrial infrastructure as their employees enjoy high quality of civic amenities.

It has been rightly observed that unity is strength. It holds true in employment relations also. It is so because the individual employed can exert a very limited influence on the employer for bettering his condition because employer's savings and resources are generally greater than those of individual employees. He (employer) can outwit the individual employees, whose services are highly perishable. Therefore, the individual employee in a free economy is at a distinct disadvantage in bargaining with his employer, who usually can better afford to delay or postpone or argue about the conditions of employment.

To gain strength, workers combine together and form trade unions in order to further common interests. Trade unions stand to safeguard this common interest of its members. As such, trade unions have become the integral part of any economic system, and their influence has become a prominent factor in almost all employment relationship today. Many employment policies are determined bilaterally, that is to say, through joint action or collective bargaining by employers and unions. In such situations, the manpower management programme includes as one major function what is generally described as labour relations, meaning the negotiation and administration of collective agreements or labour contracts.

References

Tripartite Conclusions (1942-67), Govt. of India, p. 79.

Report of the National Commission on Labor (1969), Govt. of India, p 234.

Kochan, T. and M. Weinstein (1994), "Recent Developments in US Industrial Relations," *British Journal of Industrial Relations*, Vol. 32, pp. 483-84.

D'Art, Daryl and Thomas Turner (2003), "Union recognition in Ireland: One Step forward or two steps back?, *Industrial Relations Journal*, Vol. 34, No. 3.

Saini, Debi S. and Sami A. Khan (eds.) (2003), "Dynamics of New Industrial Relations and Postulates of Industrial Justice", *The Indian Journal of Labour Economics*, Vol, 46, No. 4, Oct.-Dec.

Mishra, L. (2001), 'Economy and Labour', Manak Publications Pvt. Ltd., New Delhi.

Hyman, Richard (1999), "Imagined Solidarities: Can Trade Unions Resist Globalization?", in Leisink (ed).

Mabey, Christopher, Denise Skinner and Timothy Clark (eds.) (1998), Experiencing Human Resource Management, Sage, London.

US Department of Labour (1994), Fact Finding Report—Commission on the Future of Worker-Management Relations (also called John T. Dunlop Commission Report), Washington D.C., USA.

Business India (1998), "Clutching at Straws", *Business India*, March 9-22.

Patil, B. R. (1998), "A Contemporary Industrial Relations Scenario in India with reference to Karnataka", *The Indian Journal of Industrial Relations*, Vol. 33, No. 3.

Ramaswamy, E.A. (2000), Managing Human Resources: A Contemporary Text, Oxford University Press, New Delhi.

_______ (1994), 'The Rayo Spinners—Strategic Management of Industrial Relations' , Oxford University Press, Delhi.

Mathur, A.N. (1991), 'Industrial Restructuring and Union Power', ILO-ARTEP, New Delhi.

Mamkootam, K. (1999), "Productivity Agreements and Industrial Relations in India", *Management and Change*, Vol. 3, No. 2.

Kamoche, Ken (2000), 'Sociological Paradigms and Human Resources: An African Context', Ashgate Publishing Limited, Aldershot (UK).

Kochan, T. and M. Weinstein (1994), "Recent Developments in US Industrial Relations," *British Journal of Industrial Relations*, Vol. 32, pp. 483-84.

Venkata Ratnam, C.S. (2003), 'Negotiated Change: Collective Bargaining, Liberalisation and Restructuring in India, Response' (A Division of Sage Publications), New Delhi.

Emerging Issues in TISCO

The TISCO has witnessed many ups and downs in its whole period of life. Earlier there was the environment of non-competition and threats from the global economy. These days the global economy is posing challenges to Indian steel industries including TISCO. Consequently, many issues are emerging as the challenges for Indian steel industries along with TISCO. These emerging issues are as follows:

BUSINESS CHALLENGES

Nature of the Industry

Steel is a cyclical industry. The industry witnessed a prolonged down cycle in the recent past. Aggressive cost-cutting and a change in the product mix in favour of more value added products, which even in the lower part of the cycle yielded positive contribution, enabled the company to counter the recession. Further, in the new line of business of cold rolled coils, the company will be producing part of its products conforming to high grades of steel, which were hitherto not being locally manufactured. The company feels that it can now compete effectively both in terms of quality and price with similar materials imported from various well known steel manufacturing units in Japan, Korea and Europe. With the assistance of world renowned consultants, the company has made good progress towards its objectives of becoming the lowest cost integrated steel producer in the world.

GLOBAL ECONOMY

The world GDP, as reported by International Monetary Fund, was on an upturn, growing by 5% in 2010 as compared to a negative growth of 0.5% in 2009. While the growth in the advanced economies was 3.0% in 2010, in contrast to -3.4% in 2009, the emerging and developing economies grew by 7.3% in 2010 when compared to the growth of 2.7% in 2009. The growth in the developing and emerging economies slowed down during the end of 2010 as stimulus measures were slowly removed and policies were tightened in response to rising inflation and overheating concerns. A trend of GDP growth (%) for the last five years in the world, split up into advanced economies and emerging and developing economies, is shown below:

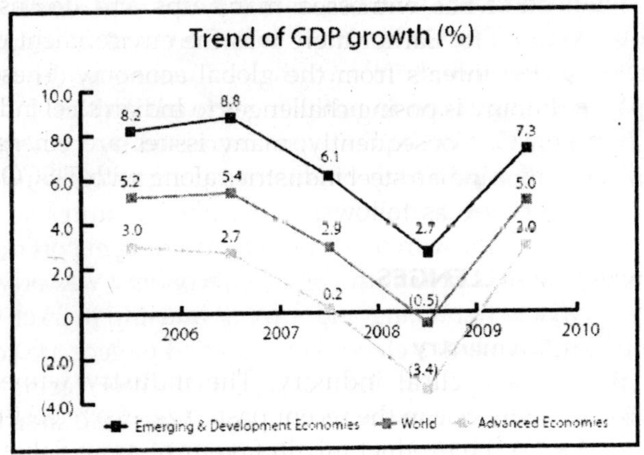

The US: The US GDP increased by 2.8% in 2010 as compared to a negative growth of 2.6% in 2009, but the country still faces large fiscal deficit. In late 2009 and early 2010 there was a deceleration in growth in the US economy as the effect of one time stimulus factors faded. However, in the second half of the year, growth picked up with a decline in the rate of unemployment and consumer spending picking up at its fastest pace in the last five years with further major stimulus measures being introduced along with tax cuts and investment incentives. The housing market, non-residential construction and overall credit growth still remained weak with tight bank lending conditions starting to ease for not only large firms but also for small and medium-sized firms.

India: As reported in the Economic Survey of 2010-11, GDP is expected to grow by 8.6% in 2010-11 as compared to the growth of 8.0% in 2009-10. The agricultural output grew by 5.4% as compared to a nominal 0.4% growth in 2009-10 when the country was hit by a deficient monsoon. Manufacturing grew by 8.8% during the year being at par with the growth noticed in the last fiscal. Overall growth in industry was 8.1% during 2010-11 compared to 8.0% in the last year. Services witnessed a decelerated growth of 9.6% as compared to a growth of 10.1% in 2009-10. Amongst the key macro-economic indicators, fiscal deficit was limited to 4.8% of GDP in 2010-11 as compared to 6.3% in 2009-10. Export and import grew positively by 29.5% and 19.0% in contrast to the negative growths experienced in the previous year. Clouds of high inflation and a temporary slowdown in the industrial growth are looming in the country as steps are being taken to mitigate such adversities.

Europe: GDP in the Eurozone increased by 1.9% in 2010-11 over 2009-10 with a high unemployment rate of around 10% and divergent performances by member countries. While Germany posted a growth of 4% driven by strong export demand and lower unemployment, the Spanish economy was adversely affected by fiscal tightening and a weak housing market with a rise in unemployment. Ireland, Portugal and Greece are seeking financial assistance from the EU and IMF after facing sharp increases in their borrowing costs and potential shortfall in funding. The UK GDP grew by 1.9% in 2010-11, continuing to recover but uneven growth, high unemployment and rising inflation has resulted in the UK household disposable income coming under pressure. There was a strong quarterly growth at the beginning of the year followed by a slowdown and winter-inflicted contraction in the December quarter. The fiscal austerity announced by the UK Government will see a 24% cut in public investment and 7% cut in real government consumption in the next five years.

TATA STEEL GROUP PERFORMANCE

Tata Steel Group steel deliveries at 23.5 million tonnes in the financial year under review were at par with the financial year 2009-10 (23.6 million tonnes). The gross steel deliveries (including the inter-group transfers) for the steel-producing entities were higher than the previous years with Tata Steel India, Tata Steel Europe, NatSteel Holdings and Tata Steel Thailand posting growth of 4%, 3%, 1% and 8% respectively. Your company's Indian operations recorded a growth of 4% in steel deliveries from 6.17 million tonnes in the financial year 2009-10 to 6.42 million tonnes in 2010-11. Along with the increase in gross steel deliveries, the steel producing entities witnessed increases in the average realisations in line with the steep increase in the raw material prices. The turnover for the Group in 2010-11 at 118,753 crores, was 16% higher than 2009-10 (Rs. 102,393 crores). While the turnover in Tata Steel India witnessed a growth of 17% from Rs. 25,022 crores in the financial year 2009-10 to Rs. 29,396 crores in the financial year 2010-11, Tata Steel Europe's turnover increased by 15% from Rs. 65,843 crores in the financial year 2009-10 to 75,991 crores in the financial year 2010-11.

The Earnings before Interest, Taxes, Depreciation and Amortisation (EBITDA) of the Group increased significantly from Rs. 9,340 crores in the fiscal year 2009-10 to Rs. 17,103 crores in the financial year 2010-11 primarily driven by the increase in prices partly off-set by the steep increase in input costs. Tata Steel India recorded an EBITDA of Rs. 12,224 crores in the financial year 2010-11 growing by 25% as compared to Rs. 9,806 crores in 2009-10. Restructuring, impairment and disposals in the current year include Rs. 2,503 crores profit on disposal of Teesside Cast Products at Tata Steel Europe. Consequently, the Group turned around with a Profit after Tax (after minority interest and share of profits of associates) for 2010-11 at Rs. 8,983 crores as compared to a loss of Rs. 2,009 crores in 2009-10.

Indian Operations: Crude steel production at 6.86 million tonnes in financial year 2010-11 was higher than the previous year (6.56 million tonnes) by 4%, thus exceeding the nameplate production capacity in the second year on enhanced capacity. There was an increase in the vessel life and heat size of the two steel melting shops enhancing their productivity to achieve the higher crude steel production of your company. Saleable steel also increased by 4% from 6.44 million tonnes recorded in financial year 2009-10 to 6.69 million tonnes in the financial year under review with higher hot metal being available from the bigger blast furnaces with higher productivity. The sales volume during the financial year 2010-11 at 6.42 million tonnes was 4% higher as compared to the previous year (6.17 million tonnes) indicating the robust growth in steel demand. Apart from the two steel melting shops, there were many units (including mines and collieries) which surpassed their respective best ever performances. Ferro Alloys and Minerals division's saleable production at 1,405k tonnes in the financial year 2010-11 was higher than financial year 2009-10 (1,350k tonnes) by 4%. The sales (including transfers to other divisions of the Company), however, at 1,464k tonnes were lower than the previous year (1,508k tonnes) by 3%. Chrome alloys exports and manganese alloys sales of the division touched new heights during the financial year under review.

Improved demand in auto and infrastructure segments led to the increase in sales and production in the Tubes division. The division recorded production of 371k tonnes in FY 2010-11, higher by 6% over FY 2009-10 (351k tonnes), while the sales improved from 349k tonnes in FY 2009-10 to 366k tonnes in 2010-11, an increase of 5%. Boosted by various improvement initiatives under 'Kar Vijay Har Shikhar' programme, the division continued to improve on its performance in various segments like 'Tata Pipes' (plumbing and irrigation), 'Tata Structura' (infrastructure) and Precision Tubes (Automotive, Process and Power sector). Sales in the Bearings division in the financial year 2010-11 at 32.95 million numbers grew by 4% against the financial year 2009-10 (31.69 million numbers), while the production at 33.14 million numbers in FY 2010-11 increased by 12% over FY 2009-10 (29.61 million numbers). The increases were primarily driven by higher demand in the domestic auto segment.

European Operations: Sales volumes of Tata Steel Europe (TSE), excluding seasonal effects, were reasonably flat for the first three quarters of the financial year 2010-11, before showing an improvement in the last quarter to the highest level of quarterly sales since financial year 2008-09. Deliveries in Tata Steel Europe during FY 2010-11 (14.9 million tonnes) increased by 3% over FY 2009-10 (14.4 million tonnes). Selling prices increased steadily through the year with the revenue per tonne increasing by around 17% over the previous year. The revenue per tonne increased relatively sharply in the first quarter of the financial year under review in anticipation of the equally sharp increase in price of raw materials, but became more modest in the second and third quarters before losing its upward momentum in the fourth quarter. Raw material prices, in contrast, peaked during the third quarter.

TSE has adopted the Tata Steel identity for trading purposes with effect from September 2010 and a progressive rebranding process is under way. The Company has also adopted a new operating model to replace the previous model of three main operating divisions (Strip Products, Long Products and Distribution and Building Systems). It is now organised into a number of business activities comprising steel-making hubs (Strip Products Mainland Europe, Strip Products UK and Long Products Europe), speciality businesses (Colours, Building Systems, Packaging, Tubes, Kalzip, Plating, Cogent Power and Speciality Steel), and a distribution and sales network (Distribution UK and Ireland, Distribution Europe and International). TSE has adopted a single sales and marketing function with eight industry-focused marketing sectors, namely, automotive, construction, packaging, rail, lifting and excavating, energy and power, industry strip and industry long products.

Europe, principally the EU, continues to be the most important market of the Company. On 24th February, 2011, Tata Steel UK Limited (TSUK), a subsidiary of TSE, signed a definitive sale agreement to sell certain assets of TCP to Sahaviriya Steel Industries Public Company Limited in a deal valuing the business at £434 million. The assets covered by the sale include the Redcar blast furnace, the Redcar and South Bank coke ovens, TCP's power generation facilities and sinter plant, and the Lackenby steel-making and casting facilities. The deal also includes TSUK and SSI entering into a joint venture to operate Redcar wharf, TCP's bulk terminal. The sale was completed on 24th March, 2011.

The 'Fit for the Future' programme initiated in response to the financial crisis continued to give results with notable reduction in the average number of employees. The deal with SSI resulted in 850 employees getting transferred to SSI and it is expected that further jobs will be created.

South-East Asian operations: NatSteel recorded an increase in steel sales by 1% in FY 2010-11 (1.80 million tonnes) over FY 2009-10 (1.78 million tonnes). The increases were most noticeable in NatSteel Singapore, the Australian units, Thailand and in trading business, while other business units in China and Vietnam witnessed decline in their respective volumes. NatSteel Singapore increased its sales volume by 106k tonnes from 738k tonnes in FY 2009-10 to 844k tonnes in FY 2010-11. Average revenue per tonne improved across all units (other than Australian units) thereby increasing the turnover of the Company. The Company sold its share in an associate company Southern Steel Berhard (SSB) during the financial year. The EBITDA of the Company, excluding the profit on sale of share of SSB in the financial year under review, reduced from the previous financial year primarily due to rise in the cost of input materials which more than off-set the increase in prices and impact of higher sales volumes.

Sales volume of Tata Steel Thailand during FY 2010-11 at 1.29 million tonnes was higher than FY 2009-10 (1.20 million tonnes) by 8%, while production increased by 6% from 1.21 million tonnes in FY 2009-10 to 1.28 million tonnes in FY 2010-11. During the financial year under review, the Company had to mothball the Mini Blast Furnace in the third quarter due to high costs of operations and low capacity utilisation, before recommencing its operations in the fourth quarter. The company incurred losses during the year primarily due to high costs of operations, low capacity utilisation and losses due to mothballing of the Mini Blast furnace partly compensated by increase in average revenue per tonne and higher sales volume.

CHINA DOMINATION IN GLOBAL STEEL TRADE

China is expected to continue to dominate the global steel trade. It has emerged as the single most important market, and its ability to sustain its rapid growth will have a fundamental impact on the global supply of steel and prices. The International Iron and Steel Institute (IISI) is cautiously optimistic that the world consumption of steel will grow by 4.6% in 2003. The international community will also watch with keen interest the ongoing efforts to shut down inefficient capacities in various countries. China's enormous consumption of steel over the past few years has been one of the main engines of the global steel industry's revival. China today is the world's largest consumer of steel, catering to its large and continuing internal infrastructural investments and also to substantial new domestic steel capacity. China's domestic steel capacity today stands at 220 million tonnes of crude steel—the largest in the world—but its consumption exceeds this level, and China still imports large tonnages of steel from international sources. Improvements in the economies of various countries have also bolstered the demand for steel, and steel prices, which have been depressed over the past seven years have firmed up on the basis of increased consumption. Availability of raw material resources in the form of iron ore and coking coal are becoming scarce and are seeing price increases also, which may result in further increases in steel prices as also protracted deliveries.

Against this backdrop, Tata Steel has understandably performed well. The various initiatives undertaken in the Company to control costs and improve productivity as also the investments made in new plant facilities have made the Company more competitive to enable the Company to focus on high value hot and cold rolled strips for sophisticated applications. Also, increased steel prices and higher demand from a buoyant Indian industry have been additional contributors towards Tata Steel registering a record performance during the year. The management team, along with employees at all levels and the union have shown a tremendous sense of teamwork and commitment in achieving this very commendable performance during the year. The challenge will undoubtedly be in sustaining, and, in fact, enhancing the level of performance of Tata Steel in the coming years, while at the same time acting responsibly by moderating the burden of price increases on its consumers. In the near future, new materials that are stronger, lighter and less expensive than steel will enter the market to compete with steel and the steel industry will need to find ways to meet these new challenges also.

EMERGING CHALLENGES OF THE FINANCE FUNCTION

The key imperative of a world class finance function is to achieve a meaningful balance of its trusteeship role in implementing effective controls and to act as a steward of the company's capital toward efficient allocation for execution of long-term strategies. The primary responsibility of a world class finance function is to achieve a meaningful balance of its trusteeship role in the oversight and implementation of effective controls as also to act as a steward of the company's capital towards efficient asset allocation for the long-term growth of the organisation. As the centres of economic activity become more distributed around the globe for an emerging market multinational like the Tata Steel Group, the organization re-orients its priorities taking into account the diversity across borders, cultures, regulatory environments and time zones. To meet these challenges, the finance function in the Tata Steel Group focuses on a value centered strategy to align its capabilities and resources most effectively with the needs of the business. This alignment is critical to enable the Company to pursue the path set by the Tata Steel Group Vision 2012 which aims to deliver significantly higher Return on Invested Capital (ROIC) to its shareholders over the next 5 years. The incremental ROIC would be generated from better margins from the existing assets through the performance improvement programmes that are currently underway, sweating of the existing capital employed in the business and efficient asset deployment in the new growth projects across the Group.

The year 2007-08 has been a historic year for Tata Steel in many ways. It was the centenary year of the company which marks a very important milestone in the company's history and we are very proud to be part of this great institution. The year also marked the completion of the Corus acquisition process on April 2, 2007 which till date is the largest transaction by an Indian company. During the year, the Company completed the long-term financing programme for the Corus acquisition. Of the total Enterprise Value of USD 14.2 billion, at the close of the Corus acquisition process on April 2, 2007, the financing included around USD 10.5 billion as bridge funding, the balance being applied out of Tata Steel's own cash and borrowings. Despite very volatile credit markets globally, the company raised around USD 6.2 billion of term debt with an average life of around 5 years at very competitive terms. This debt being non-recourse in nature was determined based on the cash flow servicing capability of our European operations and will be serviced by the Tata Steel UK (Corus) cash flows. The syndication of the above debt was completed during the year with more than 25 banks and institutions participating in the process. On the equity side, Tata Steel raised around USD 2.27 billion (Rs. 9,120 crores) of equity and convertible preference shares on a rights basis. The Company further raised around USD 875 million in Convertible Alternate Reference Securities (CARS) which is a 5 years convertible instrument with a coupon of 1% and a conversion premium of 35% to the prevailing market price in August 2007. As a result of the above, your Company raised around USD 10 billion during the year and completed the long-term financing for the Corus acquisition.

As recognition of the above, your Company won several international awards during the year for the Corus acquisition financing including the International Financing Review (IFR) Awards for the Asia Pacific Loan of the year and the Asia Pacific Leverage Loan of the year, Finance Asia award for the Best Deal of the year, AAA Asset Magazine's award for the Best Corporate Issuer amongst others.

For the finance function of the Tata Steel Group, effective Performance Management and efficient Capital Stewardship are the key enablers towards building a sustainable value centric culture. Several initiatives are currently on towards enhancing the technology effectiveness of the function of which the SAP implementation in Corus UK and South-East Asia and the Hyperion financial systems across the Group are prominent. These projects will improve the performance management process of the Company very significantly in the future.

The international financial markets have been very volatile for the last 12 months after the emergence of the sub-prime crisis in the US in mid-2007. Considering the inflationary trends and general cautiousness on the economic outlook globally, the financial markets are expected to remain weak and tentative in the near term. With general re-appraisal of risk along with increased currency volatility and firming up of the interest rates, it is very likely that the liquidity constraints will continue in the near future.

In order to finance our planned capital expenditure, the Tata Steel Group continues to follow prudent financial practices of focusing on higher generation and conservation of internal capital, improvement in the working capital management and allocation of capital to value creating projects. Our brown field expansions in India and the ongoing capital expenditure programmes globally are on track and the financing of the same are fundamentally premised on internal generations of the Group. The Company will consider raising external capital for the other growth projects as and when required based on the Company's long-term financing strategy which focuses on ensuring that the capital structure remains robust in the long-term, the financing plan provides flexibility to the balance sheet for future needs and is earnings accretive in the long-term.

RISKS, OPPORTUNITIES AND THREATS

Over the years, the Tata Steel Group (TSG) has encountered several risks and concerns during the process of its business. In keeping with the problem-solving approach that characterises the Group, it has taken several steps to counter and mitigate these, while simultaneously pursuing every underlying opportunity. Tata Steel's response to its risks, opportunities and threats have been discussed in the section below.

Growth Strategy

Since 2005, the Group embarked on an aggressive overseas acquisition strategy that added a steel capacity of 25 million tonnes across South-East Asia, the United Kingdom and Europe. An additional capacity of 3 million tonnes was added on at its existing steel plant in Jamshedpur. Enhanced capacities, new opportunities that the acquisitions generated and the benefits of the synergies have borne fruit and the Tata Steel Group today ranks amongst the top 10 steel producers in the world. With the challenges of the financial crisis of the last two years abating, the Tata Steel Group has reviewed its growth strategy. Its installed capacity in Tata Steel Europe (TSE) is sufficient to address the demand in the European market for the next 2 to 3 years, and hence the emphasis at TSE is now on capital projects that will strengthen its cost position. Additionally, there are substantial market opportunities in India and South-East Asia that warrant immediate expansion of steel capacity. There is however, a potential risk in the area of plant expansion in India, especially with green field projects, which have a longer gestation period because of possible delays that may arise on issues of land, rehabilitation, forestry and environment.

Industry Cyclicality

The steel industry is subject to cyclical swings arising from factors such as excess capacity, regional demand and supply imbalances and volatile swings in market demand. After the steep decline in steel demand in the previous year, the industry witnessed a stabilization phase followed by gradual restocking. Market confidence gradually returned and with it, we witnessed some signs of recovery in steel prices. By the end of the financial year, the industry recovery was strong in China, India and the emerging markets, while it recovered at a more modest and uneven pace in Europe and the United States. During this period, Tata Steel Europe undertook several mitigating actions, initially to align the utilisation of its installed capacity with the lower demand, and subsequently to meet the gradually rising demand by restarting idle capacity. This deliberate approach has helped to avoid new demand/supply imbalances and a double dip in prices. This, coupled with the benefits from the "Fit for the Future" initiative, is expected to enable the European operations overcome the effects of the financial crisis. In Asia, steel demand in India, China and the SEA region continued to grow and the new challenge will be to cope with the inherent risks of periodic overheating that continued rapid growth can unleash. To this end, the Group seeks to minimise any adverse consequences through appropriate sales contracting strategies and tighter procurement and working capital management.

Raw Materials Security and Price Volatility

During the financial year 2009-10, Tata Steel Group reinforced its strategy towards greater raw material security in order to insulate the Group from swings in raw material prices. This strategy was driven by several factors. These included the high raw material demand in China and India, further consolidation among the few mining majors and the recent displacement of the longstanding annual benchmarking iron ore pricing system with spot-based quarterly pricing. Quarterly contracts based on spot-pricing, if fully implemented and sustained, would imply shorter procurement cycles and greater volatility in iron ore and coking coal prices. This would give rise to a potential mismatch in timing between raw material and customer pricing for an industry that has traditionally been accustomed to long-term contracts and annual benchmark pricing for its key raw materials. TSG plans to formulate operating and hedging strategies to counter this threat.

Health, Safety and Environmental Risks

The manufacture of steel involves steps that are potentially hazardous which are likely to cause disruptions to normal operations if not executed with due care. The Group's businesses are subject to numerous laws, regulations and contractual commitments relating to health, safety and the environment in the countries in which it operates and these rules are becoming more stringent. For the ongoing 2.9 million tonnes per annum expansion in Jamshedpur, stringent, timely and intensive project management processes are being applied to ensure minimal disruptions to existing plant operations. Monitoring of dust emission levels related to the higher activity levels arising from the construction works has been stepped upto ensure they stay within permissible limits. In the mines and collieries, extra efforts are being taken to ensure workplace safety.

Technology Risks

A key challenge of the Group is to ensure that its plants are equipped with updated technologies in order to serve clients, secure cost competitiveness and maintain R&D leadership. Through the financial crisis, the Group did not cut back on investment in human resources so that it could continue to develop technologies that could advance the Group's cost competitive position, while also reducing C02 emissions from ore-based steel-making. R&D efforts are also being made to advance the Group's proprietary knowledge in order to produce new generation high strength steel, advanced and Photovoltaic coating systems, etc. For upgrading plant and equipment, funds are being made available to ensure that the Group remains technologically updated in order to meet the increasingly demanding requirements from customers across all its sectors—particularly in the fast growing automotive sector in India.

Financing

The debt for the Corus acquisition in 2008 that resides in Tata Steel Europe's Balance Sheet is a specific risk to the Group, especially in the light of the financial crisis which adversely affected its operating performance. The modified financial covenants negotiated in May 2009 have all been met in the financial year with a reduction in TSE's working capital. Nevertheless, going forward, the increasing loan amortization obligations and adherence to stricter financial covenants under the existing Senior Facility Agreement represent specific risks to TSE. Improving cash generation prospects and working capital benefits derived from initiatives taken through the entire supply chain are being closely monitored to ensure that both bank loan obligations and the business financing needs are met. Efforts are ongoing to further extend the debt maturity profile of Tata Steel Europe. The Group's operations in India and South-East Asia continue to generate cash flows and have ample headroom in committed loans to fund plant expansions and higher working capital requirements in those geographies.

References

Tata Steel, Annual Report (2000-01), p. 37.

Tata Steel, Annual Report (2002-03), p. 21.

Tata Steel, Annual Report (2003-04), pp. 14-15.

Tata Steel, Annual Report (2007-08), pp. 28-29.

Tata Steel, Annual Report (2010-11), pp. 64-67.

Tata Steel, Annual Report (2009-10), pp. 90-91.

13

Reflection

The problems of industrial relations are many, complex and highly sensitive. The maintenance of contract of service, settlement of common issues in accordance with law and the role played by the top management as a coordinator between the two groups are basic essentials of cordial relationship between the management and the labour. Preservation of the interests of the national economy by increased productivity and the satisfaction to the management and the labour are also conditions of cordial industrial relations.

The TISCO management has been alive to the problems of industrial relations right from the very beginning. The desire for a strong industrial peace, happy industrial relations and smooth human relations has always been a guiding point for their better industrial relations policy. The Tata Management has given due attention towards its employees, individually and collectively, by providing them better working and living conditions, better service conditions and establishing better understanding between them, Dorabji Tata, as early as 1917, had said: The welfare of the labouring classes must be one of the first cares of every employer. Any betterment of their conditions must proceed more from the employers downward rather than be forced up by demands from below, since labour, contented, well housed, well fed and generally well looked after, is not only as asset and advantage to the employer, but services to raise the standard of industry and labour in the country.

The evil effects of industrial revolution became apparent at Jamshedpur in spite of benevolent and humanitarian philosophy of the founder of the company. The evils of industrialization for new industrial workers were added by the problems created by the first world war, the rising prices and the consequent increasing economic hardships on the steelmen. Apart from the industrial and economic factors arousing class consciousness there were a few more forceful factors which brought the steelmen together, increased the degree of class consciousness and forced them to form their organisation. These factors were the success of the Russian Revolution and its impact on the world labour class, the establishment of the ILO, the necessity of sending labour representatives to the ILO and the stern attitude of the TISCO management with the staff association at Calcutta and Bombay in 1918. All these factors created an atmosphere favourable for emergence of class consciousness.

The labour leader, V.V. Giri, propounding the policy of "one union in one industry" set-up Metal Workers' Union in 1932 in order to streamline the steelmen movement. He started death benefit scheme for the members of the union. This new feature justified it as a welfare institution. In 1930s the Congress leaders were deputed to this important industrial centre for organising the workers. Prof. Abdul Bari, a man of passionate conviction, because the President of Labour Association in 1936. On the suggestion of many leaders its name was changed to Tata Workers' Union in 1937 with Prof. Abdul Bari as President and Michael John its secretary.

'A Tata Workers' Union quickly took up pressing problems of the steelmen. As a result of negotiation an agreement was arrived at in June 1938 accepting many demands of the steelmen. It brought a big gain for Tata steelmen.

The outbreak of the Second World War again created many labour problems. It was added by the Quit India Movement in 1942. The steelmen had gone on a strike in August 1942 which was more a political strike than economic one.

The post-war problems demanded immediate solutions to the problems of economic hardship, greater leave with wages, housing facilities, absorption of surplus hands, etc. Consequently, a fresh agreement was signed in December 1945 bringing many economic and non-economic concessions.

Before independence there was only one organisation of Tata steelmen the Tata Workers' Union, which was representing the steelmen on bargaining table. By then, the sectional feeling had come on the surface among supervisors and technicians, who set-up a separate wing within T.W.U. for protection and advancement of their sectional interests. Thus, by then there was no rival union in TISCO. After independence the political leaders started looking after this industrial centre for political objective. Amongst them the communists who had by then controlling the AITUC, soon entered in this field and set-up a rival union, the Jamshedpur Mazdoor Union in 1953.

The practice of collective bargaining, first started in 1920, was strengthened during two decades. During 1938-53 there were ten agreements reached between the TISCO and the TWU covering a large number of issues. These agreements brought many concessions for the steelmen.

The agreement of 1956 is a landmark in the history of collective bargaining. It guaranteed mutual security to union and management, provided check-off system and facilities to the elected labour representatives for attending meetings and conferences. Another important feature of that agreement is the provision of "closer association of employees with management" introducing the scheme of participative management.

Uniformity of service conditions in an industry has become a demand of the time. Consequently, in January 1962, a Central Wage Board for Iron and Steel was set-up. This provided a new forum for bargaining at industrial level. The steelmen of India and the steel plants have been benefited much by the establishment of Wage Board.

Late 1950s period was full of unrest, turmoil and violence. The long period of industrial peace had made the management slack and sleepy. The under current of unrest, then prevailing among steelmen, could not be noticed by the management. The Jamshedpur Mazdoor Union, which had gained strength the then, consolidated itself enough to call strike unparallel in the history of TISCO. The Jamshedpur Mazdoor Union called a strike starting from May 12, 1958 in support of 15 point charter of demands. The workers went on preparing for success of the strike. Appeals were made by the Chairman, Conciliation proceedings were started. In the meantime an agreement was signed between the management and the TWU. But all these failed to act as miracle in easing the industrial tension. The strike was fought by both sides. The Government deployed large number of police, military and officials to protect the plant and to maintain law and order situation. The management declared lock-out which irritated the striker, who in turn became violent. There were lathi charges, fire and arson. Strike, which had started with high morale, failed unconditionally.

The Kramcharies of TISCO preferred to have their own organisations particularly on the initiative of the industrial labour organisation. Consequently the leader of the Bhartiya Mazdoor Sangh succeeded in establishing the TISCO Karmchari Sangh in 1962. Another organisation of Karmachari, namely, the TISCO Karmchari Union was set-up in 1971 on the initiative of the leaders of Centre of Indian Trade Unions (CITU).

The two socialist leaders, associated with the HMS, succeeded in establishing a rival union, namely, the Ispat Mazdoor Sabha in 1967. This was the fifth union in series.

The contractor workers, who were left unorganised till 1970, had been subject to various exploitation. It was communist leaders who took pity upon the pitiable conditions. They worked hard to organise them under the banner of Jamshedpur Contractor Employees' Union in 1971 under the Presidentship of Kedar Das. As it was the only union of contractor workers therefore, it did not create more rivalry.

The steelmen of Tata and their associations are contented with their service conditions. It so happened when the Government was contemplating to nationalise the TISCO, the move was opposed both by the workers and their organisations. The TWU had succeeded in forcing the management to grant many concessions including wage revision through mutual negotiation. Agreement after agreement were signed during 1970s and first half of 1980s. These agreements provide a record of achievements made by the TWU.

The issues of contract labour gradually became serious. They started agitating against the non-implementation of the provisions of the Contract Labour (Regulation and Abolitions) Act, 1970. The contractor labour under the banner of their own organisation started preparation for a confrontation. Their cause was supported by the AITUC and the CITU. The management refused to yield to the genuine demands even after Government's interference. The contract labour went on a strike on February 11, 1981. The strike was fought with full morale. The management was perturbed to see the unity amongst the contract labour. There had been sit down strike and violence. The TWU showed indifference on the problem of contract labour. Their demand was fair and justified because the contract labour system had been already abolished in Jamshedpur by TISCO and the Tin Plate Company but TISCO remain adamant on its stand. As it was a legal case so it had been referred to Ranchi Labour Tribunal.

The contract labour strike has opened a new chapter. It moulded the management which granted a few concessions to contract labour such as maternity leave, medical facilities, facility of creache, bonus and payment of D.A. the greatest achievement is the job security as after end of a contract, the new contractor is persuaded to engage the labour of old contractor so that they could have security of job and security of income.

The dream to establish Iron and Steel plant in India came first to Jamsetji Nausservanji Tata. His creative mind, entrepreneurship, foresights and risk-taking-capacity shaped the whole thing, during a period when the existing environment was not at all favourable. His successful venture, direction and guidance resulted into the establishment of the first Iron and Steel Plant in the private sector in Chhotanagpur jungle of Bihar. Its construction works started in 1907. Within four years it was completed and the first ignot rolled out on February 16, 1912. Since then the factory has been expanded and modernised. Its capacity of production has been increased to the tune of 1.6 million tonnes of iron and steel every year.

The TISCO presents a fascinating picture of the old and the new blended harmoniously for optimum output. The TISCO management has a well established organization structure to administer the whole factory. It is a matter of credit to the TISCO management for providing security of job and security of income even in this age of unemployment and in face of modernization scheme.

The demand for steel in the developing world will continue

to be an important engine of growth. It will be the anchor material for construction, infrastructure, automobiles and consumer durables, China, India and Brazil, will be countries where internal demand to meet infrastructure and construction needs will continue to grow substantially in the years ahead.

India is uniquely positioned to become a major self sufficient, low cost steel manufacturing nation. Today, India annually produces only 53 million tonnes of steel, (4% of global steel production), and consumes 59 million tonnes. This works out to a per capita consumption of steel of 49 kgs. China, by contrast, currently produces 489 million tonnes of steel (36% of global steel production), and consumes 420 million tonnes to meet its development and urbanisation plans. The per capita consumption of steel in China therefore works out to be 318 kgs.—approximately 6.5 times that of India.

It is broadly recognised that over the years India has fallen behind its Asian neighbours in keeping pace with investments in infrastructure. The availability of steel would be one of the important factors in such an essential development plan. Large public works schemes and infrastructure projects would provide tens of thousands of jobs through the construction of roadways, power plants, water projects and agriculture related schemes. Evidence seems to indicate a direct correlation between the level of domestic steel production in a country and its investment level.

India is still a net importer of steel. It would not seem out of the realm of reality that India could support a domestic steel capacity of 100 million tonnes per year, with domestic consumption being, say, 85-90% of that output. Its capacity were based on maximising the use of domestic iron ore and coking coal, such self-sufficiency could help insulate the country from the runaway price spiral and currency fluctuations that impact investment in infrastructure and industrial capacity.

Tata Steel recognises that it no longer is a steel company located and operating in India above, and that it has to sustain itself in the global arena. Its long-term goals would be to continue to play a meaningful role in the economic development in India and in the overseas markets it serves. Its future growth in India and overseas will be both in steel producing facilities as also in natural resource assets. While the Company may grow and spread its geographical footprint, embracing different cultures, it will not lose sight of its great heritage of social and community responsibility.

The industrial relations policy of TISCO is based on the humanitarian approach of Jamsetji. His approach was strengthened and developed by Dorabji Tata in 1917. The management accepted that the betterment of service conditions of works should be done by the management itself rather than it be forced by the workers. The policy was further alienated by Naval H. Tata, who is known as the symbol of labour policy of the Tata house. He repeatedly advocated the policy of bipartite agreement rather than an adjudication and Government's interference. He had laid down essential features for establishing healthy industrial relations.

Industrial relations policy of TISCO has been framed, guided and amended by many top persons like J.R.D. Tata, Naval, H. Tata, R.S. Modi, R.P. Billimoria, R.S. Pande and Prof. A.D. Singh. The humanitarian approach, the desire for industrial peace and industrial harmony have helped in maintaining a cordial atmosphere for the settlement of industrial disputes.

It is a matter of credit that the management and the TWU have been practicing the method of collective bargaining, solving their all crucial issues. Collective bargaining has become the way of life. One will appreciate to know that not a single case has been referred for adjudication except the issue of contractor labour. Even services of conciliation machinery have rarely been availed. This shows their firm belief in bipartism.

The TWU had laid down a process of formulation of demand so that it could be framed taking into confidence the wishes and aspirations of the ordinary members. Proper checks and counter-checks are maintained for an agreed list of demands. The bargaining team consists of nominated persons from both sides. Both the sides nominate persons having different knowledge and skill in order to have a better team for bargaining. The management possess the services of the experts. The union team is headed by the President and the General Secretary, who are answerable to the executive committee and the general body. The scope of collective bargaining has expanding trend. New subjects have been brought on the bargaining table which shows the increasing power of the union. Gradually the prerogatives of the management are being shared by the management and the union.

The practice of *ad-hoc* agreements has been replaced by comprehensive agreements since 1970. This has helped in solving major problems in one stretch. Comprehensive agreement eliminates possibility of frequently industrial unrest. Agreement for a long period is a new trend. Previously no period was mentioned for validity of an agreement. It started first to have three years agreement in 1956 which has now become four years of period of agreement. These new practices confirm that collective bargaining practice has matured in TISCO. The long industrial peace in TISCO can be held as a fruit of collective bargaining maturity.

A changing philosophy of human relations demands replacement of conservative managerial practices by the new practice based on mutual cooperation between the capital and labour.

The genesis of participative management lies in the acceptance of the Joint Consultation Machinery as early as in 1919 in TISCO. This trend could not continue because of short comings. However, the break of the practice did not discourage forever.

The TISCO has been pioneer in this field again by establishing Works Committee in 1919, even before the statutory provision. The under current human relations policy of the company continued to flow. After a long gap again the Joint Committees were set-up in 1946. With many ups and downs, pleasant and unpleasant experiences, successes and failures this system has continued with gaining maturity.

It was in 1956 through an agreement a scheme of "Closer association of employees with management" was adopted. It laid down a three-tier structure at the base the Joint Departmental Councils, at the middle the Joint Works Council and at the top the Joint Consultative Council of Management. This scheme of participative management is a new step towards human relations.

There are at present 41 Joint Department Councils functioning in TISCO. The JDCs have been established at departmental level consisting of the equal number of representatives from both sides.

The acceptance of suggestions to the tune of 70.77% is

really a higher percentage showing satisfactory functioning of the JDCs. The two sides have learned by now to tag their group interests with the collective interests of the other side. Mutual decisions on issues like production, productivity, cost of production, method of production and improvement of quality indicate that they also keep in their mind the interests of the economy.

The Joint Works Council functions as intermediatory between the JDCs and the JCCM. It supervises the works of five committees which are the Central Canteen Managing Committee, the Welfare Committee, the Safety Committee, the Safety Appliance Committee and the Suggestion Box Committee. The JWC covers issues like works and productivity, safety, welfare and other allied issues. There had been less meetings of the JWC than prescribed one. The JWC should meet regularly. Non-holding of meetings of the JWC affects adversely in proper functioning and delays the issues which require prompt decisions. However, on the little information available it can be said that 40% of issues were accepted and implemented, the issues pending were 40% and rest 20% issues were dropped.

The JCCM, the apex body, also has less meetings. It has never met quarterly. The non-holding of the meeting might be because of various reasons. But it must have delayed the discussions and prompt decisions. In one meeting it discussed 74 issues, out of which 49 issues were accepted and implemented. In that meeting nearly 66.2% recommendations were accepted by the JCCM. The acceptance of such a high percentage of recommendations may be held as satisfactory performance. If the JCCM would have met regularly, there might have been better record of performance. Further the non-holding of regular meetings results into accumulation of issues. On the other hand, one finds that in one meeting there were 74 issues for discussions. It is not possible to discuss cooly and in detail so many issues in a few hours of one meeting. Hasty decisions may not be correct decisions. And even if the decisions were correct, for granted, it is not physically possible to give proper attention to so many issue at one time.

The nature of decisions are also a point of consideration. Though under the scheme this is called as consultative but in practice the decisions are based on mutual understanding and mutual consent. A decision arrived at the Joint Council's meeting, if under the authorised and financial control, the management accept the decisions and implement these properly. This shows the decisions taken under the jurisdictional power are decisions which can be called as final. Therefore, in such cases the nature of decision can be called as "Decision-making."

It has been the findings of this study that performance of the TISCO has not been upto the expectation for which many factors have been responsible. But the most important factor has been the neglect of human element which has led to unsatisfactory state of industrial relations. Inter and intra-union rivalries due to multiplicity of trade unions and their close attachment with political parties, bureaucratic attitude of marginal personnel, lack of adequate cooperation between management and workers, political instability in the states where plants have been located, ineffective working of grievances handling machinery, lack of discipline among workers, failure of collective bargaining machinery, etc. have adversely influenced the industrial relations in TISCO.

Suggestions

The industrial relations policy of TISCO is based on the humanitarian approach of the founder Jamsetji Nausservanji Tata which was developed by Dorabji Tata, Naval H. Tata and J.R.D. Tata in such a way that the Tata policy of industrial relations has become a model worth adoptable by other industrial establishments of India. The relationship of cooperation, initially starting from the stage of "antagonistic cooperation", has reached the stage of "closer association of employees with management." With its chequered life, it has been developed through mutual negotiation in 1956. Since then the three-tier not work of joint councils system is functioning. The functions of the joint councils are satisfactory though there are enough scope for making it more active, constructive and fruitful.

The meetings of the Joint Councils should be held regularly. Discussion should be conducted in free and frank atmosphere without status consciousness.

The other joint committees existing at present can make more contribution by toning up their way of functioning. There is a proverb "Even best can be improved." Though the joint councils and joint committees are functioning, amidst various odds, to our satisfaction still their performance can be improved if efforts are made in that direction.

A grievance procedure with its present structure of three steps ladder system supplemented by open-door policy has satisfactory record of prompt, quick and early settlement of grievances.

Collective bargaining has become life and blood of industrial relations system. It has matured with the adoption of the practice of comprehensive and long-term agreements. The parties have learned the art of negotiation, the way to remove misunderstanding and developed the desire to develop mutual understanding and mutual decisions for the good of both. The human relations approach has added to this policy to such an extent that it has celebrated longer periods of industrial peace, probably unparallel in the history of industrial relations in India.

MISSION, VISION AND VALUES

Mission of TISCO

Consistent with the vision and values of the founder Jamsetji Tata, Tata Steel strives to strengthen India's industrial base through the effective utilisation of staff and materials. The means envisaged to achieve this are high technology and productivity, consistent with modern management practices. Tata Steel recognises that while honesty and integrity are the essential ingredients of a strong and stable enterprise, profitability provides the main spark for economic activity. Overall, the Company seeks to scale the heights of excellence in all that it does in an atmosphere free from fear, and thereby reaffirms its faith in democratic values.

Vision of TISCO

- **To seize the opportunities of tomorrow and create a future that will make us an EVA positive company:** To be on the look-out for and shape the opportunities to get the first-mover advantage and remain ahead of competition. The opportunities could exist in emerging technologies, new business models, value creation, customer service, new products, services or businesses, financing options, etc. To mobilize all resources and efforts through value-based management that will help us earn returns better than the cost of capital. The equation below shows that the EVA is positive when the RONA is greater than the cost of the capital invested.

EVA = (RONA – WACC) X Invested Capital
EVA Economic Value Added
RONA Return on Net Assets (= Net Operating Profit After Tax/Net Assets)
WACC Weighted Average Cost of Capital

Our resolve to become EVA positive is significant in the context of industry structure for steel business worldwide. There are few steel companies that have returned value consistently. We believe that Tata Steel can do so based on its strengths and new initiatives.

- **To continue to improve the quality of life of our employees and the communities we serve.** Tata Steel will continue to be guided by the TATA group's endeavour to improve the quality of life of the communities we serve (e.g. Customers, customers' customers, suppliers, governments, shareholders, local community, etc.). The company has always tried to maintain a good quality of life for its employees. The company, ahead of any legislation, introduced provident fund, maternity leave, eight hour working, etc. Similar spirit will continue to guide our future efforts in improving the quality of life of our employees.
- **Revitalize the core business for a sustainable future:** The core business is sought to be revitalized by a comprehensive set of initiatives under the ASPIRE program. Aspirational initiatives will be taken in each area of our enterprise to reduce costs and enhance revenues coupled with finance prudence to galvanize the core business into an

attractive investment option. By making the core business EVA positive we wish to ensure its long-term sustainability.

- **Venture into new businesses that will own a share of our future:** By the year 2007 we expect to enter into at least one major new business that would have grown comparable in size to the core business. We also expect to continuously evaluate and expand the new businesses to compliment the cyclical nature of the steel business.
- **Uphold the spirit and values of TATAs towards nation-building:** Even as the face of the new business may be fundamentally different from our existing core businesses what will bind them together will be the spirit and the values of TATAs. It is our belief that upholding these values will continue to be the reason for our enduring success and respectability.

Strategic Goals

- **Move from commodities to Brands:** To beat the industry trend in a situation of over-supply we need to move away from selling commodities by converting them into Brands. Even as we will continue to leverage and take to greater heights the value of TATA brand, there will be efforts to create new images and associations for our services and products in current as well as new businesses.
- **EVA Positive Core Business:** At the present level of investment, we require a PBT of Rs. 800 to 1000 crore (at MAT level of taxation the PBT requirement is at Rs. 800 crore) to become EVA positive. We expect to complete this journey in about 3 years time. Our effort will be to maximize the present value of future EVA so that the investor confidence is restored and reinforced in the core business. In the context of industry structure, the company intends to make it possible through the ASPIRE program.
- **Continue to be lowest cost producer of steel:** We

acquired the status of the lowest cost producer of steel in 2001. The world outside is, however, changing fast and the lowest cost status is constantly under threat from new technologies, currency depreciation in other countries, cost escalation of raw material inputs, energy and labour, etc. Maintaining the world benchmark will be one of the greatest challenges for the core steel business.

- **Value creating partnerships with customers and suppliers:** We recognize the value of partnerships and so do our customers and suppliers whom we have helped grow in the past. We respect these relationships and wish to carry them forward by creating mutually value-adding partnerships. We hope to build the new business models by forging alliances with our customers and suppliers to strengthen the value chain helping us reduce the system costs, improve service levels, reach and offer new products and services.
- **Enthused and Happy employees:** A lot is dependent on the individual spirit and enthusiasm of the employees to realize our vision. We will accelerate our efforts to provide a work environment that will ensure a sense of purpose and personal growth for each individual. We wish to see the smile on every face every day.
- **Sustainable Growth:** We wish grow but intend to temper our ambitions for growth with financial prudence to ensure a long-term sustainable future. While we will be willing to experiment and take the risk with new business models and ideas, we wish to fuel our growth ambition on conservative financials.
- **Management of Knowledge:** We recognize and endorse the importance of knowledge as a source of innovation and competitive advantage. We wish to leverage all our associations within and outside the company to harness the ideas and provide the means for exchanging and growing knowledge. Company has started the efforts to create an atmosphere where free exchange of knowledge is

amongst its 46,000 plus employees and has created the infrastructure to enable this exchange.

- **Strategically Outsourcing:** The non-core activities and the activities that could help us grow by leveraging our brand image without parting with sources of competitive advantage would be selectively outsourced.
- **Encouragement of Innovation and Allow the Freedom to Fail:** Value-based management to make the core business EVA positive will be highly dependent on innovation. Active and visible encouragement for innovation seeking behaviour will be provided to one and all. A culture of taking calculated risks will be nurtured by allowing the Freedom to take those risks without the fear of reprimand for failure.
- **Excellence at TBEM:** The TATA Business Excellence Model, which lays stress on Results through the processes of Customer and Market Focus, Strategic planning, Information and Ananlysis, Human Resource Development, Partnerships, etc. would be our guiding model for business excellence. We will continue to leverage the model's strengths by insisting on benchmarking, Evaluation and Improvement cycles and the core values of the model to break new barriers of excellence.
- **Unleashment of people's potential and creation of leaders who will build the future:** The entrepreneurial spirit of individuals and their inherent potential will find expression in the opportunities provided by adequate stretch and nurturing. Development of individuals who can create and lead the businesses of tomorrow will be emphasized through sustained talent identification and development programs.
- **Invest in attractive new Businesses:** We will actively seek attractive new business opportunities that will expectedly have the characteristics different from the core business. The new opportunities may have less Asset intensive nature, shorter payback

period or a different business cycle that can compliment steel. The opportunities may or may not be related to steel or processing industry.

- **Ensuring Safety and Environmental Sustainability:** Safety is a key priority area for our current business. It will continue to be our priority for the new businesses as well. Using suitable processes, technology and work ethic will reinforce our concern for environment and the desire to conserve the natural resources.

Bibliography

PART A

AITUC (2001), Recent Wage Agreements, All India Trade Union Congress (AITUC), New Delhi.

Amin, Samir (2000), "The Political Economy of the Twentieth Century", *Monthly Review*, Vol. 52, No. 2, pp. 1-17.

Anderson, Perry (1978), "The Limits and Possibilities of Trade Union Action", in Clarke, Tom and Clements, Lawrie (ids.), Trade Unions Under Capitalism, Humanities Press, New Jersey, pp. 333-50.

Adler, Max (1978), "Metamorphosis of the Working Class" in Bottomore, Thomas B. and Goode, Patrick (eds.), Austro Marxism, Oxford University Press.

Bardhan, Pranav (2002), "The political Economy of Reform in India", in Mohan, Rakesh (ed.), Facets of the Indian Economy, New Delhi, pp. 123, 135.

Bhattacherjee, D. (2000), "Globalising Economy, Localising Labour", *Economic and Political Weekly*, Vol. XXXV, No. 42, October.

Bardhan, Pranab (1992), "A Political Economic Perspective in Development", in Jalan, Bimal (ed.).

Bagchi, A.K. (2002), Capital and Labour Redefined: India and the Third World, Tulika, New Delhi, pp. 233-34.

Bahl, Vinay (1995), The Making of the Indian Working Class, Sage, New Delhi.

Bengal Chambers of Commerce (BCC) (1998), Productivity on the Rise in West Bengal, BCC, Calcutta.

Business India (1998), "Clutching at Straws", *Business India*, March 9-22.

Bettelheim, Charles (1976), Class Struggles in the USSR, Monthly Review Press, New York.

Beyron, H. (1975), Working for Ford, E.P. Publishing, Wakefield.

Chandra, Bipin (1992), "The Colonial Legacy", in Jalan, Bimal (ed.).

Clyde E. Dankert, "On temporary Unionism", p. 1.

Chamberlin, W. Neil (1951): "Collective Bargaining", Mc Graw Hill, New York.

Cole, G.D.H. (1962a), A History of Socialist Thought, Vol. 1, Macmillan, London.

____(1962b), A History of Socialist Thought, Vol. 2: Marxism and Anarchism, 1850-90, Macmillan, London.

____(1962c), An Introduction to Trade Unionism, George Allen and Unwin, Third Impression, London.

Clements, Laurie (1978), "Reference Groups and Trade Union Consciousness", in Clarke, Tom and Clements, Lawrie (eds.), Trade Unions under Capitalism, Humanities Press, New Jersey, pp. 309-32.

"Compulsory Adjudication Syndrome in India: Some Implications for Workplace Relations", in Debi S. Saini (ed.) Labour Law Work and Development: Essays in Honour of P. Gopa Krishnan, Westvill, New Delhi.

D. Jarath, D. (1992), Employment and Unionism in Indian Industry, Friederick Ebert Foundation, New Delhi.

Dreze, Jean, and Sen, Amartya (2003),. Development and Participation. Oxford University Press, New Delhi.

Davala, Sarath E.A. (1992), Employment and Unionisation in Indian Industry, Friedrich Ebert Stifting, New Delhi.

Dev, Mahendra S. and Ravi, C. (2007), "Poverty and Inequality: All India and States, 1983-2005", *Economic and Political Weekly*, 10 Feb. 2007, pp. 519-20.

D'Art, Daryl and Thomas Turner (2003), "Union recognition in Ireland: One step forward or two steps back?", *Industrial Relations Journal*, Vol. 34, No. 3.

Engels, F. (1978), Socialism: Utopian and Scientific, Progress Publishers, First Printing 1954,

Fallon, Petter R. and Robert E.B. Lucas (1991), "The Impact of Job Security Regulations in India and Zimbabwe", *World Bank Economic Review*, Vol. 5, No. 3.

Frank, Jannenbaum, "The Labour Movement", p. 29.

Freeman, R. and Medoff, J. (1984), What Do Unions Do?, Basic Books, New York.

Freeman, R.B. (1992), Labour Market Institutions and Policies: Help or Hindrance, proceedings of the World Bank Annual Conference on Development Economics, supplement to the *World Bank Economic Review and World Bank Research Observer*, World Bank, Washington, D.C., pp. 117-56.

Ghosh, Jayati . (2002), "Exporting Jobs or Watching Them Disappear", in Ghosh and Chandrasekhar (eds.).

Ghosh, Jayati and Chandrasekhar, C.P. (2002), The Market That Failed, Left Word, New Delhi.

Government of India, Report of the National Commission on Labour, 1969, p. 345, para 24.14.

Government of India, Report of the Second Pay Commission, 1959, p. 551.

George, W. Jaylor, "Government Regulation of Industrial Relations", p. 20.

Gapasin, Fernando and Yates, Michael (1997), "Organising the Unorganised: Will Promises become Practices?", *Monthly Review*, Vol. 49, No. 3, pp. 46-62.

Gorz, Andre (1967), Strategy for Labour: A Radical Proposal, Beacon, Boston.

Gramsci, Antonio (1977), "The Turin Workers' Council" (trans. From L' Ordine Nuovo, 1919-20), in Robin Blackburr Revolution and Class Struggle: A Reader in Marxist Politics, Glasgow, pp. 307-409.

Globalisation and Labour-Management Relations: Dynamics of Change, Response (A Division of Sage) Publications, New Delhi.

Gramsci, Antonio (1968), "Soviets in Italy", *New Left Review*, Vol. 51.

Gramsci Antonio (1988), An Antonio Gramsci Reader, in David Frogacs (ed.), Shocken Books, New York.

Hammer, M. and J. Champy (1993), Reengineering the Corporation: A Manifesto for Business Revolution, Nicholas Brearley, London.

Harward Business Review (2003), "Capital *vs.* Talent", July.

Hobsbawm, Eric (1988), The Age of Revolution, Cardinal, London, First Published, 1962.

Hyman, Richard (1971), Marxism and the Sociology of Trade Unions, Pluto Press.

Hoxie, Robert F. (1920), Trade Unionism in the United States, D. Appleton and Company, New York.

Hyman, R. and Fryer, R.H. (1978), "Trade Unions: Sociology and Political Economy", in Clarke, Tom and Clements, Lawrie (eds.), Trade Unions under Capitalism, Humanities Press, New Jersey, pp. 152-74.

Harris, A. Millis and Royal E. Mongtomery, *The Economics of Labour,* Vol. III, Organized Labour, p. 3.

Henwood, Doug (1996), "Post What?", *Monthly Review,* Vol. 48, No. 4, pp. 1-11.

Hyman, Richard (1999), "Imagined Solidarities: Can Trade Unions Resist Globalisation?", in Leisink (ed.).

Hancke, Bob (1993), "Trade Union Membership in Europe, 1960-1990", *British Journal of Industrial Relations,* 31, No. 4, pp. 593-613.

International Labour Organisation (1991), Report of the Director General to the 78th Session, ILO, Geneva. Government of India (1996a), Agenda: 33rd Session of the Standing Labour Committee, September 13, Ministry of Labour, New Delhi.

— (1996b), Agenda: 33rd Session of the Indian Labour Conference, Ministry of Labour, New Delhi, October 23-25.

_____(1996c), Annual Report, 1995-96, Ministry of Labour (also 1998-99 Report), New Delhi.

_____(1996d), Report of the Working Group on Labour Policy: Ninth Five Year Plan (1997-2002), Ministry of Labour, New Delhi.

Irving, Bernstein, "The Growth of American Unions", *American Economics Review,* June (1954).

INTUC: Eighth Annual Conference at Surat.

ILO (1997), World Labour Report, 1997-98: Industrial Relations,

Democracy, and Social Stability, International Labour Organisation, Geneva.

Jalan, Bimal.(ed.) (1992),"The Indian Economy: Problems and Prospects, Viking, New Delhi.

Jhaveri, Narendra (2003), "India's Growth Chase", *Economic and Political Weekly*, pp. 4336-350.

Joh, T. Dunlop, "The Development of Labour Orgnisation", pp. 163-96.

Joseph, Shister, "The Logic of Union Growith", *Journal of Political Economy*.

Julius, Rezler, "Union Growth Reconsidered" (M/S).

Jhaveri, Narendra (2003), "India's Growth Chase", *Economic and Political Weekly*, pp. 4336-350.

Kochan, T., H. Katz and R. Mckersie (1986), The Transformation of American Industrial Relations, Basic Books, New York.

Kuczynski, Jurgen (1975), The Rise of the Working Class, McGraw Hill, New York.

Kamoche, Ken (2000), Sociological Paradigms and Human Resources: An African Context, Ashgate Publishing Limited, Aldershot (U.K.).

Kochan, T. and M. Weinstein (1994), "Recent Developments in U.S. Industrial Relations," *British Journal of Industrial Relations*, Vol. 32, pp. 483-84.

Kochan, T., H. Katz and R. Mckersie (1986), The Transformation of American Industrial Relations, Basic Books, New York.

Korpi, W. (1983), The Democratic Class Struggle, Routledge and Kegan, London.

Kuruvilla, Sarosh (1996), "Industrialization Strategies and National Industrial Relations Policy in Southeast Asia: Singapore, Malaysia, Philippines, and India", *Industrial and Labour Relations Review*, Vol. 49, No. 4, pp. 635-57.

Katz, Harry C. and Darbishire, Owen (2000), Converging Divergences: Worldwide Changes in Employment System, Comell University Press, Ithaca.

Lewis, J. (1992), "Gender and the Development of Gender Regimes", *Journal of European Social Policy*, Vol. 2, No. 3.

Lozovsky, A. (1975), Marx and the Trade Unions, Radical Book Club, 2nd print in India, Calcutta.

Lenin, V.I. (1960), *Collected Works*, Vol. IV, Progress Publishers, Moscow.

Lenin, V.I. (1978), What is to be Done?, Progress Publishers, First Published in 1947, Moscow.

Lipset, S.M. (1960), "The Political Process in Trade Unions: A Theoretical Statement", in W. Galenson and S.M. Lipset (eds.), Labour and Trade Unionism, Wiley, New York.

Lambert, Rob (1999), "Australia's Historic Industrial Relations Transition", in Leisink (ed.).

Mathur, A.N. (1989), Industrial Restructuring and Union Power; Micro-Economic Dimensions of Economic Restructuring and Industrial Relations in India, ILO-ARTEP, New Delhi.

_____(1992), Employment Security and Industrial Restructuring in India: Separating Facts from Folklore The Exit Policy Controversy, IIM, Calcutta.

Mukherji, Aditya (2002), Imperialism, Nationalism and the Making of the Indian Capitalist Class, 1920-47, Sage, New Delhi.

Mamkottam, K (2003), Labour and Change: Essays on Globalisation, Technological Change and Labour in India, Response (A Division of Sage), New Delhi.

Mortan, A.L. (1974), A Peoples History of England, International Publishers, 4th Impression, New York.

Marglin, S.A. (1974), "What Do Boses Do?—the Origins and Functions of Hierarchy in Capitalist Production", *Review of Radical Political Economics*, Vol. 6, pp. 60-112

Marx, Karl (1978a), *Capital*, Vol. 1, Progress Publishers, First Published in 1954, Moscow.

_____(1978b), Wages, Price and Profit, Progress Publishers, Moscow, First Published in 1947.

Michaes, R.W.E. (1966), Political Parties, Free Press, First Published in 1915, NY.

Mann, Michael (1973), Consciousness and Action among the Western Working Class, Macmillan.

Mabey, Christopher, Denise Skinner and Timothy Clark (eds.), Experiencing Human Resource Management, Sage, London.

Mathur, A.N. (1991), Industrial Restructuring and Union Power, ILO-ARTEP, New Delhi.

Mishra, L. (2001), Economy and Labour, Manak Publications Pvt. Ltd., New Delhi.

Mukherjee, Aditya (2002), Imperialism, Nationalism and the Making of the Indian Capitalist Class, 1920-47, Sage, New Delhi.

Marx, K. and Engels, F. (1977), Manifesto of the Communist Party, Progress Publishers, 2nd revised edition, reproduction of the translation made by Samuel Moore in 1888, Moscow.

Moody, Kim (1997), "American Labour: A Movement Again?", *Monthly Review*, Vol. 49, No. 3, pp. 63-79.

Nayyar, Baldev Raj (2003), "Economic Globalisation and its Advance, From Shallow to Deep Integration", *Economic and Political Weekly*, November 8, pp. 4780-82.

NCEUS (2007), Report on Condition of Work and Promotion of Livelihoods in the Unorganised Sector, National Commission on Enterprises in the Unorganised Sector, www.nceus.gov.in.

New Perspectives in Human Resource Management, Rouledge, London.

Nair, K.R. (1996), "Kerala", in Venkata Ratnam, C.S. (2000), Economic Changes and Industrial Relations in Indian States, Global Business Press, New Delhi.

Observer Research Foundation (1996), Economic Reforms: The Role of the States and the Future of Centre-State Relations, New Delhi.

Offe, Claus and Wiesenthal, Helmet (2002), "Two Logics of Collective Action", in John Kelly (ed.), Industrial Relations, Vol. II, Routledge, London.

Papola, T.S. (1994), "Employment, Growth and Social Protection of Labour in India", in P. Sinha, C.S. Venkat Ratnam and G. Botterweek (eds.), Labour and Unions in a Period of Transition, Friedrich Ebert Stiftung, Delhi.

Perrow, Charles (1992), "Organisation Theorists in a Society of Organisations", *International Sociology*, Vol. 7, No. 3, pp. 371-80.

Podur, Justin (2003), "Beyond Disillusionment", *Frontline*, Vol. 20, No. 5, March 1-14, pp. 62-63.

Panitch, Leo and Gindin, Sam (2000), "Transcending Pessimism: Rekindling Socialist Imagination", in Panitch, Leo and Leys, Colin (eds.) Socialist Register, K.P Bagchi, Calcutta, pp. 1-30.

Pateman, Carole (1970), Participation and Democratic Theory, Cambridge University Press, London.

Papola, T.S. and G. Rodgefs (eds.) (1992), Labour Institutions and Economic Development in India, International Institute for Labour Studies, Geneva.

"Productivity Agreements and Industrial Relations in India", *Management and Change*, Vol. 3, No. 2,

Rastogi, J.L., *op. cit.*, p. 9.

Robertson, D.H., "The Control of Industry."

Ramaswamy, E.A. (2000), Managing Human Resources: A Contemporary Text, Oxford University Press, New York.

Rudolph, Lloyd and Rudolph, Susanne (1987), In Pursuit of Lakshmi: The Political Economy of the Indian State, The University of Chicago Press, Chicago.

R.F. Hoxie as coated in *Ibid.*, p. 3.

Ramaswamy, E.A. (2000), Managing Human Resources: A Contemporary Text, Oxford University Press, New Delhi.

Sainsbury, D. (1954), "Dual Welfare and Sex Seggregation of Access to Social Benefits, Income Maintenance Policies in the UK, the US, the Netherlands, and Sweden", *Journal of Social Policy*, Vol. 22, No. 1.

Slichter, S.H. (1929), "The Current Labour Policies of American Industries", *Quarterly Journal of Economics*, Vol. XLII, No. 3, May.

Standing, Guy (1991), "Structural Adjustment and Labour Market Policies, Towards Social Adjustment?", in G. Standing and V. Tokman (eds.), Towards Social Adjustment Labour Market Issues in Structural Adjustment, ILO, Geneva.

Shyam Sunder, K.R. (1998), "Industrial Conflict in Tamilnadu, 1960-80", Ph.D. Thesis, Mumbai University, Mumbai.

Shyam Sunder, K.R. (1999), "Indutrial Conflict and the

Institutional Framework of the Industrial Relations System in India", *Management and Change*, Vol. 3, No. 1, pp. 53-88.

Standing, Guy (2002), "Human Security and Social Protection", in Ghosh and Chandrasekhar (eds.).

Saini, Debi S. and Pawan Budhwar (2003), "HRM in India", in Pawan Budhwar (ed.), Human Resource Management in Asia-Pacific Countries, Routledge, London.

Sidney and Beatrice Webbs, "The Histroy of Trande Unionism", p. 1.

Sirianni, Cannen (1982), Workers' Control and Socialist Democracy: The Soviet Experience, Verso, London.

Sheth, N.R. (1993), "Our Trade Unions: An Overview", *Economic and Political Weekly*, Vol. 28, No. 6, pp. 231-36.

Sciacchitano, Katherine (2000), "Unions, Organising and Democracy: Living in One's Time, Building for the Future", Dissent, Spring, pp. 75-81.

Saini, Debi S. and Sami, A. Khan (eds.) (2000), Human Resource Management: Perspectives for the New Era, Response Books (A Division of Sage), New Delhi.

Shyam Sunder, K.R., (2003), "Trade Unions and New Strategies for Organising Labour: New Wine in Old Bottle?", *The Indian Journal of Labour Economics*, Vol. 46, No. 2.

Shorter, E. and Tilly, C. (1974), Strikes in France, 1830-1968, Cambridge University Press, Cambridge.

Thakur, C.P. and Munson, Fred. C. (1969), Industrial Relations in Printing Industry, Shri Ram Centre for Industrial Relations, New Delhi.

The Economist (2001), "Survey of Globalisaiton", September 29.

T.E. Chester and Gardner Foresight, "Concept of Joint Consultation in Great Britain", *Indian Journal of Labour Economics*, Vol. II, Nos. 2-3, July-October 1959, pp.141-42.

The typical example being South Metropolitan Gas Company.

Thompson, E.P. (1980), The Making of the English Working Class, Penguin, London.

The Hindustan Times, New Delhi.

Trotsky, Leon (1969), "The Trade Unions in Britain", in Leon Trotsky on the Trade Unions, Pathfinder Press, pp. 53-57.

Thompson, E.P. (1980), The Making of the English Working Class, Penguin, London.

The Economic Times (2003), "See No Evil, Hear No Evil," November, 14. (Quotes Forbes on Hiring illegal immigrants on the sly through layers of contract by Wal-Mart and other retailers in the U.S.A.).

U.K. Industrial Relations Handbook, 1961, p. 23.

US Department of Labour (1994), Fact Finding Report—Commission on the Future of Worker-Management Relations (also called John T. Dunlop Commission Report), Washington D.C., USA.

Venkata Ratnam (1996), Welfare and Moneyfare: Collective Bargaining and Social Security, A Project of UNDP and Centre for Development Studies (Memio).

Venkata Ratnam (1991), Unusual Collective Agreements, Global Business Press, New Delhi.

Virmani, B.R. (1995), New Perspective on Industrial Relations, Fredrich Eburt Stiftung, New Delhi.

Venkata Ratnam, C.S. (2003), Negotiated Change: Collective Bargaining. Liberalisation and Restructuring in India, Response (A Division of Sage Publications), New Delhi.

_____(2001), Globalisation and Labour-Management Relations: Dynamics of Change, Response (A Division of Sage) Publications, New Delhi

Visser, Jelle (1989), European Trade Unions in Figures, Kluwer Law and Taxation Publishers, Boston.

Venkata Ratnam, C.S. (1977), Industrial Relations in Indian States, Industrial Relations Research Association and Global Business Press, New Delhi.

Venkata Ratnam, C.S. and Anil Varma (ed.) (1998), Challenge of Change—Industrial Relations in Indian Industry, Allied, New Delhi.

Venkata Ratnam, C.S., (2003), "Negotiating Flexibility", in Negotiated Change, Response Books, New Delhi.

Venkata Ratnam, C.S. (1996), Welfare to Moneyfare: A Study of Social Security Clauses in Collective Bargaining, A study sponsored by UNDP and the Centre for Development Studies, International Management Institute, New Delhi.

Whyte, W. F., and Whyte, K. K. (1988), Making Mondragon: The Growth and Dynamics of Worker Co-operative Complex, ILR Press, Ithaca, NY.

Wallerstein, Immanuel (2002), "New Revolts Against The System", *New Left Review*, 18, Nov.-Dec.

World Bank (1995), World Development Report—Workers in an Integrated World, World Bank and Oxford University Press.

Yodder, Dale (1957): "personnel Management and Industrial Relations, Prentice Hall INC, New York.

Yates, Michael D. (1999), "Braverman and the Class Struggle", *Monthly Review*, Vol. 50, No. 8, pp. 2-11.

PART B

Business India (1998), "Clutching at Straws", *Business India*, March 9-22.

Chester, T.E. and Gardner, foresight (1959): "Concept of Joint consultation in Great Britain", *Indian Journal of Labor Economics*, Vol. II, Nos. 2-3, July- October, p. 142.

Chamberlin, W. Neil, Collective Bargaining, Mc Graw-Hill, New York, 1951, p. 121.

Dunlop, John T. (1958), 'Industrial Relations Systems', Hennry Hott and Company, New York.

D'Art, Daryl and Thomas Turner (2003), "Union recognition in Ireland: One Step forward or two steps back?, *Industrial Relations Journal*, Vol. 34, No. 3.

Flanders, Allen, "Bargaining Theory: The Classical Model Reconsidered," Industrial Relations—Contemporary Issues, Edited by B.C. Roberts, Macmillan, London, 1968, p. 25.

Hyman, Richard (1999), "Imagined Solidarities: Can Trade Unions Resist Globalization?", in Leisink (ed).

Kamoche, Ken (2000), 'Sociological Paradigms and Human Resources: An African Context', Ashgate Publishing Limited, Aldershot (UK).

Kochan, T. and M. Weinstein (1994), "Recent Developments in US Industrial Relations," *British Journal of Industrial Relations*, Vol. 32, pp. 483-84.

Lala, R.M., 'The Creation of Wealth', p. 125.

Lambert, Rob (1999), "Australia's Historic Industrial Relations Transition", in Leisink (ed.).

Mamkoottam, K. (2003), Labour and Change: Essays on Globalisation, Technological Change and Labor in India, Response (A Division of Sage), New Delhi.

Mishra, L. (2001), 'Economy and Labour', Manak Publications Pvt. Ltd., New Delhi.

Mabey, Christopher, Denise Skinner and Timothy Clark (eds.) (1998), Experiencing Human Resource Management, Sage, London.

Mathur, A.N. (1991), 'Industrial Restructuring and Union Power', ILO-ARTEP, New Delhi.

Mamkootam, K. (1999), "Productivity Agreements and Industrial Relations in India", *Management and Change,* Vol. 3, No. 2.

'National Commission on Labour' (1969): Government of India, Report, p. 345, par. 24.14.

Nayyar, Baldev Raj (2003), "Economic Globalization and its Advance, From Shallow to Deep Integration", *Economic and Political Weekly,* November 8, pp. 4780-82.

Pande, R.S., "Changing Pattern of Industrial Relations", Man-Management in Tata Steel, p. 10.

Pandey, R.N., "Industrial Relations in Major Industrial Units at Jamshedpur", (Ph.D. Thesis submitted in Bhagalpur University), 1970, p. 18.

Patil, B.R. (1998), "A Contemporary Industrial Relations Scenario in India with reference to Karnataka", *The Indian Journal of Industrial Relations,* Vol. 33, No. 3.

Rastogi, J.L. (1958): 'Casselman's Labour Dictionary', Industrial Relations in Uttar Pradesh, Kitab Printing, Lucknow.

Report of the National Commission on Labor (1969), Govt. of India, p. 234.

Ramaswamy, E.A. (2000), Managing Human Resources: A Contemporary Text, Oxford University Press, New Delhi.

________ (1994), 'The Rayo Spinners—Strategic Management of Industrial Relations' , Oxford University Press, Delhi.

'Second Pay Commission Report' (1959), Govt. of India.

Singh, A.D., "Welcome Address", Seminar on Man-Management For Peace, Productivity and Progress, p. 5.

Shyam Sunder, K.R. (2003), "Trade Unions and New Strategies for Organising Labour: New Wine in Old Bottle?", *The Indian Journal of Labour Economics*, Vol. 46, No. 2.

Saini, Debi S. and Sami, A. Khan (eds.) (2000), Human Resource Management: Perspectives for the New Era, Response Books (A Division of Sage), New Delhi.

Saini, Debi S. (2003): "Dynamics of New Industrial Relations and Postulates of Industrial Justice", *The Indian Journal of Labour Economics*, Vol. 46, No. 4, Oct.-Dec.

Saini, Debi S. and Sami A. Khan (eds.) (2003), "Dynamics of New Industrial Relations and Postulates of Industrial Justice", *The Indian Journal of Labour Economics*, Vol. 46, No. 4, Oct.-Dec.

Tata Steel, Annual Report (2000-01).

Tata Steel, Annual Report (2001-02).

Tata Steel, Annual Report (2002-03).

Tata Steel, Annual Report (2003-04).

Tata Steel, Annual Report (2004-05).

Tata Steel, Annual Report (2005-06).

Tata Steel, Annual Report (2006-07).

Tata Steel, Annual Report (2007-08).

Tata Steel, Annual Report (2008-09).

Tata Steel, Annual Report (2009-10).

Tata Steel, Annual Report (2010-11).

Tata Steel, Annual Report (2000-01), p. 37.

Tata Steel, Annual Report (2002-03), p. 21.

Tata Steel, Annual Report (2003-04), pp. 14-15.

Tata Steel, Annual Report (2007-08), pp. 28-29.

Tata Steel, Annual Report (2010-11), pp. 64-67.

Tata Steel, Annual Report (2009-10), pp. 90-91

Tata, Naval H., "Industrial Relations", Man-Management in Tata Steel, p. 1.

TISCO, Man Management in Tata Steel, p. Introductory page.

TISCO, "Seminar on Man-Management for Peace", 'Productivity and Progress,' Proceeding of the Seminar, p. 20.

TISCO, 'Man -Management in Tata Steel'.

The Economic Times (2003), "See No Evil, Hear No Evil," November 14. (Quotes Forbes on Hiring Illegal immigrants on the sly through layers of contract by Wal-Mart and other retailers in the U.S.A.).

Tripartite Conclusions (1942-67): Govt. of India, p. 79.

'UK Industrial Relations Handbook' (1961).

US Department of Labour (1994), Fact Finding Report—Commission on the Future of Worker-Management Relations (also called John T. Dunlop Commission Report), Washington D.C., USA.

Venkata Ratnam, C.S. (2003), "Negotiating Flexibility", in Negotiated Change, Response Books, New Delhi.

Venkata Ratnam, C.S. (2003), 'Negotiated Change: Collective Bargaining.

Index